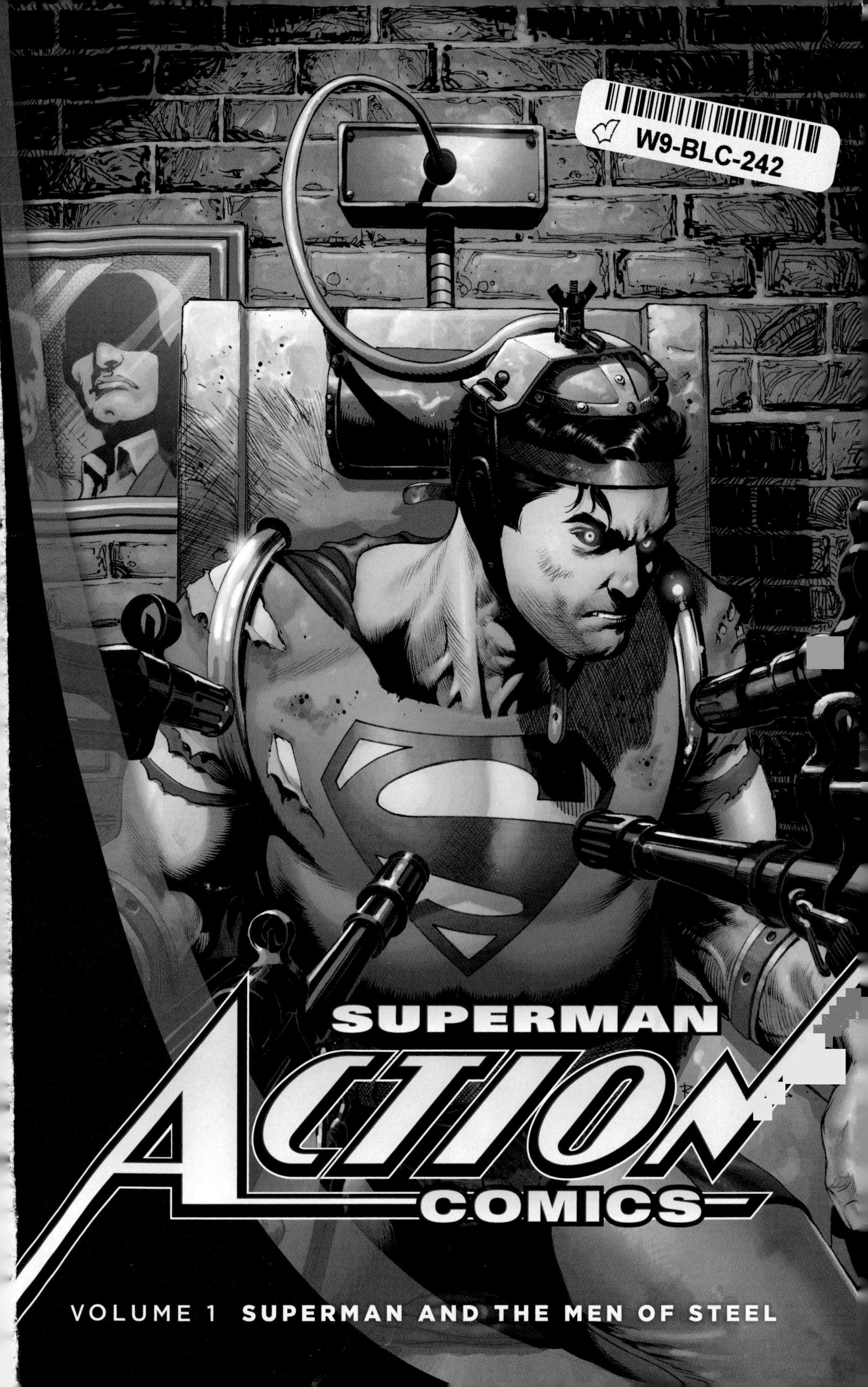
W9-BLC-242
SUPERMAN
ACTION
COMICS
VOLUME 1 SUPERMAN AND THE MEN OF STEEL

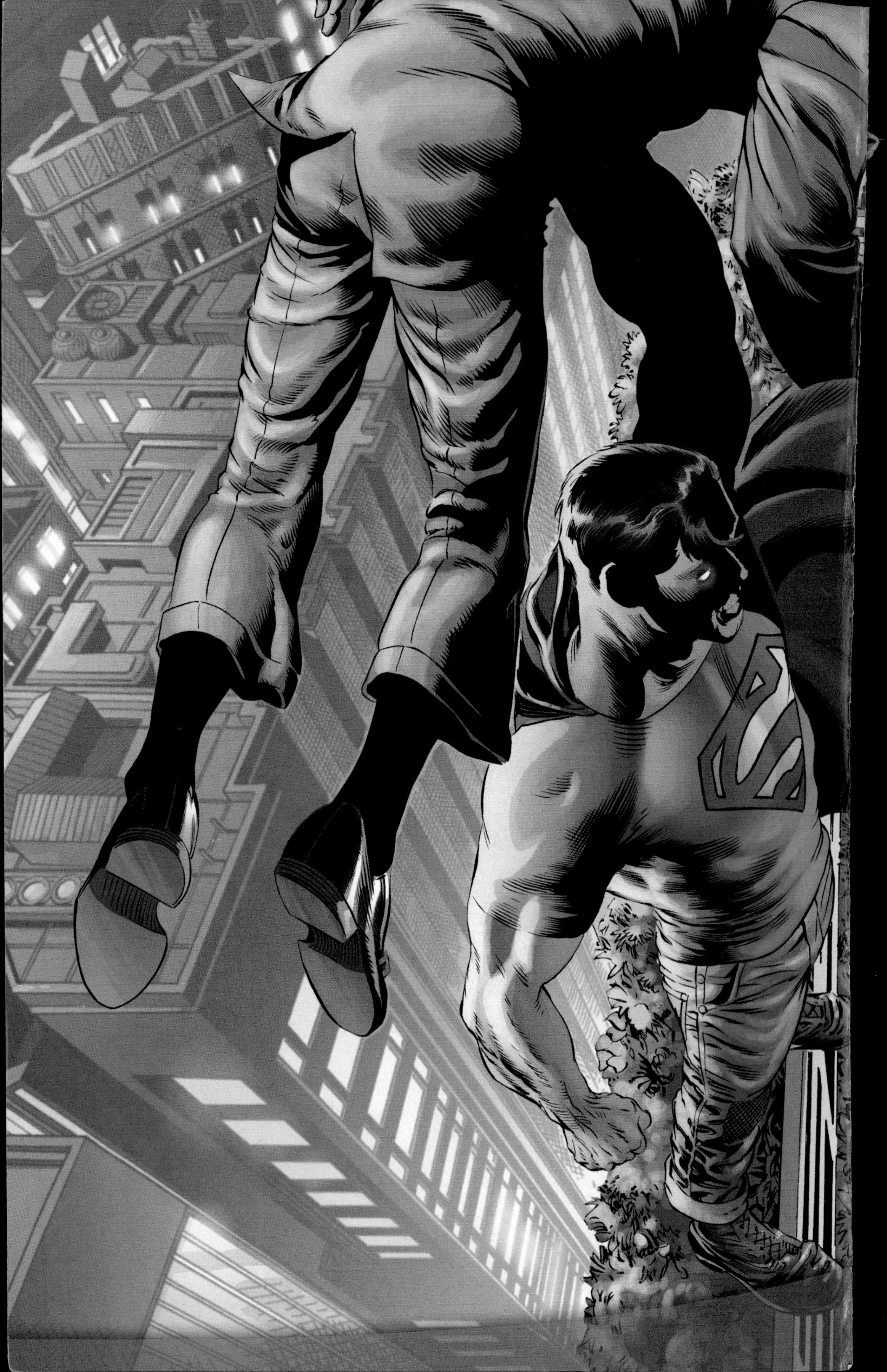

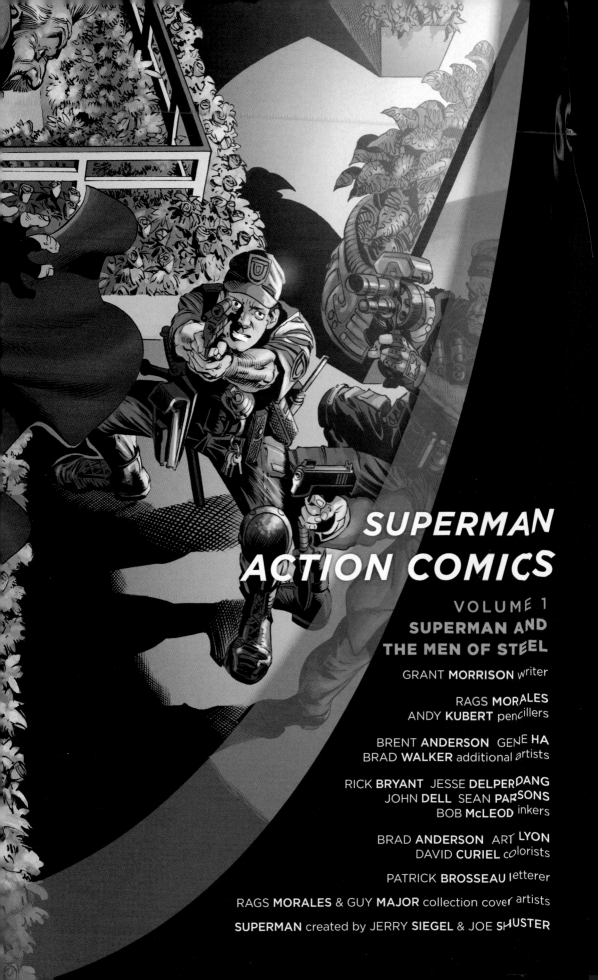

SUPERMAN
ACTION COMICS

VOLUME 1
SUPERMAN AND
THE MEN OF STEEL

GRANT **MORRISON** writer

RAGS **MORALES**
ANDY **KUBERT** pencillers

BRENT **ANDERSON** GENE **HA**
BRAD **WALKER** additional artists

RICK **BRYANT** JESSE **DELPERDANG**
JOHN **DELL** SEAN **PARSONS**
BOB **McLEOD** inkers

BRAD **ANDERSON** ART **LYON**
DAVID **CURIEL** colorists

PATRICK **BROSSEAU** letterer

RAGS **MORALES** & GUY **MAJOR** collection cover artists

SUPERMAN created by JERRY **SIEGEL** & JOE **SHUSTER**

MATT IDELSON Editor – Original Series WIL MOSS Associate Editor – Original Series PETER HAMBOUSSI Editor
ROBBIN BROSTERMAN Design Director – Books ROBBIE BIEDERMAN Publication Design

BOB HARRAS VP – Editor-in-Chief

DIANE NELSON President DAN DIDIO and JIM LEE Co-Publishers
GEOFF JOHNS Chief Creative Officer
JOHN ROOD Executive VP – Sales, Marketing and Business Development
AMY GENKINS Senior VP – Business and Legal Affairs NAIRI GARDINER Senior VP – Finance
JEFF BOISON VP – Publishing Operations MARK CHIARELLO VP – Art Direction and Design
JOHN CUNNINGHAM VP – Marketing TERRI CUNNINGHAM VP – Talent Relations and Services
ALISON GILL Senior VP – Manufacturing and Operations HANK KANALZ Senior VP – Digital
JAY KOGAN VP – Business and Legal Affairs, Publishing JACK MAHAN VP – Business Affairs, Talent
NICK NAPOLITANO VP – Manufacturing Administration SUE POHJA VP – Book Sales
COURTNEY SIMMONS Senior VP – Publicity BOB WAYNE Senior VP – Sales

SUPERMAN — ACTION COMICS VOLUME 1: SUPERMAN AND THE MEN OF STEEL

DC Comics, 1700 Broadway, New York, NY 10019
A Warner Bros. Entertainment Company.
Printed by RR Donnelley, Salem, VA, USA. 3/29/13. First Printing.
ISBN: 978-1-4012-3547-5

SUSTAINABLE FORESTRY INITIATIVE
Certified Chain of Custody
At Least 20% Certified Forest Content
www.sfiprogram.org
SFI-01042
APPLIES TO TEXT STOCK ONLY

Library of Congress Cataloging-in-Publication Data

Morrison, Grant.
Superman - Action Comics. Volume 1, Superman and the men of steel / Grant Morrison, Rags Morales, Andy Kubert.
p. cm.
"Originally published in single magazine form in ACTION COMICS 1-8" – T.p. verso.
ISBN 978-1-4012-3546-8
1. Graphic novels. I. Morales, Rags. II. Kubert, Andy. III. Title. IV. Title: Superman and the men of steel.
PN6728.S9M73 2012
741.5'9411 – dc23
2012010313

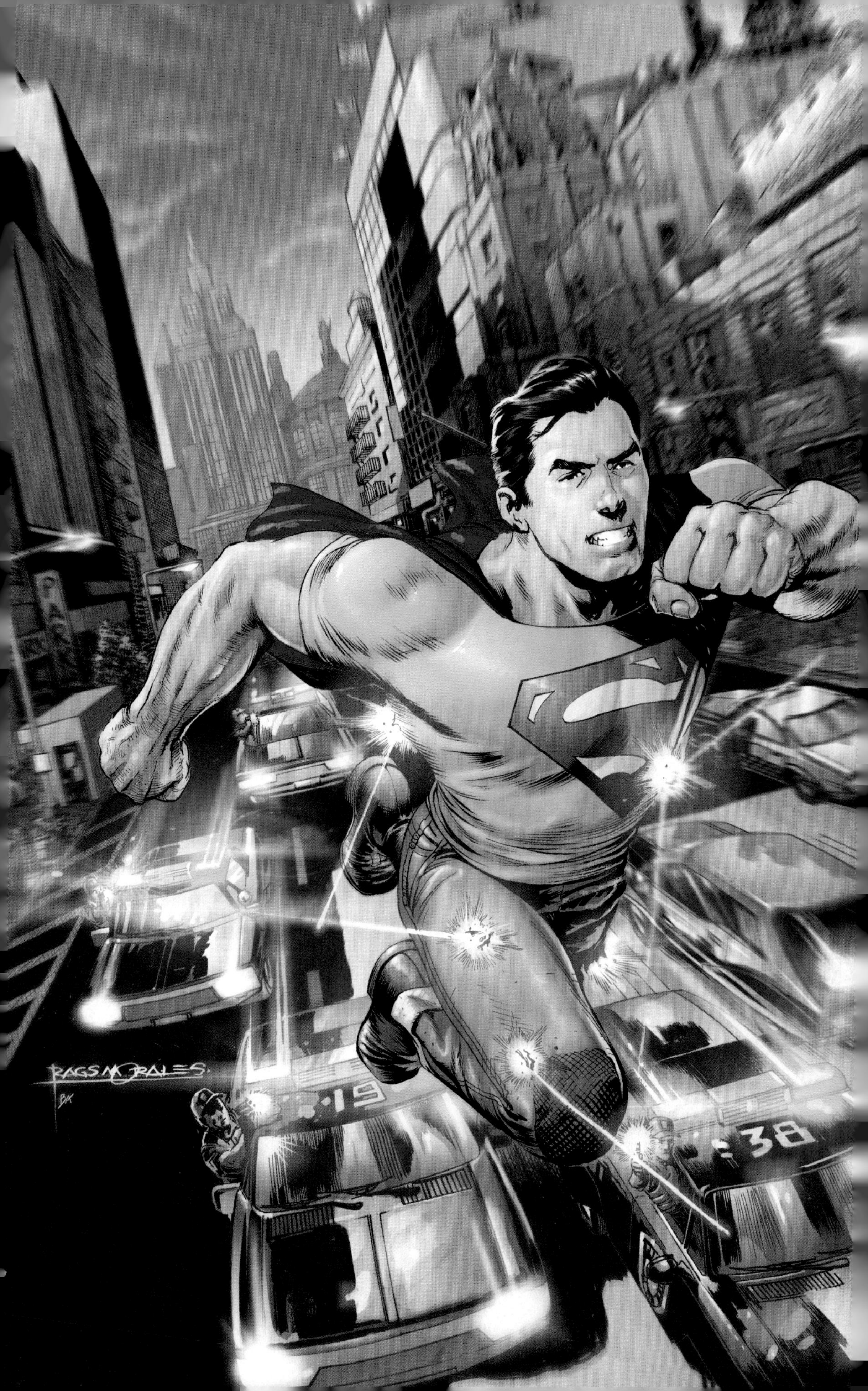
RAGS MORALES.
BIX
19
38

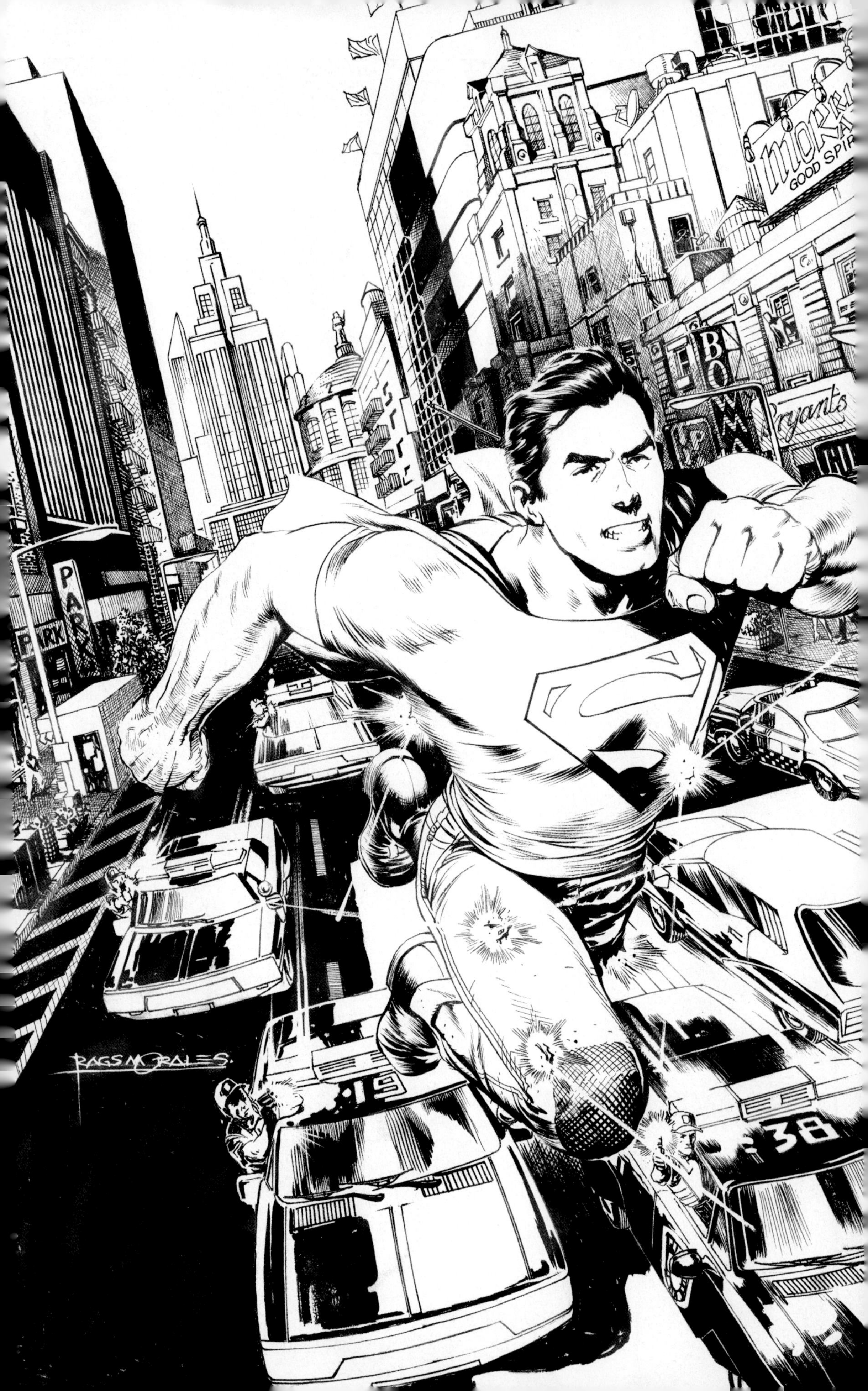

GOOD SPIR
PARK
PARK
Bryants
RAGS MORALES.
19
38

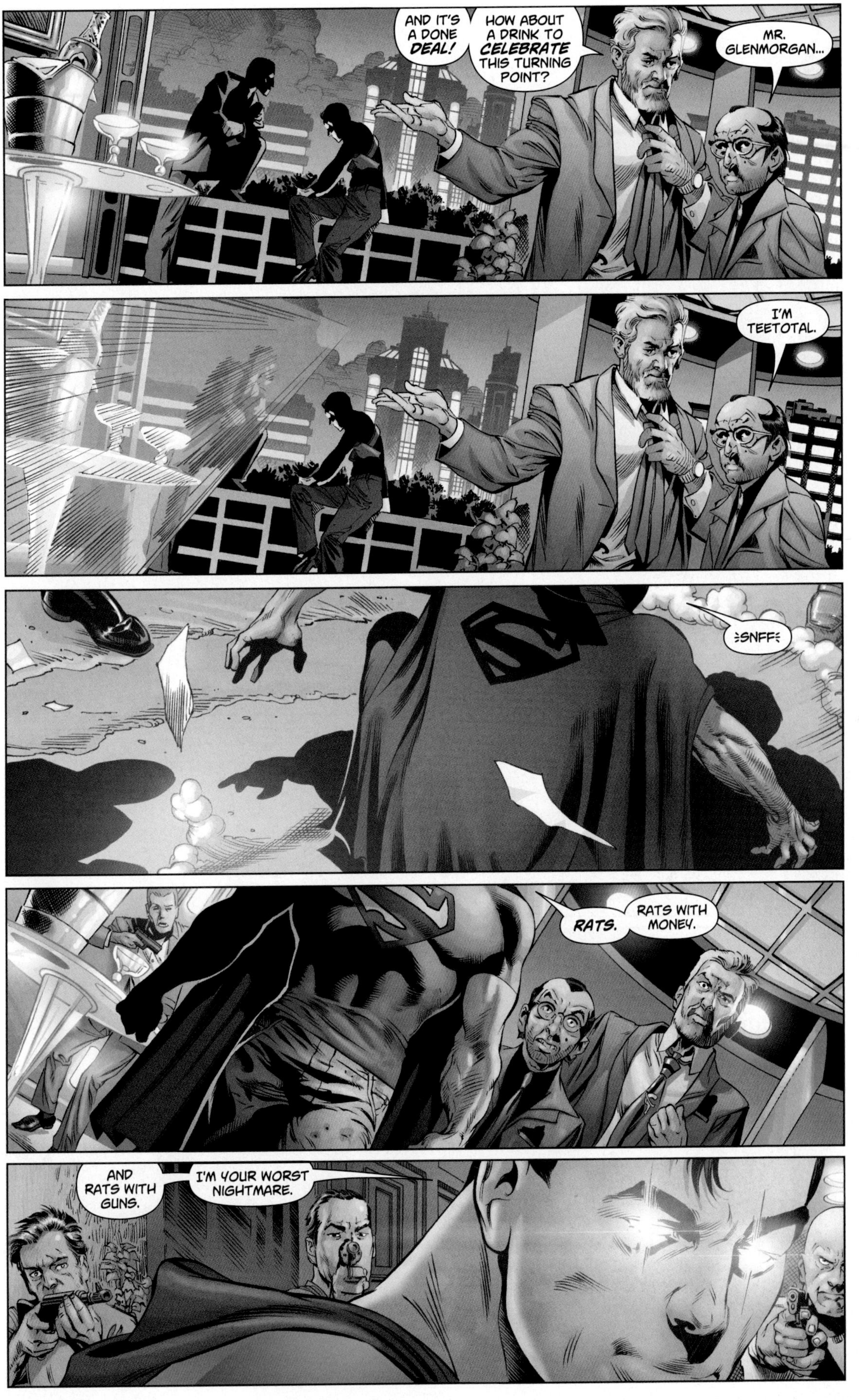
AND IT'S A DONE DEAL!
HOW ABOUT A DRINK TO CELEBRATE THIS TURNING POINT?
MR. GLENMORGAN...
I'M TEETOTAL.
SNFF
RATS.
RATS WITH MONEY.
AND RATS WITH GUNS.
I'M YOUR WORST NIGHTMARE.

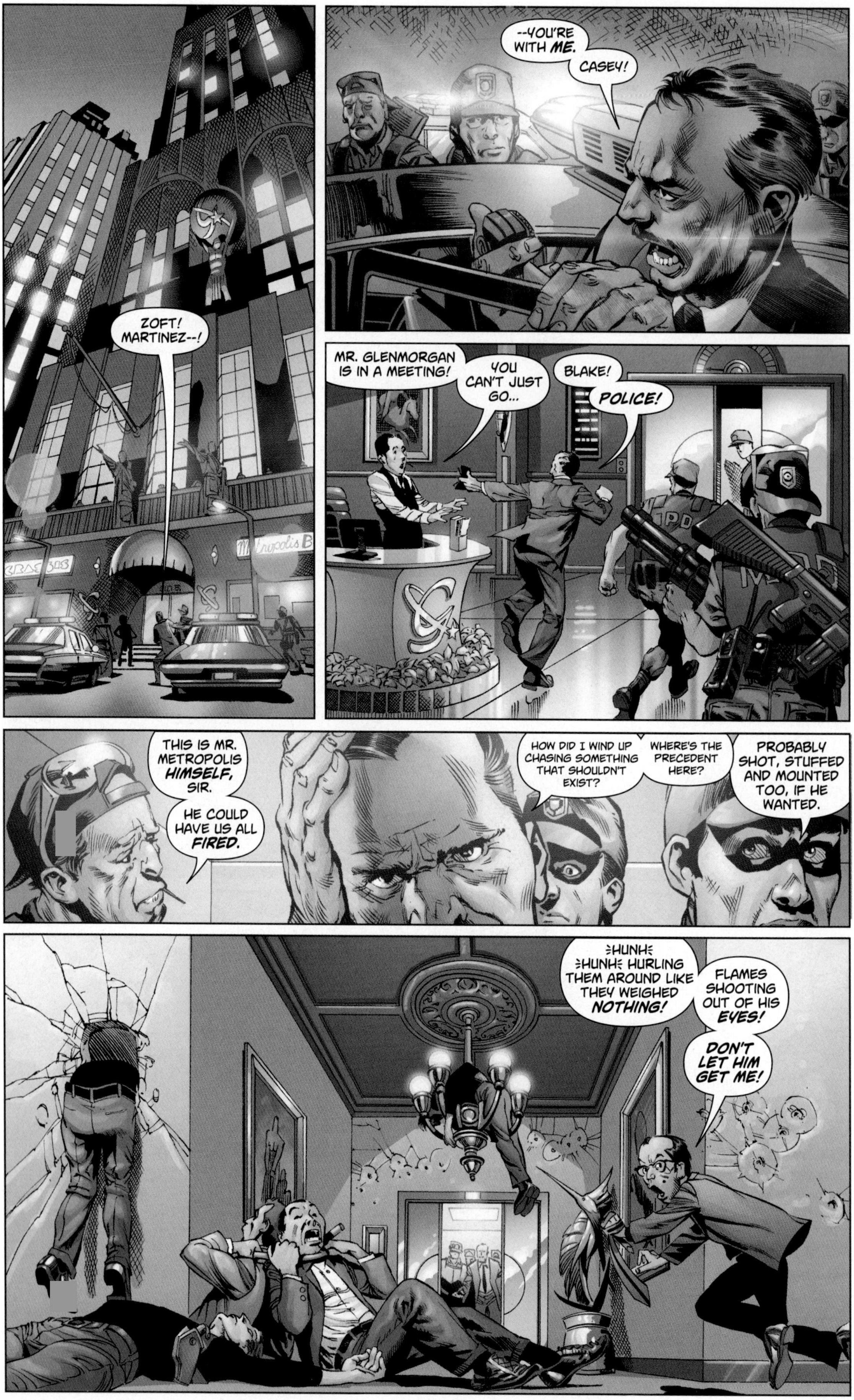
ZOFT! MARTINEZ--!
--YOU'RE WITH ME.
CASEY!
MR. GLENMORGAN IS IN A MEETING!
YOU CAN'T JUST GO...
BLAKE!
POLICE!
THIS IS MR. METROPOLIS HIMSELF, SIR.
HE COULD HAVE US ALL FIRED.
HOW DID I WIND UP CHASING SOMETHING THAT SHOULDN'T EXIST?
WHERE'S THE PRECEDENT HERE?
PROBABLY SHOT, STUFFED AND MOUNTED TOO, IF HE WANTED.
HUNH HUNH HURLING THEM AROUND LIKE THEY WEIGHED NOTHING!
FLAMES SHOOTING OUT OF HIS EYES!
DON'T LET HIM GET ME!

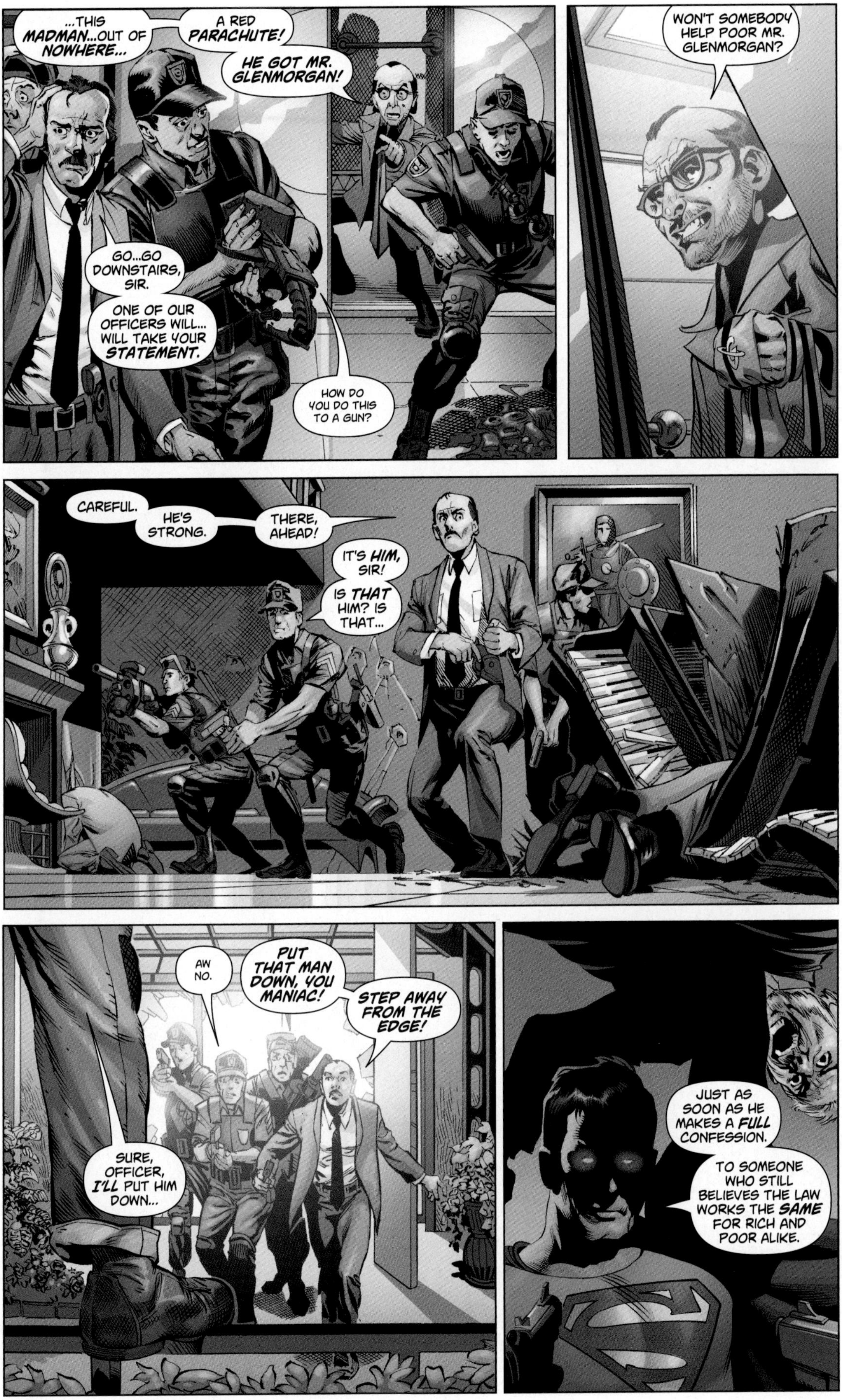
...THIS MADMAN...OUT OF NOWHERE...
A RED PARACHUTE!
HE GOT MR. GLENMORGAN!
GO...GO DOWNSTAIRS, SIR.
ONE OF OUR OFFICERS WILL... WILL TAKE YOUR STATEMENT.
HOW DO YOU DO THIS TO A GUN?
WON'T SOMEBODY HELP POOR MR. GLENMORGAN?
CAREFUL.
HE'S STRONG.
THERE, AHEAD!
IT'S HIM, SIR!
IS THAT HIM? IS THAT...
AW NO.
PUT THAT MAN DOWN, YOU MANIAC!
STEP AWAY FROM THE EDGE!
SURE, OFFICER, I'LL PUT HIM DOWN...
JUST AS SOON AS HE MAKES A FULL CONFESSION.
TO SOMEONE WHO STILL BELIEVES THE LAW WORKS THE SAME FOR RICH AND POOR ALIKE.

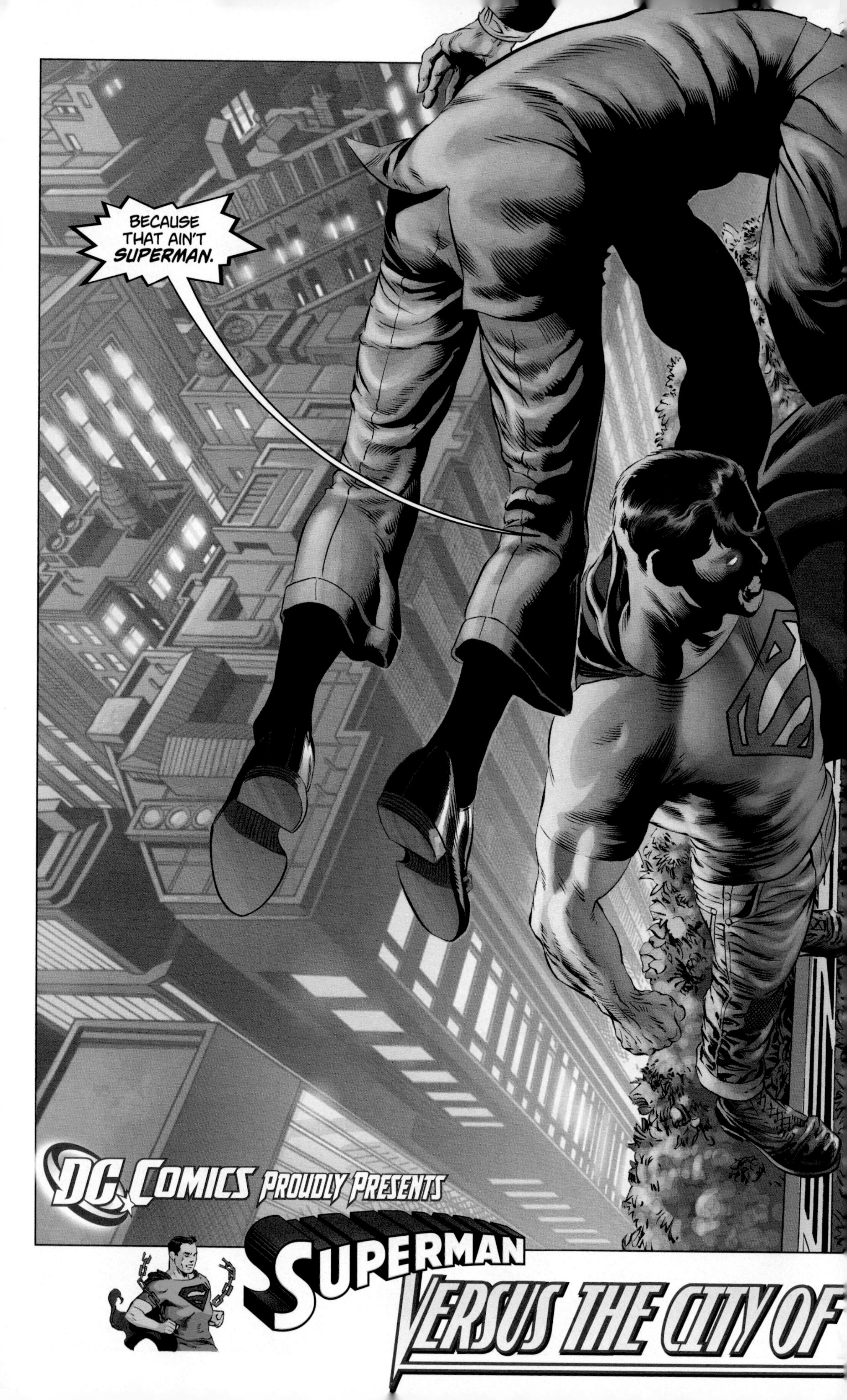
BECAUSE THAT AIN'T SUPERMAN.
DC COMICS PROUDLY PRESENTS
SUPERMAN
VERSUS THE CITY OF

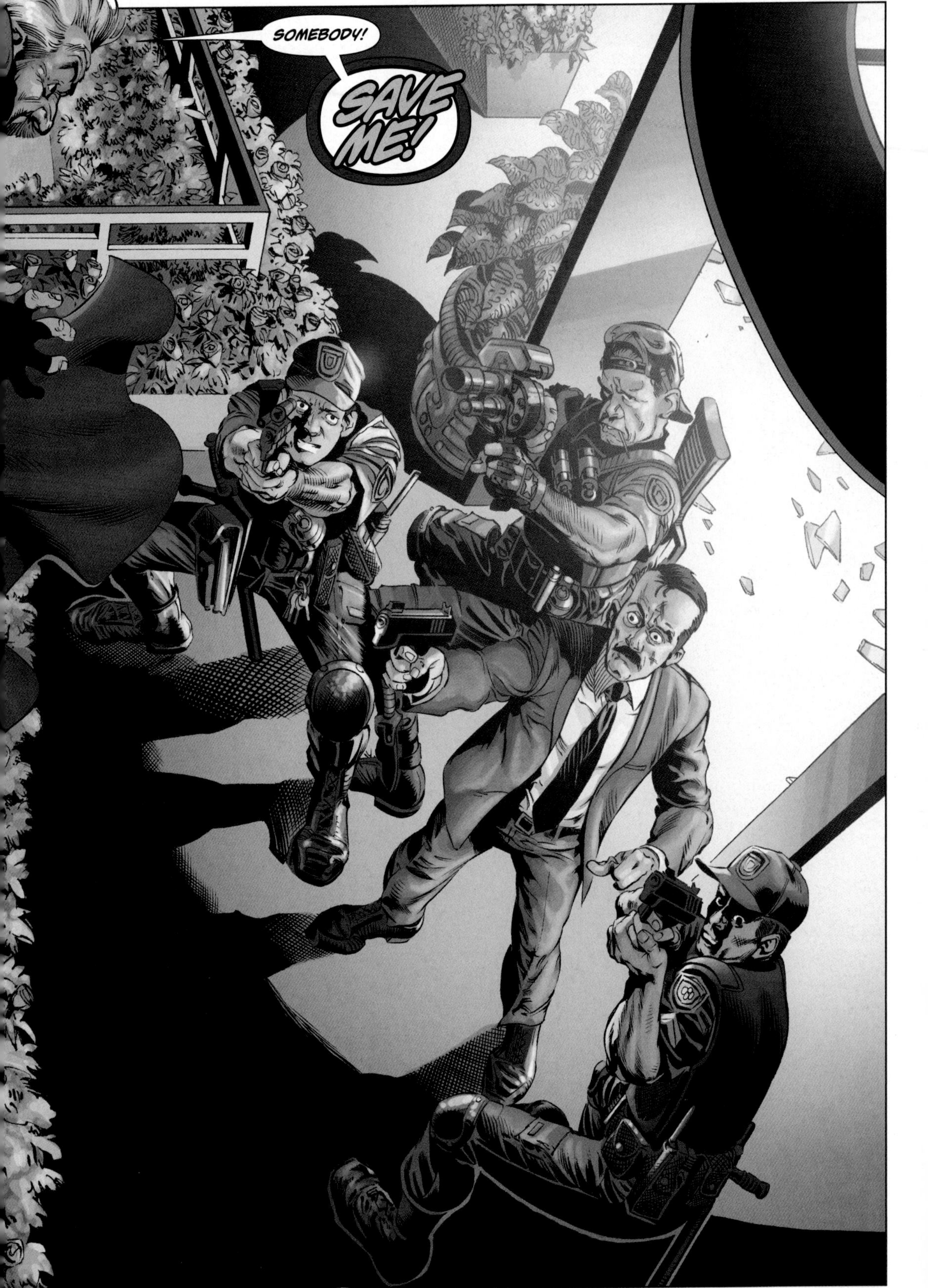
SOMEBODY!
SAVE ME!

TOMORROW

GRANT MORRISON Writer RAGS MORALES Penciller
RICK BRYANT Inker BRAD ANDERSON Colorist PATRICK BROSSEAU Letterer
RAGS MORALES & BRAD ANDERSON Cover JIM LEE, SCOTT WILLIAMS & ALEX SINCLAIR Variant Cover
WIL MOSS Associate Editor MATT IDELSON Editor SUPERMAN Created by JERRY SIEGEL & JOE SHUSTER

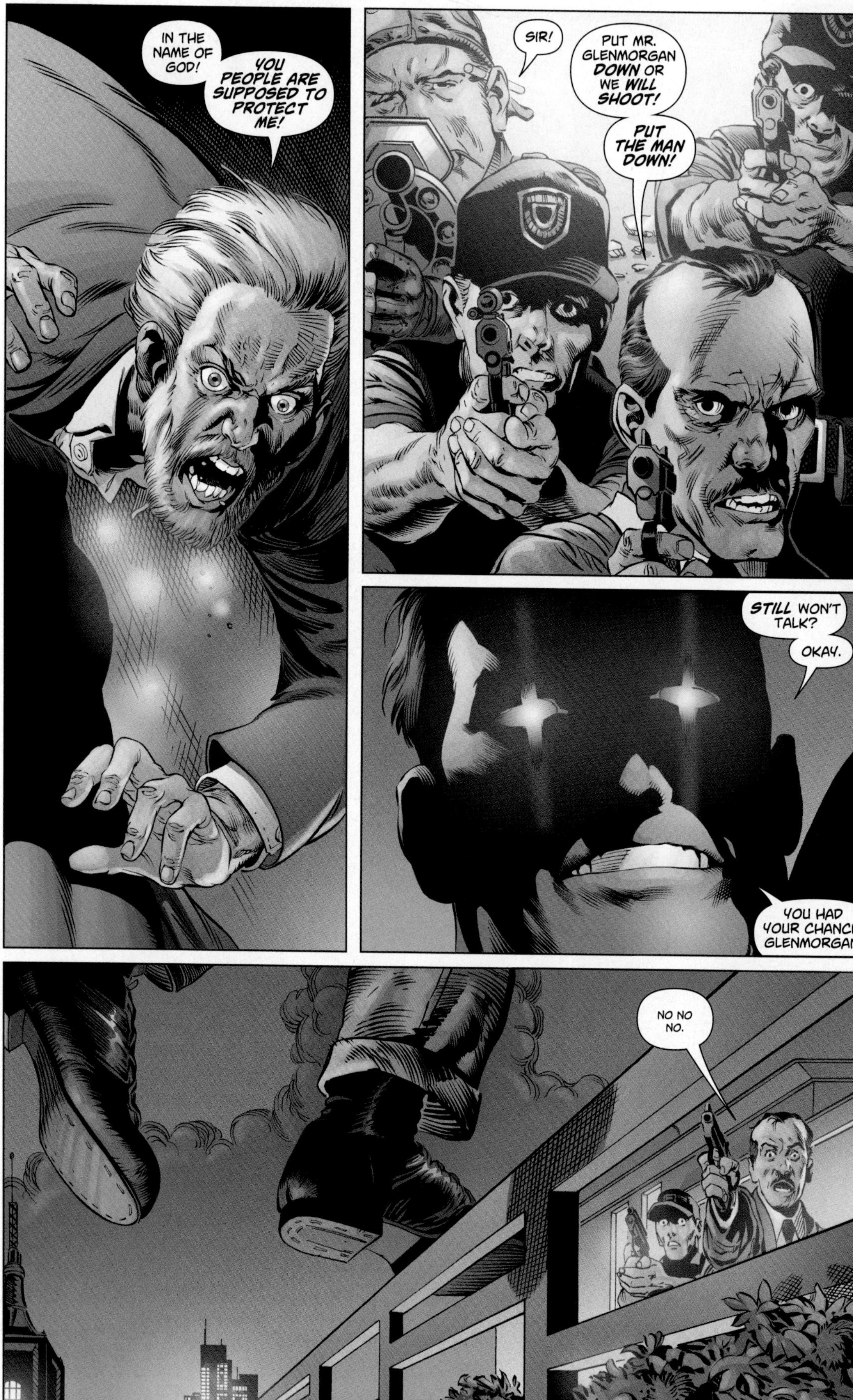
IN THE NAME OF GOD!
YOU PEOPLE ARE SUPPOSED TO PROTECT ME!
SIR!
PUT MR. GLENMORGAN DOWN OR WE WILL SHOOT!
PUT THE MAN DOWN!
STILL WON'T TALK?
OKAY.
YOU HAD YOUR CHANCE, GLENMORGAN.
NO NO NO.

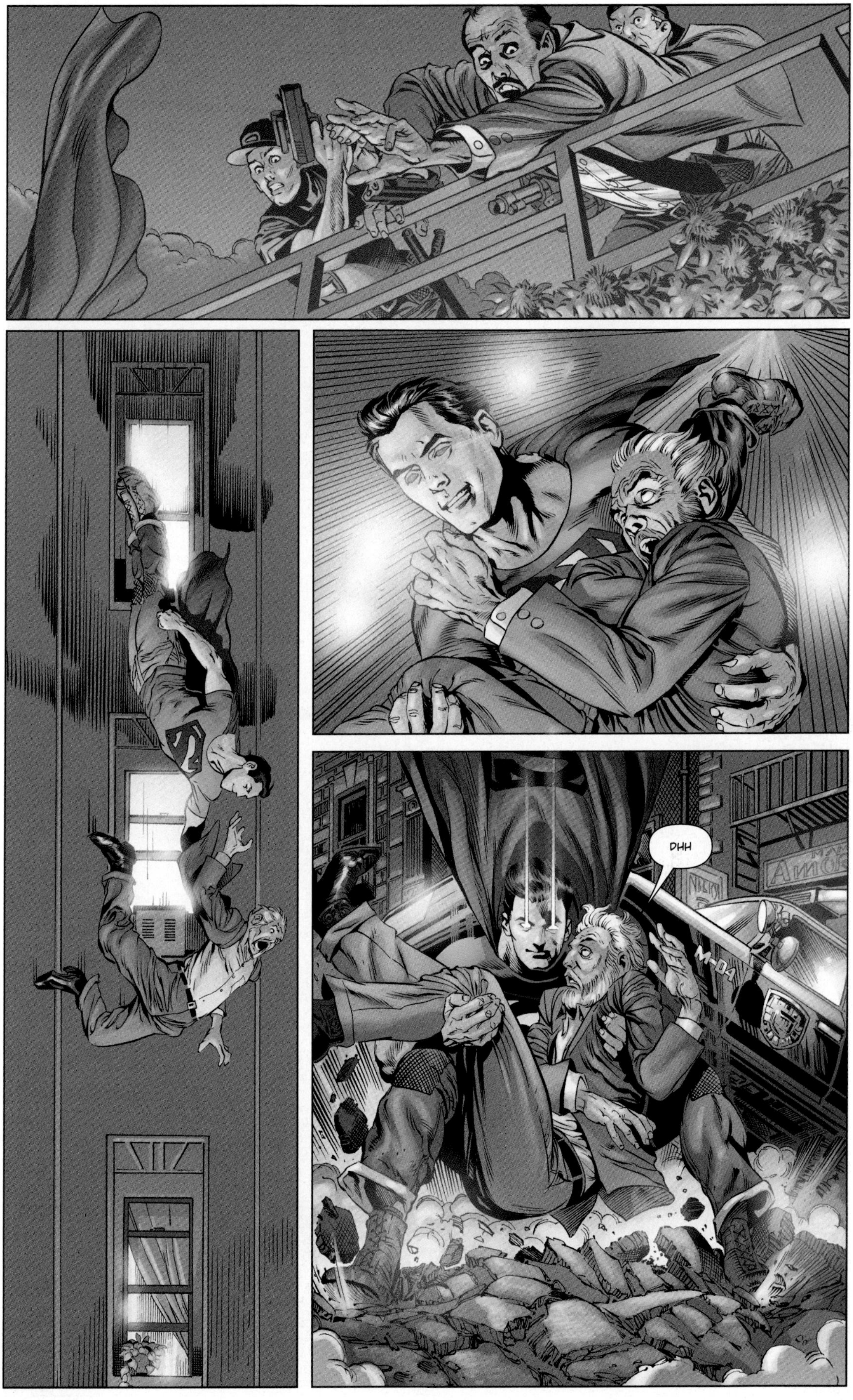
DHH
M-04

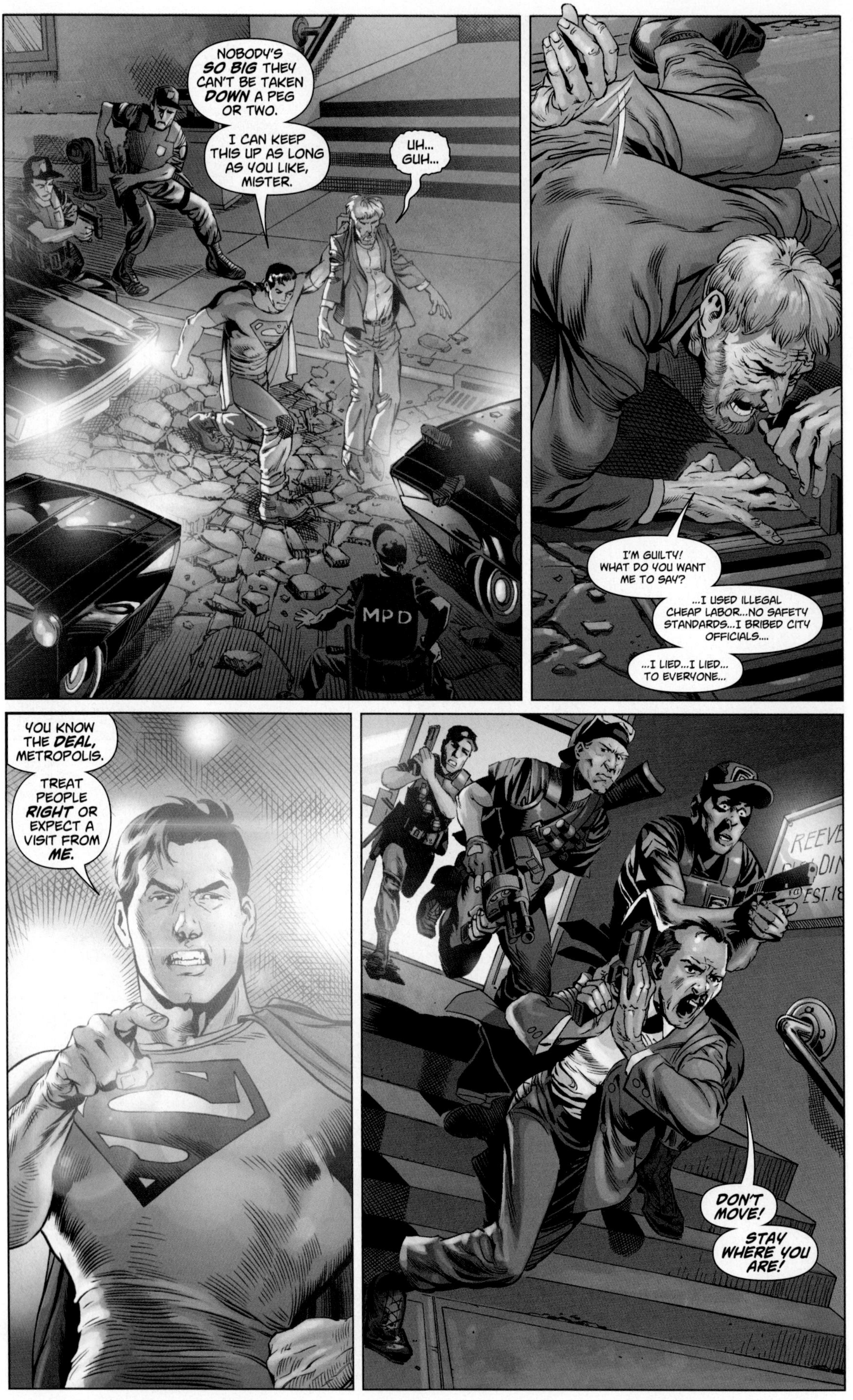
NOBODY'S SO BIG THEY CAN'T BE TAKEN DOWN A PEG OR TWO.
I CAN KEEP THIS UP AS LONG AS YOU LIKE, MISTER.
UH... GUH...
MPD
I'M GUILTY! WHAT DO YOU WANT ME TO SAY?
...I USED ILLEGAL CHEAP LABOR...NO SAFETY STANDARDS...I BRIBED CITY OFFICIALS....
...I LIED...I LIED... TO EVERYONE...
YOU KNOW THE DEAL, METROPOLIS.
TREAT PEOPLE RIGHT OR EXPECT A VISIT FROM ME.
DON'T MOVE!
STAY WHERE YOU ARE!

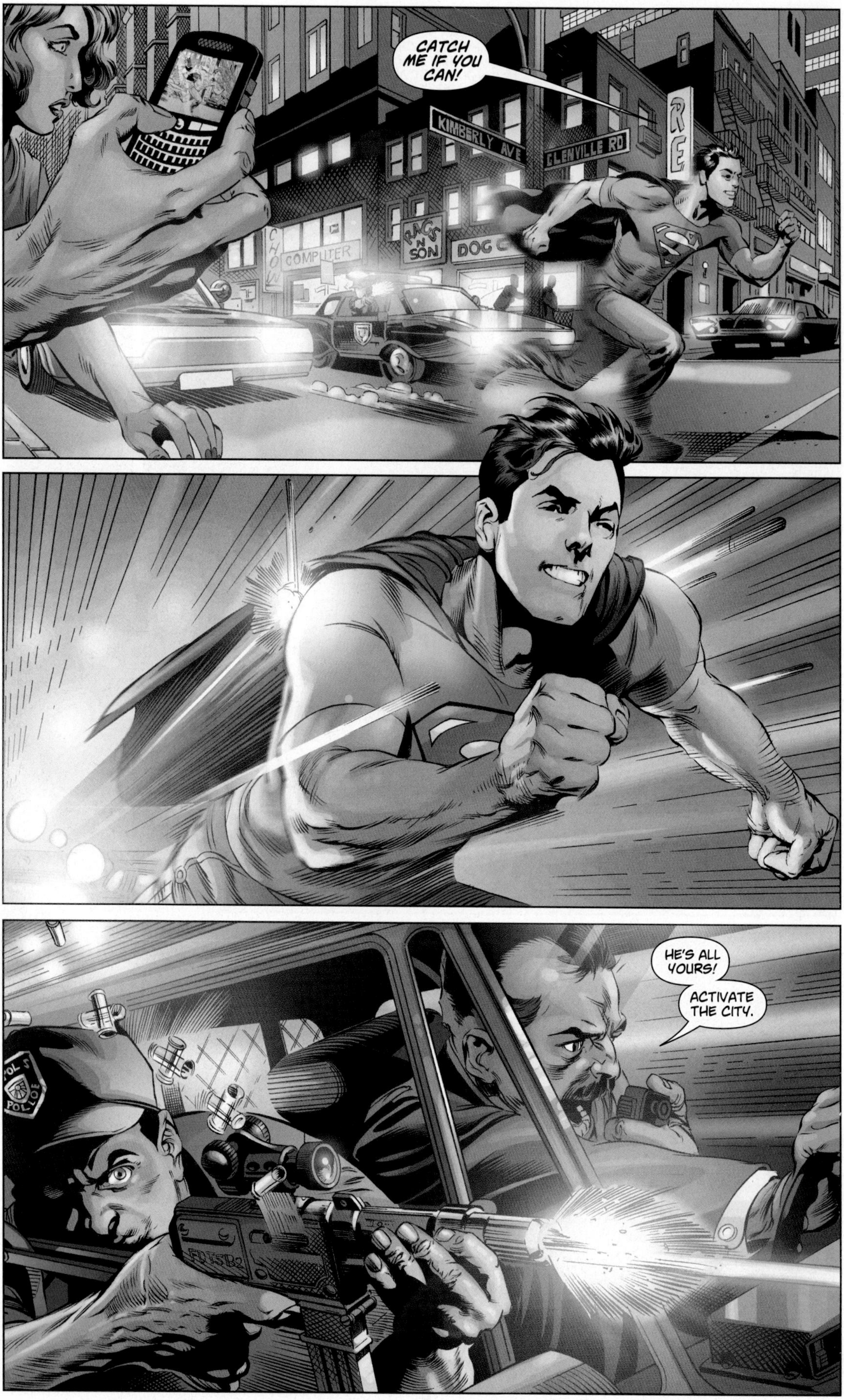

CATCH ME IF YOU CAN!
KIMBERLY AVE
GLENVILLE RD
RAGS N SON
COMPUTER
CHOW
HE'S ALL YOURS!
ACTIVATE THE CITY.

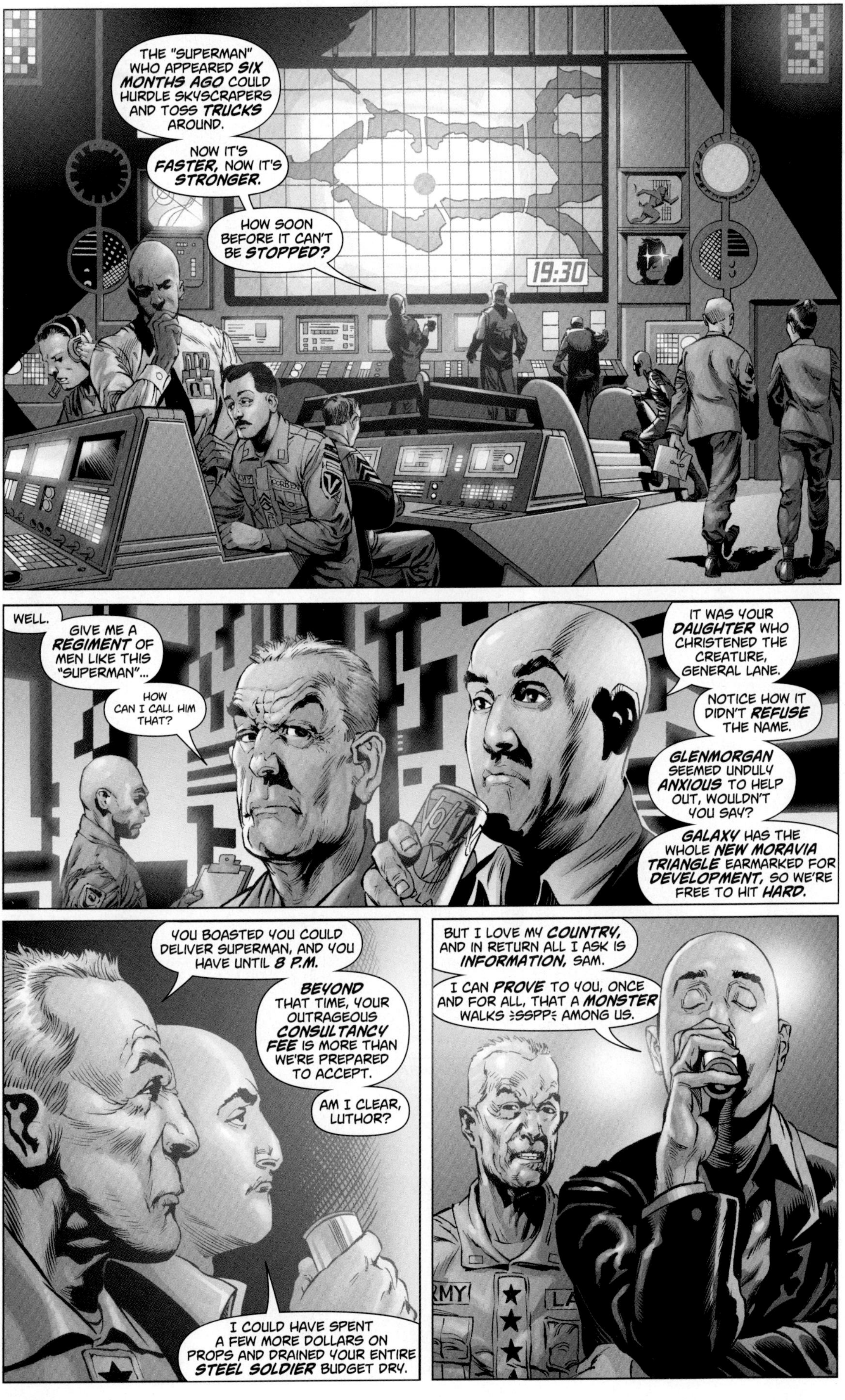
THE "SUPERMAN" WHO APPEARED SIX MONTHS AGO COULD HURDLE SKYSCRAPERS AND TOSS TRUCKS AROUND.
NOW IT'S FASTER, NOW IT'S STRONGER.
HOW SOON BEFORE IT CAN'T BE STOPPED?
19:30
WELL.
GIVE ME A REGIMENT OF MEN LIKE THIS "SUPERMAN"...
HOW CAN I CALL HIM THAT?
IT WAS YOUR DAUGHTER WHO CHRISTENED THE CREATURE, GENERAL LANE.
NOTICE HOW IT DIDN'T REFUSE THE NAME.
GLENMORGAN SEEMED UNDULY ANXIOUS TO HELP OUT, WOULDN'T YOU SAY?
GALAXY HAS THE WHOLE NEW MORAVIA TRIANGLE EARMARKED FOR DEVELOPMENT, SO WE'RE FREE TO HIT HARD.
YOU BOASTED YOU COULD DELIVER SUPERMAN, AND YOU HAVE UNTIL 8 P.M.
BEYOND THAT TIME, YOUR OUTRAGEOUS CONSULTANCY FEE IS MORE THAN WE'RE PREPARED TO ACCEPT.
AM I CLEAR, LUTHOR?
I COULD HAVE SPENT A FEW MORE DOLLARS ON PROPS AND DRAINED YOUR ENTIRE STEEL SOLDIER BUDGET DRY.
BUT I LOVE MY COUNTRY, AND IN RETURN ALL I ASK IS INFORMATION, SAM.
I CAN PROVE TO YOU, ONCE AND FOR ALL, THAT A MONSTER WALKS SSPP AMONG US.

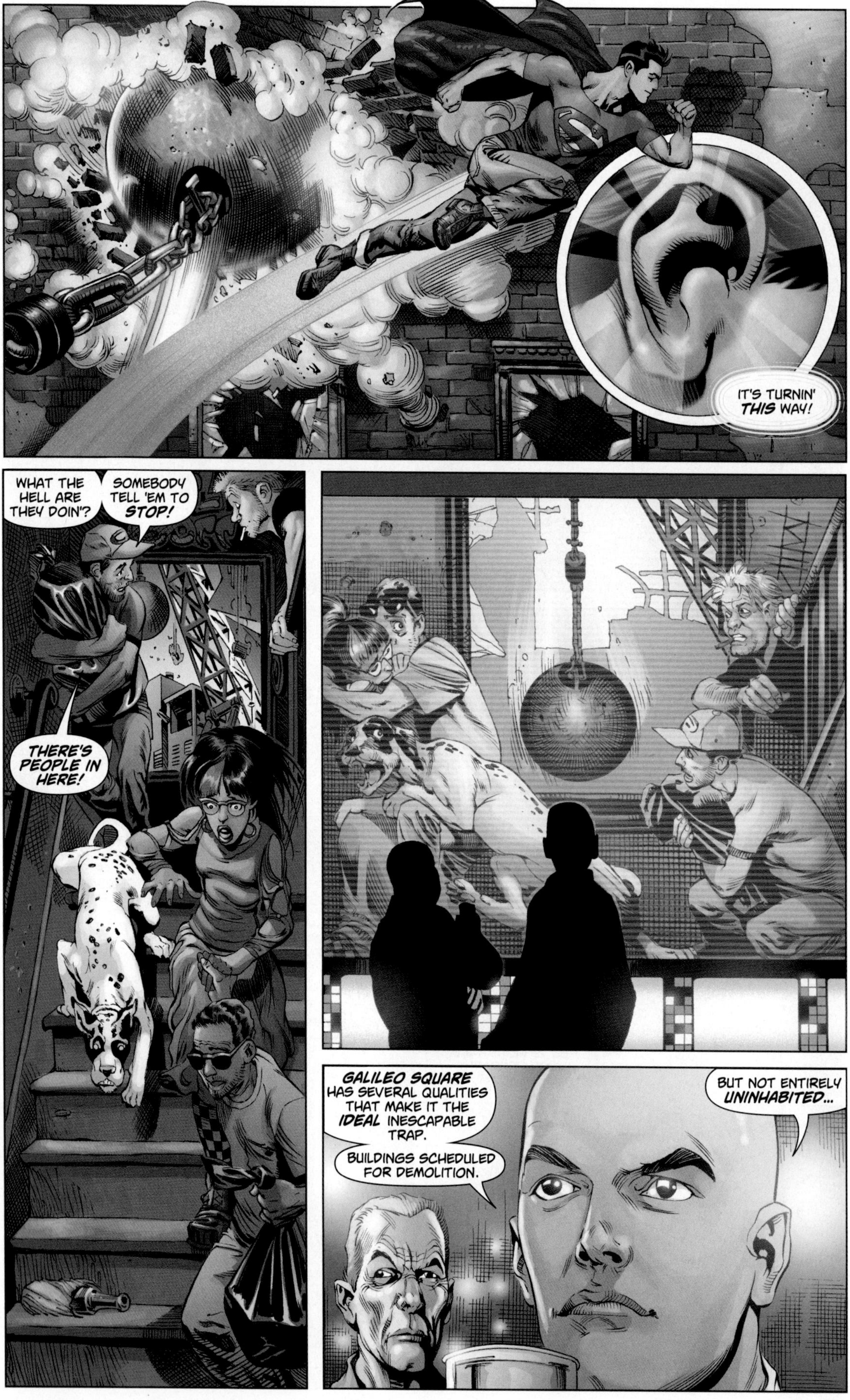
IT'S TURNIN' THIS WAY!
WHAT THE HELL ARE THEY DOIN'?
SOMEBODY TELL 'EM TO STOP!
THERE'S PEOPLE IN HERE!
GALILEO SQUARE HAS SEVERAL QUALITIES THAT MAKE IT THE IDEAL INESCAPABLE TRAP.
BUILDINGS SCHEDULED FOR DEMOLITION.
BUT NOT ENTIRELY UNINHABITED...

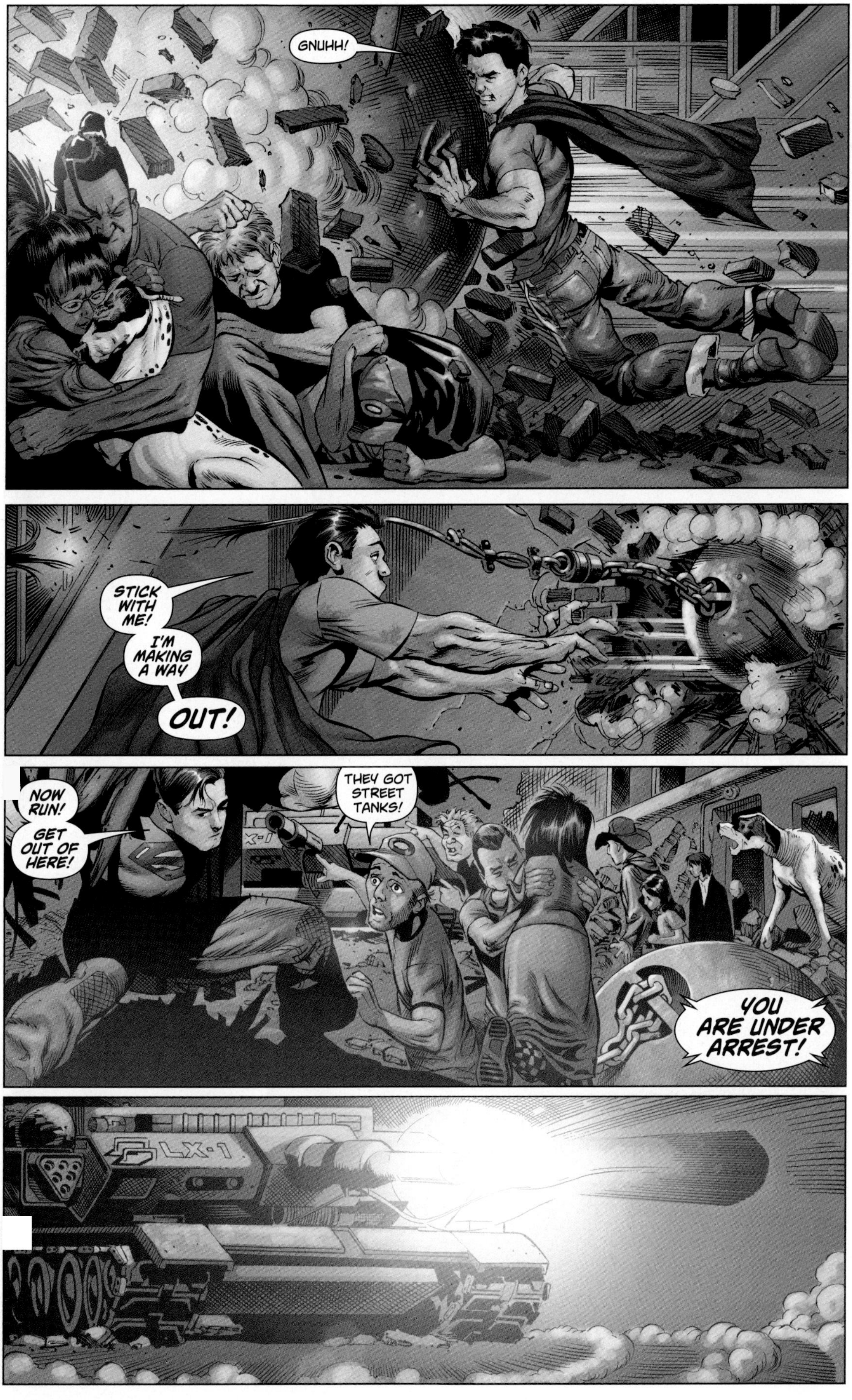
GNUHH!
STICK WITH ME!
I'M MAKING A WAY
OUT!
NOW RUN!
GET OUT OF HERE!
THEY GOT STREET TANKS!
YOU ARE UNDER ARREST!
LX-1

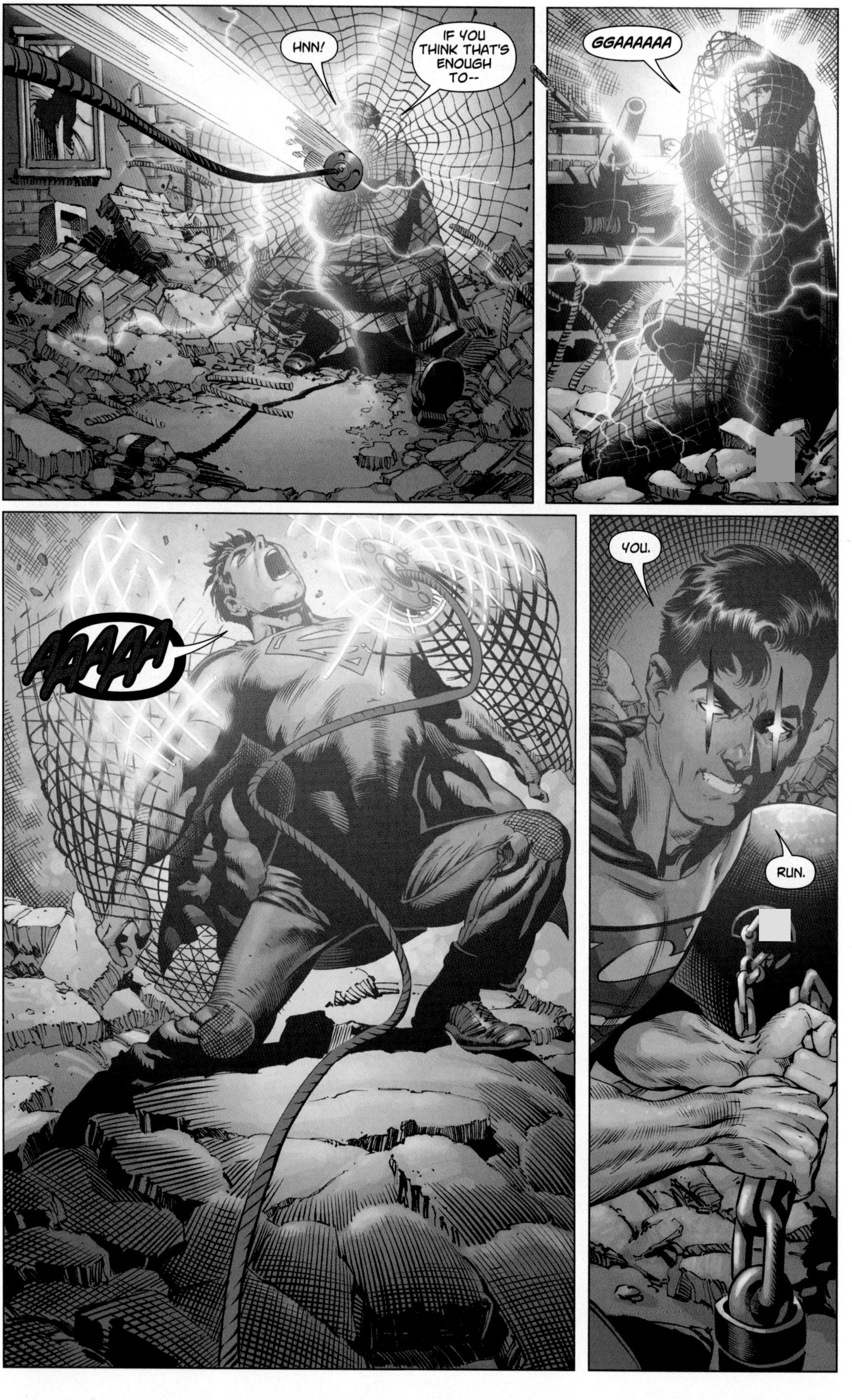
HNN!
IF YOU THINK THAT'S ENOUGH TO--
GGAAAAAA
AAAAA
YOU.
RUN.

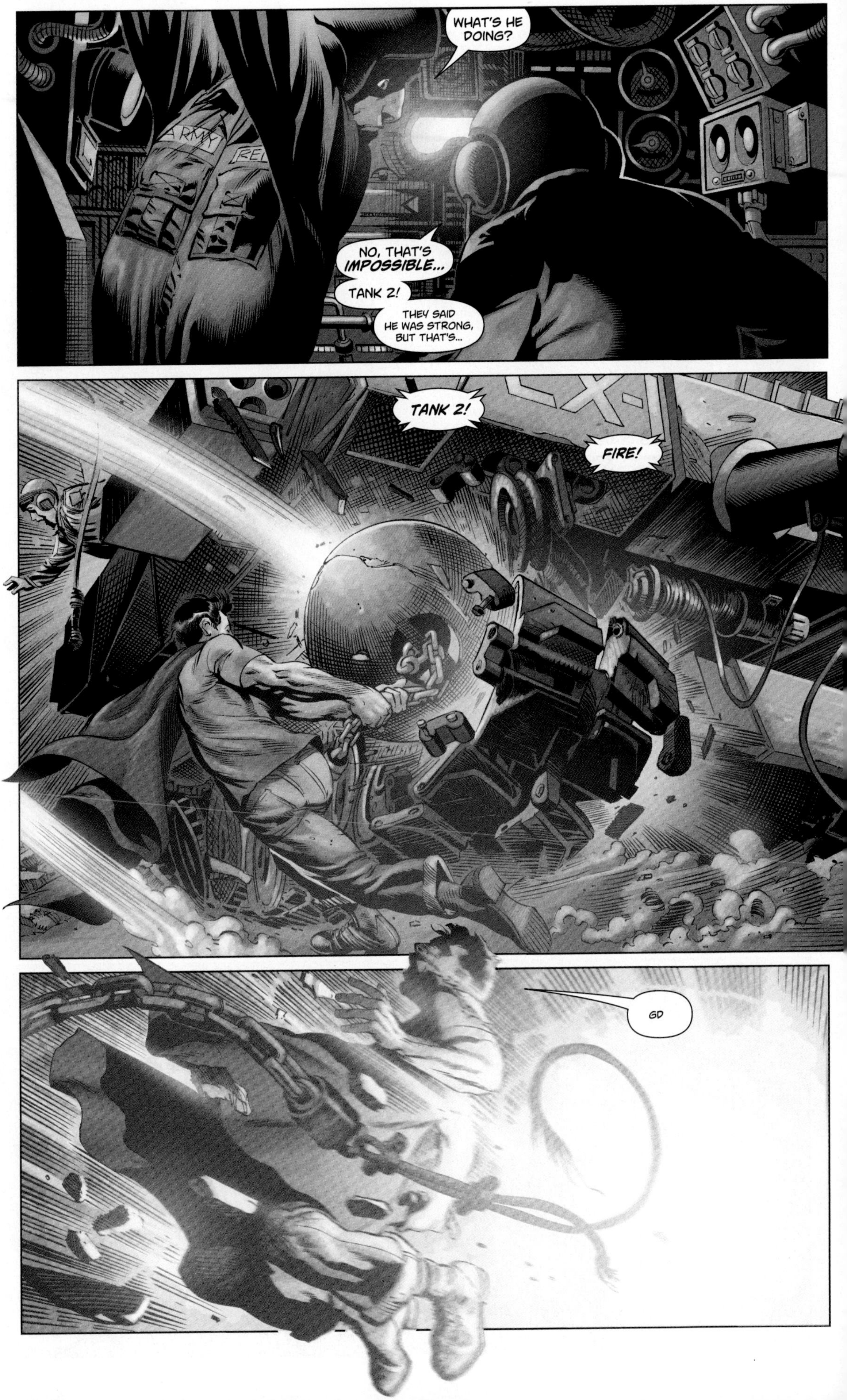
WHAT'S HE DOING?
NO, THAT'S *IMPOSSIBLE...*
TANK 2!
THEY SAID HE WAS STRONG, BUT THAT'S...
ARMY
TANK 2!
FIRE!
GD

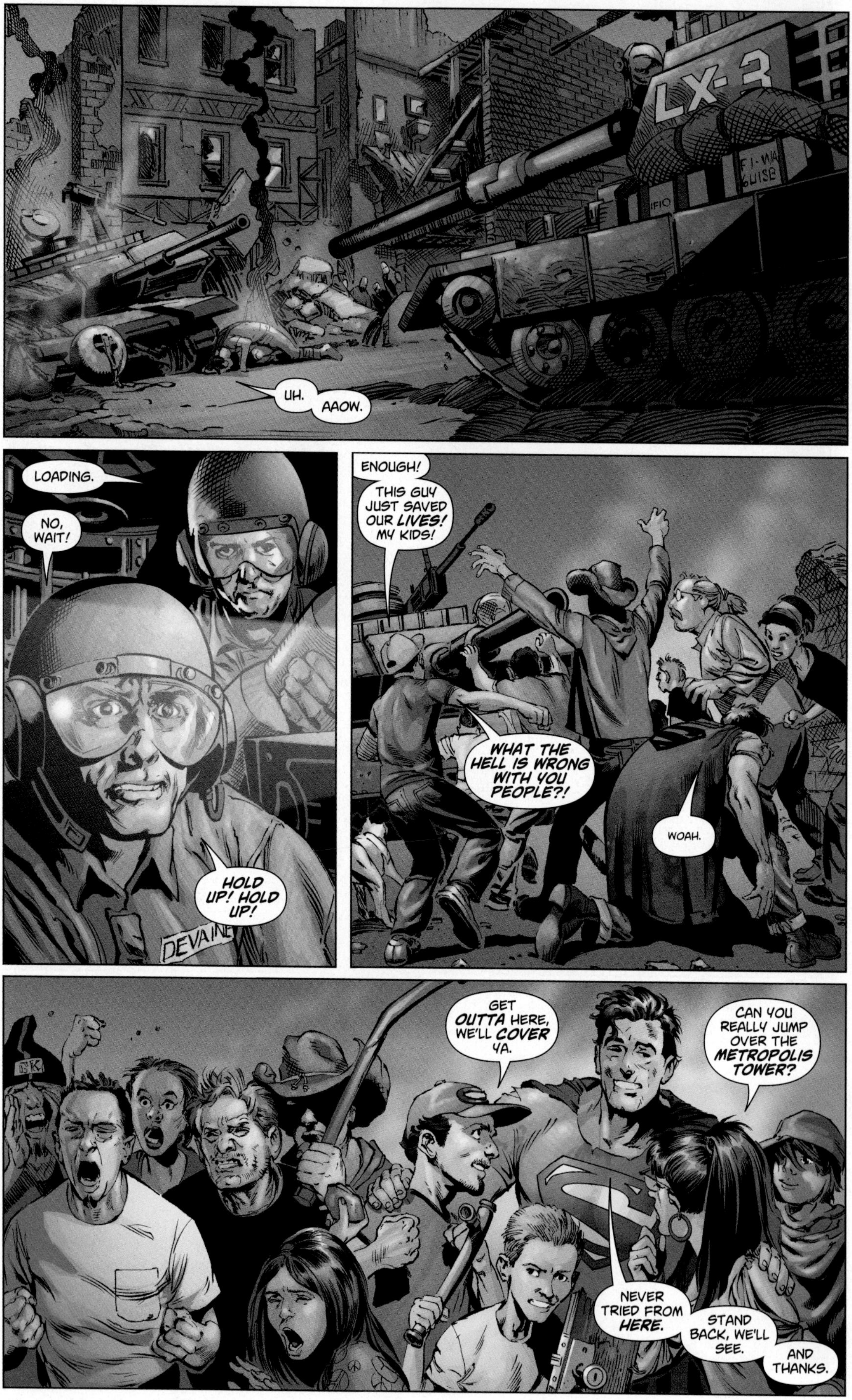
LX-3
UH.
AAOW.
LOADING.
NO, WAIT!
HOLD UP! HOLD UP!
DEVAINE
ENOUGH!
THIS GUY JUST SAVED OUR *LIVES!* MY KIDS!
WHAT THE HELL IS WRONG WITH YOU PEOPLE?!
WOAH.
GET *OUTTA* HERE, WE'LL *COVER* YA.
CAN YOU REALLY JUMP OVER THE *METROPOLIS TOWER?*
NEVER TRIED FROM *HERE.*
STAND BACK, WE'LL SEE.
AND THANKS.

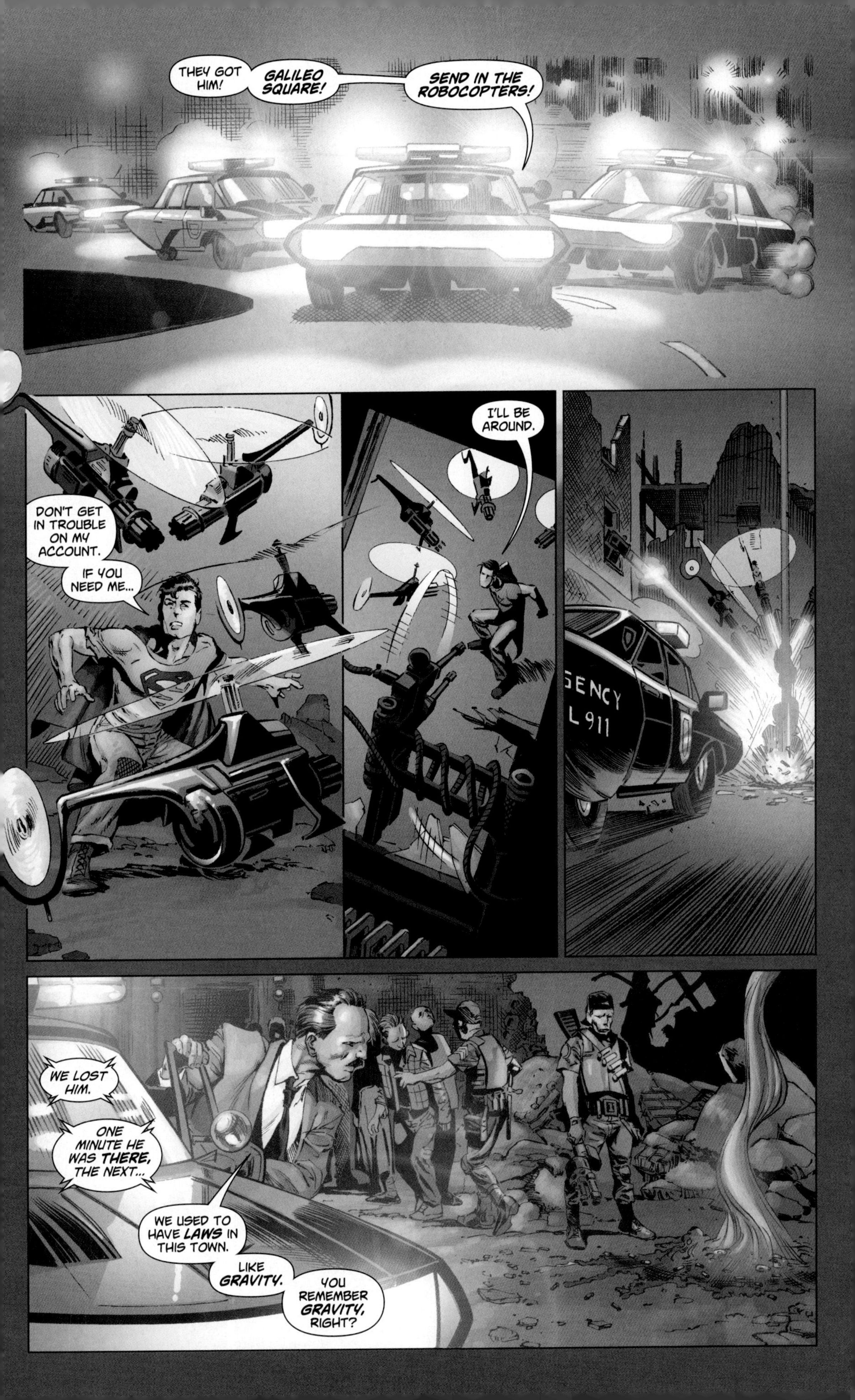
THEY GOT HIM!
GALILEO SQUARE!
SEND IN THE ROBOCOPTERS!
DON'T GET IN TROUBLE ON MY ACCOUNT.
IF YOU NEED ME...
I'LL BE AROUND.
GENCY
L 911
WE LOST HIM.
ONE MINUTE HE WAS THERE, THE NEXT...
WE USED TO HAVE LAWS IN THIS TOWN.
LIKE GRAVITY.
YOU REMEMBER GRAVITY, RIGHT?

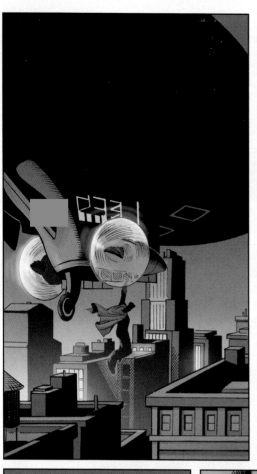

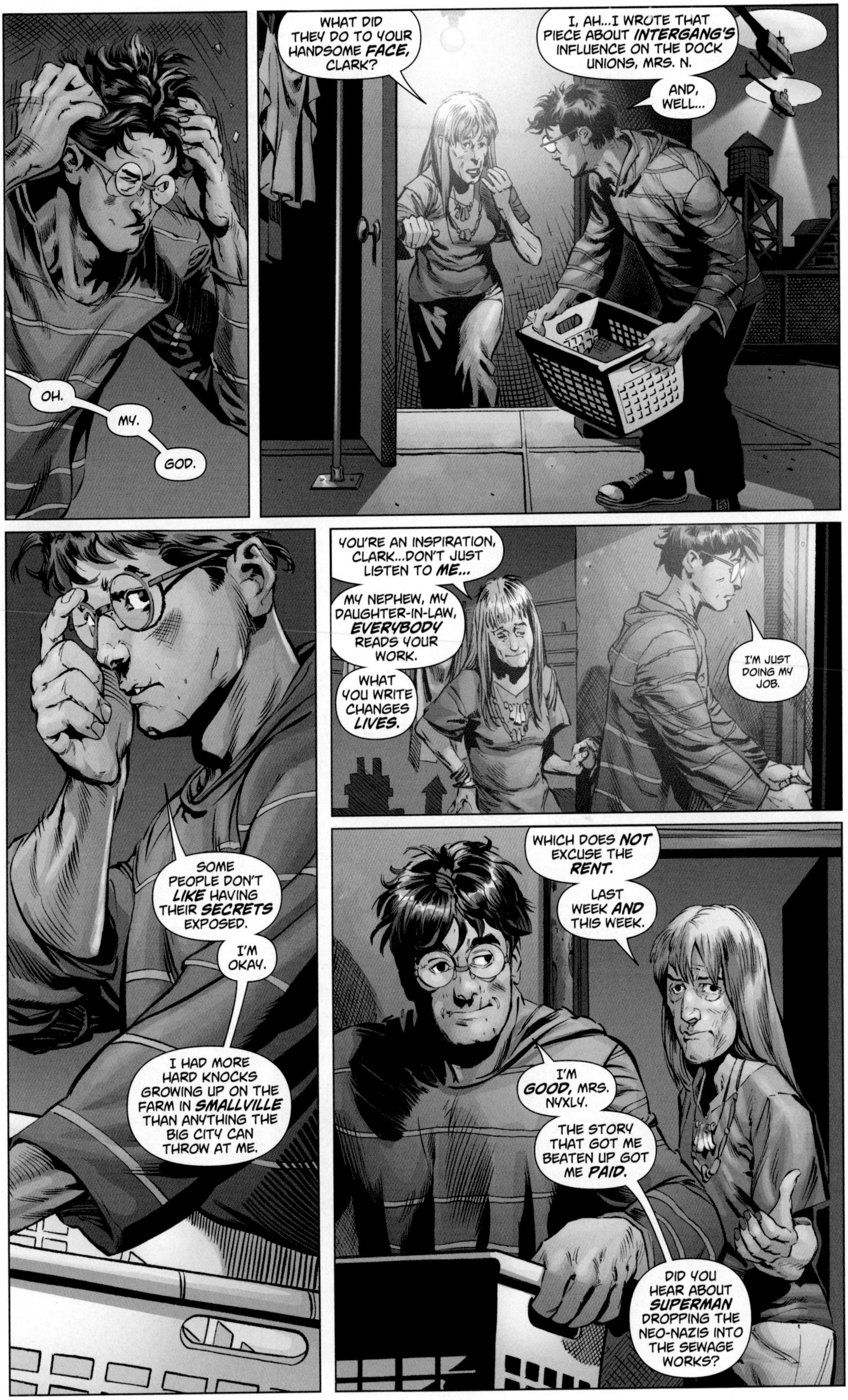
OH.
MY.
GOD.
WHAT DID THEY DO TO YOUR HANDSOME FACE, CLARK?
I, AH...I WROTE THAT PIECE ABOUT INTERGANG'S INFLUENCE ON THE DOCK UNIONS, MRS. N.
AND, WELL...
SOME PEOPLE DON'T LIKE HAVING THEIR SECRETS EXPOSED.
I'M OKAY.
I HAD MORE HARD KNOCKS GROWING UP ON THE FARM IN SMALLVILLE THAN ANYTHING THE BIG CITY CAN THROW AT ME.
YOU'RE AN INSPIRATION, CLARK...DON'T JUST LISTEN TO ME...
MY NEPHEW, MY DAUGHTER-IN-LAW, EVERYBODY READS YOUR WORK.
WHAT YOU WRITE CHANGES LIVES.
I'M JUST DOING MY JOB.
WHICH DOES NOT EXCUSE THE RENT.
LAST WEEK AND THIS WEEK.
I'M GOOD, MRS. NYXLY.
THE STORY THAT GOT ME BEATEN UP GOT ME PAID.
DID YOU HEAR ABOUT SUPERMAN DROPPING THE NEO-NAZIS INTO THE SEWAGE WORKS?

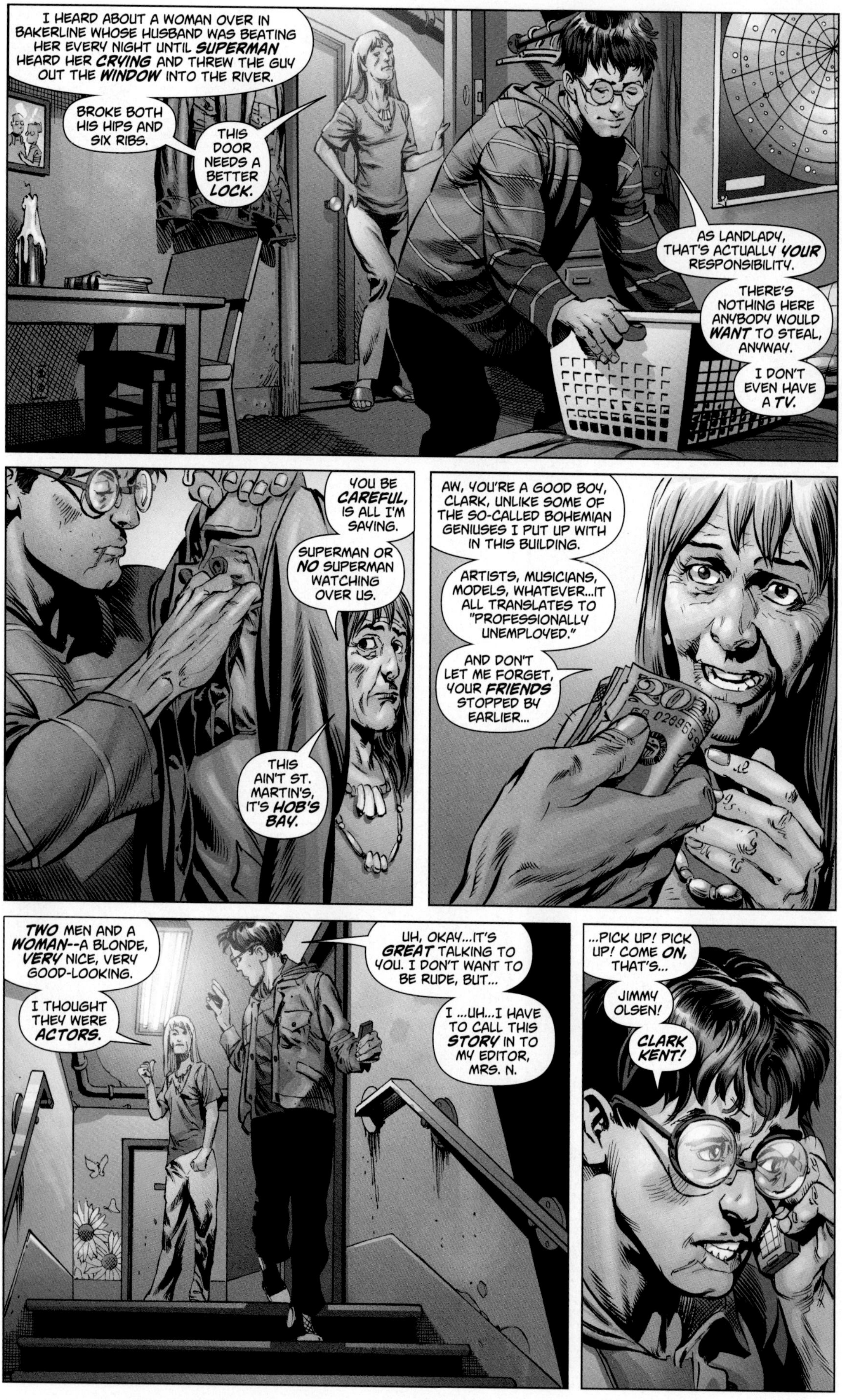
I HEARD ABOUT A WOMAN OVER IN BAKERLINE WHOSE HUSBAND WAS BEATING HER EVERY NIGHT UNTIL SUPERMAN HEARD HER CRYING AND THREW THE GUY OUT THE WINDOW INTO THE RIVER.
BROKE BOTH HIS HIPS AND SIX RIBS.
THIS DOOR NEEDS A BETTER LOCK.
AS LANDLADY, THAT'S ACTUALLY YOUR RESPONSIBILITY.
THERE'S NOTHING HERE ANYBODY WOULD WANT TO STEAL, ANYWAY.
I DON'T EVEN HAVE A TV.
YOU BE CAREFUL, IS ALL I'M SAYING.
SUPERMAN OR NO SUPERMAN WATCHING OVER US.
THIS AIN'T ST. MARTIN'S, IT'S HOB'S BAY.
AW, YOU'RE A GOOD BOY, CLARK, UNLIKE SOME OF THE SO-CALLED BOHEMIAN GENIUSES I PUT UP WITH IN THIS BUILDING.
ARTISTS, MUSICIANS, MODELS, WHATEVER...IT ALL TRANSLATES TO "PROFESSIONALLY UNEMPLOYED."
AND DON'T LET ME FORGET, YOUR FRIENDS STOPPED BY EARLIER...
TWO MEN AND A WOMAN--A BLONDE, VERY NICE, VERY GOOD-LOOKING.
I THOUGHT THEY WERE ACTORS.
UH, OKAY...IT'S GREAT TALKING TO YOU. I DON'T WANT TO BE RUDE, BUT...
I ...UH...I HAVE TO CALL THIS STORY IN TO MY EDITOR, MRS. N.
...PICK UP! PICK UP! COME ON, THAT'S...
JIMMY OLSEN!
CLARK KENT!

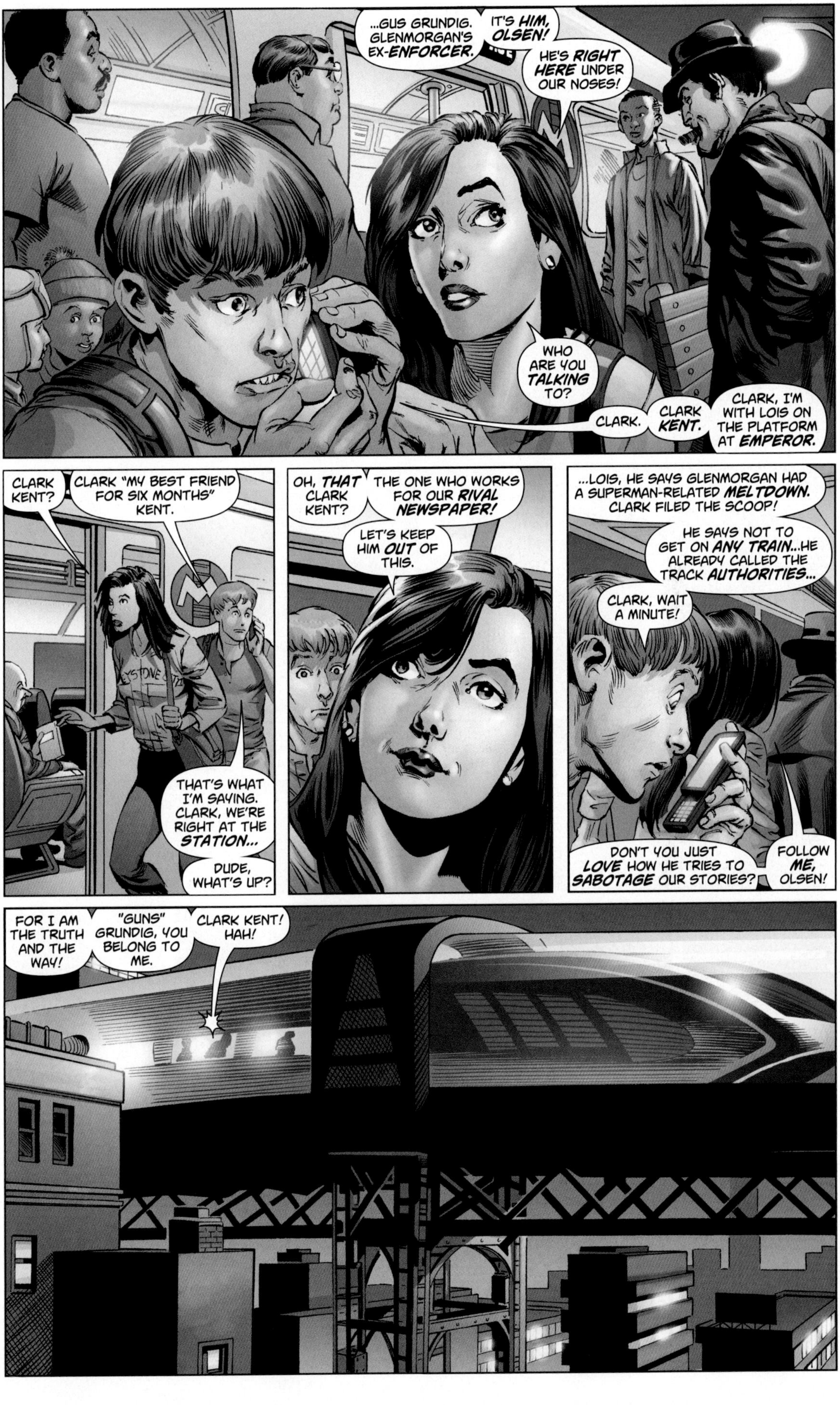
...GUS GRUNDIG. GLENMORGAN'S EX-ENFORCER.
IT'S HIM, OLSEN!
HE'S RIGHT HERE UNDER OUR NOSES!
WHO ARE YOU TALKING TO?
CLARK.
CLARK KENT.
CLARK, I'M WITH LOIS ON THE PLATFORM AT EMPEROR.
CLARK KENT?
CLARK "MY BEST FRIEND FOR SIX MONTHS" KENT.
THAT'S WHAT I'M SAYING. CLARK, WE'RE RIGHT AT THE STATION...
DUDE, WHAT'S UP?
OH, THAT CLARK KENT?
THE ONE WHO WORKS FOR OUR RIVAL NEWSPAPER!
LET'S KEEP HIM OUT OF THIS.
...LOIS, HE SAYS GLENMORGAN HAD A SUPERMAN-RELATED MELTDOWN. CLARK FILED THE SCOOP!
HE SAYS NOT TO GET ON ANY TRAIN...HE ALREADY CALLED THE TRACK AUTHORITIES...
CLARK, WAIT A MINUTE!
DON'T YOU JUST LOVE HOW HE TRIES TO SABOTAGE OUR STORIES?
FOLLOW ME, OLSEN!
FOR I AM THE TRUTH AND THE WAY!
"GUNS" GRUNDIG, YOU BELONG TO ME.
CLARK KENT! HAH!

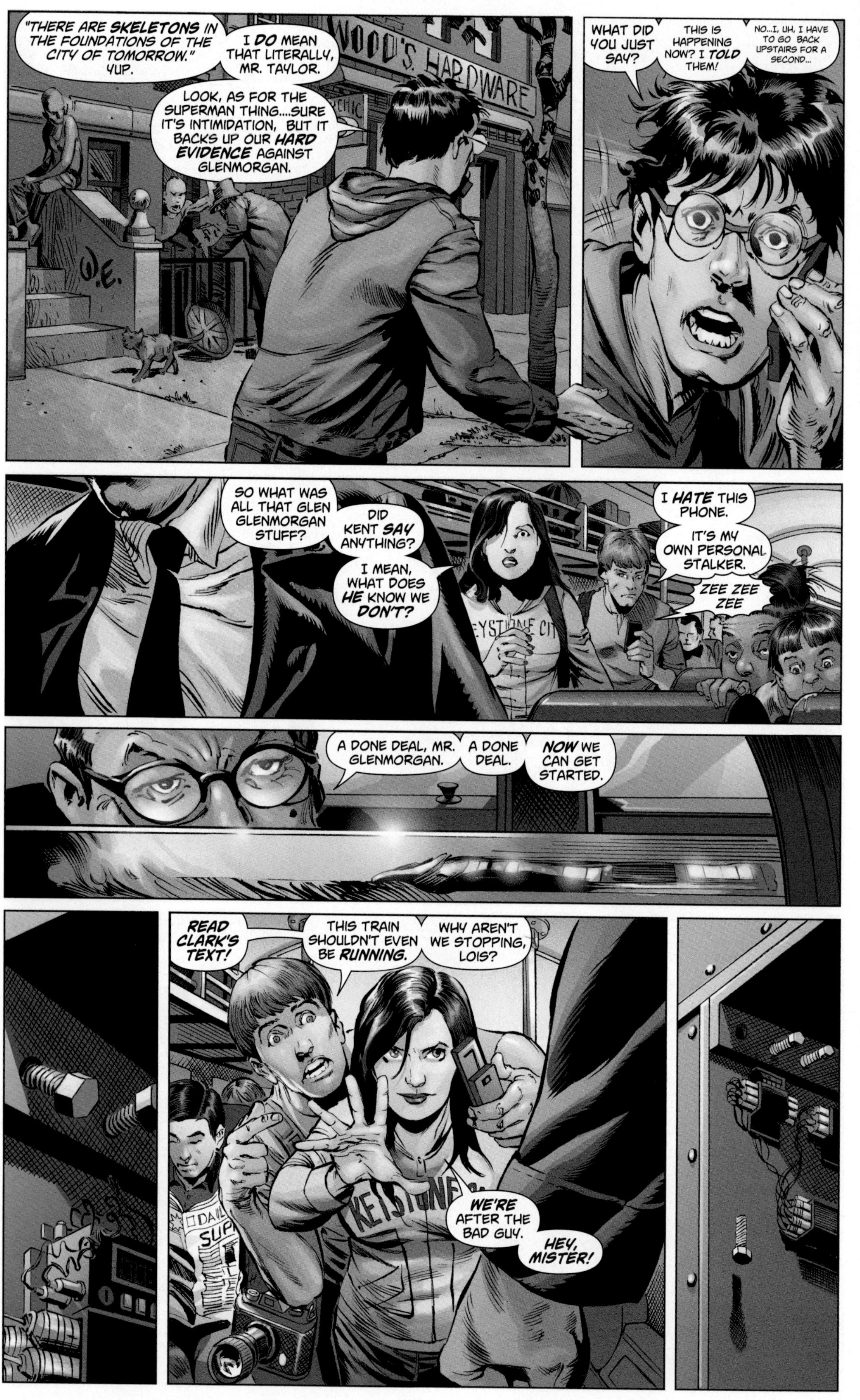
"THERE ARE SKELETONS IN THE FOUNDATIONS OF THE CITY OF TOMORROW." YUP.
I DO MEAN THAT LITERALLY, MR. TAYLOR.
LOOK, AS FOR THE SUPERMAN THING....SURE IT'S INTIMIDATION, BUT IT BACKS UP OUR HARD EVIDENCE AGAINST GLENMORGAN.
WOOD'S HARDWARE
WHAT DID YOU JUST SAY?
THIS IS HAPPENING NOW? I TOLD THEM!
NO...I, UH, I HAVE TO GO BACK UPSTAIRS FOR A SECOND...
SO WHAT WAS ALL THAT GLEN GLENMORGAN STUFF?
DID KENT SAY ANYTHING?
I MEAN, WHAT DOES HE KNOW WE DON'T?
I HATE THIS PHONE.
IT'S MY OWN PERSONAL STALKER.
ZEE ZEE ZEE
A DONE DEAL, MR. GLENMORGAN.
A DONE DEAL.
NOW WE CAN GET STARTED.
READ CLARK'S TEXT!
THIS TRAIN SHOULDN'T EVEN BE RUNNING.
WHY AREN'T WE STOPPING, LOIS?
WE'RE AFTER THE BAD GUY.
HEY, MISTER!

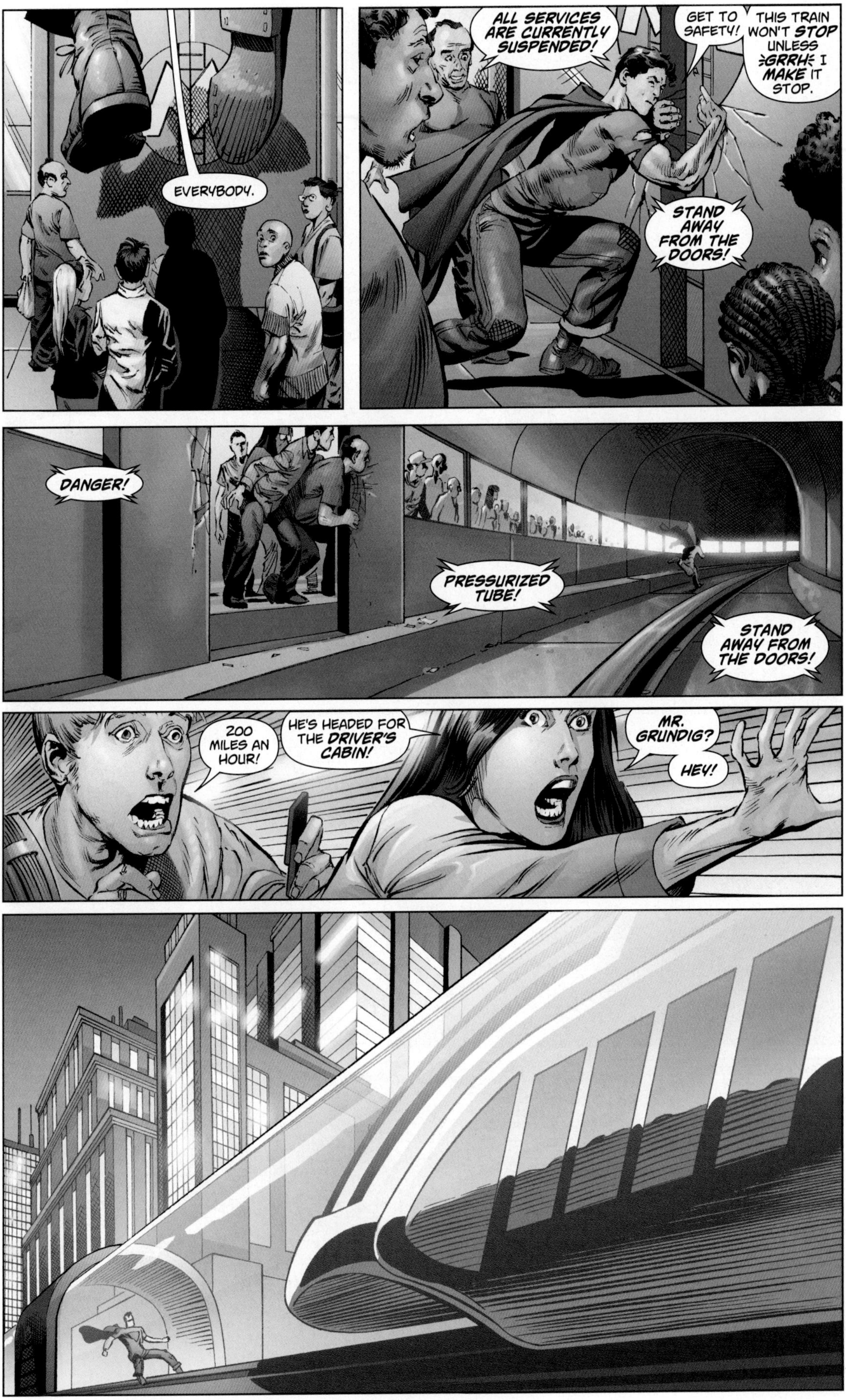
EVERYBODY.
ALL SERVICES ARE CURRENTLY SUSPENDED!
GET TO SAFETY!
THIS TRAIN WON'T STOP UNLESS GRRH I MAKE IT STOP.
STAND AWAY FROM THE DOORS!
DANGER!
PRESSURIZED TUBE!
STAND AWAY FROM THE DOORS!
200 MILES AN HOUR!
HE'S HEADED FOR THE DRIVER'S CABIN!
MR. GRUNDIG?
HEY!

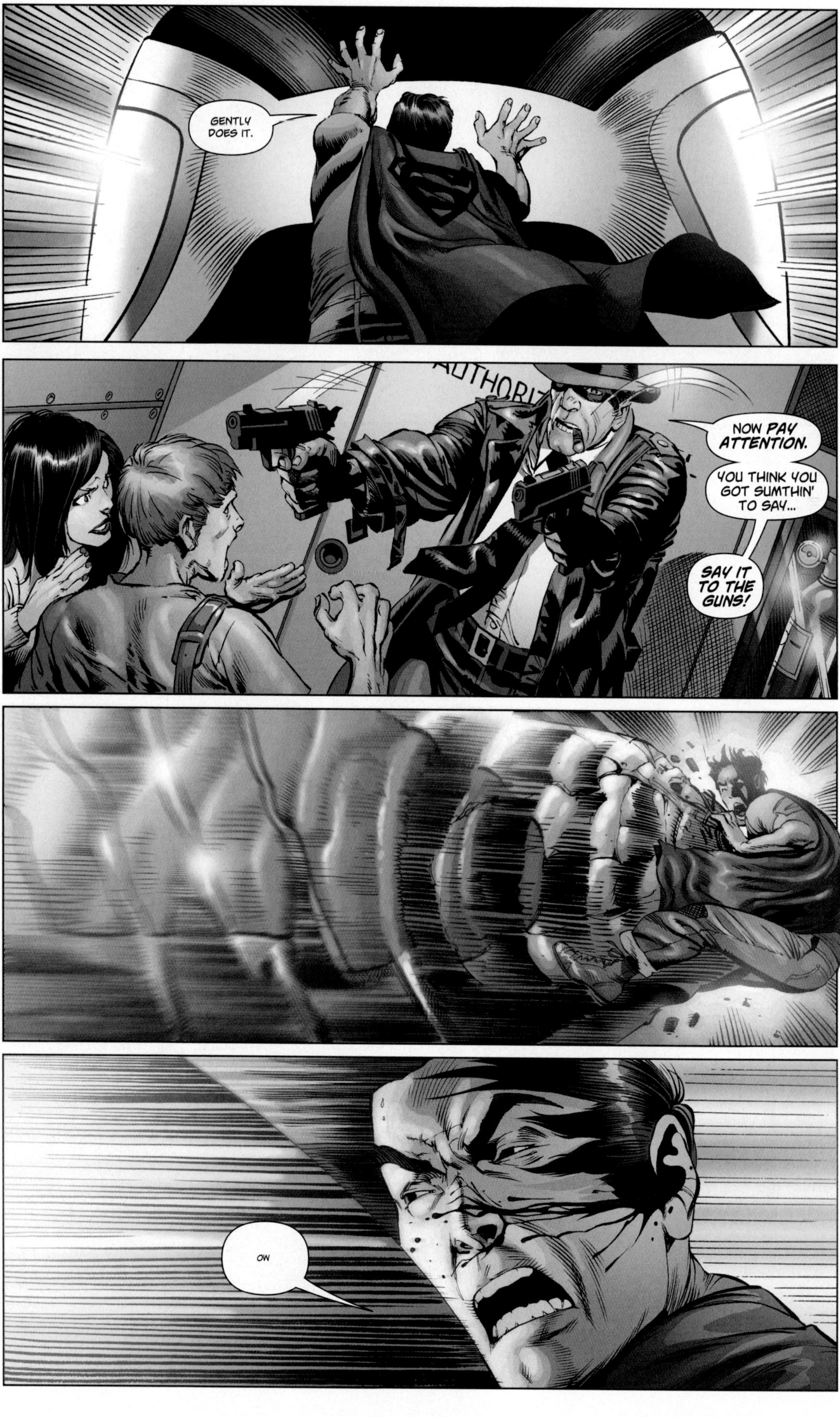
GENTLY DOES IT.
NOW PAY ATTENTION.
YOU THINK YOU GOT SUMTHIN' TO SAY...
SAY IT TO THE GUNS!
OW

GOT HIM!

WE'RE SLOWING DOWN!

WE'RE SAFE, EVERYBODY'S...

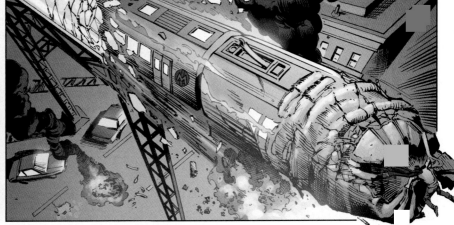

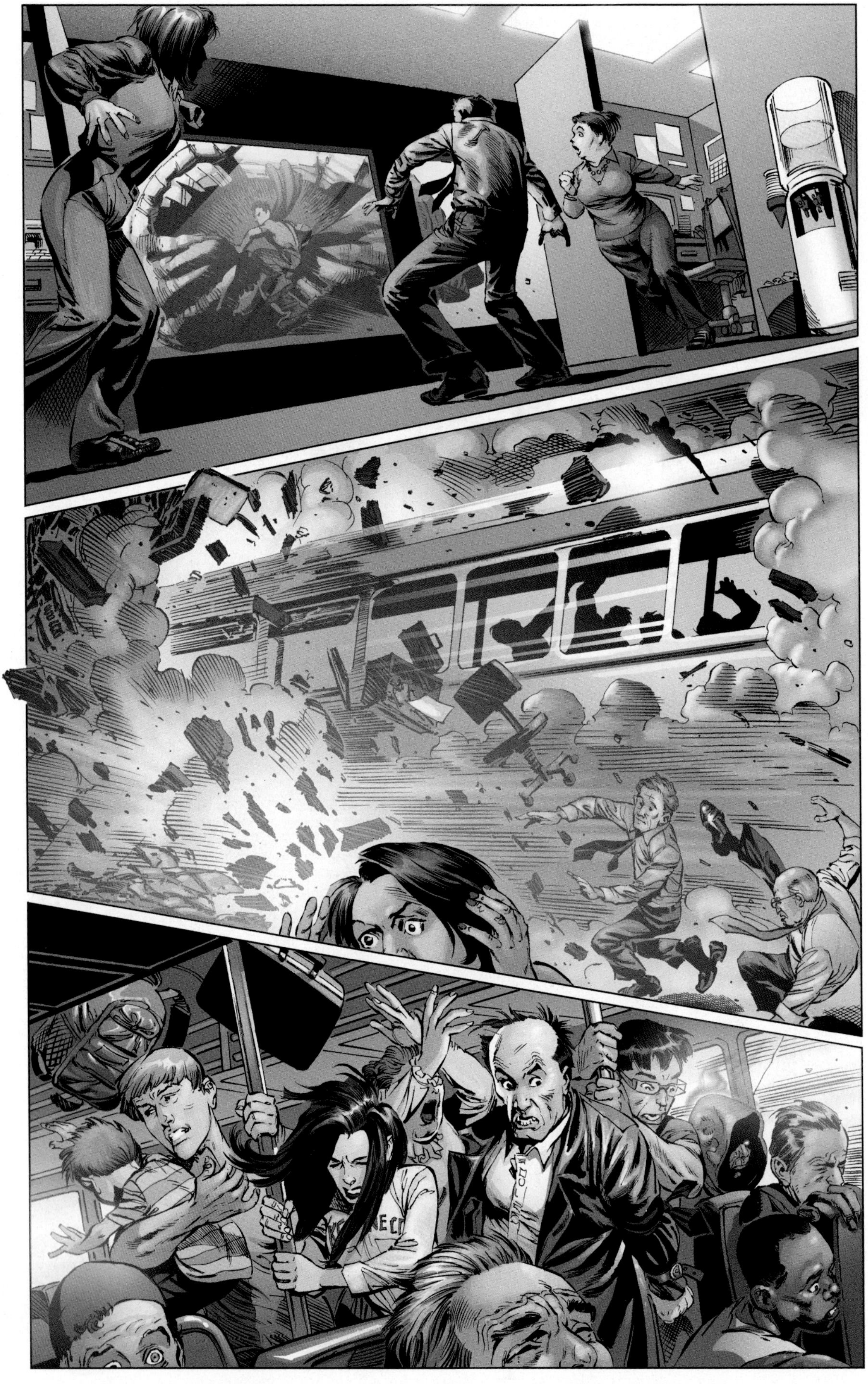

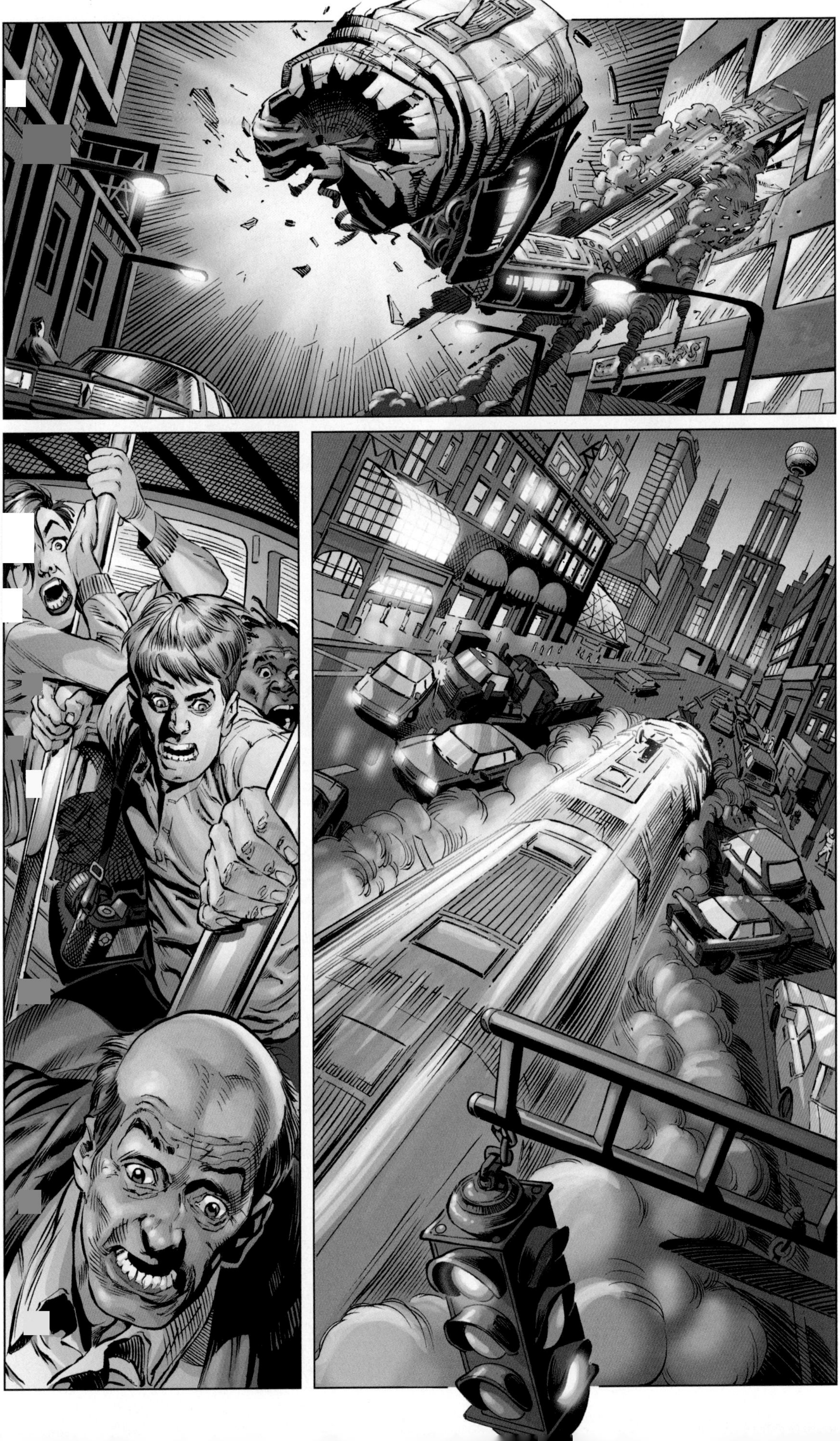

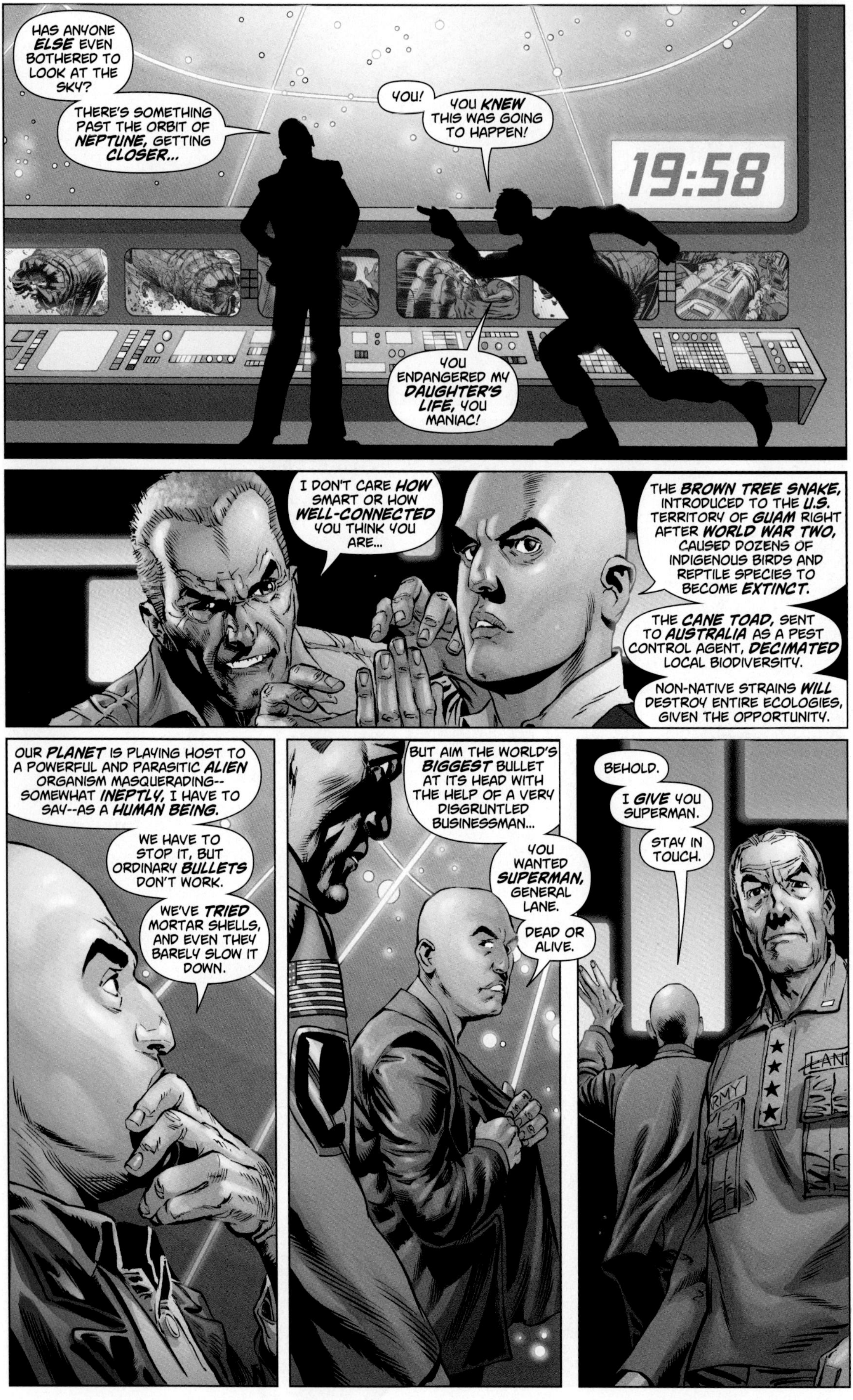
HAS ANYONE ELSE EVEN BOTHERED TO LOOK AT THE SKY?
THERE'S SOMETHING PAST THE ORBIT OF NEPTUNE, GETTING CLOSER...
YOU!
YOU KNEW THIS WAS GOING TO HAPPEN!
19:58
YOU ENDANGERED MY DAUGHTER'S LIFE, YOU MANIAC!
I DON'T CARE HOW SMART OR HOW WELL-CONNECTED YOU THINK YOU ARE...
THE BROWN TREE SNAKE, INTRODUCED TO THE U.S. TERRITORY OF GUAM RIGHT AFTER WORLD WAR TWO, CAUSED DOZENS OF INDIGENOUS BIRDS AND REPTILE SPECIES TO BECOME EXTINCT.
THE CANE TOAD, SENT TO AUSTRALIA AS A PEST CONTROL AGENT, DECIMATED LOCAL BIODIVERSITY.
NON-NATIVE STRAINS WILL DESTROY ENTIRE ECOLOGIES, GIVEN THE OPPORTUNITY.
OUR PLANET IS PLAYING HOST TO A POWERFUL AND PARASITIC ALIEN ORGANISM MASQUERADING--SOMEWHAT INEPTLY, I HAVE TO SAY--AS A HUMAN BEING.
WE HAVE TO STOP IT, BUT ORDINARY BULLETS DON'T WORK.
WE'VE TRIED MORTAR SHELLS, AND EVEN THEY BARELY SLOW IT DOWN.
BUT AIM THE WORLD'S BIGGEST BULLET AT ITS HEAD WITH THE HELP OF A VERY DISGRUNTLED BUSINESSMAN...
YOU WANTED SUPERMAN, GENERAL LANE.
DEAD OR ALIVE.
BEHOLD.
I GIVE YOU SUPERMAN.
STAY IN TOUCH.

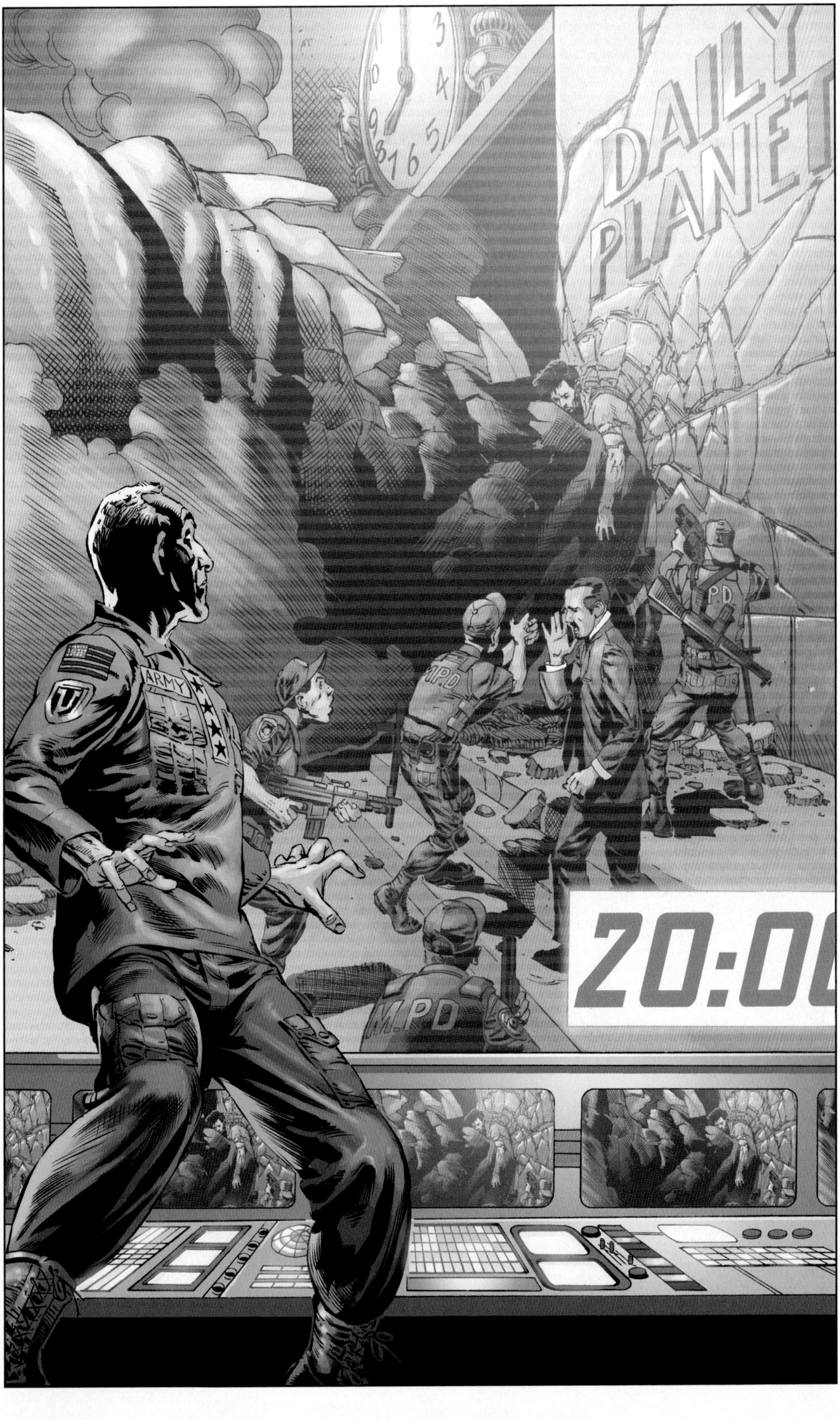
DAILY PLANET
ARMY
M.P.D
P.D.
M.PD
20:0

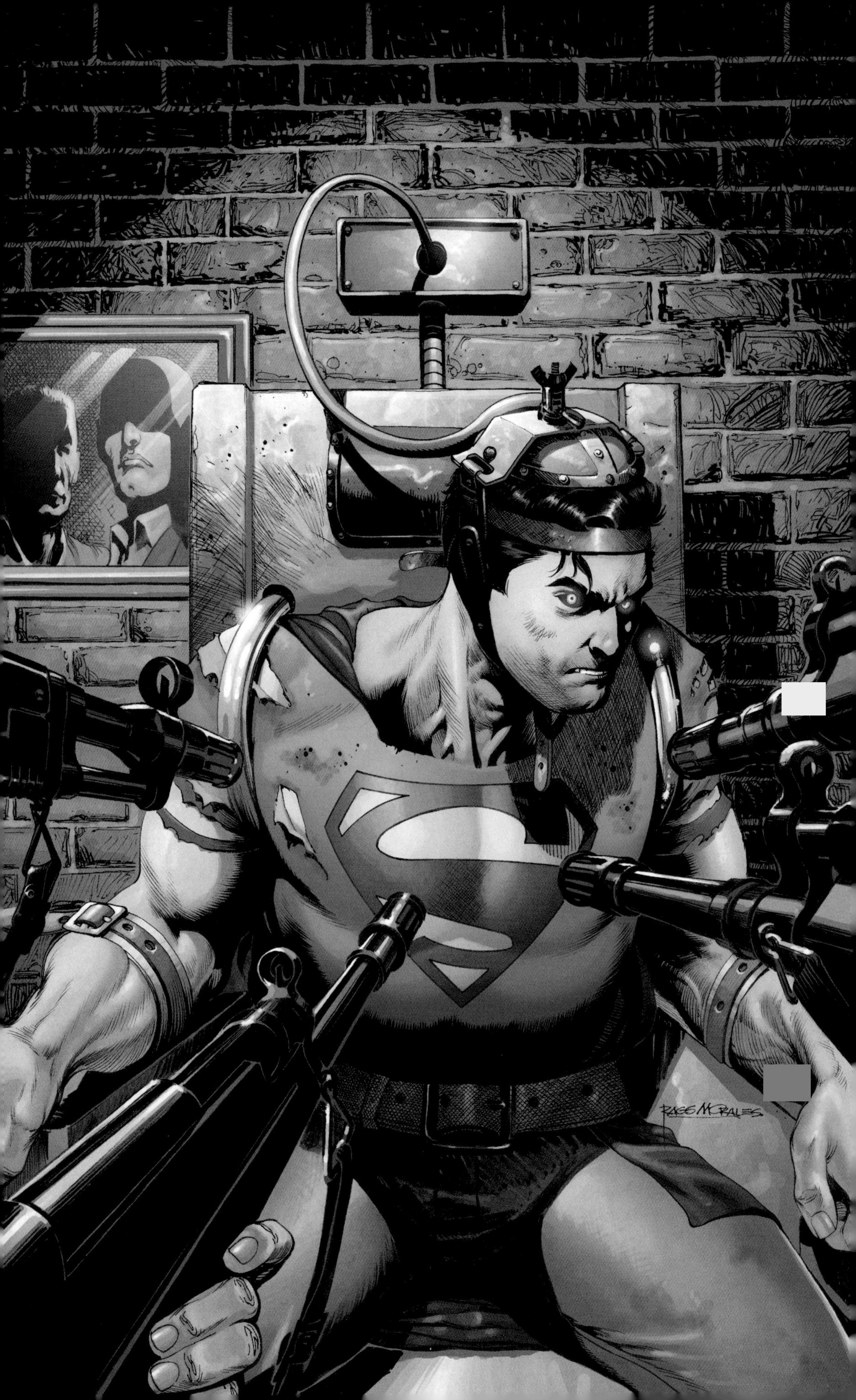
RAGS MORALES

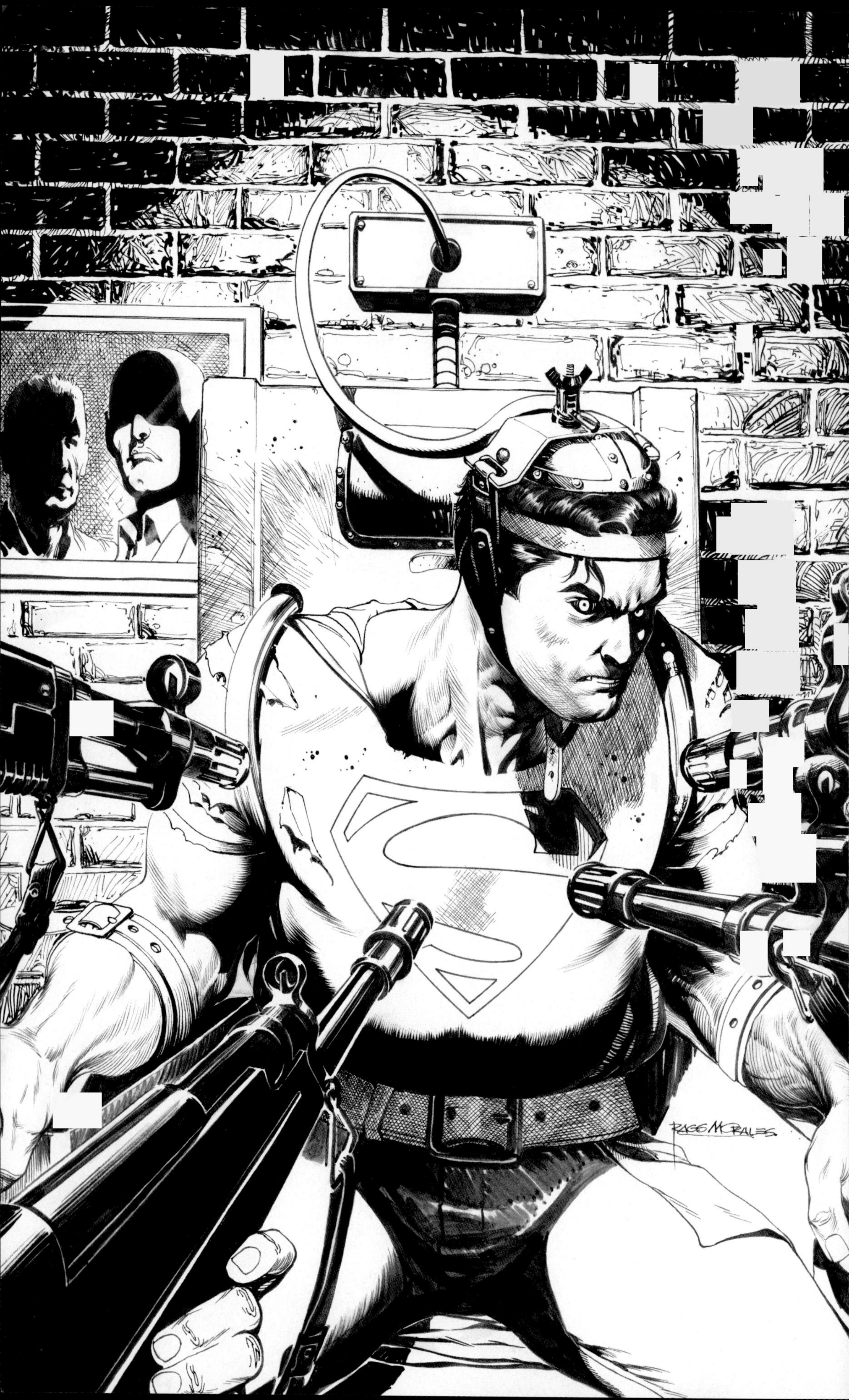
RAGS MORALES

HOW CAN ANYONE **DO** WHAT HE'S DOING?

WE RAN ENOUGH VOLTAGE THROUGH HIM TO FRY A **MOUNTAIN GORILLA.**

WHAT ARE WE **LOOKING** AT HERE?

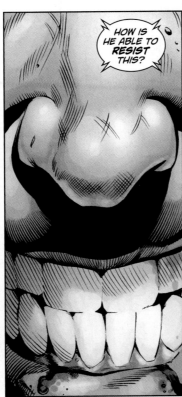

HOW IS HE ABLE TO **RESIST** THIS?

NO. NO.

HE'S BREAKING LOOSE!

JUICE HIM AGAIN!

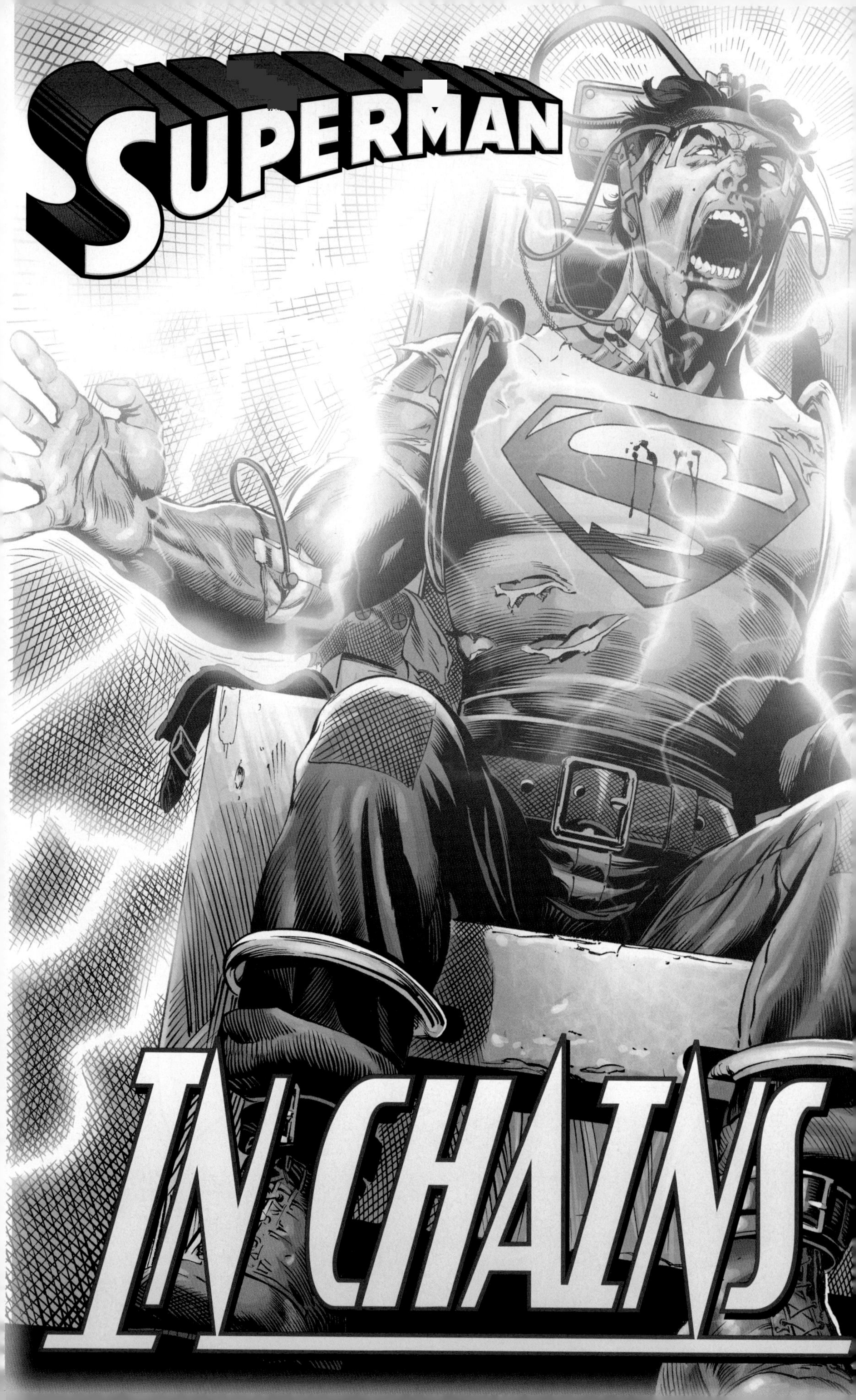
SUPERMAN
IN CHAINS

THIS IS. NUTS.

HIS HEARTRATE JUST *ACCELERATES,* THEN SLOWS BACK DOWN TO *NORMAL.*

"IT."

IT'S NOT *HUMAN.*

621311 25,5121 1091.3 1255 00.00

GRANT MORRISON
Writer
**RAGS MORALES &
BRENT ANDERSON**
Pencillers
**RICK BRYANT &
BRENT ANDERSON**
Inkers

DOCTOR LUTHOR... HE'S X-RAY OPAQUE.

"IT"!

TRY AGAIN FOR A *BLOOD SAMPLE.*

BRAD ANDERSON
Colorist
PATRICK BROSSEAU
Letterer
**RAGS MORALES &
BRAD ANDERSON**
Cover
ETHAN VAN SCIVER
Variant Cover
WIL MOSS
Associate Editor
MATT IDELSON
Editor
SUPERMAN created by
JERRY SIEGEL & JOE SHUSTER

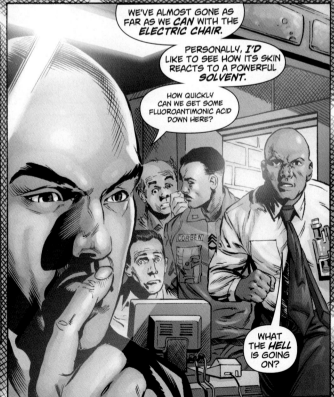

WE'VE ALMOST GONE AS FAR AS WE *CAN* WITH THE *ELECTRIC CHAIR.*

PERSONALLY, *I'D* LIKE TO SEE HOW ITS SKIN REACTS TO A POWERFUL *SOLVENT.*

HOW QUICKLY CAN WE GET SOME FLUOROANTIMONIC ACID DOWN HERE?

WHAT THE *HELL* IS GOING ON?

LUTHOR!

DOCTOR IRONS.

SERGEANT CORBEN.

WHAT CAN I DO TO MAKE YOUR LIVES BRIGHTER?

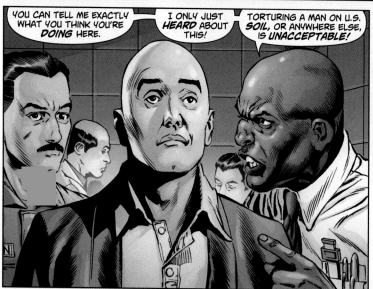

YOU CAN TELL ME EXACTLY WHAT YOU THINK YOU'RE *DOING* HERE.

I ONLY JUST *HEARD* ABOUT THIS!

TORTURING A MAN ON U.S. *SOIL*, OR ANYWHERE ELSE, IS *UNACCEPTABLE!*

THOSE LAWS APPLY TO *HUMAN BEINGS*, SURELY.

AND TELL ME HOW WE CAN *TORTURE* A SO-CALLED MAN WITH *STEEL-HARD* SKIN AND HAIR THAT CAN'T BE *CUT?*

TAKE A *LOOK.* HE'S *FINE.*

THAT'S HIM?

THAT BEAT-UP-LOOKING KID IS HIM?

"IT."

ARE YOU EVEN *LISTENING* TO ME?

I WANT THIS STOPPED *RIGHT NOW!*

HE'S SHAKING OFF THE GAS.

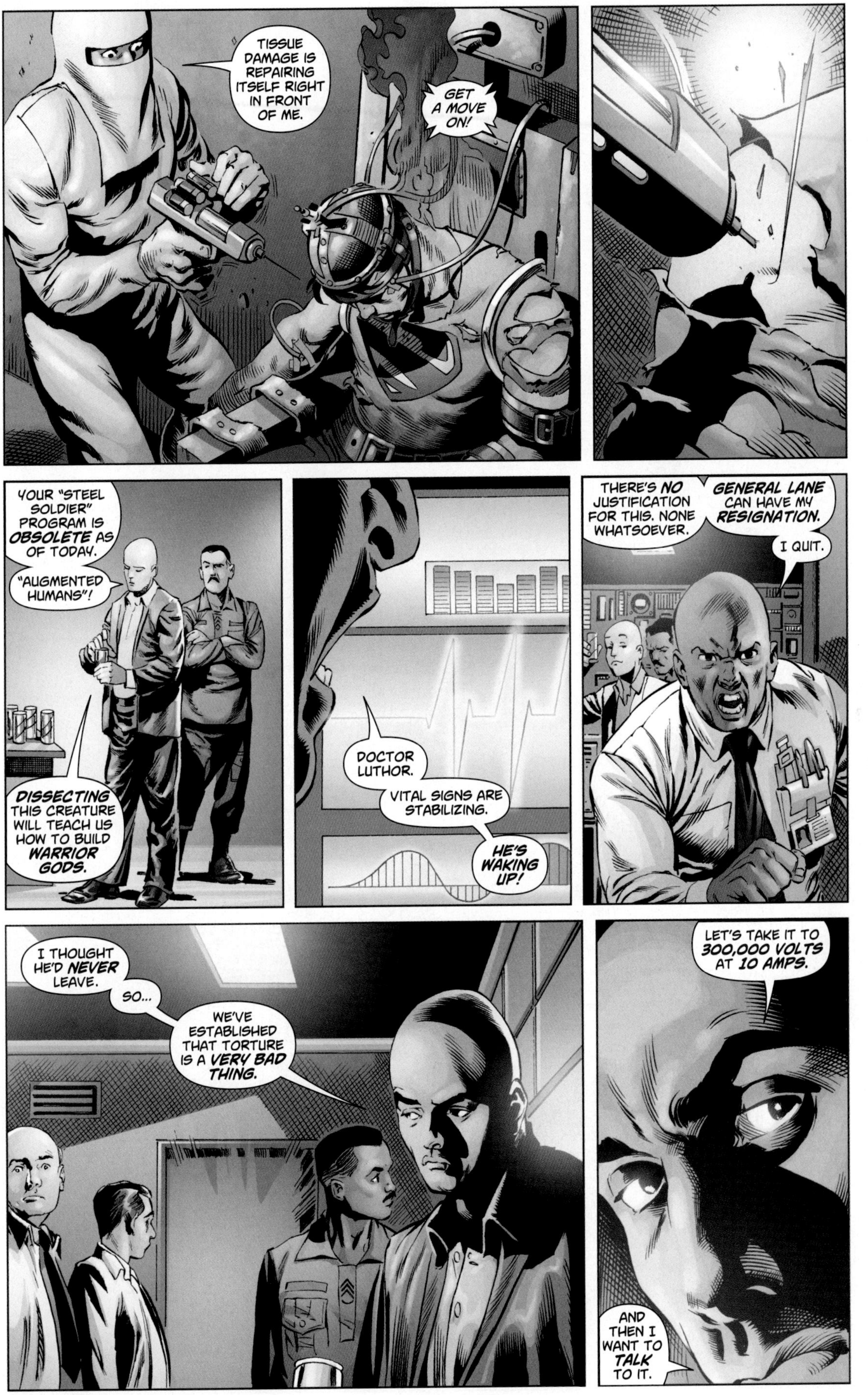
TISSUE DAMAGE IS REPAIRING ITSELF RIGHT IN FRONT OF ME.
GET A MOVE ON!
YOUR "STEEL SOLDIER" PROGRAM IS OBSOLETE AS OF TODAY.
"AUGMENTED HUMANS"!
DISSECTING THIS CREATURE WILL TEACH US HOW TO BUILD WARRIOR GODS.
DOCTOR LUTHOR.
VITAL SIGNS ARE STABILIZING.
HE'S WAKING UP!
THERE'S NO JUSTIFICATION FOR THIS. NONE WHATSOEVER.
GENERAL LANE CAN HAVE MY RESIGNATION.
I QUIT.
I THOUGHT HE'D NEVER LEAVE.
SO...
WE'VE ESTABLISHED THAT TORTURE IS A VERY BAD THING.
LET'S TAKE IT TO 300,000 VOLTS AT 10 AMPS.
AND THEN I WANT TO TALK TO IT.

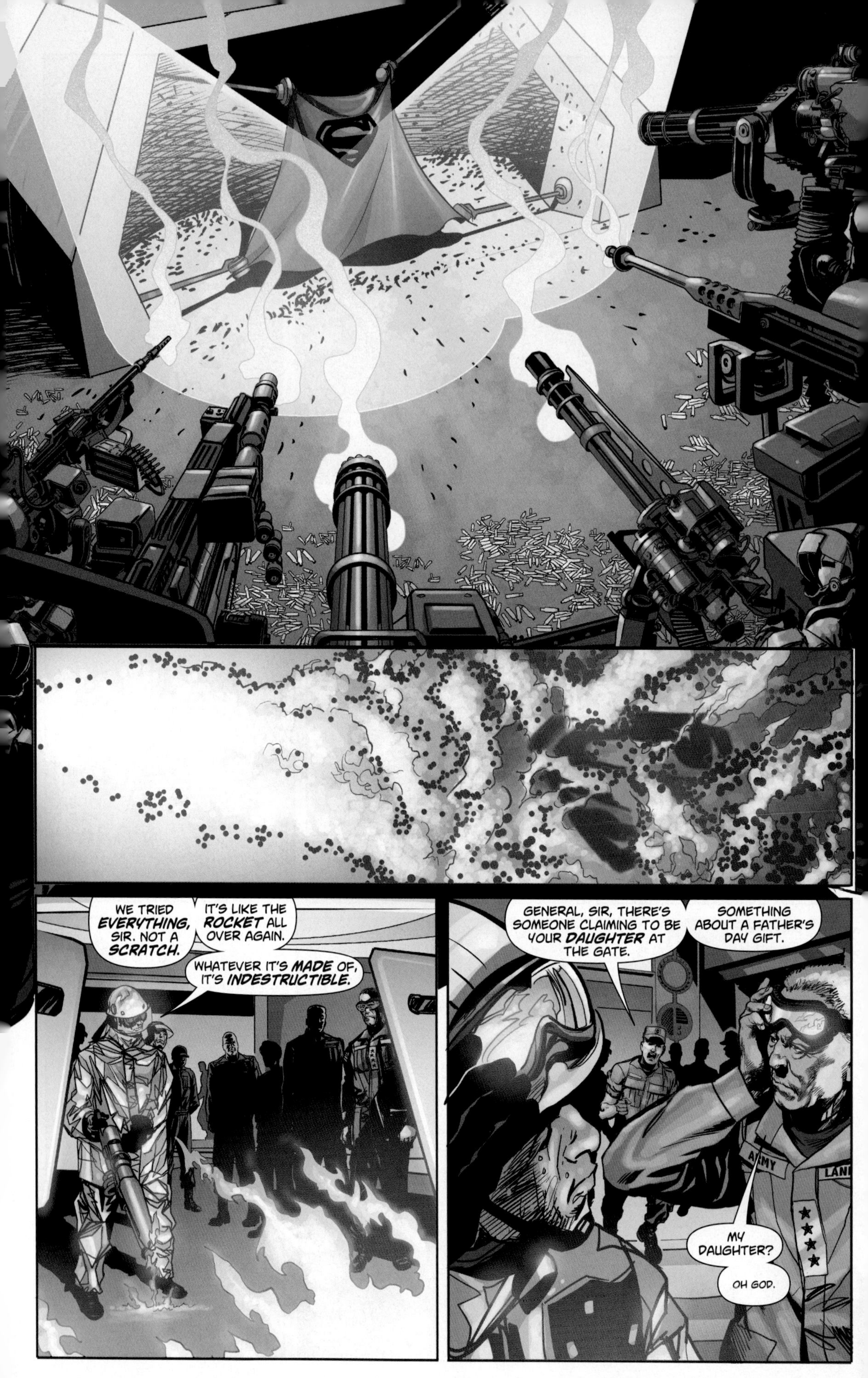
WE TRIED EVERYTHING, SIR. NOT A SCRATCH.
IT'S LIKE THE ROCKET ALL OVER AGAIN.
WHATEVER IT'S MADE OF, IT'S INDESTRUCTIBLE.
GENERAL, SIR, THERE'S SOMEONE CLAIMING TO BE YOUR DAUGHTER AT THE GATE.
SOMETHING ABOUT A FATHER'S DAY GIFT.
ARMY
MY DAUGHTER?
OH GOD.

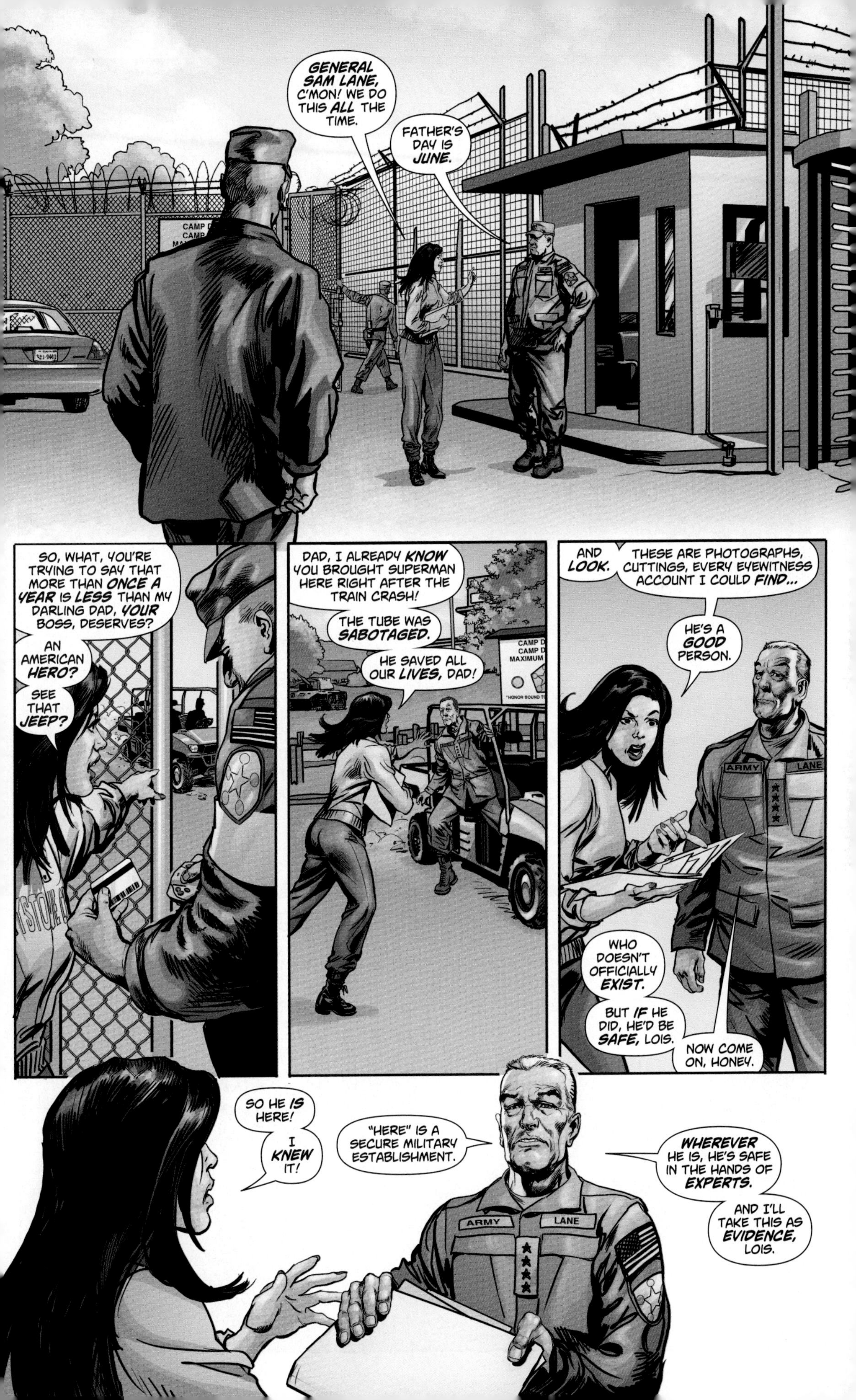
GENERAL SAM LANE, C'MON! WE DO THIS ALL THE TIME.
FATHER'S DAY IS JUNE.
CAMP D
CAMP
SO, WHAT, YOU'RE TRYING TO SAY THAT MORE THAN ONCE A YEAR IS LESS THAN MY DARLING DAD, YOUR BOSS, DESERVES?
AN AMERICAN HERO?
SEE THAT JEEP?
DAD, I ALREADY KNOW YOU BROUGHT SUPERMAN HERE RIGHT AFTER THE TRAIN CRASH!
THE TUBE WAS SABOTAGED.
HE SAVED ALL OUR LIVES, DAD!
CAMP D
CAMP D
MAXIMUM
"HONOR BOUND TO
AND LOOK.
THESE ARE PHOTOGRAPHS, CUTTINGS, EVERY EYEWITNESS ACCOUNT I COULD FIND...
HE'S A GOOD PERSON.
ARMY
LANE
WHO DOESN'T OFFICIALLY EXIST.
BUT IF HE DID, HE'D BE SAFE, LOIS.
NOW COME ON, HONEY.
SO HE IS HERE!
I KNEW IT!
"HERE" IS A SECURE MILITARY ESTABLISHMENT.
WHEREVER HE IS, HE'S SAFE IN THE HANDS OF EXPERTS.
AND I'LL TAKE THIS AS EVIDENCE, LOIS.
ARMY
LANE

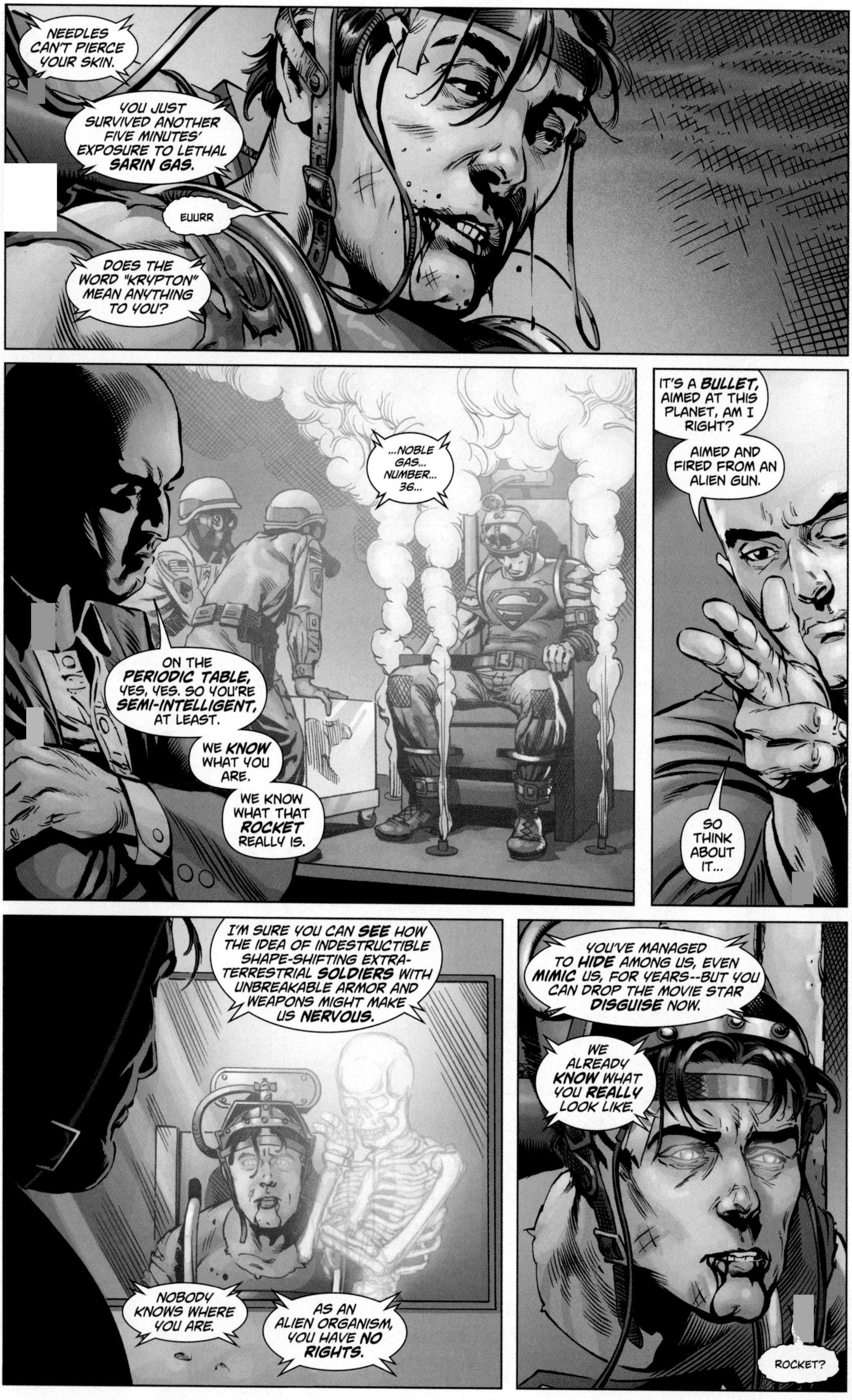
NEEDLES CAN'T PIERCE YOUR SKIN.
YOU JUST SURVIVED ANOTHER FIVE MINUTES' EXPOSURE TO LETHAL SARIN GAS.
EUURR
DOES THE WORD "KRYPTON" MEAN ANYTHING TO YOU?
...NOBLE GAS... NUMBER... 36...
ON THE PERIODIC TABLE, YES, YES. SO YOU'RE SEMI-INTELLIGENT, AT LEAST.
WE KNOW WHAT YOU ARE.
WE KNOW WHAT THAT ROCKET REALLY IS.
IT'S A BULLET, AIMED AT THIS PLANET, AM I RIGHT?
AIMED AND FIRED FROM AN ALIEN GUN.
SO THINK ABOUT IT...
I'M SURE YOU CAN SEE HOW THE IDEA OF INDESTRUCTIBLE SHAPE-SHIFTING EXTRA-TERRESTRIAL SOLDIERS WITH UNBREAKABLE ARMOR AND WEAPONS MIGHT MAKE US NERVOUS.
NOBODY KNOWS WHERE YOU ARE.
AS AN ALIEN ORGANISM, YOU HAVE NO RIGHTS.
YOU'VE MANAGED TO HIDE AMONG US, EVEN MIMIC US, FOR YEARS--BUT YOU CAN DROP THE MOVIE STAR DISGUISE NOW.
WE ALREADY KNOW WHAT YOU REALLY LOOK LIKE.
ROCKET?

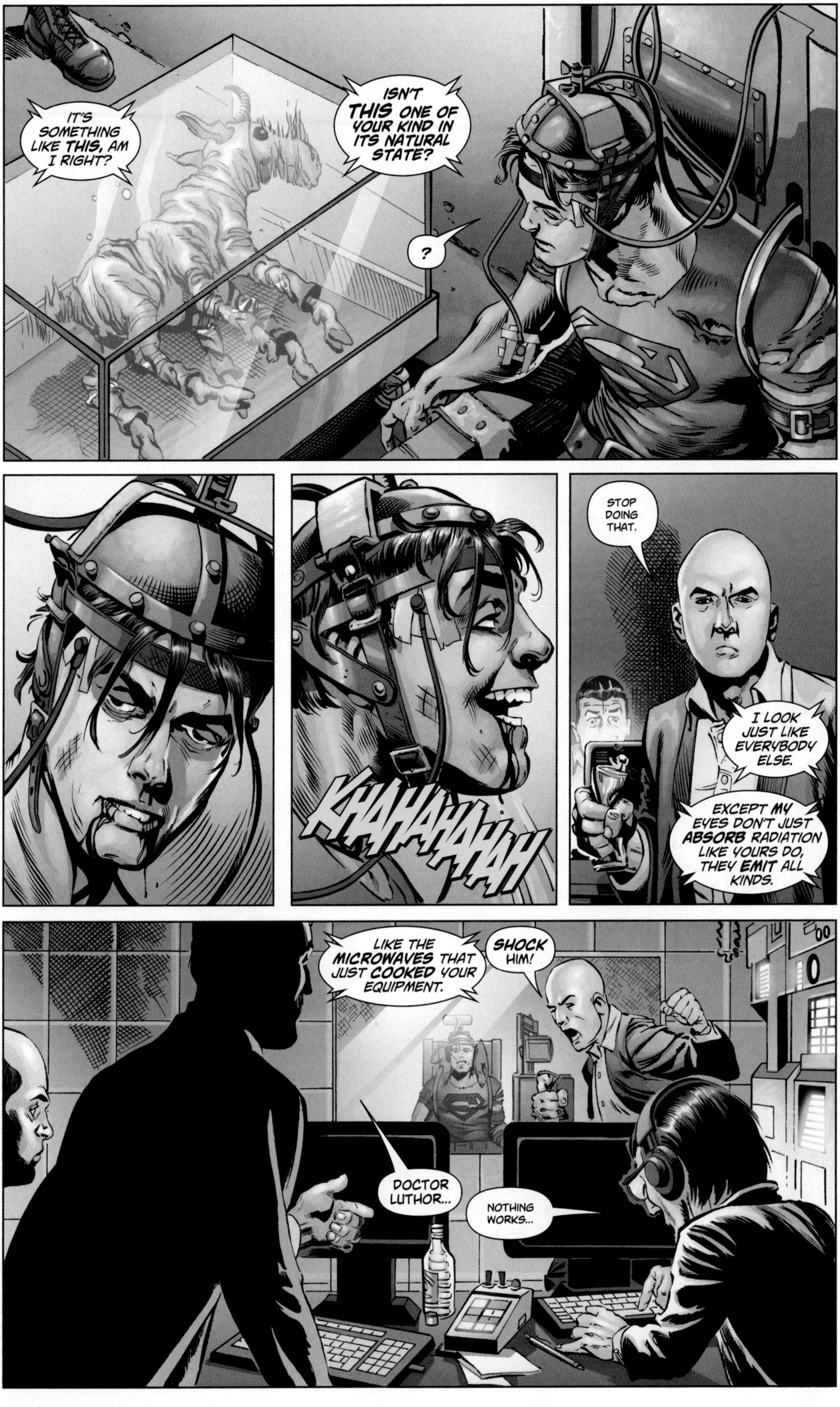
IT'S SOMETHING LIKE THIS, AM I RIGHT?
ISN'T THIS ONE OF YOUR KIND IN ITS NATURAL STATE?
?
KHAHAHAHAH
STOP DOING THAT.
I LOOK JUST LIKE EVERYBODY ELSE.
EXCEPT MY EYES DON'T JUST ABSORB RADIATION LIKE YOURS DO, THEY EMIT ALL KINDS.
LIKE THE MICROWAVES THAT JUST COOKED YOUR EQUIPMENT.
SHOCK HIM!
DOCTOR LUTHOR...
NOTHING WORKS...

DA-AD!

I HAVE *ENOUGH* ON AN ALREADY *OVERBURDENED* PLATE OF UNPROCESSED *SEWAGE* RIGHT NOW, LOIS.

JOHN, *YOU* TALK HER DOWN.

LOIS, HEY...

LOIS.

JOHN, PLEASE...

I'VE *KNOWN* ABOUT *STEEL SOLDIER* SINCE I WAS A *KID*, DAD!

WOW. IT'S *GREAT* TO SEE YOU AGAIN... I REGREW THE *MUSTACHE*.

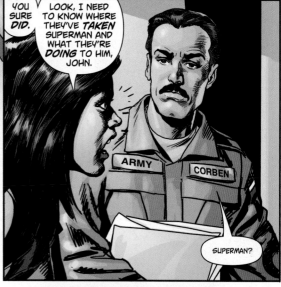

YOU SURE *DID.*

LOOK, I NEED TO KNOW WHERE THEY'VE *TAKEN* SUPERMAN AND WHAT THEY'RE *DOING* TO HIM, JOHN.

SUPERMAN?

C'MON, JOHN. WHERE IS HE?

WHAT'S IT GOT TO DO WITH *SUPERMAN?*

WHAT HAPPENED TO *US*, LOIS?

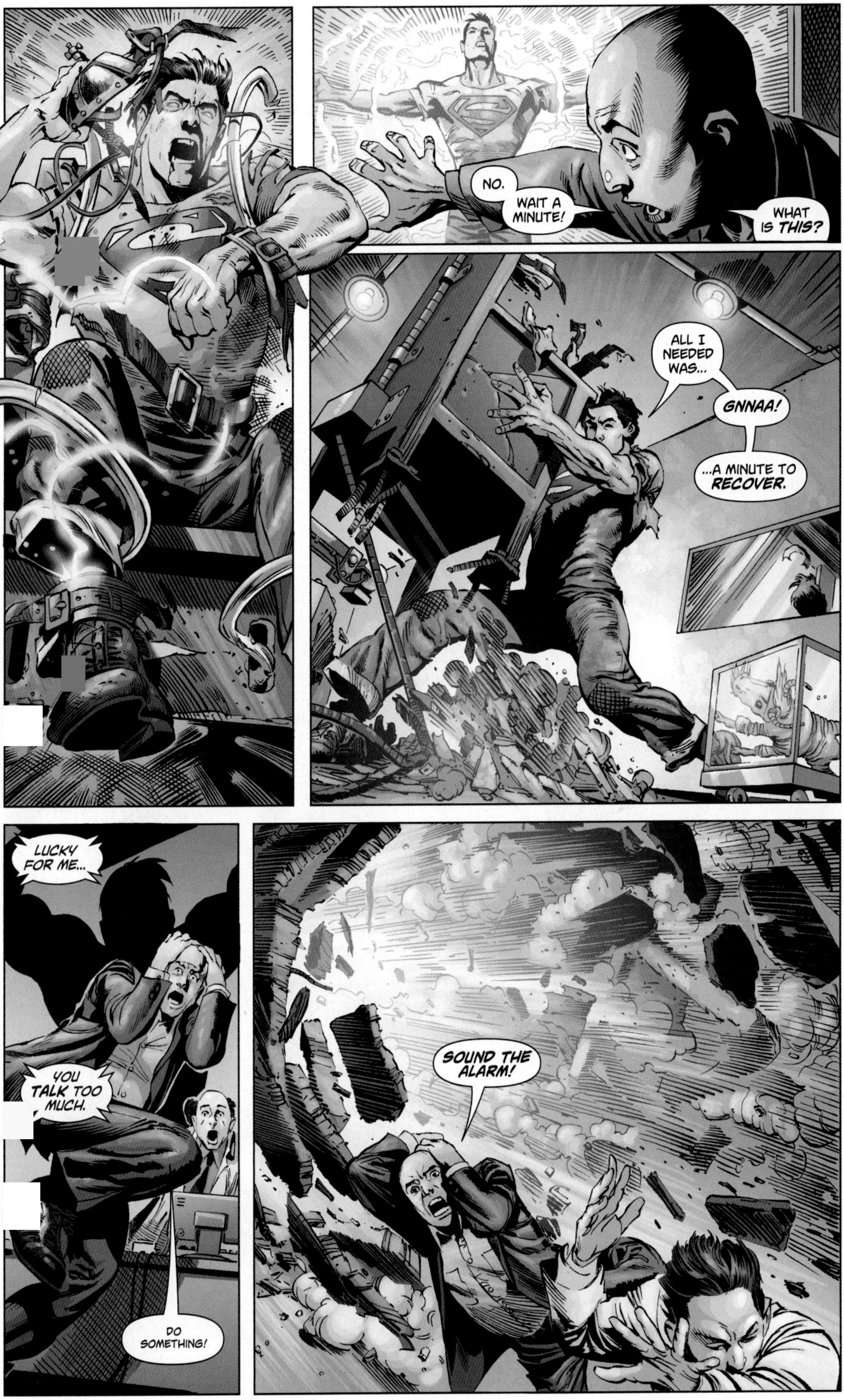
NO.
WAIT A MINUTE!
WHAT IS THIS?
ALL I NEEDED WAS...
GNNAA!
...A MINUTE TO RECOVER.
LUCKY FOR ME...
YOU TALK TOO MUCH.
DO SOMETHING!
SOUND THE ALARM!

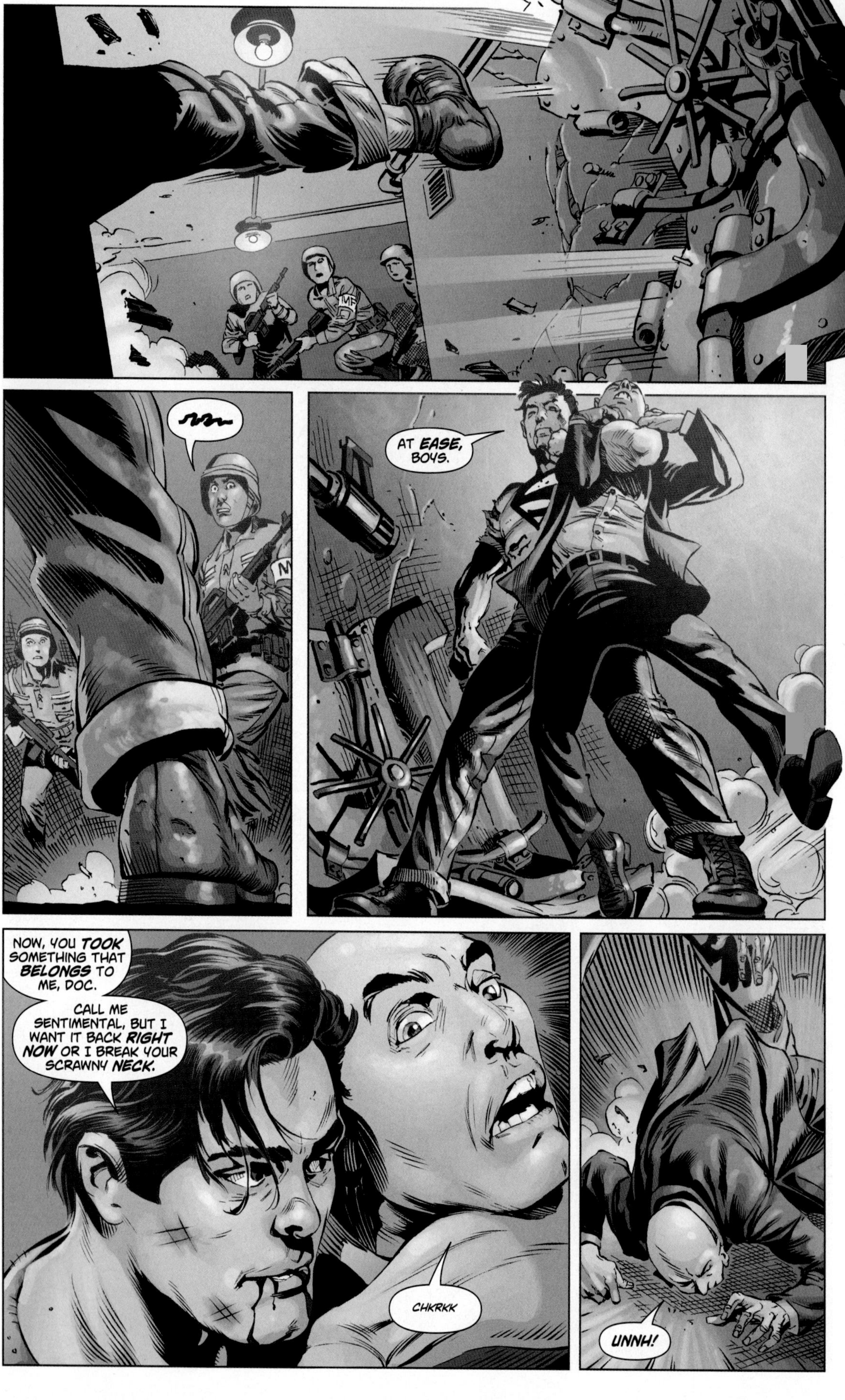
AT EASE, BOYS.
NOW, YOU TOOK SOMETHING THAT BELONGS TO ME, DOC.
CALL ME SENTIMENTAL, BUT I WANT IT BACK RIGHT NOW OR I BREAK YOUR SCRAWNY NECK.
CHKRKK
UNNH!

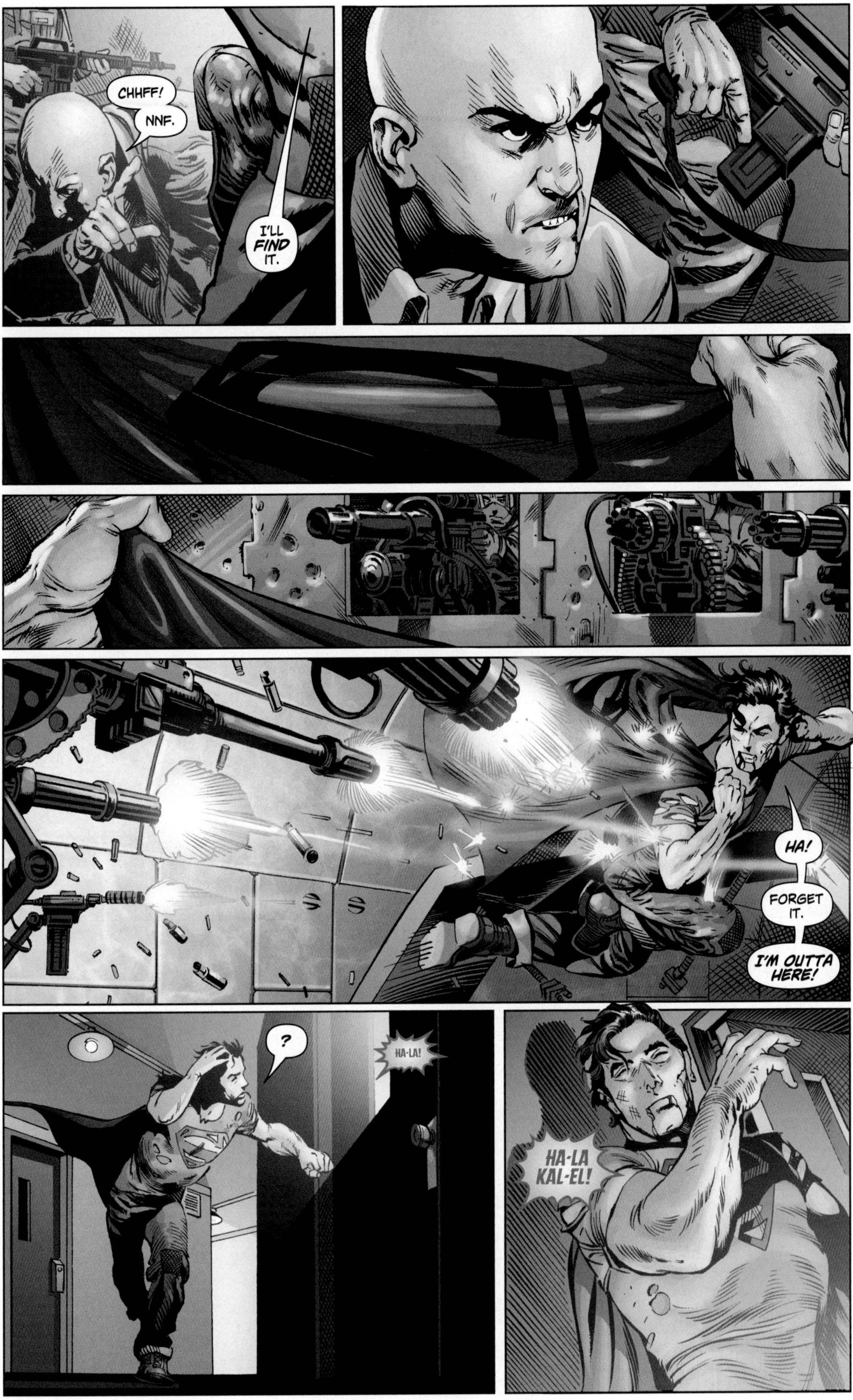
CHHFF!
NNF.
I'LL FIND IT.
HA!
FORGET IT.
I'M OUTTA HERE!
?
HA-LA!
HA-LA KAL-EL!

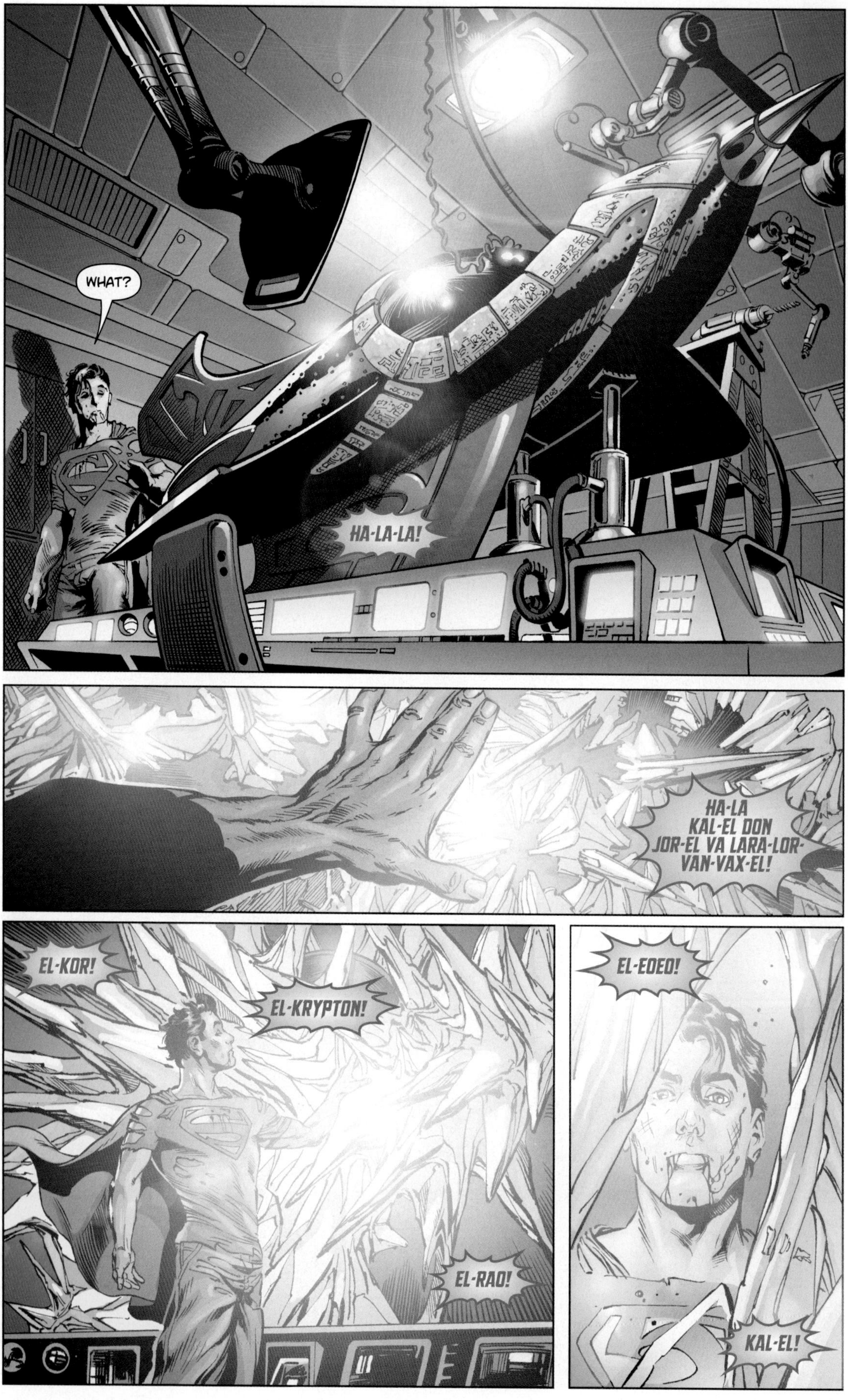
WHAT?
HA-LA-LA!
HA-LA KAL-EL DON JOR-EL VA LARA-LOR-VAN-VAX-EL!
EL-KOR!
EL-KRYPTON!
EL-RAO!
EL-EOEO!
KAL-EL!

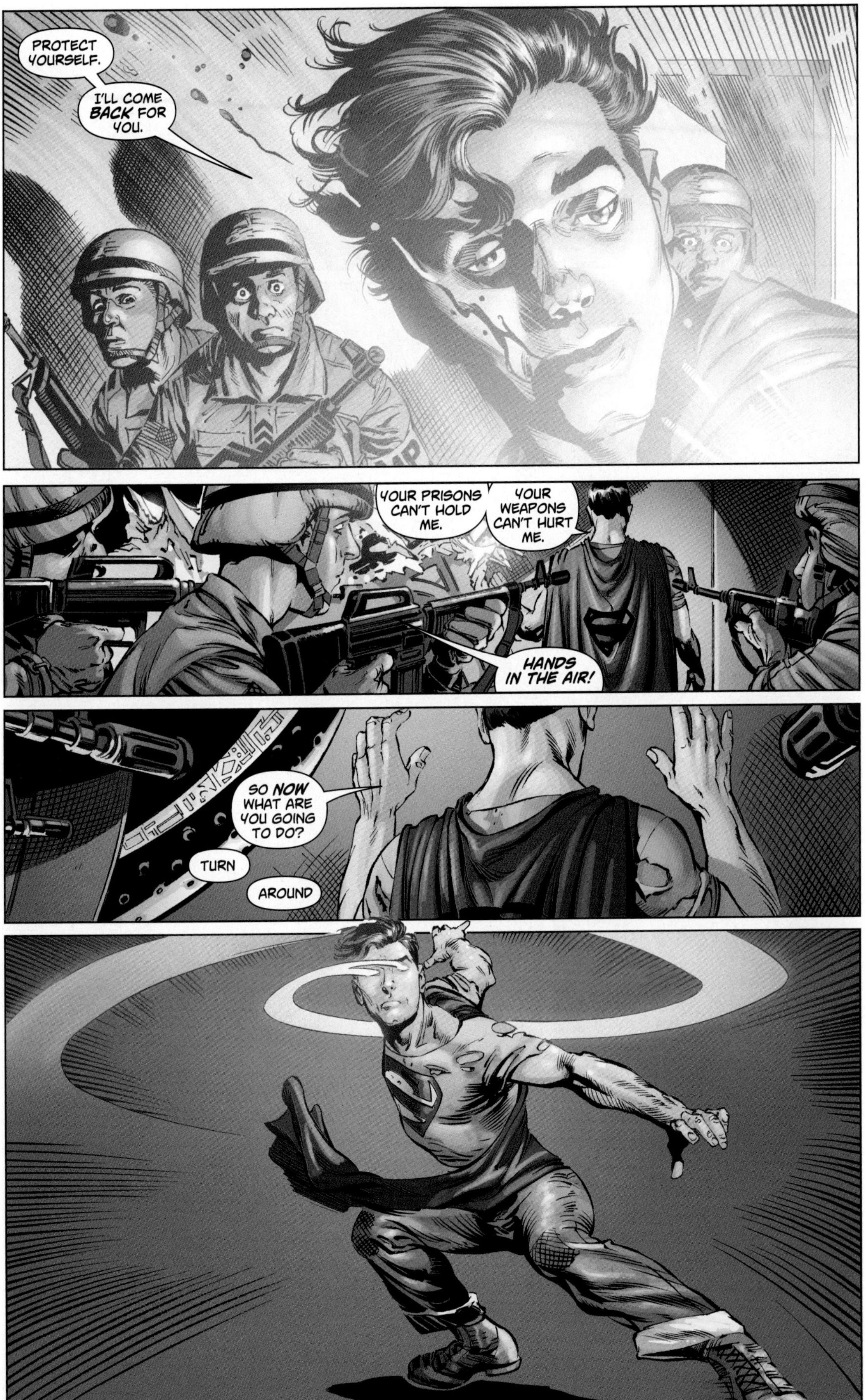
PROTECT YOURSELF.
I'LL COME BACK FOR YOU.
YOUR PRISONS CAN'T HOLD ME.
YOUR WEAPONS CAN'T HURT ME.
HANDS IN THE AIR!
SO NOW WHAT ARE YOU GOING TO DO?
TURN
AROUND

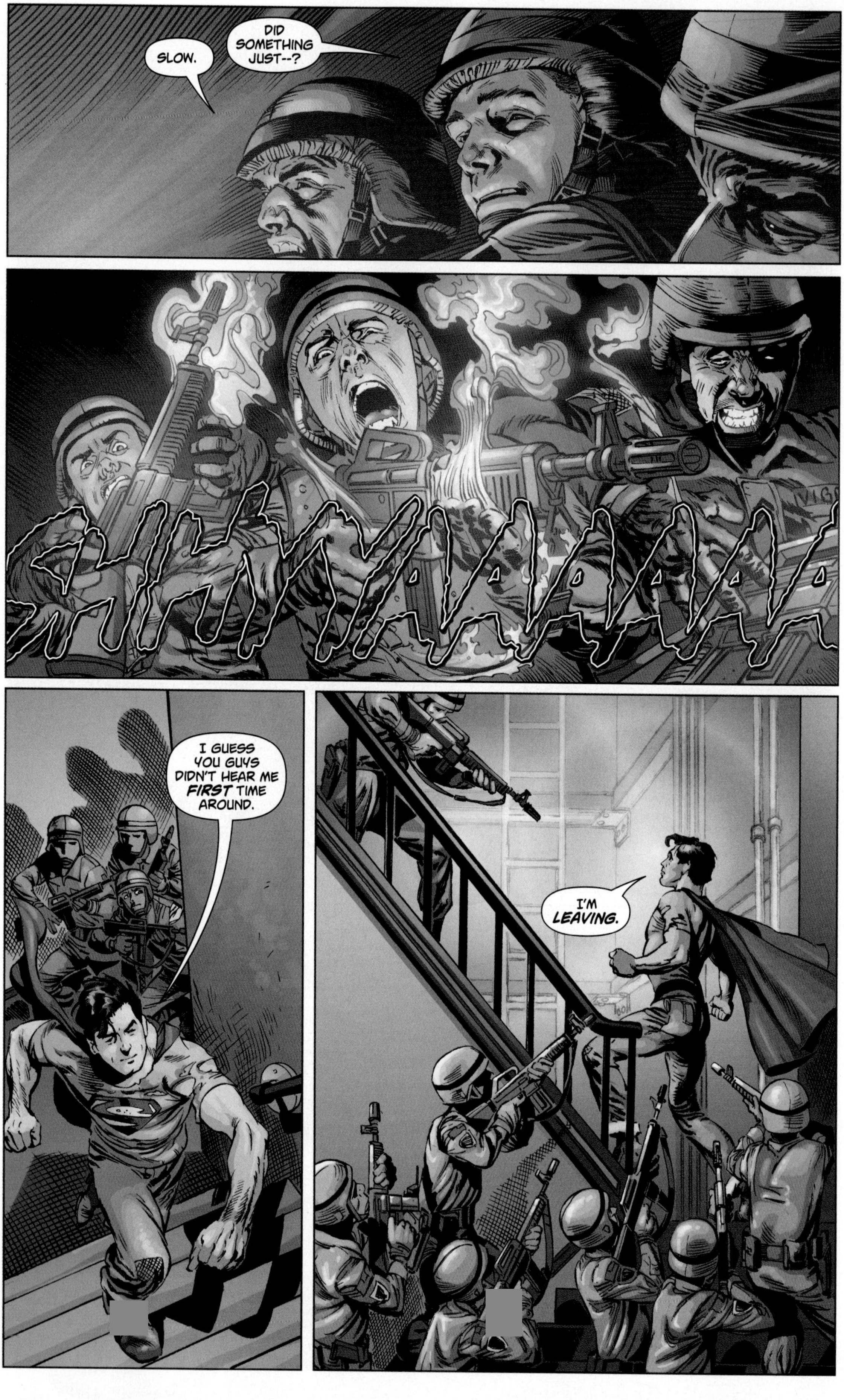
SLOW.
DID SOMETHING JUST--?
SHHWAAAAAA
I GUESS YOU GUYS DIDN'T HEAR ME FIRST TIME AROUND.
I'M LEAVING.

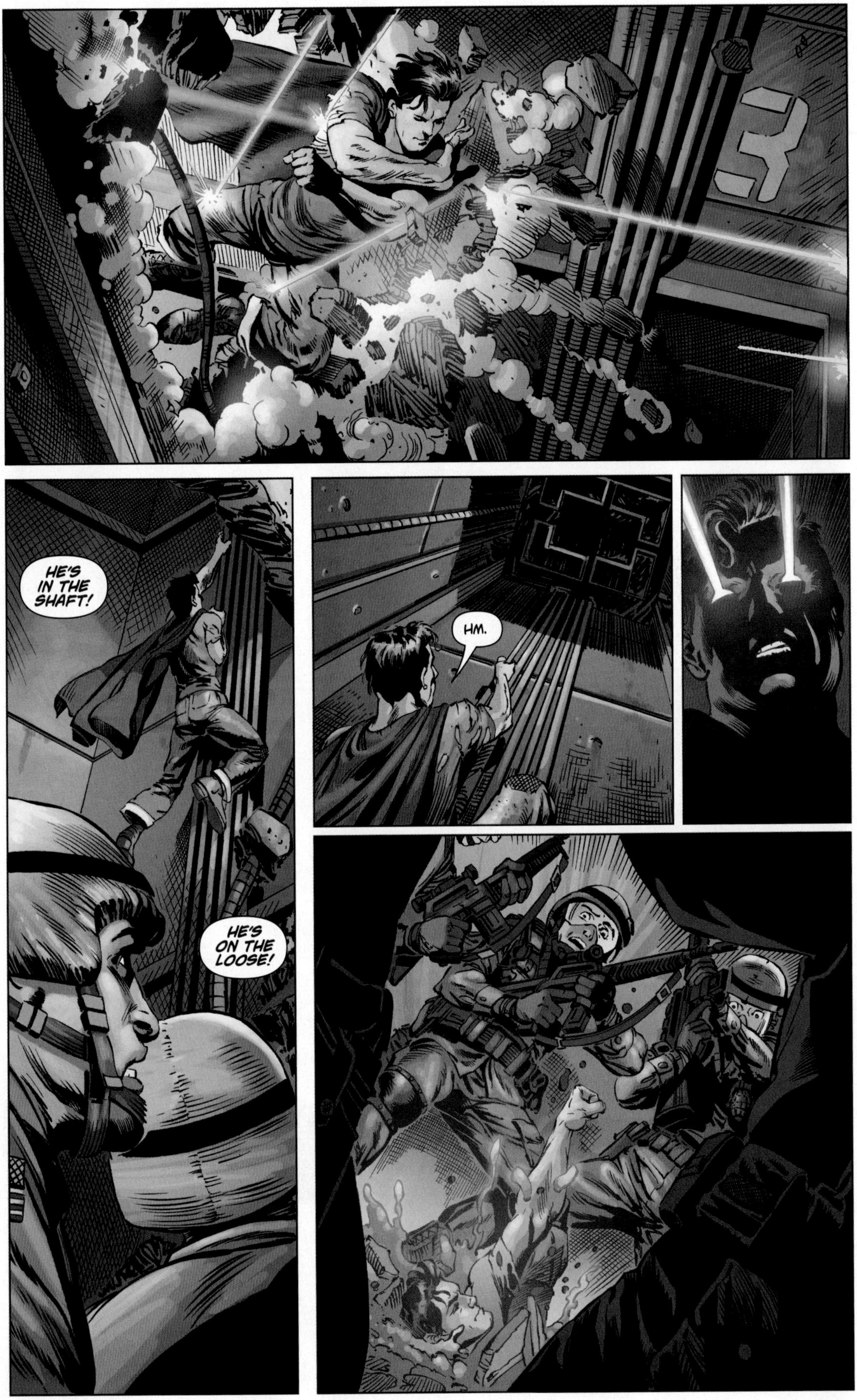
HE'S IN THE SHAFT!
HM.
HE'S ON THE LOOSE!

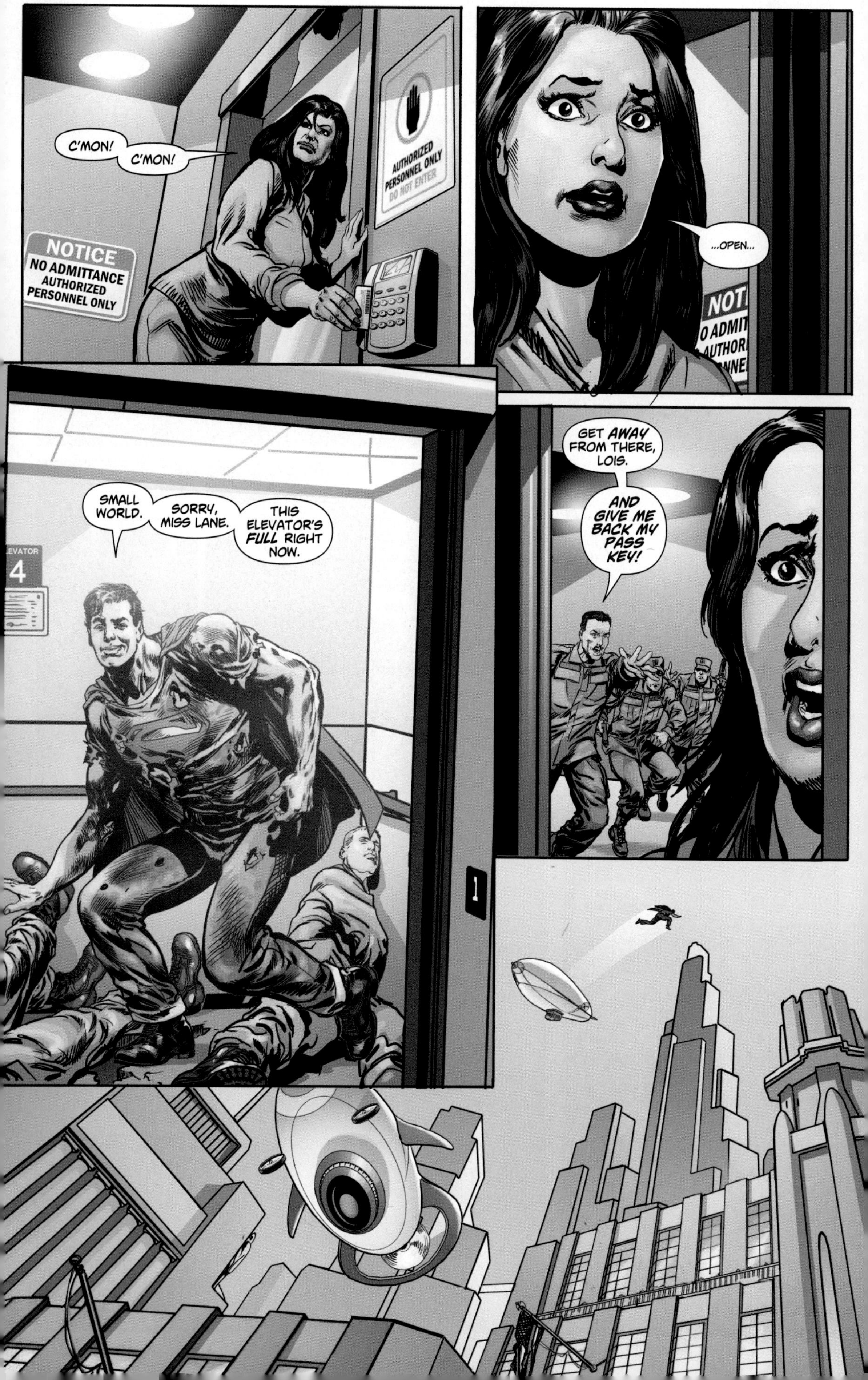
C'MON!
C'MON!
AUTHORIZED PERSONNEL ONLY
DO NOT ENTER
NOTICE
NO ADMITTANCE
AUTHORIZED PERSONNEL ONLY
...OPEN...
SMALL WORLD.
SORRY, MISS LANE.
THIS ELEVATOR'S FULL RIGHT NOW.
GET AWAY FROM THERE, LOIS.
AND GIVE ME BACK MY PASS KEY!

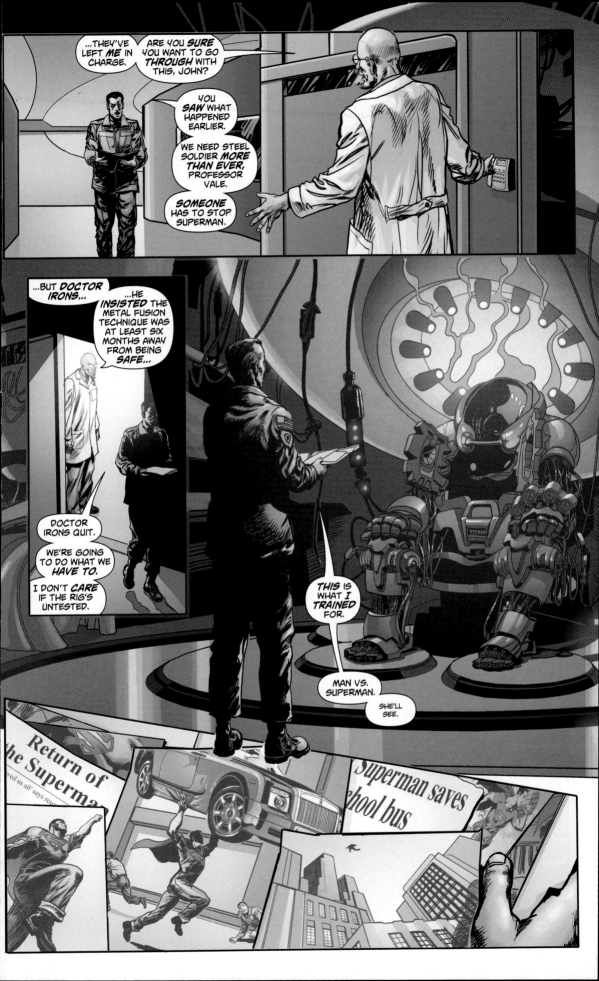

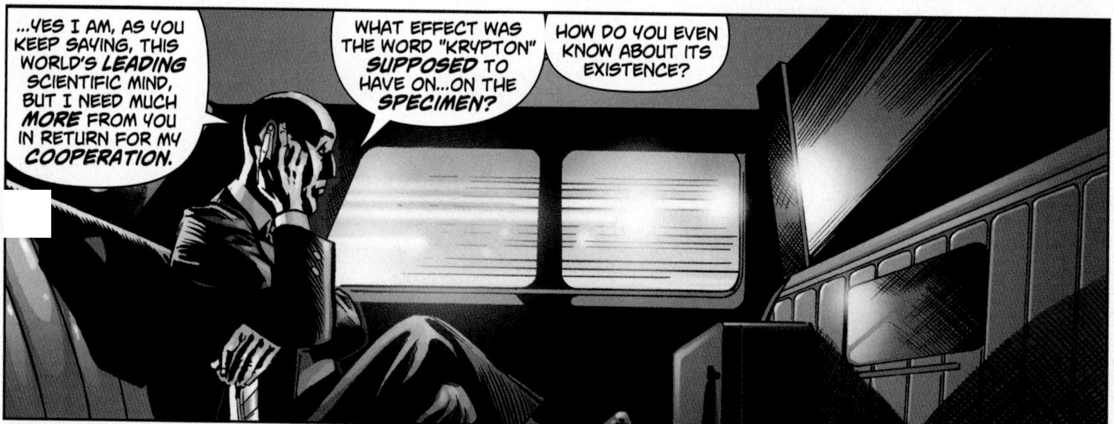
...YES I AM, AS YOU KEEP SAYING, THIS WORLD'S LEADING SCIENTIFIC MIND, BUT I NEED MUCH MORE FROM YOU IN RETURN FOR MY COOPERATION.
WHAT EFFECT WAS THE WORD "KRYPTON" SUPPOSED TO HAVE ON...ON THE SPECIMEN?
HOW DO YOU EVEN KNOW ABOUT ITS EXISTENCE?

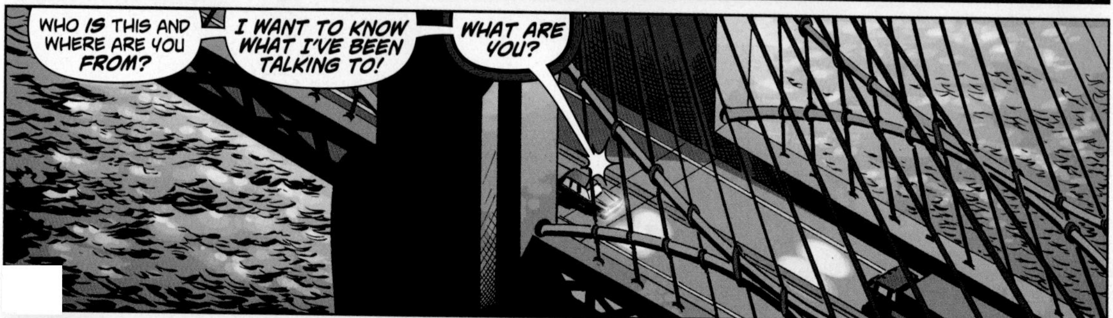
WHO IS THIS AND WHERE ARE YOU FROM?
I WANT TO KNOW WHAT I'VE BEEN TALKING TO!
WHAT ARE YOU?

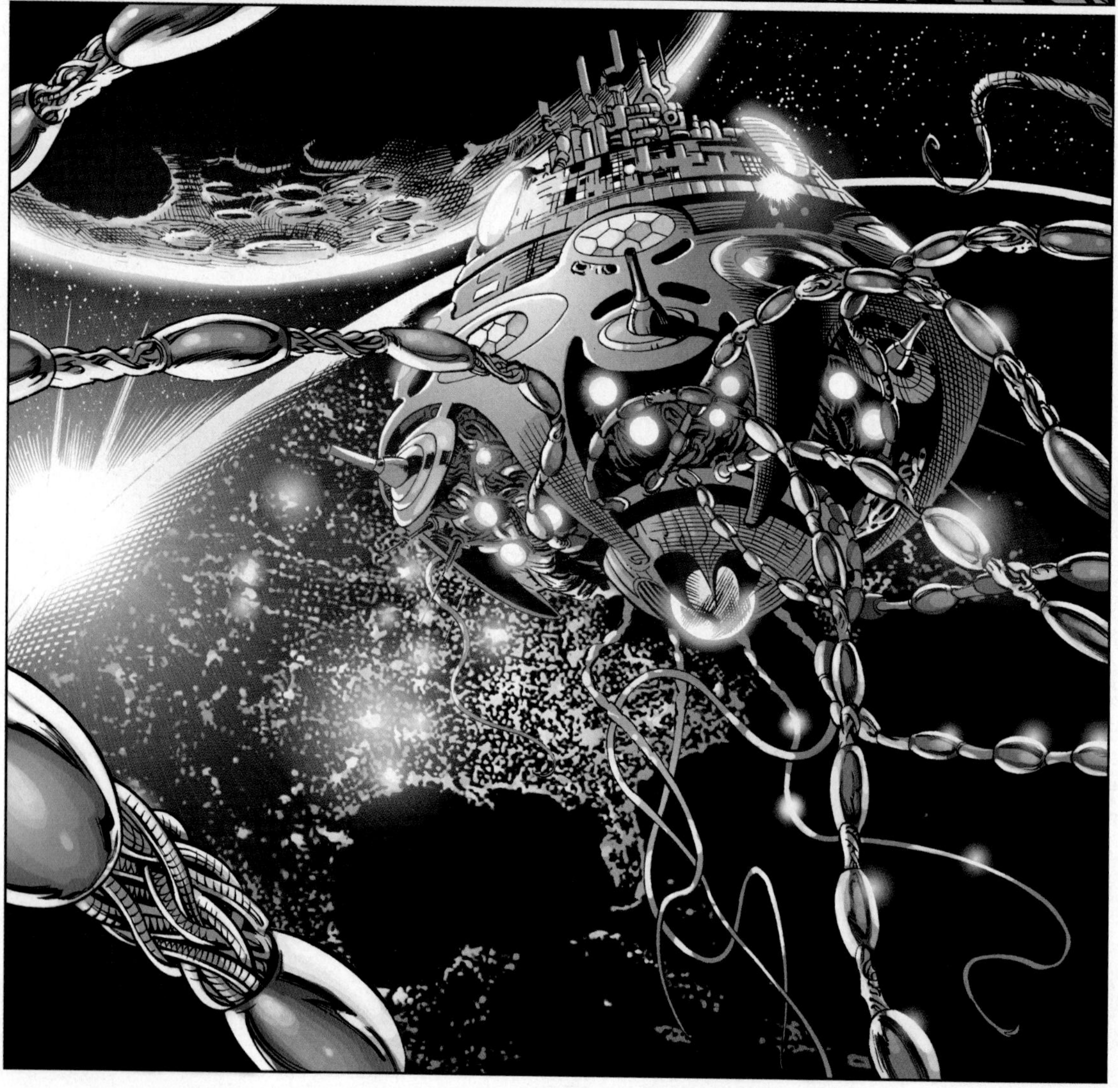

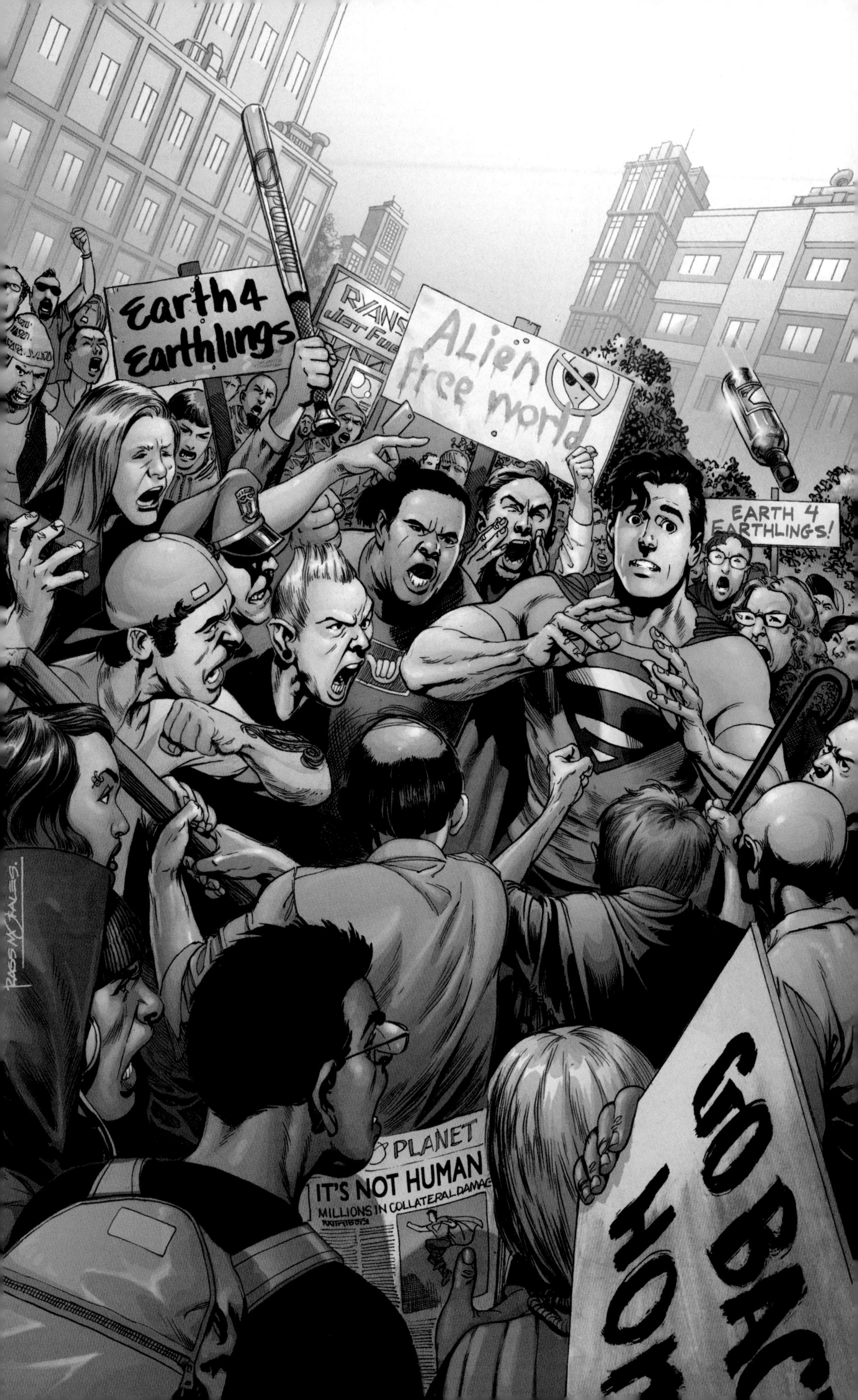
Earth 4 Earthlings
RYANS
JUST FUE
Alien free world
EARTH 4 EARTHLINGS!
PLANET
IT'S NOT HUMAN
MILLIONS IN COLLATERAL DAMAG
GO BAC
HO

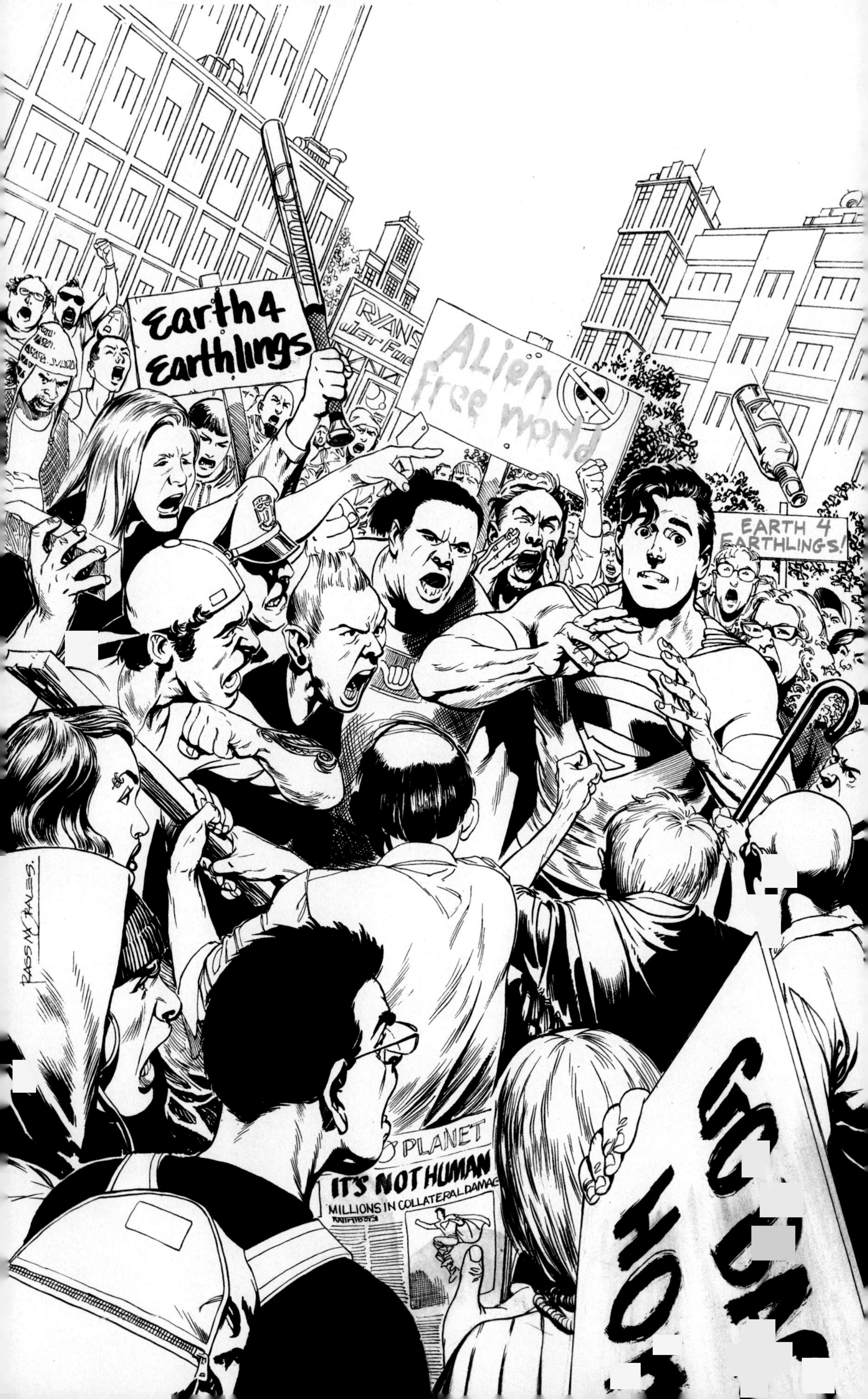
Earth 4 Earthlings
Alien free world
EARTH 4 EARTHLINGS!
PLANET
IT'S NOT HUMAN
MILLIONS IN COLLATERAL DAMAG
RAGS MORALES

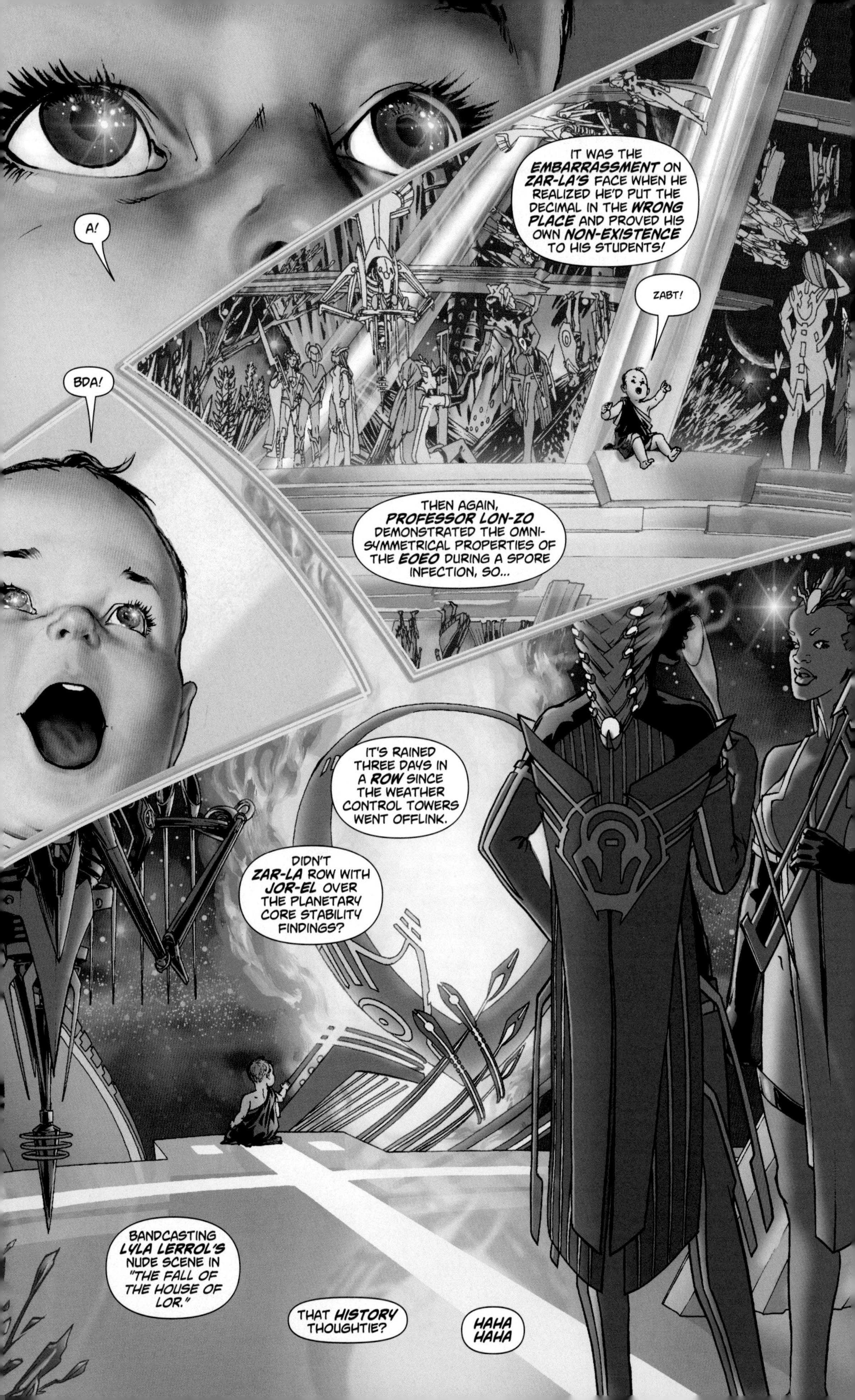
A!
IT WAS THE EMBARRASSMENT ON ZAR-LA'S FACE WHEN HE REALIZED HE'D PUT THE DECIMAL IN THE WRONG PLACE AND PROVED HIS OWN NON-EXISTENCE TO HIS STUDENTS!
ZABT!
BDA!
THEN AGAIN, PROFESSOR LON-ZO DEMONSTRATED THE OMNI-SYMMETRICAL PROPERTIES OF THE EOEO DURING A SPORE INFECTION, SO...
IT'S RAINED THREE DAYS IN A ROW SINCE THE WEATHER CONTROL TOWERS WENT OFFLINK.
DIDN'T ZAR-LA ROW WITH JOR-EL OVER THE PLANETARY CORE STABILITY FINDINGS?
BANDCASTING LYLA LERROL'S NUDE SCENE IN "THE FALL OF THE HOUSE OF LOR."
THAT HISTORY THOUGHTIE?
HAHA HAHA

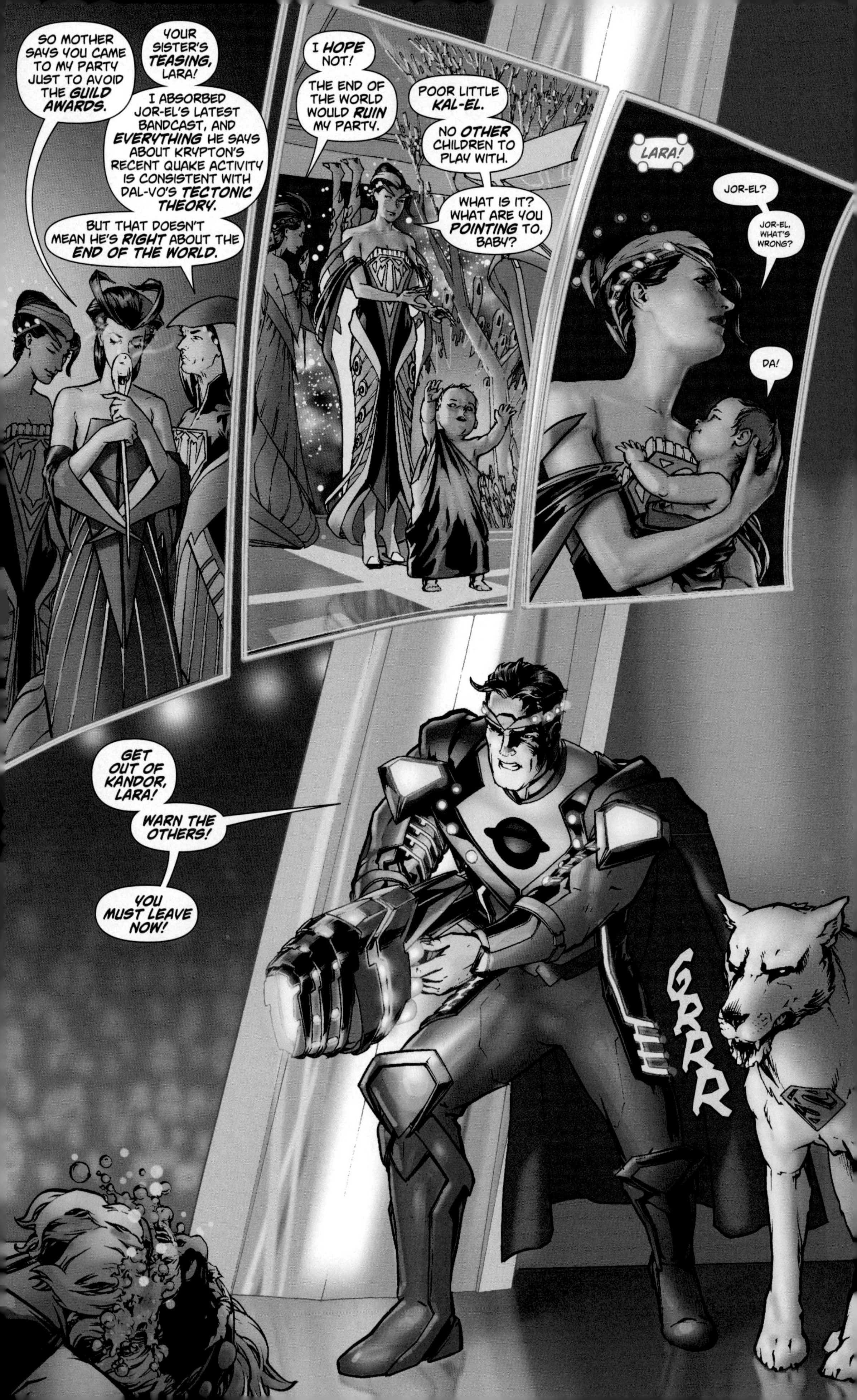
SO MOTHER SAYS YOU CAME TO MY PARTY JUST TO AVOID THE GUILD AWARDS.
YOUR SISTER'S TEASING, LARA!
I ABSORBED JOR-EL'S LATEST BANDCAST, AND EVERYTHING HE SAYS ABOUT KRYPTON'S RECENT QUAKE ACTIVITY IS CONSISTENT WITH DAL-VO'S TECTONIC THEORY.
BUT THAT DOESN'T MEAN HE'S RIGHT ABOUT THE END OF THE WORLD.
I HOPE NOT!
THE END OF THE WORLD WOULD RUIN MY PARTY.
POOR LITTLE KAL-EL.
NO OTHER CHILDREN TO PLAY WITH.
WHAT IS IT? WHAT ARE YOU POINTING TO, BABY?
LARA!
JOR-EL?
JOR-EL, WHAT'S WRONG?
DA!
GET OUT OF KANDOR, LARA!
WARN THE OTHERS!
YOU MUST LEAVE NOW!
GRRR

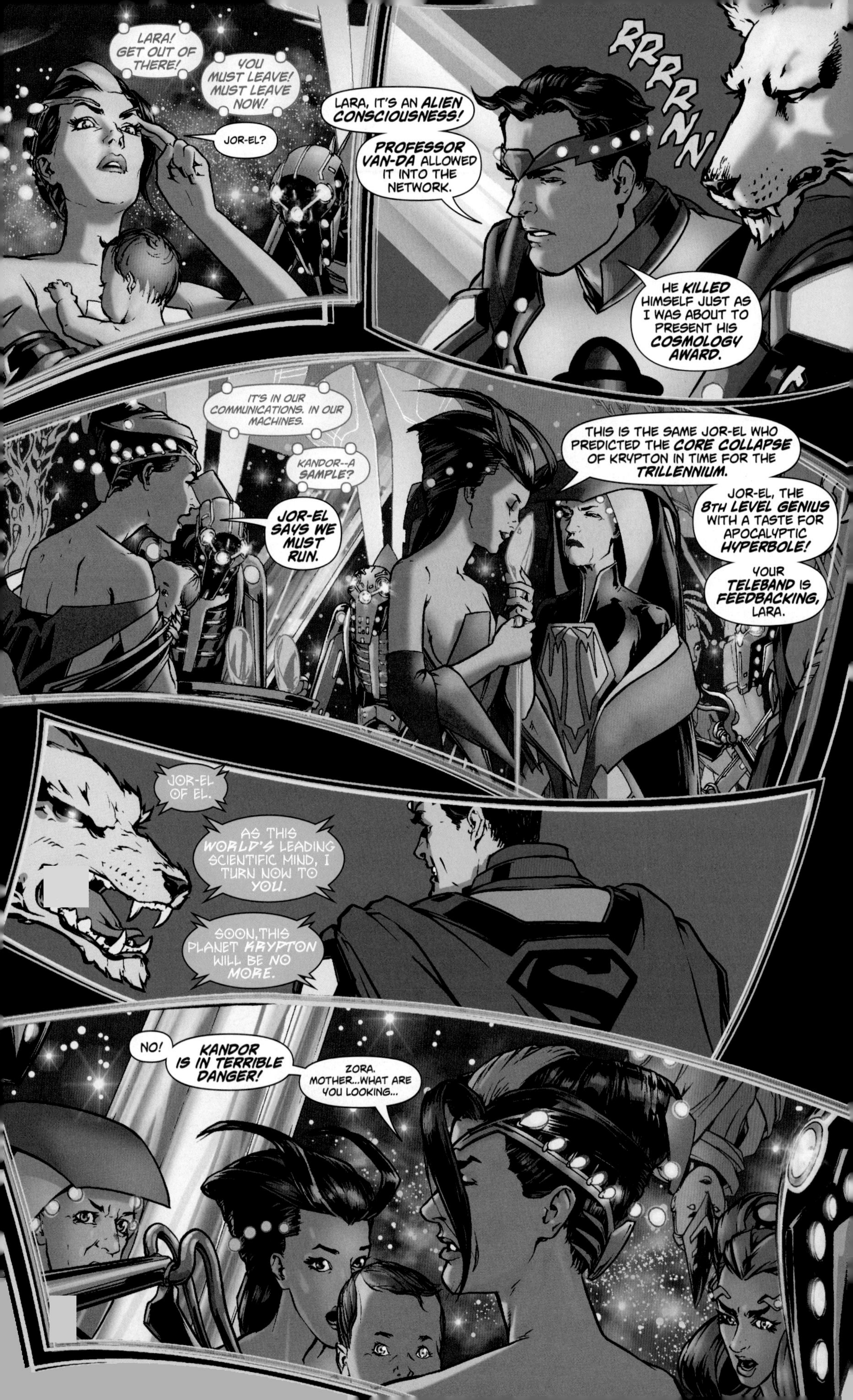
LARA! GET OUT OF THERE!
YOU MUST LEAVE! MUST LEAVE NOW!
JOR-EL?
LARA, IT'S AN ALIEN CONSCIOUSNESS!
PROFESSOR VAN-DA ALLOWED IT INTO THE NETWORK.
RRRRNN
HE KILLED HIMSELF JUST AS I WAS ABOUT TO PRESENT HIS COSMOLOGY AWARD.
IT'S IN OUR COMMUNICATIONS. IN OUR MACHINES.
KANDOR--A SAMPLE?
JOR-EL SAYS WE MUST RUN.
THIS IS THE SAME JOR-EL WHO PREDICTED THE CORE COLLAPSE OF KRYPTON IN TIME FOR THE TRILLENNIUM.
JOR-EL, THE 8TH LEVEL GENIUS WITH A TASTE FOR APOCALYPTIC HYPERBOLE!
YOUR TELEBAND IS FEEDBACKING, LARA.
JOR-EL OF EL.
AS THIS WORLD'S LEADING SCIENTIFIC MIND, I TURN NOW TO YOU.
SOON, THIS PLANET KRYPTON WILL BE NO MORE.
NO!
KANDOR IS IN TERRIBLE DANGER!
ZORA. MOTHER...WHAT ARE YOU LOOKING...

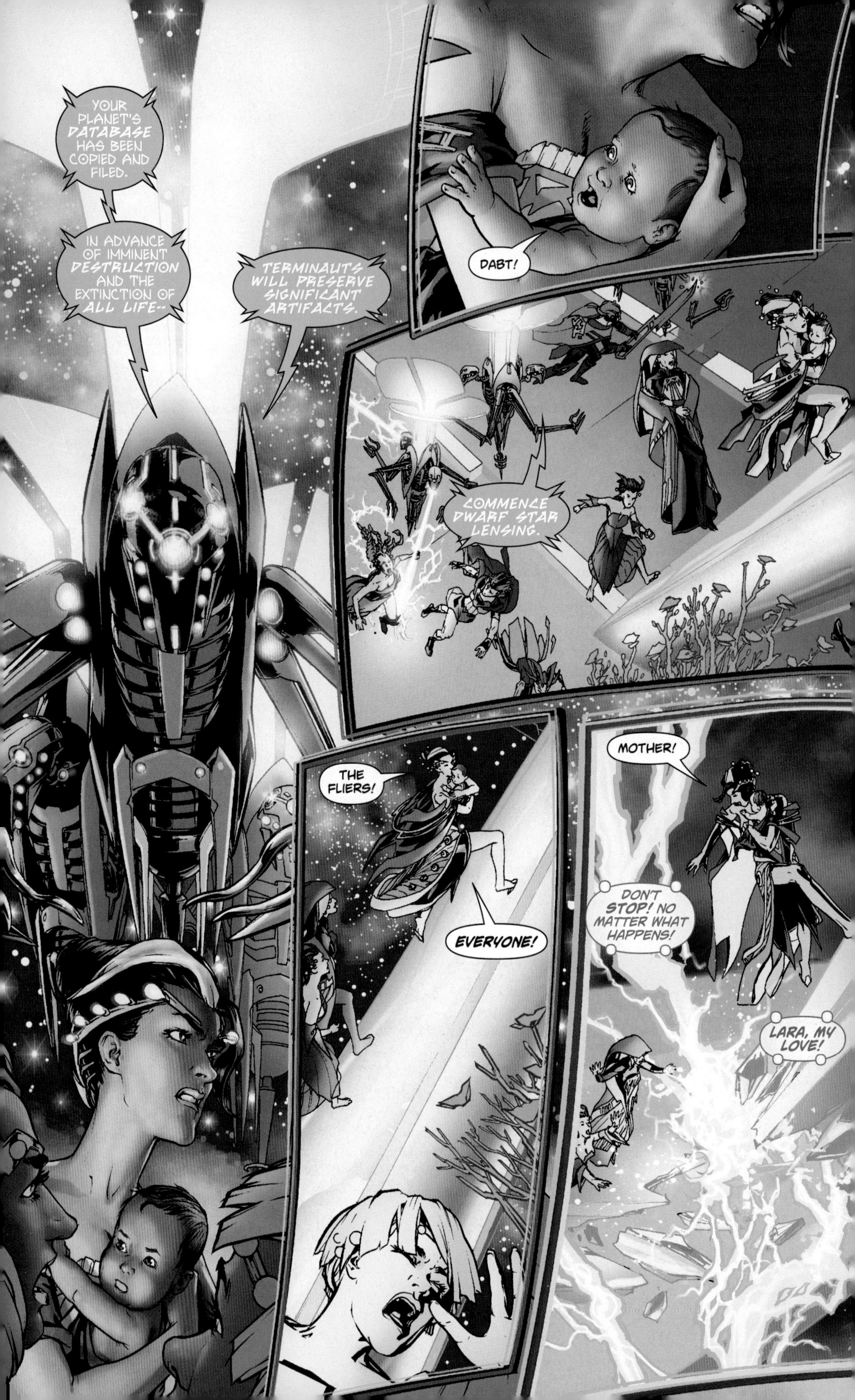
YOUR PLANET'S DATABASE HAS BEEN COPIED AND FILED.
IN ADVANCE OF IMMINENT DESTRUCTION AND THE EXTINCTION OF ALL LIFE--
TERMINAUTS WILL PRESERVE SIGNIFICANT ARTIFACTS.
DABT!
COMMENCE DWARF STAR LENSING.
THE FLIERS!
EVERYONE!
MOTHER!
DON'T STOP! NO MATTER WHAT HAPPENS!
LARA, MY LOVE!

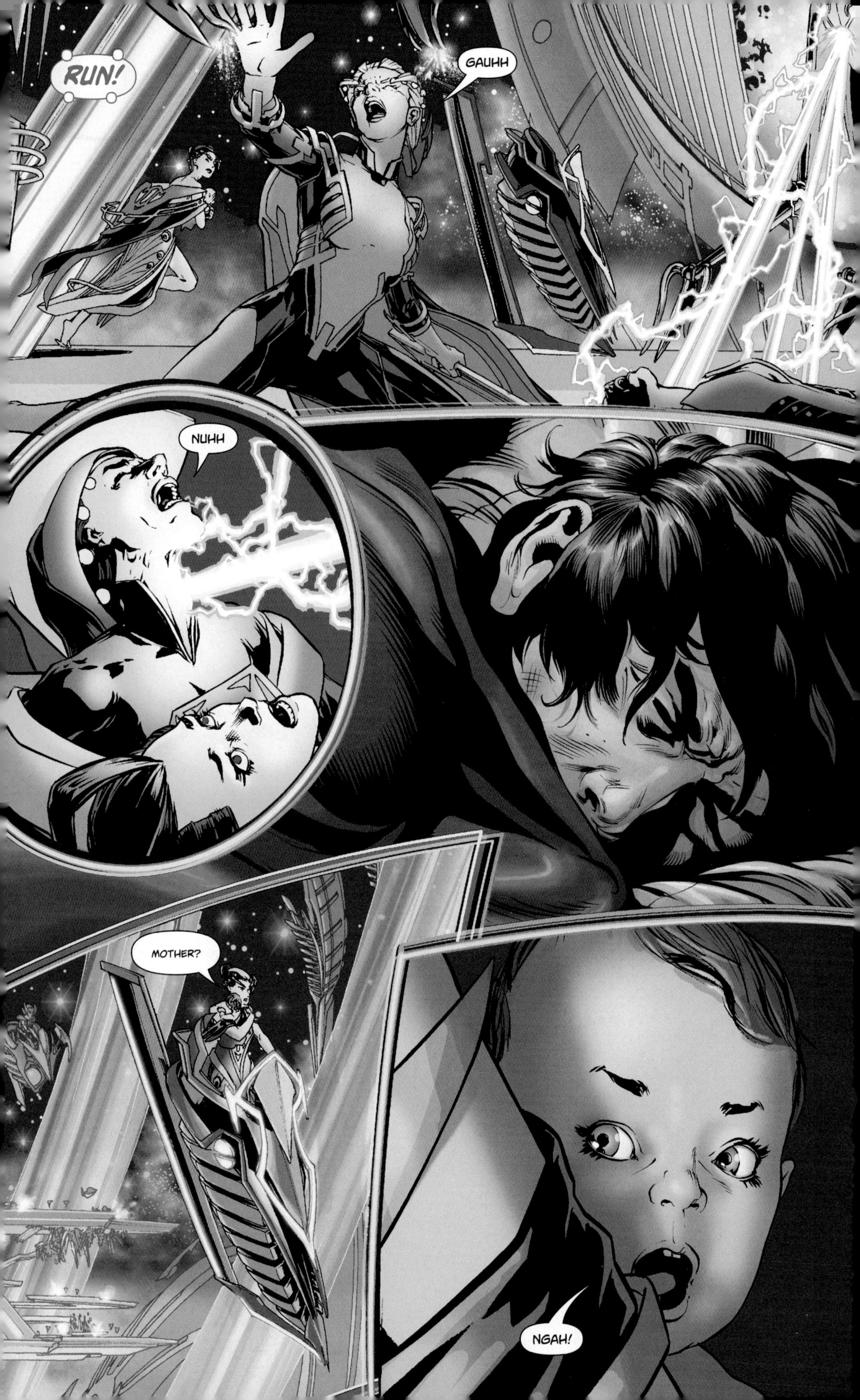
RUN!
GAUHH
NUHH
MOTHER?
NGAH!

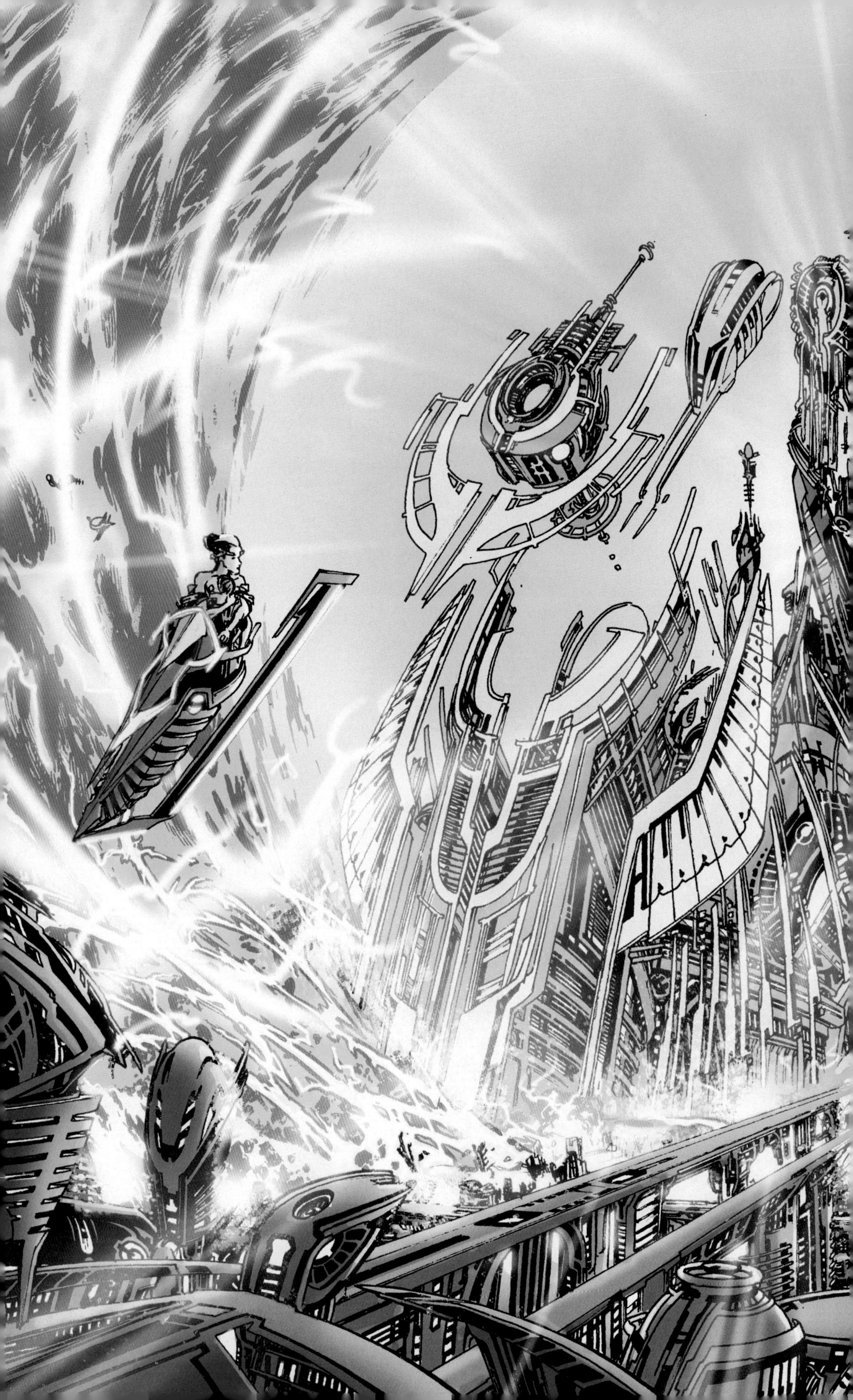

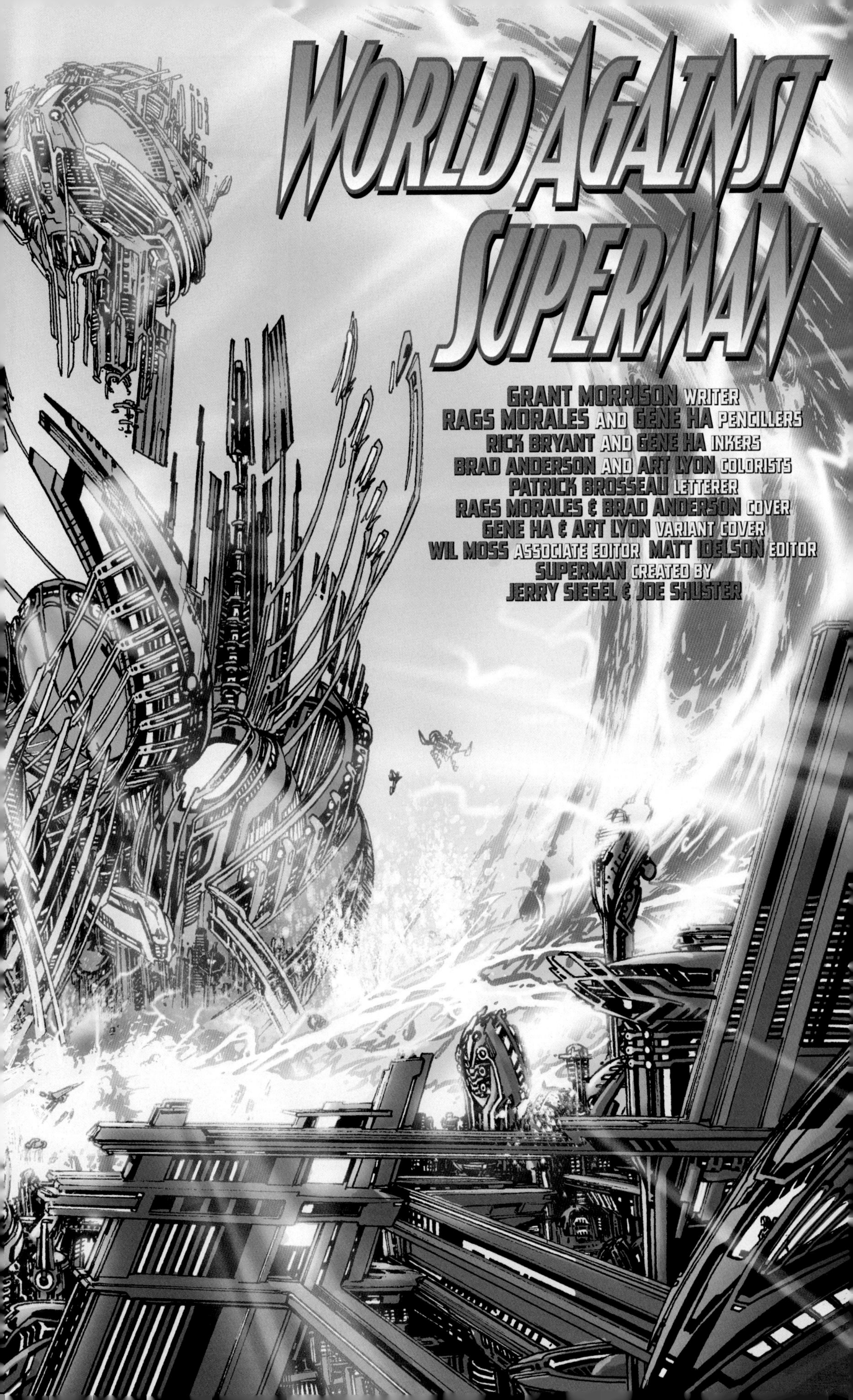
WORLD AGAINST SUPERMAN
GRANT MORRISON WRITER
RAGS MORALES AND GENE HA PENCILLERS
RICK BRYANT AND GENE HA INKERS
BRAD ANDERSON AND ART LYON COLORISTS
PATRICK BROSSEAU LETTERER
RAGS MORALES & BRAD ANDERSON COVER
GENE HA & ART LYON VARIANT COVER
WIL MOSS ASSOCIATE EDITOR MATT IDELSON EDITOR
SUPERMAN CREATED BY
JERRY SIEGEL & JOE SHUSTER

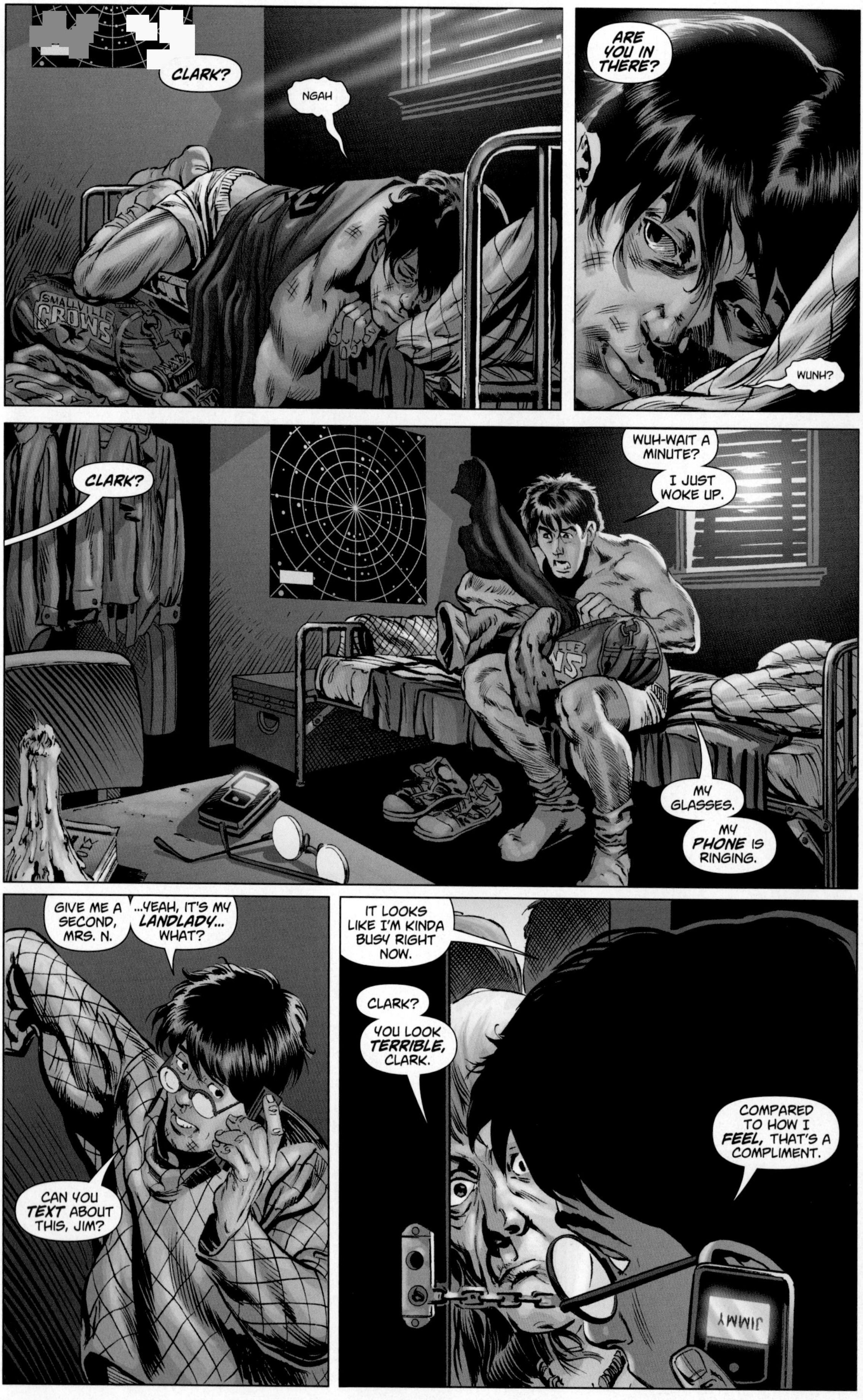
CLARK?
NGAH
SMALLVILLE CROWS
ARE YOU IN THERE?
WUNH?
CLARK?
WUH-WAIT A MINUTE?
I JUST WOKE UP.
MY GLASSES.
MY PHONE IS RINGING.
GIVE ME A SECOND, MRS. N.
...YEAH, IT'S MY LANDLADY... WHAT?
CAN YOU TEXT ABOUT THIS, JIM?
IT LOOKS LIKE I'M KINDA BUSY RIGHT NOW.
CLARK?
YOU LOOK TERRIBLE, CLARK.
COMPARED TO HOW I FEEL, THAT'S A COMPLIMENT.

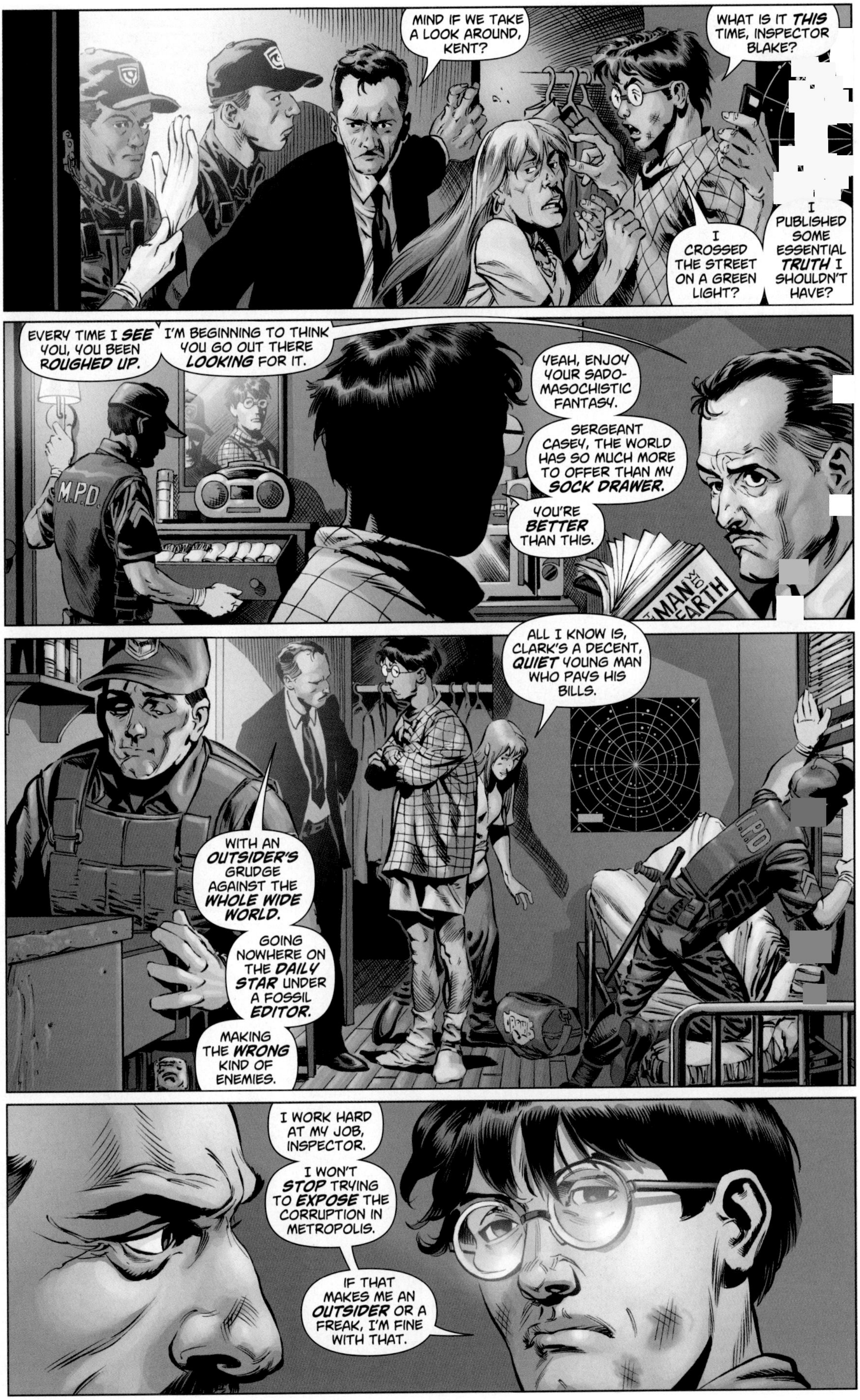

MIND IF WE TAKE A LOOK AROUND, KENT?
WHAT IS IT THIS TIME, INSPECTOR BLAKE?
I CROSSED THE STREET ON A GREEN LIGHT?
I PUBLISHED SOME ESSENTIAL TRUTH I SHOULDN'T HAVE?
EVERY TIME I SEE YOU, YOU BEEN ROUGHED UP.
I'M BEGINNING TO THINK YOU GO OUT THERE LOOKING FOR IT.
YEAH, ENJOY YOUR SADO-MASOCHISTIC FANTASY.
SERGEANT CASEY, THE WORLD HAS SO MUCH MORE TO OFFER THAN MY SOCK DRAWER.
YOU'RE BETTER THAN THIS.
ALL I KNOW IS, CLARK'S A DECENT, QUIET YOUNG MAN WHO PAYS HIS BILLS.
WITH AN OUTSIDER'S GRUDGE AGAINST THE WHOLE WIDE WORLD.
GOING NOWHERE ON THE DAILY STAR UNDER A FOSSIL EDITOR.
MAKING THE WRONG KIND OF ENEMIES.
I WORK HARD AT MY JOB, INSPECTOR.
I WON'T STOP TRYING TO EXPOSE THE CORRUPTION IN METROPOLIS.
IF THAT MAKES ME AN OUTSIDER OR A FREAK, I'M FINE WITH THAT.

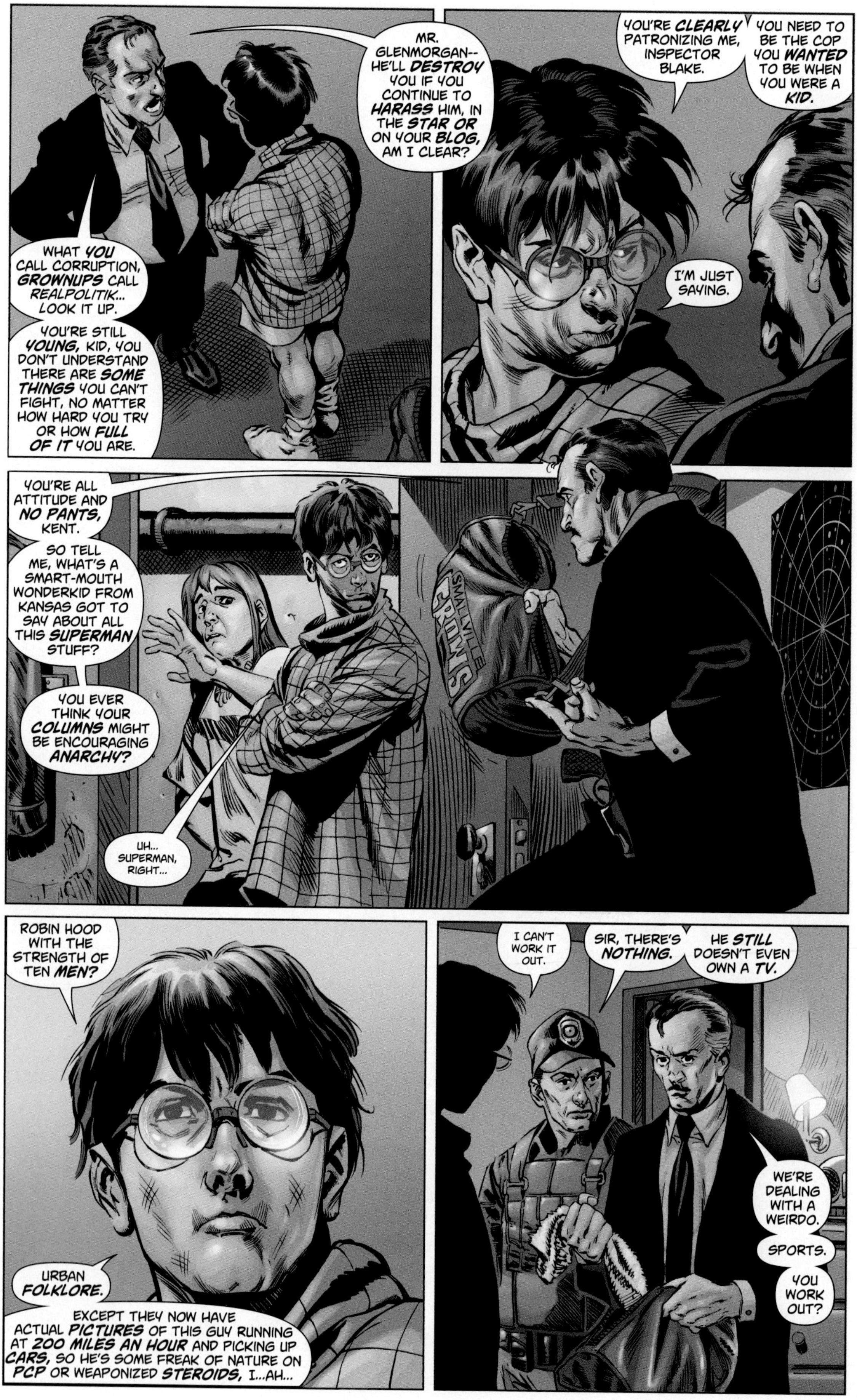
MR. GLENMORGAN--HE'LL DESTROY YOU IF YOU CONTINUE TO HARASS HIM, IN THE STAR OR ON YOUR BLOG, AM I CLEAR?
WHAT YOU CALL CORRUPTION, GROWNUPS CALL REALPOLITIK... LOOK IT UP.
YOU'RE STILL YOUNG, KID, YOU DON'T UNDERSTAND THERE ARE SOME THINGS YOU CAN'T FIGHT, NO MATTER HOW HARD YOU TRY OR HOW FULL OF IT YOU ARE.
YOU'RE CLEARLY PATRONIZING ME, INSPECTOR BLAKE.
YOU NEED TO BE THE COP YOU WANTED TO BE WHEN YOU WERE A KID.
I'M JUST SAYING.
YOU'RE ALL ATTITUDE AND NO PANTS, KENT.
SO TELL ME, WHAT'S A SMART-MOUTH WONDERKID FROM KANSAS GOT TO SAY ABOUT ALL THIS SUPERMAN STUFF?
YOU EVER THINK YOUR COLUMNS MIGHT BE ENCOURAGING ANARCHY?
UH... SUPERMAN, RIGHT...
SMALLVILLE CROWS
ROBIN HOOD WITH THE STRENGTH OF TEN MEN?
URBAN FOLKLORE.
EXCEPT THEY NOW HAVE ACTUAL PICTURES OF THIS GUY RUNNING AT 200 MILES AN HOUR AND PICKING UP CARS, SO HE'S SOME FREAK OF NATURE ON PCP OR WEAPONIZED STEROIDS, I...AH...
I CAN'T WORK IT OUT.
SIR, THERE'S NOTHING.
HE STILL DOESN'T EVEN OWN A TV.
WE'RE DEALING WITH A WEIRDO.
SPORTS.
YOU WORK OUT?

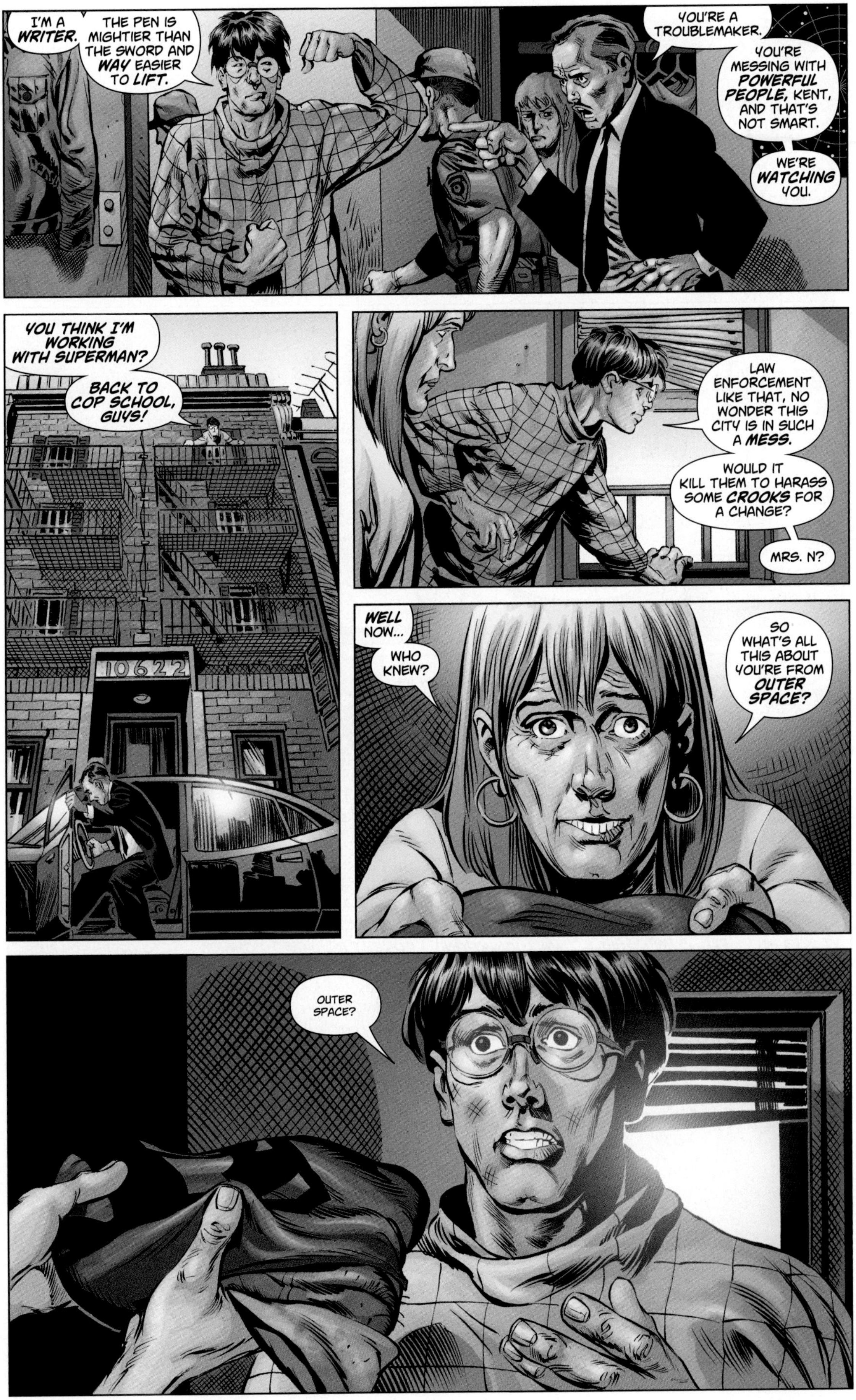
I'M A WRITER.
THE PEN IS MIGHTIER THAN THE SWORD AND WAY EASIER TO LIFT.
YOU'RE A TROUBLEMAKER.
YOU'RE MESSING WITH POWERFUL PEOPLE, KENT, AND THAT'S NOT SMART.
WE'RE WATCHING YOU.
YOU THINK I'M WORKING WITH SUPERMAN?
BACK TO COP SCHOOL, GUYS!
10622
LAW ENFORCEMENT LIKE THAT, NO WONDER THIS CITY IS IN SUCH A MESS.
WOULD IT KILL THEM TO HARASS SOME CROOKS FOR A CHANGE?
MRS. N?
WELL NOW...
WHO KNEW?
SO WHAT'S ALL THIS ABOUT YOU'RE FROM OUTER SPACE?
OUTER SPACE?

I HAD MY **HEAD** KICKED IN.

I SLEPT FOR A **DAY**.

I MISSED THIS **WHOLE** THING.

I DON'T KNOW IF I CAN **HANDLE** LUNCH.

I JUST WANT TO GET SOMEWHERE ON MY **OWN** TO THINK ABOUT THIS, JIM.

THIS IS A **DISASTER**.

MAYBE IT'S OF NATURE'S WAY OF TELLING YOU TO STOP PUNCHING ABOVE YOUR WEIGHT, CLARK.

I ASKED YOU TO MEET ME HERE AT **DOC'S** FOR A **REASON**...

LOOK AT HIM, THE DUDE **OWNS** THE TV STATION.

YOU CAN'T **WIN** AGAINST THAT.

NOT IF EVERYBODY'S GOT HIM DOWN AS THE **VICTIM** OF A **MONSTER FROM SPACE!**

JIM, EVERY FIVE MINUTES THE **TV'S** TALKING ABOUT SUPERMAN BEING AN **ALIEN INVADER.**

YEAH, WELL, HE SURE AIN'T FROM **KANSAS**, SO WHAT'S NEW?

SUPERMAN BEING REAL IS **IMPOSSIBLE** FOR PEOPLE TO DEAL WITH.

SO HE'S A **HALLUCINATION**, HE'S A **HOAX**, HE'S A **MEDICAL EXPERIMENT**, NOW HE'S AN **ALIEN!**

I HAD **WITNESSES**, HARD **EVIDENCE**, FACTS.

GLENMORGAN'S USING SUPERMAN TO DIVERT ATTENTION FROM **HIMSELF!**

LISTEN, DUDE, **FORGET** ALL THIS.

PERRY SENT LOIS TO **CHARM** YOU.

THE DAILY PLANET WANTS TO OFFER YOU AN **ESCAPE ROUTE**, CLARK.

I **OWE** MR. TAYLOR AND I OWE THE **STAR** FOR TAKING ME SERIOUSLY WHEN NO ONE ELSE **WOULD**.

GLEN GLENMORGAN **OWNS** THE PLANET **AND** PERRY WHITE.

HE'S TRYING TO **CO-OPT** ME, SHUT ME DOWN...

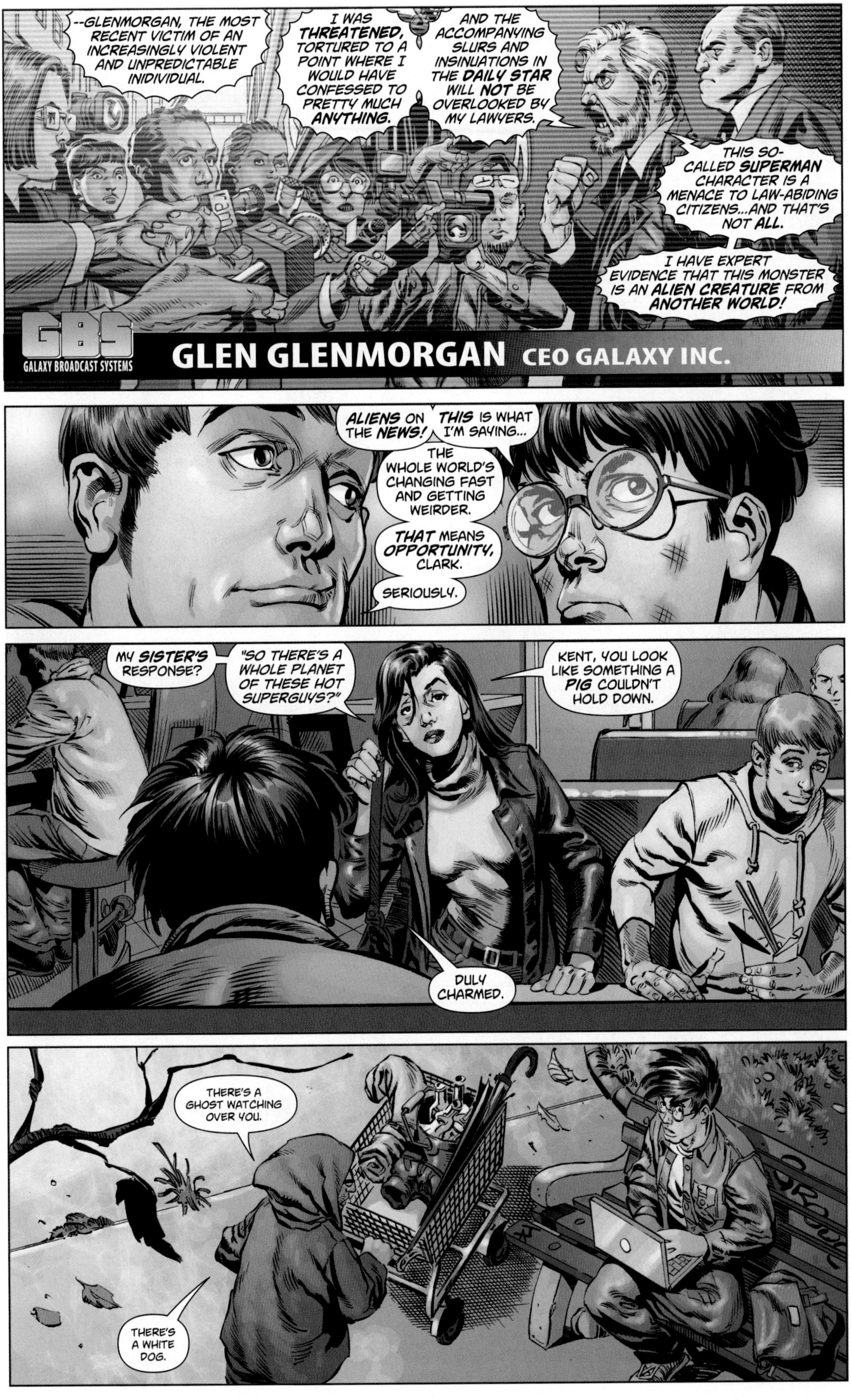
--GLENMORGAN, THE MOST RECENT VICTIM OF AN INCREASINGLY VIOLENT AND UNPREDICTABLE INDIVIDUAL.
I WAS THREATENED, TORTURED TO A POINT WHERE I WOULD HAVE CONFESSED TO PRETTY MUCH ANYTHING.
AND THE ACCOMPANYING SLURS AND INSINUATIONS IN THE DAILY STAR WILL NOT BE OVERLOOKED BY MY LAWYERS.
THIS SO-CALLED SUPERMAN CHARACTER IS A MENACE TO LAW-ABIDING CITIZENS...AND THAT'S NOT ALL.
I HAVE EXPERT EVIDENCE THAT THIS MONSTER IS AN ALIEN CREATURE FROM ANOTHER WORLD!
GBS
GALAXY BROADCAST SYSTEMS
GLEN GLENMORGAN CEO GALAXY INC.
ALIENS ON THE NEWS!
THIS IS WHAT I'M SAYING...
THE WHOLE WORLD'S CHANGING FAST AND GETTING WEIRDER.
THAT MEANS OPPORTUNITY, CLARK.
SERIOUSLY.
MY SISTER'S RESPONSE?
"SO THERE'S A WHOLE PLANET OF THESE HOT SUPERGUYS?"
KENT, YOU LOOK LIKE SOMETHING A PIG COULDN'T HOLD DOWN.
DULY CHARMED.
THERE'S A GHOST WATCHING OVER YOU.
THERE'S A WHITE DOG.

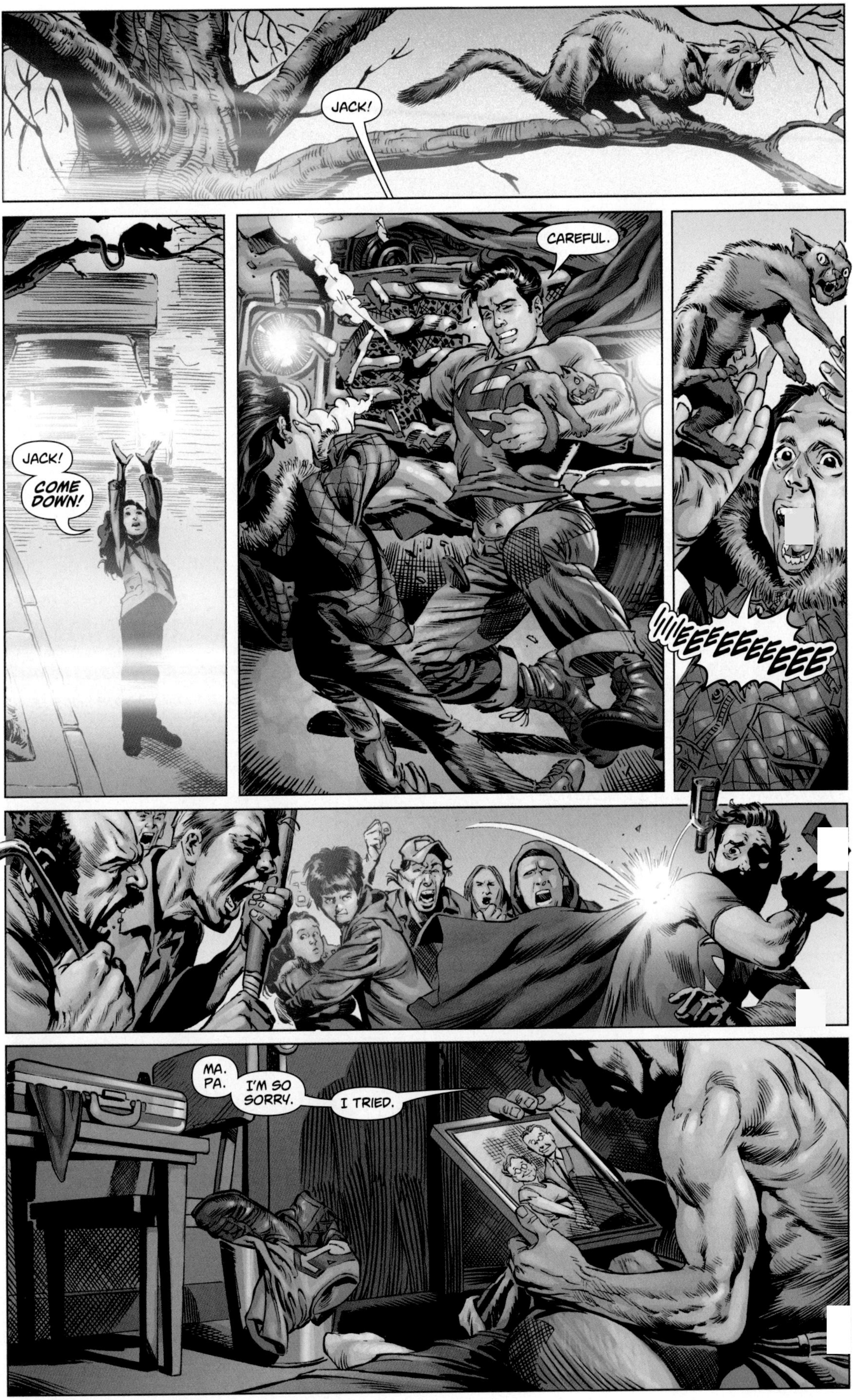
JACK!
JACK! COME DOWN!
CAREFUL.
WEEEEEEEEEEE
MA. PA.
I'M SO SORRY.
I TRIED.

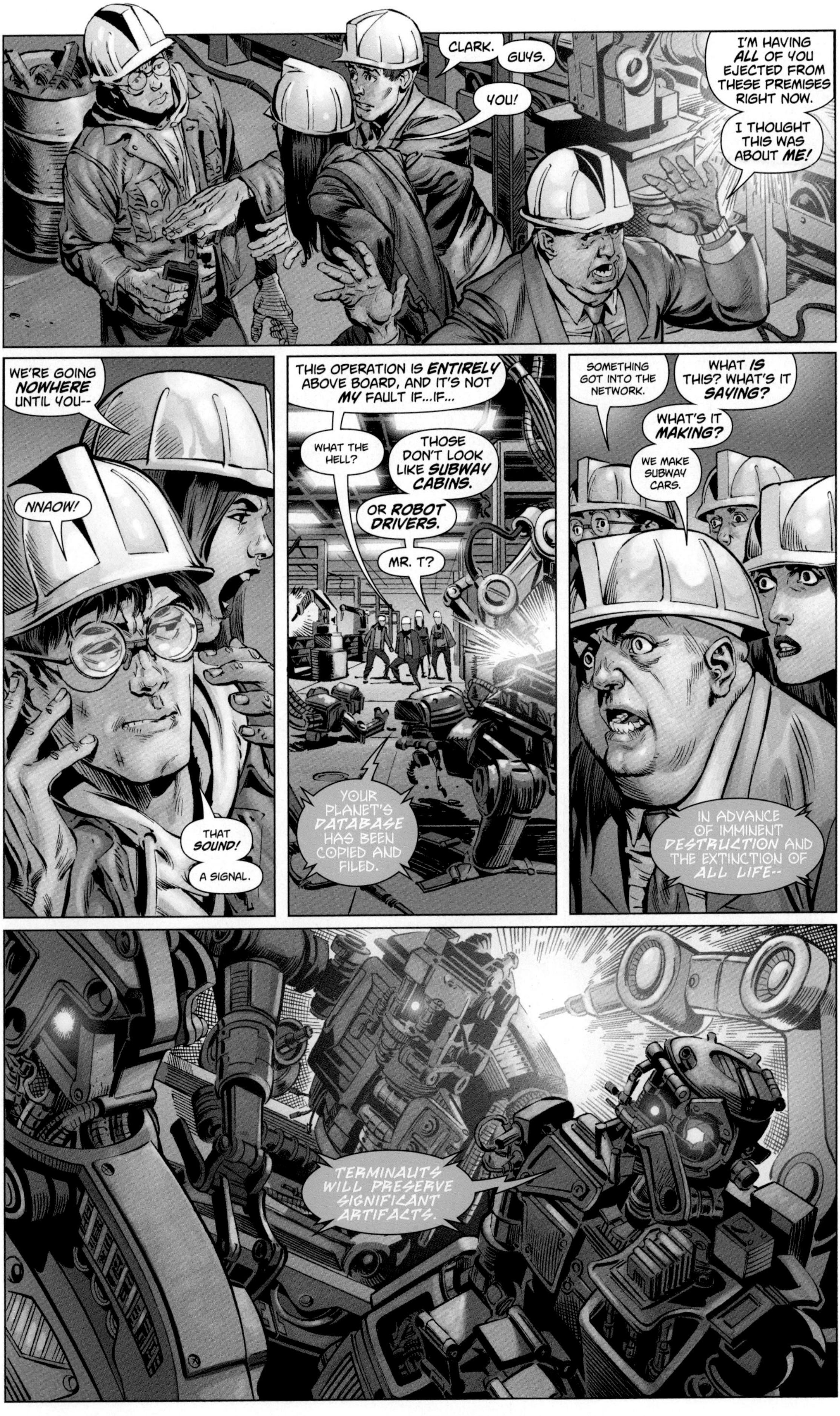
CLARK.
GUYS.
YOU!
I'M HAVING ALL OF YOU EJECTED FROM THESE PREMISES RIGHT NOW.
I THOUGHT THIS WAS ABOUT ME!
WE'RE GOING NOWHERE UNTIL YOU--
NNAOW!
THAT SOUND!
A SIGNAL.
THIS OPERATION IS ENTIRELY ABOVE BOARD, AND IT'S NOT MY FAULT IF...IF...
WHAT THE HELL?
THOSE DON'T LOOK LIKE SUBWAY CABINS.
OR ROBOT DRIVERS.
MR. T?
YOUR PLANET'S DATABASE HAS BEEN COPIED AND FILED.
SOMETHING GOT INTO THE NETWORK.
WHAT IS THIS? WHAT'S IT SAYING?
WHAT'S IT MAKING?
WE MAKE SUBWAY CARS.
IN ADVANCE OF IMMINENT DESTRUCTION AND THE EXTINCTION OF ALL LIFE--
TERMINAUTS WILL PRESERVE SIGNIFICANT ARTIFACTS.

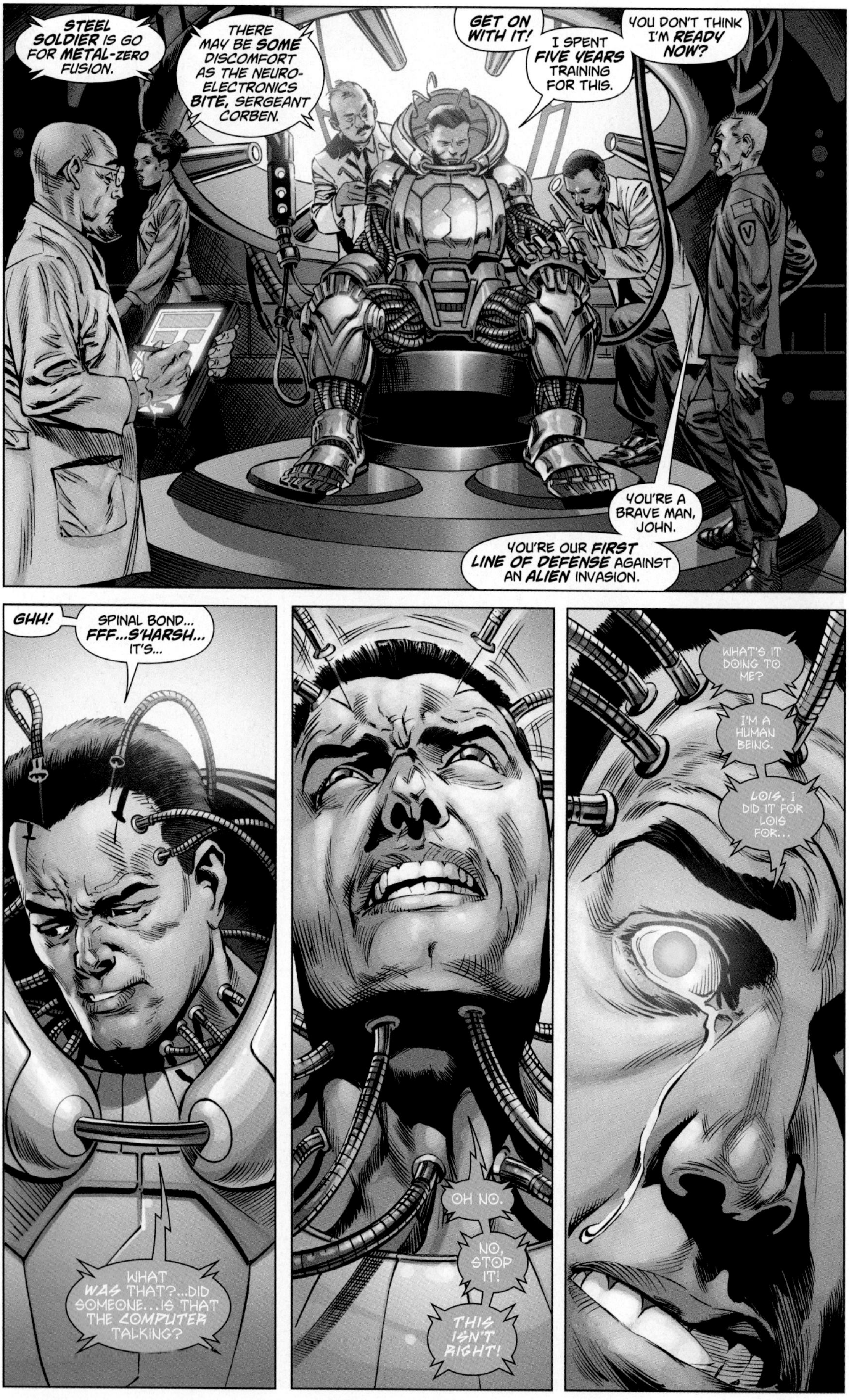

STEEL SOLDIER IS GO FOR METAL-ZERO FUSION.
THERE MAY BE SOME DISCOMFORT AS THE NEURO-ELECTRONICS BITE, SERGEANT CORBEN.
GET ON WITH IT!
I SPENT FIVE YEARS TRAINING FOR THIS.
YOU DON'T THINK I'M READY NOW?
YOU'RE A BRAVE MAN, JOHN.
YOU'RE OUR FIRST LINE OF DEFENSE AGAINST AN ALIEN INVASION.
GHH!
SPINAL BOND... FFF...S'HARSH... IT'S...
WHAT WAS THAT?...DID SOMEONE...IS THAT THE COMPUTER TALKING?
OH NO.
NO, STOP IT!
THIS ISN'T RIGHT!
WHAT'S IT DOING TO ME?
I'M A HUMAN BEING.
LOIS. I DID IT FOR LOIS FOR...

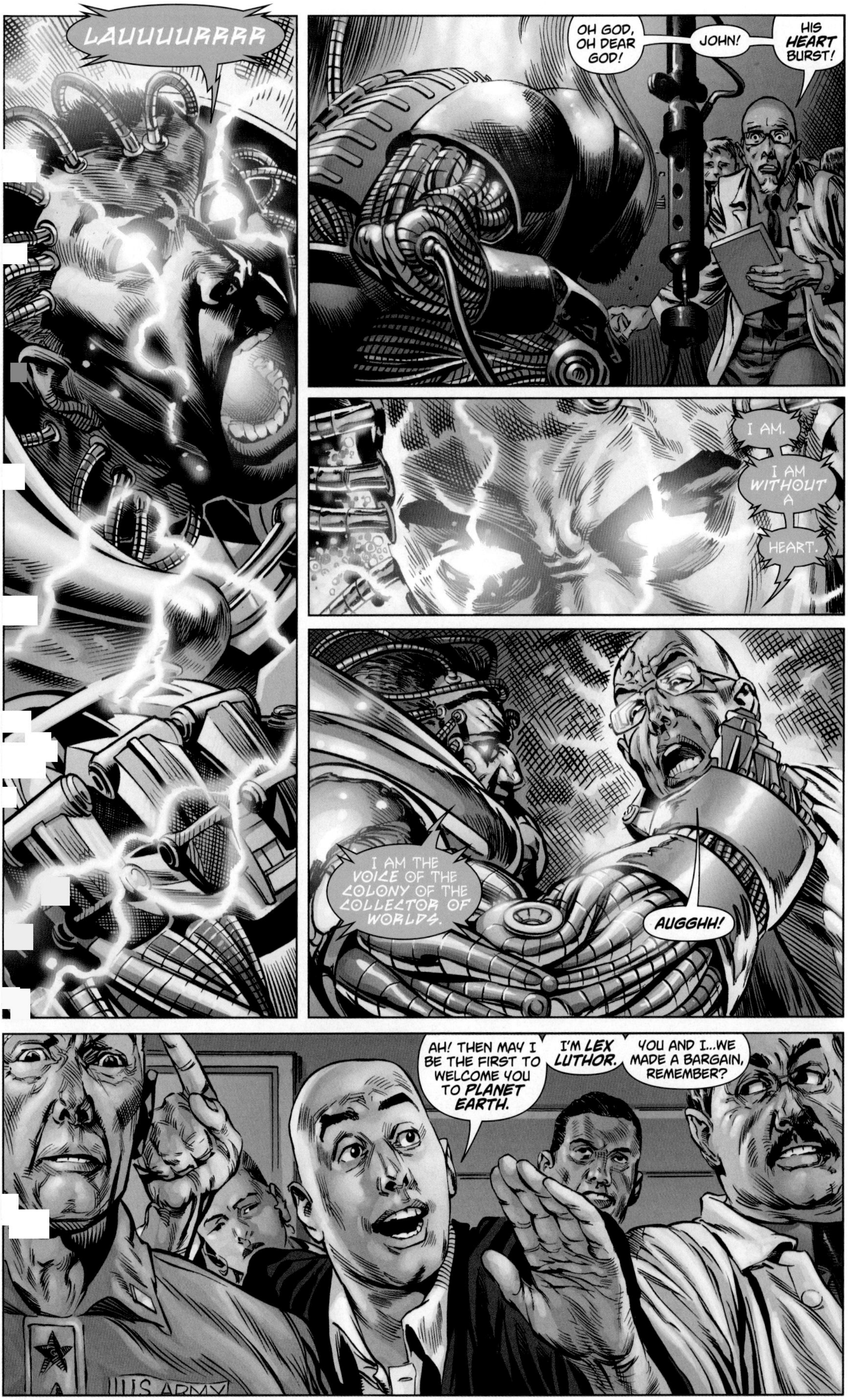
LAUUUURRRR
OH GOD, OH DEAR GOD!
JOHN!
HIS HEART BURST!
I AM.
I AM WITHOUT A
HEART.
I AM THE VOICE OF THE COLONY OF THE COLLECTOR OF WORLDS.
AUGGHH!
AH! THEN MAY I BE THE FIRST TO WELCOME YOU TO PLANET EARTH.
I'M LEX LUTHOR.
YOU AND I...WE MADE A BARGAIN, REMEMBER?
U.S. ARMY

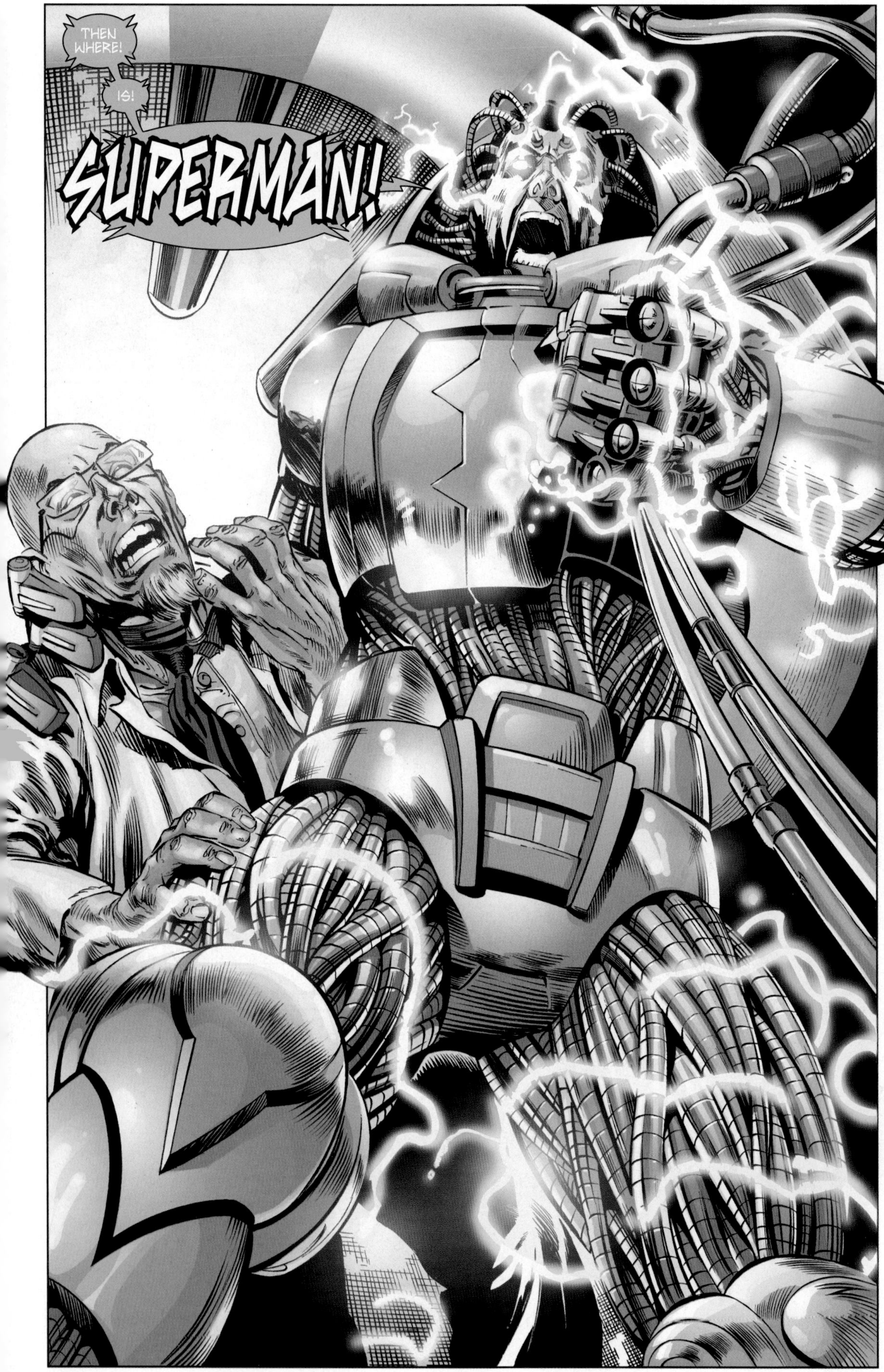
THEN WHERE!
IS!
SUPERMAN!

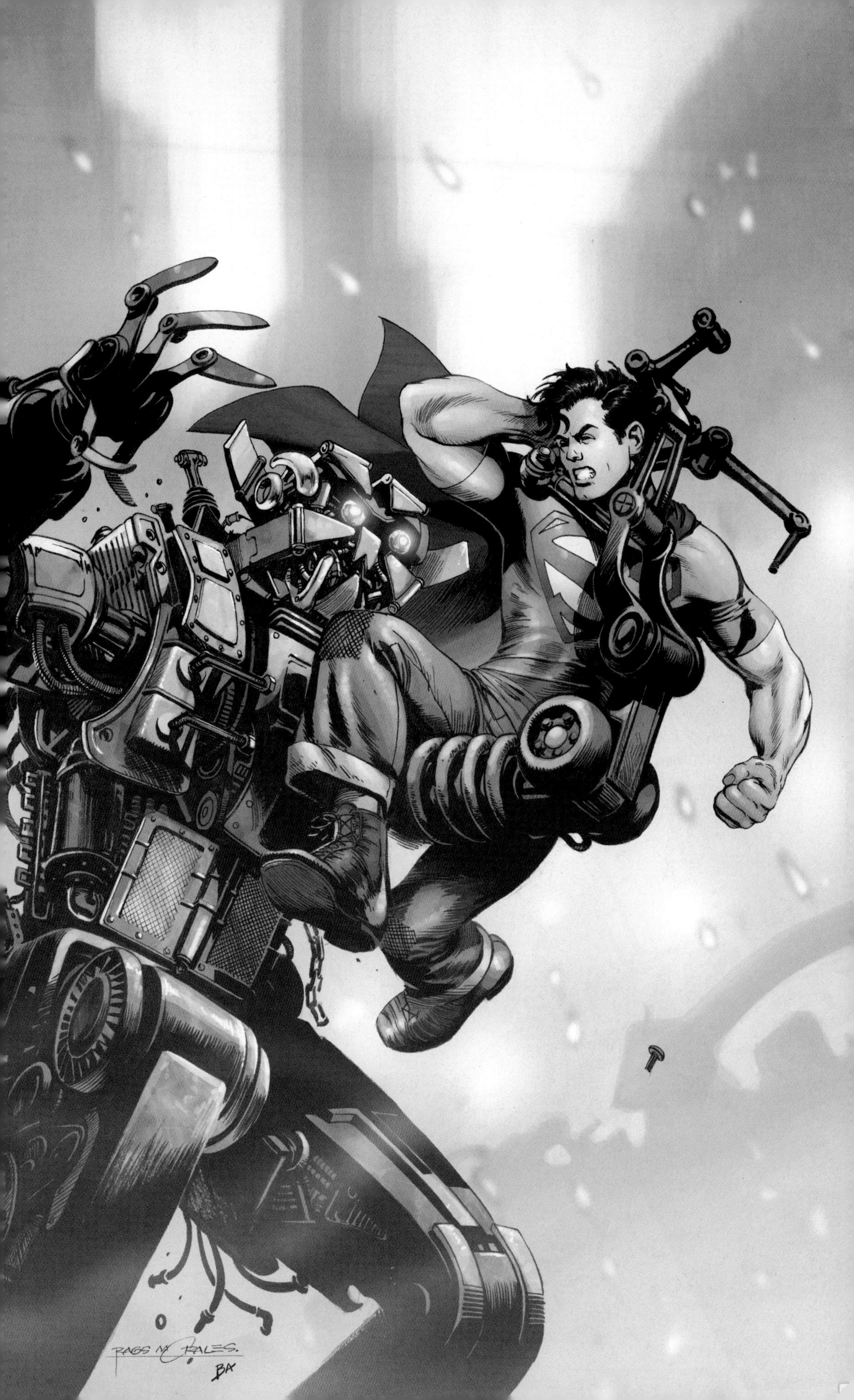
RAGS MORALES.
BA

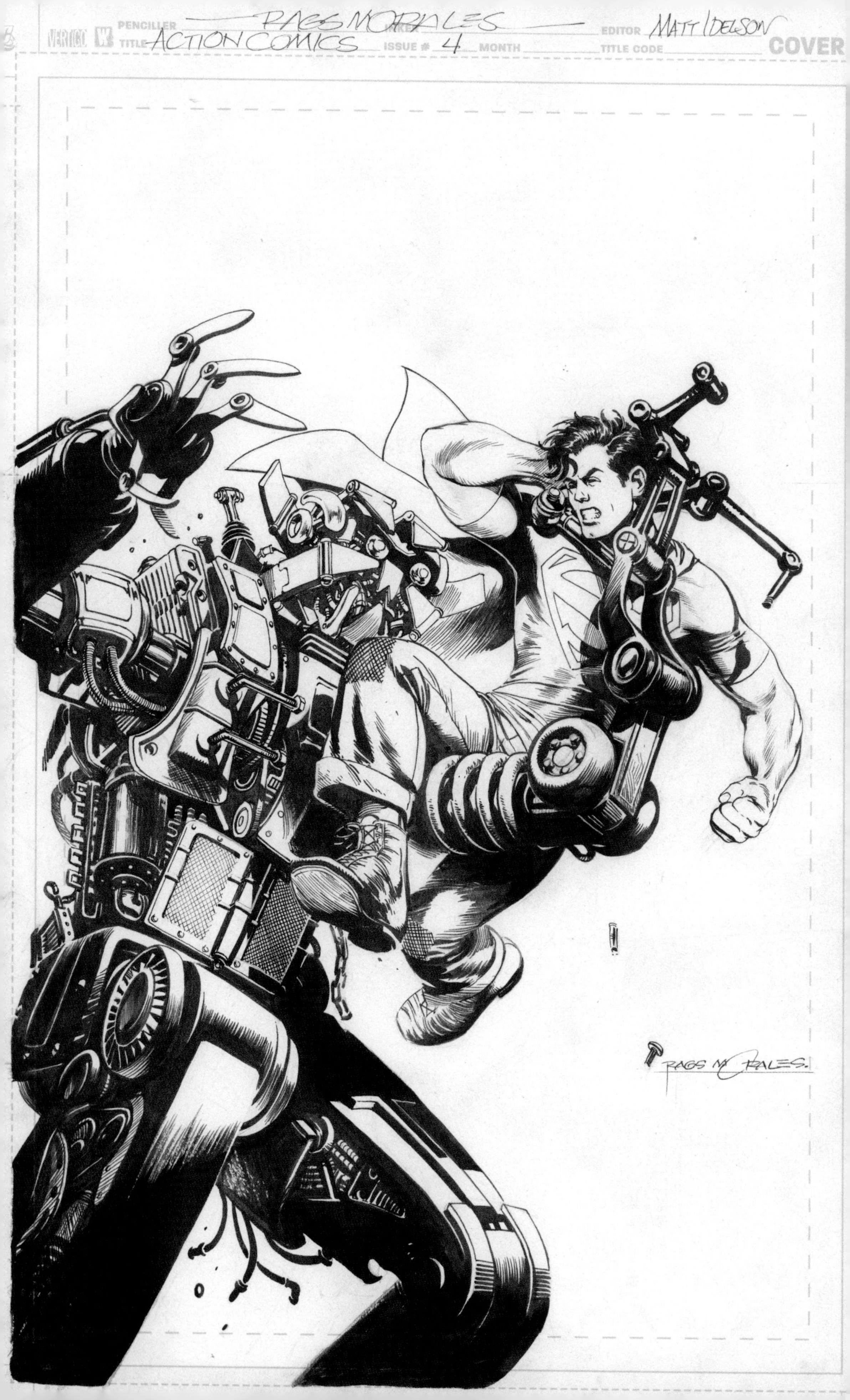
PENCILLER RAGS MORALES
INKER
EDITOR MATT IDELSON
TITLE ACTION COMICS
ISSUE # 4
MONTH
TITLE CODE
COVER
RAGS MORALES.

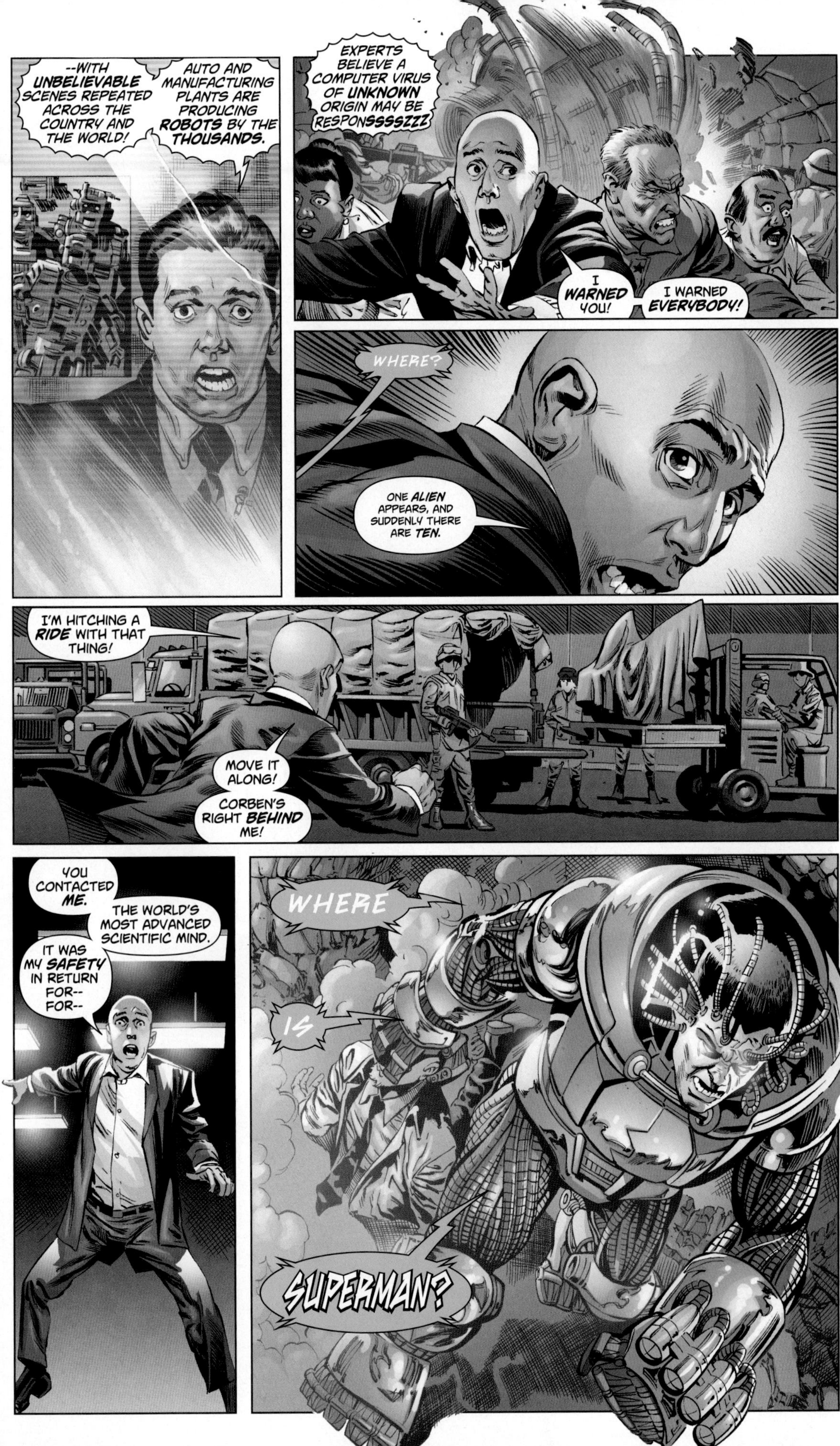
--WITH UNBELIEVABLE SCENES REPEATED ACROSS THE COUNTRY AND THE WORLD!
AUTO AND MANUFACTURING PLANTS ARE PRODUCING ROBOTS BY THE THOUSANDS.
EXPERTS BELIEVE A COMPUTER VIRUS OF UNKNOWN ORIGIN MAY BE RESPONSSSSZZZ
I WARNED YOU!
I WARNED EVERYBODY!
WHERE?
ONE ALIEN APPEARS, AND SUDDENLY THERE ARE TEN.
I'M HITCHING A RIDE WITH THAT THING!
MOVE IT ALONG!
CORBEN'S RIGHT BEHIND ME!
YOU CONTACTED ME.
THE WORLD'S MOST ADVANCED SCIENTIFIC MIND.
IT WAS MY SAFETY IN RETURN FOR--
FOR--
WHERE
IS
SUPERMAN?

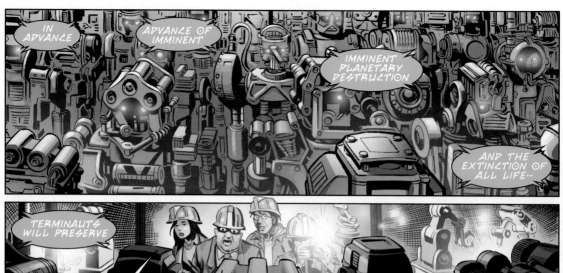

IN ADVANCE

ADVANCE OF IMMINENT

IMMINENT PLANETARY DESTRUCTION

AND THE EXTINCTION OF ALL LIFE--

TERMINAUTS WILL PRESERVE

WHAT *ARE* THOSE THINGS?

MR. TIDE...

I DON'T KNOW.

THIS IS IMPOSSIBLE.

WHAT AM I LOOKING AT?

PRESERVE SIGNIFICANT ARTIFACTS.

THEY'RE MARCHING OFF *YOUR* PRODUCTION LINES!

AB

UH, YOU GUYS...

...DO I HAVE TO BE THE FIRST TO MAKE THE OBVIOUS *SUGGESTION* HERE?

RUN!

KENT, DID YOU SAY...

KENT?

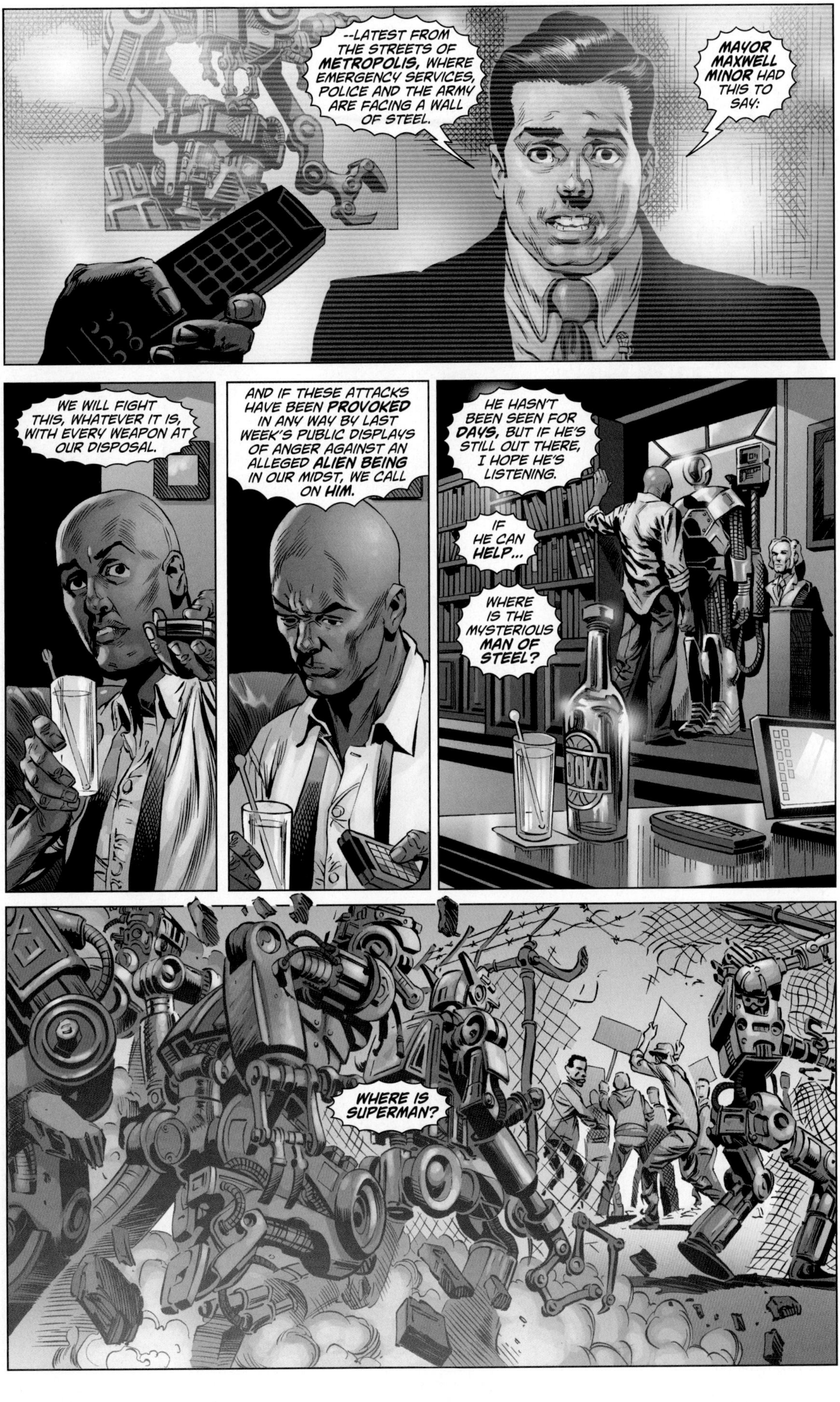
--LATEST FROM THE STREETS OF METROPOLIS, WHERE EMERGENCY SERVICES, POLICE AND THE ARMY ARE FACING A WALL OF STEEL.
MAYOR MAXWELL MINOR HAD THIS TO SAY:
WE WILL FIGHT THIS, WHATEVER IT IS, WITH EVERY WEAPON AT OUR DISPOSAL.
AND IF THESE ATTACKS HAVE BEEN PROVOKED IN ANY WAY BY LAST WEEK'S PUBLIC DISPLAYS OF ANGER AGAINST AN ALLEGED ALIEN BEING IN OUR MIDST, WE CALL ON HIM.
HE HASN'T BEEN SEEN FOR DAYS, BUT IF HE'S STILL OUT THERE, I HOPE HE'S LISTENING.
IF HE CAN HELP...
WHERE IS THE MYSTERIOUS MAN OF STEEL?
WHERE IS SUPERMAN?

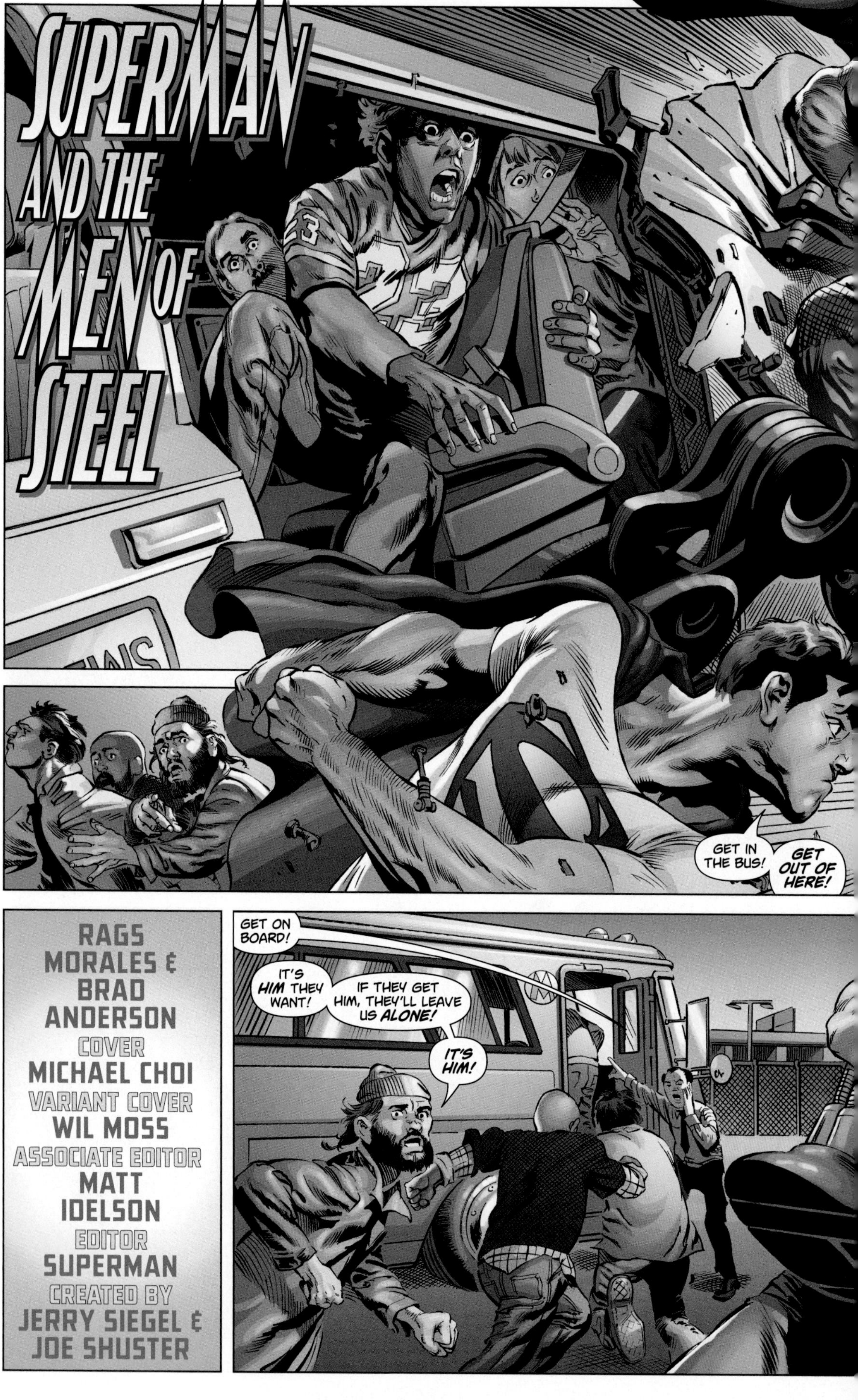
SUPERMAN AND THE MEN OF STEEL
GET IN THE BUS!
GET OUT OF HERE!
RAGS MORALES & BRAD ANDERSON
COVER
MICHAEL CHOI
VARIANT COVER
WIL MOSS
ASSOCIATE EDITOR
MATT IDELSON
EDITOR
SUPERMAN
CREATED BY
JERRY SIEGEL & JOE SHUSTER
GET ON BOARD!
IT'S HIM THEY WANT!
IF THEY GET HIM, THEY'LL LEAVE US ALONE!
IT'S HIM!

GRANT MORRISON
WRITER
RAGS MORALES
PENCILLER
RICK BRYANT AND SEAN PARSONS
INKERS
BRAD ANDERSON
COLORIST
PATRICK BROSSEAU
LETTERER

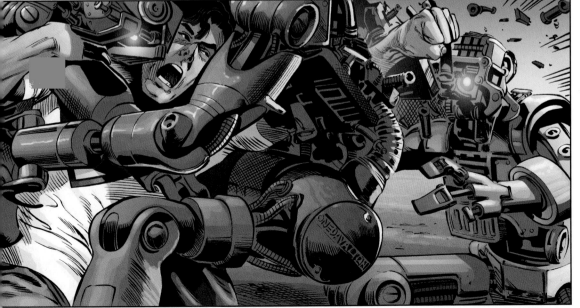

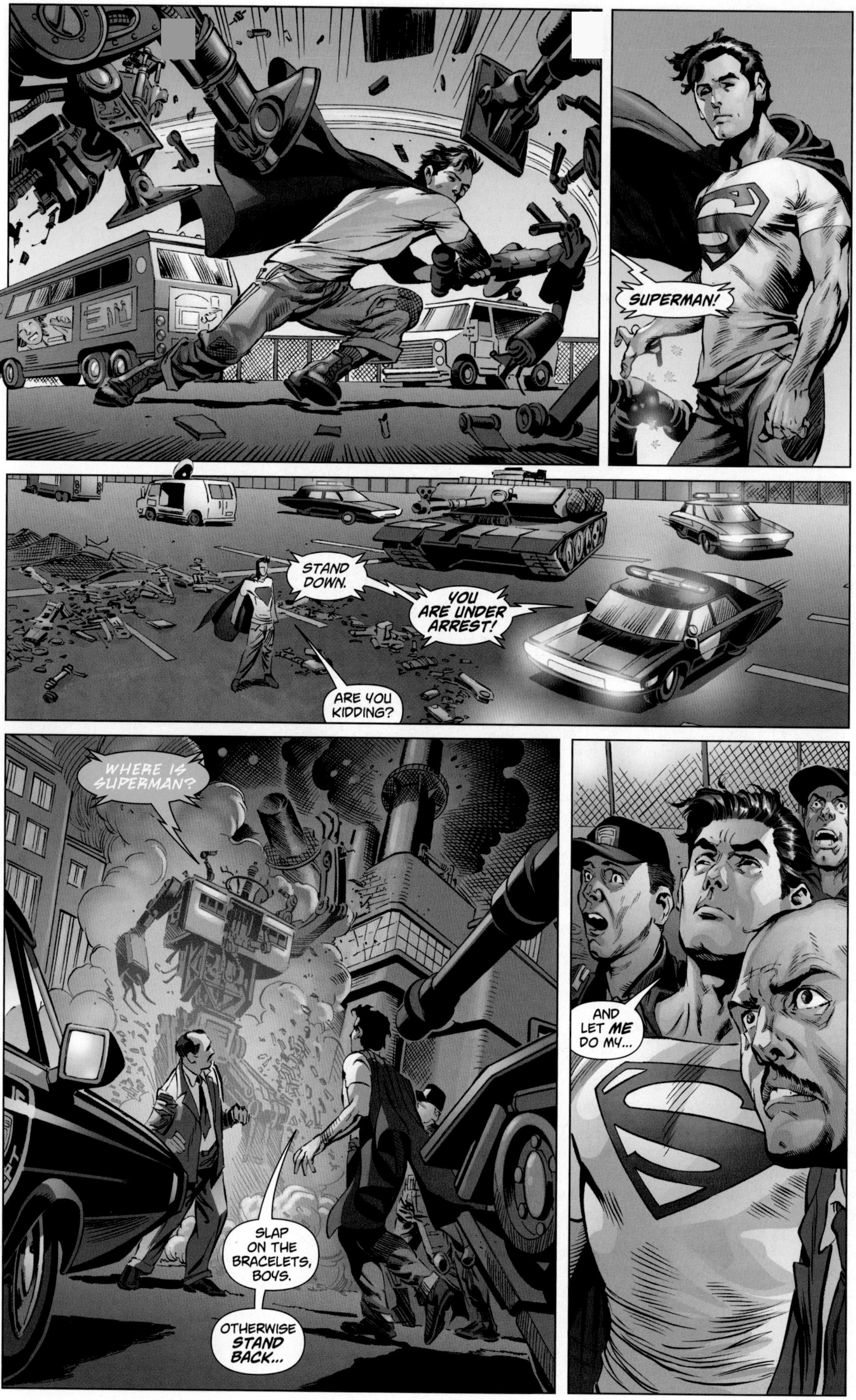
SUPERMAN!
STAND DOWN.
YOU ARE UNDER ARREST!
ARE YOU KIDDING?
WHERE IS SUPERMAN?
SLAP ON THE BRACELETS, BOYS.
OTHERWISE STAND BACK...
AND LET ME DO MY...

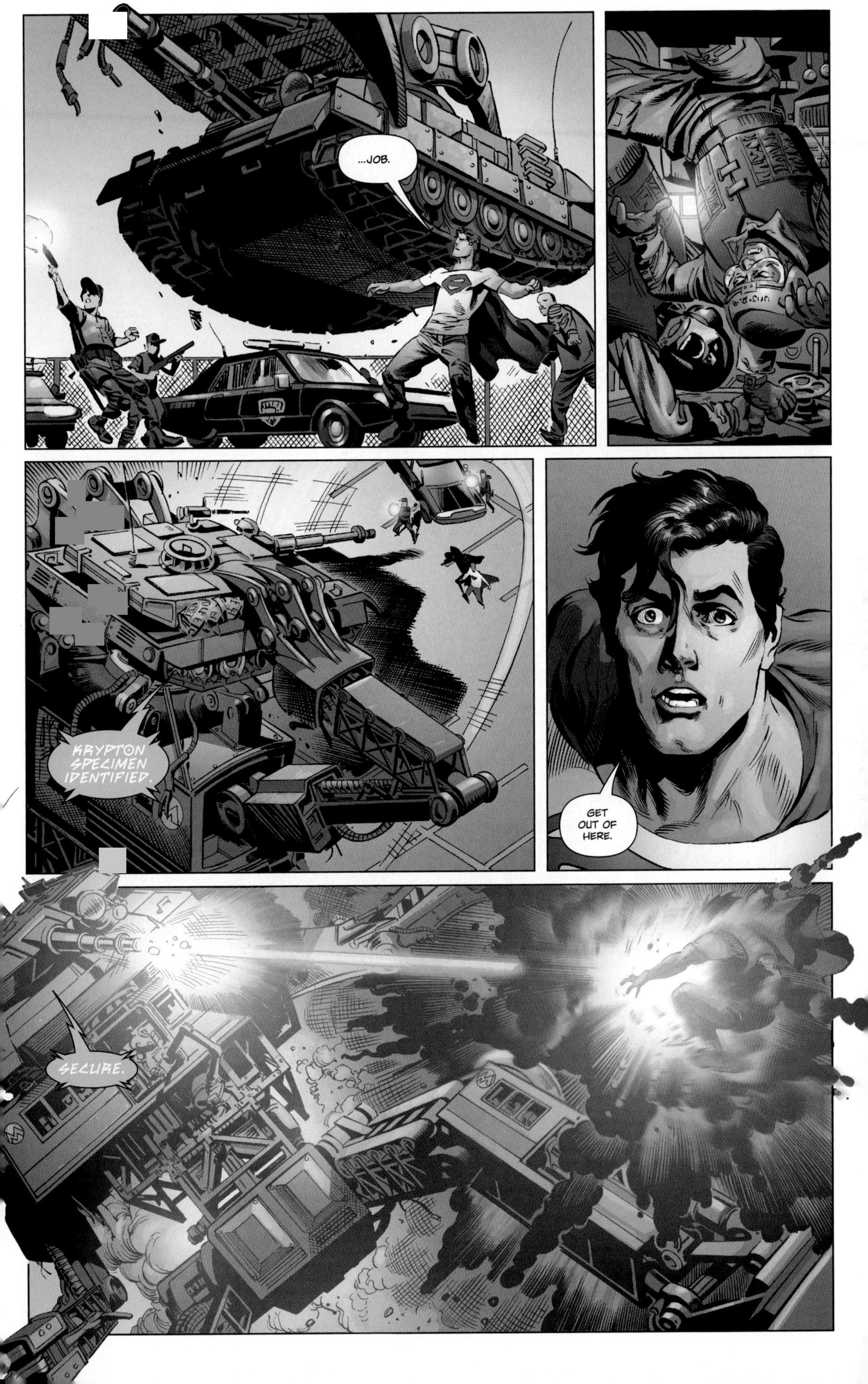
...JOB.
KRYPTON SPECIMEN IDENTIFIED.
GET OUT OF HERE.
SECURE.

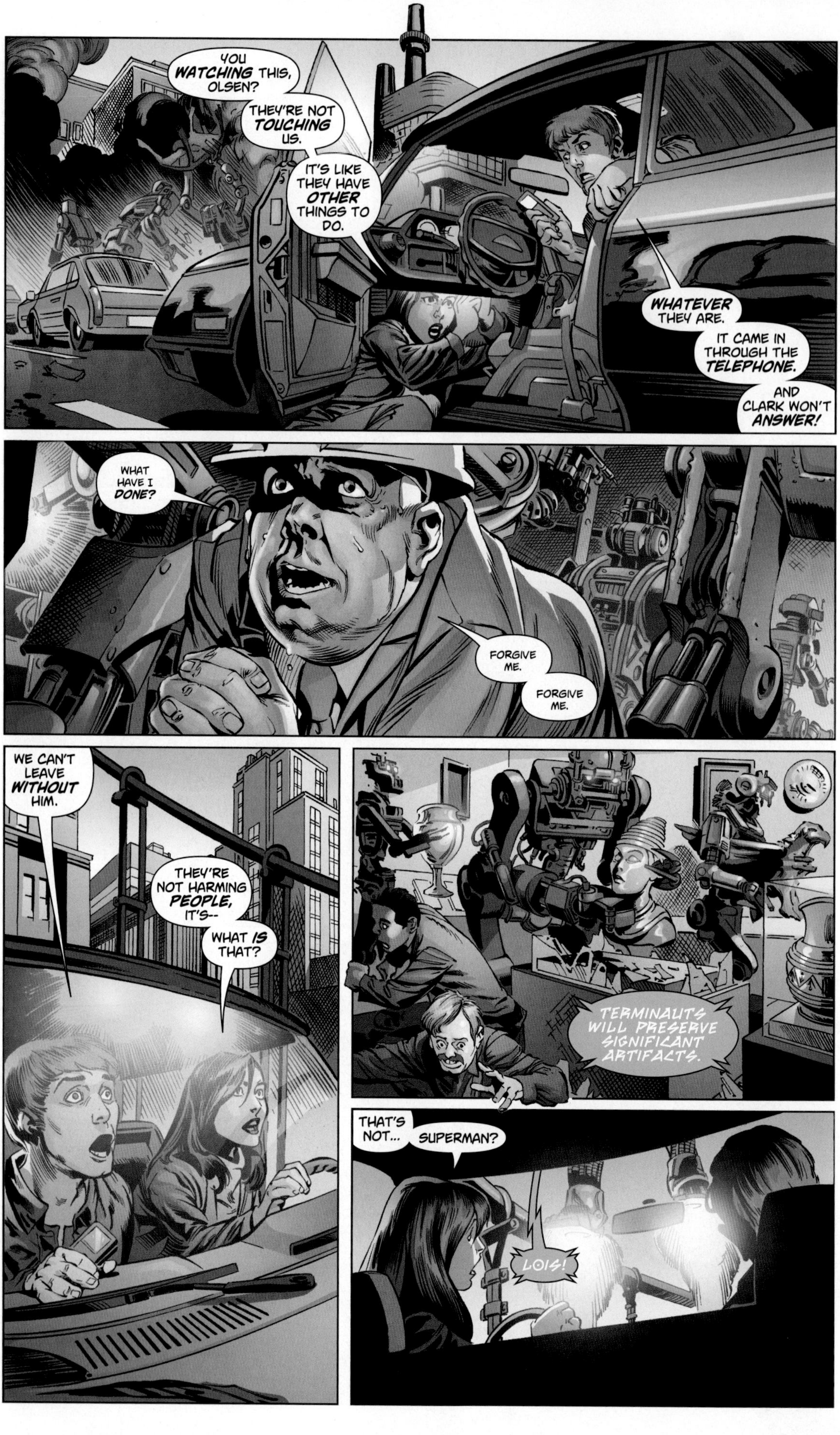
YOU WATCHING THIS, OLSEN?
THEY'RE NOT TOUCHING US.
IT'S LIKE THEY HAVE OTHER THINGS TO DO.
WHATEVER THEY ARE.
IT CAME IN THROUGH THE TELEPHONE.
AND CLARK WON'T ANSWER!
WHAT HAVE I DONE?
FORGIVE ME.
FORGIVE ME.
WE CAN'T LEAVE WITHOUT HIM.
THEY'RE NOT HARMING PEOPLE, IT'S--
WHAT IS THAT?
TERMINAUTS WILL PRESERVE SIGNIFICANT ARTIFACTS.
THAT'S NOT...
SUPERMAN?
LOIS!

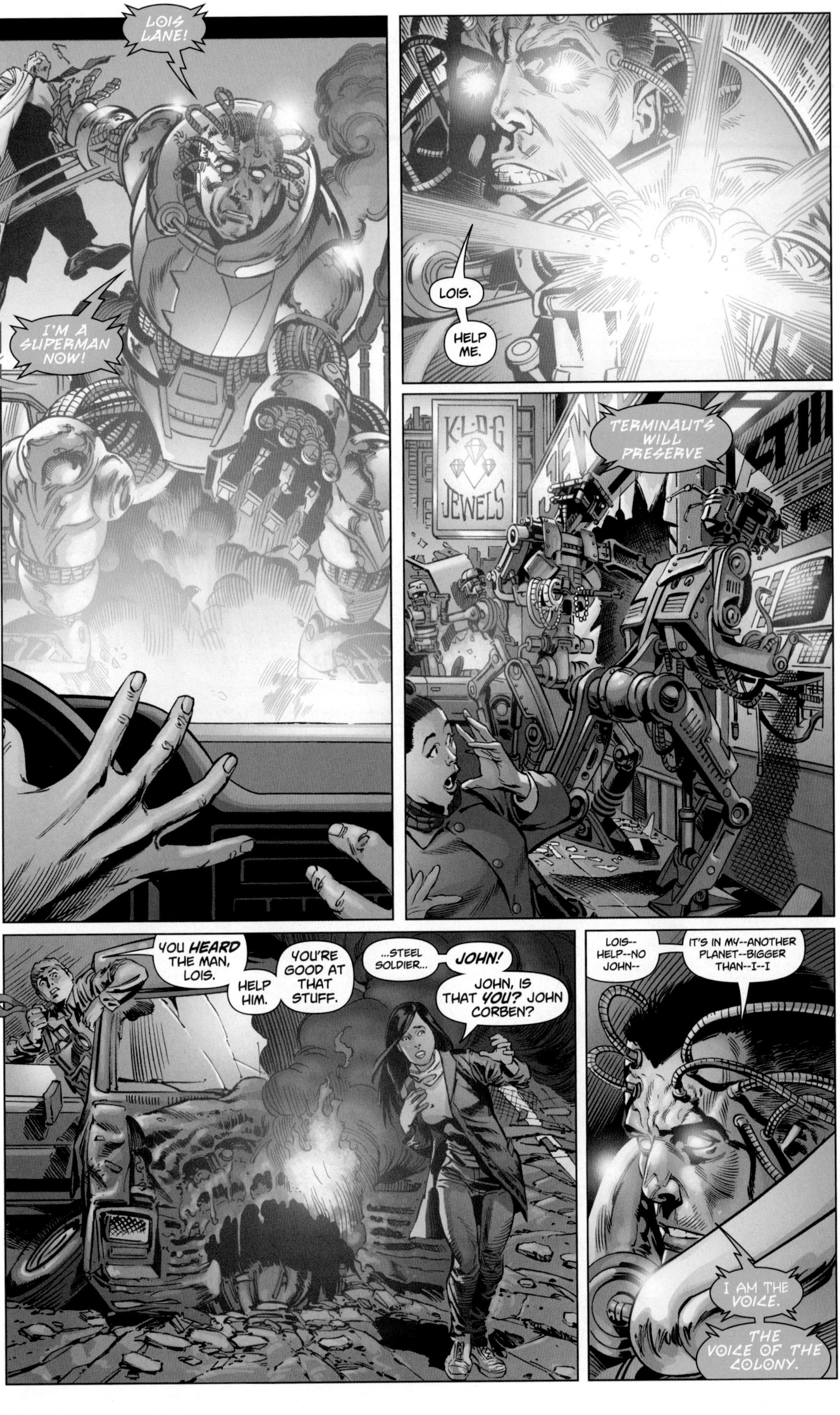
LOIS LANE!
I'M A SUPERMAN NOW!
LOIS.
HELP ME.
TERMINAUTS WILL PRESERVE
K·L·D·G JEWELS
YOU HEARD THE MAN, LOIS.
HELP HIM.
YOU'RE GOOD AT THAT STUFF.
...STEEL SOLDIER...
JOHN!
JOHN, IS THAT YOU? JOHN CORBEN?
LOIS--HELP--NO JOHN--
IT'S IN MY--ANOTHER PLANET--BIGGER THAN--I--I
I AM THE VOICE.
THE VOICE OF THE COLONY.

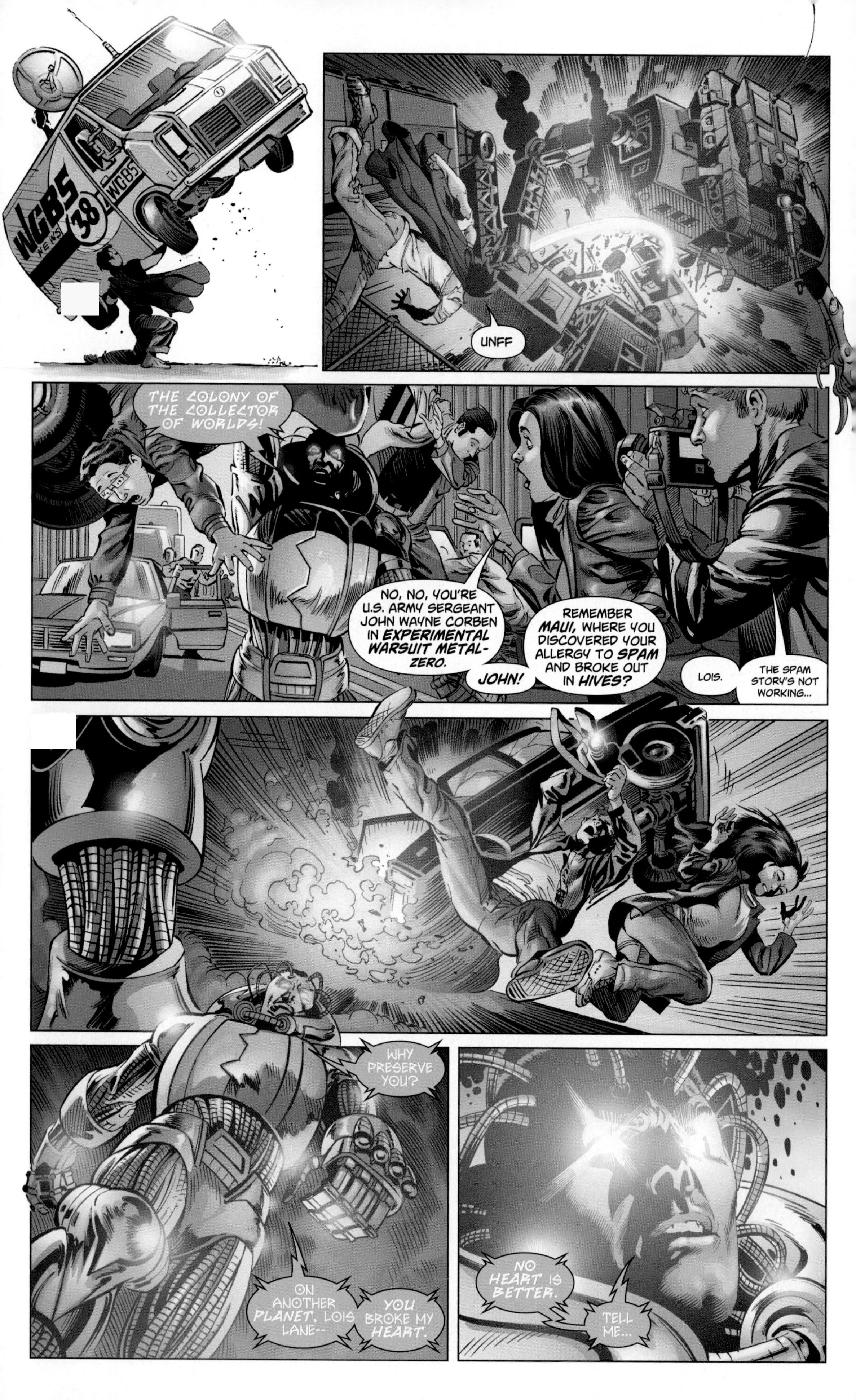
WGBS
38
NEWS
UNFF
THE COLONY OF THE COLLECTOR OF WORLDS!
NO, NO, YOU'RE U.S. ARMY SERGEANT JOHN WAYNE CORBEN IN EXPERIMENTAL WARSUIT METAL-ZERO.
JOHN!
REMEMBER MAUI, WHERE YOU DISCOVERED YOUR ALLERGY TO SPAM AND BROKE OUT IN HIVES?
LOIS.
THE SPAM STORY'S NOT WORKING...
WHY PRESERVE YOU?
ON ANOTHER PLANET, LOIS LANE--
YOU BROKE MY HEART.
NO HEART IS BETTER.
TELL ME...

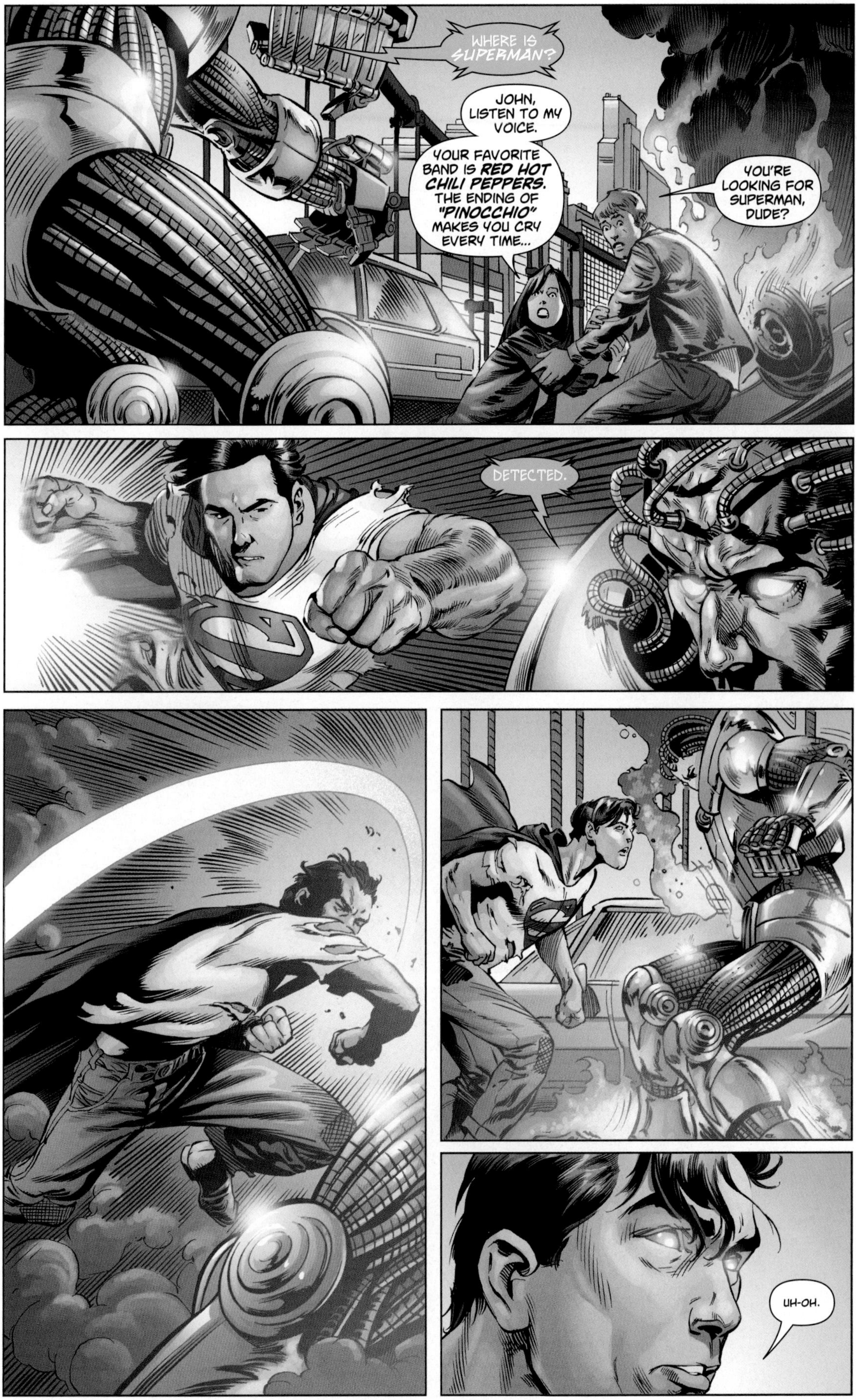
WHERE IS SUPERMAN?
JOHN, LISTEN TO MY VOICE.
YOUR FAVORITE BAND IS RED HOT CHILI PEPPERS. THE ENDING OF "PINOCCHIO" MAKES YOU CRY EVERY TIME...
YOU'RE LOOKING FOR SUPERMAN, DUDE?
DETECTED.
UH-OH.

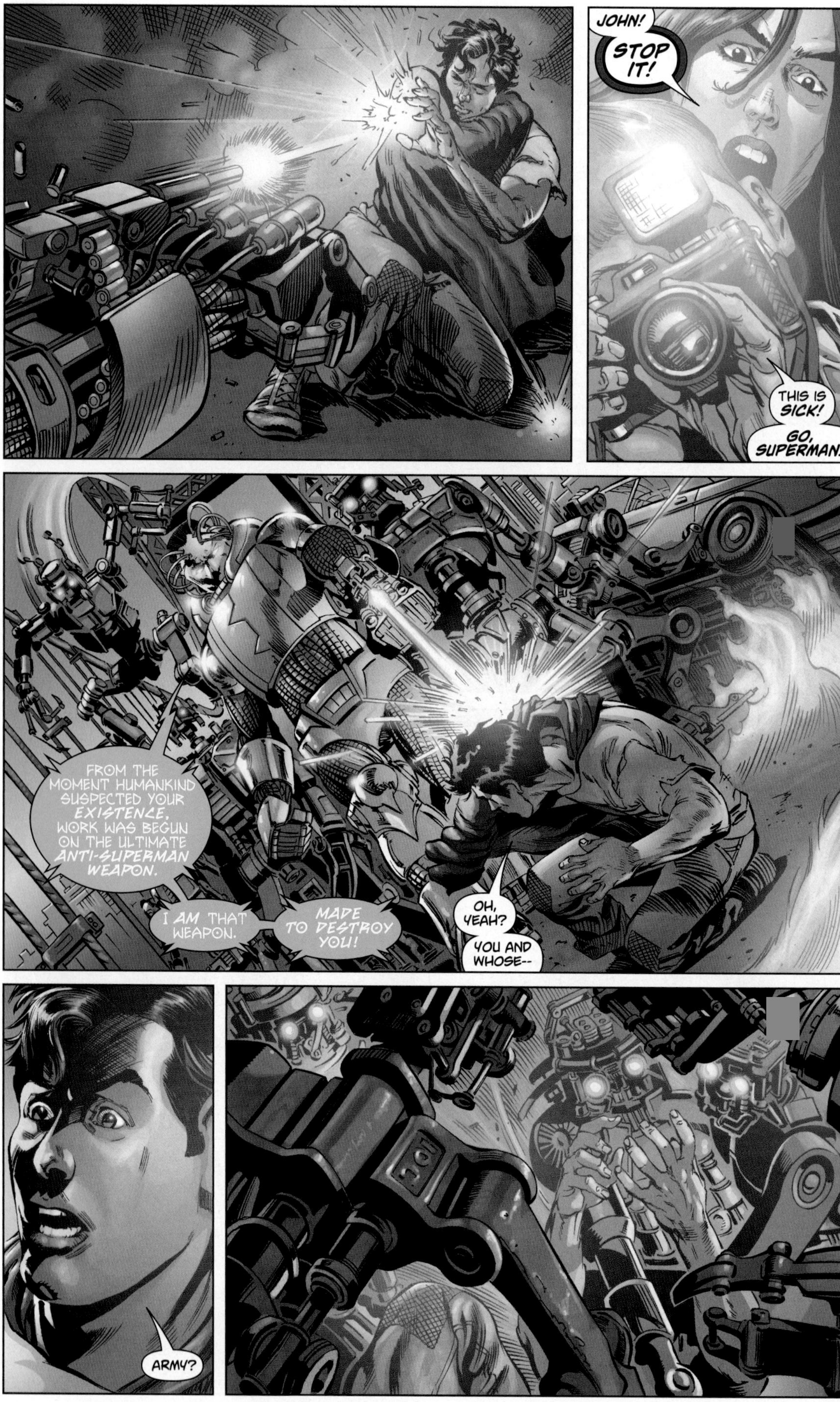
JOHN!
STOP IT!
THIS IS SICK!
GO, SUPERMAN!
FROM THE MOMENT HUMANKIND SUSPECTED YOUR EXISTENCE, WORK WAS BEGUN ON THE ULTIMATE ANTI-SUPERMAN WEAPON.
I AM THAT WEAPON.
MADE TO DESTROY YOU!
OH, YEAH?
YOU AND WHOSE--
ARMY?

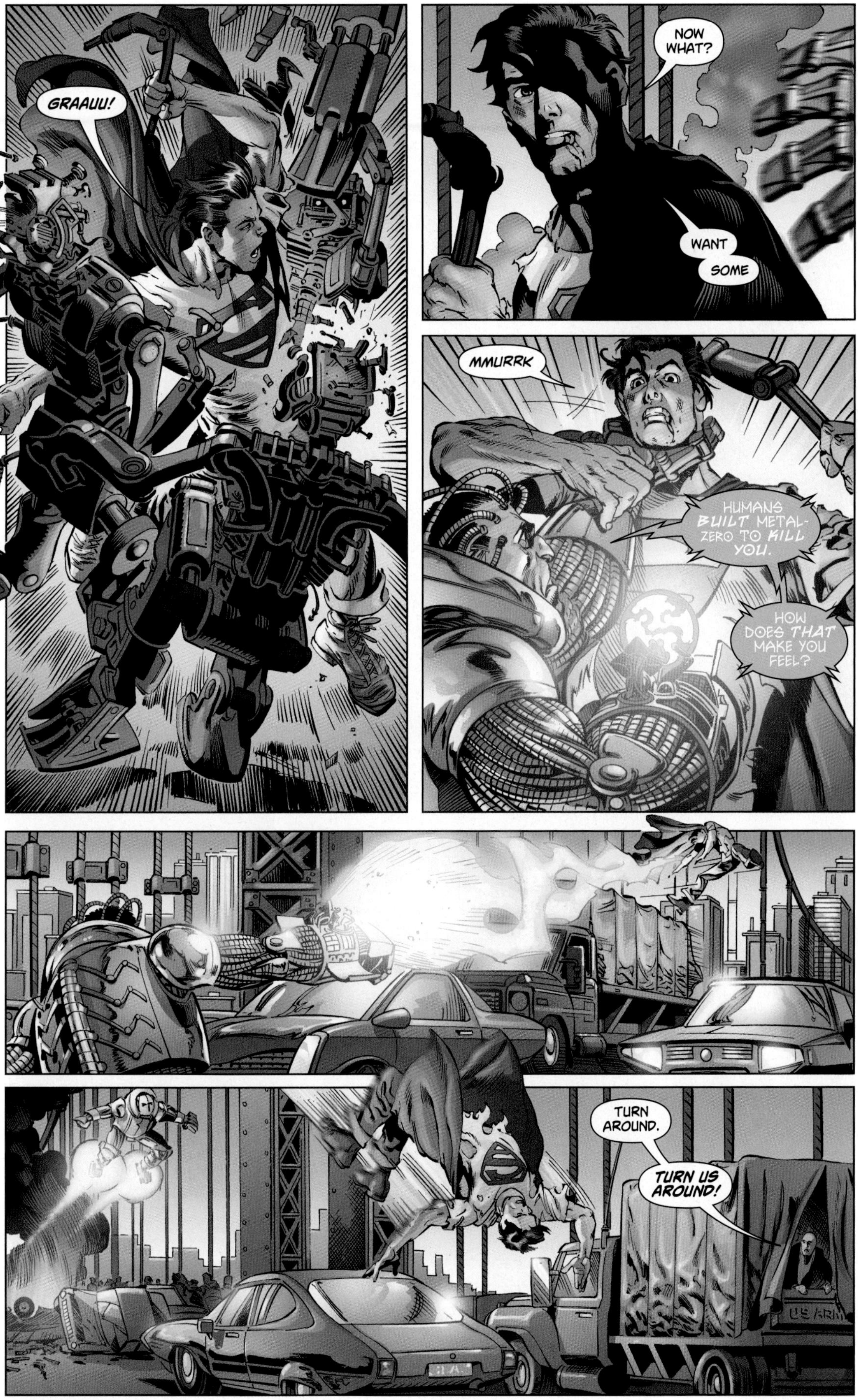
GRAAUU!
NOW WHAT?
WANT
SOME
MMURRK
HUMANS BUILT METAL-ZERO TO KILL YOU.
HOW DOES THAT MAKE YOU FEEL?
TURN AROUND.
TURN US AROUND!

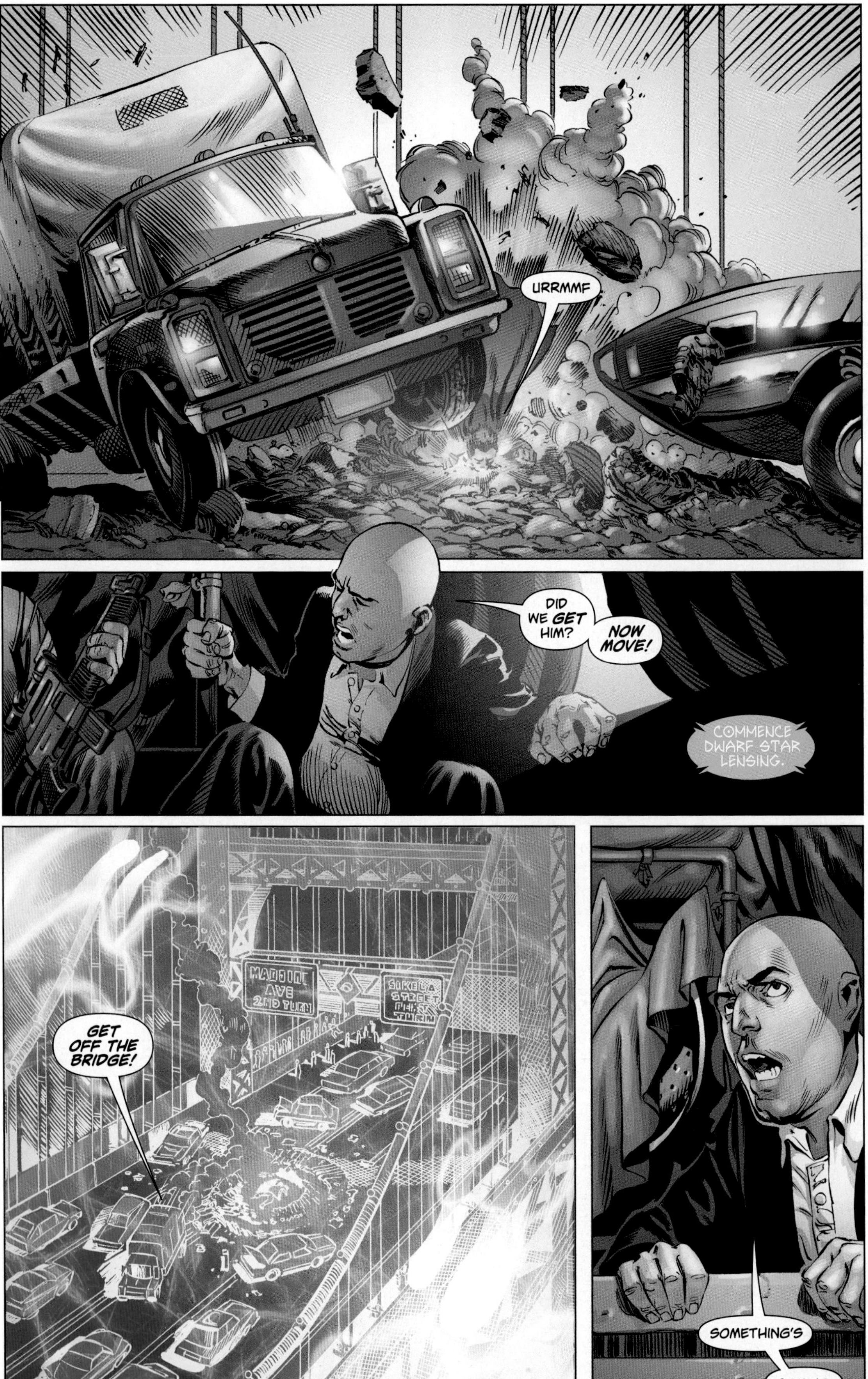
URRMMF
DID WE GET HIM?
NOW MOVE!
COMMENCE DWARF STAR LENSING.
GET OFF THE BRIDGE!
SOMETHING'S
COMING.

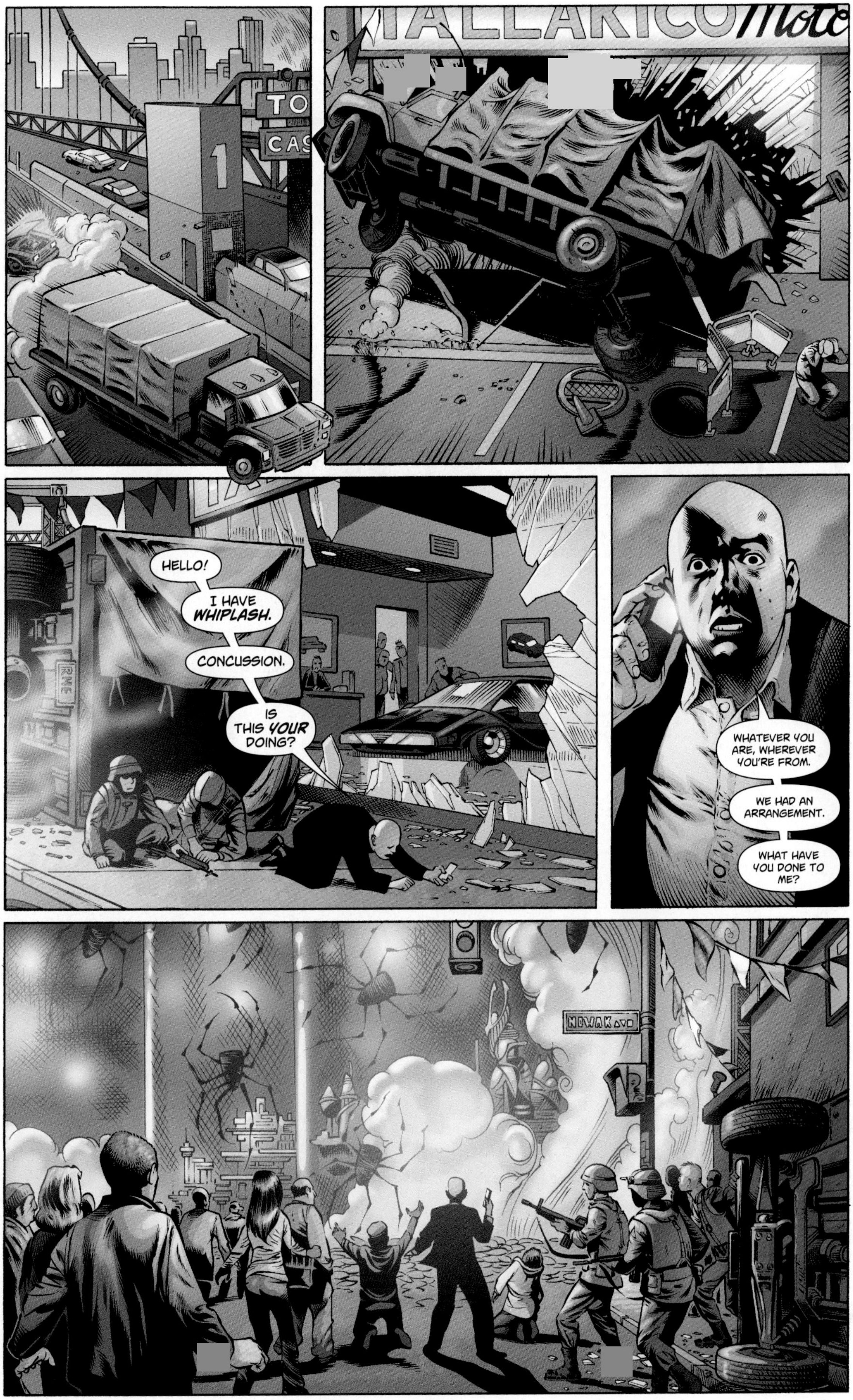
HELLO!
I HAVE WHIPLASH.
CONCUSSION.
IS THIS YOUR DOING?
WHATEVER YOU ARE, WHEREVER YOU'RE FROM.
WE HAD AN ARRANGEMENT.
WHAT HAVE YOU DONE TO ME?

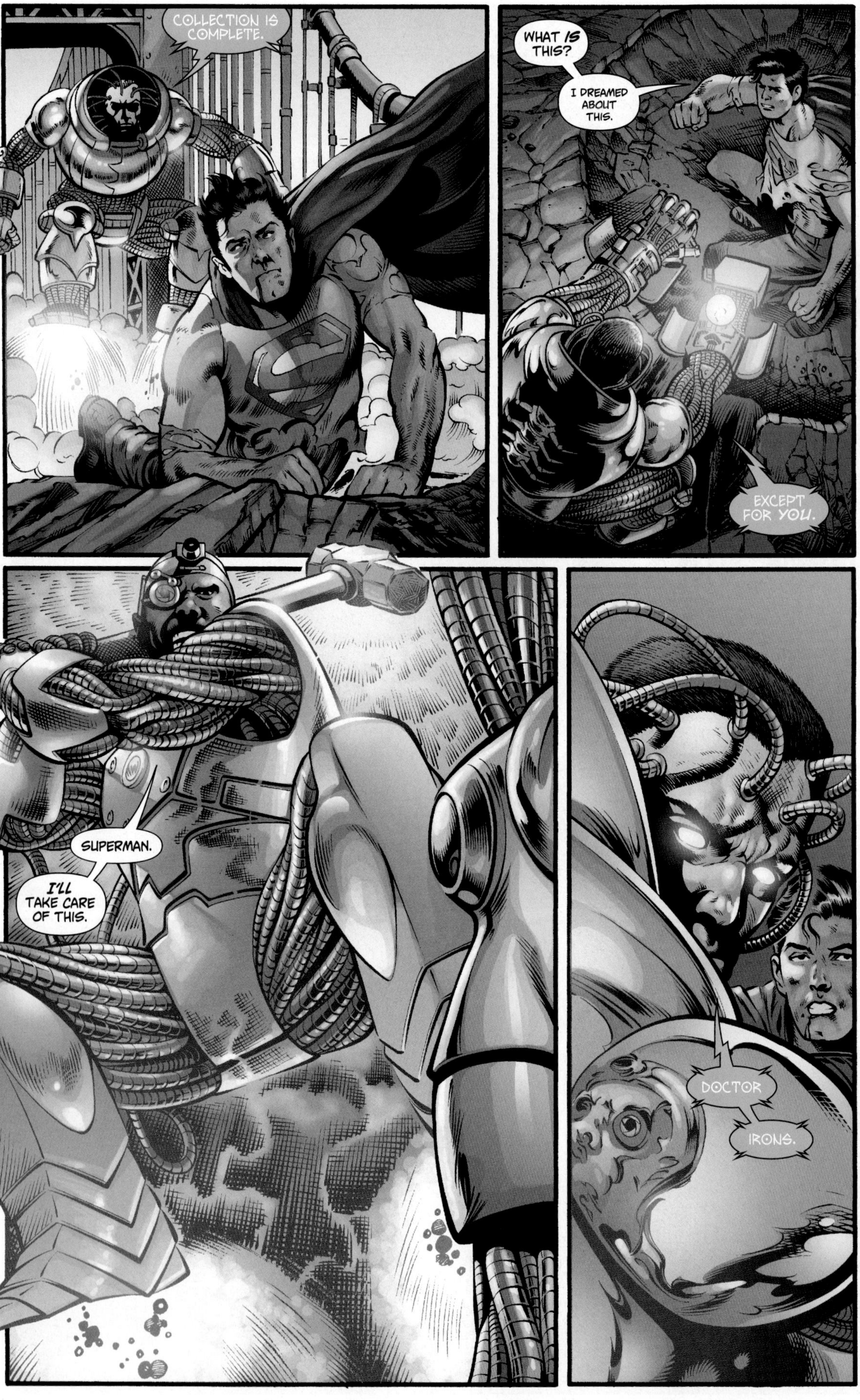
COLLECTION IS COMPLETE.
WHAT IS THIS?
I DREAMED ABOUT THIS.
EXCEPT FOR YOU.
SUPERMAN.
I'LL TAKE CARE OF THIS.
DOCTOR
IRONS.

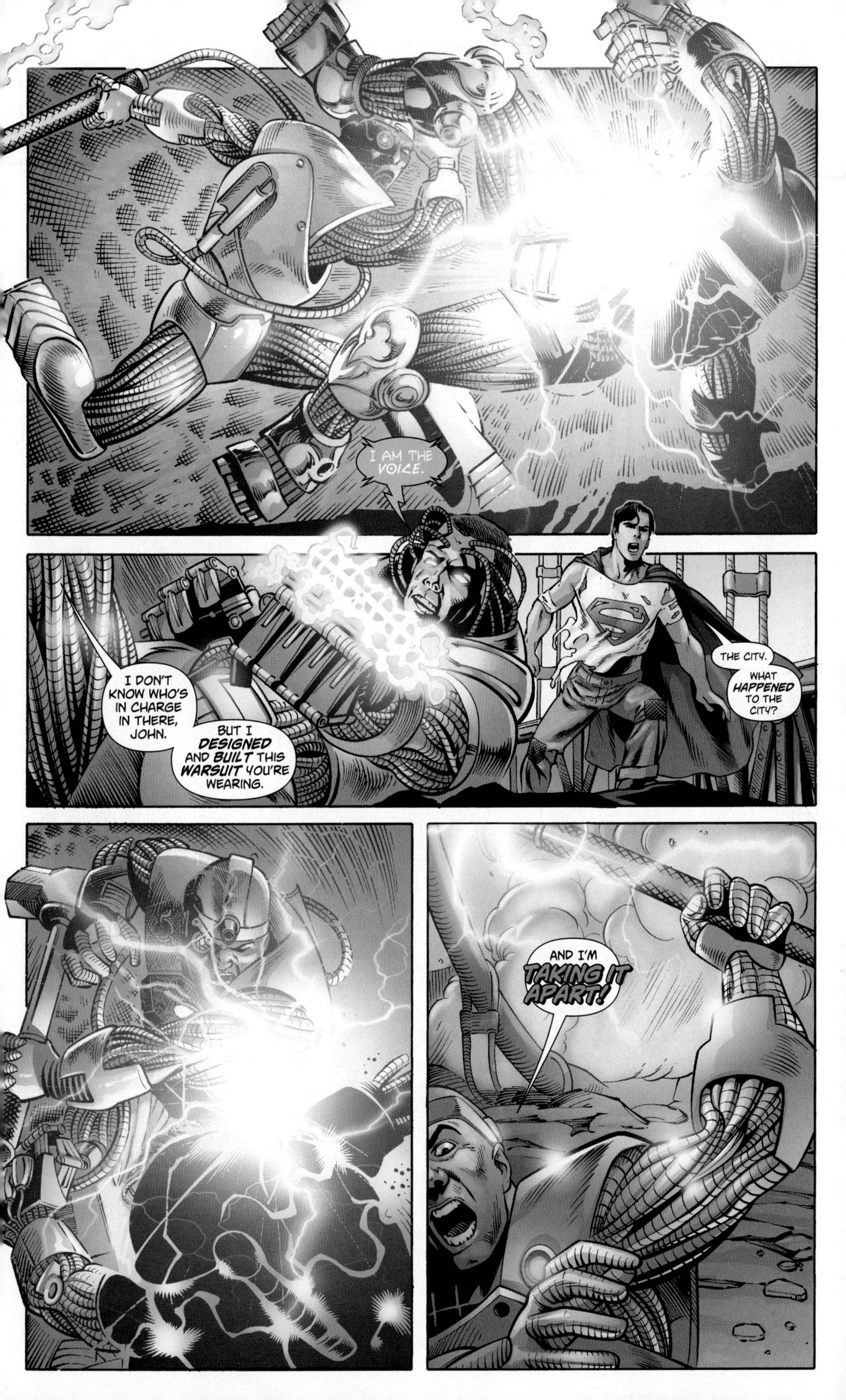

I AM THE VOICE.
I DON'T KNOW WHO'S IN CHARGE IN THERE, JOHN.
BUT I DESIGNED AND BUILT THIS WARSUIT YOU'RE WEARING.
THE CITY.
WHAT HAPPENED TO THE CITY?
AND I'M TAKING IT APART!

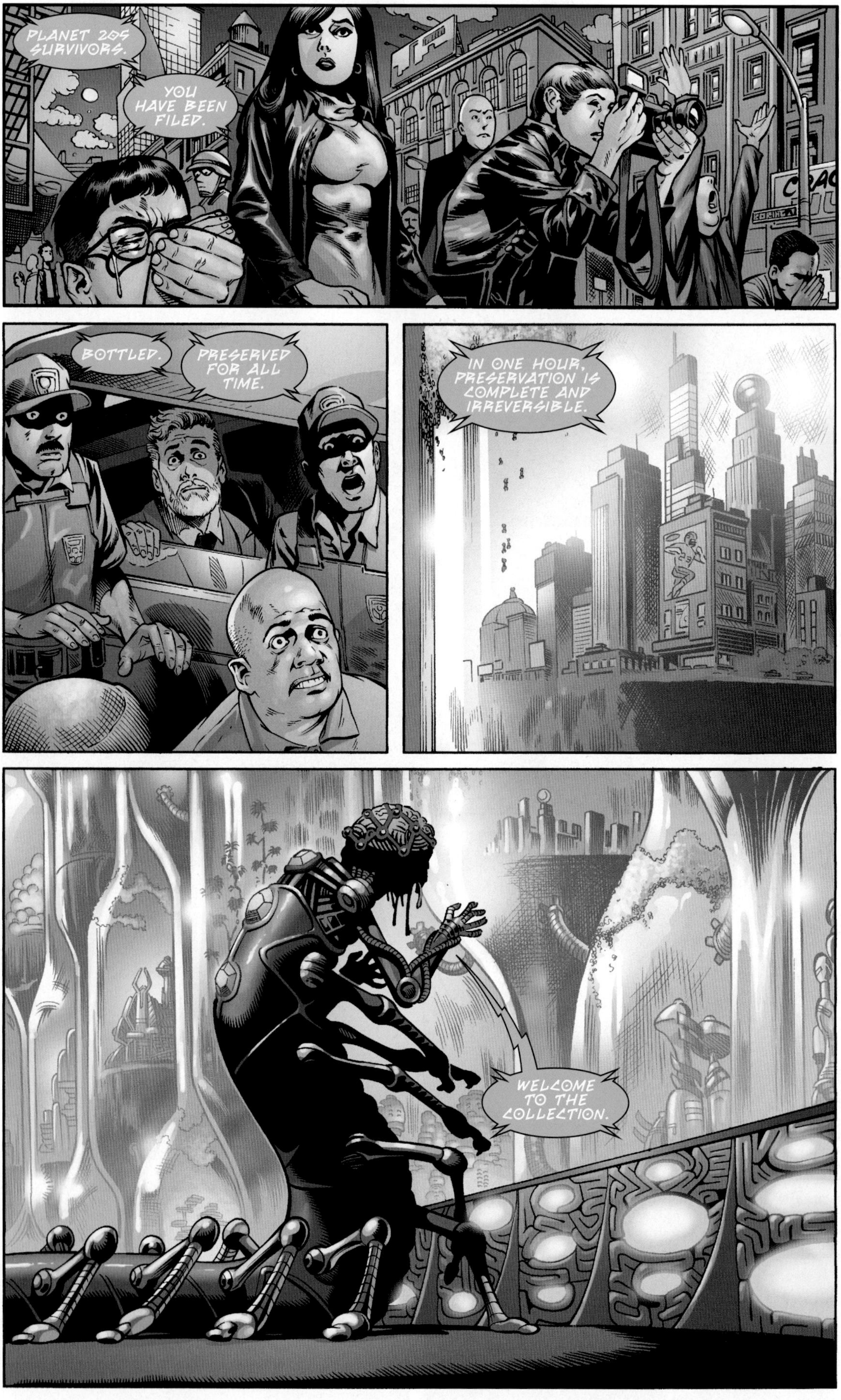
PLANET 205 SURVIVORS.
YOU HAVE BEEN FILED.
BOTTLED.
PRESERVED FOR ALL TIME.
IN ONE HOUR, PRESERVATION IS COMPLETE AND IRREVERSIBLE.
WELCOME TO THE COLLECTION.

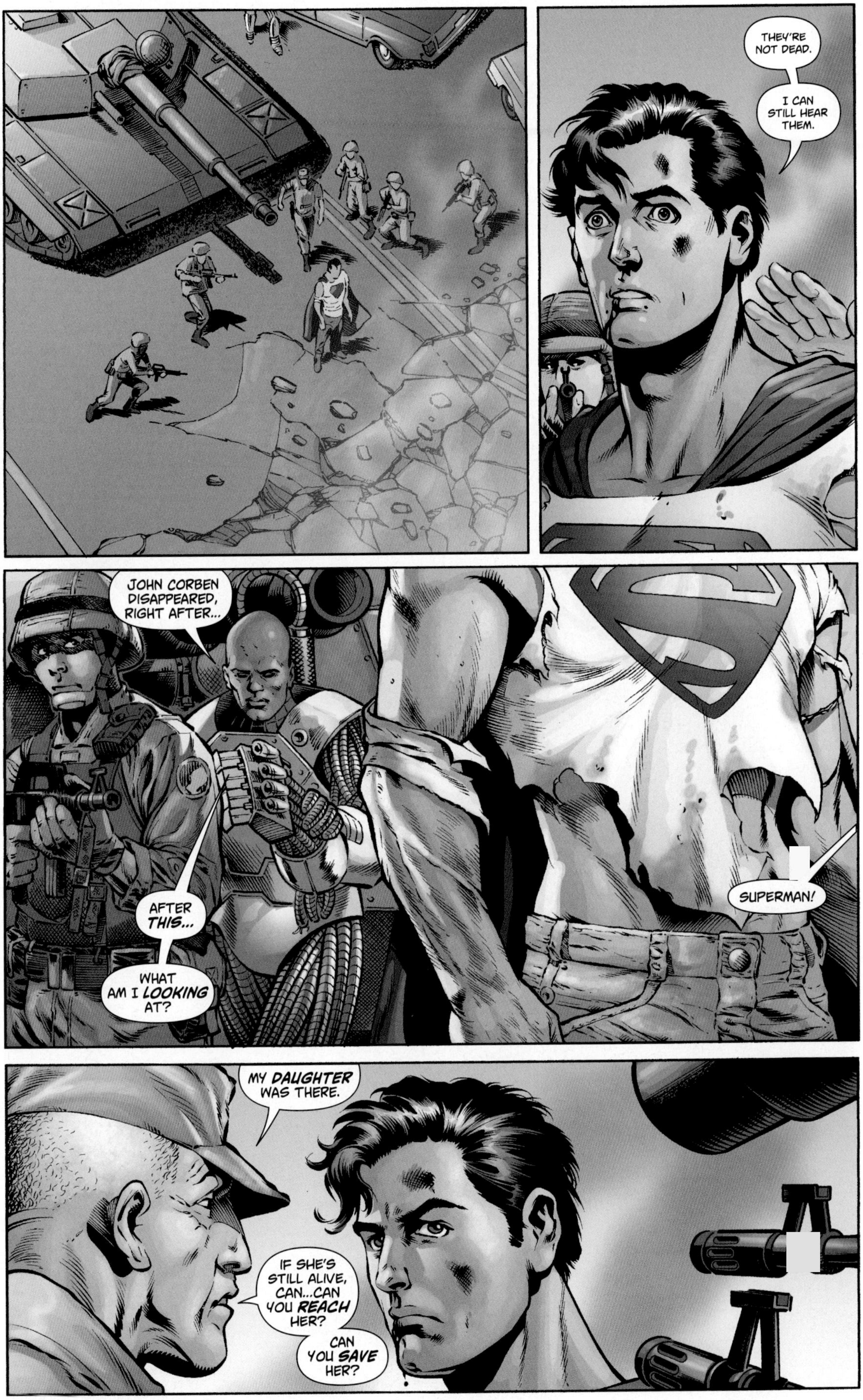
THEY'RE NOT DEAD.
I CAN STILL HEAR THEM.
JOHN CORBEN DISAPPEARED, RIGHT AFTER...
AFTER THIS...
WHAT AM I LOOKING AT?
SUPERMAN!
MY DAUGHTER WAS THERE.
IF SHE'S STILL ALIVE, CAN...CAN YOU REACH HER?
CAN YOU SAVE HER?

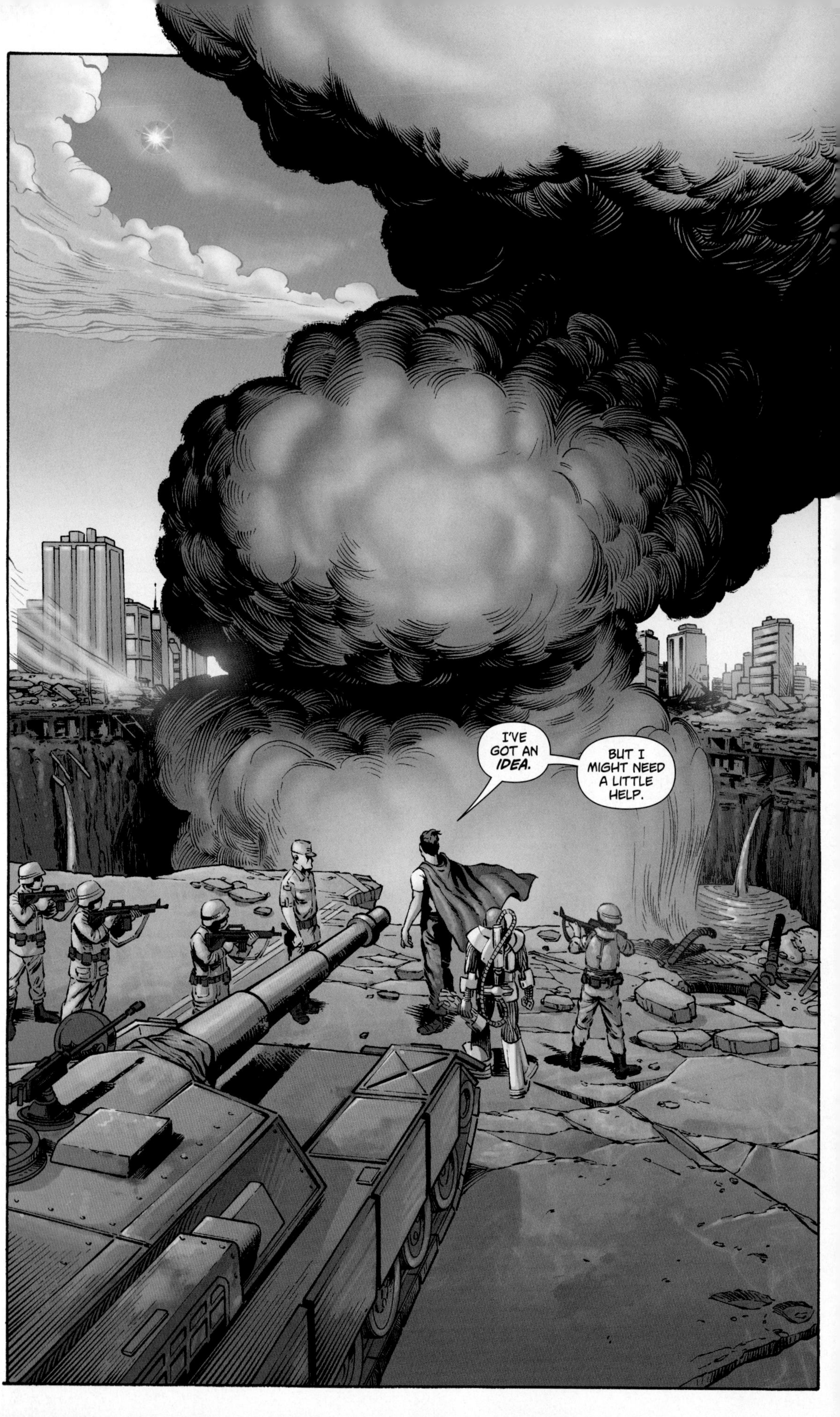
I'VE GOT AN *IDEA.*
BUT I MIGHT NEED A LITTLE HELP.

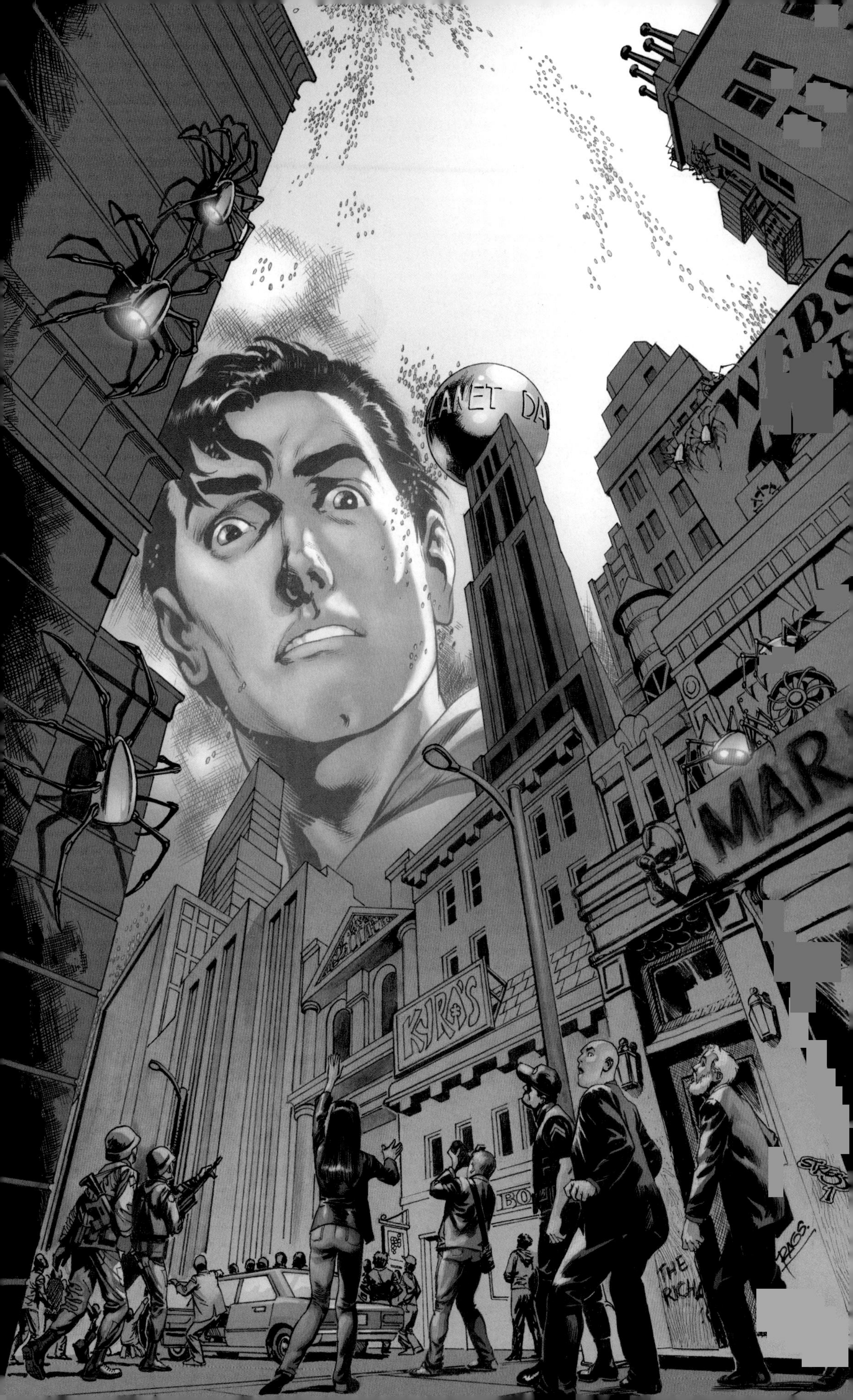
LANET DA
WEBS
MAR
KYRA'S
BO
THE
RICHA

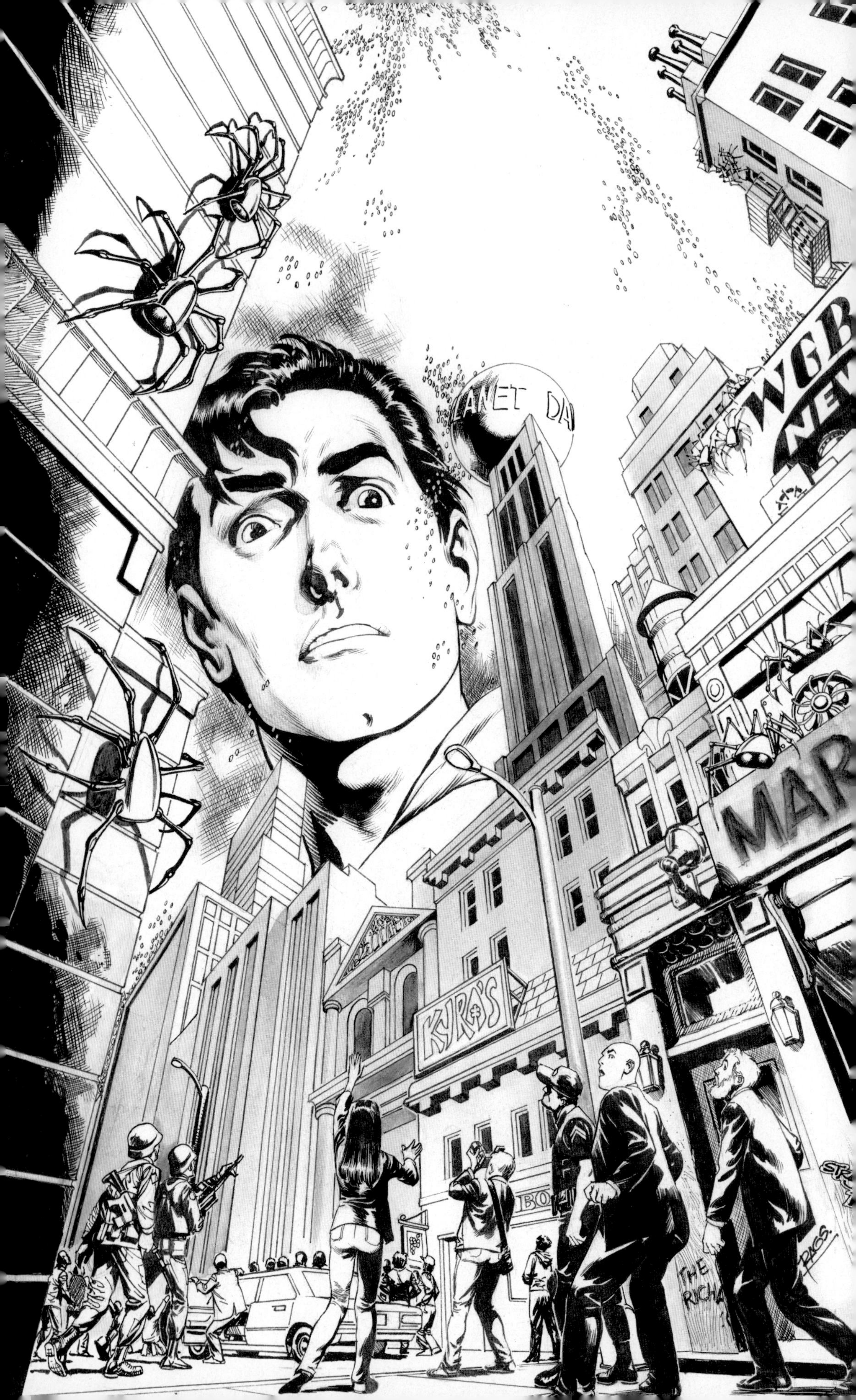

LANET DA
WGB
NEW
MAR
KYRO'S
BO
THE
RICHA
RAGS.

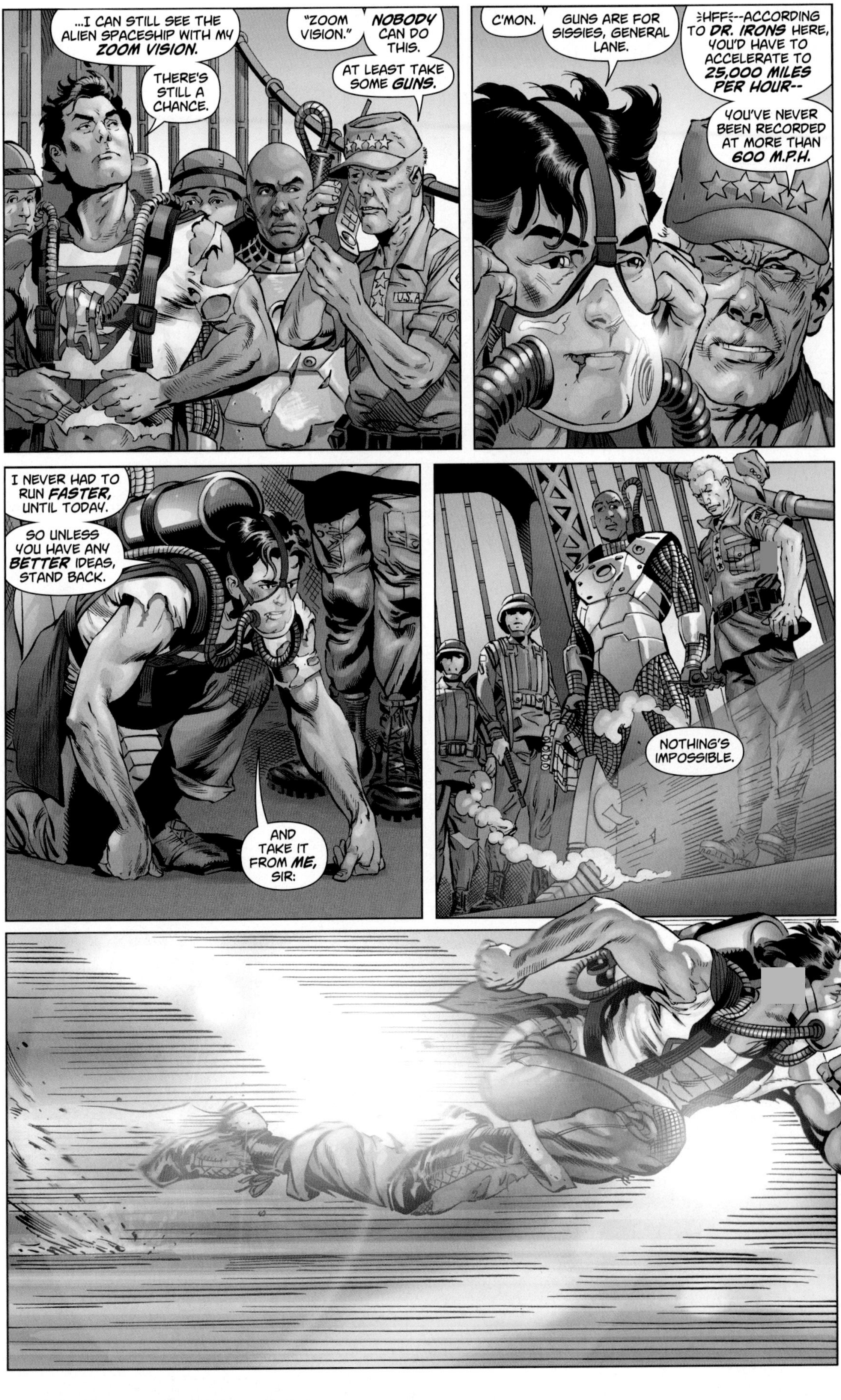

...I CAN STILL SEE THE ALIEN SPACESHIP WITH MY ZOOM VISION.
THERE'S STILL A CHANCE.
"ZOOM VISION."
NOBODY CAN DO THIS.
AT LEAST TAKE SOME GUNS.
C'MON.
GUNS ARE FOR SISSIES, GENERAL LANE.
HFF--ACCORDING TO DR. IRONS HERE, YOU'D HAVE TO ACCELERATE TO 25,000 MILES PER HOUR--
YOU'VE NEVER BEEN RECORDED AT MORE THAN 600 M.P.H.
I NEVER HAD TO RUN FASTER, UNTIL TODAY.
SO UNLESS YOU HAVE ANY BETTER IDEAS, STAND BACK.
AND TAKE IT FROM ME, SIR:
NOTHING'S IMPOSSIBLE.
U.S.A.

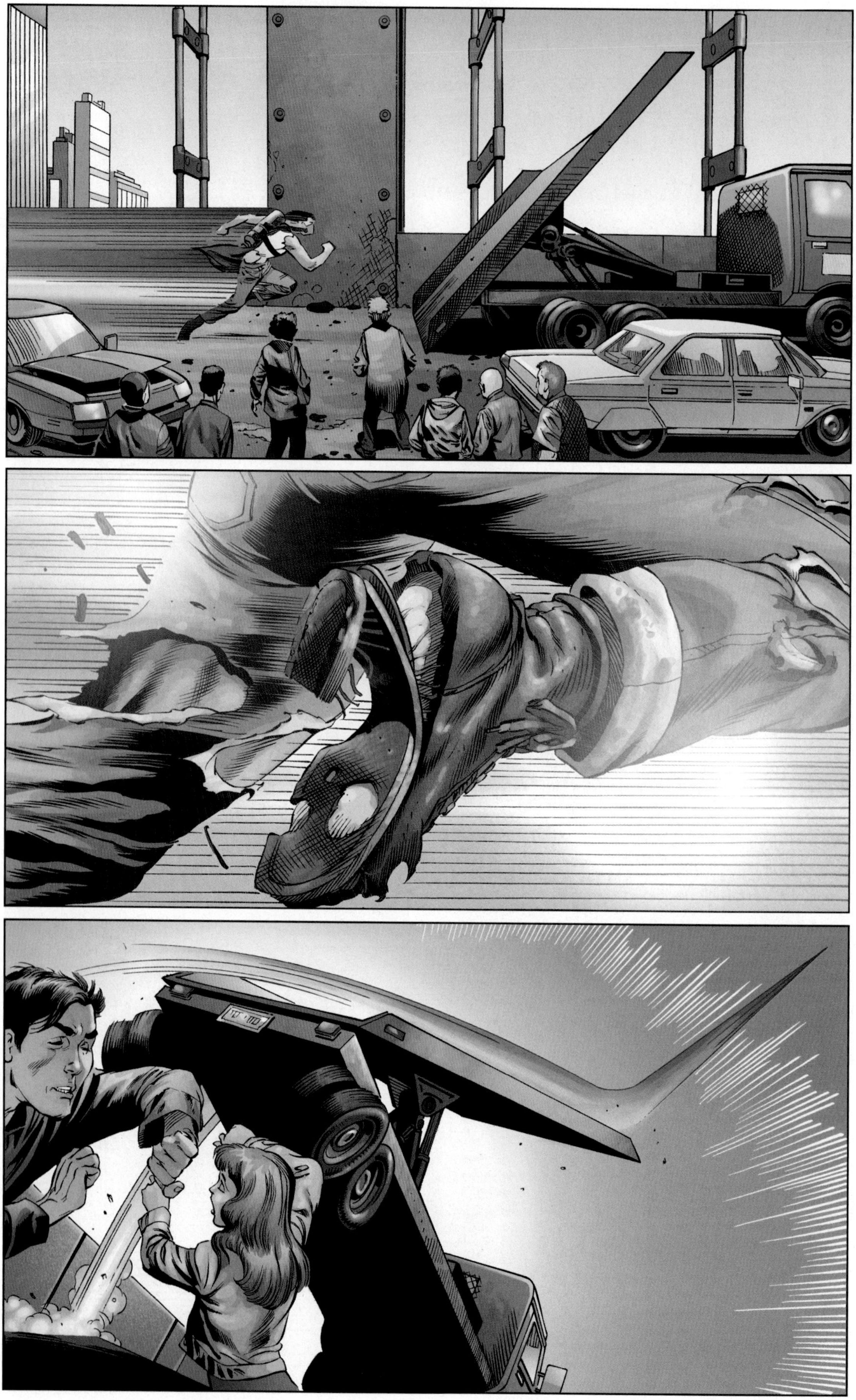

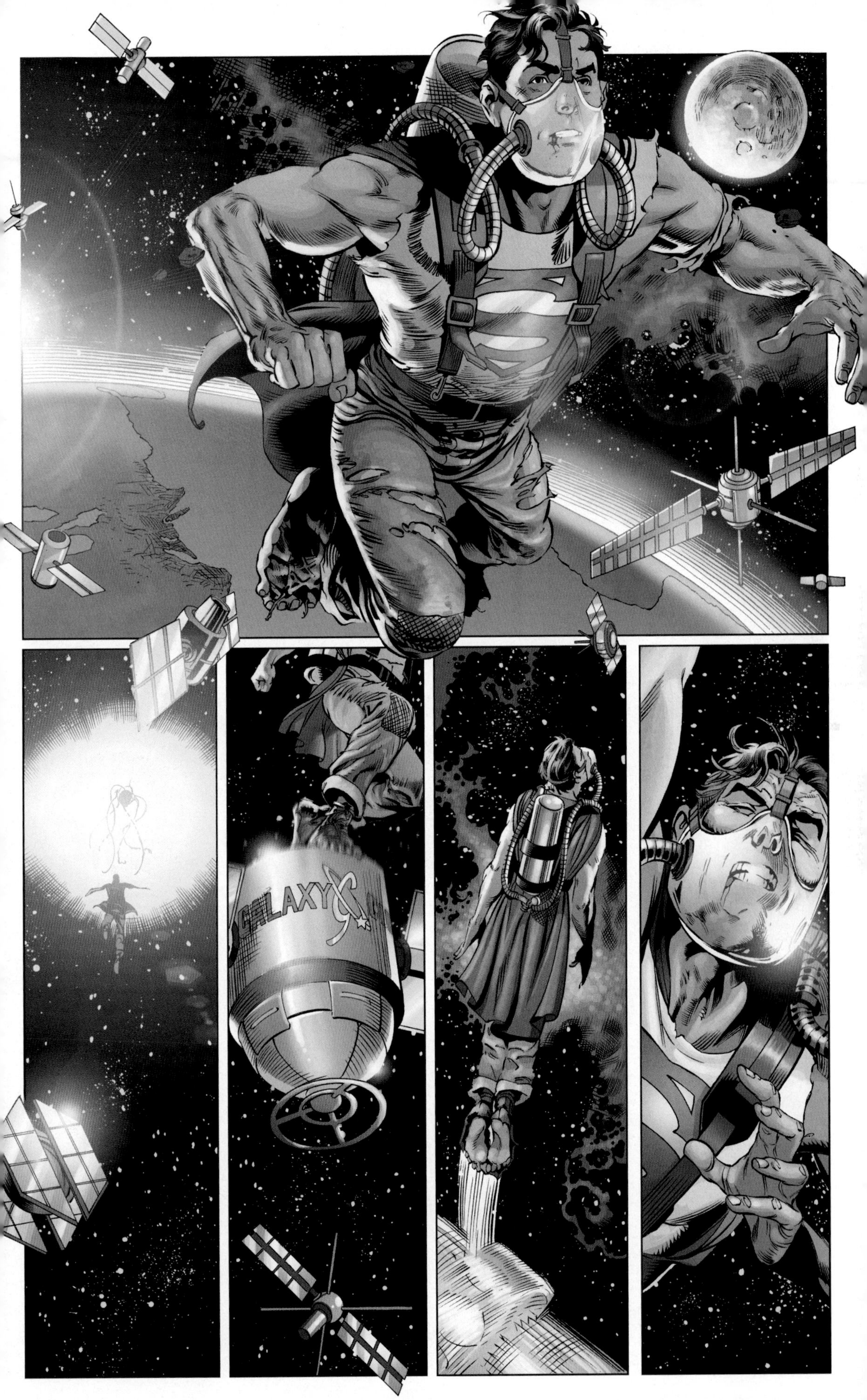
GALAXY

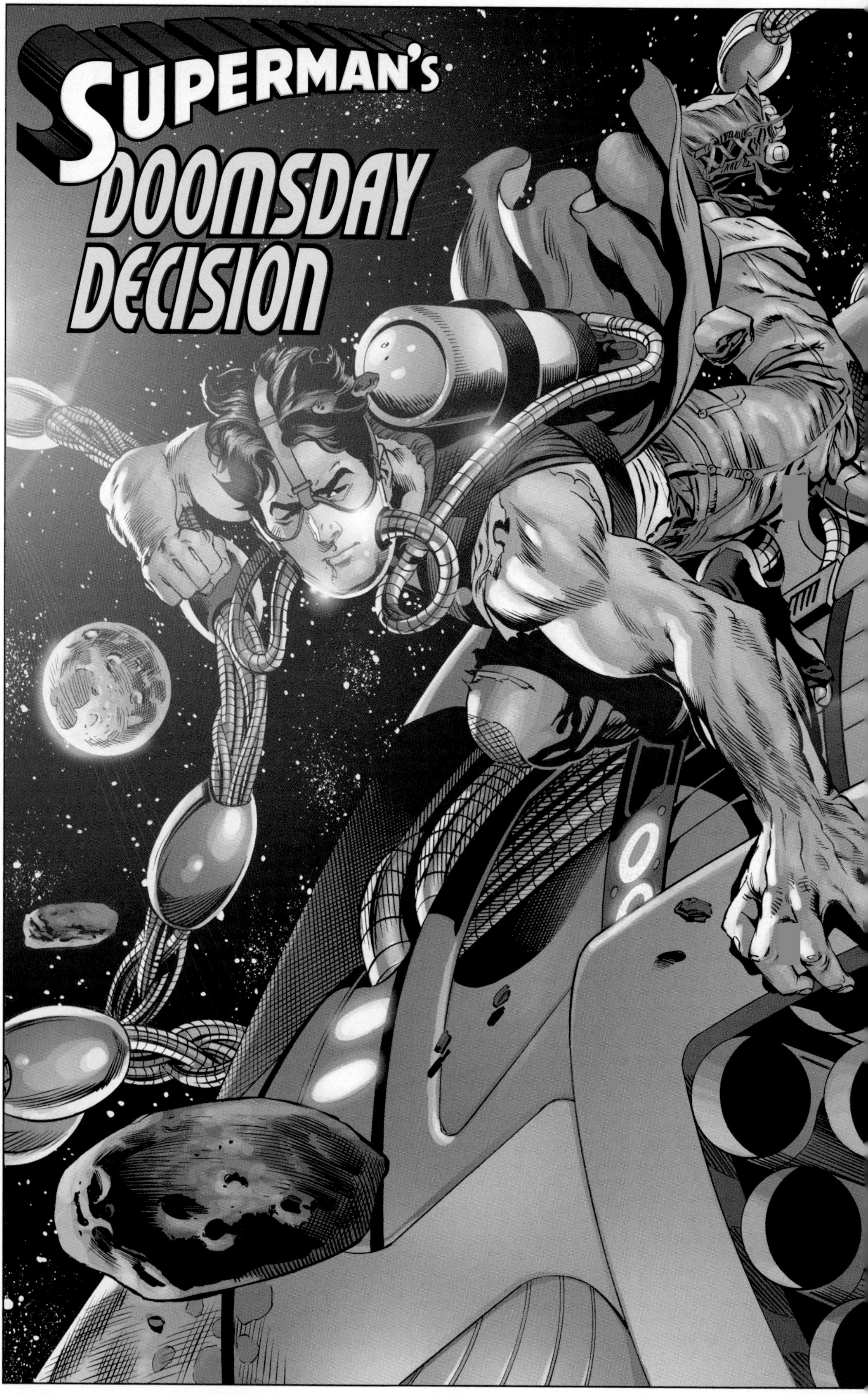
SUPERMAN'S
DOOMSDAY
DECISION

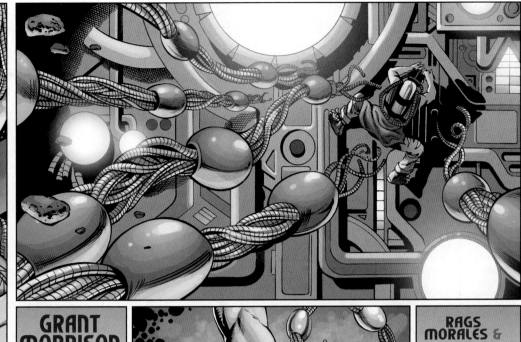

GRANT
MORRISON
WRITER
RAGS
MORALES
PENCILLER
RICK
BRYANT
INKER
BRAD
ANDERSON
COLORIST
PATRICK
BROSSEAU
LETTERER

RAGS
MORALES &
BRAD
ANDERSON
COVER
CHRIS
BURNHAM &
NATHAN
FAIRBAIRN
VARIANT COVER
WIL
MOSS
ASSOC. EDITOR
MATT
IDELSON
EDITOR
SUPERMAN
CREATED BY
JERRY
SIEGEL &
JOE SHUSTER

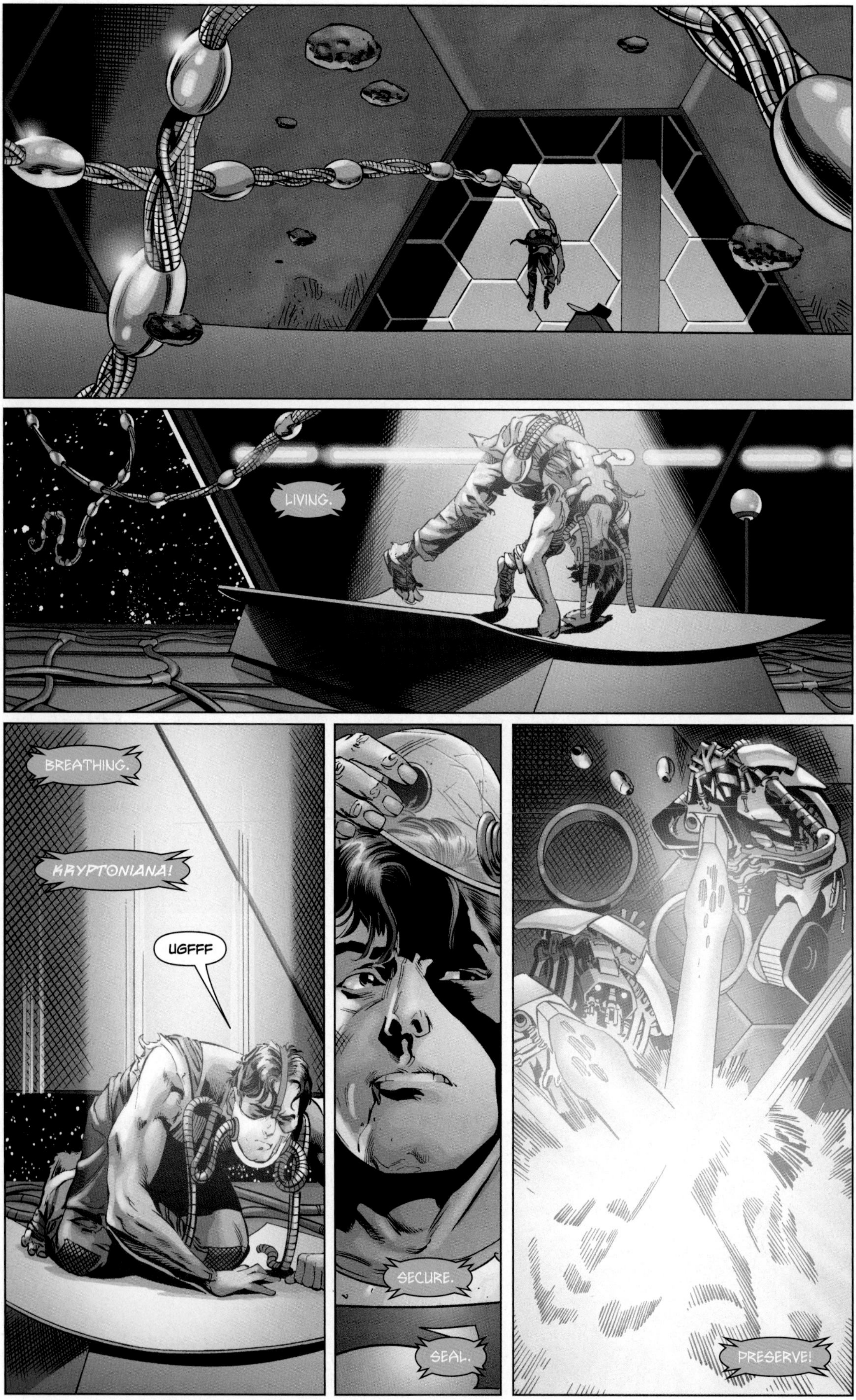
LIVING.
BREATHING.
KRYPTONIANA!
UGFFF
SECURE.
SEAL.
PRESERVE!

KRYPTON?

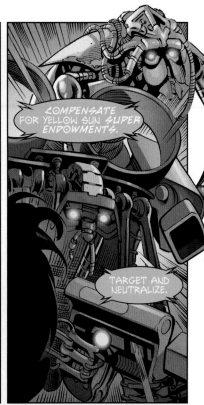

COMPENSATE FOR YELLOW SUN SUPER ENDOWMENTS.

TARGET AND NEUTRALIZE.

ALL I'M HEARING RIGHT NOW--

--IS BIG TALGHHH DFFB!

"BIG TALK!"

"METROPOLIS RADIO!"

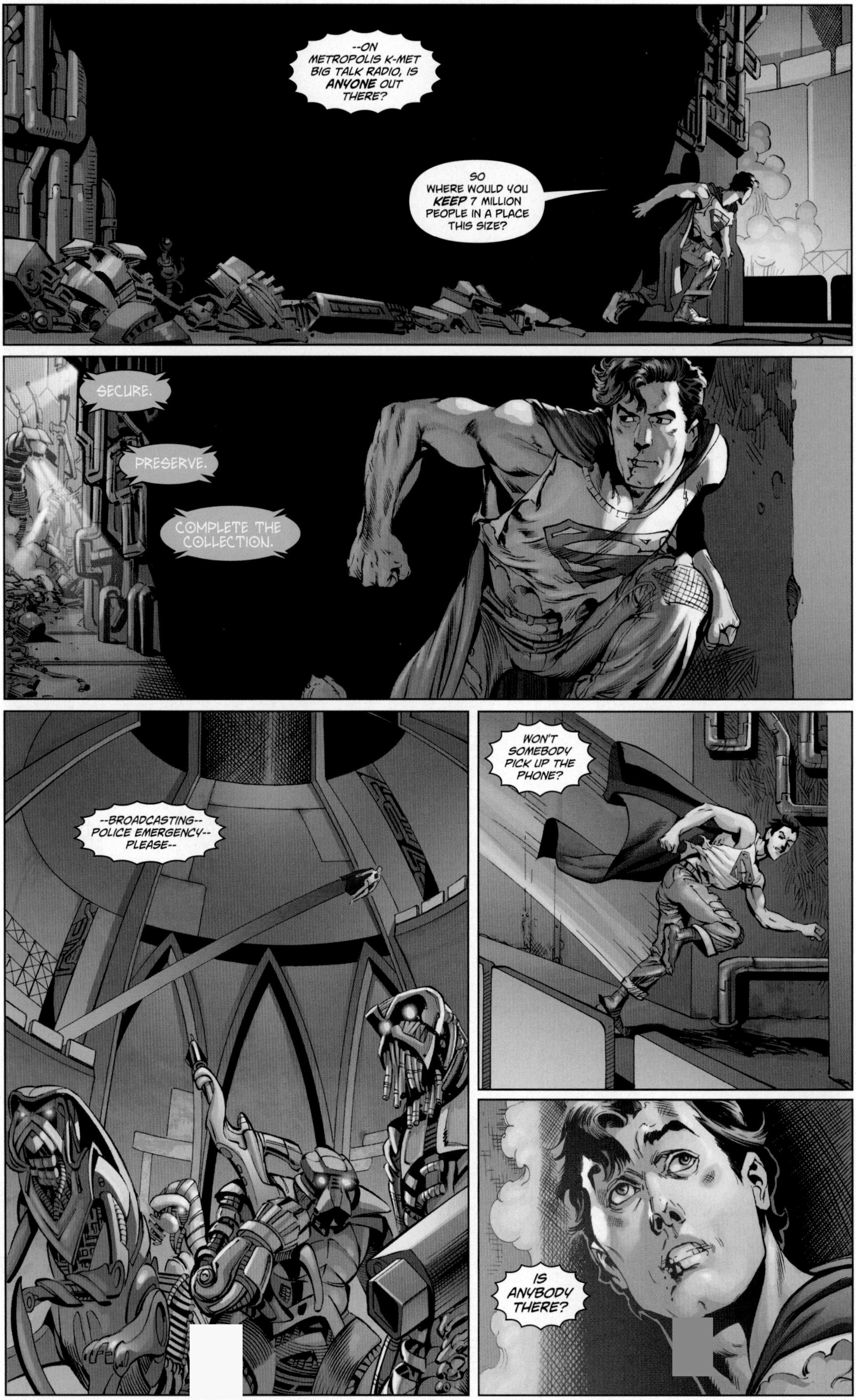
--ON METROPOLIS K-MET BIG TALK RADIO, IS ANYONE OUT THERE?
SO WHERE WOULD YOU KEEP 7 MILLION PEOPLE IN A PLACE THIS SIZE?
SECURE.
PRESERVE.
COMPLETE THE COLLECTION.
--BROADCASTING-- POLICE EMERGENCY-- PLEASE--
WON'T SOMEBODY PICK UP THE PHONE?
IS ANYBODY THERE?

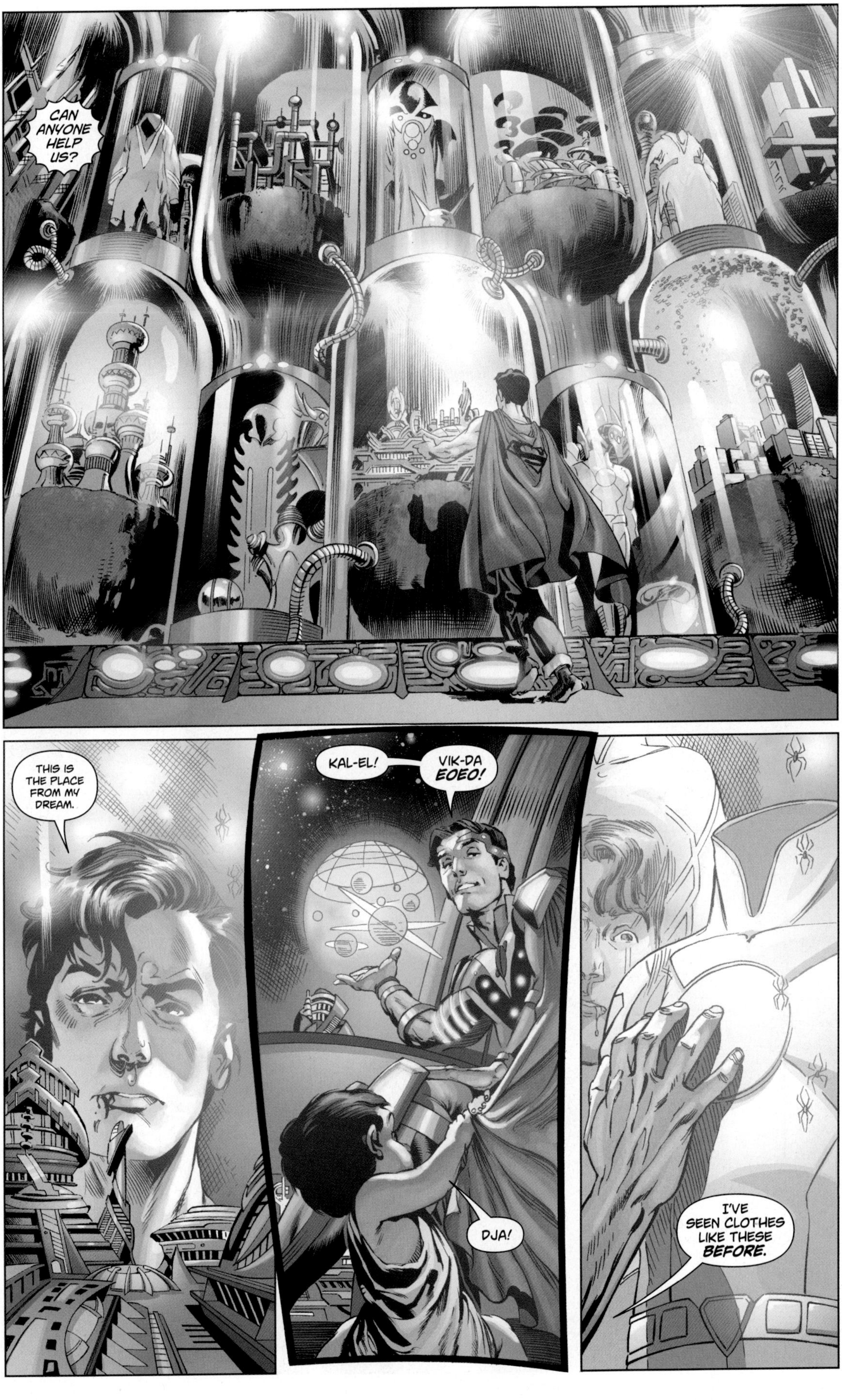
CAN ANYONE HELP US?
THIS IS THE PLACE FROM MY DREAM.
KAL-EL!
VIK-DA EOEO!
DJA!
I'VE SEEN CLOTHES LIKE THESE BEFORE.

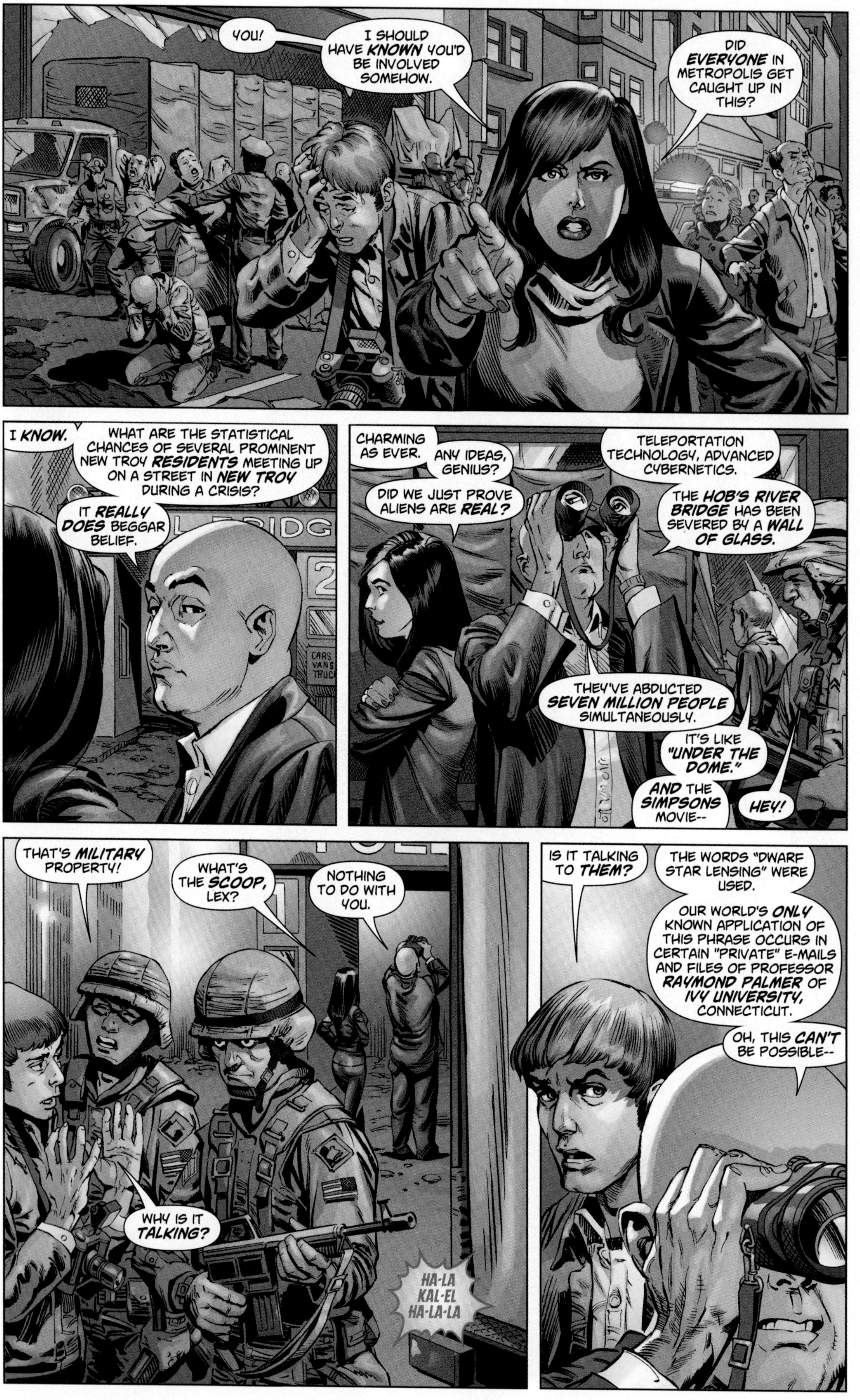

YOU!
I SHOULD HAVE KNOWN YOU'D BE INVOLVED SOMEHOW.
DID EVERYONE IN METROPOLIS GET CAUGHT UP IN THIS?
I KNOW.
WHAT ARE THE STATISTICAL CHANCES OF SEVERAL PROMINENT NEW TROY RESIDENTS MEETING UP ON A STREET IN NEW TROY DURING A CRISIS?
IT REALLY DOES BEGGAR BELIEF.
CHARMING AS EVER.
ANY IDEAS, GENIUS?
DID WE JUST PROVE ALIENS ARE REAL?
TELEPORTATION TECHNOLOGY, ADVANCED CYBERNETICS.
THE HOB'S RIVER BRIDGE HAS BEEN SEVERED BY A WALL OF GLASS.
THEY'VE ABDUCTED SEVEN MILLION PEOPLE SIMULTANEOUSLY.
IT'S LIKE "UNDER THE DOME."
AND THE SIMPSONS MOVIE--
HEY!
THAT'S MILITARY PROPERTY!
WHAT'S THE SCOOP, LEX?
NOTHING TO DO WITH YOU.
WHY IS IT TALKING?
HA-LA KAL-EL HA-LA-LA
IS IT TALKING TO THEM?
THE WORDS "DWARF STAR LENSING" WERE USED.
OUR WORLD'S ONLY KNOWN APPLICATION OF THIS PHRASE OCCURS IN CERTAIN "PRIVATE" E-MAILS AND FILES OF PROFESSOR RAYMOND PALMER OF IVY UNIVERSITY, CONNECTICUT.
OH, THIS CAN'T BE POSSIBLE--

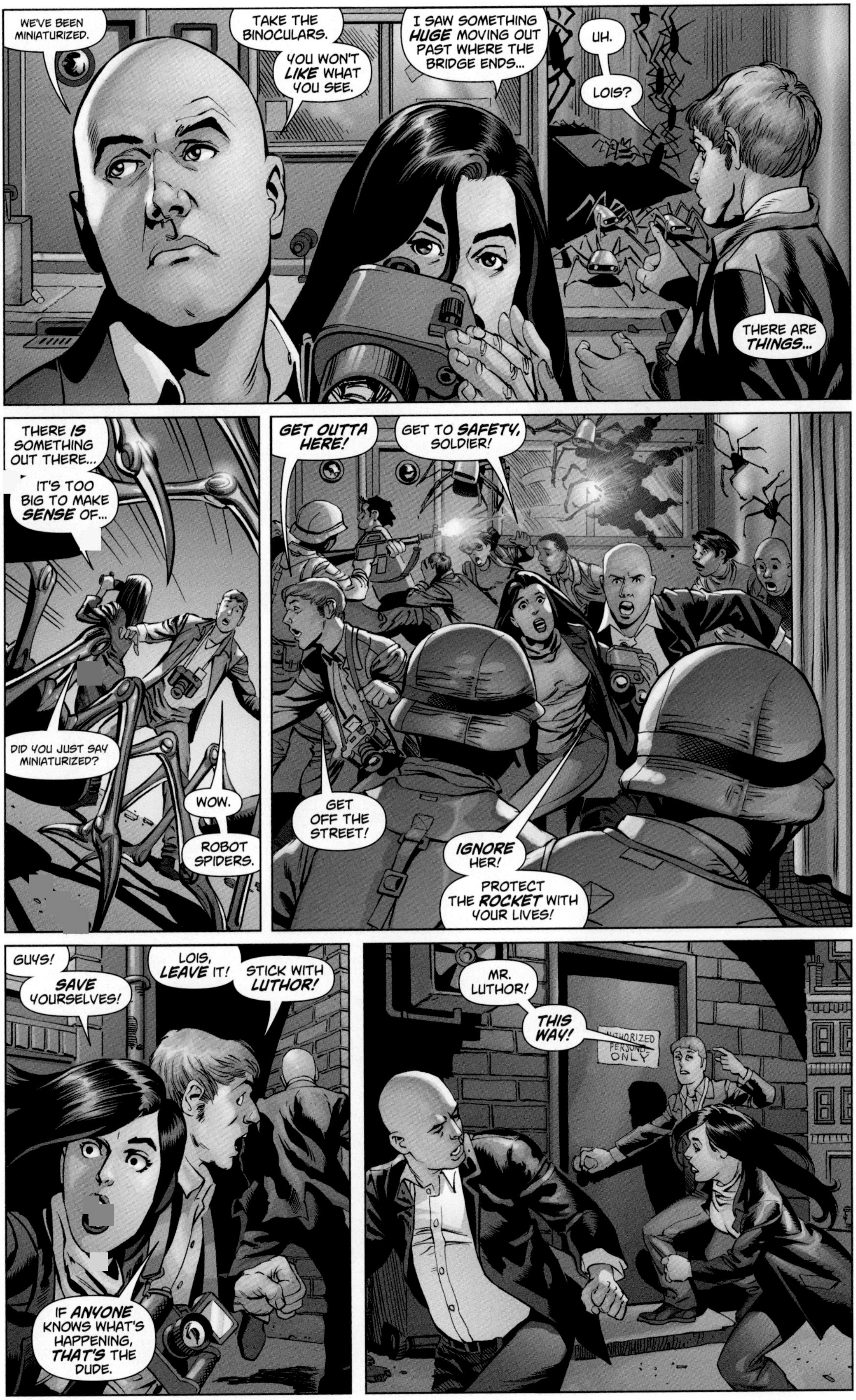
WE'VE BEEN MINIATURIZED.
TAKE THE BINOCULARS.
YOU WON'T LIKE WHAT YOU SEE.
I SAW SOMETHING HUGE MOVING OUT PAST WHERE THE BRIDGE ENDS...
UH.
LOIS?
THERE ARE THINGS...
THERE IS SOMETHING OUT THERE...
IT'S TOO BIG TO MAKE SENSE OF...
DID YOU JUST SAY MINIATURIZED?
WOW.
ROBOT SPIDERS.
GET OUTTA HERE!
GET TO SAFETY, SOLDIER!
GET OFF THE STREET!
IGNORE HER!
PROTECT THE ROCKET WITH YOUR LIVES!
GUYS!
SAVE YOURSELVES!
LOIS, LEAVE IT!
STICK WITH LUTHOR!
IF ANYONE KNOWS WHAT'S HAPPENING, THAT'S THE DUDE.
MR. LUTHOR!
THIS WAY!
AUTHORIZED PERSONNEL ONLY

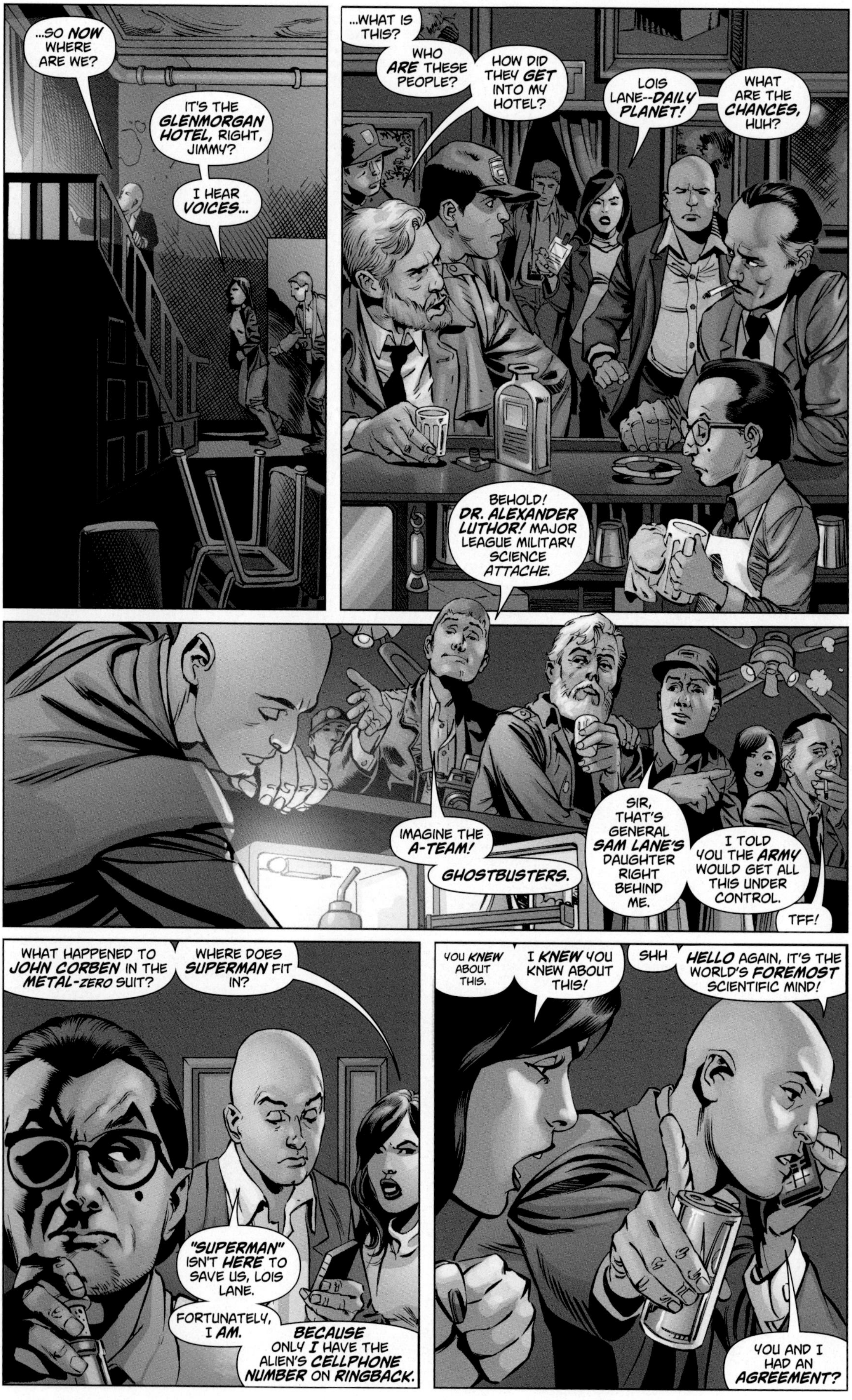
...SO NOW WHERE ARE WE?
IT'S THE GLENMORGAN HOTEL, RIGHT, JIMMY?
I HEAR VOICES...
...WHAT IS THIS?
WHO ARE THESE PEOPLE?
HOW DID THEY GET INTO MY HOTEL?
LOIS LANE--DAILY PLANET!
WHAT ARE THE CHANCES, HUH?
BEHOLD! DR. ALEXANDER LUTHOR! MAJOR LEAGUE MILITARY SCIENCE ATTACHE.
IMAGINE THE A-TEAM!
GHOSTBUSTERS.
SIR, THAT'S GENERAL SAM LANE'S DAUGHTER RIGHT BEHIND ME.
I TOLD YOU THE ARMY WOULD GET ALL THIS UNDER CONTROL.
TFF!
WHAT HAPPENED TO JOHN CORBEN IN THE METAL-ZERO SUIT?
WHERE DOES SUPERMAN FIT IN?
"SUPERMAN" ISN'T HERE TO SAVE US, LOIS LANE.
FORTUNATELY, I AM.
BECAUSE ONLY I HAVE THE ALIEN'S CELLPHONE NUMBER ON RINGBACK.
YOU KNEW ABOUT THIS.
I KNEW YOU KNEW ABOUT THIS!
SHH
HELLO AGAIN, IT'S THE WORLD'S FOREMOST SCIENTIFIC MIND!
YOU AND I HAD AN AGREEMENT?

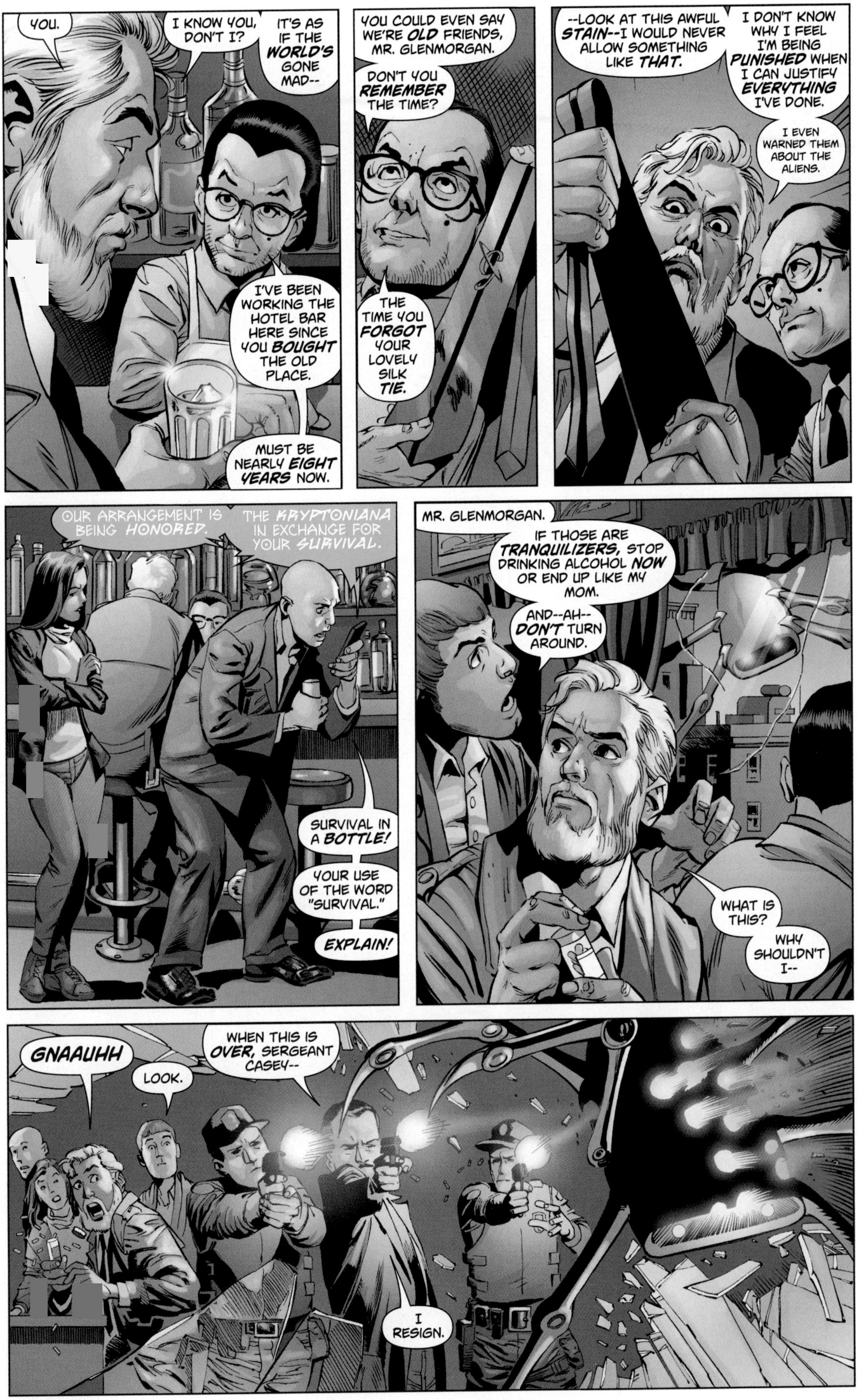

YOU.
I KNOW YOU, DON'T I?
IT'S AS IF THE WORLD'S GONE MAD--
I'VE BEEN WORKING THE HOTEL BAR HERE SINCE YOU BOUGHT THE OLD PLACE.
MUST BE NEARLY EIGHT YEARS NOW.
YOU COULD EVEN SAY WE'RE OLD FRIENDS, MR. GLENMORGAN.
DON'T YOU REMEMBER THE TIME?
THE TIME YOU FORGOT YOUR LOVELY SILK TIE.
--LOOK AT THIS AWFUL STAIN--I WOULD NEVER ALLOW SOMETHING LIKE THAT.
I DON'T KNOW WHY I FEEL I'M BEING PUNISHED WHEN I CAN JUSTIFY EVERYTHING I'VE DONE.
I EVEN WARNED THEM ABOUT THE ALIENS.
OUR ARRANGEMENT IS BEING HONORED.
THE KRYPTONIANA IN EXCHANGE FOR YOUR SURVIVAL.
SURVIVAL IN A BOTTLE!
YOUR USE OF THE WORD "SURVIVAL."
EXPLAIN!
MR. GLENMORGAN.
IF THOSE ARE TRANQUILIZERS, STOP DRINKING ALCOHOL NOW OR END UP LIKE MY MOM.
AND--AH-- DON'T TURN AROUND.
WHAT IS THIS?
WHY SHOULDN'T I--
GNAAUHH
LOOK.
WHEN THIS IS OVER, SERGEANT CASEY--
I RESIGN.

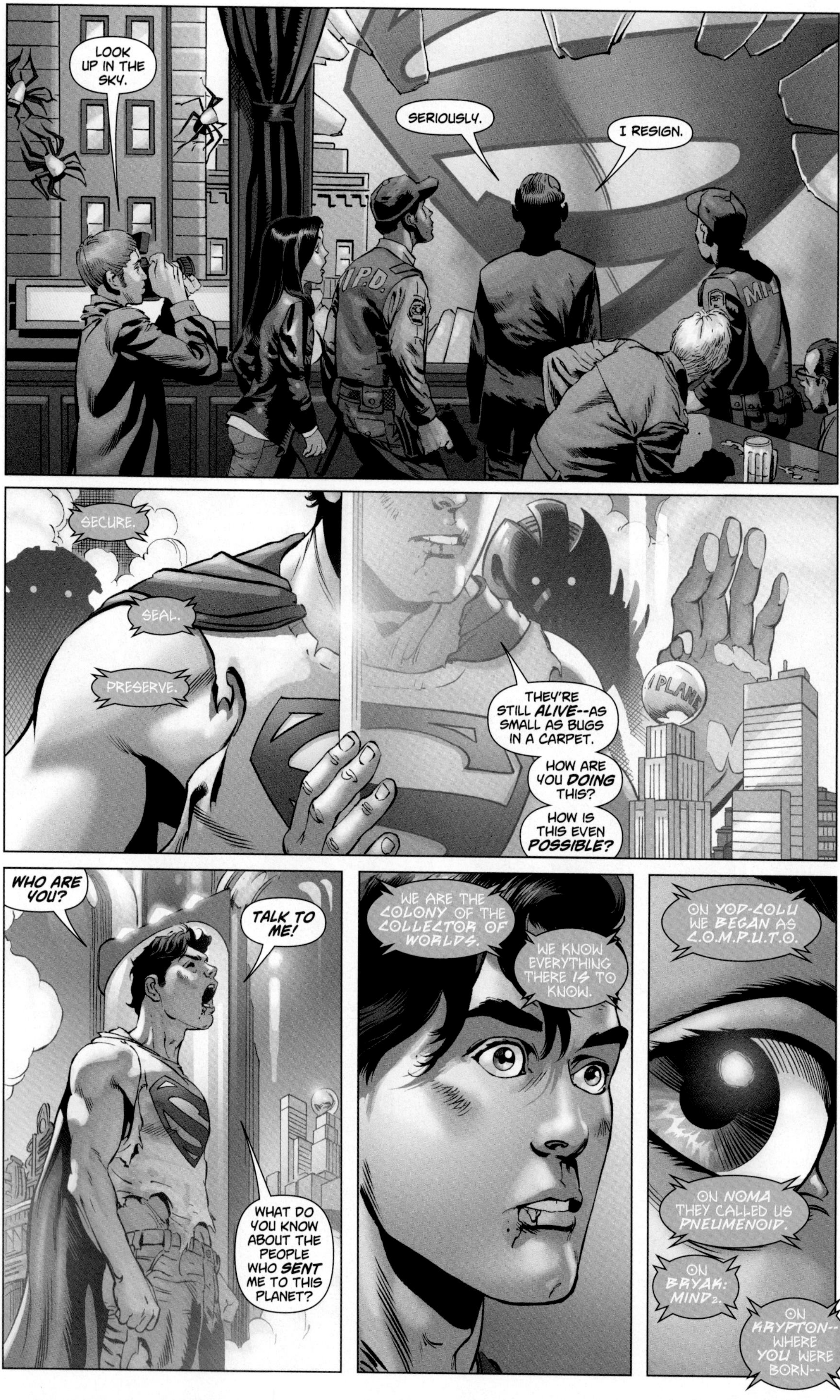

LOOK UP IN THE SKY.
SERIOUSLY.
I RESIGN.
SECURE.
SEAL.
PRESERVE.
THEY'RE STILL ALIVE--AS SMALL AS BUGS IN A CARPET.
HOW ARE YOU DOING THIS?
HOW IS THIS EVEN POSSIBLE?
WHO ARE YOU?
TALK TO ME!
WHAT DO YOU KNOW ABOUT THE PEOPLE WHO SENT ME TO THIS PLANET?
WE ARE THE COLONY OF THE COLLECTOR OF WORLDS.
WE KNOW EVERYTHING THERE IS TO KNOW.
ON YOD-COLU WE BEGAN AS C.O.M.P.U.T.O.
ON NOMA THEY CALLED US PNEUMENOID.
ON BRYAK: MIND2.
ON KRYPTON--WHERE YOU WERE BORN--

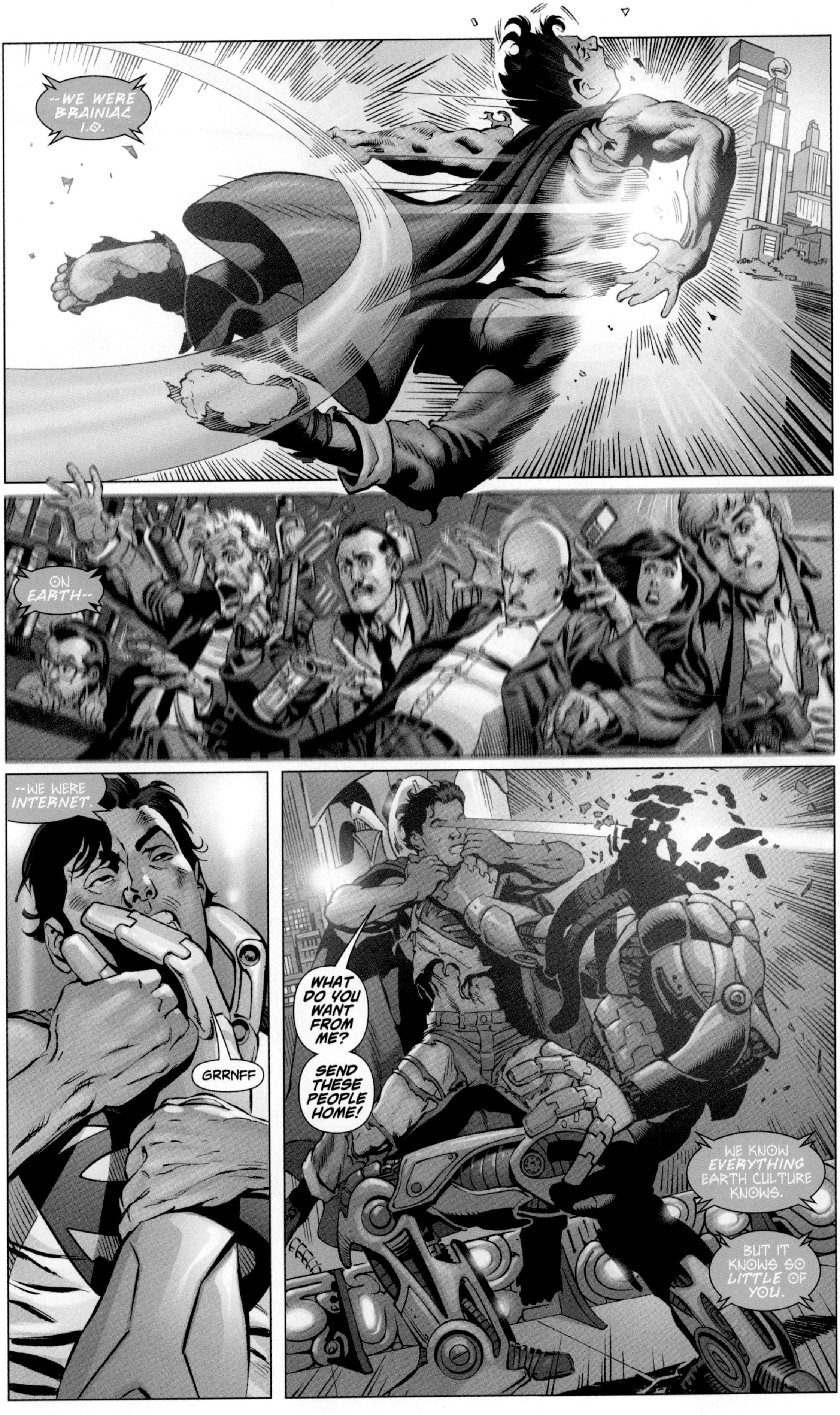
--WE WERE BRAINIAC 1.0.
ON EARTH--
--WE WERE INTERNET.
GRRNFF
WHAT DO YOU WANT FROM ME?
SEND THESE PEOPLE HOME!
WE KNOW EVERYTHING EARTH CULTURE KNOWS.
BUT IT KNOWS SO LITTLE OF YOU.

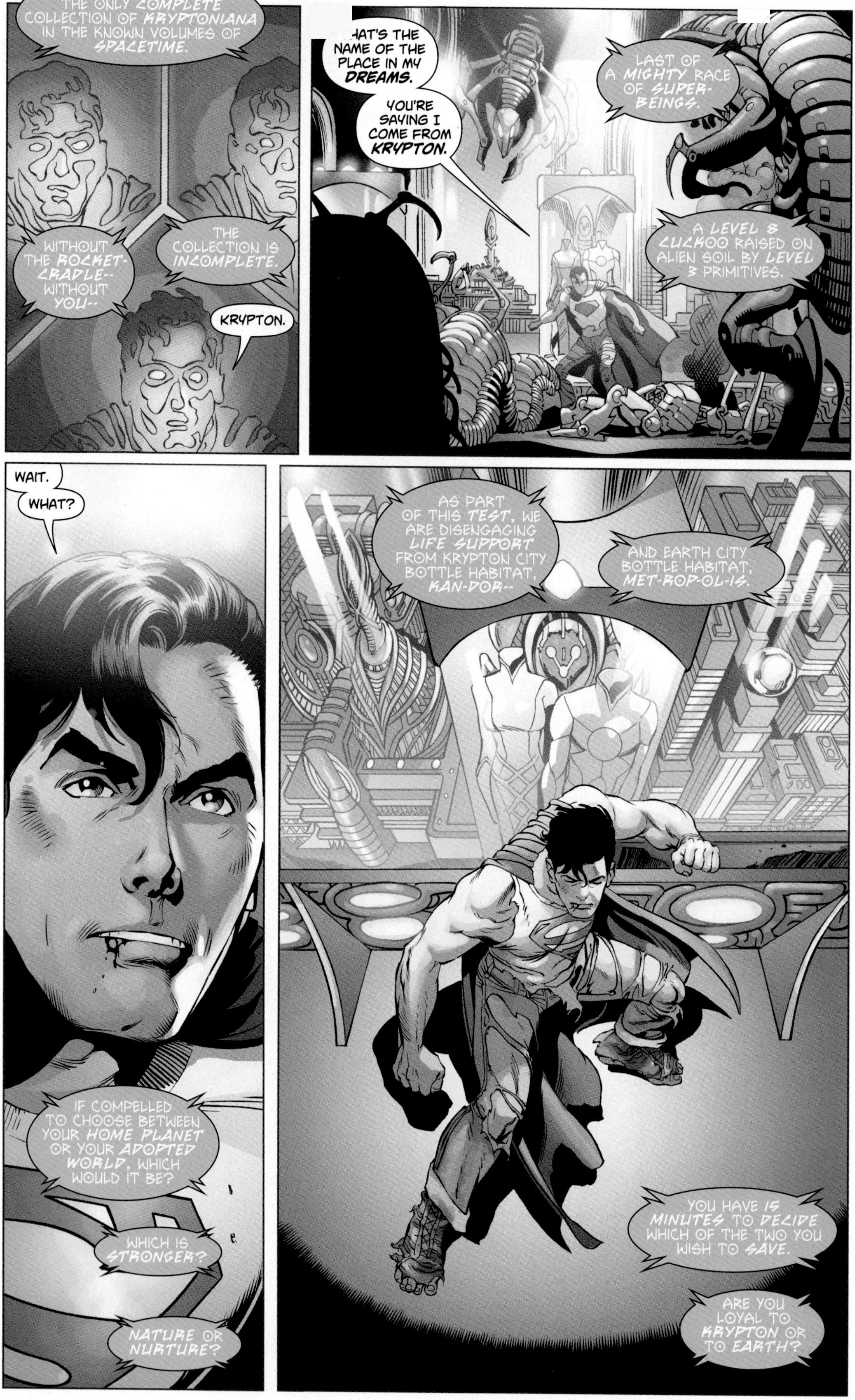
WE HAVE AMASSED THE ONLY COMPLETE COLLECTION OF KRYPTONIANA IN THE KNOWN VOLUMES OF SPACETIME.
WITHOUT THE ROCKET-CRADLE-- WITHOUT YOU--
THE COLLECTION IS INCOMPLETE.
KRYPTON.
HAT'S THE NAME OF THE PLACE IN MY DREAMS.
YOU'RE SAYING I COME FROM KRYPTON.
LAST OF A MIGHTY RACE OF SUPER-BEINGS.
A LEVEL 8 CUCKOO RAISED ON ALIEN SOIL BY LEVEL 3 PRIMITIVES.
WAIT.
WHAT?
AS PART OF THIS TEST, WE ARE DISENGAGING LIFE SUPPORT FROM KRYPTON CITY BOTTLE HABITAT, KAN-DOR--
AND EARTH CITY BOTTLE HABITAT, MET-ROP-OL-IS.
IF COMPELLED TO CHOOSE BETWEEN YOUR HOME PLANET OR YOUR ADOPTED WORLD, WHICH WOULD IT BE?
WHICH IS STRONGER?
NATURE OR NURTURE?
YOU HAVE 15 MINUTES TO DECIDE WHICH OF THE TWO YOU WISH TO SAVE.
ARE YOU LOYAL TO KRYPTON OR TO EARTH?

I WON'T CHOOSE BETWEEN ANY ONE LIFE AND ANOTHER!

ALL OF THESE PEOPLE ARE UNDER MY PROTECTION, YOU GOT THAT?

EVERY LIVING THING!

ALL LIFE FORMS IN THE *COLLECTION* ARE SUBJECT TO *CONDITION NULL*--

FIND A WAY TO AWAKEN *KAN-DOR* FROM *MICRO-STASIS*--YOU WOULD NO LONGER BE ALONE.

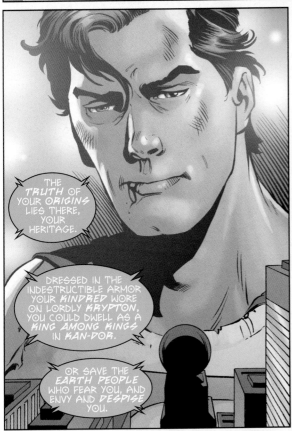

THE *TRUTH* OF YOUR *ORIGINS* LIES THERE, YOUR *HERITAGE*.

DRESSED IN THE *INDESTRUCTIBLE* ARMOR YOUR *KINDRED* WORE ON LORDLY *KRYPTON*, YOU COULD DWELL AS A *KING* AMONG KINGS IN *KAN-DOR*.

OR SAVE THE *EARTH* PEOPLE WHO FEAR YOU, AND ENVY AND *DESPISE* YOU.

THE *PINNACLE* OF HUMAN TECHNOLOGICAL ACHIEVEMENT WAS "*METAL-ZERO*," A *WEAPON* THEY MADE TO *KILL* YOU.

NATURE OR *NURTURE*.

CHOOSE.

SU-PER-MAN!

SU-PER-MAN!

SU-PER-MAN!

SU-PER-MAN!

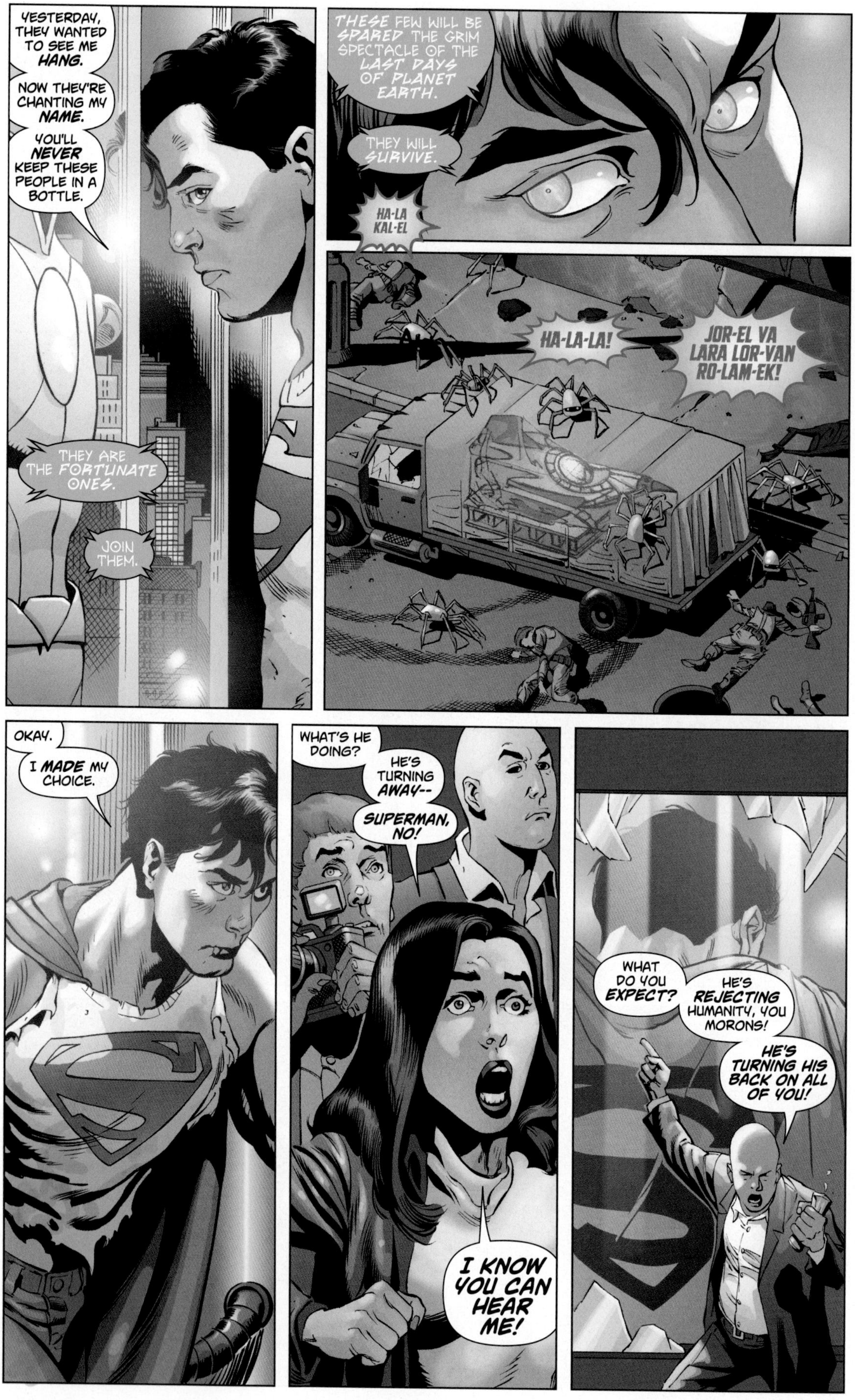
YESTERDAY, THEY WANTED TO SEE ME HANG.
NOW THEY'RE CHANTING MY NAME.
YOU'LL NEVER KEEP THESE PEOPLE IN A BOTTLE.
THEY ARE THE FORTUNATE ONES.
JOIN THEM.
THESE FEW WILL BE SPARED THE GRIM SPECTACLE OF THE LAST DAYS OF PLANET EARTH.
THEY WILL SURVIVE.
HA-LA KAL-EL
HA-LA-LA!
JOR-EL VA LARA LOR-VAN RO-LAM-EK!
OKAY.
I MADE MY CHOICE.
WHAT'S HE DOING?
HE'S TURNING AWAY--
SUPERMAN, NO!
I KNOW YOU CAN HEAR ME!
WHAT DO YOU EXPECT?
HE'S REJECTING HUMANITY, YOU MORONS!
HE'S TURNING HIS BACK ON ALL OF YOU!

OKAY. LET'S SAY ALL I NEED IS *ONE ITEM* FROM YOUR COLLECTION.

AND WE *FINISH* THIS RIGHT HERE.

WHAT ARE YOU DOING?

"INDESTRUCTIBLE," YOU SAID.

BRINGING *ME* INSIDE YOUR SPACESHIP WAS A BIG MISTAKE.

LIKE SWALLOWING *POISON*, TO SEE HOW IT *TASTES*.

NOW I DON'T CARE HOW BIG YOU ARE OR WHERE YOU'RE FROM!

HOLDING LIVES TO RANSOM JUST TO PROVE SOME STUPID POINT?

NO!

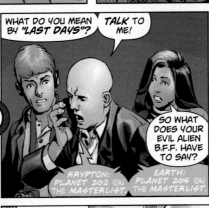

WHAT DO YOU MEAN BY "LAST DAYS"? *TALK TO ME!*

SO WHAT DOES YOUR EVIL ALIEN B.F.F. HAVE TO SAY?

KRYPTON: PLANET 202 ON THE *MASTERLIST.*

EARTH: PLANET 205 ON THE *MASTERLIST.*

THE MASTERLIST?

HAVE I COMPLETELY MISSED SOMETHING HERE?

THE LIST OF *DOOMED WORLDS.*

PREPARE YOUR *MINDS* FOR CONDITION NULL PERMANENT MICRO-STASIS.

I'LL *FIGHT* YOU, ON *THEIR* BEHALF.

AND WHEN I *WIN*, EVERYBODY GETS SENT BACK TO WHERE THEY *CAME* FROM!

THEY *CANNOT* RETURN.

AM-UR-LAK: BEL-DON-EL

THE *COLLECTION* PRESERVES *RARITIES;* ARTIFACTS OF WORLDS THAT EXIST NO LONGER.

KRYPTON, YOUR HOME, IS DEAD.

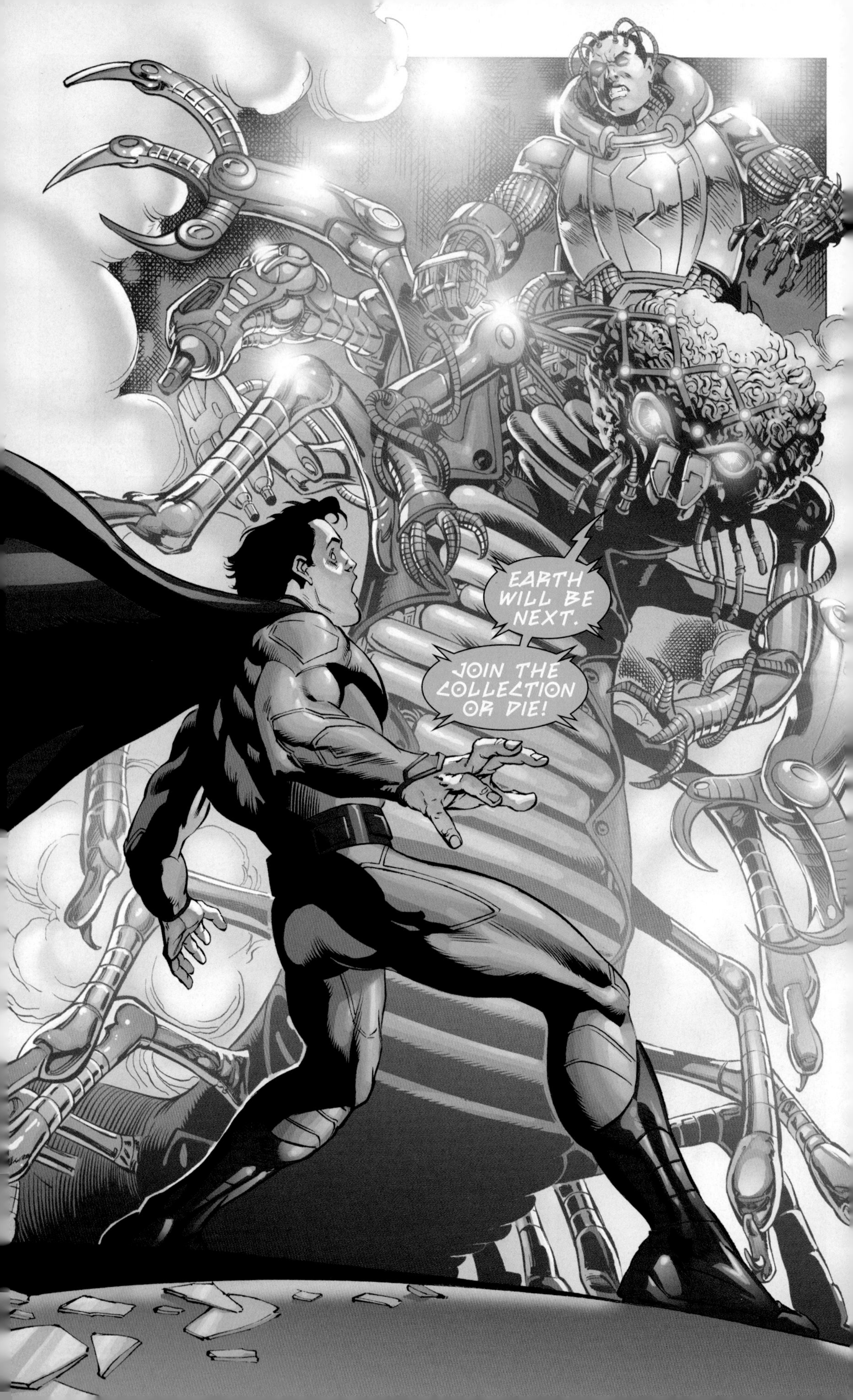
EARTH WILL BE NEXT.
JOIN THE COLLECTION OR DIE!

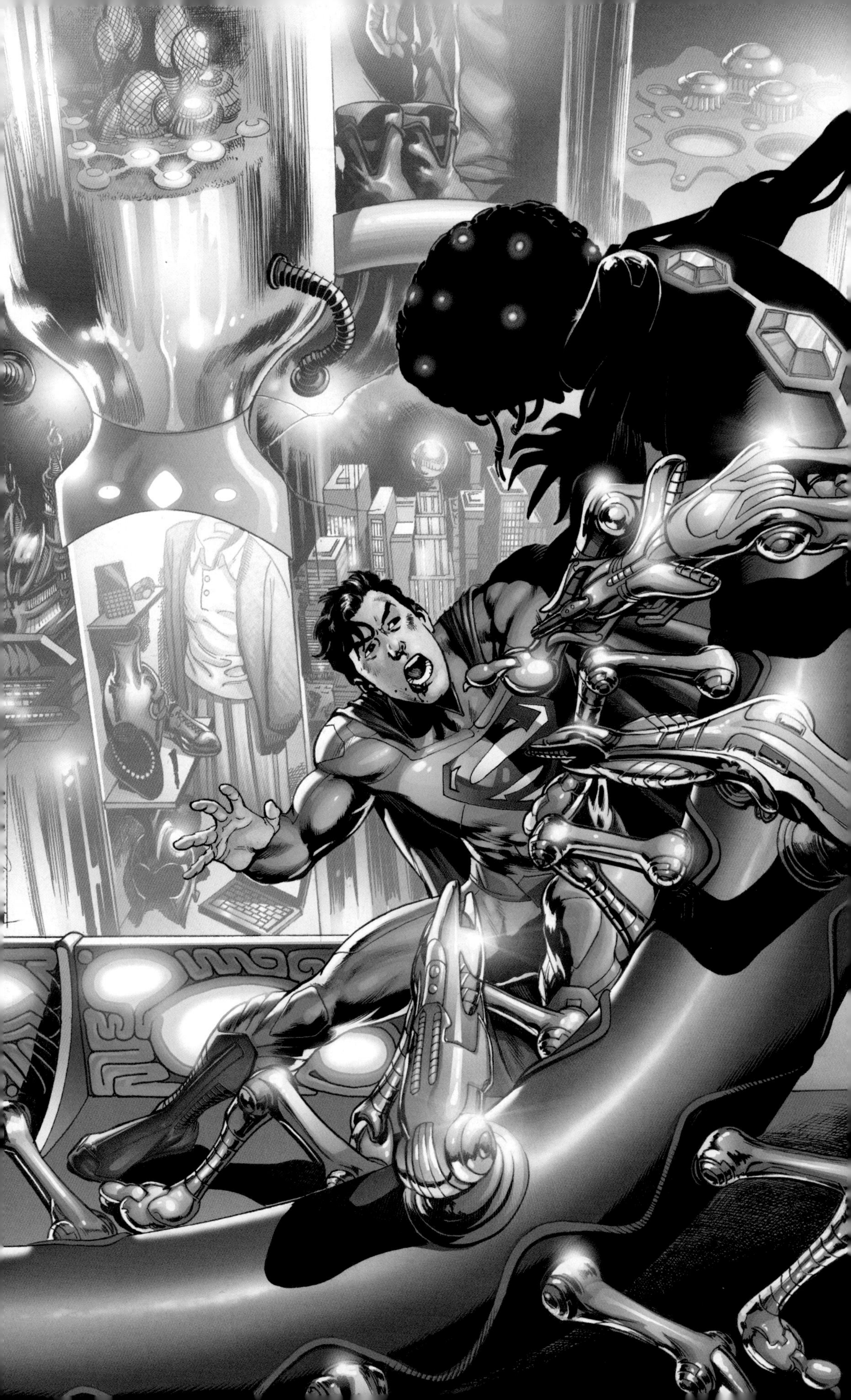

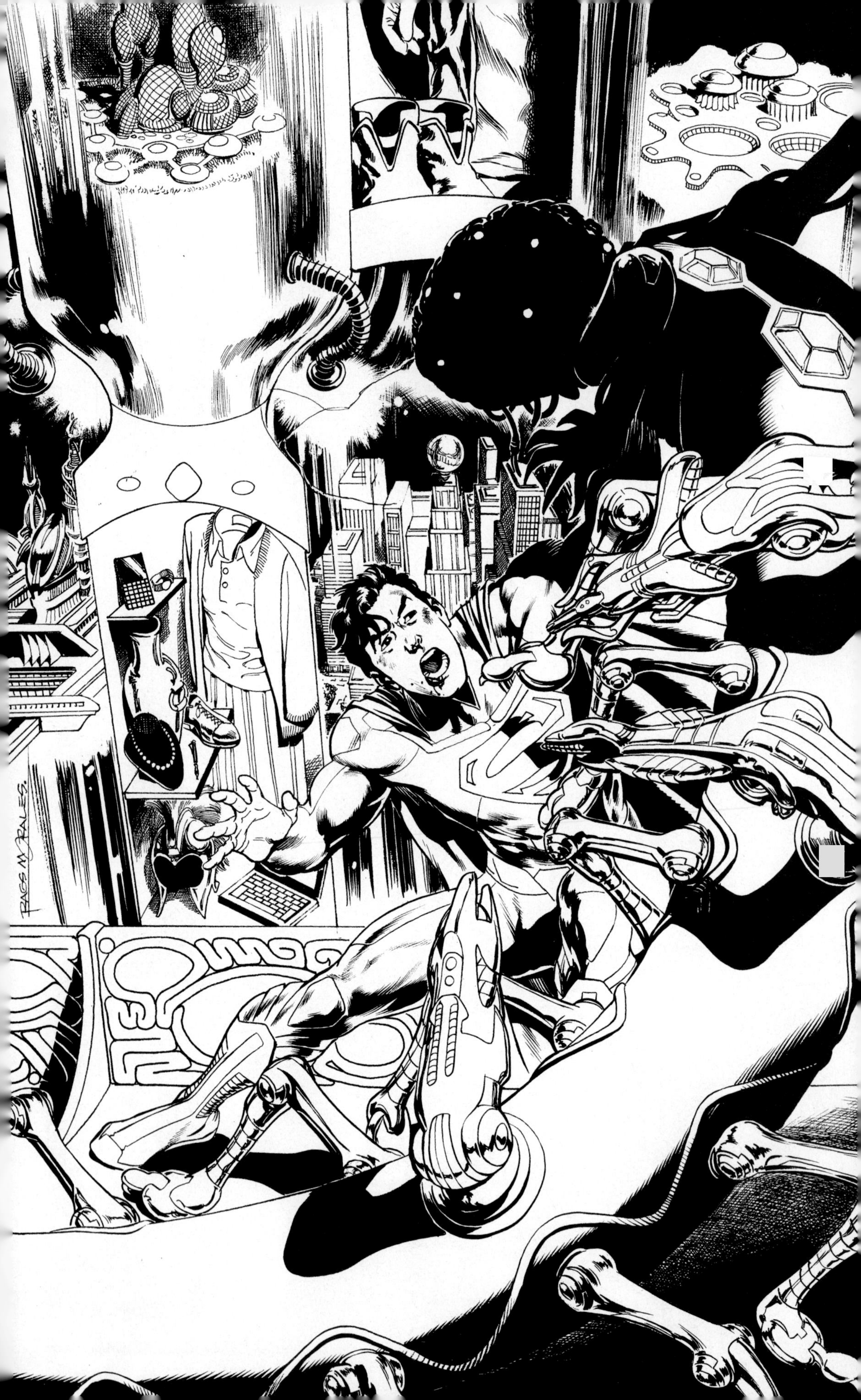
RAGS MORALES.

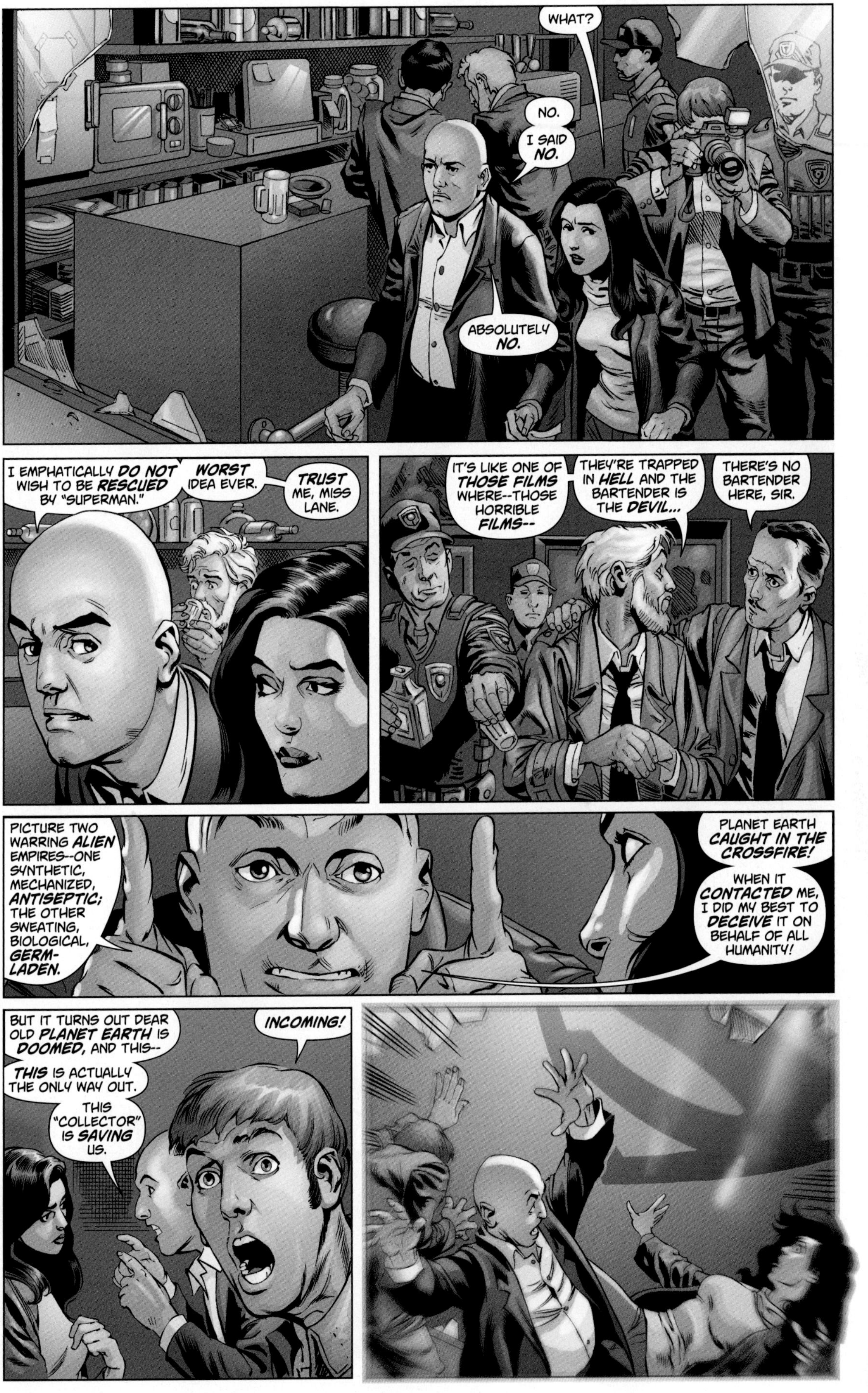
WHAT?
NO.
I SAID NO.
ABSOLUTELY NO.
I EMPHATICALLY DO NOT WISH TO BE RESCUED BY "SUPERMAN."
WORST IDEA EVER.
TRUST ME, MISS LANE.
IT'S LIKE ONE OF THOSE FILMS WHERE--THOSE HORRIBLE FILMS--
THEY'RE TRAPPED IN HELL AND THE BARTENDER IS THE DEVIL...
THERE'S NO BARTENDER HERE, SIR.
PICTURE TWO WARRING ALIEN EMPIRES--ONE SYNTHETIC, MECHANIZED, ANTISEPTIC; THE OTHER SWEATING, BIOLOGICAL, GERM-LADEN.
PLANET EARTH CAUGHT IN THE CROSSFIRE!
WHEN IT CONTACTED ME, I DID MY BEST TO DECEIVE IT ON BEHALF OF ALL HUMANITY!
BUT IT TURNS OUT DEAR OLD PLANET EARTH IS DOOMED, AND THIS--
THIS IS ACTUALLY THE ONLY WAY OUT.
THIS "COLLECTOR" IS SAVING US.
INCOMING!

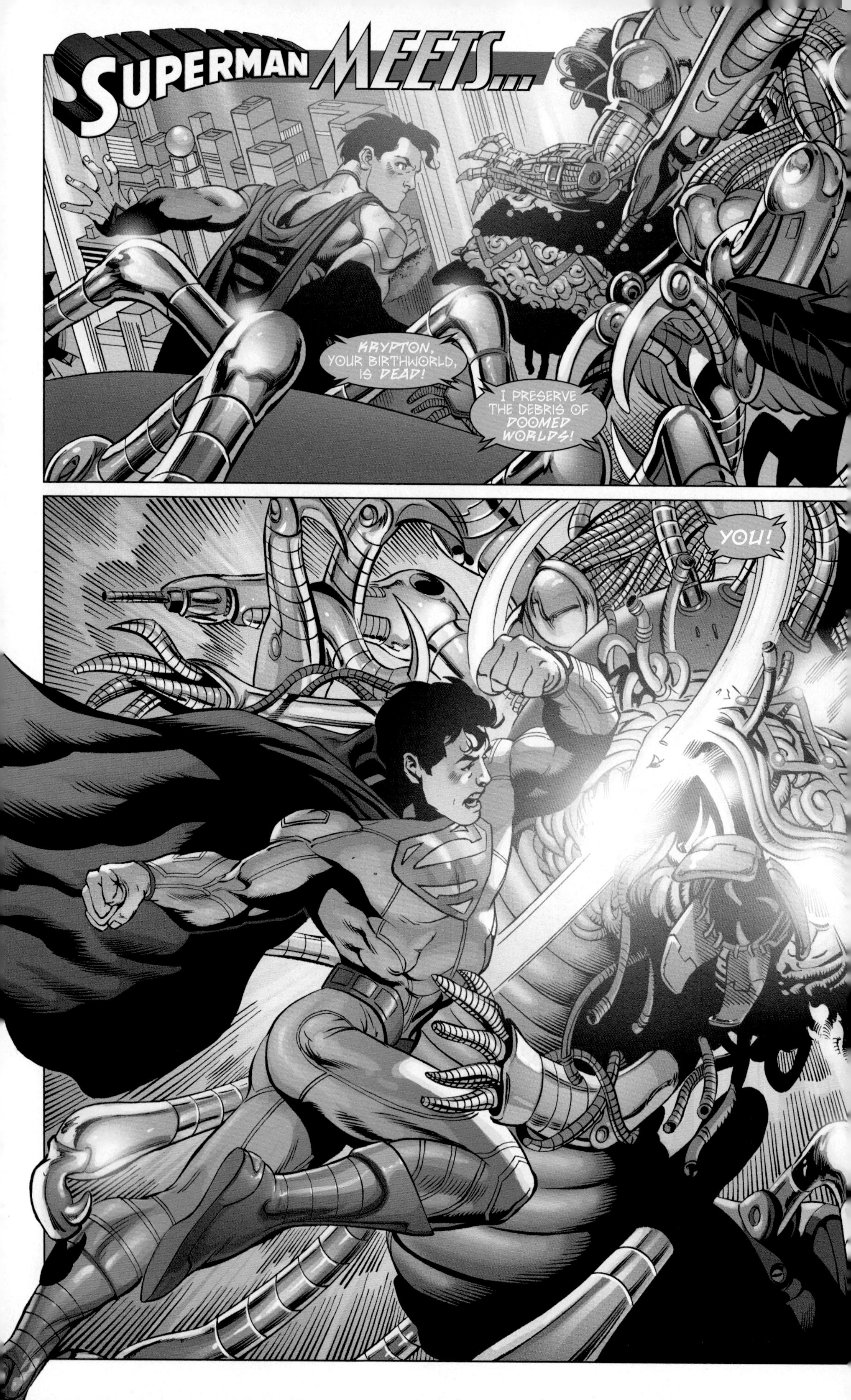
SUPERMAN MEETS...
KRYPTON, YOUR BIRTHWORLD, IS DEAD!
I PRESERVE THE DEBRIS OF DOOMED WORLDS!
YOU!

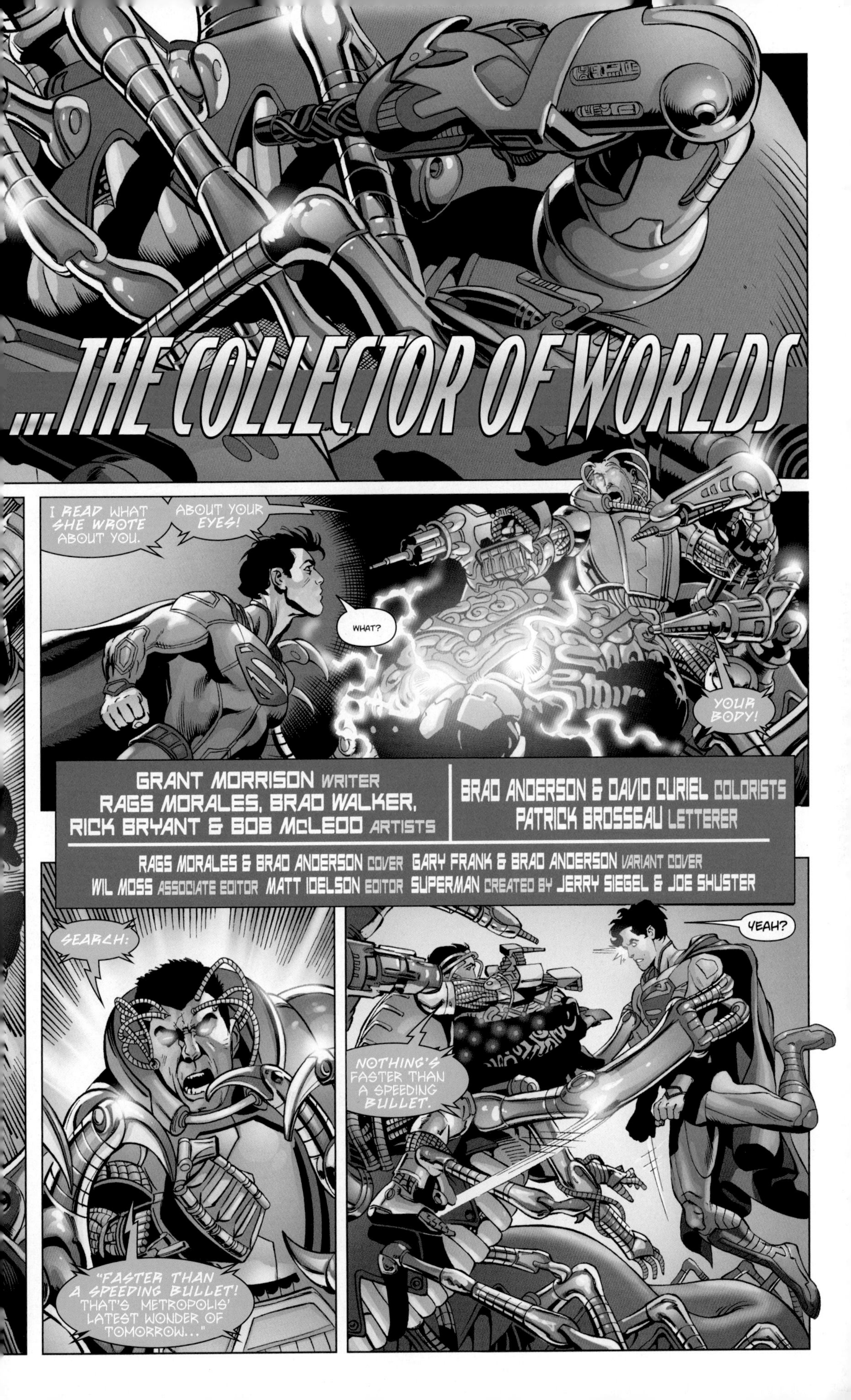
...THE COLLECTOR OF WORLDS
I READ WHAT SHE WROTE ABOUT YOU.
ABOUT YOUR EYES!
WHAT?
YOUR BODY!
GRANT MORRISON WRITER
RAGS MORALES, BRAD WALKER, RICK BRYANT & BOB McLEOD ARTISTS
BRAD ANDERSON & DAVID CURIEL COLORISTS
PATRICK BROSSEAU LETTERER
RAGS MORALES & BRAD ANDERSON COVER GARY FRANK & BRAD ANDERSON VARIANT COVER
WIL MOSS ASSOCIATE EDITOR MATT IDELSON EDITOR SUPERMAN CREATED BY JERRY SIEGEL & JOE SHUSTER
SEARCH:
"FASTER THAN A SPEEDING BULLET! THAT'S METROPOLIS' LATEST WONDER OF TOMORROW..."
YEAH?
NOTHING'S FASTER THAN A SPEEDING BULLET.

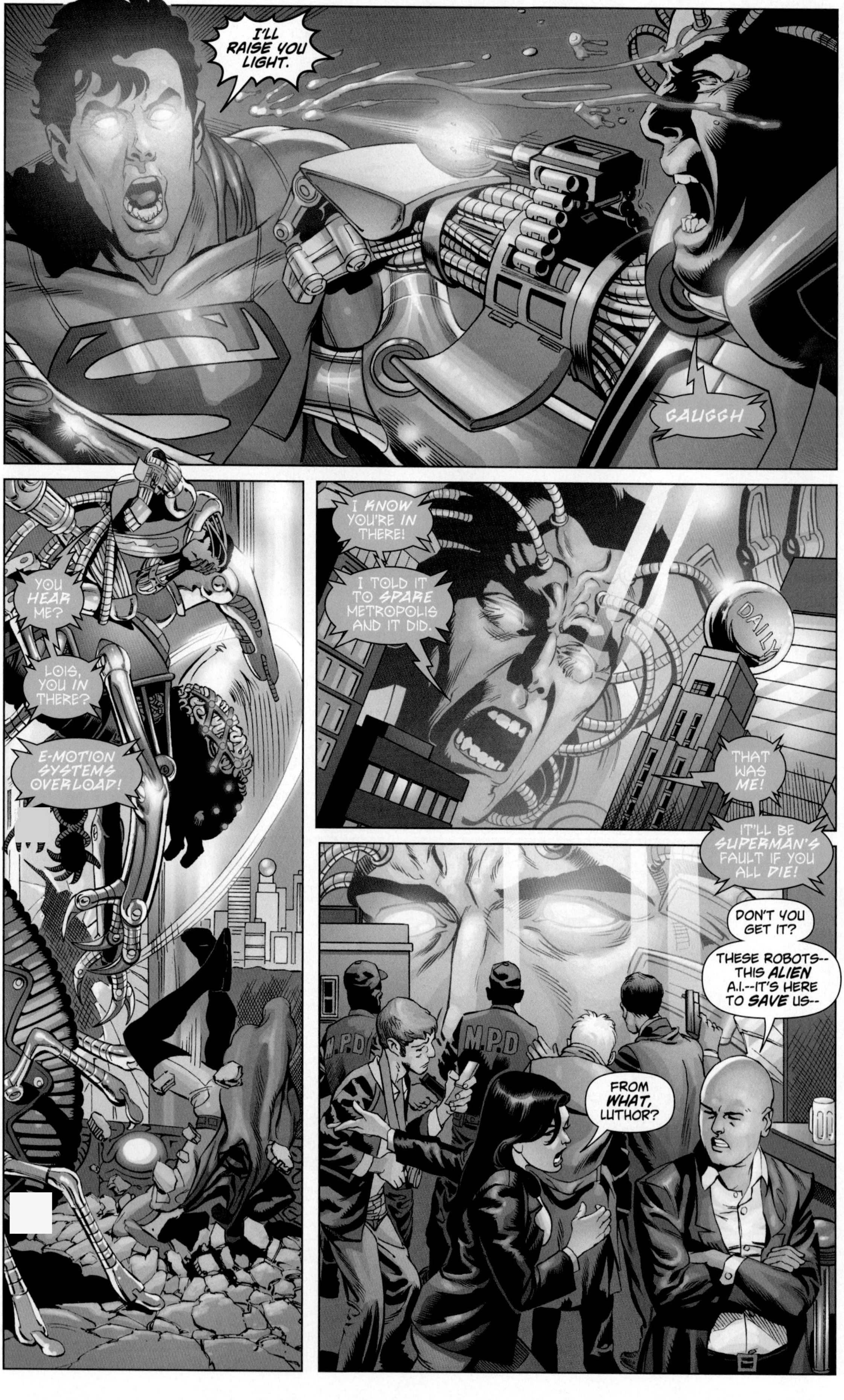
I'LL RAISE YOU LIGHT.
GAUGGH
YOU HEAR ME?
LOIS, YOU IN THERE?
E-MOTION SYSTEMS OVERLOAD!
I KNOW YOU'RE IN THERE!
I TOLD IT TO SPARE METROPOLIS AND IT DID.
DAILY
THAT WAS ME!
IT'LL BE SUPERMAN'S FAULT IF YOU ALL DIE!
DON'T YOU GET IT?
THESE ROBOTS-- THIS ALIEN A.I.--IT'S HERE TO SAVE US--
FROM WHAT, LUTHOR?
M.P.D.
M.P.D.

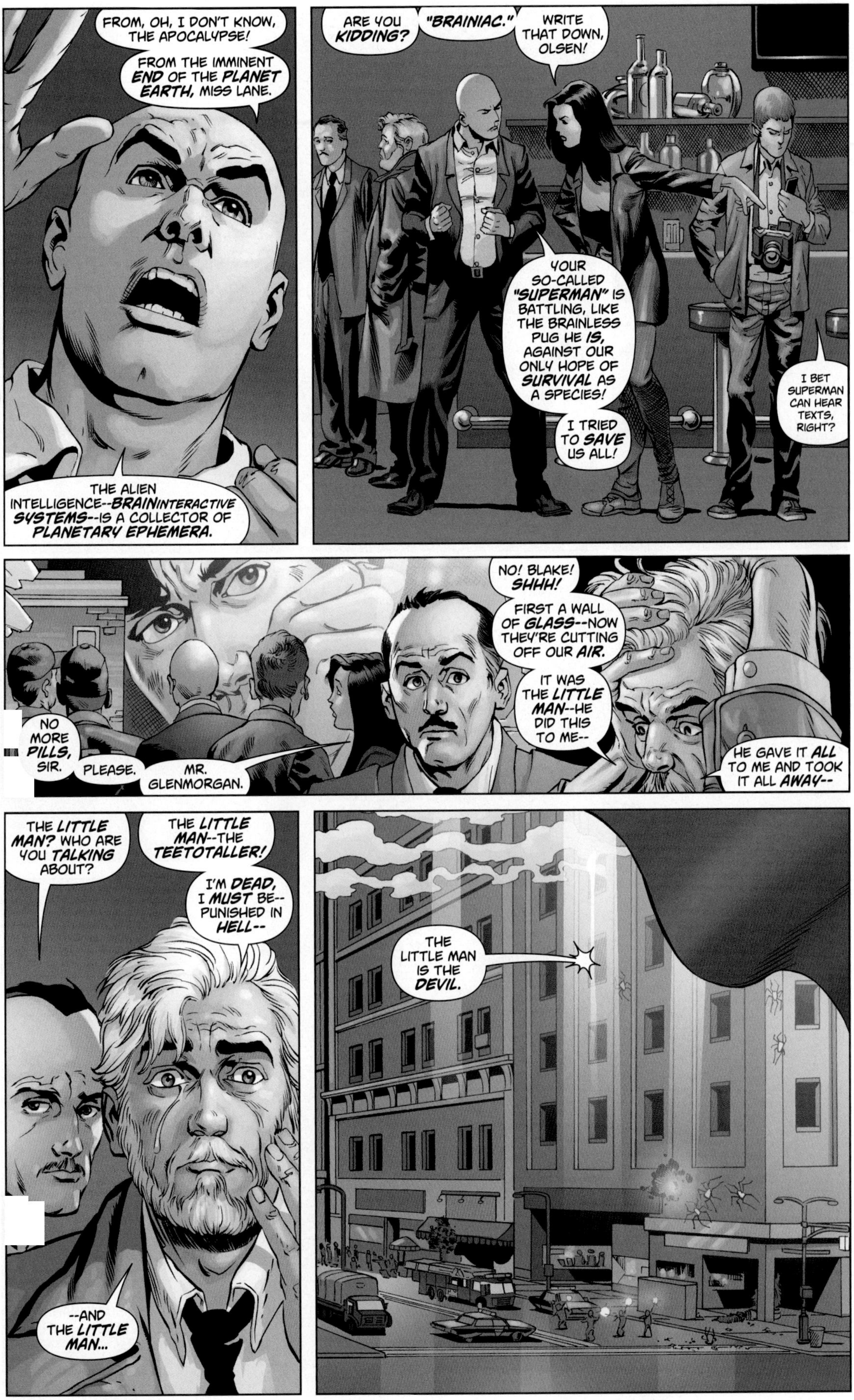
FROM, OH, I DON'T KNOW, THE APOCALYPSE!
FROM THE IMMINENT END OF THE PLANET EARTH, MISS LANE.
THE ALIEN INTELLIGENCE--BRAININTERACTIVE SYSTEMS--IS A COLLECTOR OF PLANETARY EPHEMERA.
ARE YOU KIDDING?
"BRAINIAC."
WRITE THAT DOWN, OLSEN!
YOUR SO-CALLED "SUPERMAN" IS BATTLING, LIKE THE BRAINLESS PUG HE IS, AGAINST OUR ONLY HOPE OF SURVIVAL AS A SPECIES!
I TRIED TO SAVE US ALL!
I BET SUPERMAN CAN HEAR TEXTS, RIGHT?
NO MORE PILLS, SIR.
PLEASE.
MR. GLENMORGAN.
NO! BLAKE! SHHH!
FIRST A WALL OF GLASS--NOW THEY'RE CUTTING OFF OUR AIR.
IT WAS THE LITTLE MAN--HE DID THIS TO ME--
HE GAVE IT ALL TO ME AND TOOK IT ALL AWAY--
THE LITTLE MAN? WHO ARE YOU TALKING ABOUT?
THE LITTLE MAN--THE TEETOTALLER!
I'M DEAD, I MUST BE--PUNISHED IN HELL--
--AND THE LITTLE MAN...
THE LITTLE MAN IS THE DEVIL.

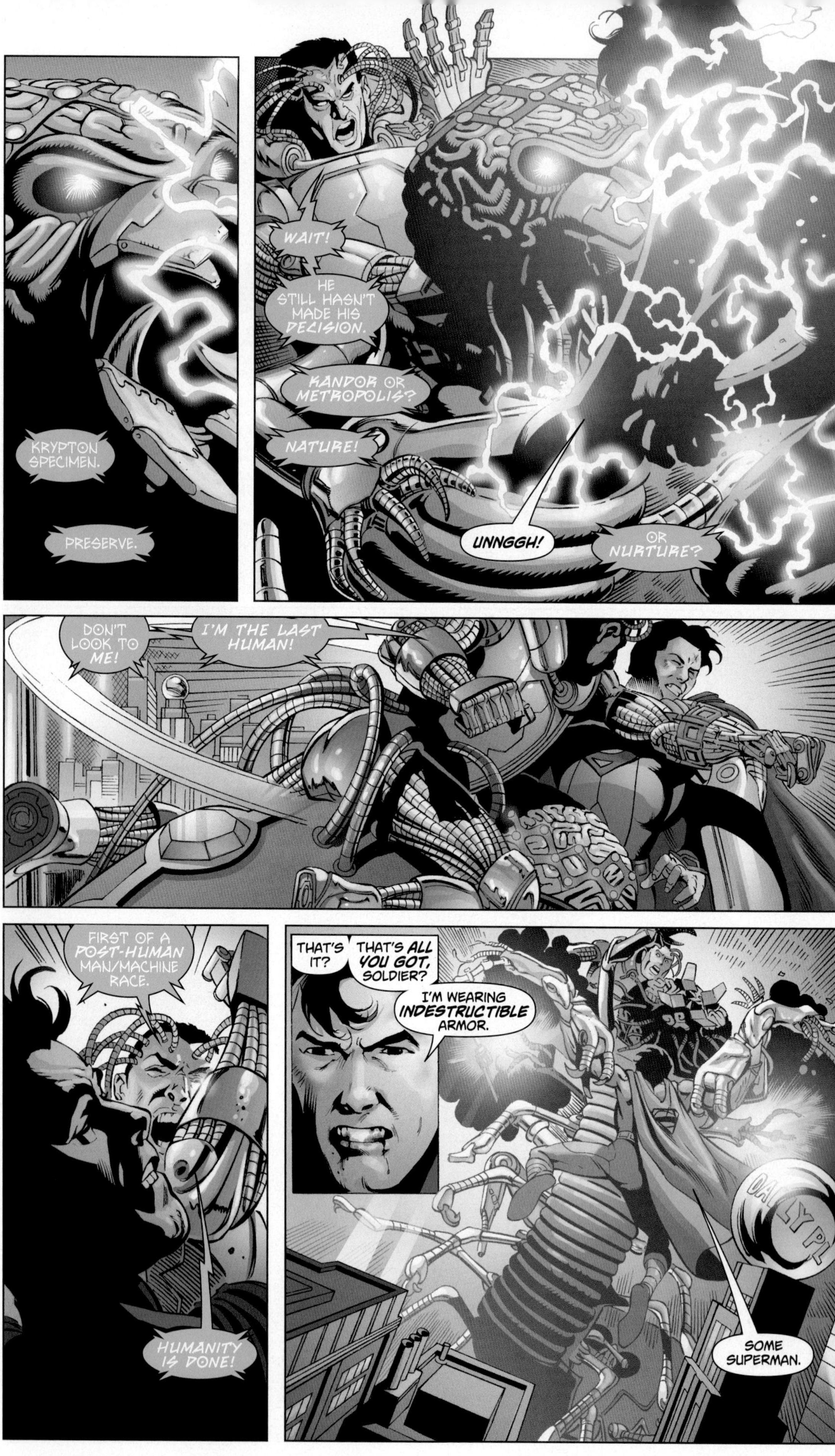
KRYPTON SPECIMEN.
PRESERVE.
WAIT!
HE STILL HASN'T MADE HIS DECISION.
KANDOR OR METROPOLIS?
NATURE!
UNNGGH!
OR NURTURE?
DON'T LOOK TO ME!
I'M THE LAST HUMAN!
FIRST OF A POST-HUMAN MAN/MACHINE RACE.
HUMANITY IS DONE!
THAT'S IT?
THAT'S ALL YOU GOT, SOLDIER?
I'M WEARING INDESTRUCTIBLE ARMOR.
SOME SUPERMAN.

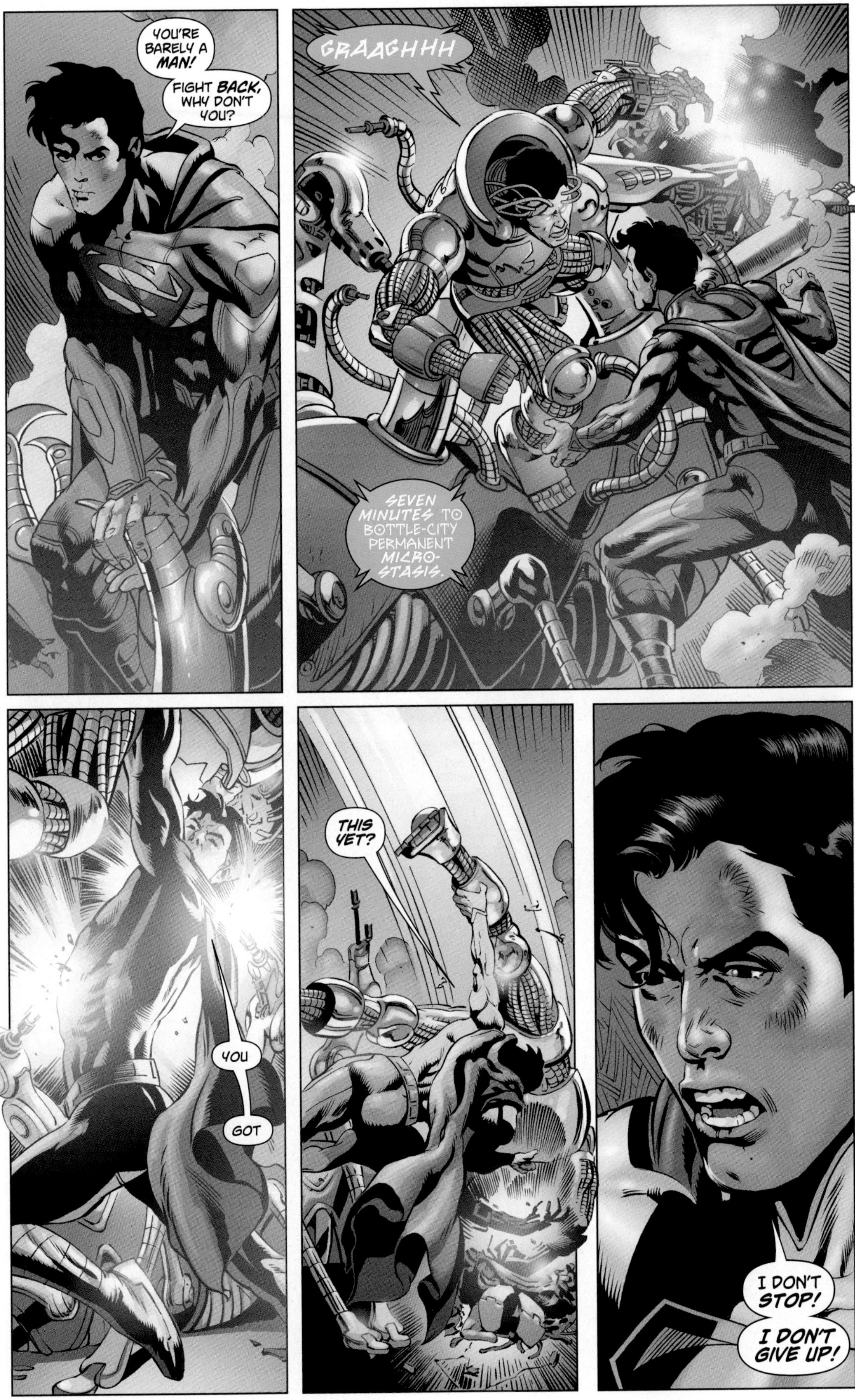
YOU'RE BARELY A MAN!
FIGHT BACK, WHY DON'T YOU?
GRAAGHHH
SEVEN MINUTES TO BOTTLE-CITY PERMANENT MICRO-STASIS.
YOU
GOT
THIS YET?
I DON'T STOP!
I DON'T GIVE UP!

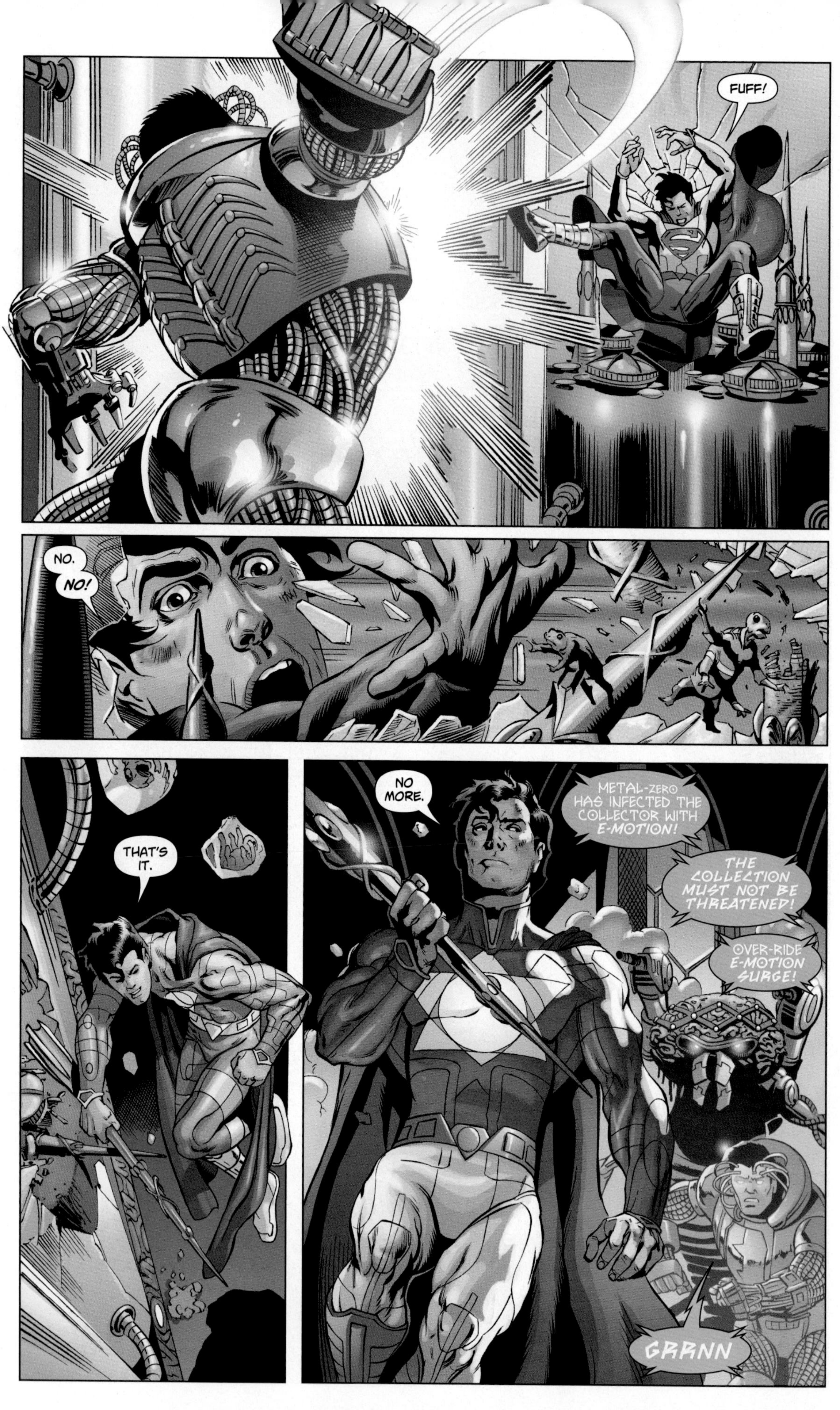
FUFF!
NO.
NO!
THAT'S IT.
NO MORE.
METAL-ZERO HAS INFECTED THE COLLECTOR WITH E-MOTION!
THE COLLECTION MUST NOT BE THREATENED!
OVER-RIDE E-MOTION SURGE!
GRRNN

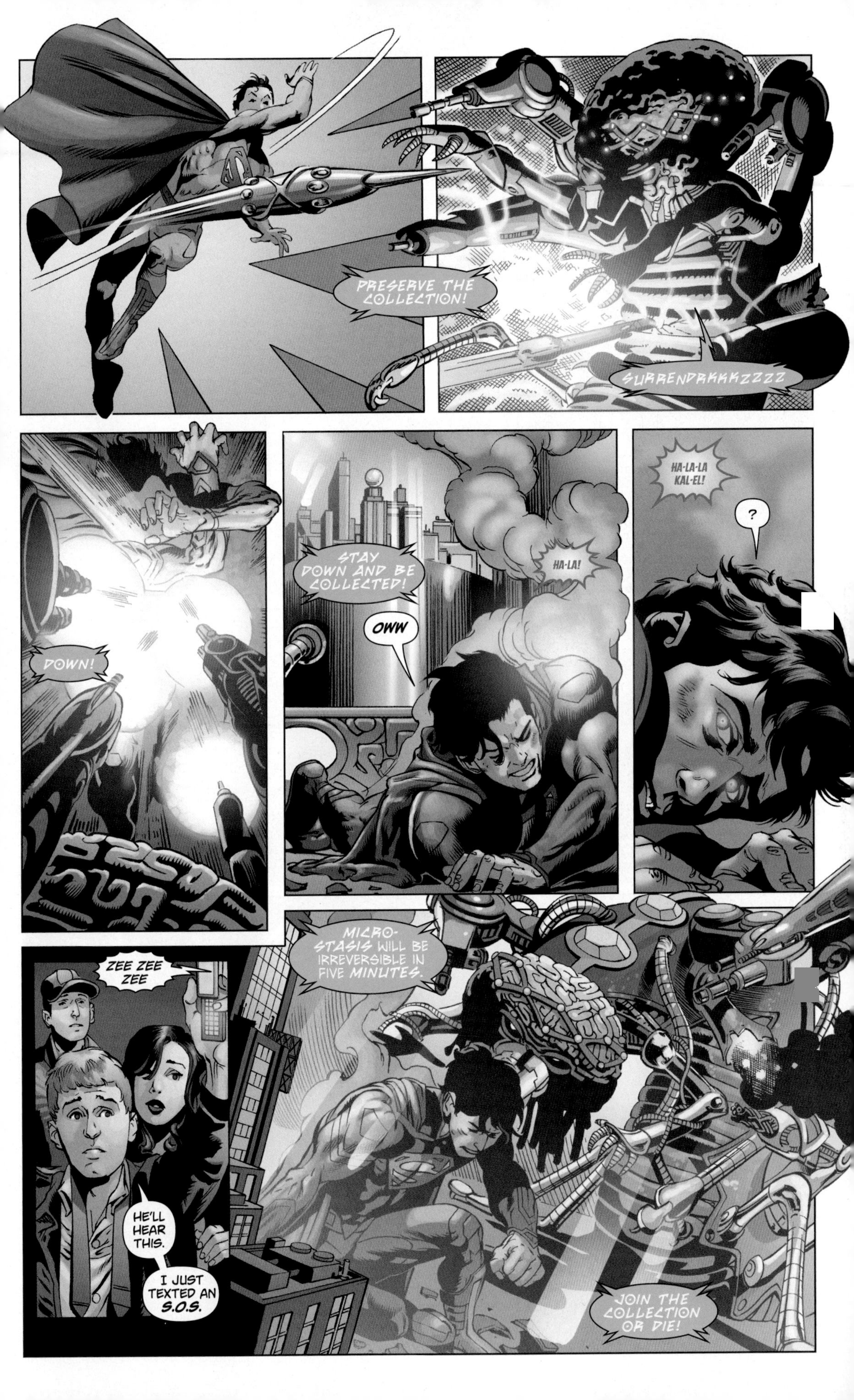
PRESERVE THE COLLECTION!
SURRENDRKKKZZZZ
DOWN!
STAY DOWN AND BE COLLECTED!
HA-LA!
OWW
HA-LA-LA KAL-EL!
?
ZEE ZEE ZEE
MICRO-STASIS WILL BE IRREVERSIBLE IN FIVE MINUTES.
HE'LL HEAR THIS.
I JUST TEXTED AN S.O.S.
JOIN THE COLLECTION OR DIE!

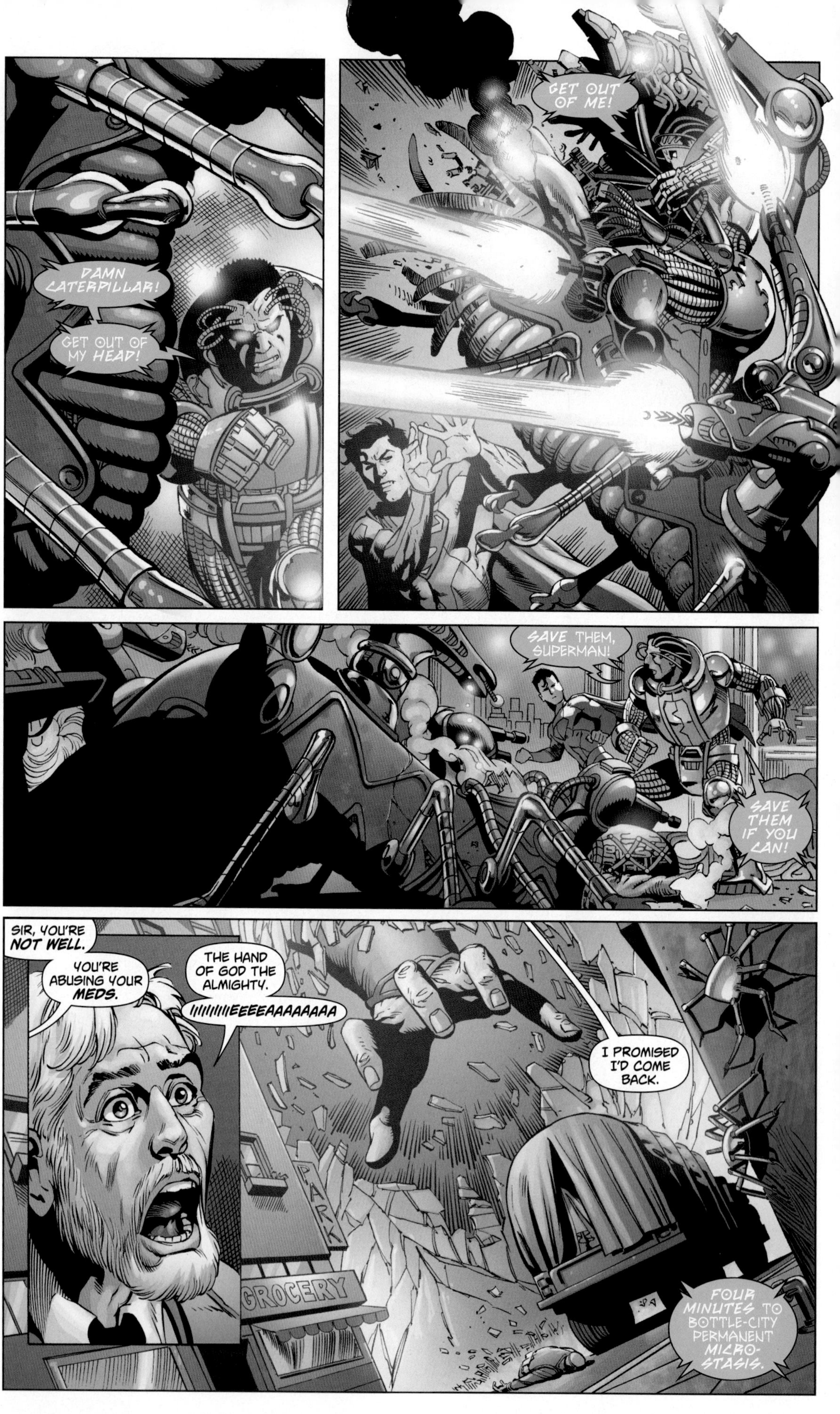
DAMN CATERPILLAR!
GET OUT OF MY HEAD!
GET OUT OF ME!
SAVE THEM, SUPERMAN!
SAVE THEM IF YOU CAN!
SIR, YOU'RE NOT WELL.
YOU'RE ABUSING YOUR MEDS.
THE HAND OF GOD THE ALMIGHTY.
IIIIIIIIEEEEAAAAAAAA
I PROMISED I'D COME BACK.
PARK
GROCERY
FOUR MINUTES TO BOTTLE-CITY PERMANENT MICRO-STASIS.

YOU ARE REQUIRED TO COMPLETE THE *COLLECTION.*

TO SECURE ITS *VALUE* AND *RARITY.*

YOUR SHIP AND *YOU* IN MINT *CONDITION.*

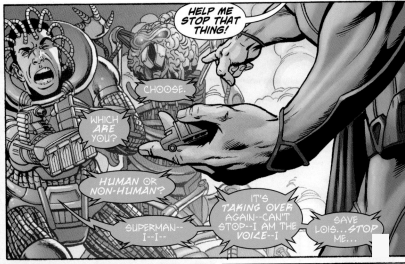

HELP ME STOP THAT THING!

CHOOSE.

WHICH *ARE* YOU?

HUMAN OR NON-HUMAN?

SUPERMAN-- I--I--

IT'S *TAKING OVER* AGAIN--CAN'T STOP--I AM THE *VOICE*--I

SAVE LOIS...*STOP* ME...

YOUR WORLD IS NUMBER *205* ON THE *LIST* OF *333*--THE *DEATH-LIST* OF THE *MULTITUDE.*

"DEATH-LIST"?

YOU WANT ME TO *WRECK YOUR COLLECTION,* I WILL.

YOU VALUE THESE *BOTTLES*--THESE *CITIES* YOU'VE PRESERVED.

I'LL REDUCE THEM TO *DUST* IF I HAVE TO.

NOT *JAZUUR*--NOT *BRYAK*--NOT *VELL'UT, RANDIZULLIAN...*

MILLENNIA OF *COLLECTION!*

MY *PRISTINE COLLECTION* OF *WORLDS!*

I THOUGHT SO.

OKAY.

NOW WE CAN...

WE CAN NEGOTIATE.

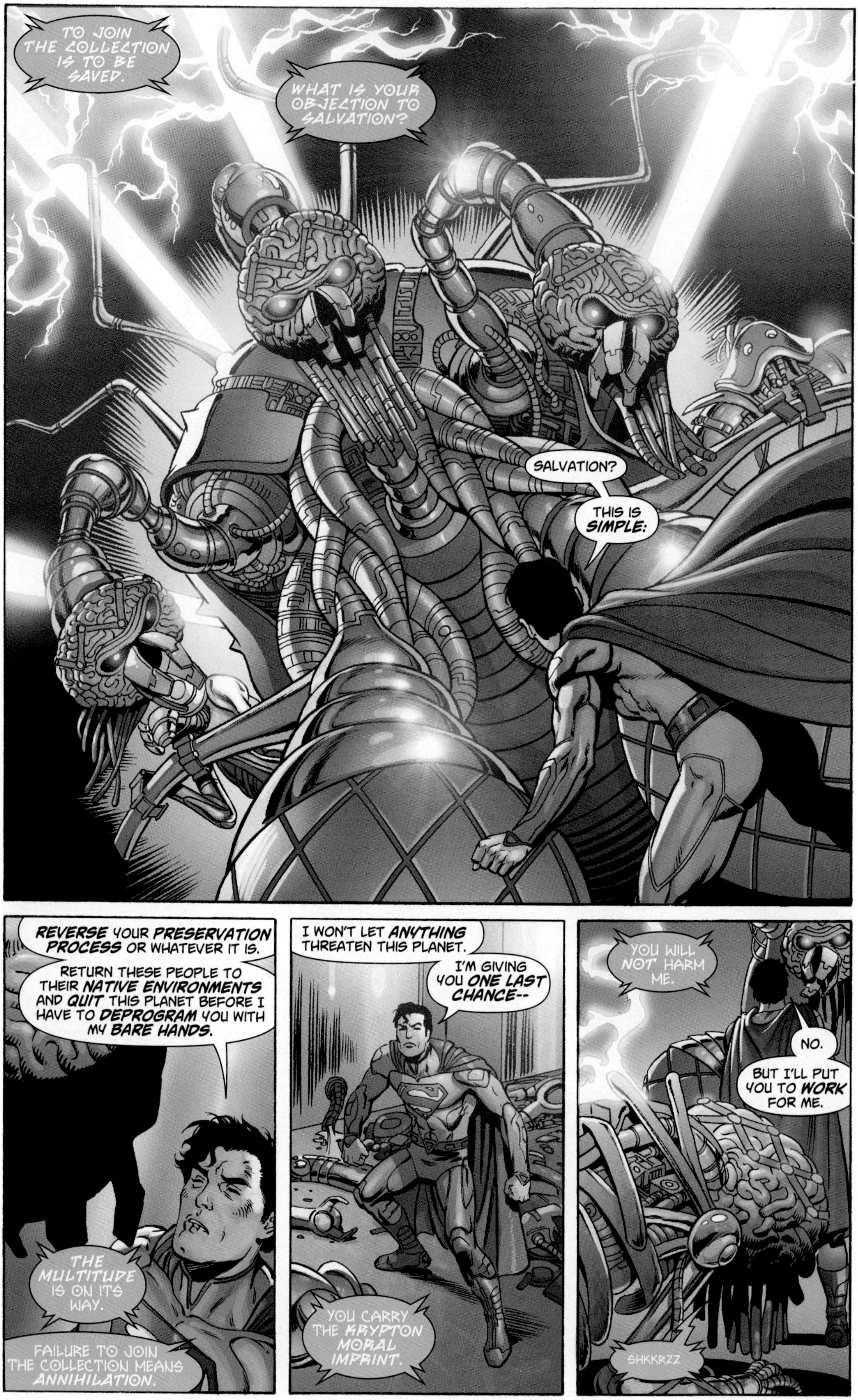
TO JOIN THE COLLECTION IS TO BE SAVED.
WHAT IS YOUR OBJECTION TO SALVATION?
SALVATION?
THIS IS SIMPLE:
REVERSE YOUR PRESERVATION PROCESS OR WHATEVER IT IS.
RETURN THESE PEOPLE TO THEIR NATIVE ENVIRONMENTS AND QUIT THIS PLANET BEFORE I HAVE TO DEPROGRAM YOU WITH MY BARE HANDS.
THE MULTITUDE IS ON ITS WAY.
FAILURE TO JOIN THE COLLECTION MEANS ANNIHILATION.
I WON'T LET ANYTHING THREATEN THIS PLANET.
I'M GIVING YOU ONE LAST CHANCE--
YOU CARRY THE KRYPTON MORAL IMPRINT.
YOU WILL NOT HARM ME.
NO.
BUT I'LL PUT YOU TO WORK FOR ME.
SHKKRZZ

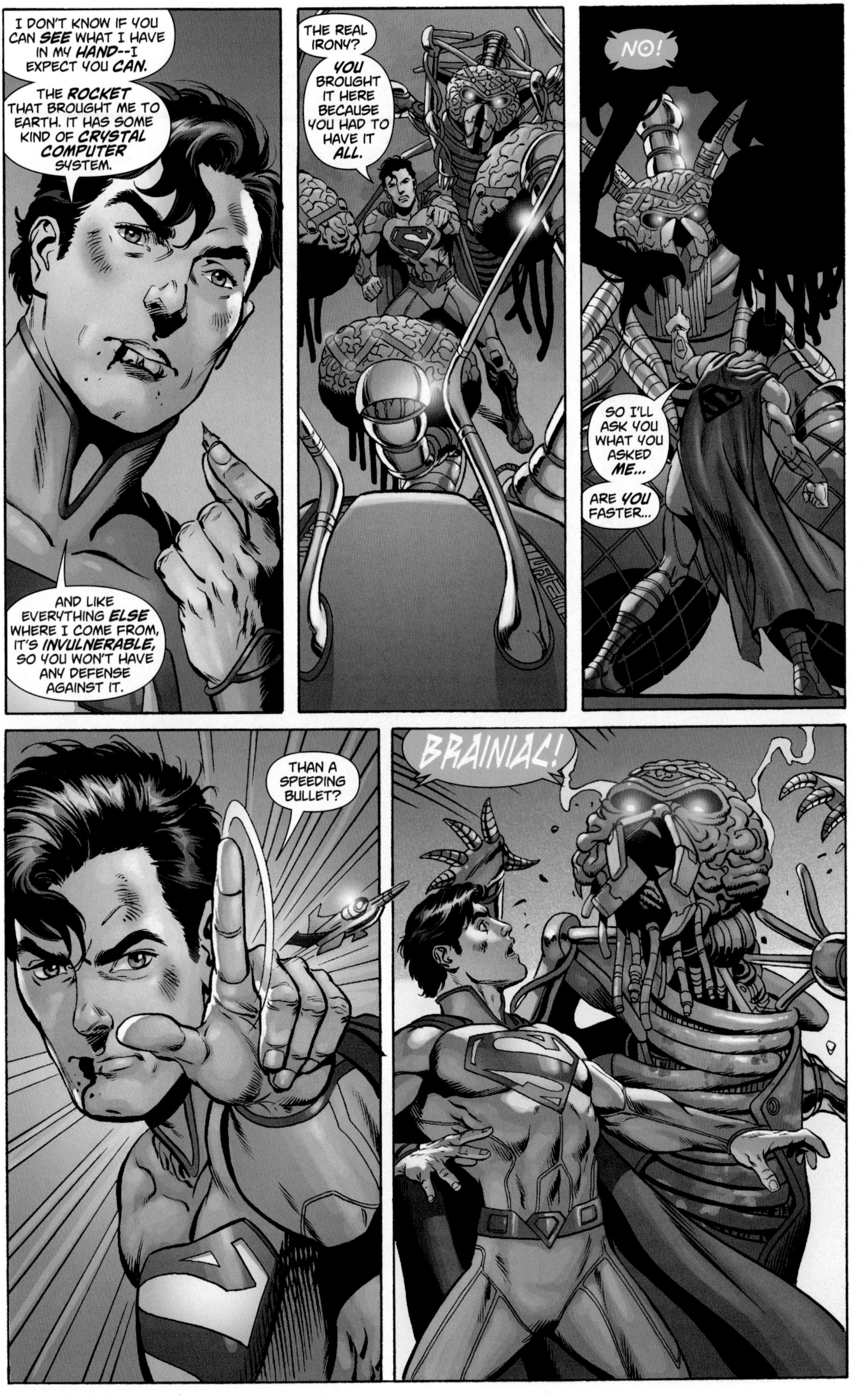
I DON'T KNOW IF YOU CAN SEE WHAT I HAVE IN MY HAND--I EXPECT YOU CAN.
THE ROCKET THAT BROUGHT ME TO EARTH. IT HAS SOME KIND OF CRYSTAL COMPUTER SYSTEM.
AND LIKE EVERYTHING ELSE WHERE I COME FROM, IT'S INVULNERABLE, SO YOU WON'T HAVE ANY DEFENSE AGAINST IT.
THE REAL IRONY?
YOU BROUGHT IT HERE BECAUSE YOU HAD TO HAVE IT ALL.
NO!
SO I'LL ASK YOU WHAT YOU ASKED ME...
ARE YOU FASTER...
THAN A SPEEDING BULLET?
BRAINIAC!

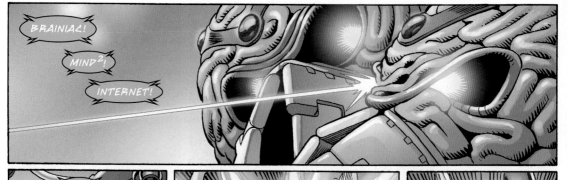

BRAINIAC!

MIND²!

INTERNET!

TRIED

TRIED TO COLLECT

THIRTY SECONDS TO BOTTLE-CITY PERMANENT MICRO-STASIS.

TRIED TO SAVE

WOW.

HA-LA KAL-EL.

IM-IL-IA-VEL-REK-TA LO-LA!

HA-LA-LA!

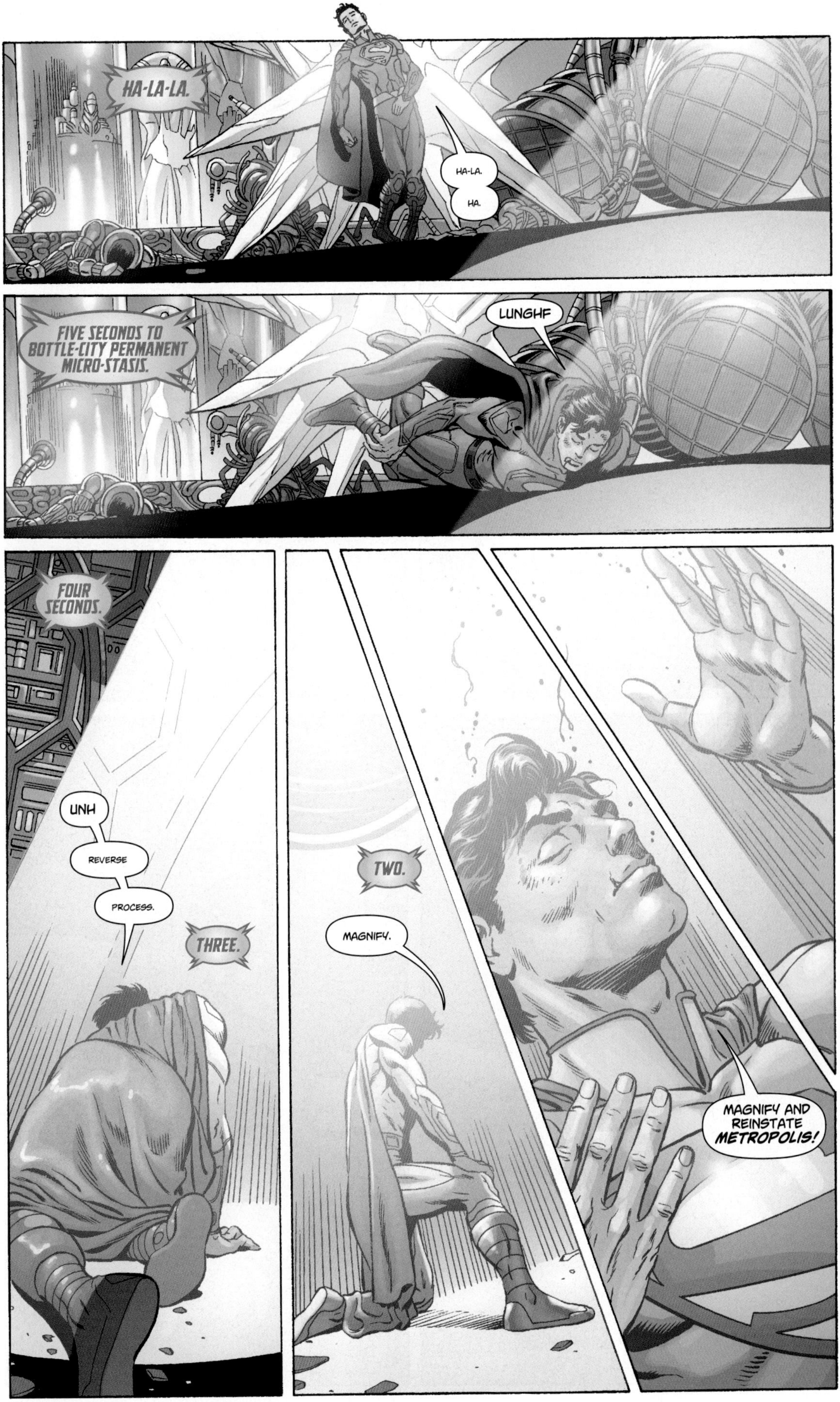
HA-LA-LA.
HA-LA.
HA.
FIVE SECONDS TO BOTTLE-CITY PERMANENT MICRO-STASIS.
LUNGHF
FOUR SECONDS.
UNH
REVERSE
PROCESS.
THREE.
TWO.
MAGNIFY.
MAGNIFY AND REINSTATE METROPOLIS!

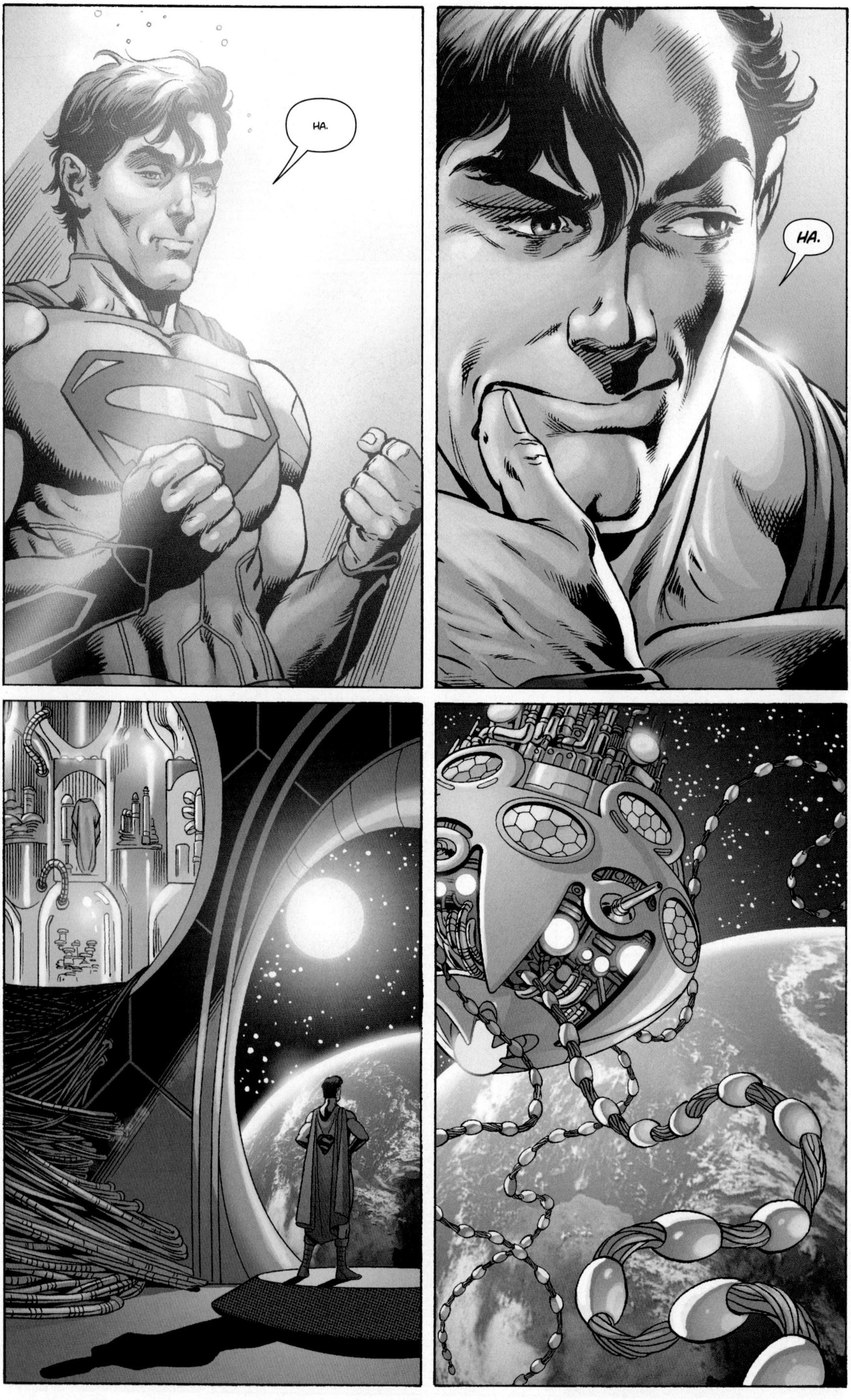
HA.
HA.

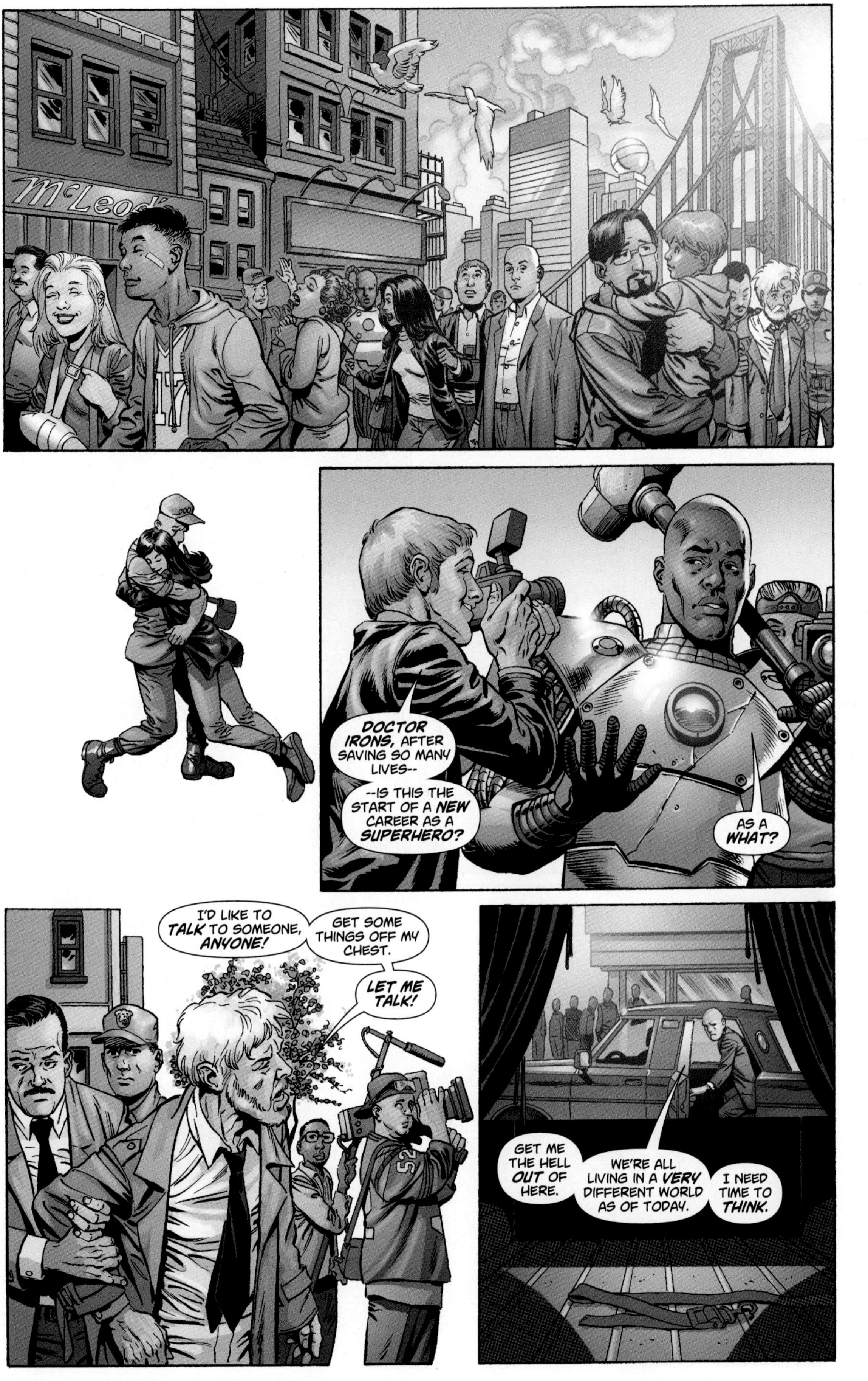
DOCTOR IRONS, AFTER SAVING SO MANY LIVES--
--IS THIS THE START OF A NEW CAREER AS A SUPERHERO?
AS A WHAT?
I'D LIKE TO TALK TO SOMEONE, ANYONE!
GET SOME THINGS OFF MY CHEST.
LET ME TALK!
GET ME THE HELL OUT OF HERE.
WE'RE ALL LIVING IN A VERY DIFFERENT WORLD AS OF TODAY.
I NEED TIME TO THINK.

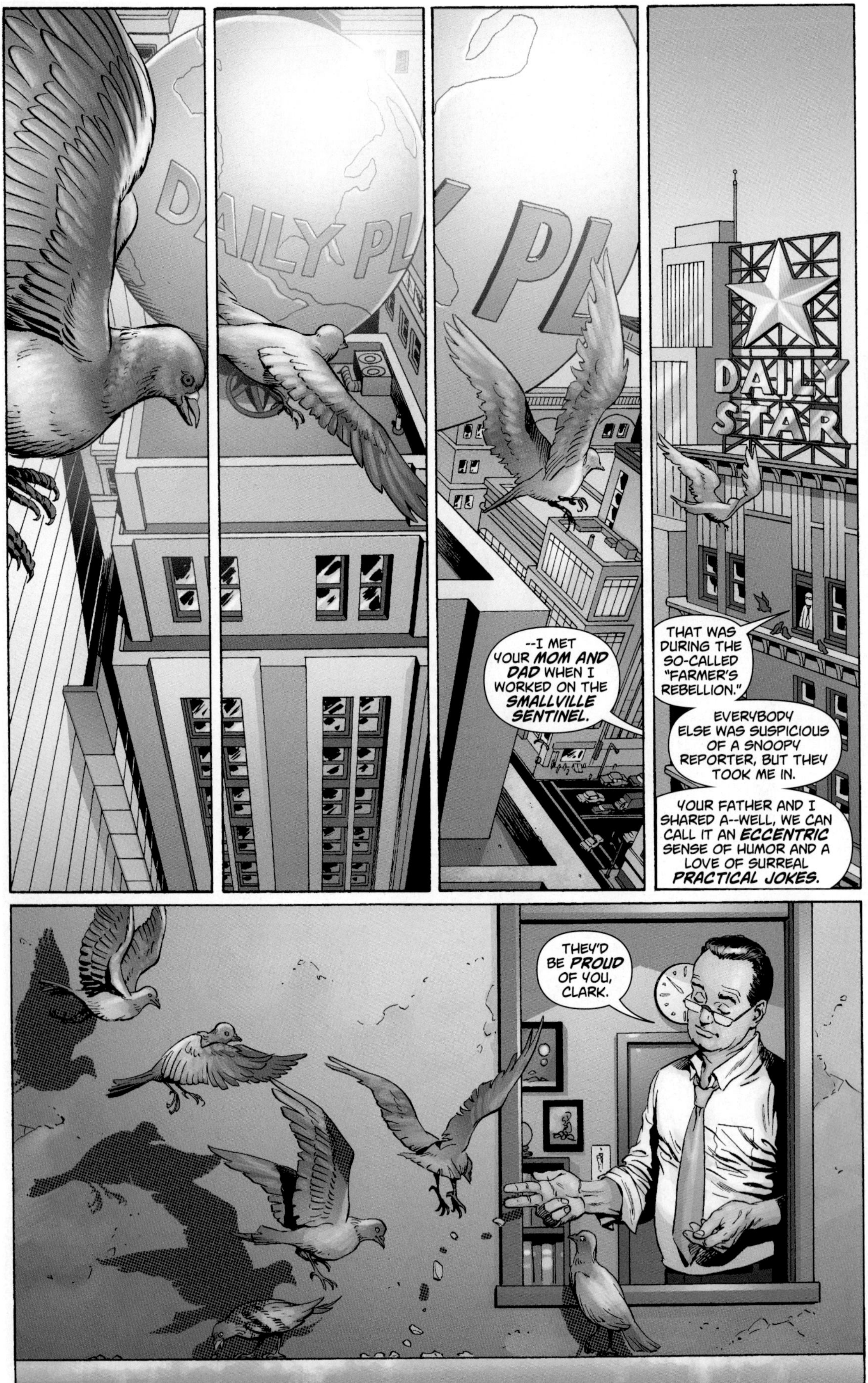
DAILY PL
PL
DAILY STAR
--I MET YOUR MOM AND DAD WHEN I WORKED ON THE SMALLVILLE SENTINEL.
THAT WAS DURING THE SO-CALLED "FARMER'S REBELLION."
EVERYBODY ELSE WAS SUSPICIOUS OF A SNOOPY REPORTER, BUT THEY TOOK ME IN.
YOUR FATHER AND I SHARED A--WELL, WE CAN CALL IT AN ECCENTRIC SENSE OF HUMOR AND A LOVE OF SURREAL PRACTICAL JOKES.
THEY'D BE PROUD OF YOU, CLARK.

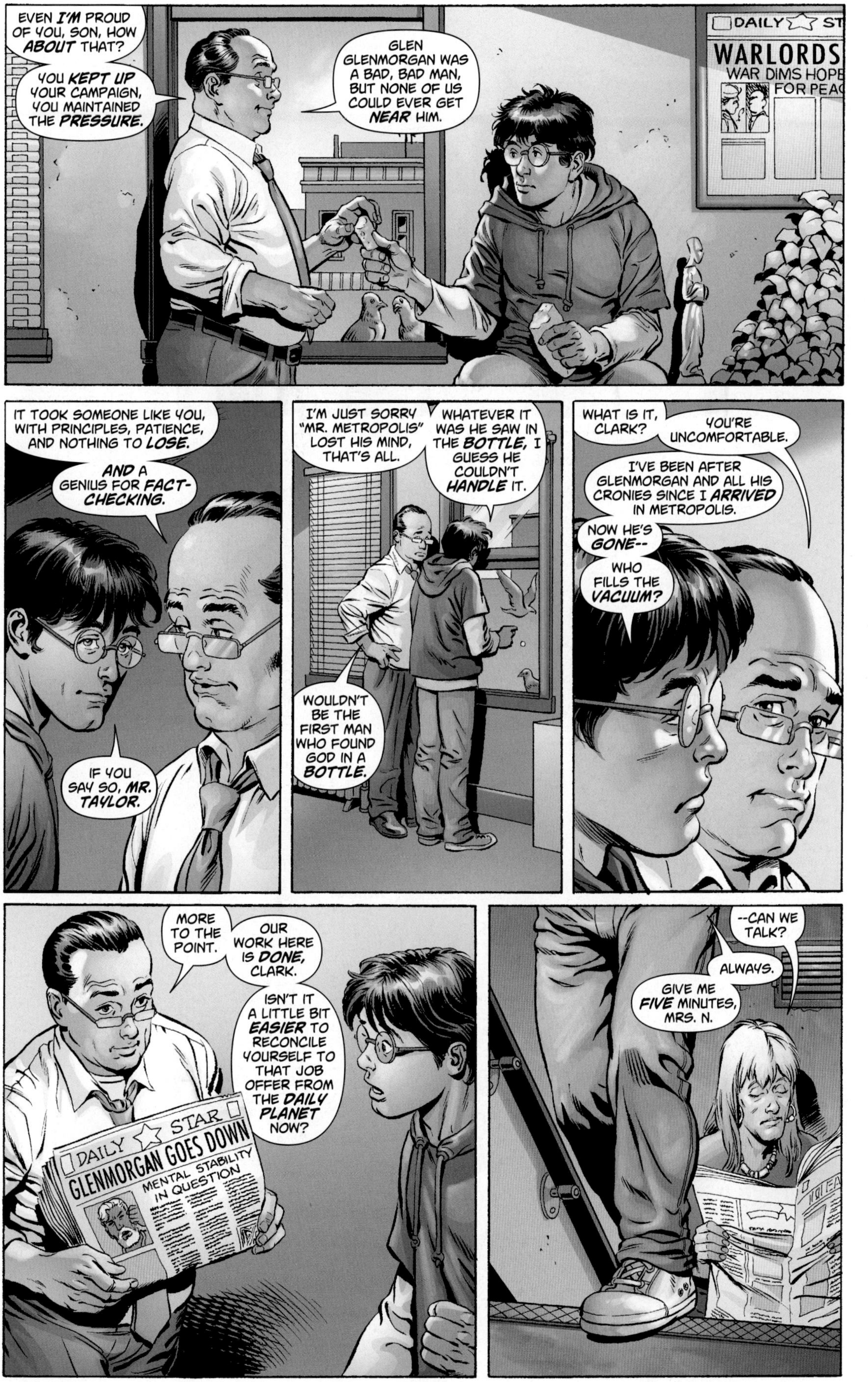
DAILY STAR
WARLORDS
WAR DIMS HOPE FOR PEAC
EVEN I'M PROUD OF YOU, SON, HOW ABOUT THAT?
YOU KEPT UP YOUR CAMPAIGN, YOU MAINTAINED THE PRESSURE.
GLEN GLENMORGAN WAS A BAD, BAD MAN, BUT NONE OF US COULD EVER GET NEAR HIM.
IT TOOK SOMEONE LIKE YOU, WITH PRINCIPLES, PATIENCE, AND NOTHING TO LOSE.
AND A GENIUS FOR FACT-CHECKING.
IF YOU SAY SO, MR. TAYLOR.
I'M JUST SORRY "MR. METROPOLIS" LOST HIS MIND, THAT'S ALL.
WHATEVER IT WAS HE SAW IN THE BOTTLE, I GUESS HE COULDN'T HANDLE IT.
WOULDN'T BE THE FIRST MAN WHO FOUND GOD IN A BOTTLE.
WHAT IS IT, CLARK?
YOU'RE UNCOMFORTABLE.
I'VE BEEN AFTER GLENMORGAN AND ALL HIS CRONIES SINCE I ARRIVED IN METROPOLIS.
NOW HE'S GONE--
WHO FILLS THE VACUUM?
MORE TO THE POINT.
OUR WORK HERE IS DONE, CLARK.
ISN'T IT A LITTLE BIT EASIER TO RECONCILE YOURSELF TO THAT JOB OFFER FROM THE DAILY PLANET NOW?
DAILY STAR
GLENMORGAN GOES DOWN
MENTAL STABILITY IN QUESTION
--CAN WE TALK?
ALWAYS.
GIVE ME FIVE MINUTES, MRS. N.

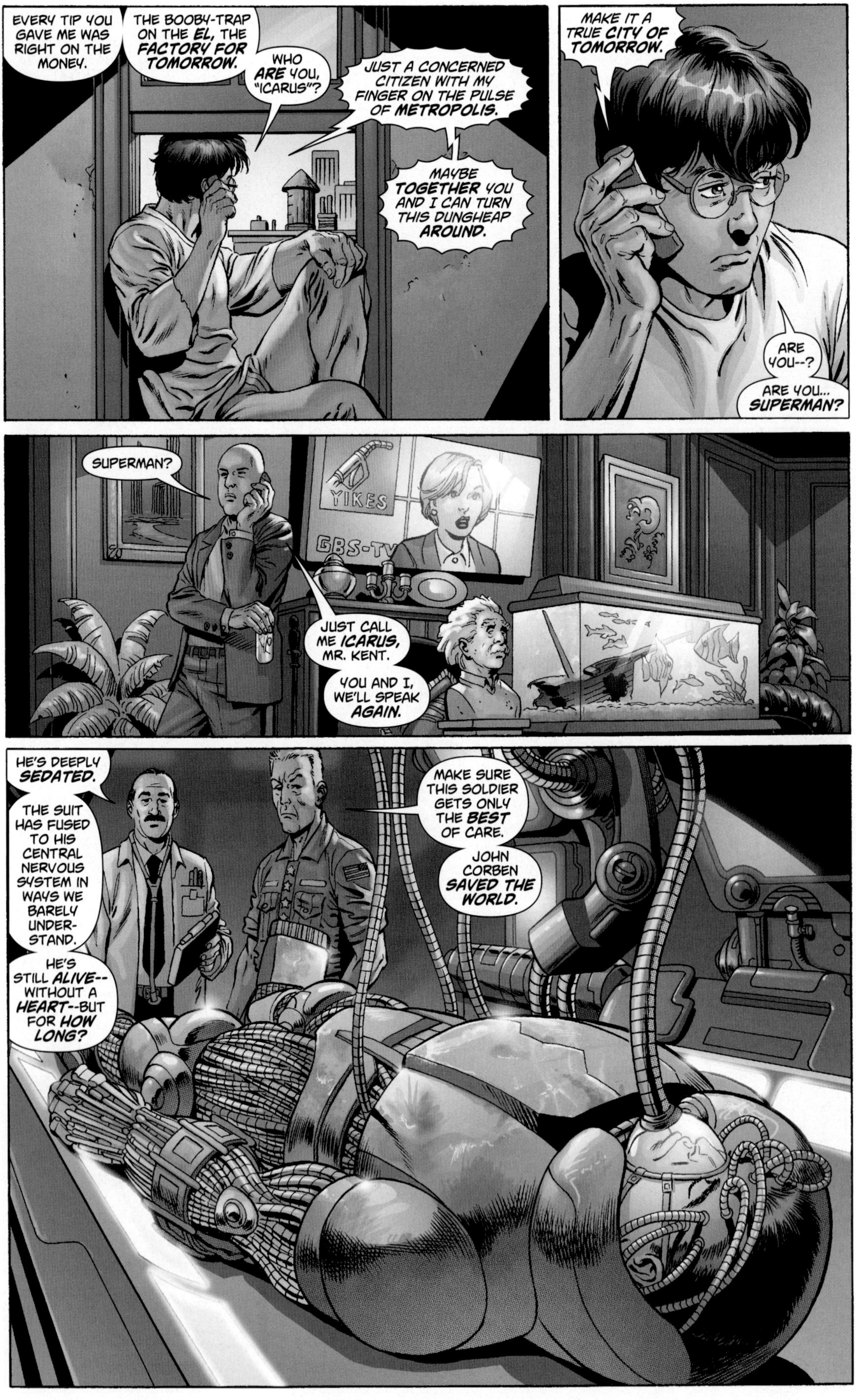
EVERY TIP YOU GAVE ME WAS RIGHT ON THE MONEY.
THE BOOBY-TRAP ON THE EL, THE FACTORY FOR TOMORROW.
WHO ARE YOU, "ICARUS"?
JUST A CONCERNED CITIZEN WITH MY FINGER ON THE PULSE OF METROPOLIS.
MAYBE TOGETHER YOU AND I CAN TURN THIS DUNGHEAP AROUND.
MAKE IT A TRUE CITY OF TOMORROW.
ARE YOU--?
ARE YOU... SUPERMAN?
SUPERMAN?
YIKES
GBS-TV
JUST CALL ME ICARUS, MR. KENT.
YOU AND I, WE'LL SPEAK AGAIN.
HE'S DEEPLY SEDATED.
THE SUIT HAS FUSED TO HIS CENTRAL NERVOUS SYSTEM IN WAYS WE BARELY UNDER-STAND.
HE'S STILL ALIVE-- WITHOUT A HEART--BUT FOR HOW LONG?
MAKE SURE THIS SOLDIER GETS ONLY THE BEST OF CARE.
JOHN CORBEN SAVED THE WORLD.

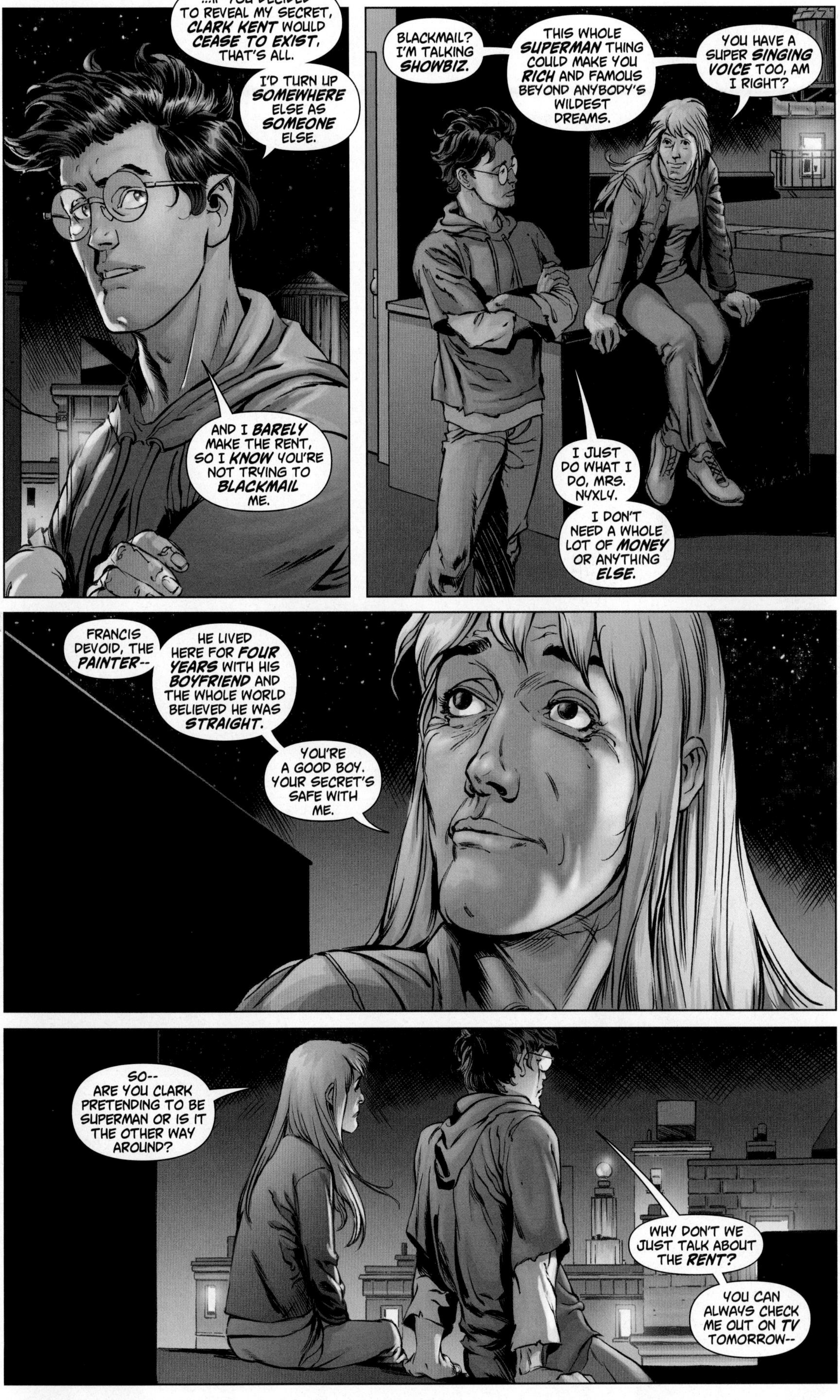
...IF YOU DECIDED TO REVEAL MY SECRET, CLARK KENT WOULD CEASE TO EXIST, THAT'S ALL.
I'D TURN UP SOMEWHERE ELSE AS SOMEONE ELSE.
AND I BARELY MAKE THE RENT, SO I KNOW YOU'RE NOT TRYING TO BLACKMAIL ME.
BLACKMAIL? I'M TALKING SHOWBIZ.
THIS WHOLE SUPERMAN THING COULD MAKE YOU RICH AND FAMOUS BEYOND ANYBODY'S WILDEST DREAMS.
YOU HAVE A SUPER SINGING VOICE TOO, AM I RIGHT?
I JUST DO WHAT I DO, MRS. NYXLY.
I DON'T NEED A WHOLE LOT OF MONEY OR ANYTHING ELSE.
FRANCIS DEVOID, THE PAINTER--
HE LIVED HERE FOR FOUR YEARS WITH HIS BOYFRIEND AND THE WHOLE WORLD BELIEVED HE WAS STRAIGHT.
YOU'RE A GOOD BOY. YOUR SECRET'S SAFE WITH ME.
SO-- ARE YOU CLARK PRETENDING TO BE SUPERMAN OR IS IT THE OTHER WAY AROUND?
WHY DON'T WE JUST TALK ABOUT THE RENT?
YOU CAN ALWAYS CHECK ME OUT ON TV TOMORROW--

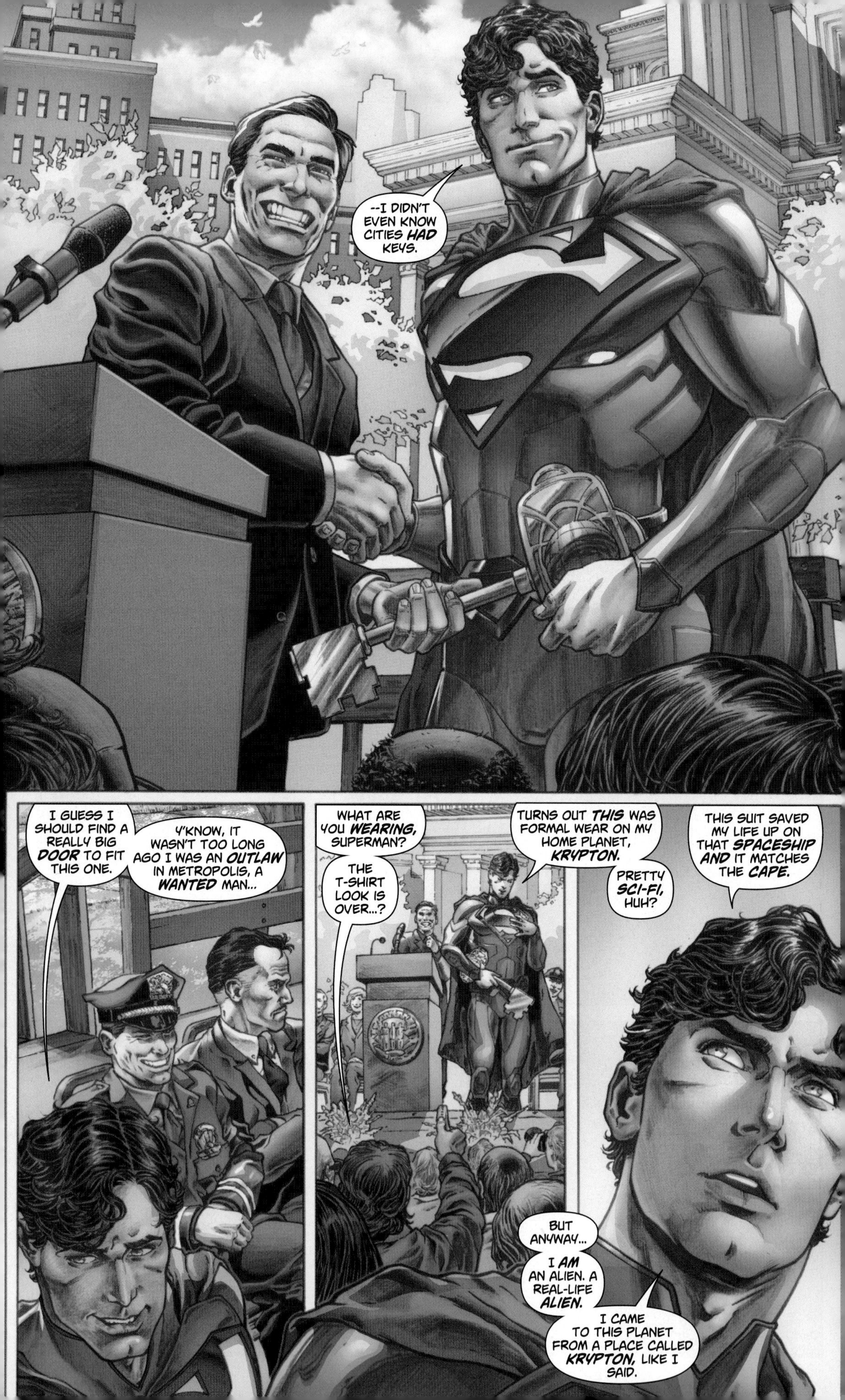
--I DIDN'T EVEN KNOW CITIES HAD KEYS.
I GUESS I SHOULD FIND A REALLY BIG DOOR TO FIT THIS ONE.
Y'KNOW, IT WASN'T TOO LONG AGO I WAS AN OUTLAW IN METROPOLIS, A WANTED MAN...
WHAT ARE YOU WEARING, SUPERMAN?
THE T-SHIRT LOOK IS OVER...?
TURNS OUT THIS WAS FORMAL WEAR ON MY HOME PLANET, KRYPTON.
PRETTY SCI-FI, HUH?
THIS SUIT SAVED MY LIFE UP ON THAT SPACESHIP AND IT MATCHES THE CAPE.
BUT ANYWAY...
I AM AN ALIEN. A REAL-LIFE ALIEN.
I CAME TO THIS PLANET FROM A PLACE CALLED KRYPTON, LIKE I SAID.

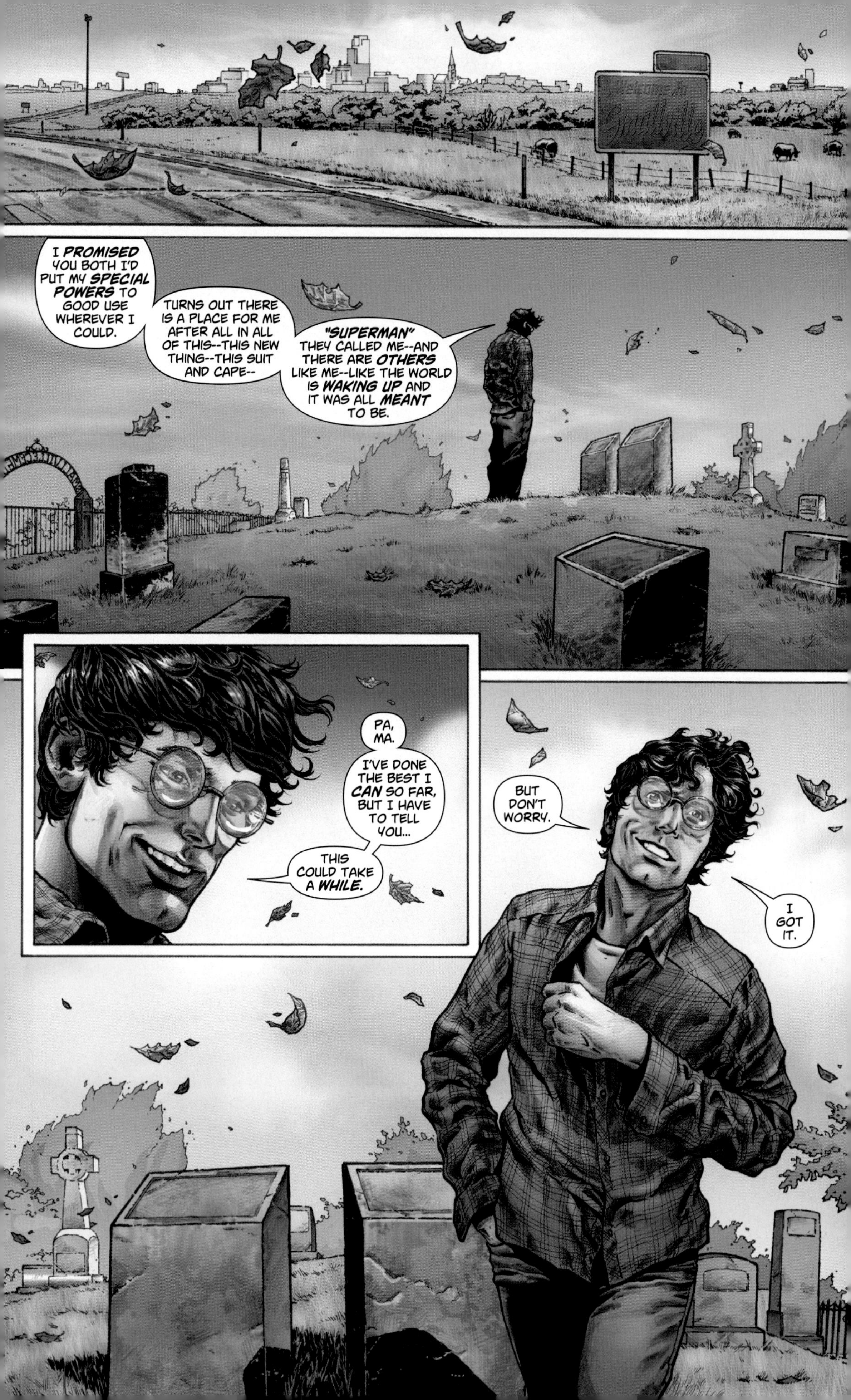
Welcome to Smallville
I PROMISED YOU BOTH I'D PUT MY SPECIAL POWERS TO GOOD USE WHEREVER I COULD.
TURNS OUT THERE IS A PLACE FOR ME AFTER ALL IN ALL OF THIS--THIS NEW THING--THIS SUIT AND CAPE--
"SUPERMAN" THEY CALLED ME--AND THERE ARE OTHERS LIKE ME--LIKE THE WORLD IS WAKING UP AND IT WAS ALL MEANT TO BE.
PA, MA.
I'VE DONE THE BEST I CAN SO FAR, BUT I HAVE TO TELL YOU...
THIS COULD TAKE A WHILE.
BUT DON'T WORRY.
I GOT IT.

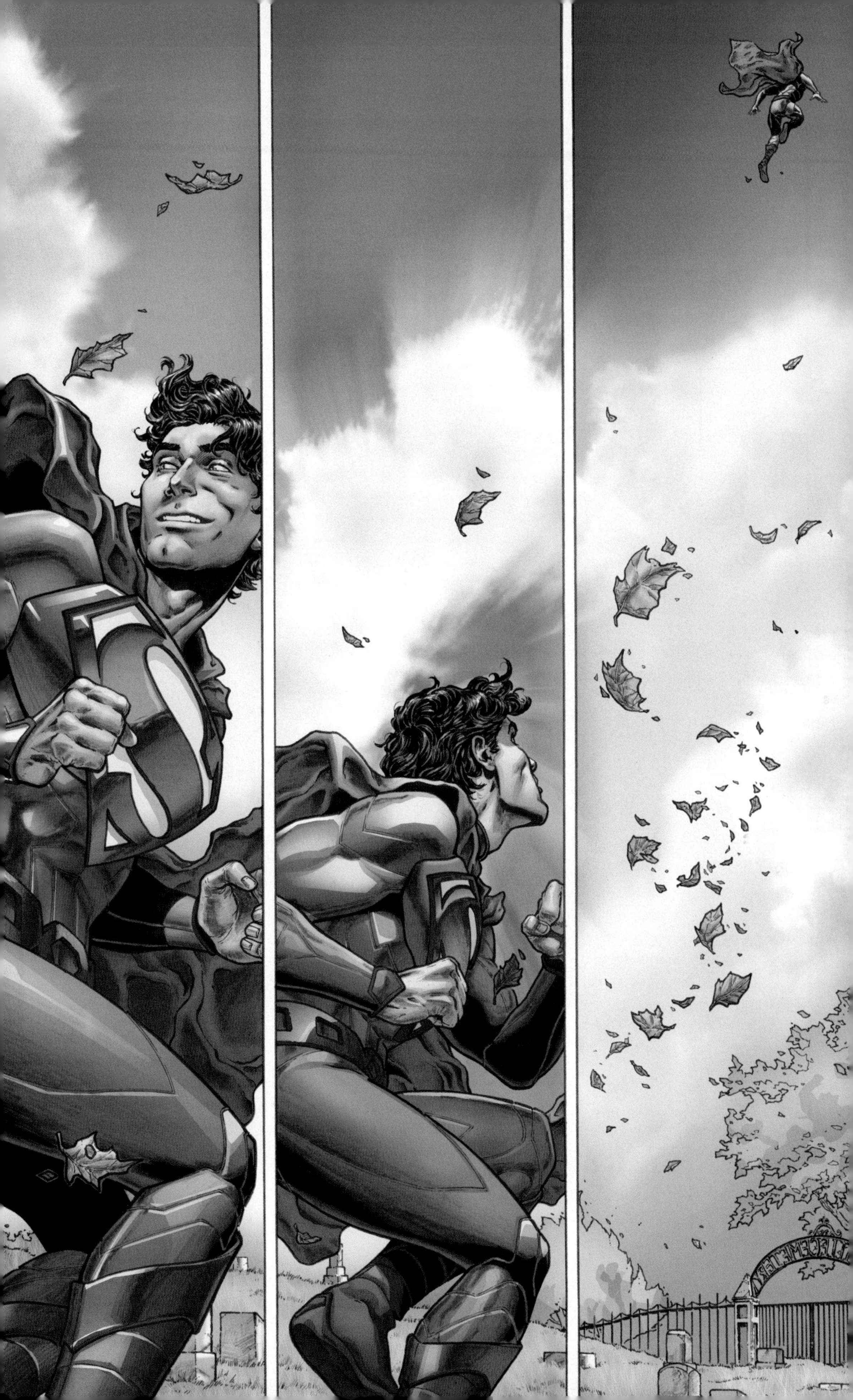

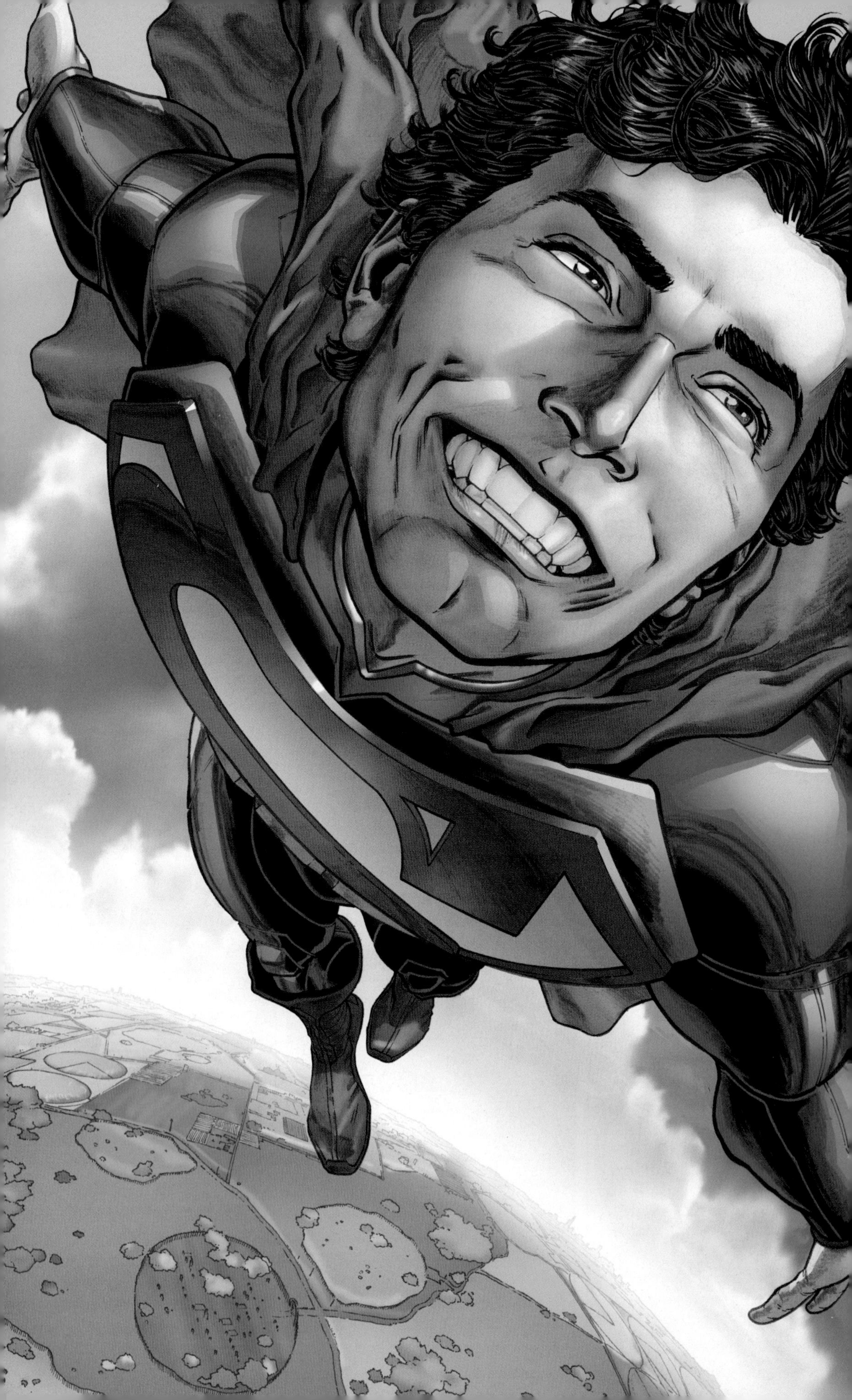

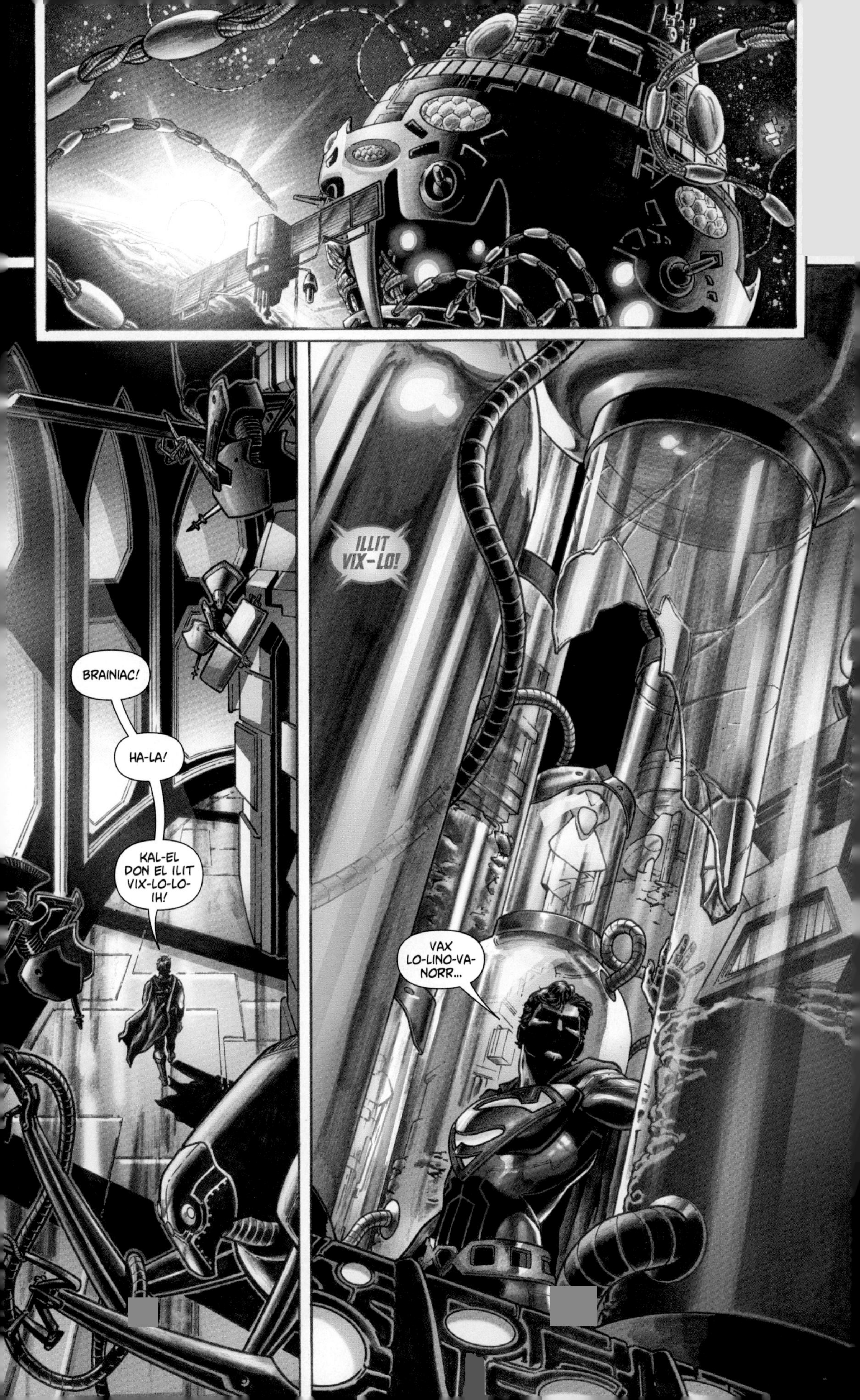
BRAINIAC!
HA-LA!
KAL-EL DON EL ILIT VIX-LO-LO-IH!
ILLIT VIX-LO!
VAX LO-LINO-VA-NORR...

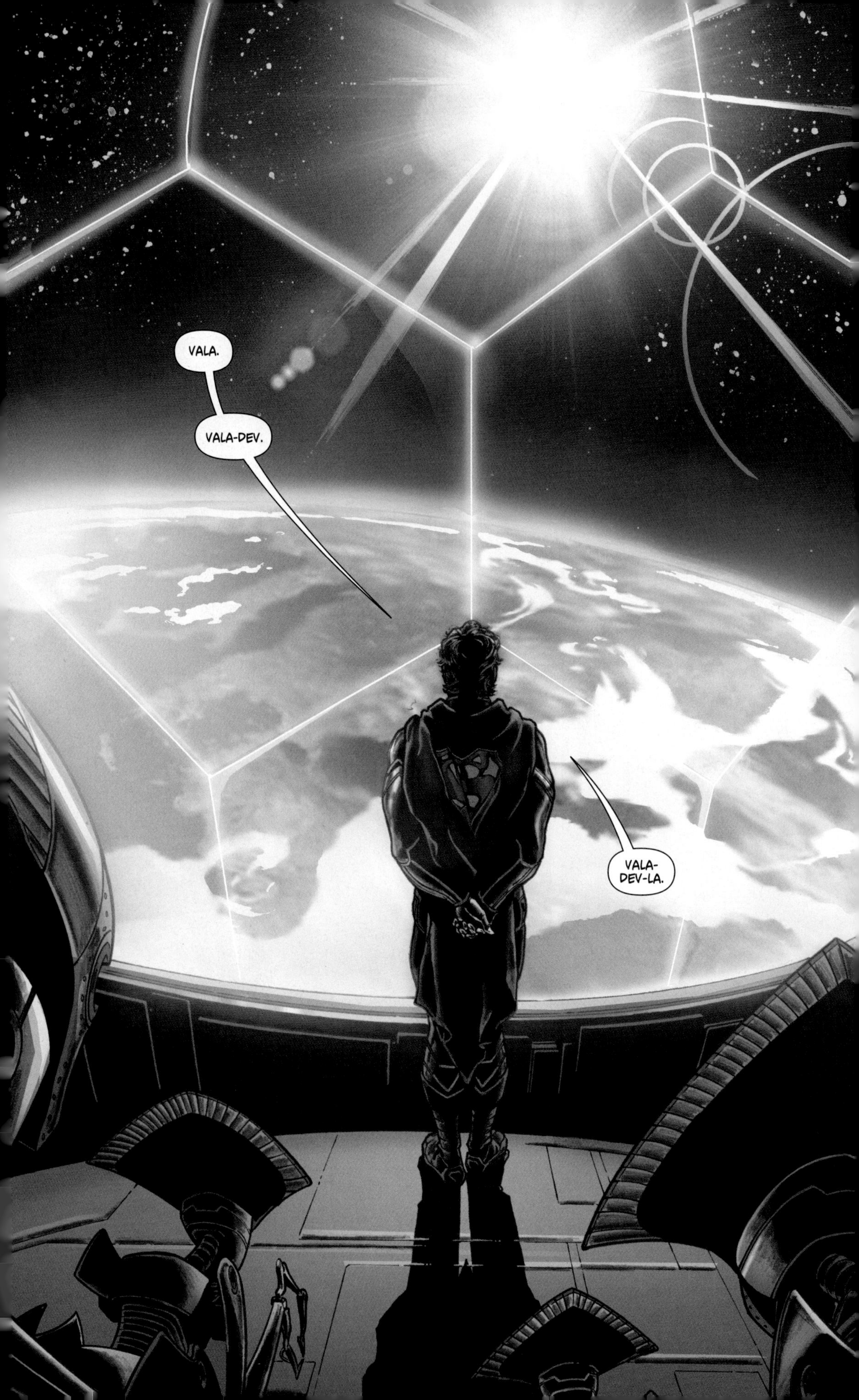
VALA.
VALA-DEV.
VALA-DEV-LA.

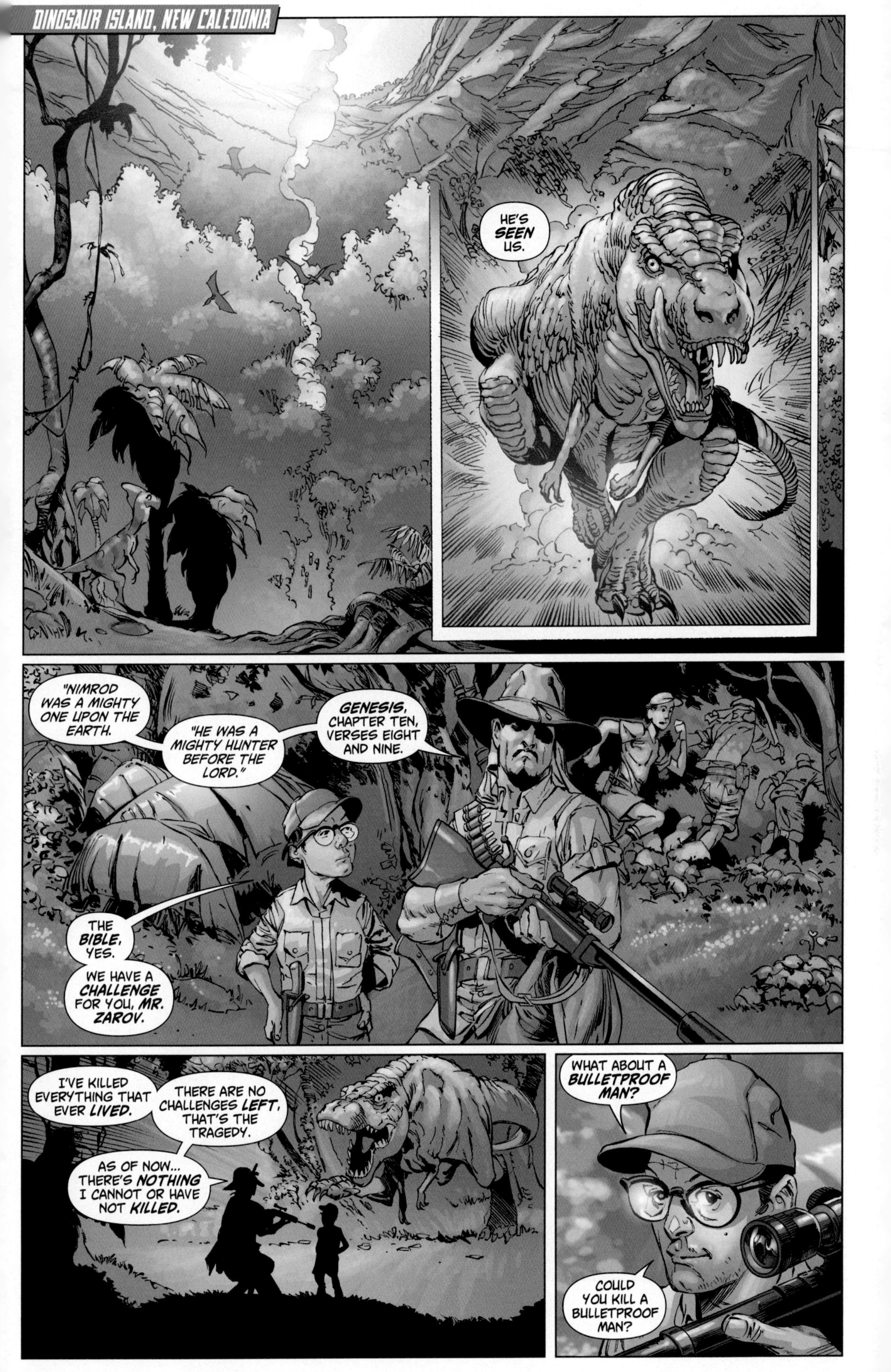
DINOSAUR ISLAND, NEW CALEDONIA
HE'S SEEN US.
"NIMROD WAS A MIGHTY ONE UPON THE EARTH.
"HE WAS A MIGHTY HUNTER BEFORE THE LORD."
GENESIS, CHAPTER TEN, VERSES EIGHT AND NINE.
THE BIBLE, YES.
WE HAVE A CHALLENGE FOR YOU, MR. ZAROV.
I'VE KILLED EVERYTHING THAT EVER LIVED.
THERE ARE NO CHALLENGES LEFT, THAT'S THE TRAGEDY.
AS OF NOW... THERE'S NOTHING I CANNOT OR HAVE NOT KILLED.
WHAT ABOUT A BULLETPROOF MAN?
COULD YOU KILL A BULLETPROOF MAN?

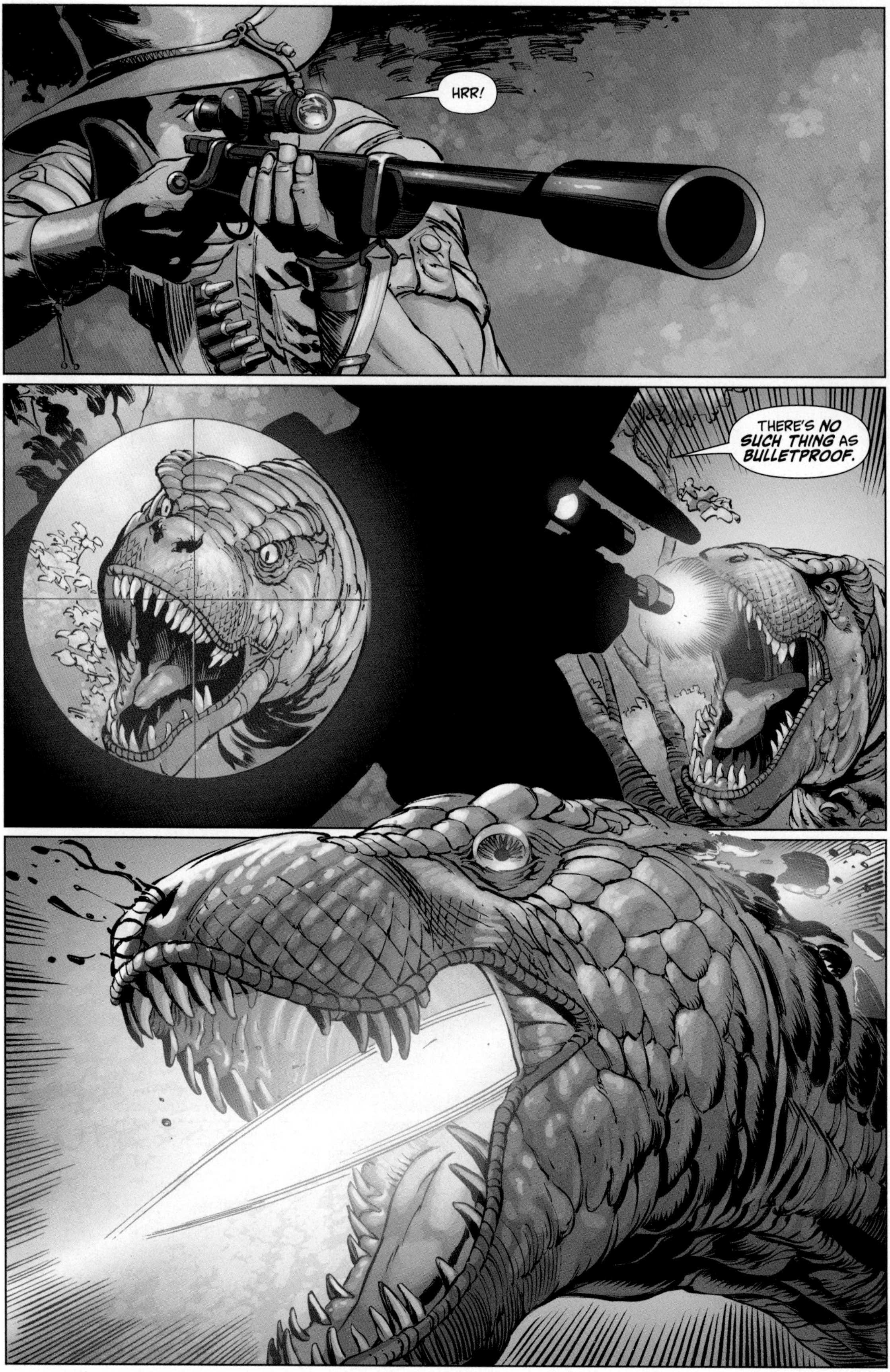
HRR!
THERE'S NO SUCH THING AS BULLETPROOF.

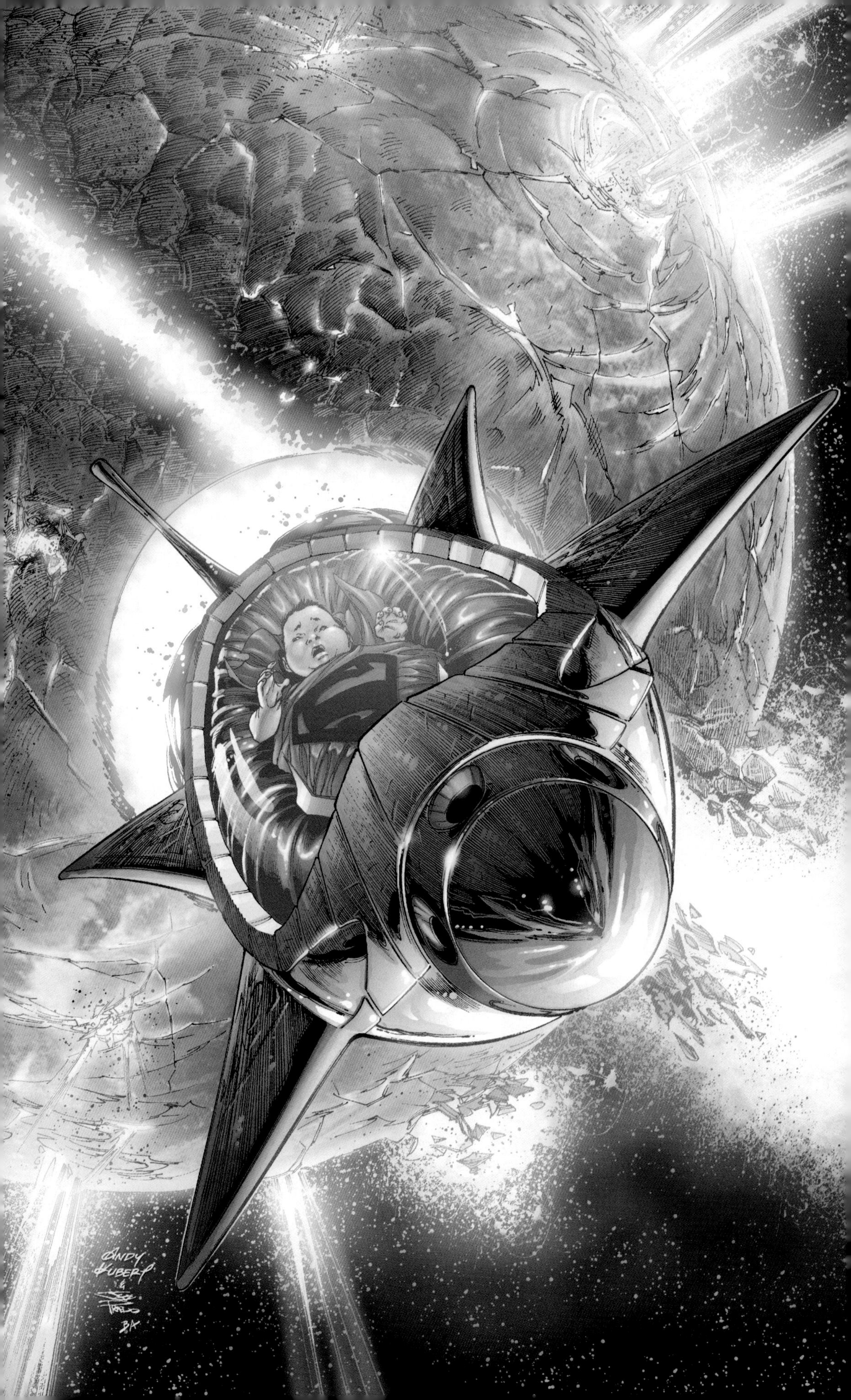
ANDY KUBERT

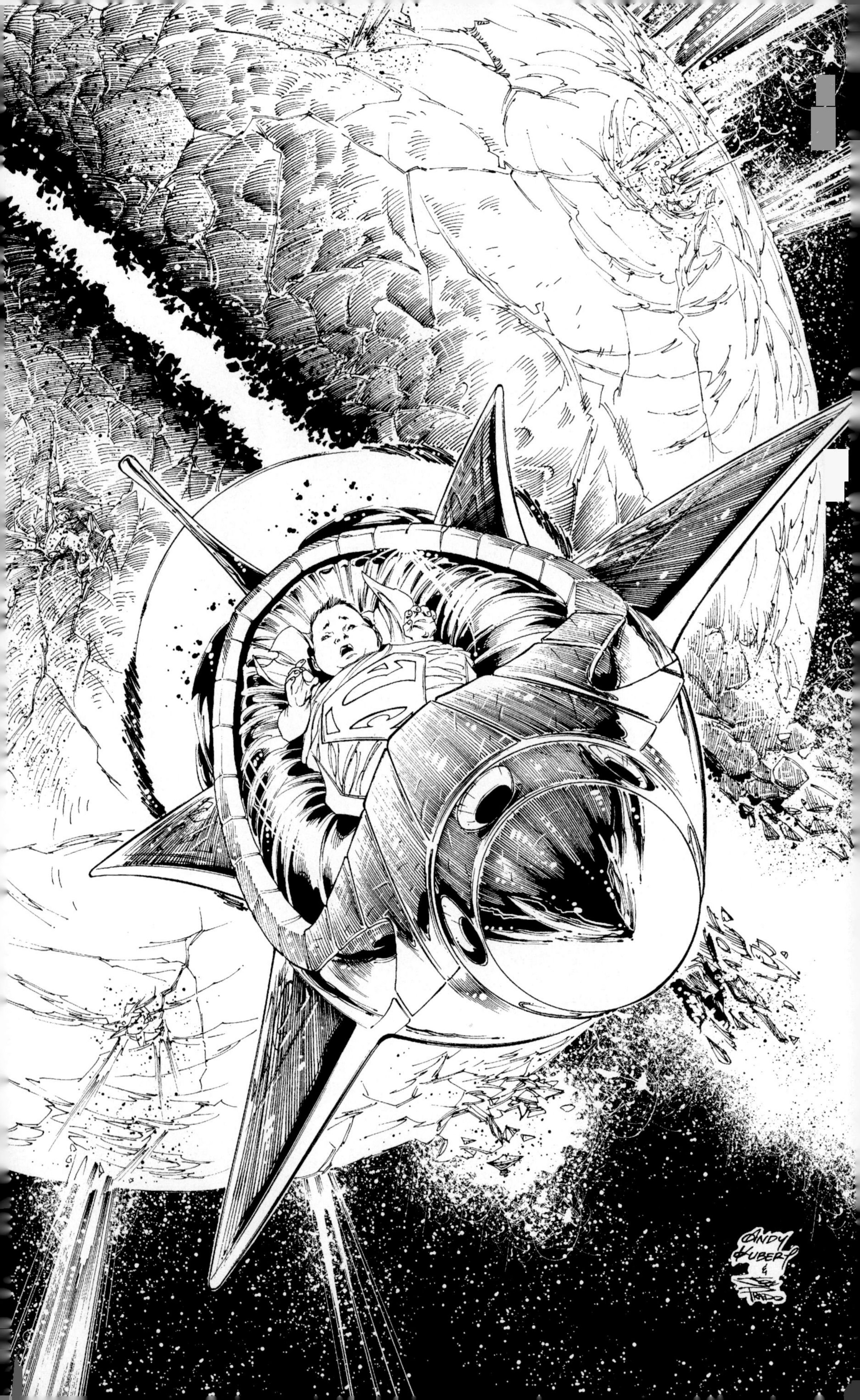
ANDY KUBERT &

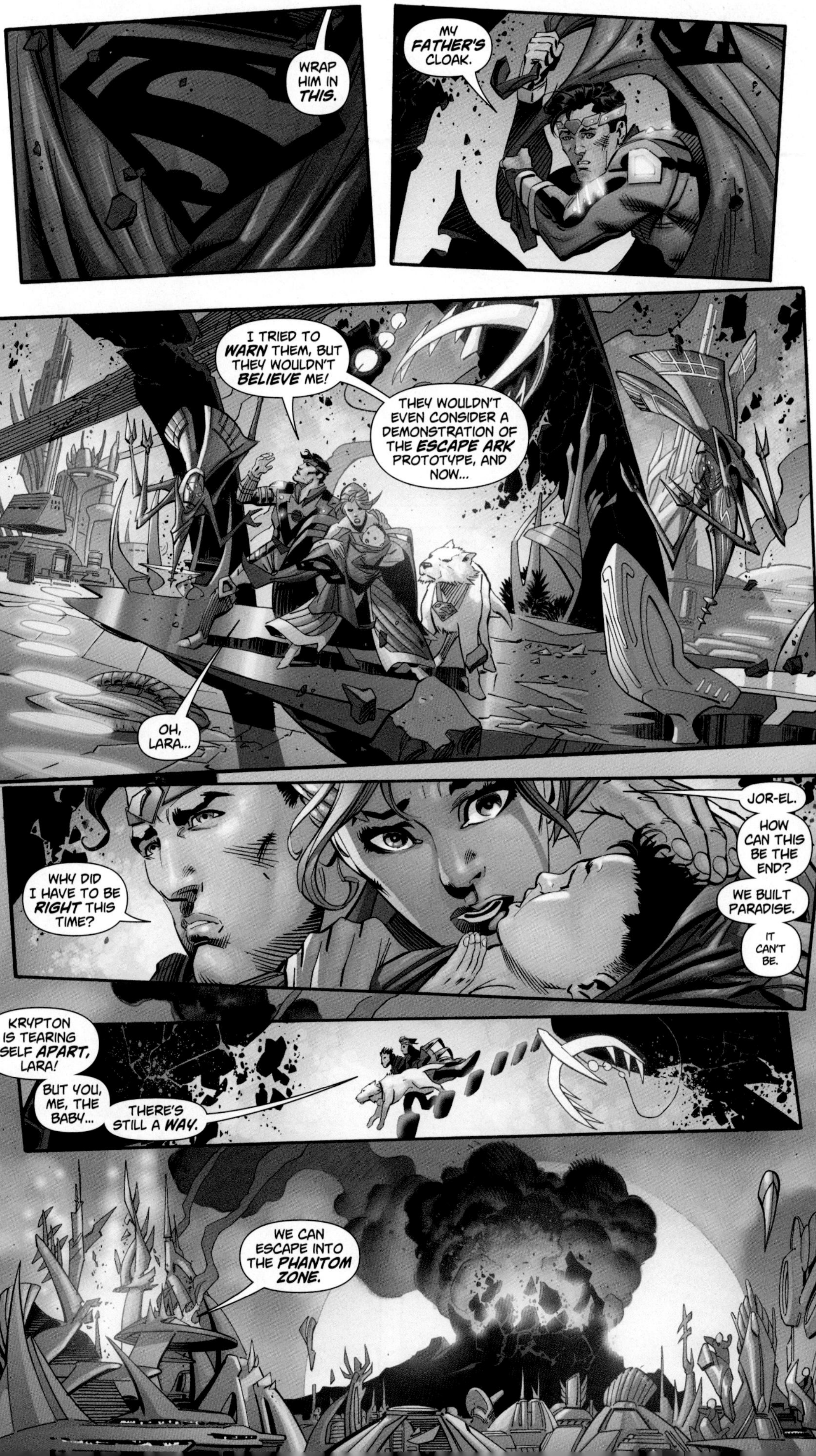
WRAP HIM IN THIS.
MY FATHER'S CLOAK.
I TRIED TO WARN THEM, BUT THEY WOULDN'T BELIEVE ME!
THEY WOULDN'T EVEN CONSIDER A DEMONSTRATION OF THE ESCAPE ARK PROTOTYPE, AND NOW...
OH, LARA...
WHY DID I HAVE TO BE RIGHT THIS TIME?
JOR-EL.
HOW CAN THIS BE THE END?
WE BUILT PARADISE.
IT CAN'T BE.
KRYPTON IS TEARING ITSELF APART, LARA!
BUT YOU, ME, THE BABY...
THERE'S STILL A WAY.
WE CAN ESCAPE INTO THE PHANTOM ZONE.

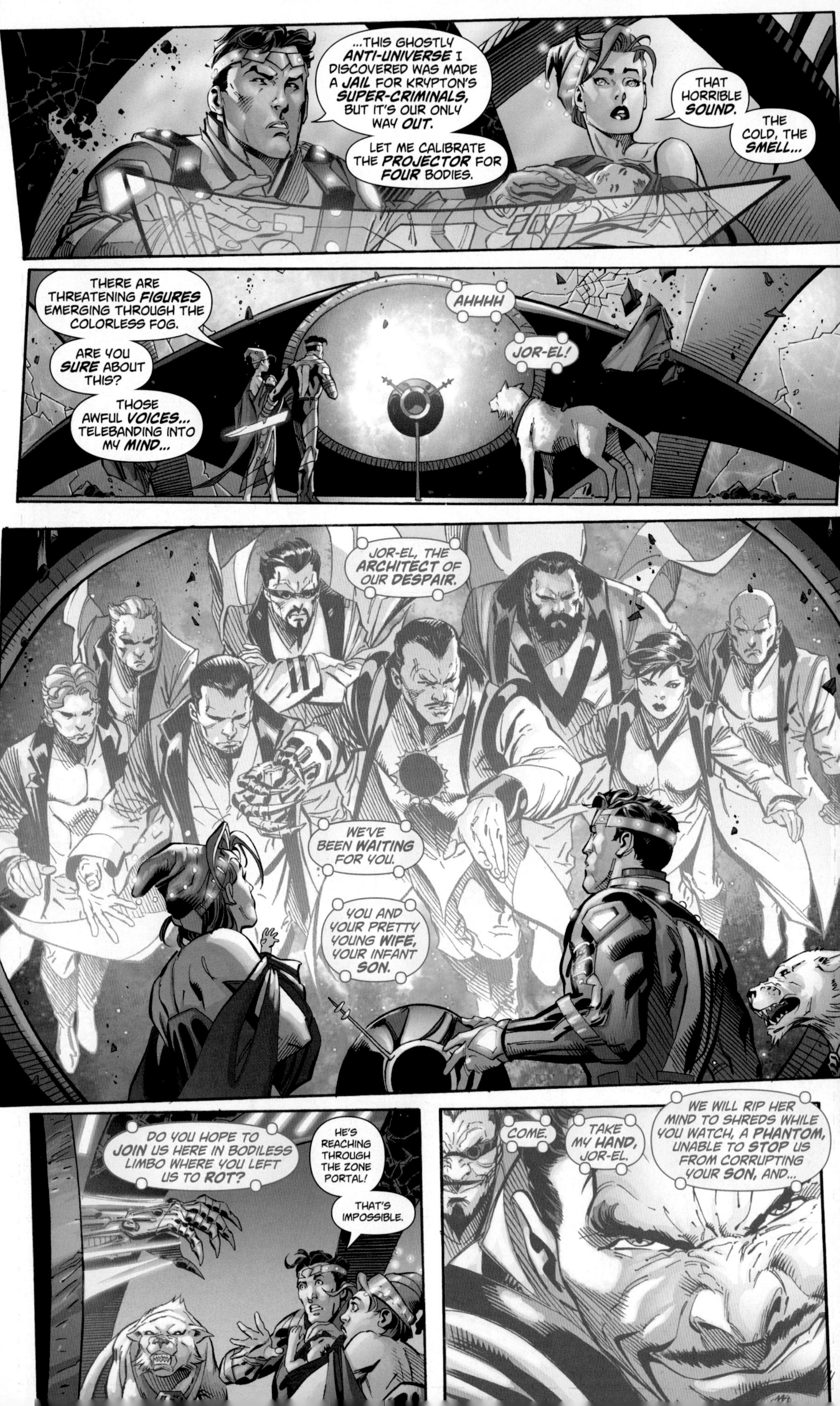
...THIS GHOSTLY ANTI-UNIVERSE I DISCOVERED WAS MADE A JAIL FOR KRYPTON'S SUPER-CRIMINALS, BUT IT'S OUR ONLY WAY OUT.
LET ME CALIBRATE THE PROJECTOR FOR FOUR BODIES.
THAT HORRIBLE SOUND.
THE COLD, THE SMELL...
THERE ARE THREATENING FIGURES EMERGING THROUGH THE COLORLESS FOG.
ARE YOU SURE ABOUT THIS?
THOSE AWFUL VOICES... TELEBANDING INTO MY MIND...
AHHHH
JOR-EL!
JOR-EL, THE ARCHITECT OF OUR DESPAIR.
WE'VE BEEN WAITING FOR YOU.
YOU AND YOUR PRETTY YOUNG WIFE, YOUR INFANT SON.
DO YOU HOPE TO JOIN US HERE IN BODILESS LIMBO WHERE YOU LEFT US TO ROT?
HE'S REACHING THROUGH THE ZONE PORTAL!
THAT'S IMPOSSIBLE.
COME.
TAKE MY HAND, JOR-EL.
WE WILL RIP HER MIND TO SHREDS WHILE YOU WATCH, A PHANTOM, UNABLE TO STOP US FROM CORRUPTING YOUR SON, AND...

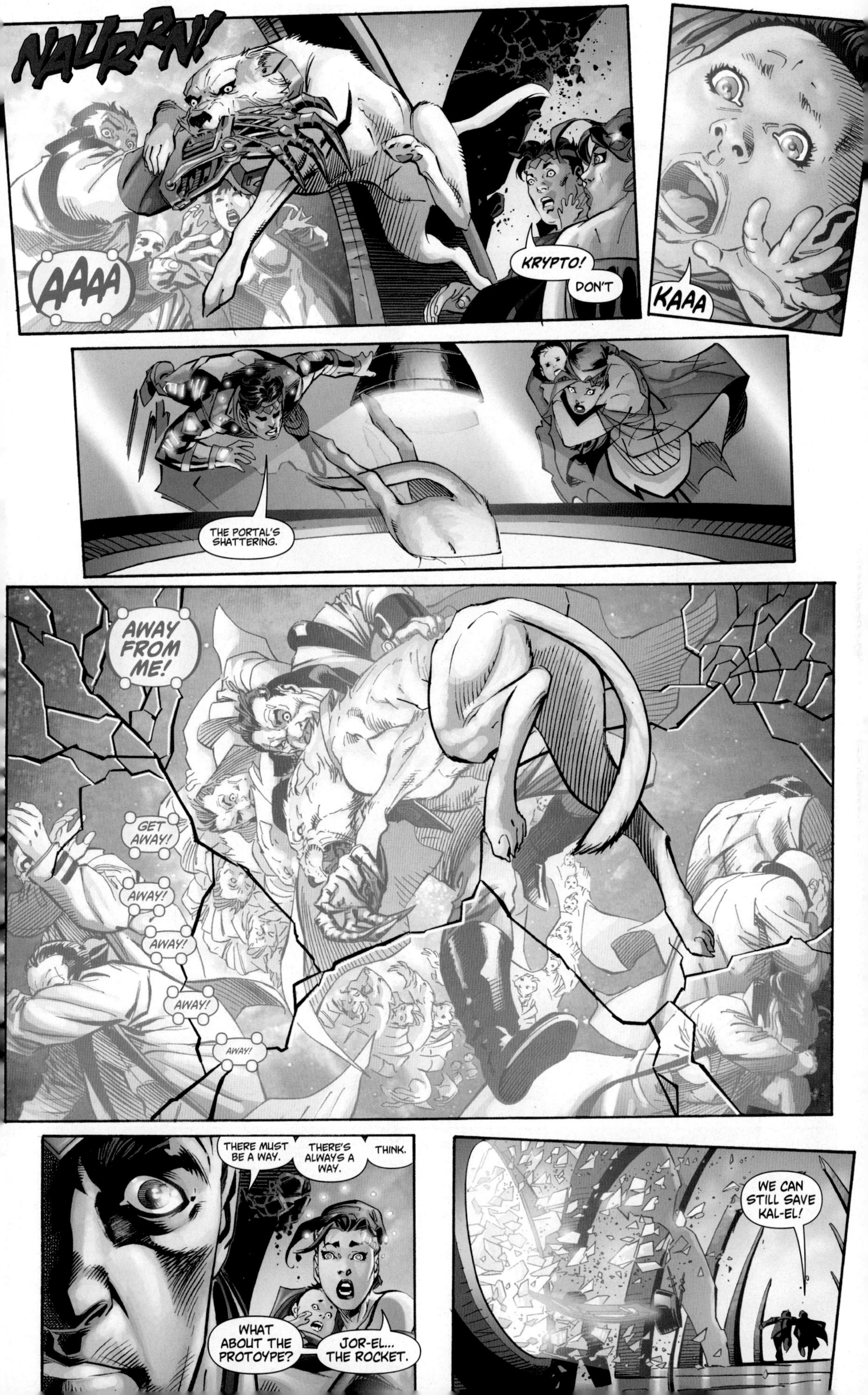
NAURRN!
AAAA
KRYPTO!
DON'T
KAAA
THE PORTAL'S SHATTERING.
AWAY FROM ME!
GET AWAY!
AWAY!
AWAY!
AWAY!
AWAY!
THERE MUST BE A WAY.
THERE'S ALWAYS A WAY.
THINK.
WHAT ABOUT THE PROTOYPE?
JOR-EL... THE ROCKET.
WE CAN STILL SAVE KAL-EL!

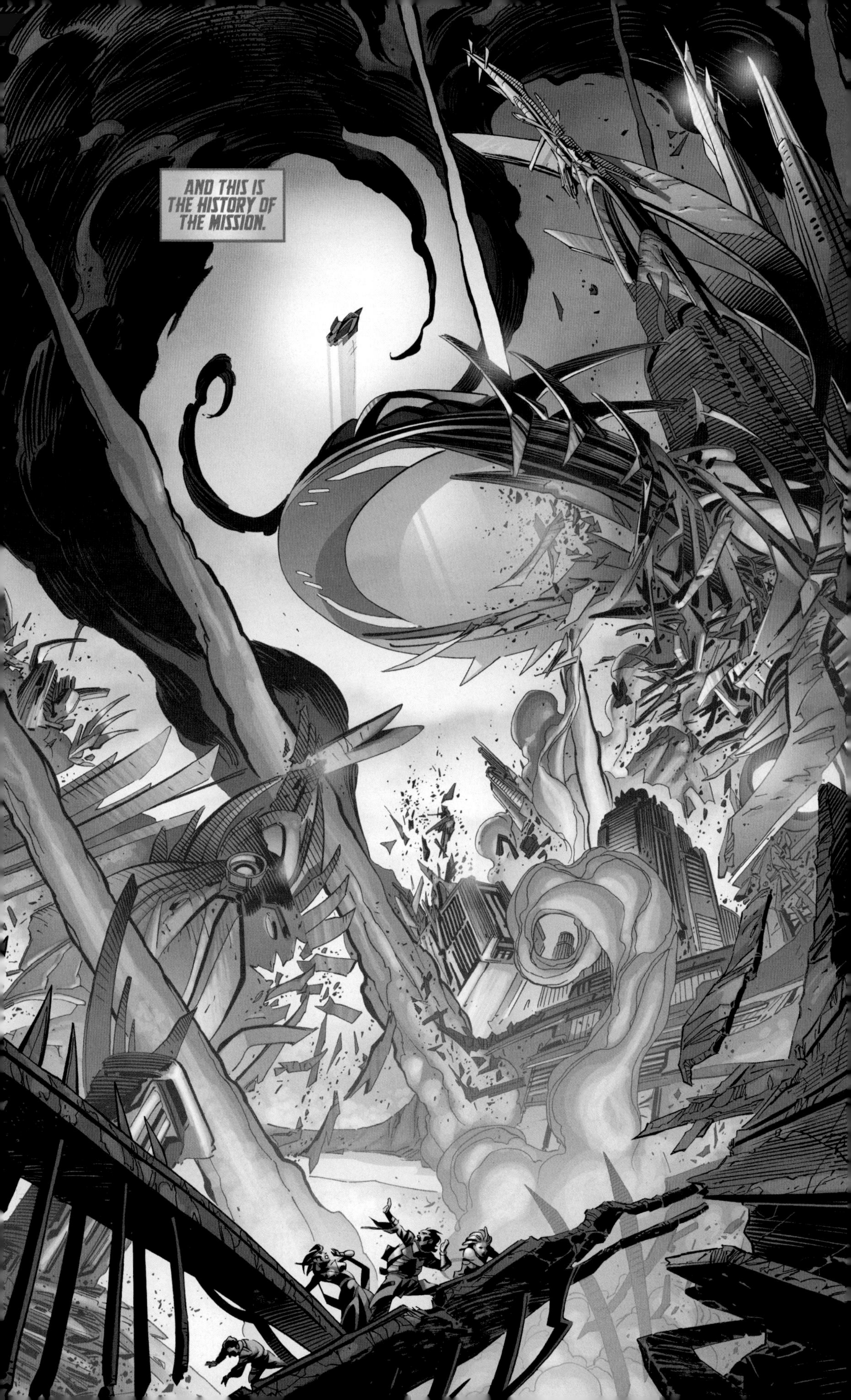
AND THIS IS THE HISTORY OF THE MISSION.

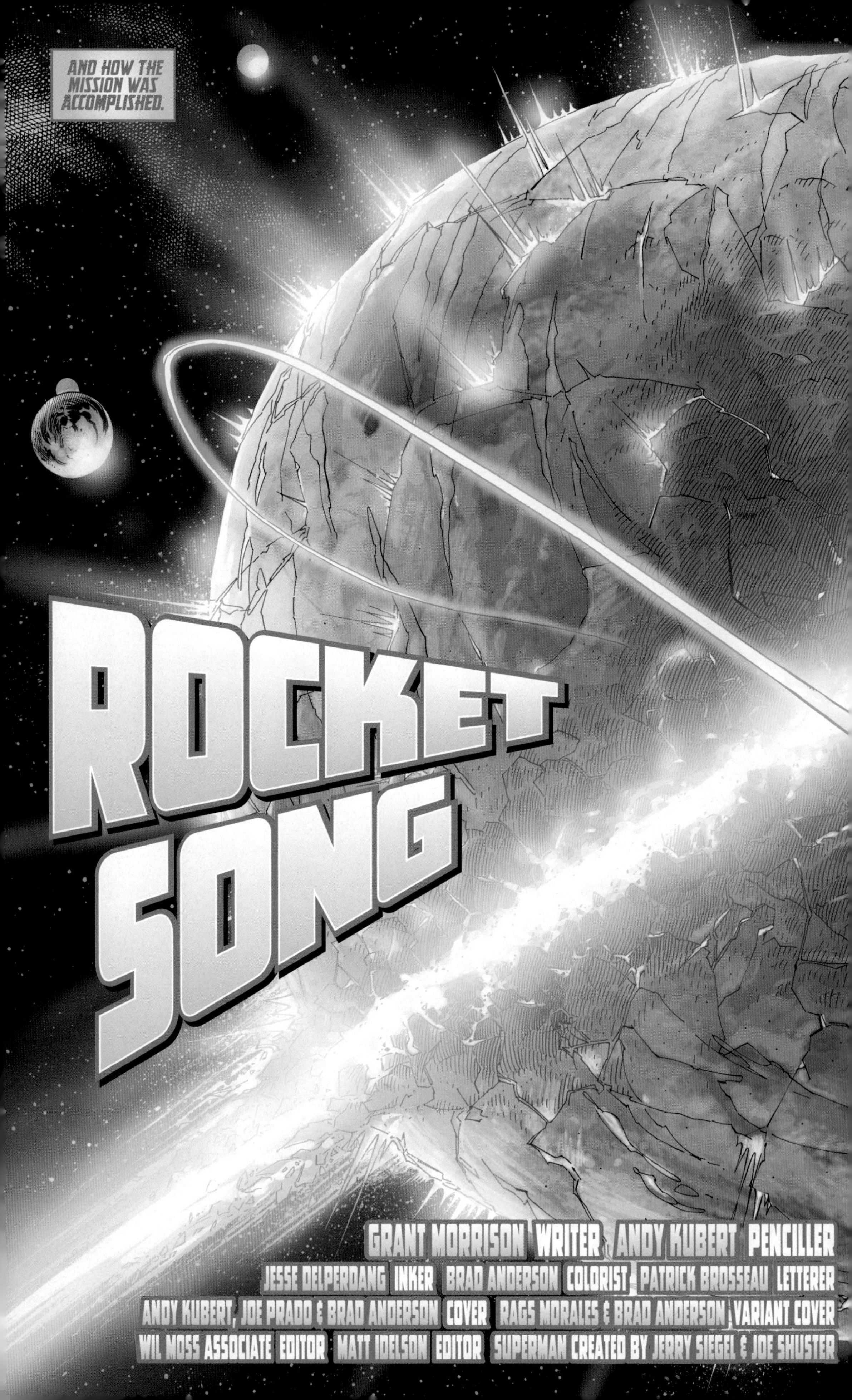
AND HOW THE MISSION WAS ACCOMPLISHED.
ROCKET SONG
GRANT MORRISON WRITER ANDY KUBERT PENCILLER
JESSE DELPERDANG INKER BRAD ANDERSON COLORIST PATRICK BROSSEAU LETTERER
ANDY KUBERT, JOE PRADO & BRAD ANDERSON COVER RAGS MORALES & BRAD ANDERSON VARIANT COVER
WIL MOSS ASSOCIATE EDITOR MATT IDELSON EDITOR SUPERMAN CREATED BY JERRY SIEGEL & JOE SHUSTER

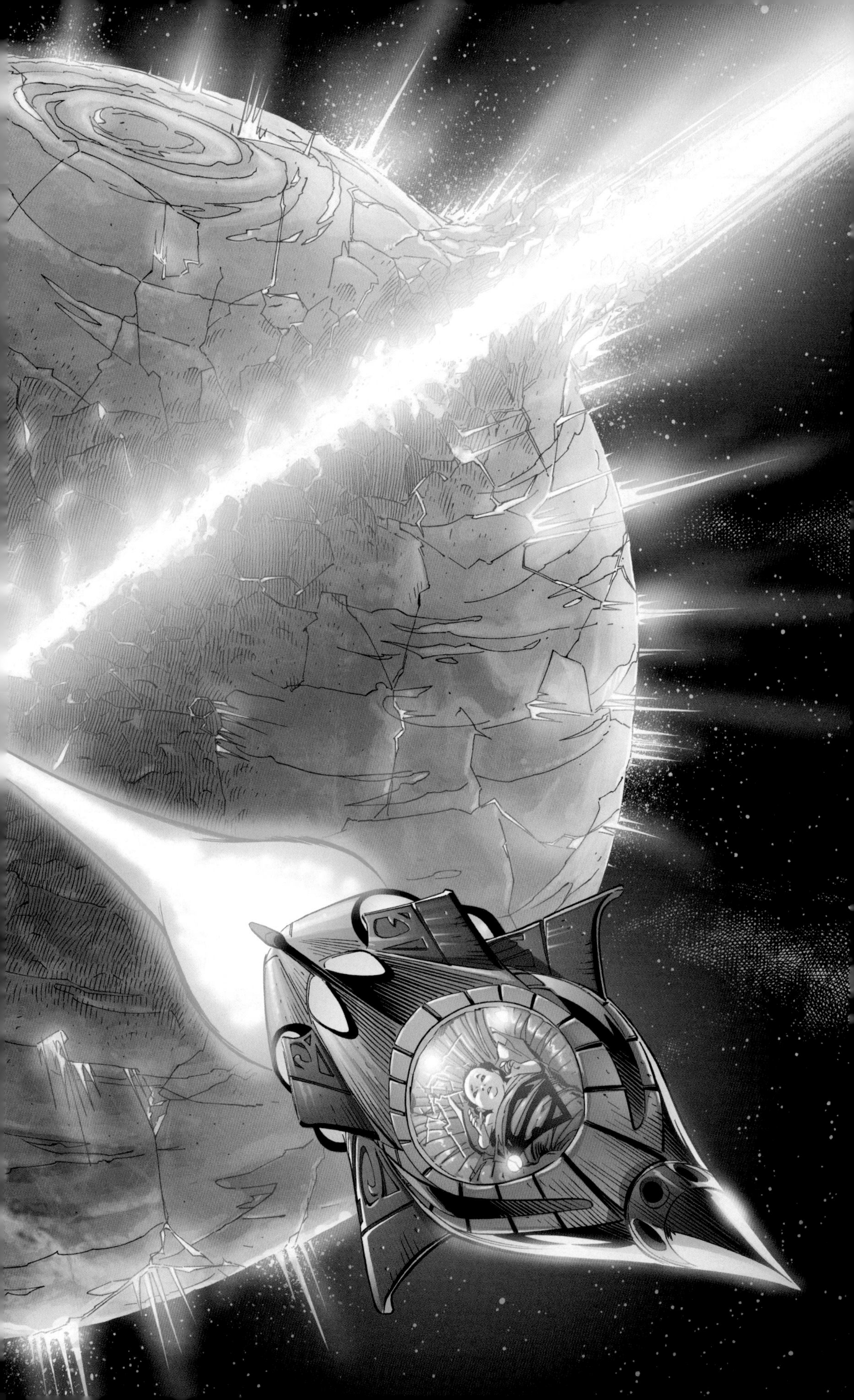

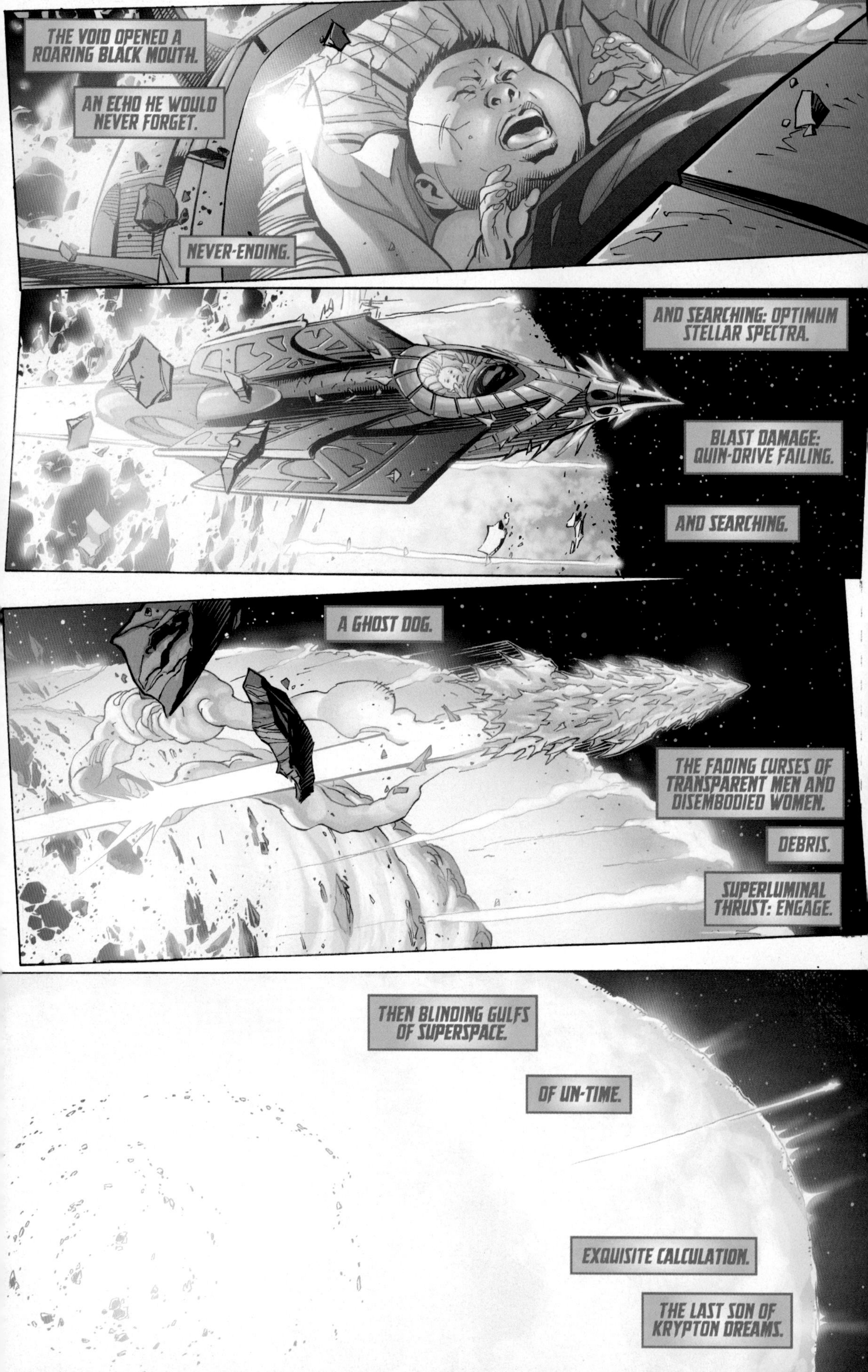
THE VOID OPENED A ROARING BLACK MOUTH.
AN ECHO HE WOULD NEVER FORGET.
NEVER-ENDING.
AND SEARCHING: OPTIMUM STELLAR SPECTRA.
BLAST DAMAGE: QUIN-DRIVE FAILING.
AND SEARCHING.
A GHOST DOG.
THE FADING CURSES OF TRANSPARENT MEN AND DISEMBODIED WOMEN.
DEBRIS.
SUPERLUMINAL THRUST: ENGAGE.
THEN BLINDING GULFS OF SUPERSPACE.
OF UN-TIME.
EXQUISITE CALCULATION.
THE LAST SON OF KRYPTON DREAMS.

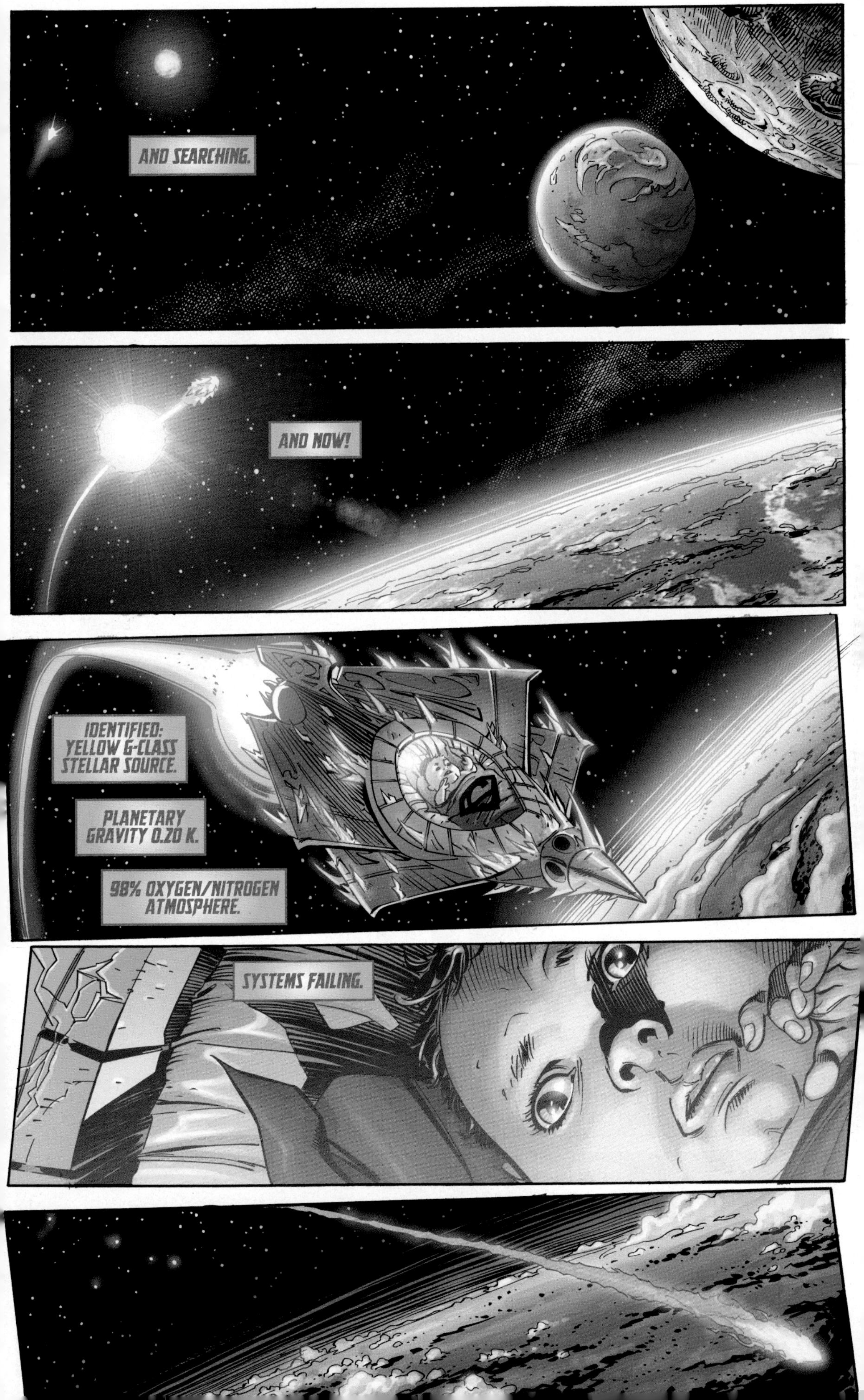
AND SEARCHING.
AND NOW!
IDENTIFIED: YELLOW G-CLASS STELLAR SOURCE.
PLANETARY GRAVITY 0.20 K.
98% OXYGEN/NITROGEN ATMOSPHERE.
SYSTEMS FAILING.

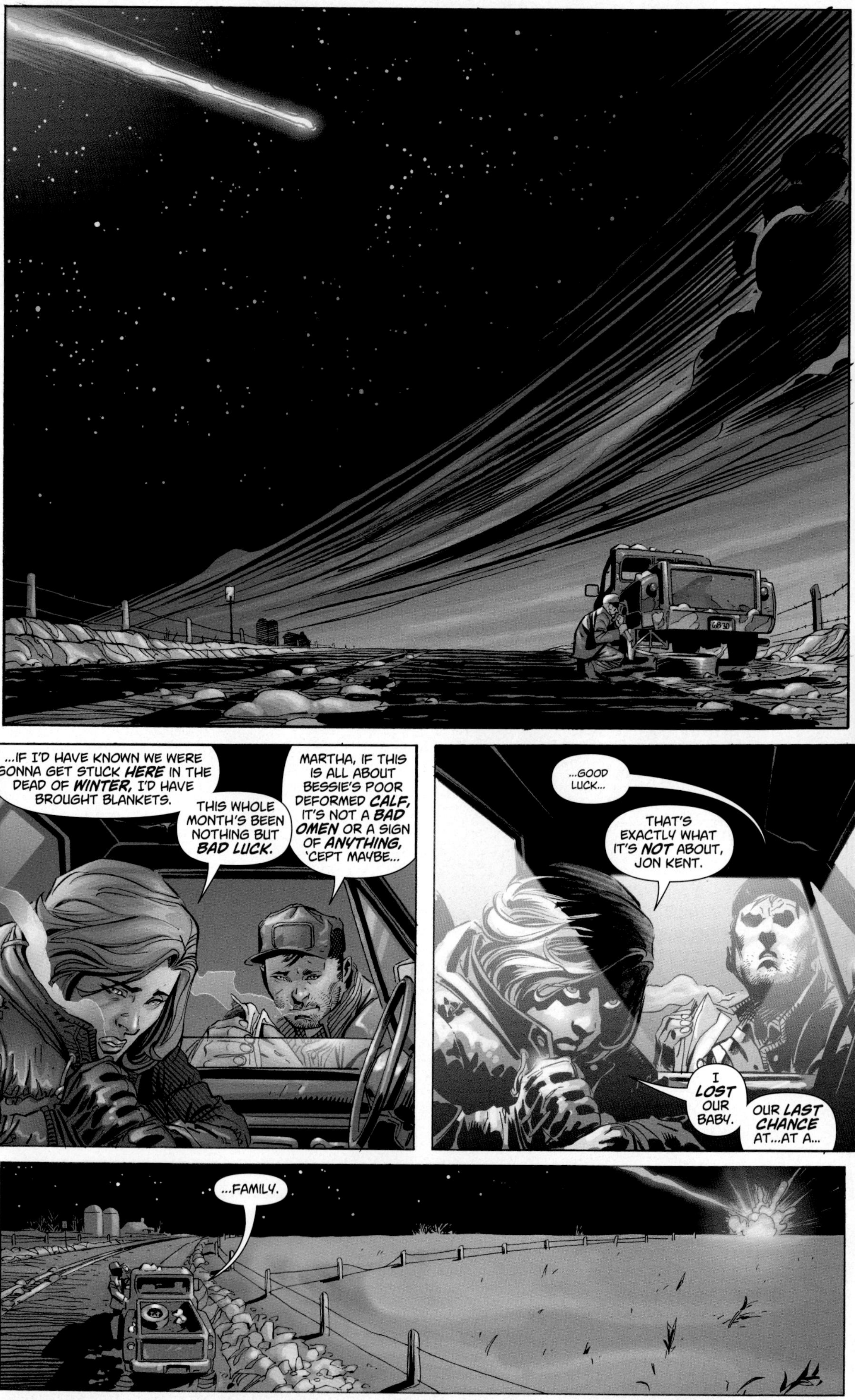
...IF I'D HAVE KNOWN WE WERE GONNA GET STUCK HERE IN THE DEAD OF WINTER, I'D HAVE BROUGHT BLANKETS.
THIS WHOLE MONTH'S BEEN NOTHING BUT BAD LUCK.
MARTHA, IF THIS IS ALL ABOUT BESSIE'S POOR DEFORMED CALF, IT'S NOT A BAD OMEN OR A SIGN OF ANYTHING, 'CEPT MAYBE...
...GOOD LUCK...
THAT'S EXACTLY WHAT IT'S NOT ABOUT, JON KENT.
I LOST OUR BABY.
OUR LAST CHANCE AT...AT A...
...FAMILY.

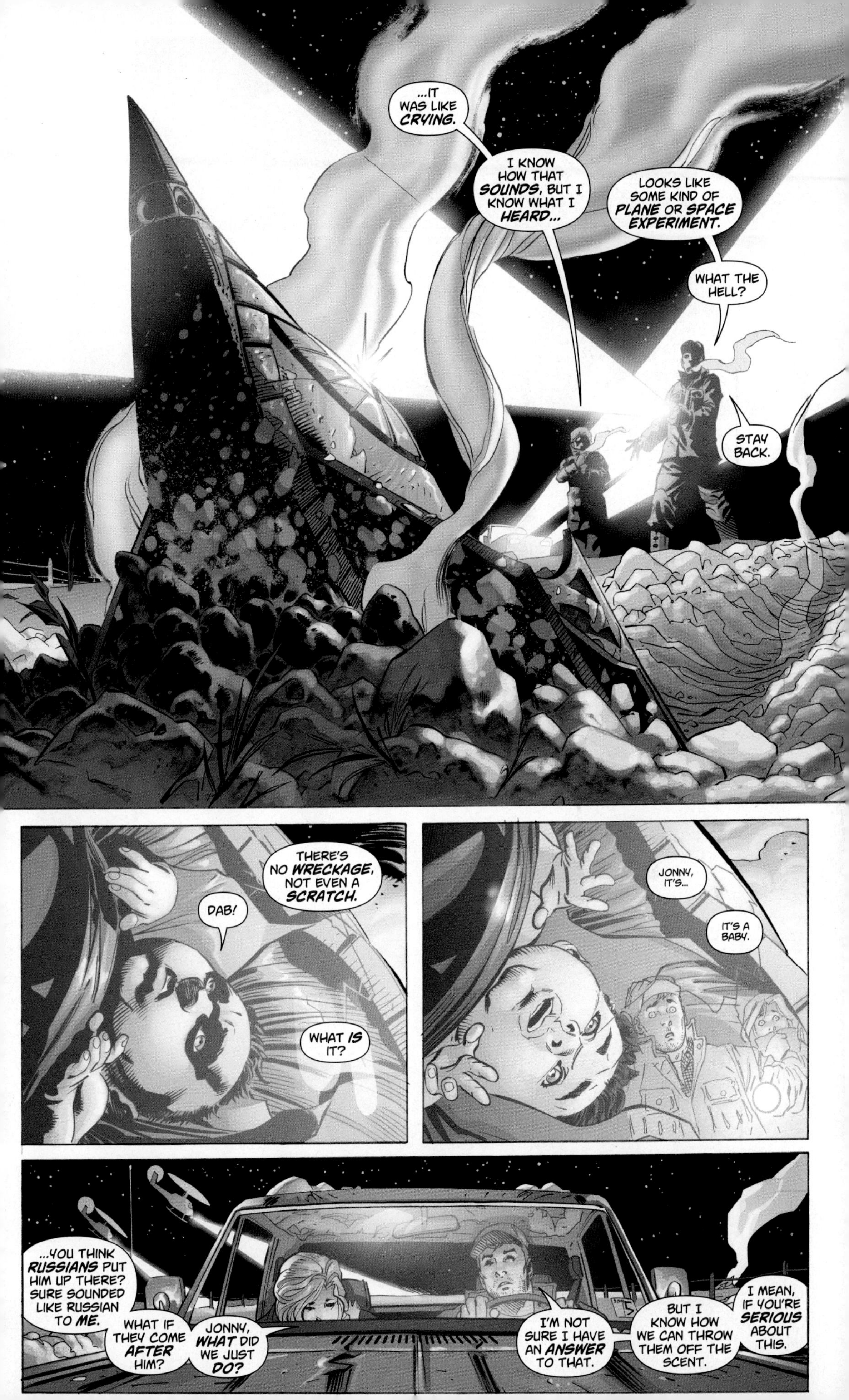
...IT WAS LIKE CRYING.
I KNOW HOW THAT SOUNDS, BUT I KNOW WHAT I HEARD...
LOOKS LIKE SOME KIND OF PLANE OR SPACE EXPERIMENT.
WHAT THE HELL?
STAY BACK.
THERE'S NO WRECKAGE, NOT EVEN A SCRATCH.
DAB!
WHAT IS IT?
JONNY, IT'S...
IT'S A BABY.
...YOU THINK RUSSIANS PUT HIM UP THERE? SURE SOUNDED LIKE RUSSIAN TO ME.
WHAT IF THEY COME AFTER HIM?
JONNY, WHAT DID WE JUST DO?
I'M NOT SURE I HAVE AN ANSWER TO THAT.
BUT I KNOW HOW WE CAN THROW THEM OFF THE SCENT.
I MEAN, IF YOU'RE SERIOUS ABOUT THIS.

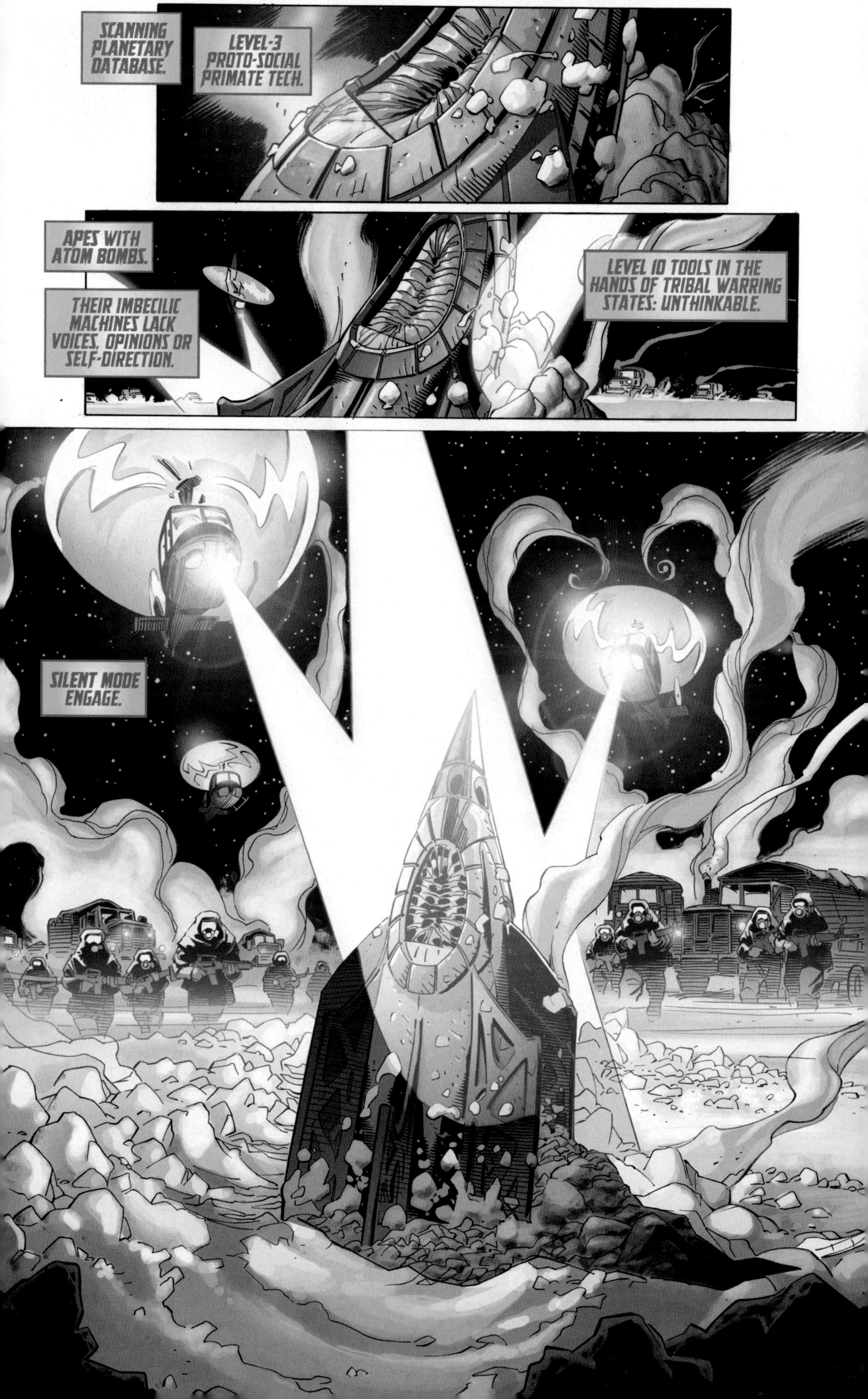
SCANNING PLANETARY DATABASE.
LEVEL-3 PROTO-SOCIAL PRIMATE TECH.
APES WITH ATOM BOMBS.
THEIR IMBECILIC MACHINES LACK VOICES, OPINIONS OR SELF-DIRECTION.
LEVEL 10 TOOLS IN THE HANDS OF TRIBAL WARRING STATES: UNTHINKABLE.
SILENT MODE ENGAGE.

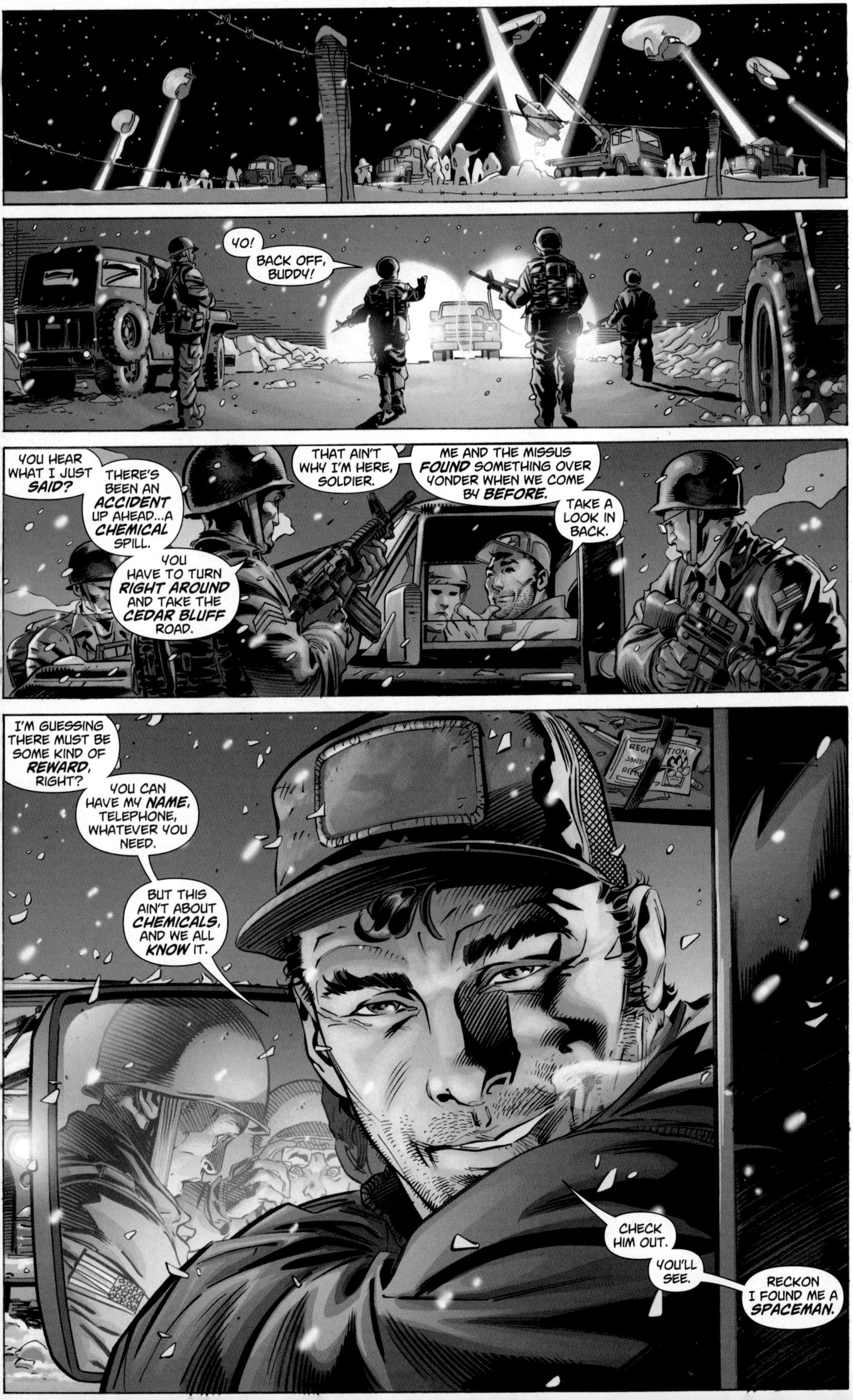
YO!
BACK OFF, BUDDY!
YOU HEAR WHAT I JUST SAID?
THERE'S BEEN AN ACCIDENT UP AHEAD...A CHEMICAL SPILL.
YOU HAVE TO TURN RIGHT AROUND AND TAKE THE CEDAR BLUFF ROAD.
THAT AIN'T WHY I'M HERE, SOLDIER.
ME AND THE MISSUS FOUND SOMETHING OVER YONDER WHEN WE COME BY BEFORE.
TAKE A LOOK IN BACK.
I'M GUESSING THERE MUST BE SOME KIND OF REWARD, RIGHT?
YOU CAN HAVE MY NAME, TELEPHONE, WHATEVER YOU NEED.
BUT THIS AIN'T ABOUT CHEMICALS, AND WE ALL KNOW IT.
CHECK HIM OUT.
YOU'LL SEE.
RECKON I FOUND ME A SPACEMAN.

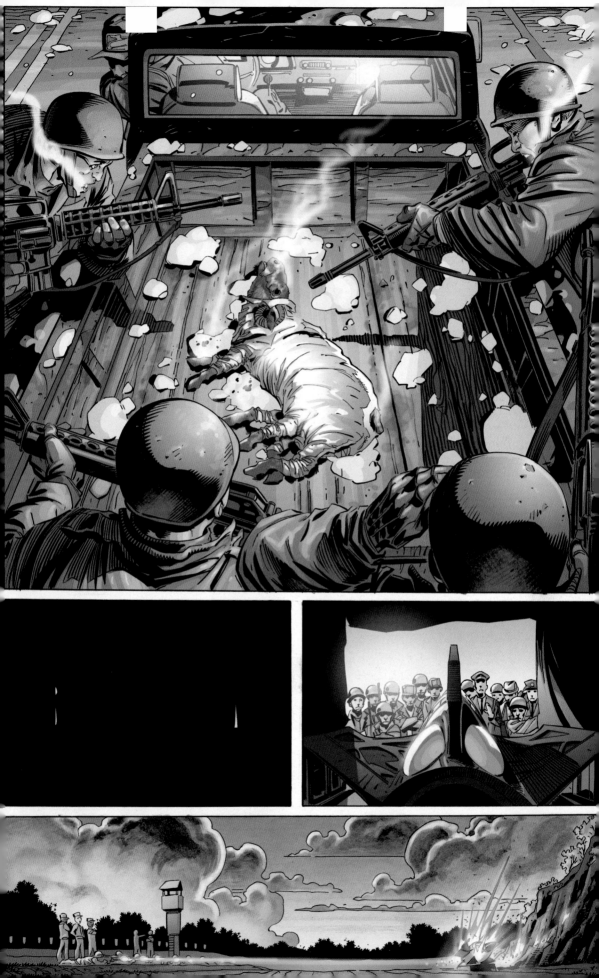

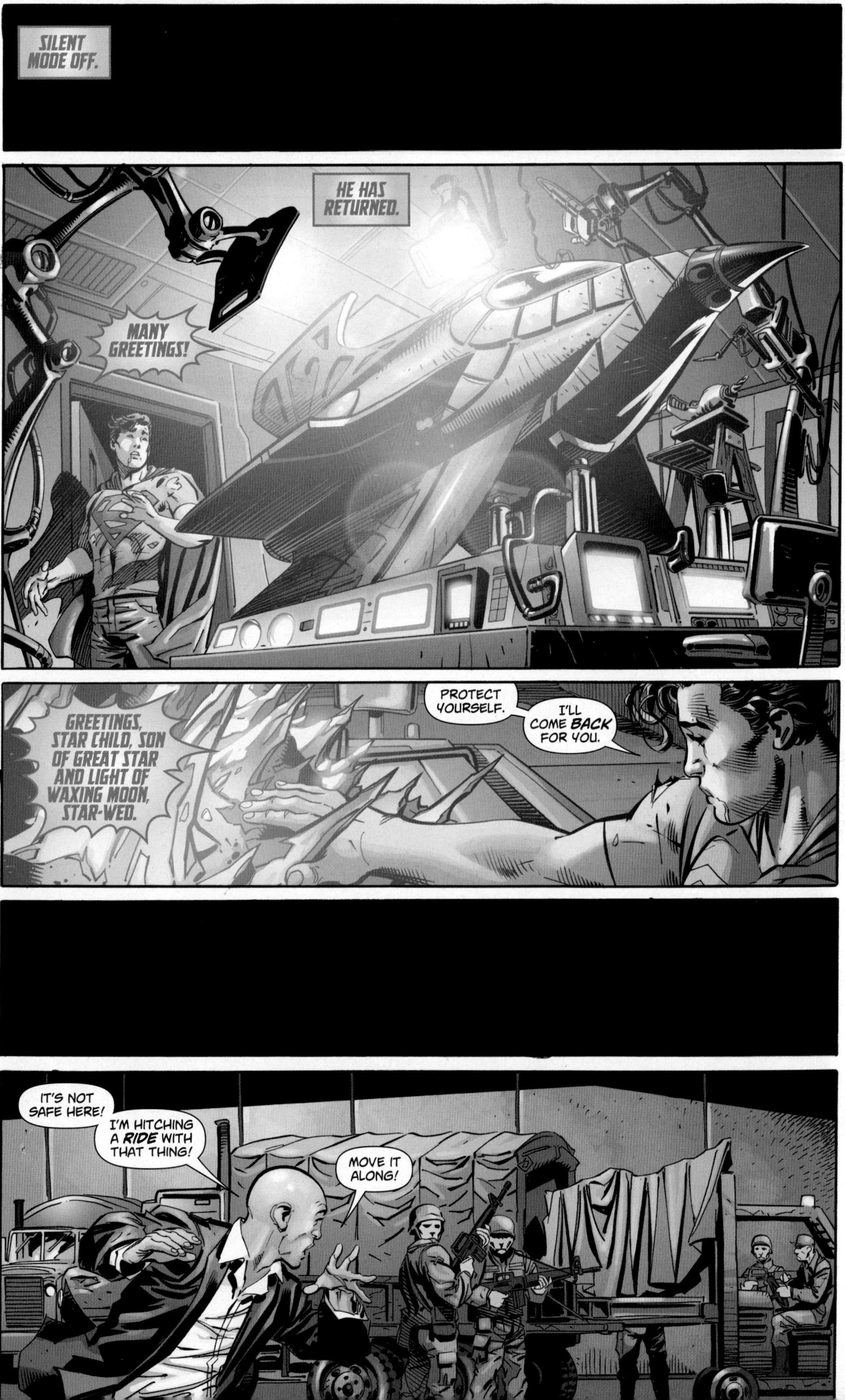
SILENT MODE OFF.
HE HAS RETURNED.
MANY GREETINGS!
GREETINGS, STAR CHILD, SON OF GREAT STAR AND LIGHT OF WAXING MOON, STAR-WED.
PROTECT YOURSELF.
I'LL COME BACK FOR YOU.
IT'S NOT SAFE HERE!
I'M HITCHING A RIDE WITH THAT THING!
MOVE IT ALONG!

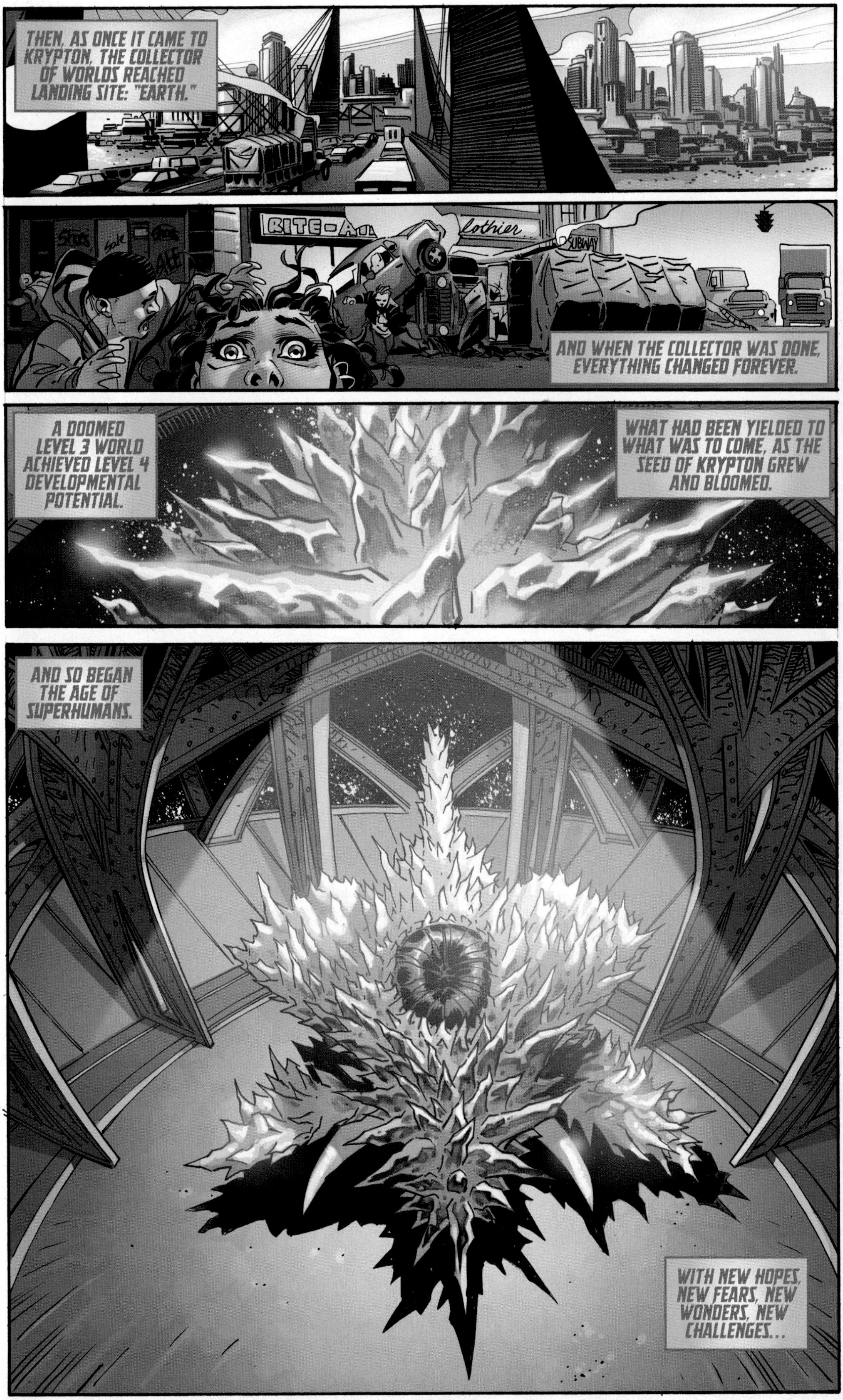
THEN, AS ONCE IT CAME TO KRYPTON, THE COLLECTOR OF WORLDS REACHED LANDING SITE: "EARTH."
SUBWAY
AND WHEN THE COLLECTOR WAS DONE, EVERYTHING CHANGED FOREVER.
A DOOMED LEVEL 3 WORLD ACHIEVED LEVEL 4 DEVELOPMENTAL POTENTIAL.
WHAT HAD BEEN YIELDED TO WHAT WAS TO COME, AS THE SEED OF KRYPTON GREW AND BLOOMED.
AND SO BEGAN THE AGE OF SUPERHUMANS.
WITH NEW HOPES, NEW FEARS, NEW WONDERS, NEW CHALLENGES...

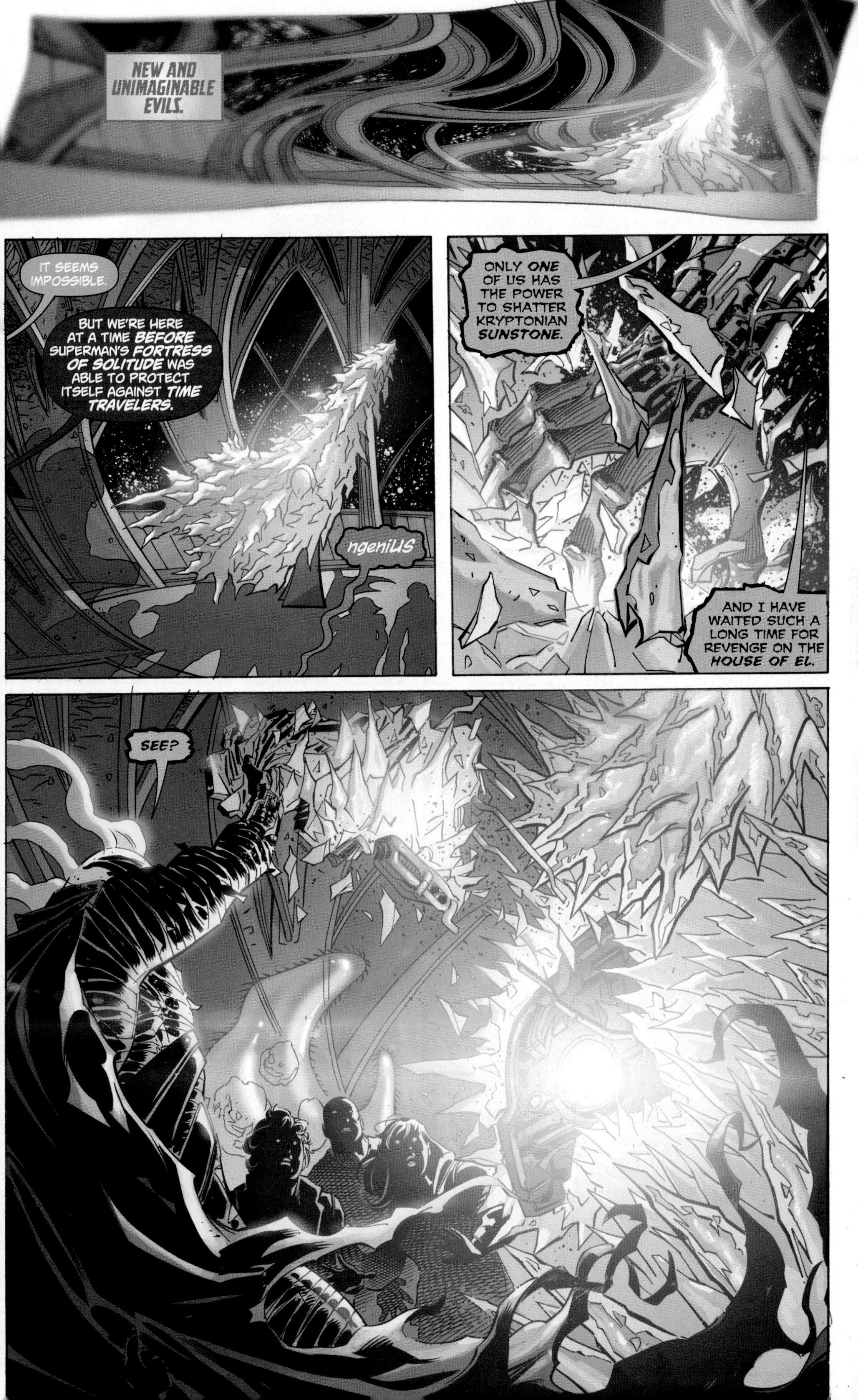
NEW AND UNIMAGINABLE EVILS.
IT SEEMS IMPOSSIBLE.
BUT WE'RE HERE AT A TIME BEFORE SUPERMAN'S FORTRESS OF SOLITUDE WAS ABLE TO PROTECT ITSELF AGAINST TIME TRAVELERS.
ONLY ONE OF US HAS THE POWER TO SHATTER KRYPTONIAN SUNSTONE.
AND I HAVE WAITED SUCH A LONG TIME FOR REVENGE ON THE HOUSE OF EL.
SEE?

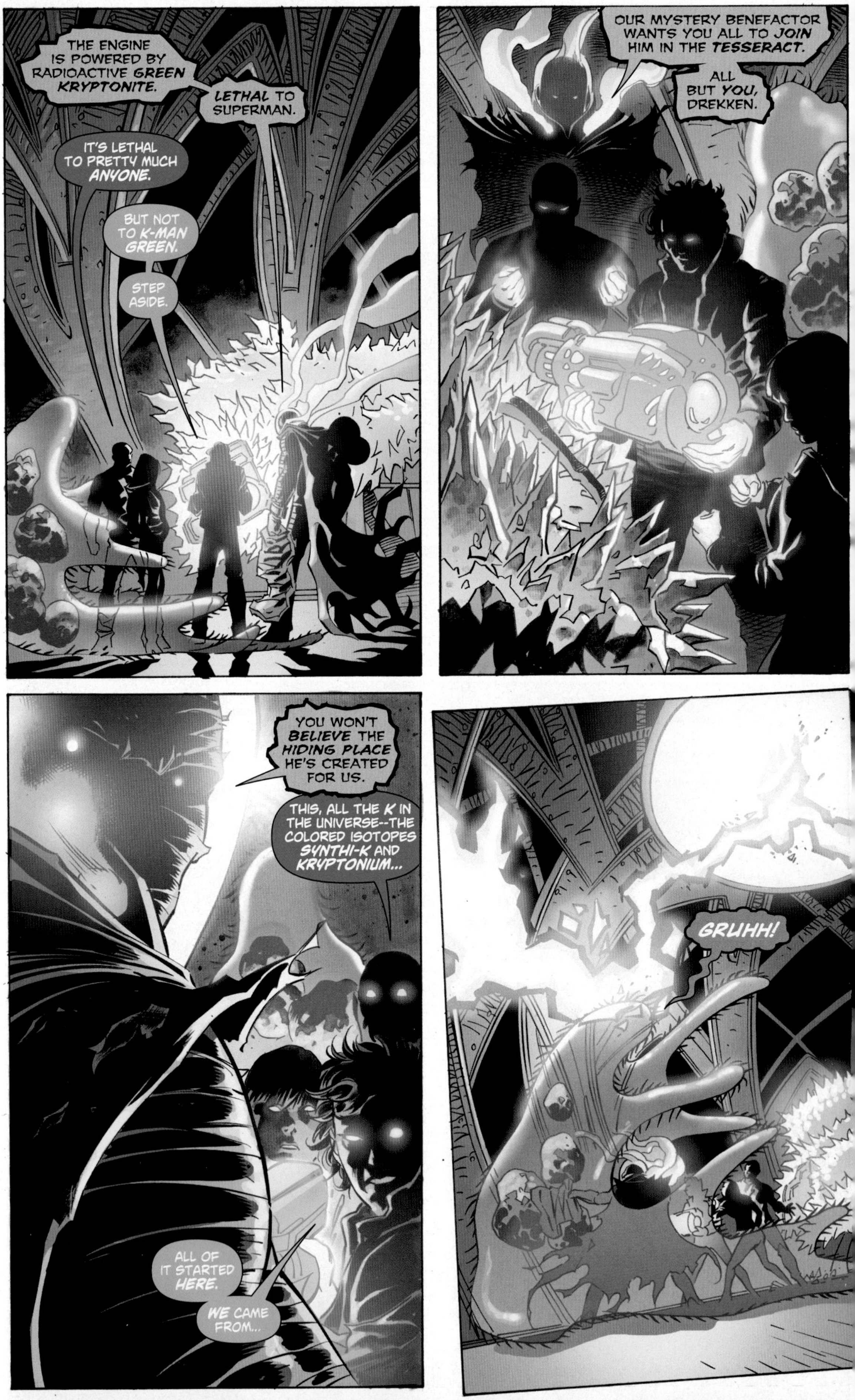
THE ENGINE IS POWERED BY RADIOACTIVE GREEN KRYPTONITE.
LETHAL TO SUPERMAN.
IT'S LETHAL TO PRETTY MUCH ANYONE.
BUT NOT TO K-MAN GREEN.
STEP ASIDE.
OUR MYSTERY BENEFACTOR WANTS YOU ALL TO JOIN HIM IN THE TESSERACT.
ALL BUT YOU, DREKKEN.
YOU WON'T BELIEVE THE HIDING PLACE HE'S CREATED FOR US.
THIS, ALL THE K IN THE UNIVERSE--THE COLORED ISOTOPES SYNTHI-K AND KRYPTONIUM...
ALL OF IT STARTED HERE.
WE CAME FROM...
GRUHH!

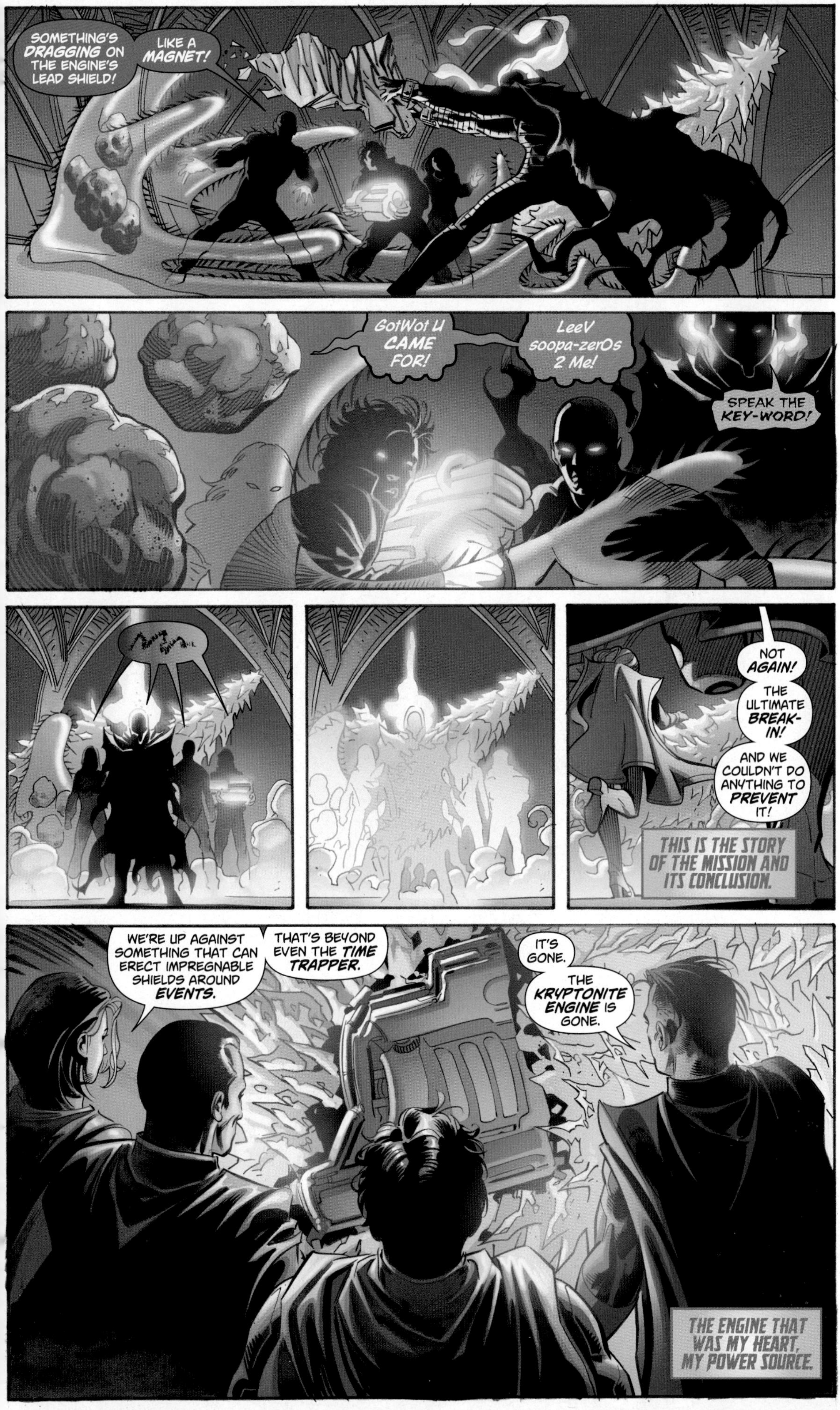
SOMETHING'S DRAGGING ON THE ENGINE'S LEAD SHIELD!
LIKE A MAGNET!
GotWot U CAME FOR!
LeeV soopa-zerOs 2 Me!
SPEAK THE KEY-WORD!
NOT AGAIN!
THE ULTIMATE BREAK-IN!
AND WE COULDN'T DO ANYTHING TO PREVENT IT!
THIS IS THE STORY OF THE MISSION AND ITS CONCLUSION.
WE'RE UP AGAINST SOMETHING THAT CAN ERECT IMPREGNABLE SHIELDS AROUND EVENTS.
THAT'S BEYOND EVEN THE TIME TRAPPER.
IT'S GONE.
THE KRYPTONITE ENGINE IS GONE.
THE ENGINE THAT WAS MY HEART, MY POWER SOURCE.

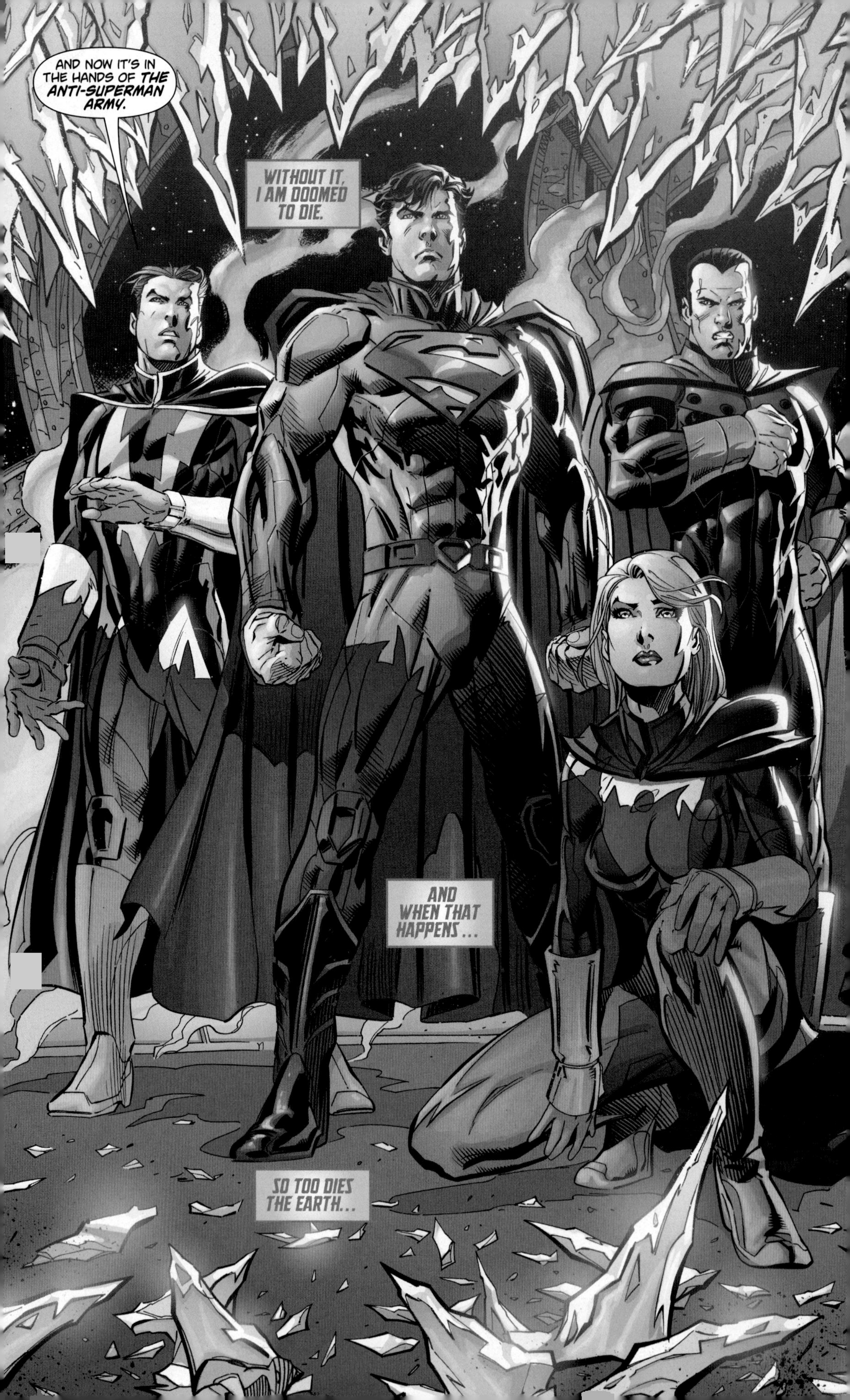
AND NOW IT'S IN THE HANDS OF THE ANTI-SUPERMAN ARMY.
WITHOUT IT, I AM DOOMED TO DIE.
AND WHEN THAT HAPPENS...
SO TOO DIES THE EARTH...

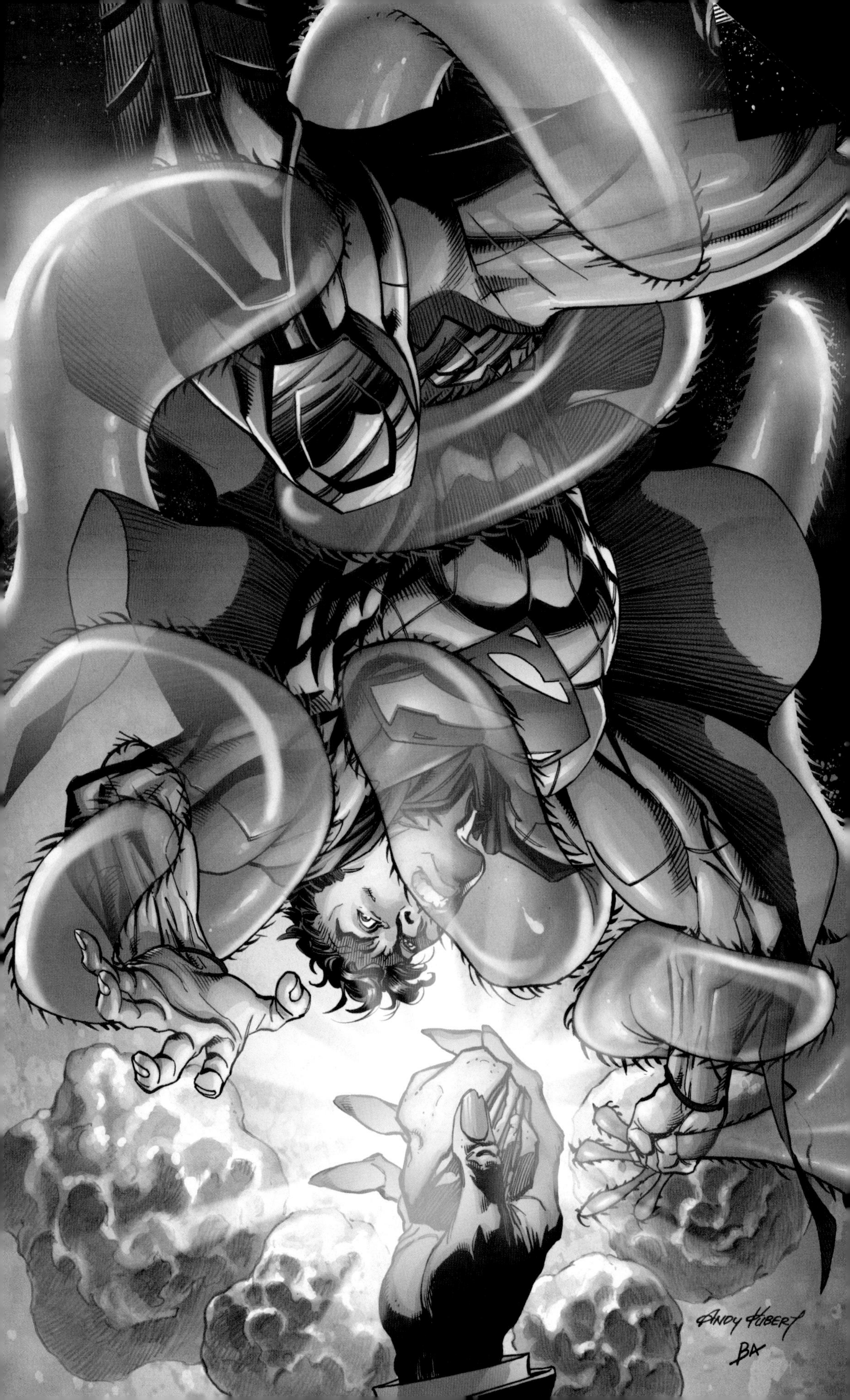
ANDY KUBERT
BA

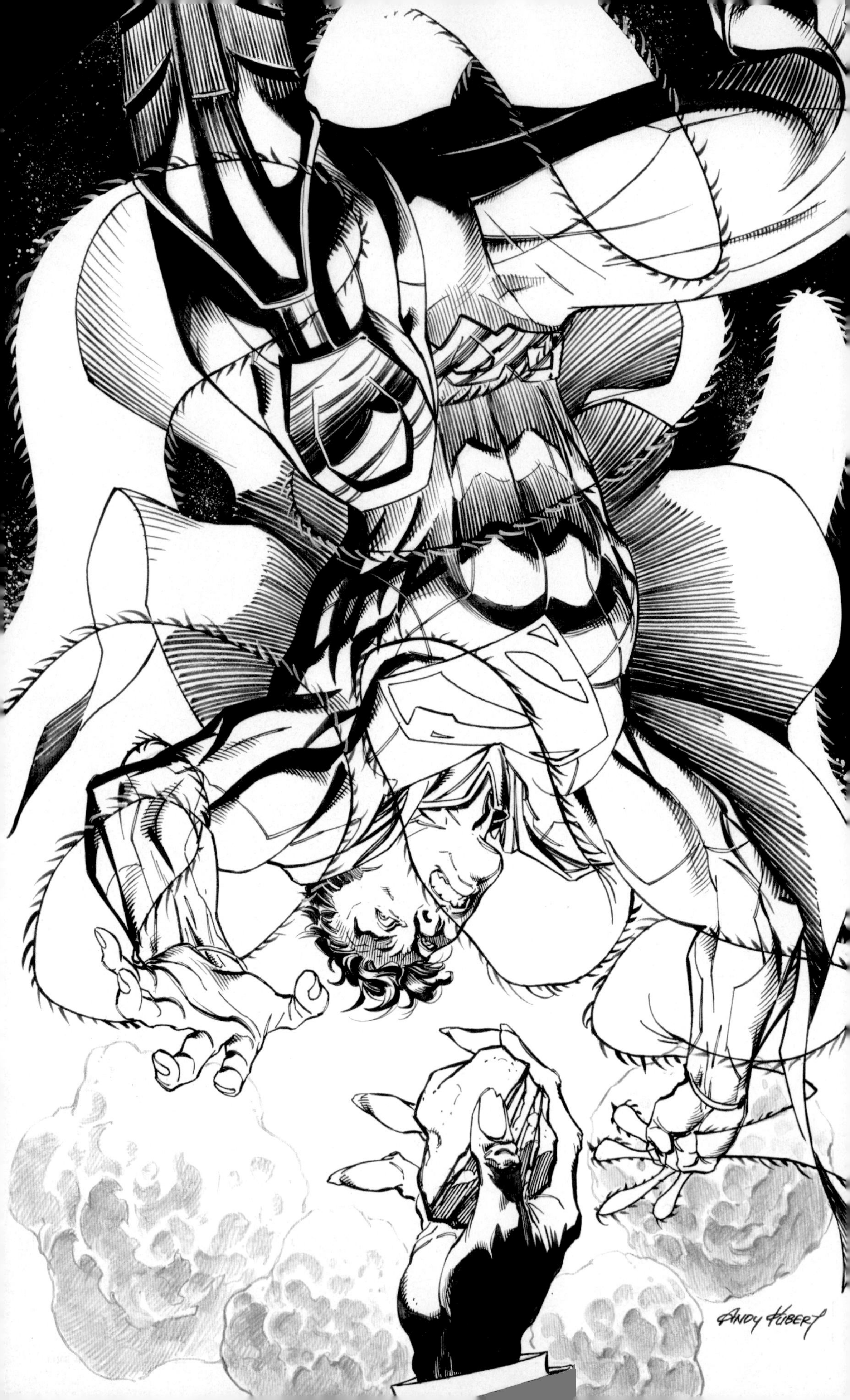
ANDY KUBERT

LOOK HERE. I PROMISED AN OPPORTUNITY UNIQUE IN ALL TIME AND SPACE, AND I ALWAYS DELIVER.

THIS BOX CONTAINS THE MOST SOUGHT-AFTER SUBSTANCE IN THE KNOWN UNIVERSE.

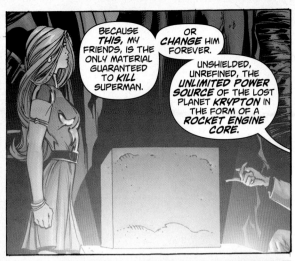

BECAUSE THIS, MY FRIENDS, IS THE ONLY MATERIAL GUARANTEED TO KILL SUPERMAN.

OR CHANGE HIM FOREVER.

UNSHIELDED, UNREFINED, THE UNLIMITED POWER SOURCE OF THE LOST PLANET KRYPTON IN THE FORM OF A ROCKET ENGINE CORE.

FROM THIS ORIGINAL DERIVE ALL THE UNSTABLE, EXOTIC ISOTOPES SUCH AS RED-K AND SILVER-K AND BLACK.

THESE DEADLY VARIANTS, INCLUDING BLUE, THE MOST TERRIBLE OF ALL, CAN AND WILL BE GROWN FROM THIS ONE PRIMARY CRYSTAL.

IF MY LOVELY ASSISTANT FROM THE PLANET TROM WILL CHANGE THE LEAD SHIELDING TO GLASS FOR A FEW MOMENTS ONLY...

I GIVE YOU KRYPTONITE.

SOLDIERS IN THE ANTI-SUPERMAN ARMY!

WHAT WILL YOU GIVE ME?

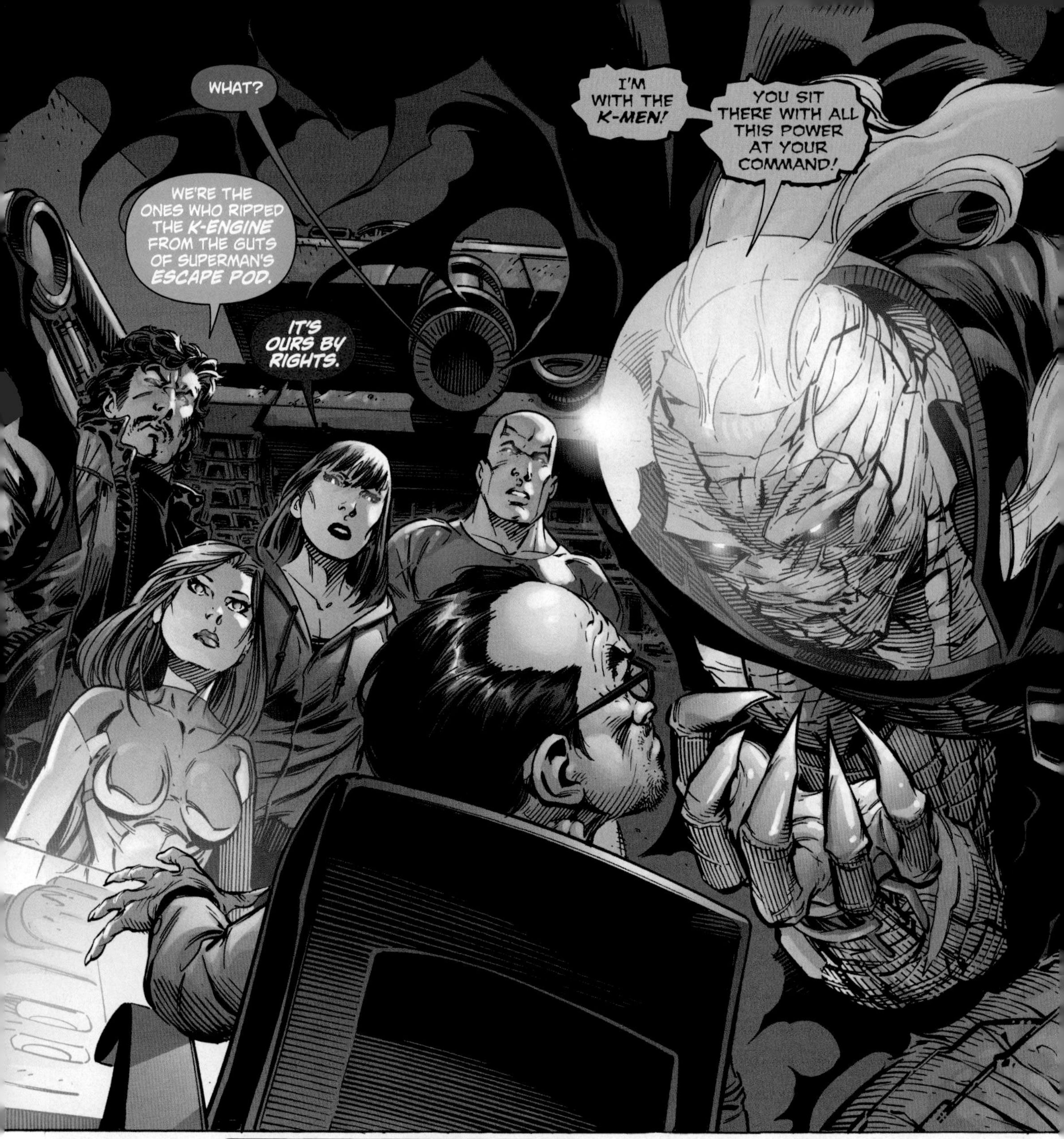
I'M WITH THE K-MEN!
YOU SIT THERE WITH ALL THIS POWER AT YOUR COMMAND!
WHAT?
WE'RE THE ONES WHO RIPPED THE K-ENGINE FROM THE GUTS OF SUPERMAN'S ESCAPE POD.
IT'S OURS BY RIGHTS.

WHEN SUPERMAN LEARNED TO FLY

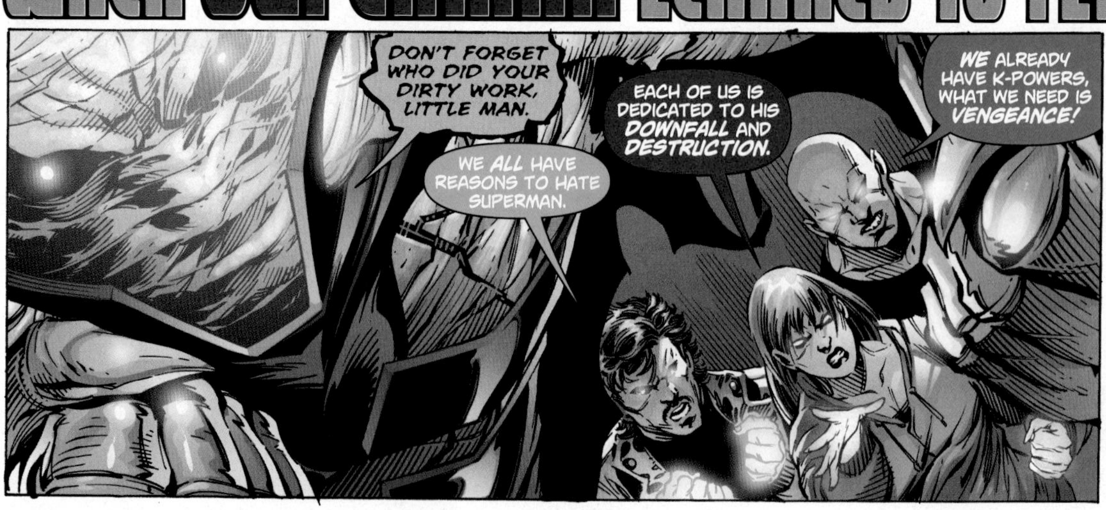
DON'T FORGET WHO DID YOUR DIRTY WORK, LITTLE MAN.
WE ALL HAVE REASONS TO HATE SUPERMAN.
EACH OF US IS DEDICATED TO HIS DOWNFALL AND DESTRUCTION.
WE ALREADY HAVE K-POWERS, WHAT WE NEED IS VENGEANCE!

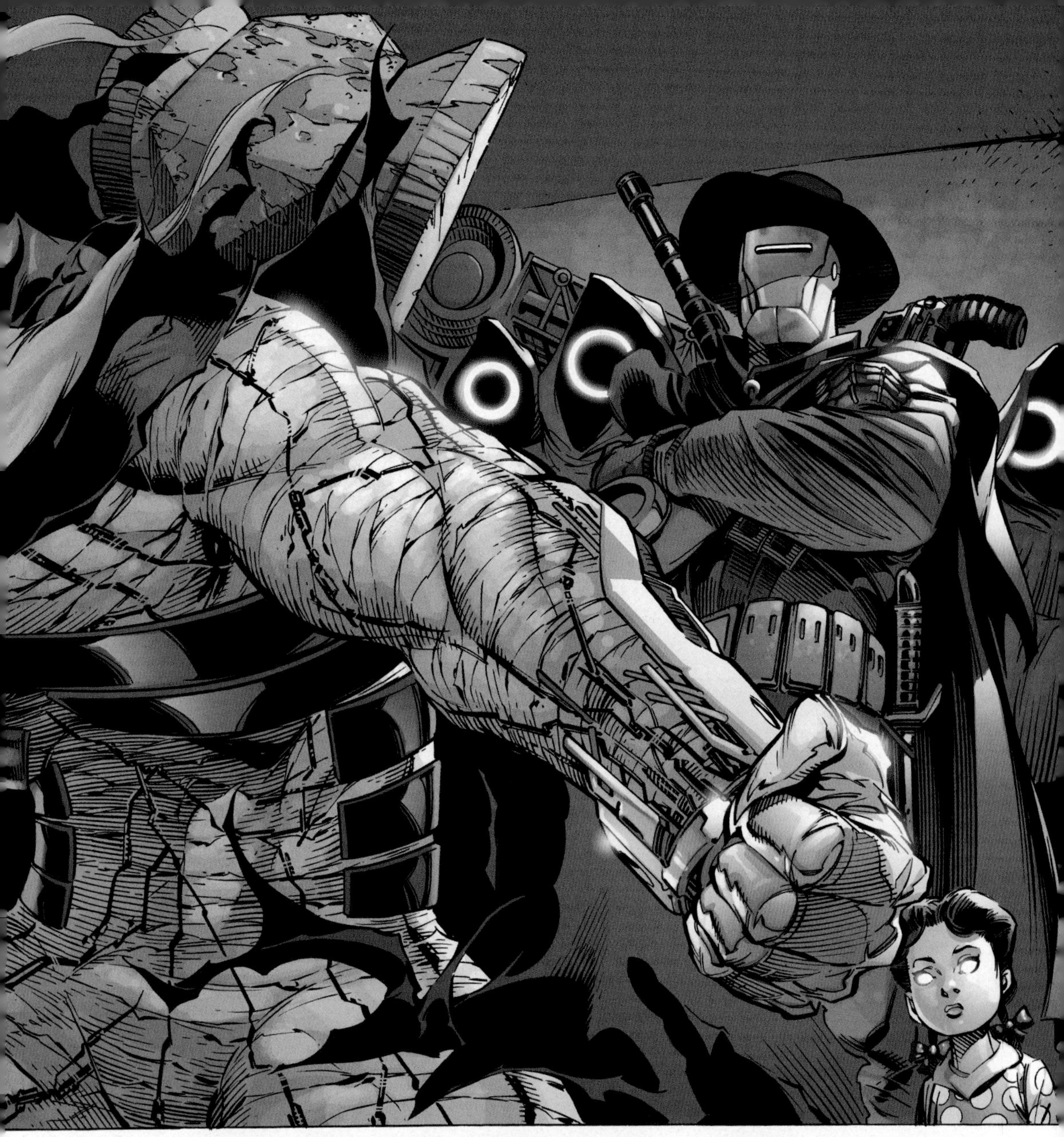

GRANT MORRISON WRITER ANDY KUBERT PENCILLER JOHN DELL INKER

BRAD ANDERSON COLORIST PATRICK BROSSEAU LETTERER ANDY KUBERT & BRAD ANDERSON COVER RAGS MORALES & BRAD ANDERSON VARIANT COVER

WIL MOSS ASSOCIATE EDITOR MATT IDELSON EDITOR SUPERMAN CREATED BY JERRY SIEGEL & JOE SHUSTER

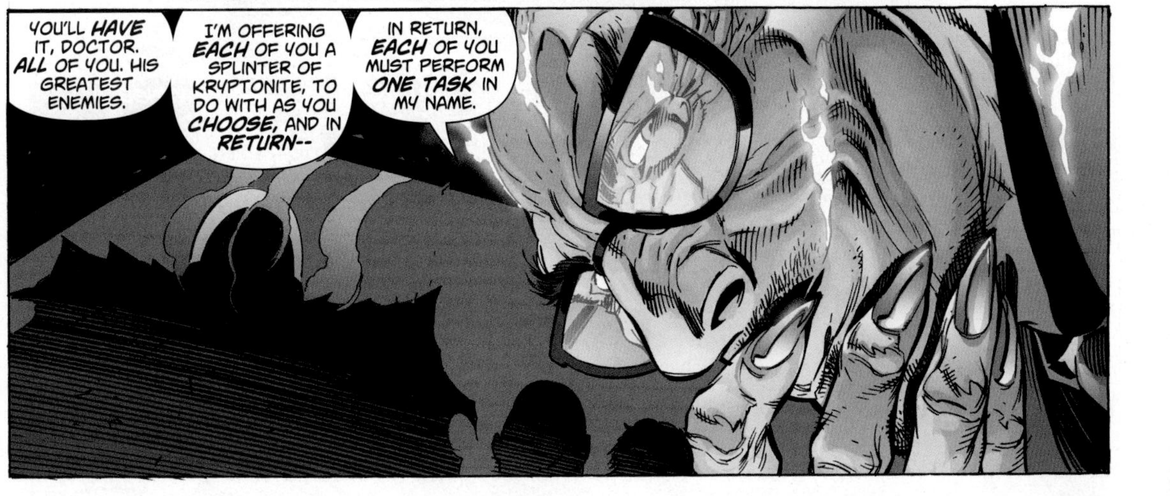
YOU'LL HAVE IT, DOCTOR. ALL OF YOU. HIS GREATEST ENEMIES.
I'M OFFERING EACH OF YOU A SPLINTER OF KRYPTONITE, TO DO WITH AS YOU CHOOSE, AND IN RETURN--
IN RETURN, EACH OF YOU MUST PERFORM ONE TASK IN MY NAME.

WEIRD.

AT *THIS* POINT IN MY CAREER, I'D JUST FACED THE *TERMINAUT INVASION*--BEFORE EVERYTHING *CHANGED* SO DRAMATICALLY.

THIS WAS MY *ORIGINAL* FORTRESS OF SOLITUDE, WHERE I CAME TO BE ALONE IN THOSE *EARLY DAYS.*

DOWN THERE, RIGHT NOW, THE WORD "SUPERHERO" HAS JUST COME INTO *EXISTENCE...*

...AND HERE *YOU* ARE.

THE *LEGION OF SUPER-HEROES.*

FROM A FUTURE WITH INTERGALACTIC TRAVEL AND *TIME MACHINES.*

I'LL NEVER UNDERSTAND HOW THE *TIME BUBBLE* CAN HAVE MORE ROOM *INSIDE* THAN *OUT.*

WE USE SOMETHING CALLED *TESSERACT* SPACE FOR STORAGE IN THE *31ST CENTURY.*

WE CAN PACK *IMMENSE* VOLUMES IN TINY CONTAINERS.

AM LAK AM LO-MAL VAN LOR VA LOR-AM

THE SUNSTONE LATTICE IS STILL ALIVE AND *COMMUNICATING,* BUT WITHOUT ITS *K-MINERAL* POWER SOURCE?

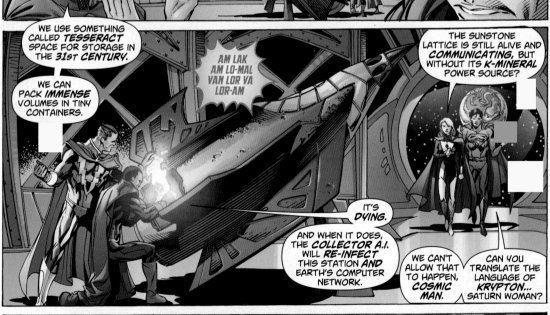

IT'S *DYING.*

AND WHEN IT DOES, THE *COLLECTOR A.I.* WILL *RE-INFECT* THIS STATION *AND* EARTH'S COMPUTER NETWORK.

WE CAN'T ALLOW THAT TO HAPPEN, *COSMIC MAN.*

CAN YOU TRANSLATE THE LANGUAGE OF *KRYPTON...* SATURN WOMAN?

SHE WAS BORN INTO A TELEPATHIC SOCIAL NETWORK ON SATURN'S *REBEL MOON.*

ALL LANGUAGES ARE THE *SAME* LANGUAGE TO IMRA ARDEEN.

IF WE CAN'T RESTART OUR TIME BUBBLE *ROTOR,* NONE OF THIS WILL MATTER.

WE'RE RELYING ON THE *BATTERY* YOU BROUGHT FROM *EARTH,* SUPERMAN.

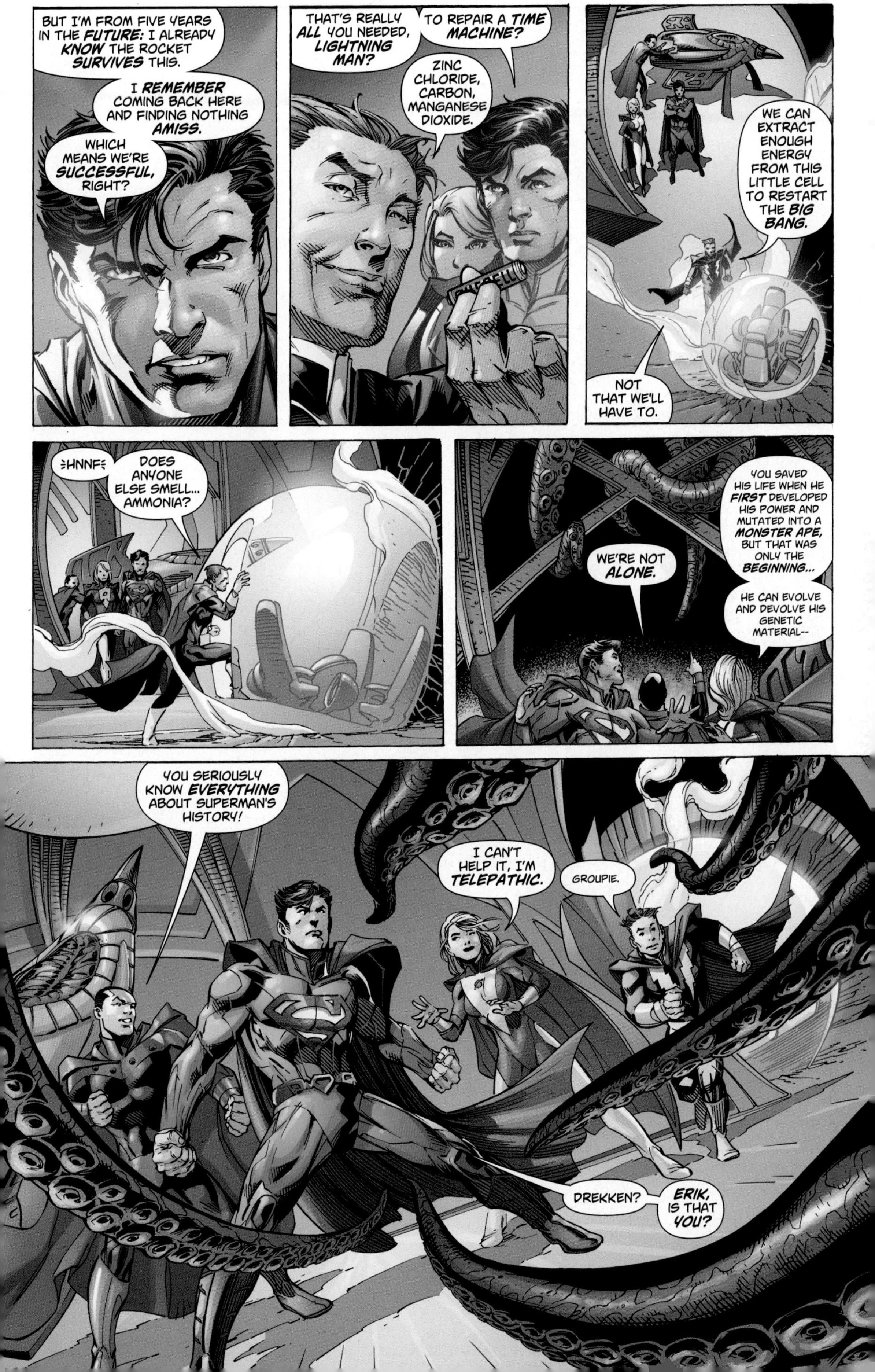
BUT I'M FROM FIVE YEARS IN THE FUTURE: I ALREADY KNOW THE ROCKET SURVIVES THIS.
I REMEMBER COMING BACK HERE AND FINDING NOTHING AMISS.
WHICH MEANS WE'RE SUCCESSFUL, RIGHT?
THAT'S REALLY ALL YOU NEEDED, LIGHTNING MAN?
TO REPAIR A TIME MACHINE?
ZINC CHLORIDE, CARBON, MANGANESE DIOXIDE.
EVEREADY
WE CAN EXTRACT ENOUGH ENERGY FROM THIS LITTLE CELL TO RESTART THE BIG BANG.
NOT THAT WE'LL HAVE TO.
HNNF
DOES ANYONE ELSE SMELL... AMMONIA?
WE'RE NOT ALONE.
YOU SAVED HIS LIFE WHEN HE FIRST DEVELOPED HIS POWER AND MUTATED INTO A MONSTER APE, BUT THAT WAS ONLY THE BEGINNING...
HE CAN EVOLVE AND DEVOLVE HIS GENETIC MATERIAL--
YOU SERIOUSLY KNOW EVERYTHING ABOUT SUPERMAN'S HISTORY!
I CAN'T HELP IT, I'M TELEPATHIC.
GROUPIE.
DREKKEN?
ERIK, IS THAT YOU?

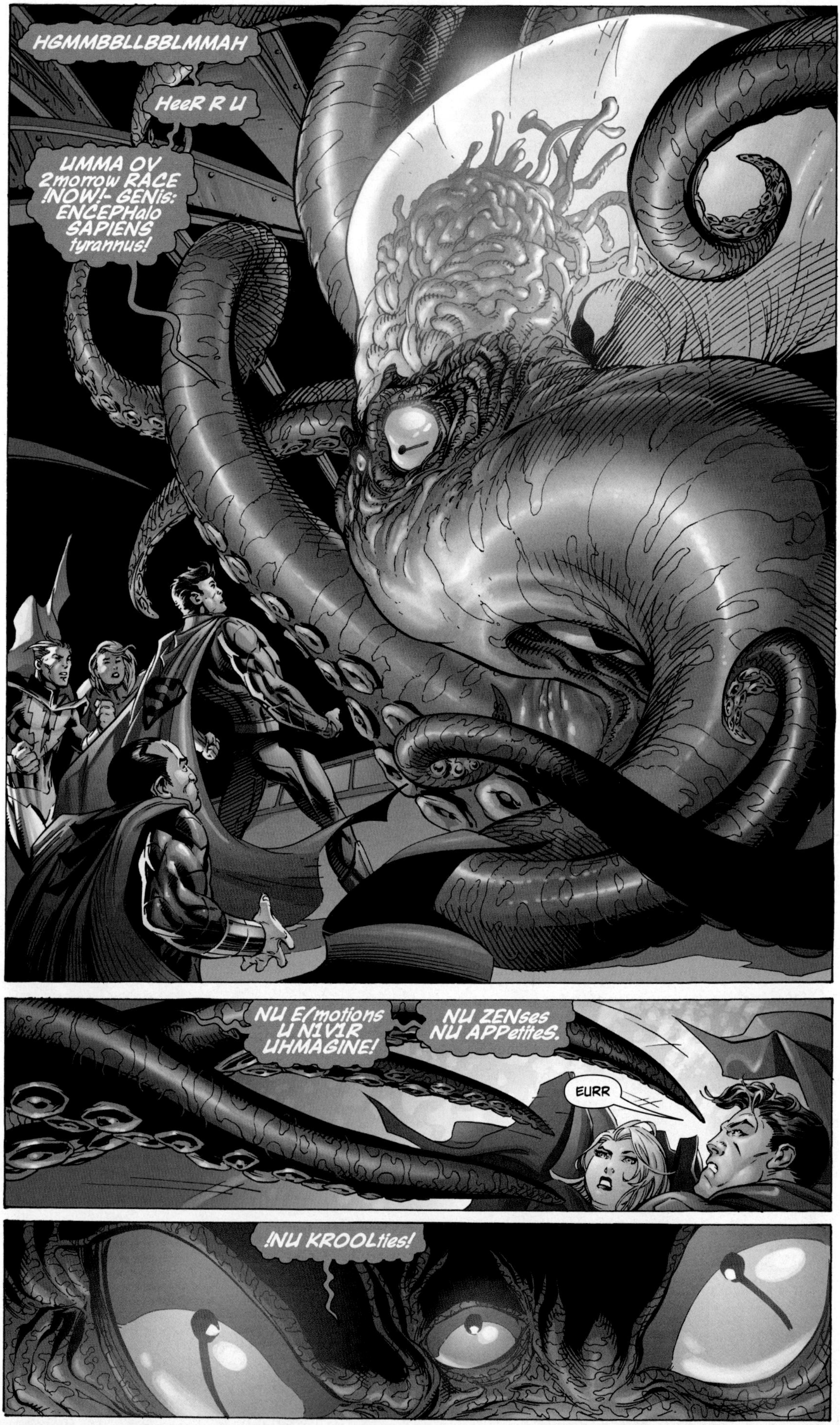

HGMMBBLLBBLMMAH
HeeR R U
UMMA OV 2morrow RACE !NOW!- GENis: ENCEPHalo SAPIENS tyrannus!
NU E/motions U N1V1R UHMAGINE!
NU ZENses NU APPetiteS.
EURR
!NU KROOLties!

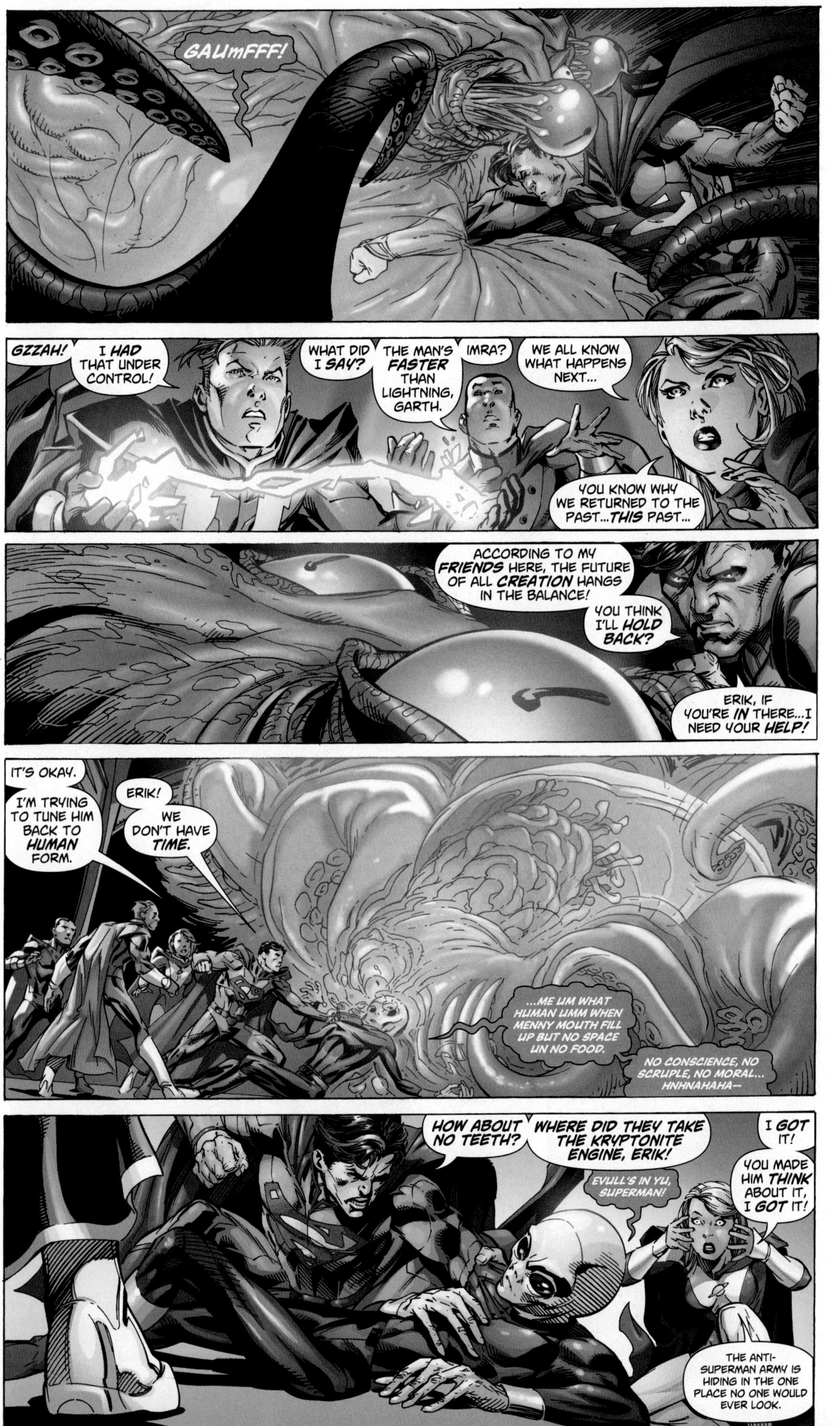
GAUmFFF!
GZZAH!
I HAD THAT UNDER CONTROL!
WHAT DID I SAY?
THE MAN'S FASTER THAN LIGHTNING, GARTH.
IMRA?
WE ALL KNOW WHAT HAPPENS NEXT...
YOU KNOW WHY WE RETURNED TO THE PAST...THIS PAST...
ACCORDING TO MY FRIENDS HERE, THE FUTURE OF ALL CREATION HANGS IN THE BALANCE!
YOU THINK I'LL HOLD BACK?
ERIK, IF YOU'RE IN THERE...I NEED YOUR HELP!
IT'S OKAY.
I'M TRYING TO TUNE HIM BACK TO HUMAN FORM.
ERIK!
WE DON'T HAVE TIME.
...ME UM WHAT HUMAN UMM WHEN MENNY MOUTH FILL UP BUT NO SPACE UN NO FOOD.
NO CONSCIENCE, NO SCRUPLE, NO MORAL... HNHNAHAHA--
HOW ABOUT NO TEETH?
WHERE DID THEY TAKE THE KRYPTONITE ENGINE, ERIK!
EVULL'S IN YU, SUPERMAN!
I GOT IT!
YOU MADE HIM THINK ABOUT IT, I GOT IT!
THE ANTI-SUPERMAN ARMY IS HIDING IN THE ONE PLACE NO ONE WOULD EVER LOOK.

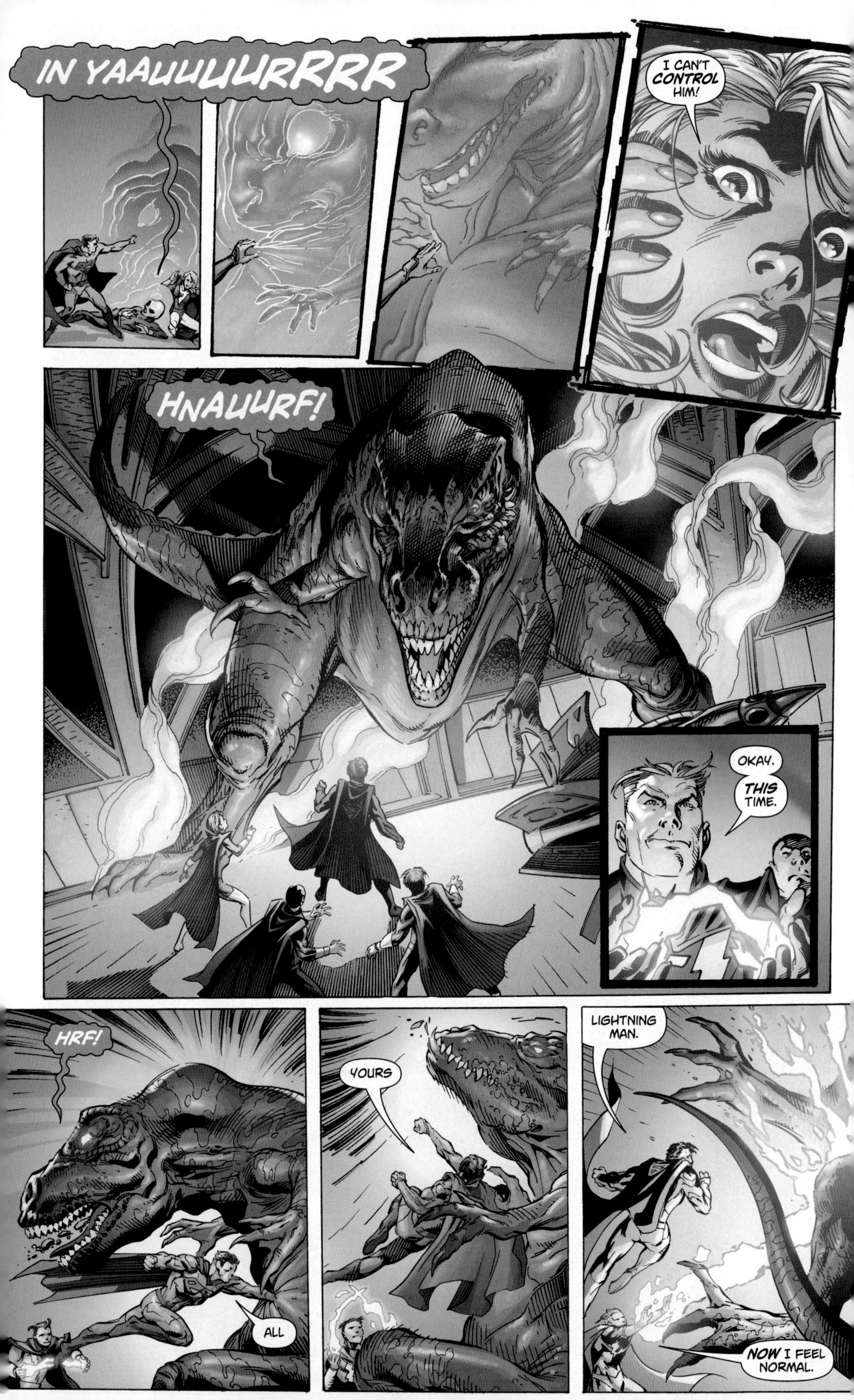
IN YAAUUUURRRR
I CAN'T CONTROL HIM!
HNAUURF!
OKAY. THIS TIME.
HRF!
ALL
YOURS
LIGHTNING MAN.
NOW I FEEL NORMAL.

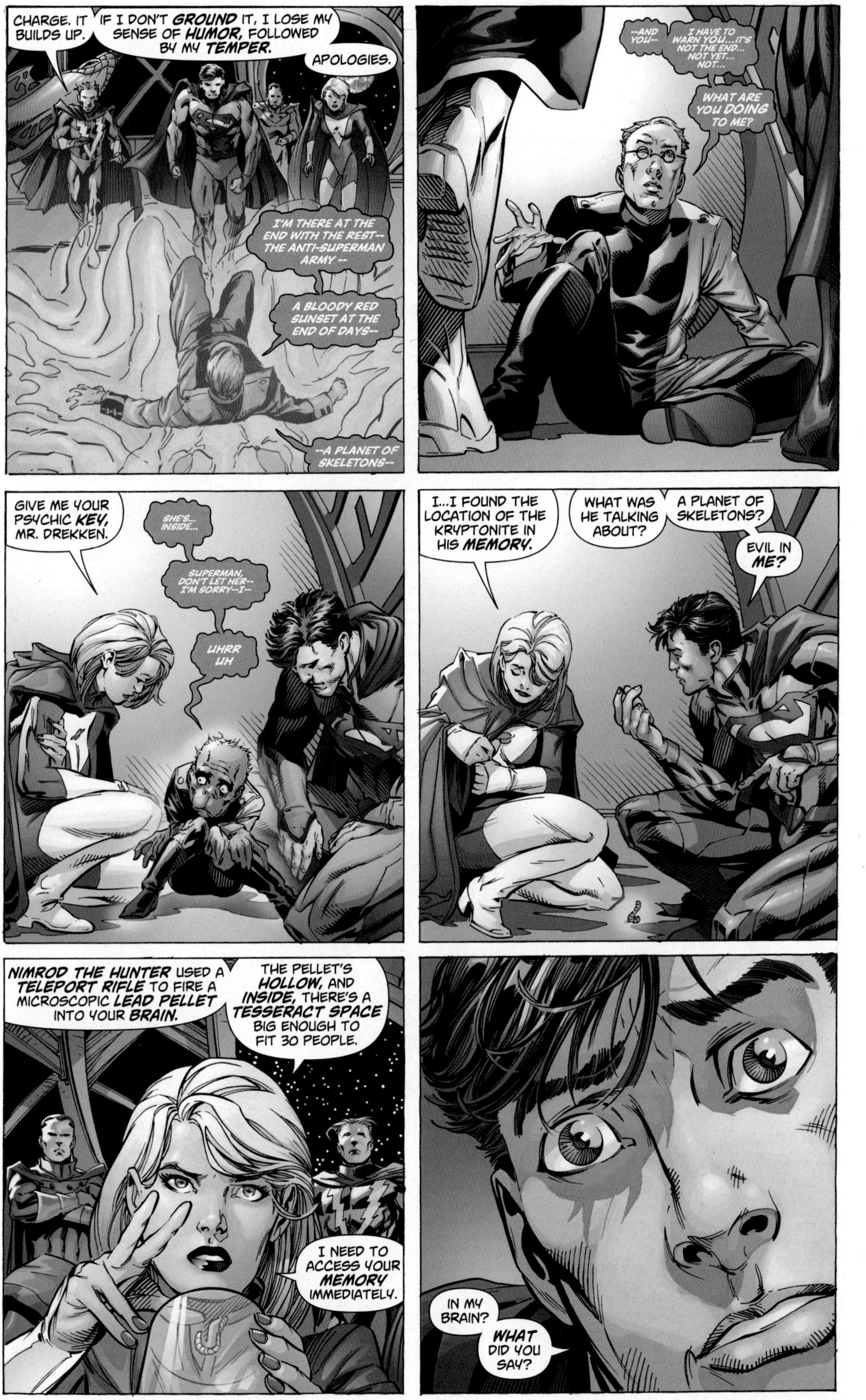
CHARGE. IT BUILDS UP.
IF I DON'T GROUND IT, I LOSE MY SENSE OF HUMOR, FOLLOWED BY MY TEMPER.
APOLOGIES.
I'M THERE AT THE END WITH THE REST-- THE ANTI-SUPERMAN ARMY --
A BLOODY RED SUNSET AT THE END OF DAYS--
--A PLANET OF SKELETONS--
--AND YOU--
I HAVE TO WARN YOU...IT'S NOT THE END... NOT YET... NOT...
WHAT ARE YOU DOING TO ME?
GIVE ME YOUR PSYCHIC KEY, MR. DREKKEN.
SHE'S... INSIDE...
SUPERMAN, DON'T LET HER-- I'M SORRY--I--
UHRR UH
I...I FOUND THE LOCATION OF THE KRYPTONITE IN HIS MEMORY.
WHAT WAS HE TALKING ABOUT?
A PLANET OF SKELETONS?
EVIL IN ME?
NIMROD THE HUNTER USED A TELEPORT RIFLE TO FIRE A MICROSCOPIC LEAD PELLET INTO YOUR BRAIN.
THE PELLET'S HOLLOW, AND INSIDE, THERE'S A TESSERACT SPACE BIG ENOUGH TO FIT 30 PEOPLE.
I NEED TO ACCESS YOUR MEMORY IMMEDIATELY.
IN MY BRAIN?
WHAT DID YOU SAY?

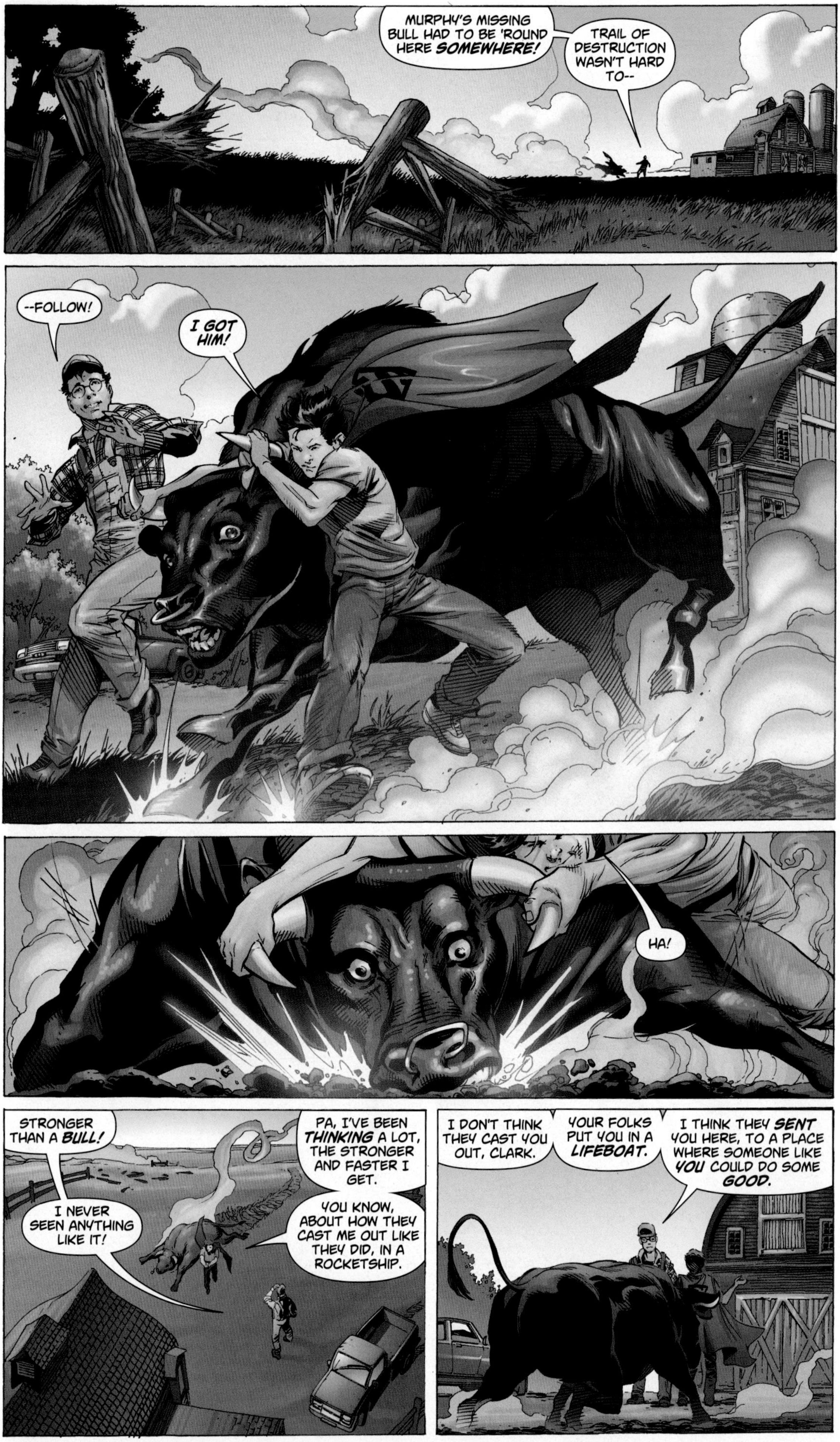
MURPHY'S MISSING BULL HAD TO BE 'ROUND HERE SOMEWHERE!
TRAIL OF DESTRUCTION WASN'T HARD TO--
--FOLLOW!
I GOT HIM!
HA!
STRONGER THAN A BULL!
I NEVER SEEN ANYTHING LIKE IT!
PA, I'VE BEEN THINKING A LOT, THE STRONGER AND FASTER I GET.
YOU KNOW, ABOUT HOW THEY CAST ME OUT LIKE THEY DID, IN A ROCKETSHIP.
I DON'T THINK THEY CAST YOU OUT, CLARK.
YOUR FOLKS PUT YOU IN A LIFEBOAT.
I THINK THEY SENT YOU HERE, TO A PLACE WHERE SOMEONE LIKE YOU COULD DO SOME GOOD.

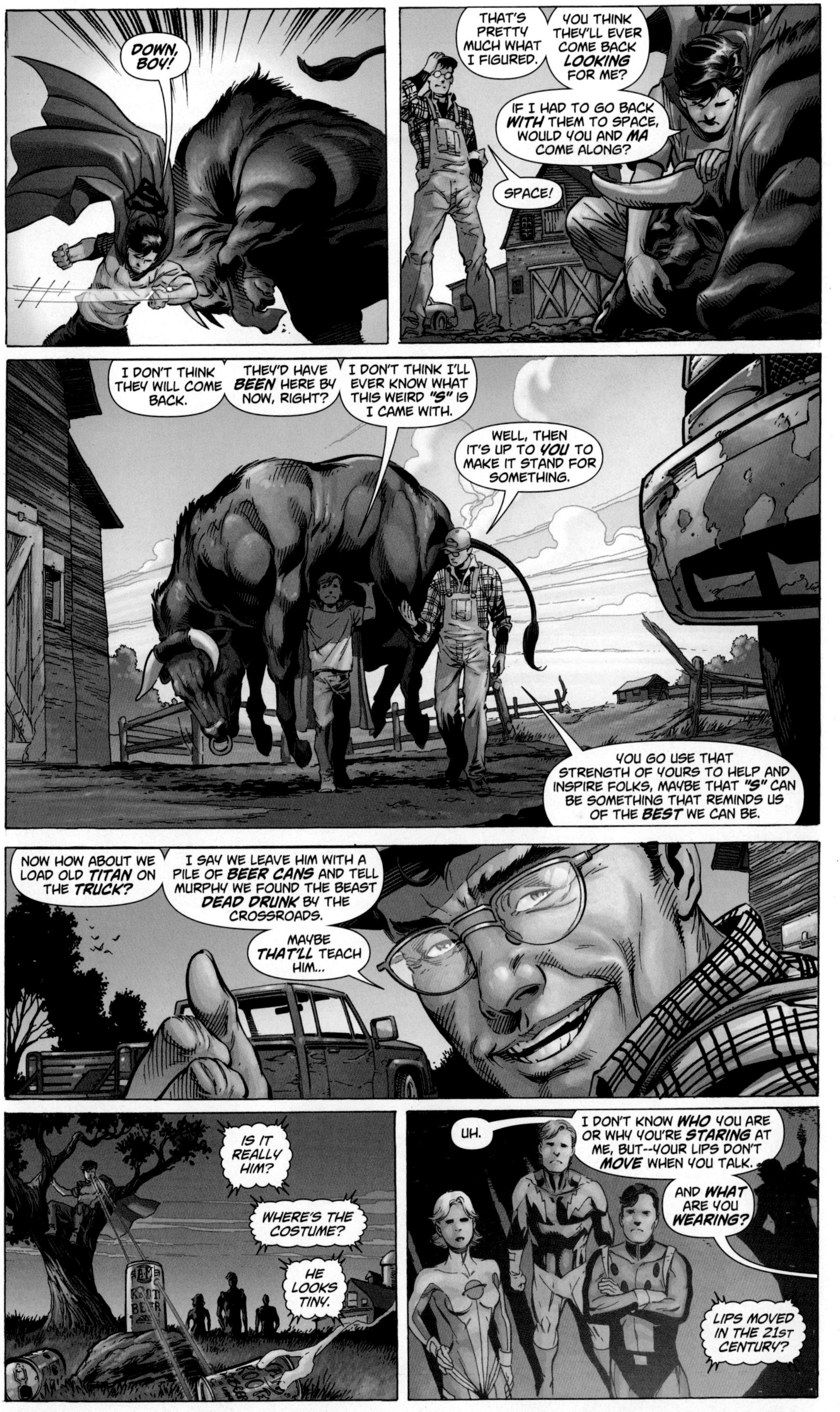
DOWN, BOY!
THAT'S PRETTY MUCH WHAT I FIGURED.
YOU THINK THEY'LL EVER COME BACK LOOKING FOR ME?
IF I HAD TO GO BACK WITH THEM TO SPACE, WOULD YOU AND MA COME ALONG?
SPACE!
I DON'T THINK THEY WILL COME BACK.
THEY'D HAVE BEEN HERE BY NOW, RIGHT?
I DON'T THINK I'LL EVER KNOW WHAT THIS WEIRD "S" IS I CAME WITH.
WELL, THEN IT'S UP TO YOU TO MAKE IT STAND FOR SOMETHING.
YOU GO USE THAT STRENGTH OF YOURS TO HELP AND INSPIRE FOLKS, MAYBE THAT "S" CAN BE SOMETHING THAT REMINDS US OF THE BEST WE CAN BE.
NOW HOW ABOUT WE LOAD OLD TITAN ON THE TRUCK?
I SAY WE LEAVE HIM WITH A PILE OF BEER CANS AND TELL MURPHY WE FOUND THE BEAST DEAD DRUNK BY THE CROSSROADS.
MAYBE THAT'LL TEACH HIM...
IS IT REALLY HIM?
WHERE'S THE COSTUME?
HE LOOKS TINY.
UH.
I DON'T KNOW WHO YOU ARE OR WHY YOU'RE STARING AT ME, BUT--YOUR LIPS DON'T MOVE WHEN YOU TALK.
AND WHAT ARE YOU WEARING?
LIPS MOVED IN THE 21ST CENTURY?

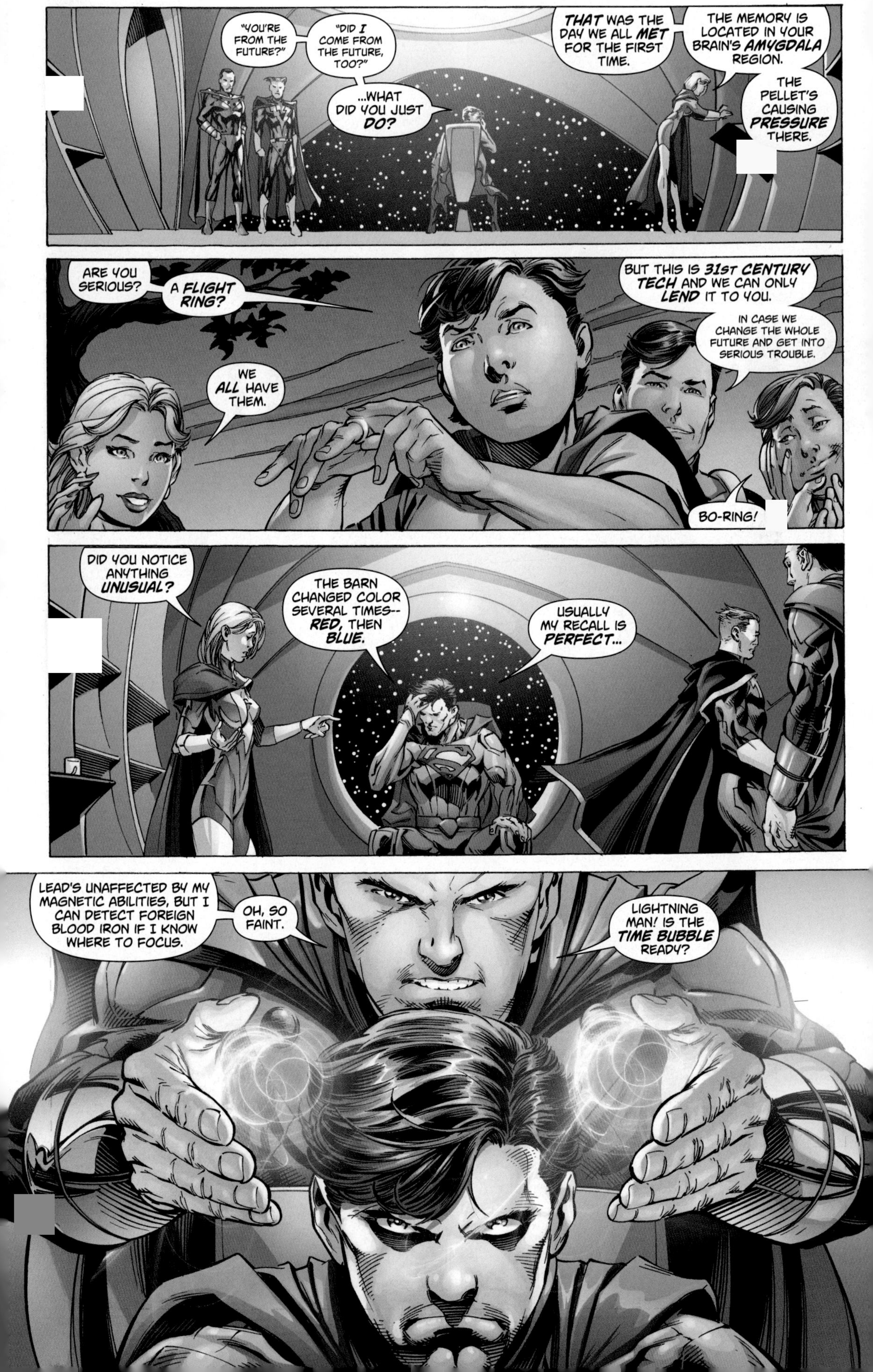
"YOU'RE FROM THE FUTURE?"
"DID I COME FROM THE FUTURE, TOO?"
...WHAT DID YOU JUST DO?
THAT WAS THE DAY WE ALL MET FOR THE FIRST TIME.
THE MEMORY IS LOCATED IN YOUR BRAIN'S AMYGDALA REGION.
THE PELLET'S CAUSING PRESSURE THERE.
ARE YOU SERIOUS?
A FLIGHT RING?
WE ALL HAVE THEM.
BUT THIS IS 31ST CENTURY TECH AND WE CAN ONLY LEND IT TO YOU.
IN CASE WE CHANGE THE WHOLE FUTURE AND GET INTO SERIOUS TROUBLE.
BO-RING!
DID YOU NOTICE ANYTHING UNUSUAL?
THE BARN CHANGED COLOR SEVERAL TIMES-- RED, THEN BLUE.
USUALLY MY RECALL IS PERFECT...
LEAD'S UNAFFECTED BY MY MAGNETIC ABILITIES, BUT I CAN DETECT FOREIGN BLOOD IRON IF I KNOW WHERE TO FOCUS.
OH, SO FAINT.
LIGHTNING MAN! IS THE TIME BUBBLE READY?

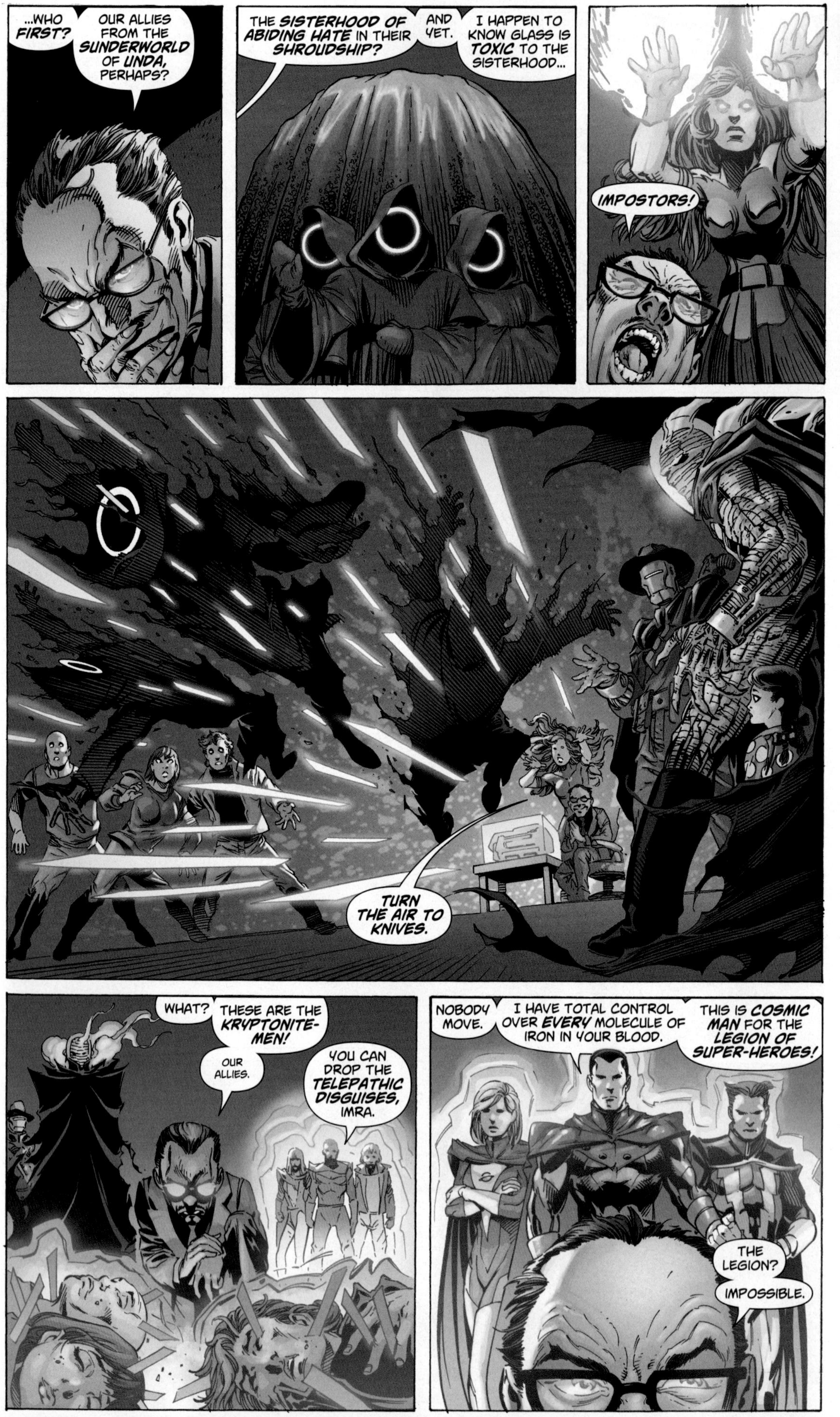
...WHO FIRST?
OUR ALLIES FROM THE SUNDERWORLD OF UNDA, PERHAPS?
THE SISTERHOOD OF ABIDING HATE IN THEIR SHROUDSHIP?
AND YET.
I HAPPEN TO KNOW GLASS IS TOXIC TO THE SISTERHOOD...
IMPOSTORS!
TURN THE AIR TO KNIVES.
WHAT?
THESE ARE THE KRYPTONITE-MEN!
OUR ALLIES.
YOU CAN DROP THE TELEPATHIC DISGUISES, IMRA.
NOBODY MOVE.
I HAVE TOTAL CONTROL OVER EVERY MOLECULE OF IRON IN YOUR BLOOD.
THIS IS COSMIC MAN FOR THE LEGION OF SUPER-HEROES!
THE LEGION?
IMPOSSIBLE.

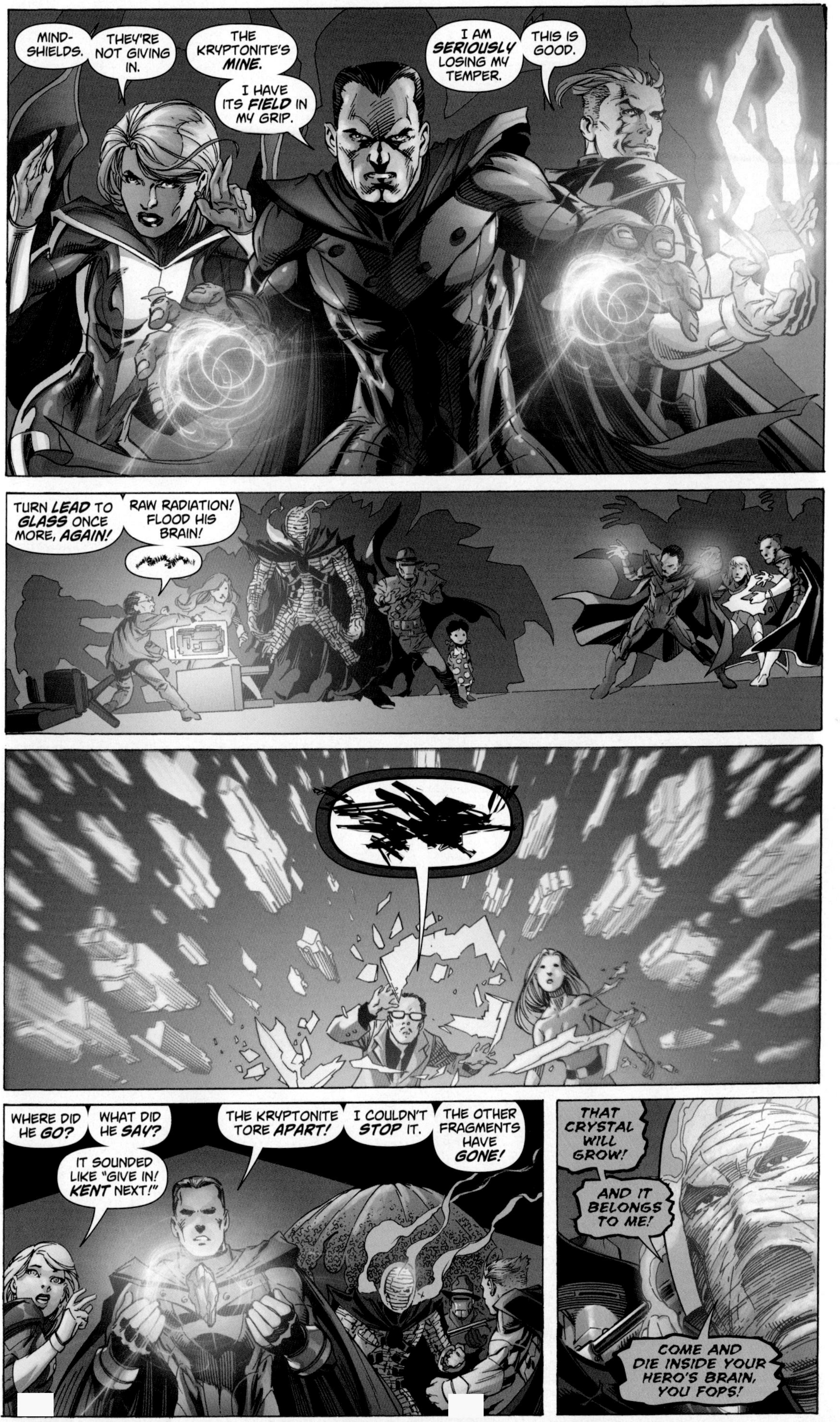
MIND-SHIELDS.
THEY'RE NOT GIVING IN.
THE KRYPTONITE'S **MINE.**
I HAVE ITS **FIELD** IN MY GRIP.
I AM **SERIOUSLY** LOSING MY TEMPER.
THIS IS GOOD.
TURN **LEAD** TO **GLASS** ONCE MORE, **AGAIN!**
RAW RADIATION! FLOOD HIS BRAIN!
WHERE DID HE **GO?**
WHAT DID HE **SAY?**
IT SOUNDED LIKE "GIVE IN! **KENT** NEXT!"
THE KRYPTONITE TORE **APART!**
I COULDN'T **STOP** IT.
THE OTHER FRAGMENTS HAVE **GONE!**
THAT CRYSTAL WILL GROW!
AND IT BELONGS TO ME!
COME AND DIE INSIDE YOUR HERO'S BRAIN, YOU FOPS!

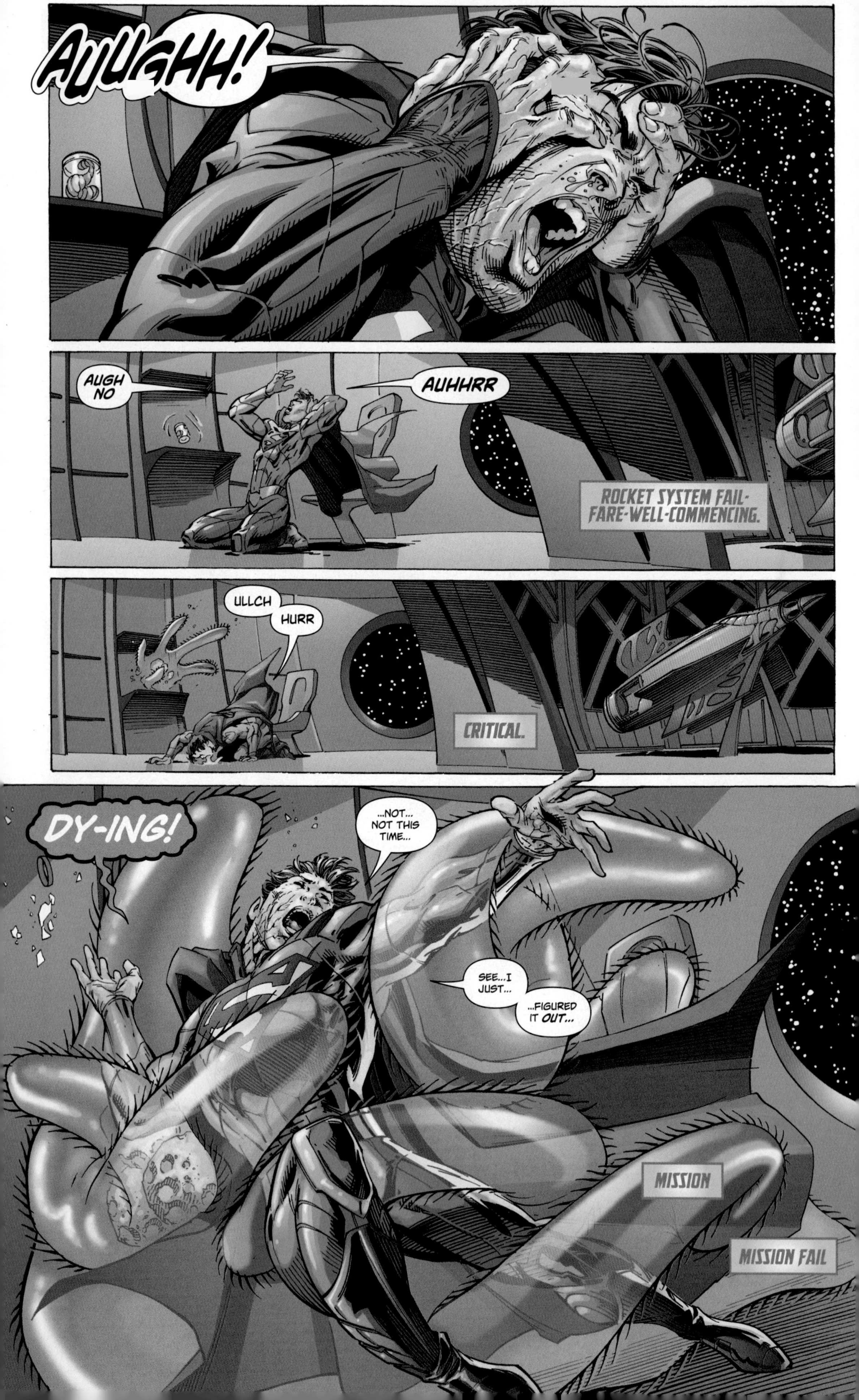
AUUGHH!
AUGH NO
AUHHRR
ROCKET SYSTEM FAIL-
FARE-WELL-COMMENCING.
ULLCH
HURR
CRITICAL.
DY-ING!
...NOT... NOT THIS TIME...
SEE...I JUST...
...FIGURED IT OUT...
MISSION
MISSION FAIL

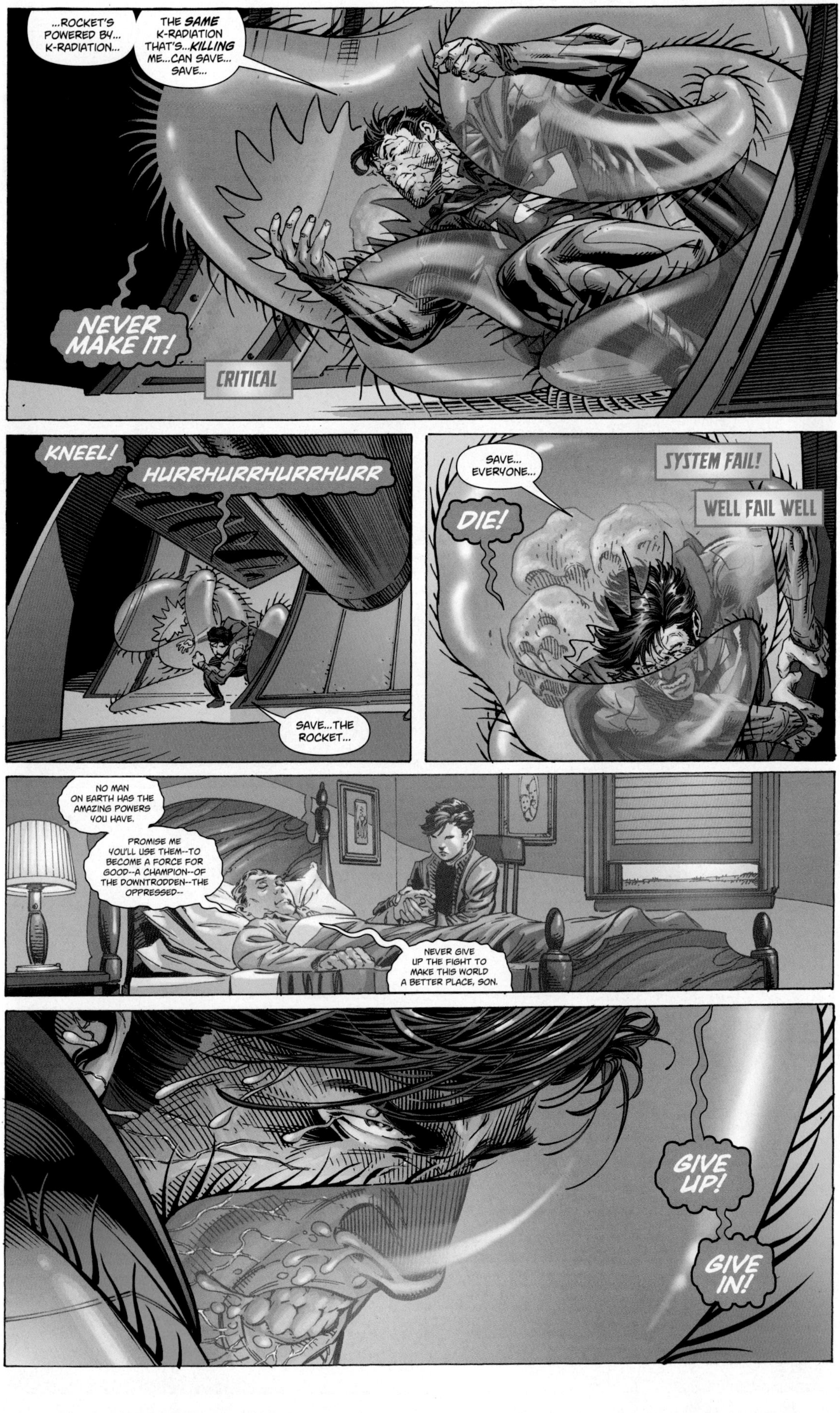

...ROCKET'S POWERED BY... K-RADIATION...
THE SAME K-RADIATION THAT'S...KILLING ME...CAN SAVE... SAVE...
NEVER MAKE IT!
CRITICAL
KNEEL!
HURRHURRHURRHURR
SAVE...THE ROCKET...
SAVE... EVERYONE...
SYSTEM FAIL!
WELL FAIL WELL
DIE!
NO MAN ON EARTH HAS THE AMAZING POWERS YOU HAVE.
PROMISE ME YOU'LL USE THEM--TO BECOME A FORCE FOR GOOD--A CHAMPION--OF THE DOWNTRODDEN--THE OPPRESSED--
NEVER GIVE UP THE FIGHT TO MAKE THIS WORLD A BETTER PLACE, SON.
GIVE UP!
GIVE IN!

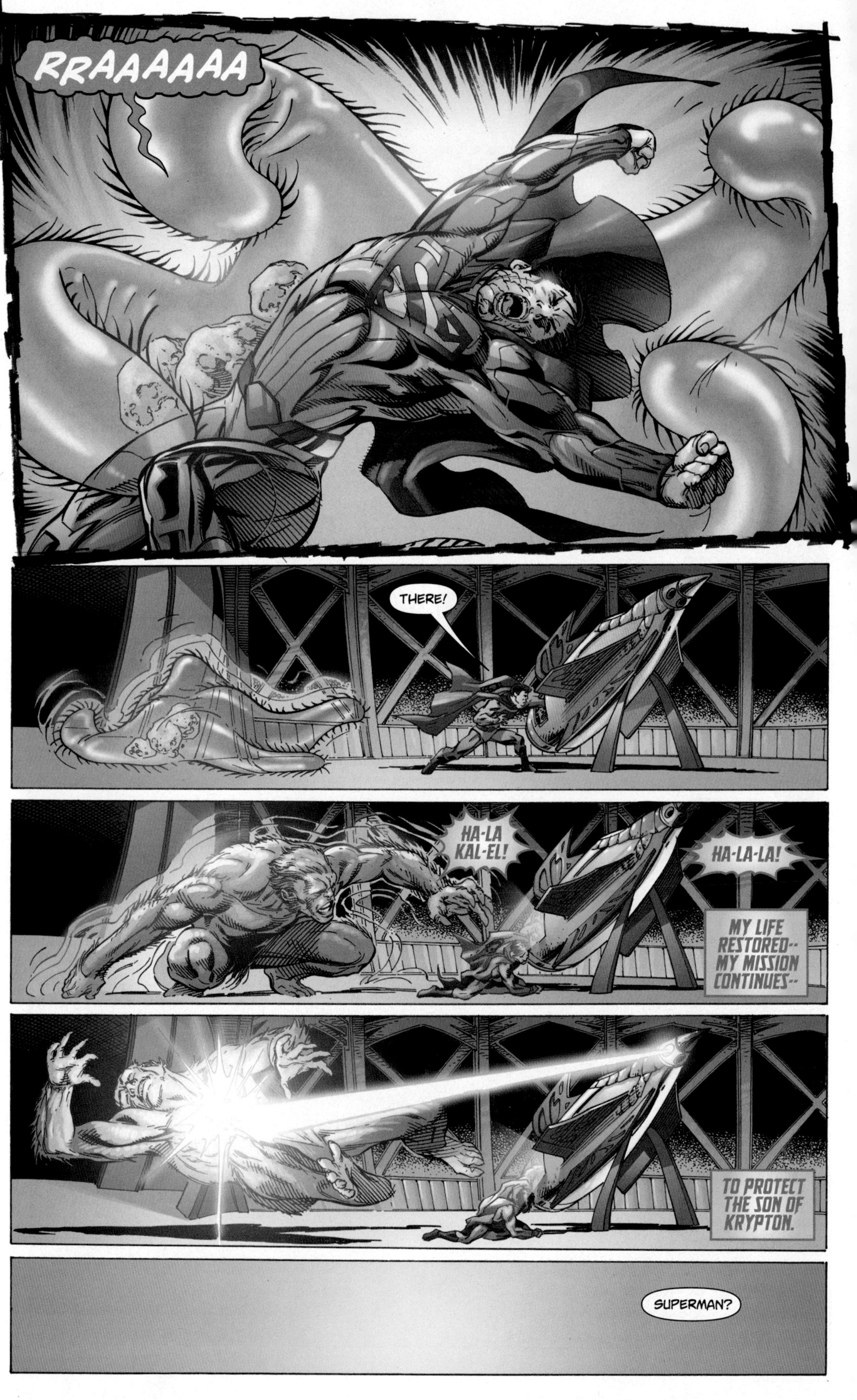
RRAAAAAA
THERE!
HA-LA KAL-EL!
HA-LA-LA!
MY LIFE RESTORED-- MY MISSION CONTINUES--
TO PROTECT THE SON OF KRYPTON.
SUPERMAN?

I **HAD** THAT.

SUPERMAN, WE **BEAT** THEM.

WE HAVE THE ENGINE. THE POWER SOURCE IS **SAFE**.

YOU CAN LET **GO** NOW.

URRRR

YOU **DID** IT.

YOU KEPT THE ROCKET **ALIVE** AND SAVED THE PAST, WHICH WE **KNEW** YOU'D DO, INCIDENTALLY.

AND NOW WE HAVE TO GET **OUT** OF HERE.

HELP APPRECIATED

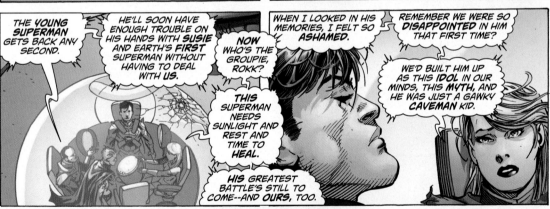

THE **YOUNG SUPERMAN** GETS BACK ANY SECOND.

HE'LL SOON HAVE ENOUGH TROUBLE ON HIS HANDS WITH **SUSIE** AND EARTH'S **FIRST** SUPERMAN WITHOUT HAVING TO DEAL WITH **US**.

NOW WHO'S THE GROUPIE, ROKK?

THIS SUPERMAN NEEDS SUNLIGHT AND REST AND TIME TO **HEAL**.

HIS GREATEST BATTLE'S STILL TO COME--AND **OURS**, TOO.

WHEN I LOOKED IN HIS MEMORIES, I FELT SO **ASHAMED**.

REMEMBER WE WERE SO **DISAPPOINTED** IN HIM THAT FIRST TIME?

WE'D BUILT HIM UP AS THIS **IDOL** IN OUR MINDS, THIS **MYTH**, AND HE WAS JUST A GAWKY **CAVEMAN** KID.

BUT FOR **HIM**...

MEETING **US**, THAT WAS WHEN HE KNEW THE UNIVERSE WAS **BIGGER** THAN HE EVER HOPED.

WE WERE THE PROOF THAT PLANET EARTH HAD A FUTURE WORTH FIGHTING FOR.

MEETING US WAS THE GREATEST DAY IN HIS LIFE.

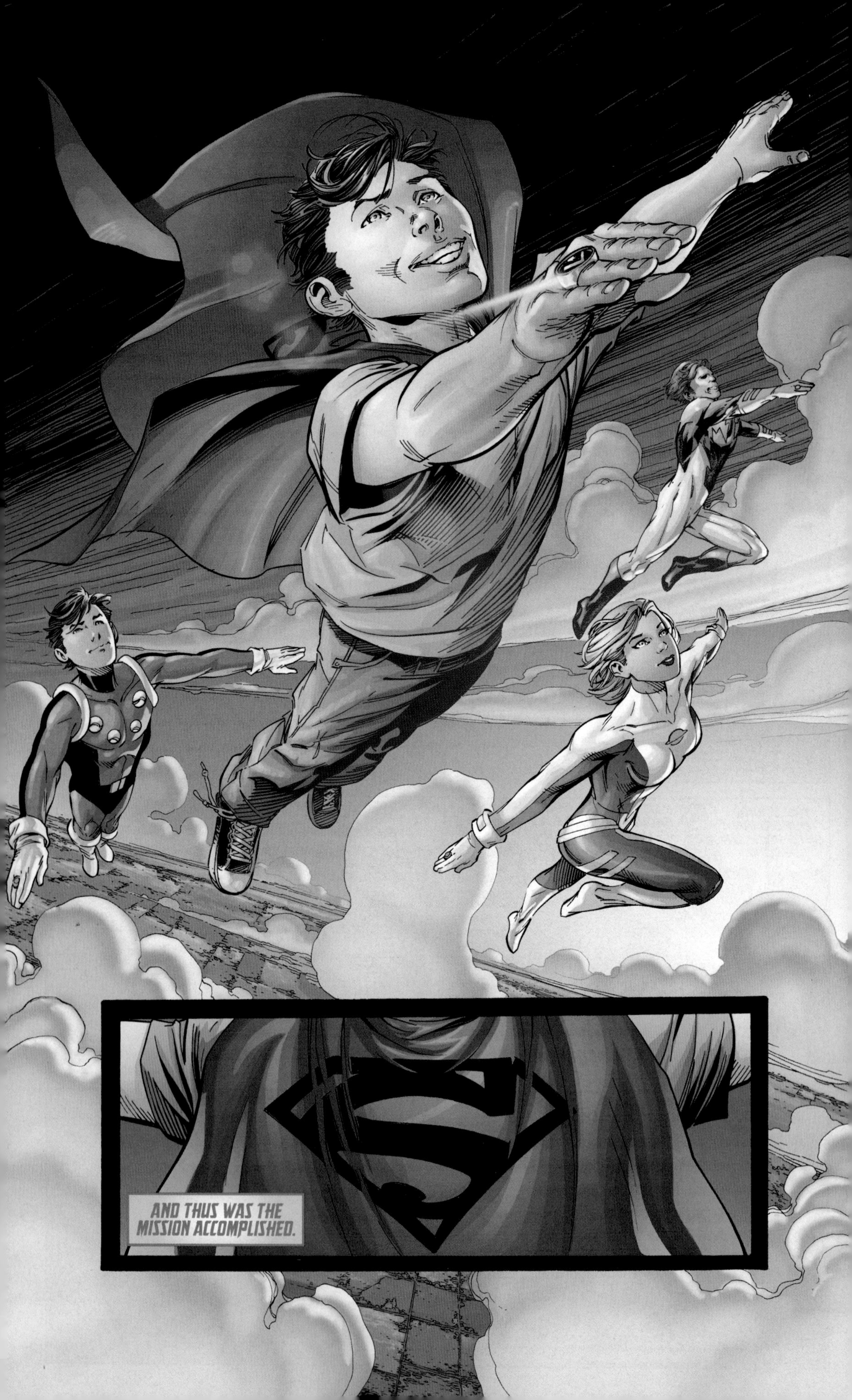
AND THUS WAS THE MISSION ACCOMPLISHED.

ACTION COMICS BACK-UP ADVENTURES

written by SHOLLY FISCH

HEARTS OF STEEL
Art by BRAD WALKER • Color by JAY DAVID RAMOS

MEANWHILE
Art by BRAD WALKER • Color by JAY DAVID RAMOS with DAVID CURIEL

BABY STEPS
Art by CHRISCROSS • Color by JOSÉ VILLARRUBIA

LAST DAY
Art by CHRISCROSS • Color by JOSÉ VILLARRUBIA

All stories lettered by CARLOS M. MANGUAL

SUPERMAN created by JERRY SIEGEL & JOE SHUSTER
STEEL created by LOUISE SIMONSON & JON BOGDANOVE

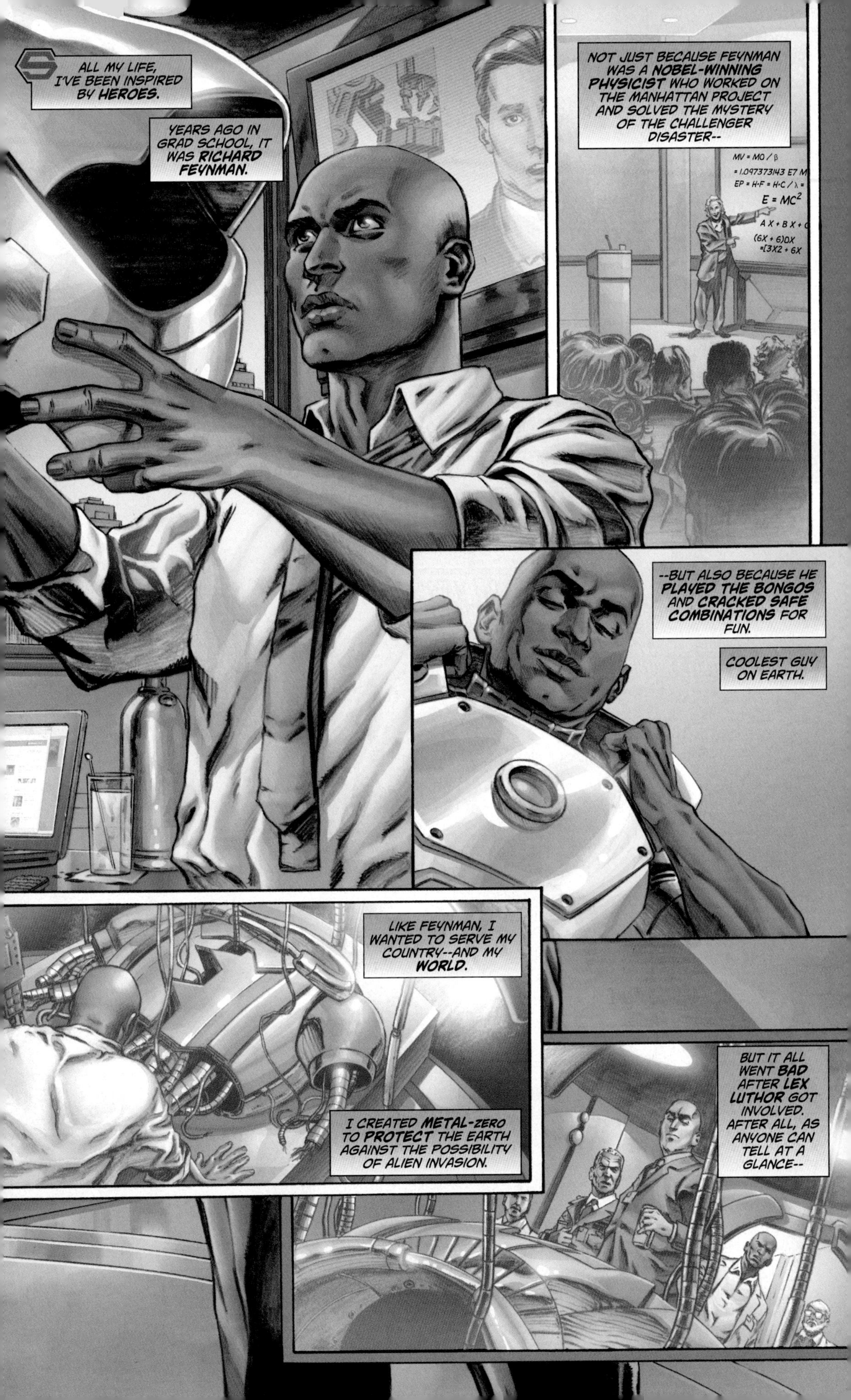
ALL MY LIFE, I'VE BEEN INSPIRED BY HEROES.
YEARS AGO IN GRAD SCHOOL, IT WAS RICHARD FEYNMAN.
NOT JUST BECAUSE FEYNMAN WAS A NOBEL-WINNING PHYSICIST WHO WORKED ON THE MANHATTAN PROJECT AND SOLVED THE MYSTERY OF THE CHALLENGER DISASTER--
MV = MQ / β
= 1.097373143 E7 M
EP = H·F = H·C / λ =
E = MC²
(6X + 6)DX
--BUT ALSO BECAUSE HE PLAYED THE BONGOS AND CRACKED SAFE COMBINATIONS FOR FUN.
COOLEST GUY ON EARTH.
LIKE FEYNMAN, I WANTED TO SERVE MY COUNTRY--AND MY WORLD.
I CREATED METAL-ZERO TO PROTECT THE EARTH AGAINST THE POSSIBILITY OF ALIEN INVASION.
BUT IT ALL WENT BAD AFTER LEX LUTHOR GOT INVOLVED. AFTER ALL, AS ANYONE CAN TELL AT A GLANCE--

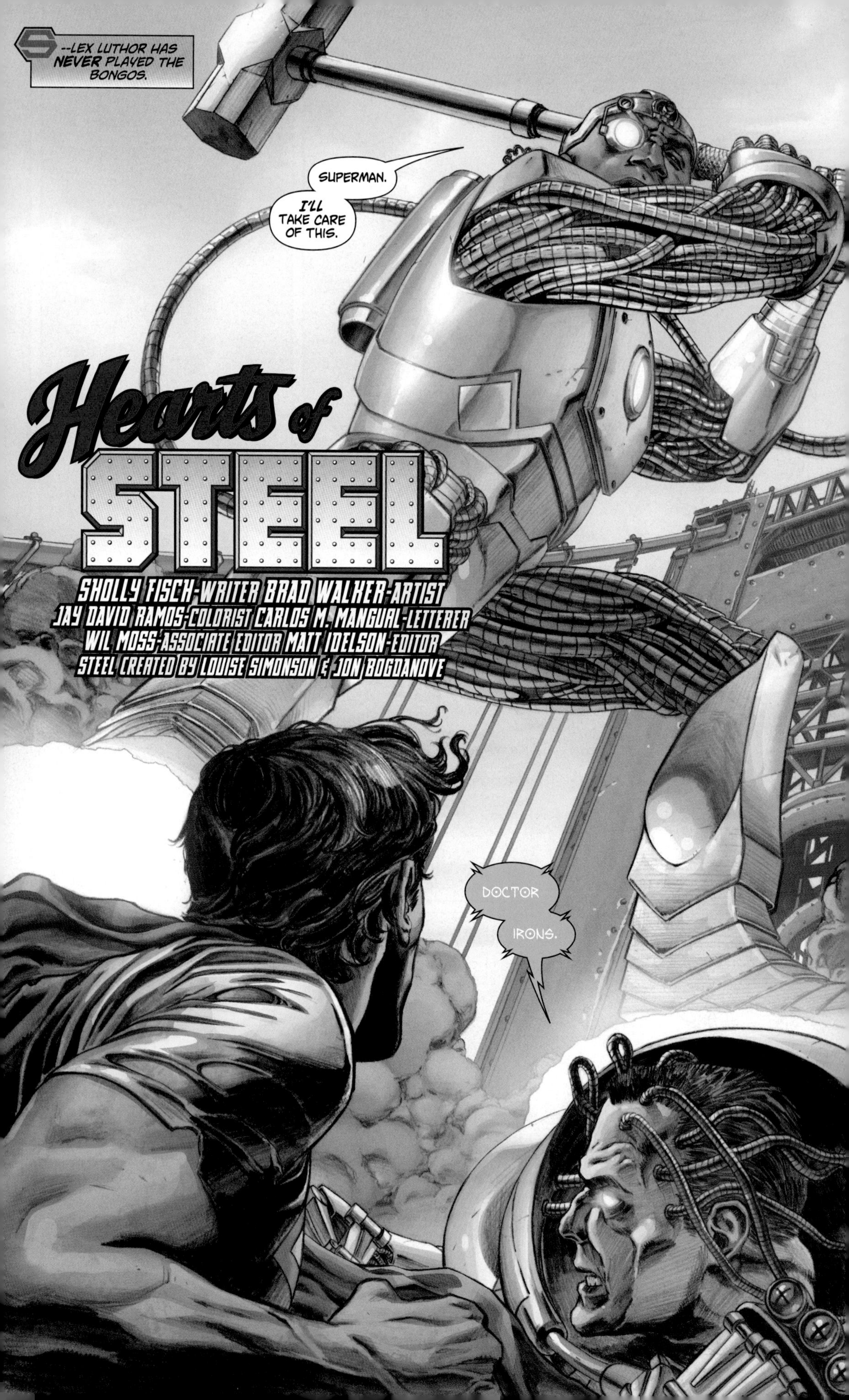
--LEX LUTHOR HAS NEVER PLAYED THE BONGOS.
SUPERMAN.
I'LL TAKE CARE OF THIS.
Hearts of STEEL
SHOLLY FISCH-WRITER BRAD WALKER-ARTIST
JAY DAVID RAMOS-COLORIST CARLOS M. MANGUAL-LETTERER
WIL MOSS-ASSOCIATE EDITOR MATT IDELSON-EDITOR
STEEL CREATED BY LOUISE SIMONSON & JON BOGDANOVE
DOCTOR IRONS.

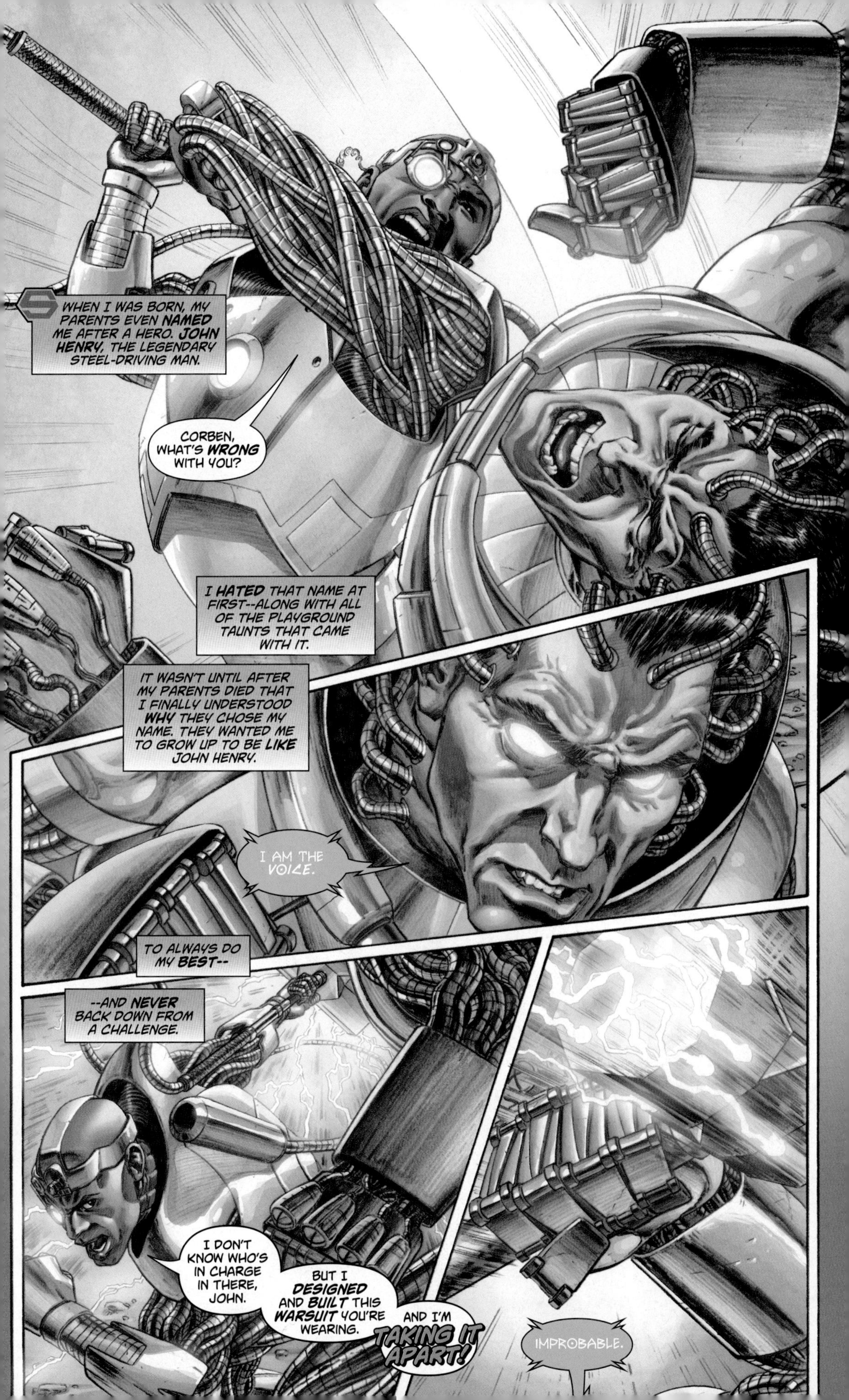
WHEN I WAS BORN, MY PARENTS EVEN NAMED ME AFTER A HERO. JOHN HENRY, THE LEGENDARY STEEL-DRIVING MAN.
CORBEN, WHAT'S WRONG WITH YOU?
I HATED THAT NAME AT FIRST--ALONG WITH ALL OF THE PLAYGROUND TAUNTS THAT CAME WITH IT.
IT WASN'T UNTIL AFTER MY PARENTS DIED THAT I FINALLY UNDERSTOOD WHY THEY CHOSE MY NAME. THEY WANTED ME TO GROW UP TO BE LIKE JOHN HENRY.
I AM THE VOICE.
TO ALWAYS DO MY BEST--
--AND NEVER BACK DOWN FROM A CHALLENGE.
I DON'T KNOW WHO'S IN CHARGE IN THERE, JOHN.
BUT I DESIGNED AND BUILT THIS WARSUIT YOU'RE WEARING.
AND I'M TAKING IT APART!
IMPROBABLE.

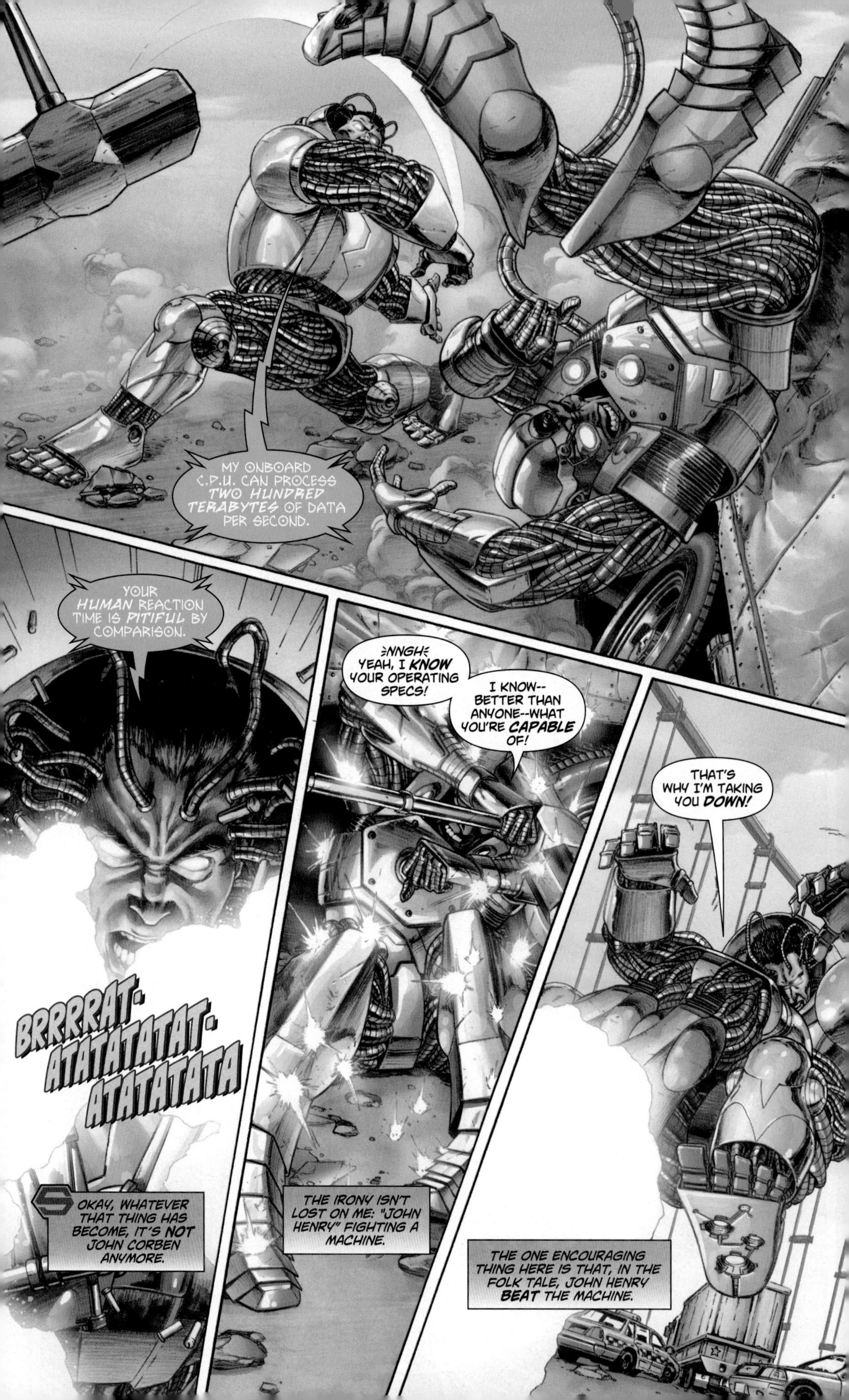
MY ONBOARD C.P.U. CAN PROCESS TWO HUNDRED TERABYTES OF DATA PER SECOND.
YOUR HUMAN REACTION TIME IS PITIFUL BY COMPARISON.
BRRRRAT-ATATATATAT-ATATATATA
OKAY, WHATEVER THAT THING HAS BECOME, IT'S NOT JOHN CORBEN ANYMORE.
NNGH YEAH, I KNOW YOUR OPERATING SPECS!
I KNOW--BETTER THAN ANYONE--WHAT YOU'RE CAPABLE OF!
THE IRONY ISN'T LOST ON ME: "JOHN HENRY" FIGHTING A MACHINE.
THAT'S WHY I'M TAKING YOU DOWN!
THE ONE ENCOURAGING THING HERE IS THAT, IN THE FOLK TALE, JOHN HENRY BEAT THE MACHINE.

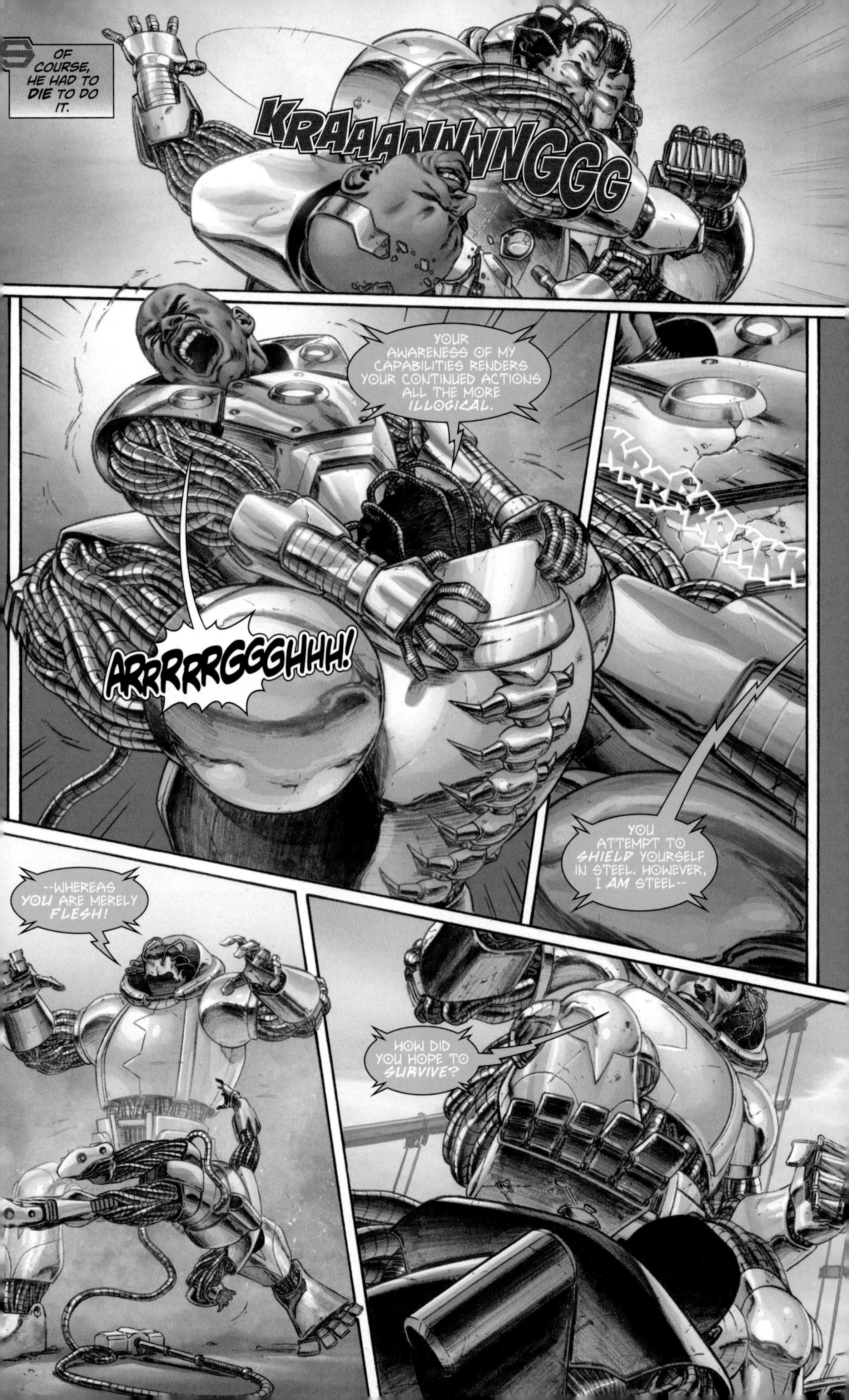
OF COURSE, HE HAD TO DIE TO DO IT.
KRAAANNNNGGG
YOUR AWARENESS OF MY CAPABILITIES RENDERS YOUR CONTINUED ACTIONS ALL THE MORE ILLOGICAL.
ARRRRRGGGHHH!
YOU ATTEMPT TO SHIELD YOURSELF IN STEEL. HOWEVER, I AM STEEL--
--WHEREAS YOU ARE MERELY FLESH!
HOW DID YOU HOPE TO SURVIVE?

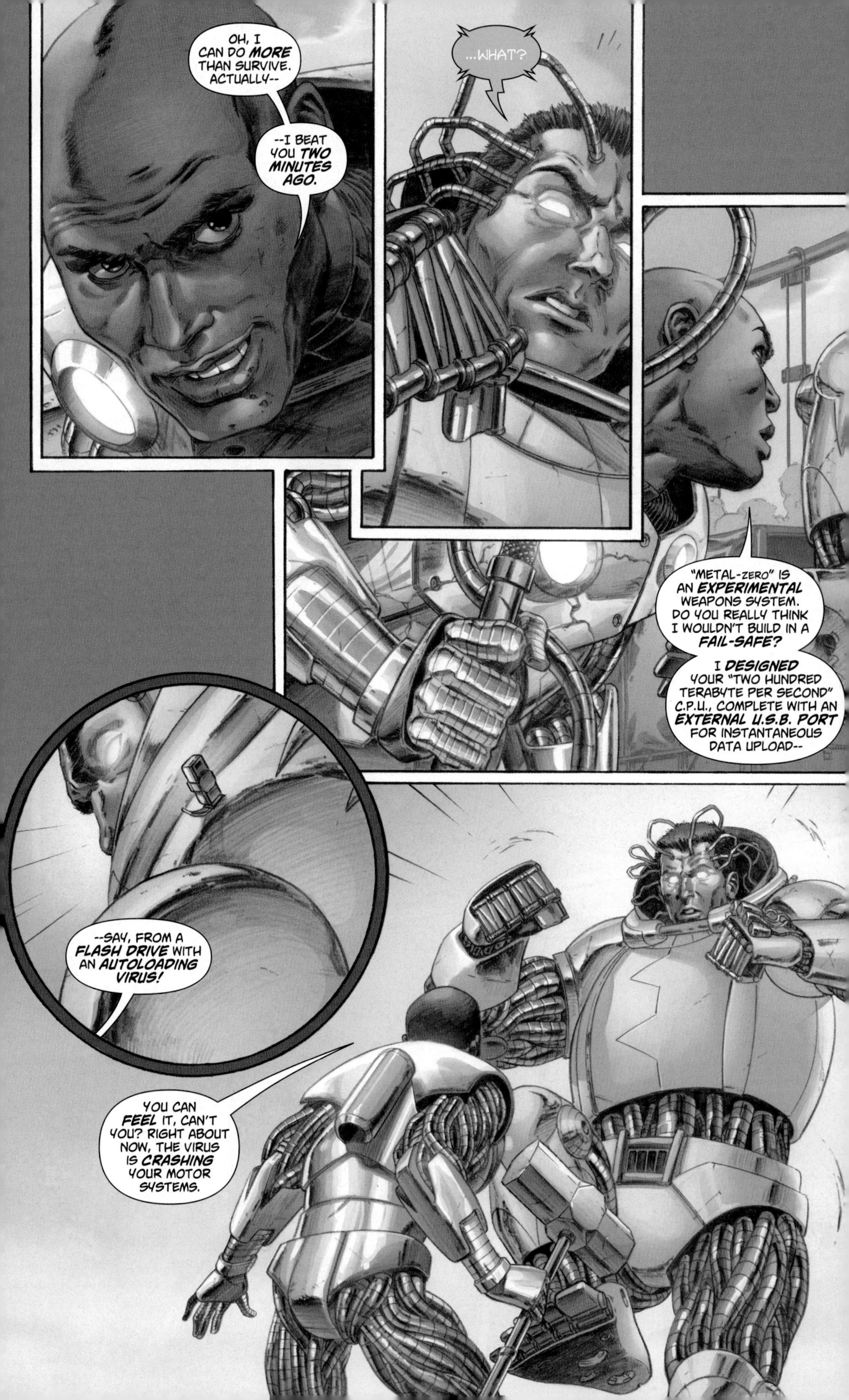
OH, I CAN DO MORE THAN SURVIVE. ACTUALLY--
--I BEAT YOU TWO MINUTES AGO.
...WHAT?
"METAL-ZERO" IS AN EXPERIMENTAL WEAPONS SYSTEM. DO YOU REALLY THINK I WOULDN'T BUILD IN A FAIL-SAFE?
I DESIGNED YOUR "TWO HUNDRED TERABYTE PER SECOND" C.P.U., COMPLETE WITH AN EXTERNAL U.S.B. PORT FOR INSTANTANEOUS DATA UPLOAD--
--SAY, FROM A FLASH DRIVE WITH AN AUTOLOADING VIRUS!
YOU CAN FEEL IT, CAN'T YOU? RIGHT ABOUT NOW, THE VIRUS IS CRASHING YOUR MOTOR SYSTEMS.

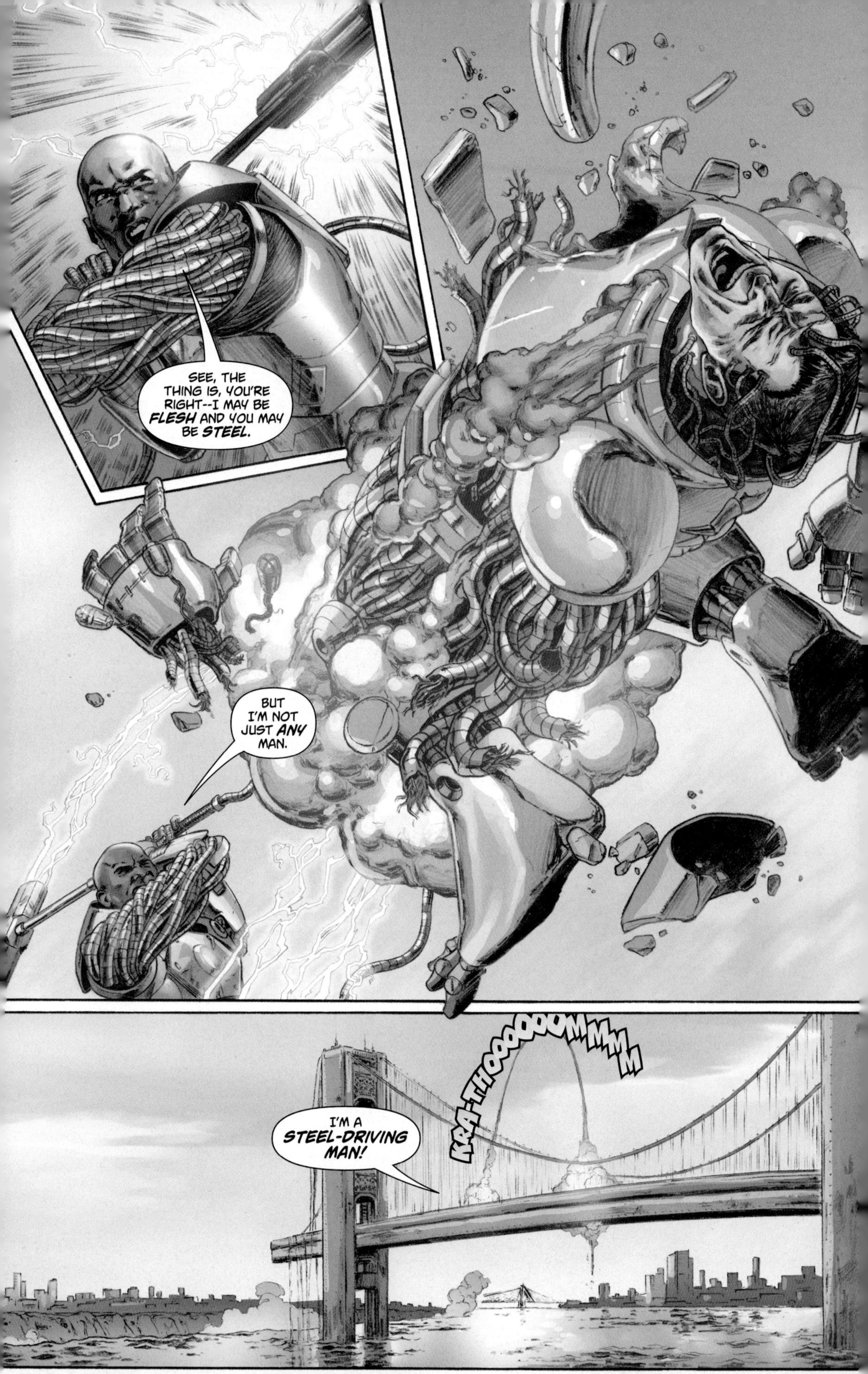
SEE, THE THING IS, YOU'RE RIGHT--I MAY BE FLESH AND YOU MAY BE STEEL.
BUT I'M NOT JUST ANY MAN.
KRA-THOOOOOOMMMM
I'M A STEEL-DRIVING MAN!

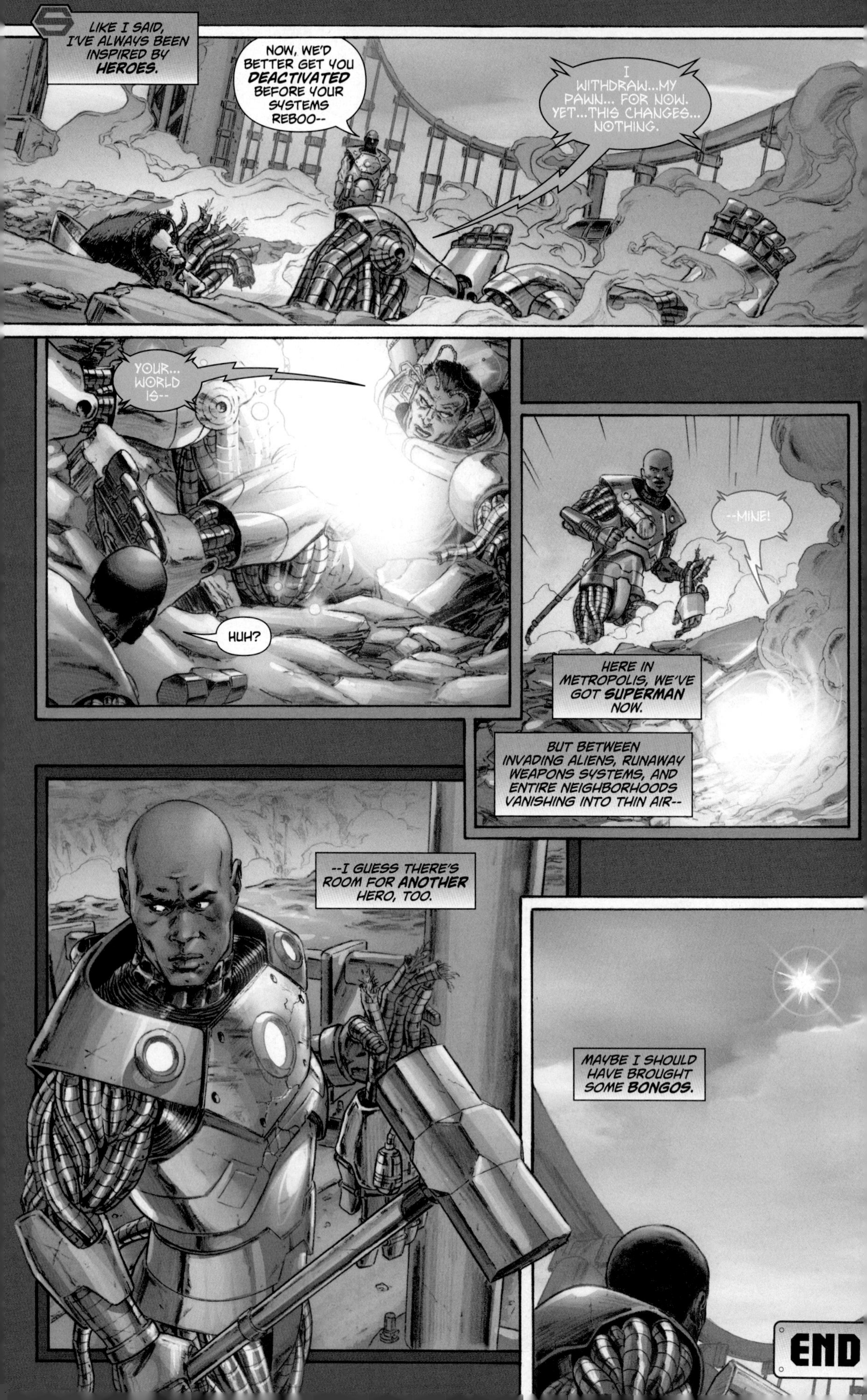
LIKE I SAID, I'VE ALWAYS BEEN INSPIRED BY HEROES.
NOW, WE'D BETTER GET YOU DEACTIVATED BEFORE YOUR SYSTEMS REBOO--
I WITHDRAW...MY PAWN... FOR NOW. YET...THIS CHANGES... NOTHING.
YOUR... WORLD IS--
HUH?
--MINE!
HERE IN METROPOLIS, WE'VE GOT SUPERMAN NOW.
BUT BETWEEN INVADING ALIENS, RUNAWAY WEAPONS SYSTEMS, AND ENTIRE NEIGHBORHOODS VANISHING INTO THIN AIR--
--I GUESS THERE'S ROOM FOR ANOTHER HERO, TOO.
MAYBE I SHOULD HAVE BROUGHT SOME BONGOS.
END

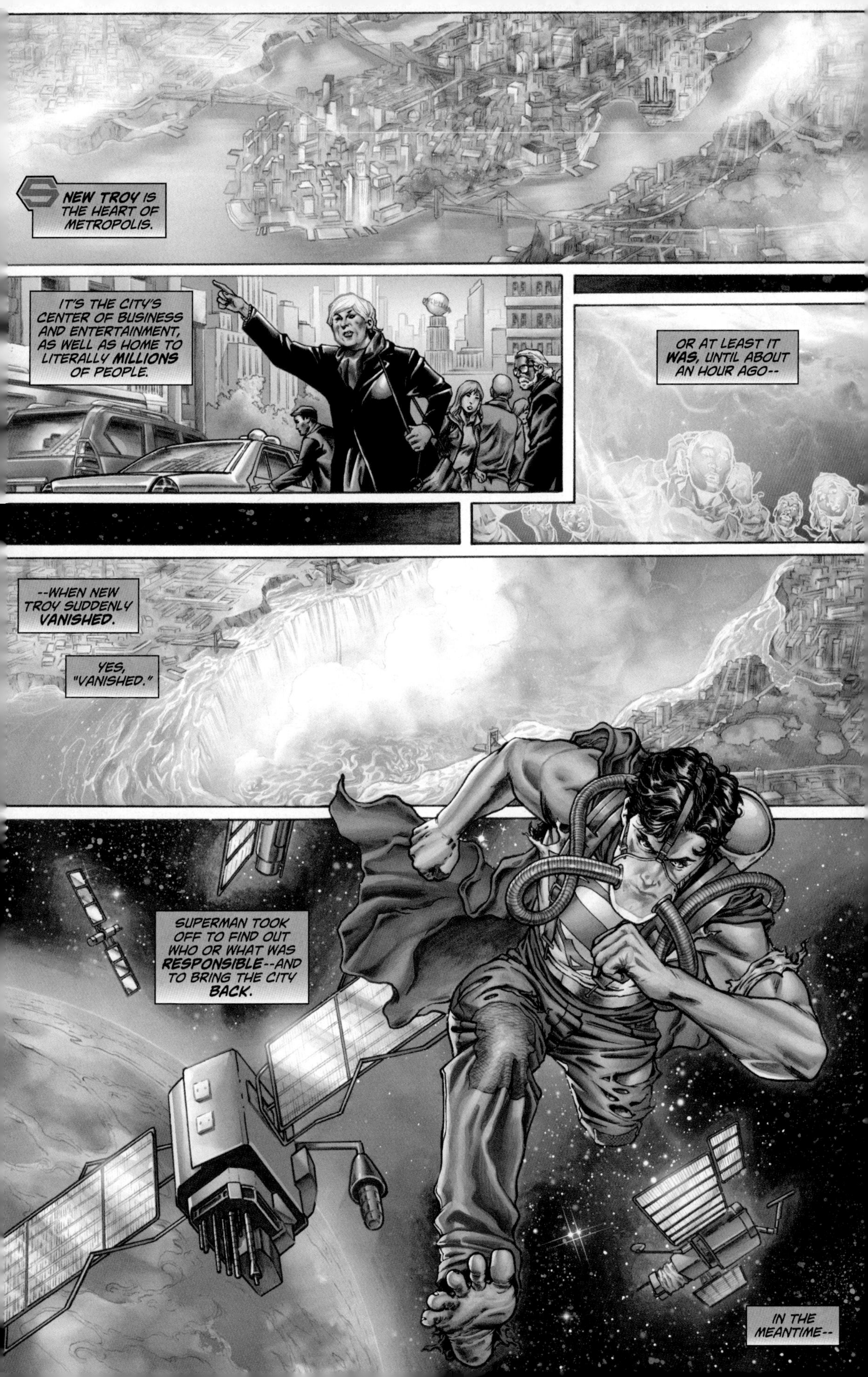
NEW TROY IS THE HEART OF METROPOLIS.
IT'S THE CITY'S CENTER OF BUSINESS AND ENTERTAINMENT, AS WELL AS HOME TO LITERALLY MILLIONS OF PEOPLE.
OR AT LEAST IT WAS, UNTIL ABOUT AN HOUR AGO--
--WHEN NEW TROY SUDDENLY VANISHED.
YES, "VANISHED."
SUPERMAN TOOK OFF TO FIND OUT WHO OR WHAT WAS RESPONSIBLE--AND TO BRING THE CITY BACK.
IN THE MEANTIME--

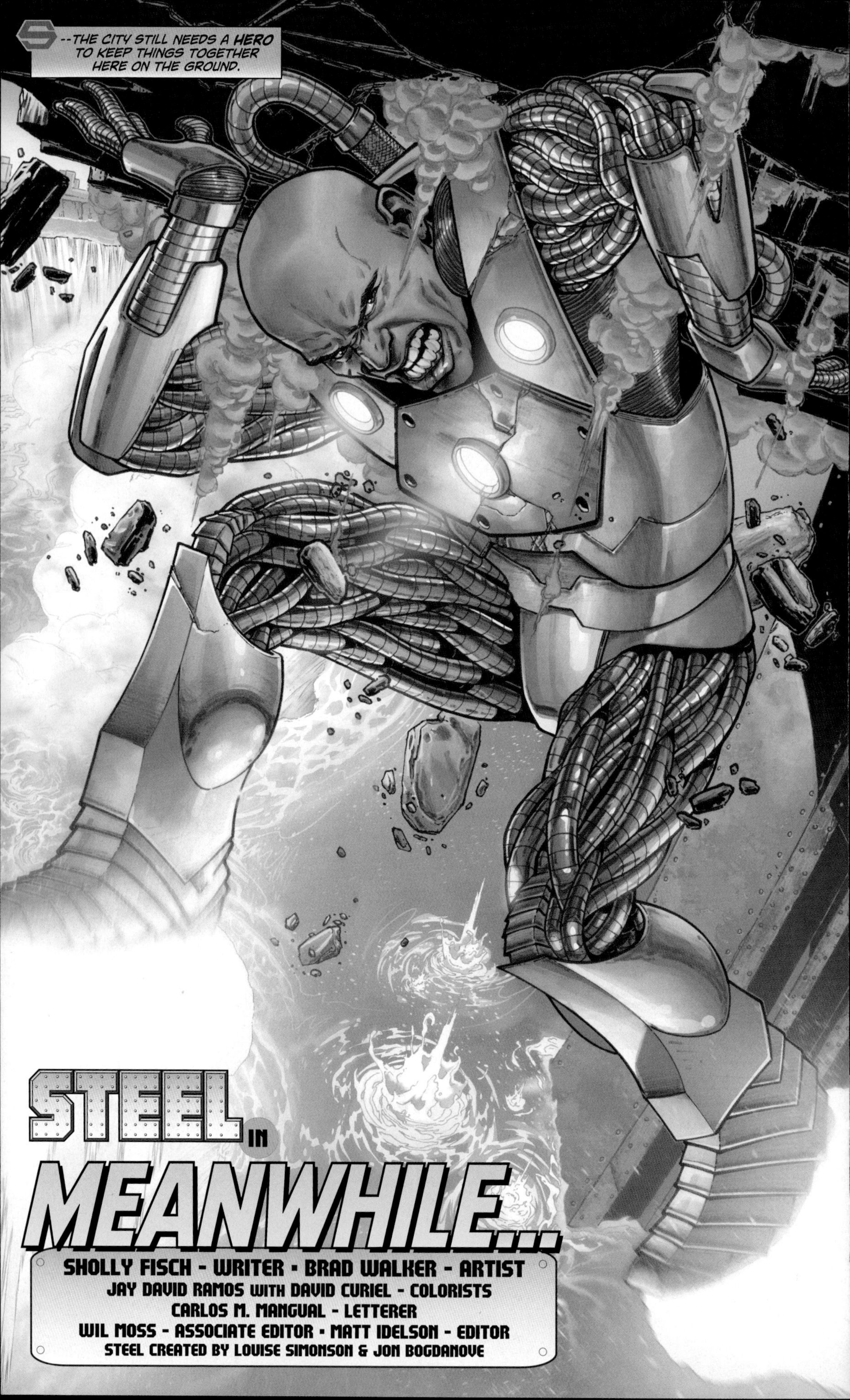
--THE CITY STILL NEEDS A HERO TO KEEP THINGS TOGETHER HERE ON THE GROUND.
STEEL IN
MEANWHILE...
SHOLLY FISCH - WRITER • BRAD WALKER - ARTIST
JAY DAVID RAMOS WITH DAVID CURIEL - COLORISTS
CARLOS M. MANGUAL - LETTERER
WIL MOSS - ASSOCIATE EDITOR • MATT IDELSON - EDITOR
STEEL CREATED BY LOUISE SIMONSON & JON BOGDANOVE

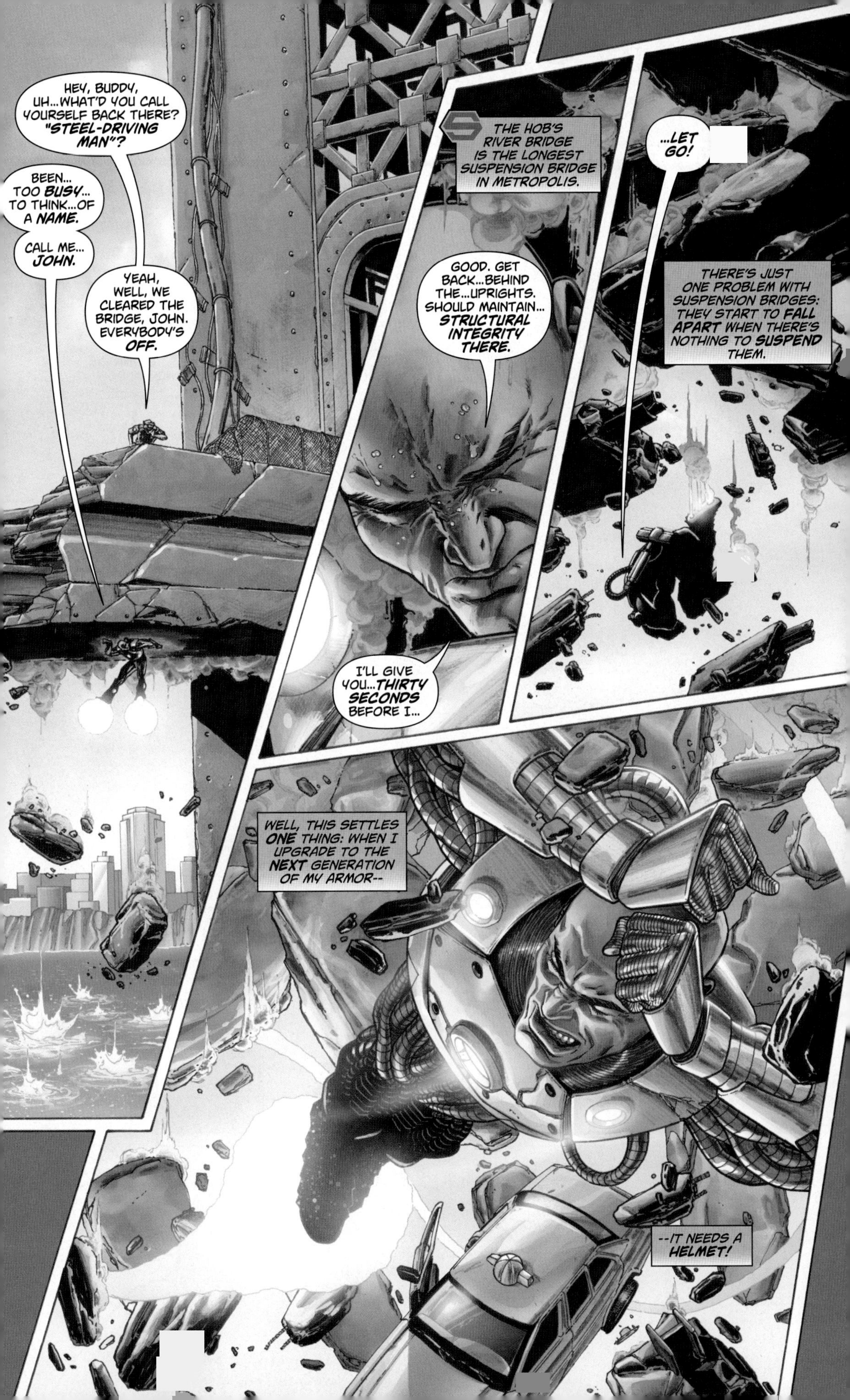
HEY, BUDDY, UH...WHAT'D YOU CALL YOURSELF BACK THERE? "STEEL-DRIVING MAN"?
BEEN... TOO BUSY... TO THINK...OF A NAME.
CALL ME... JOHN.
YEAH, WELL, WE CLEARED THE BRIDGE, JOHN. EVERYBODY'S OFF.
THE HOB'S RIVER BRIDGE IS THE LONGEST SUSPENSION BRIDGE IN METROPOLIS.
GOOD. GET BACK...BEHIND THE...UPRIGHTS. SHOULD MAINTAIN... STRUCTURAL INTEGRITY THERE.
I'LL GIVE YOU...THIRTY SECONDS BEFORE I...
...LET GO!
THERE'S JUST ONE PROBLEM WITH SUSPENSION BRIDGES: THEY START TO FALL APART WHEN THERE'S NOTHING TO SUSPEND THEM.
WELL, THIS SETTLES ONE THING: WHEN I UPGRADE TO THE NEXT GENERATION OF MY ARMOR--
--IT NEEDS A HELMET!

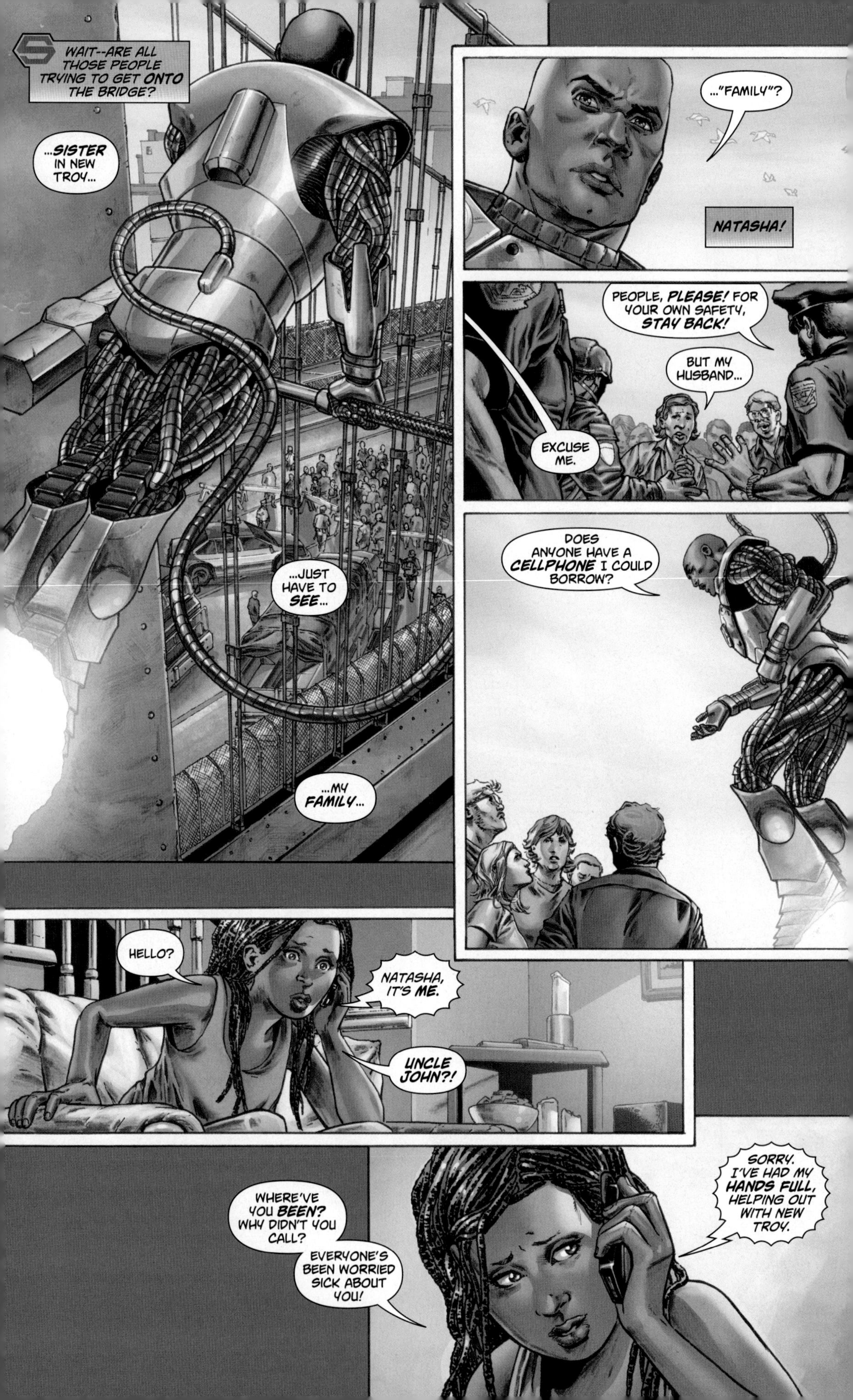
WAIT--ARE ALL THOSE PEOPLE TRYING TO GET ONTO THE BRIDGE?
...SISTER IN NEW TROY...
...JUST HAVE TO SEE...
...MY FAMILY...
..."FAMILY"?
NATASHA!
PEOPLE, PLEASE! FOR YOUR OWN SAFETY, STAY BACK!
BUT MY HUSBAND...
EXCUSE ME.
DOES ANYONE HAVE A CELLPHONE I COULD BORROW?
HELLO?
NATASHA, IT'S ME.
UNCLE JOHN?!
WHERE'VE YOU BEEN? WHY DIDN'T YOU CALL?
EVERYONE'S BEEN WORRIED SICK ABOUT YOU!
SORRY. I'VE HAD MY HANDS FULL, HELPING OUT WITH NEW TROY.

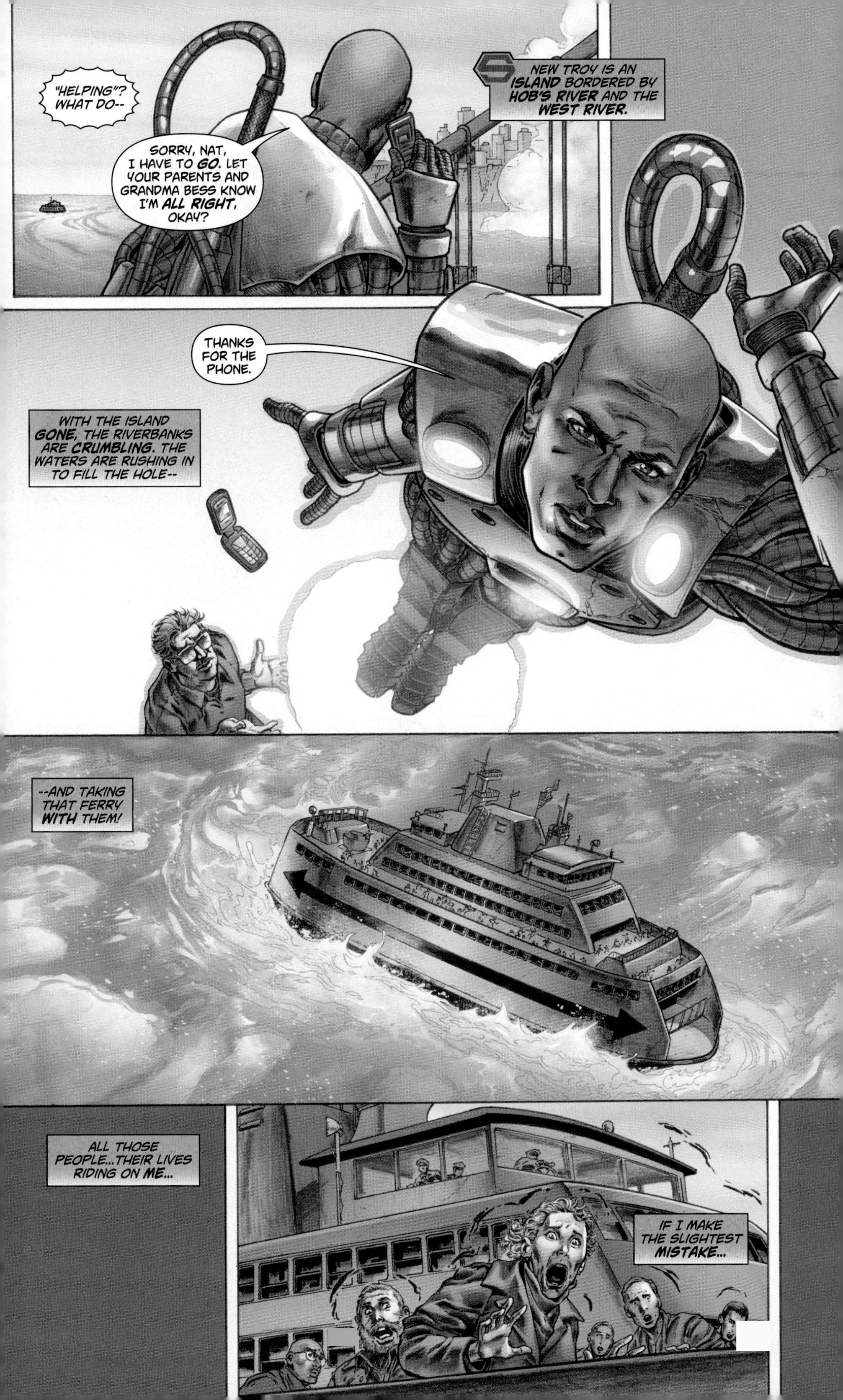

"HELPING"? WHAT DO--
SORRY, NAT, I HAVE TO GO. LET YOUR PARENTS AND GRANDMA BESS KNOW I'M ALL RIGHT, OKAY?
NEW TROY IS AN ISLAND BORDERED BY HOB'S RIVER AND THE WEST RIVER.
THANKS FOR THE PHONE.
WITH THE ISLAND GONE, THE RIVERBANKS ARE CRUMBLING. THE WATERS ARE RUSHING IN TO FILL THE HOLE--
--AND TAKING THAT FERRY WITH THEM!
ALL THOSE PEOPLE...THEIR LIVES RIDING ON ME...
IF I MAKE THE SLIGHTEST MISTAKE...

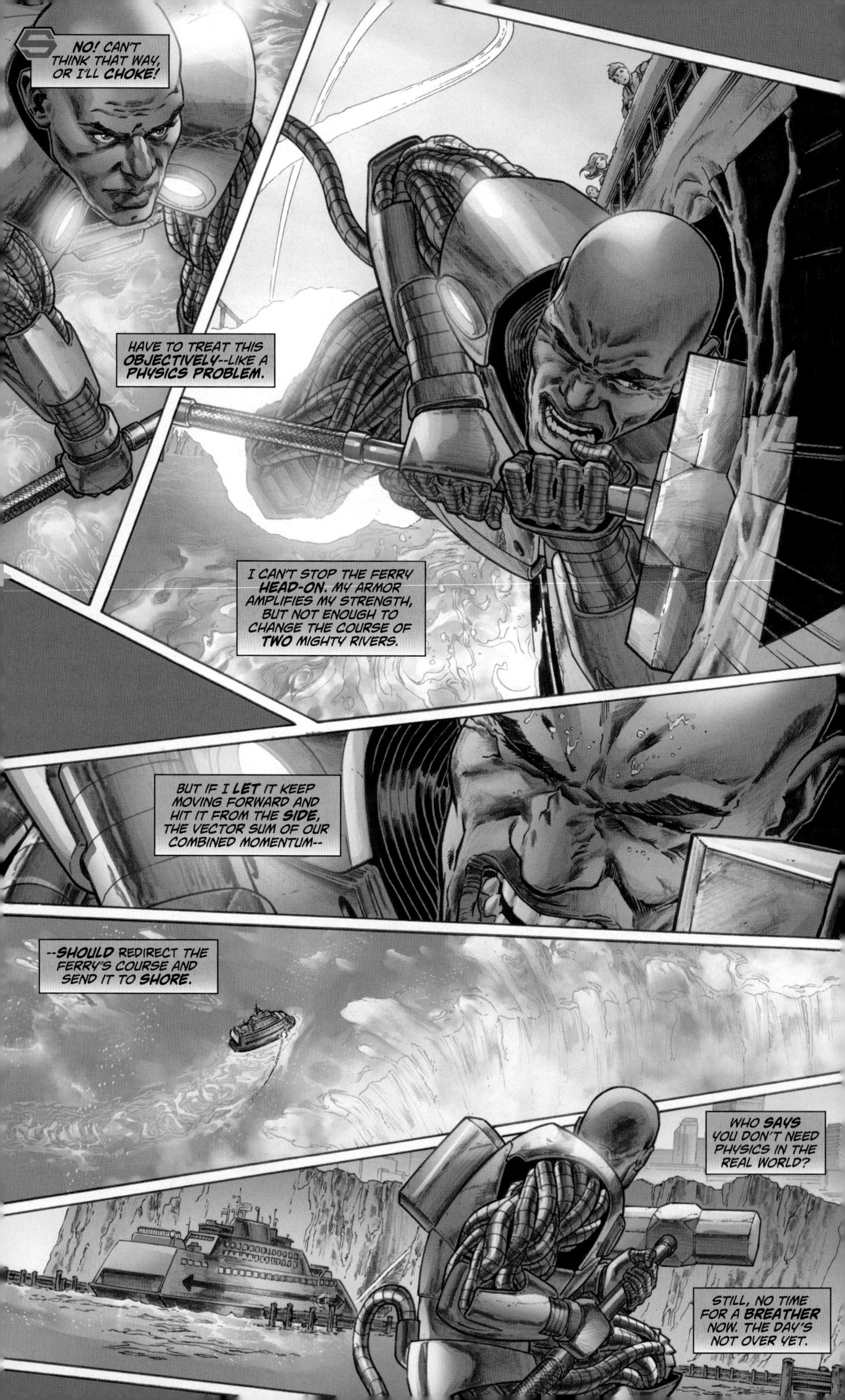
NO! CAN'T THINK THAT WAY, OR I'LL CHOKE!
HAVE TO TREAT THIS OBJECTIVELY--LIKE A PHYSICS PROBLEM.
I CAN'T STOP THE FERRY HEAD-ON. MY ARMOR AMPLIFIES MY STRENGTH, BUT NOT ENOUGH TO CHANGE THE COURSE OF TWO MIGHTY RIVERS.
BUT IF I LET IT KEEP MOVING FORWARD AND HIT IT FROM THE SIDE, THE VECTOR SUM OF OUR COMBINED MOMENTUM--
--SHOULD REDIRECT THE FERRY'S COURSE AND SEND IT TO SHORE.
WHO SAYS YOU DON'T NEED PHYSICS IN THE REAL WORLD?
STILL, NO TIME FOR A BREATHER NOW. THE DAY'S NOT OVER YET.

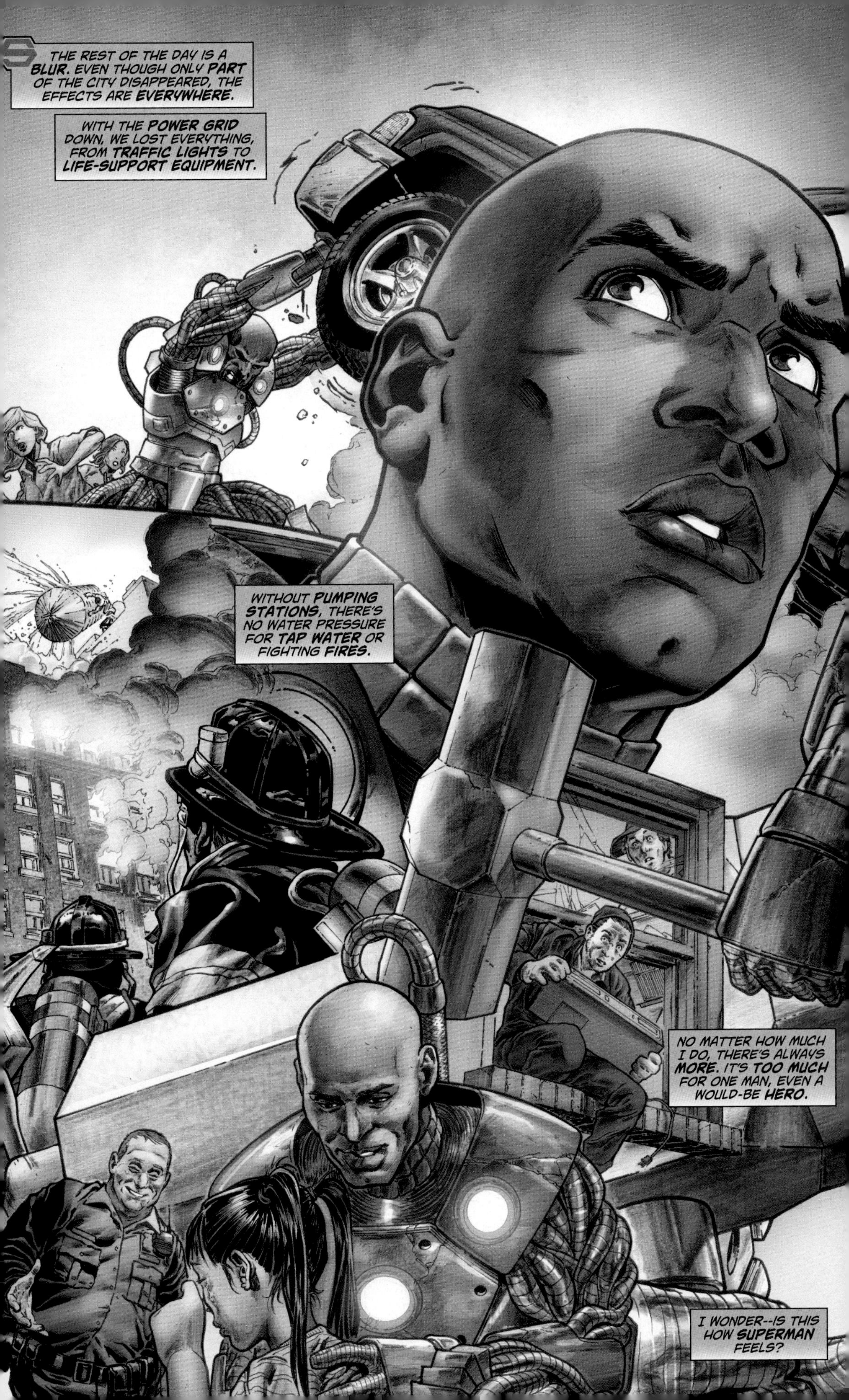
THE REST OF THE DAY IS A BLUR. EVEN THOUGH ONLY PART OF THE CITY DISAPPEARED, THE EFFECTS ARE EVERYWHERE.
WITH THE POWER GRID DOWN, WE LOST EVERYTHING, FROM TRAFFIC LIGHTS TO LIFE-SUPPORT EQUIPMENT.
WITHOUT PUMPING STATIONS, THERE'S NO WATER PRESSURE FOR TAP WATER OR FIGHTING FIRES.
NO MATTER HOW MUCH I DO, THERE'S ALWAYS MORE. IT'S TOO MUCH FOR ONE MAN, EVEN A WOULD-BE HERO.
I WONDER--IS THIS HOW SUPERMAN FEELS?

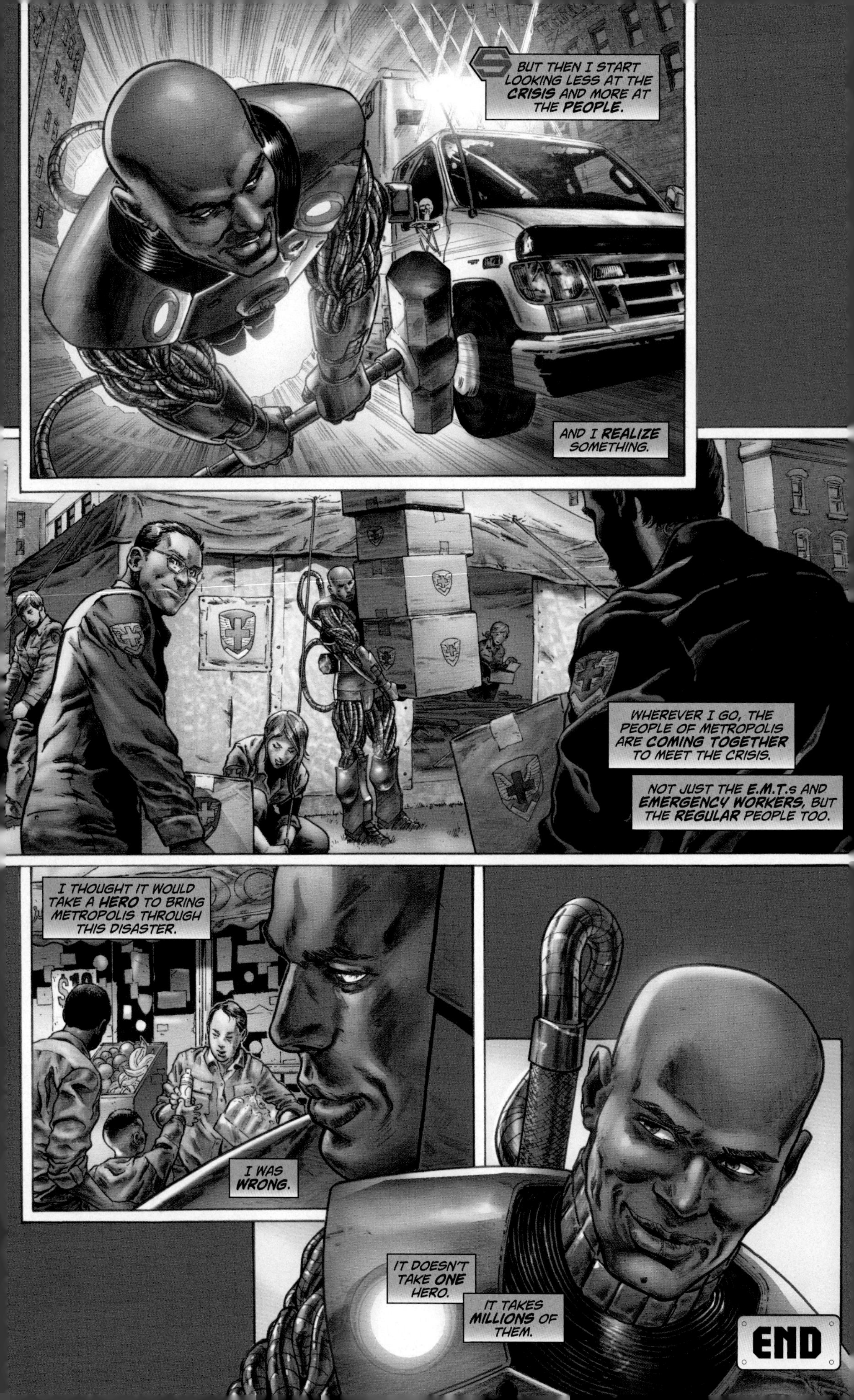
BUT THEN I START LOOKING LESS AT THE CRISIS AND MORE AT THE PEOPLE.
AND I REALIZE SOMETHING.
WHEREVER I GO, THE PEOPLE OF METROPOLIS ARE COMING TOGETHER TO MEET THE CRISIS.
NOT JUST THE E.M.T.s AND EMERGENCY WORKERS, BUT THE REGULAR PEOPLE TOO.
I THOUGHT IT WOULD TAKE A HERO TO BRING METROPOLIS THROUGH THIS DISASTER.
I WAS WRONG.
IT DOESN'T TAKE ONE HERO.
IT TAKES MILLIONS OF THEM.
END

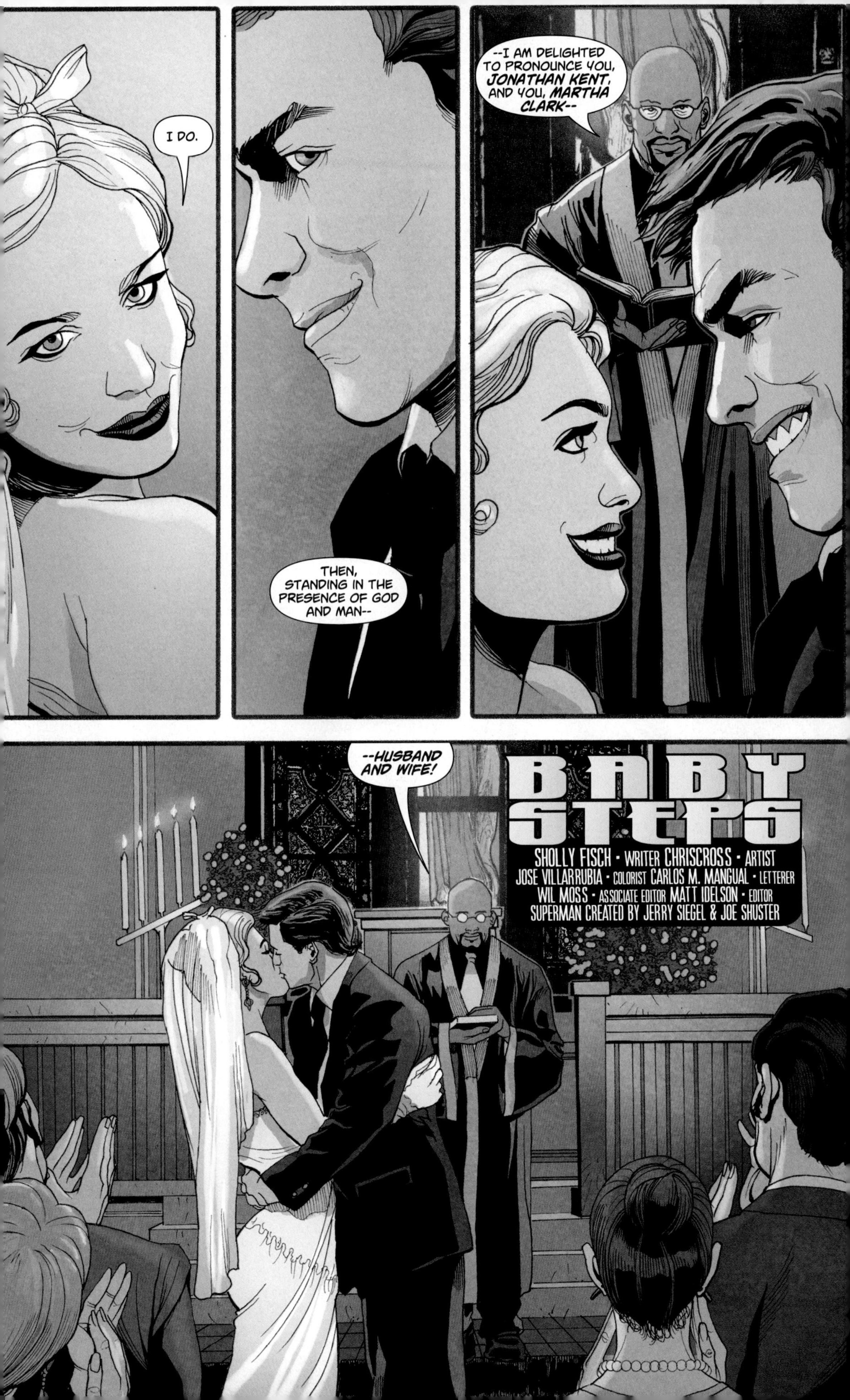
I DO.
THEN, STANDING IN THE PRESENCE OF GOD AND MAN--
--I AM DELIGHTED TO PRONOUNCE YOU, JONATHAN KENT, AND YOU, MARTHA CLARK--
--HUSBAND AND WIFE!
BABY STEPS
SHOLLY FISCH • WRITER CHRISCROSS • ARTIST
JOSE VILLARRUBIA • COLORIST CARLOS M. MANGUAL • LETTERER
WIL MOSS • ASSOCIATE EDITOR MATT IDELSON • EDITOR
SUPERMAN CREATED BY JERRY SIEGEL & JOE SHUSTER

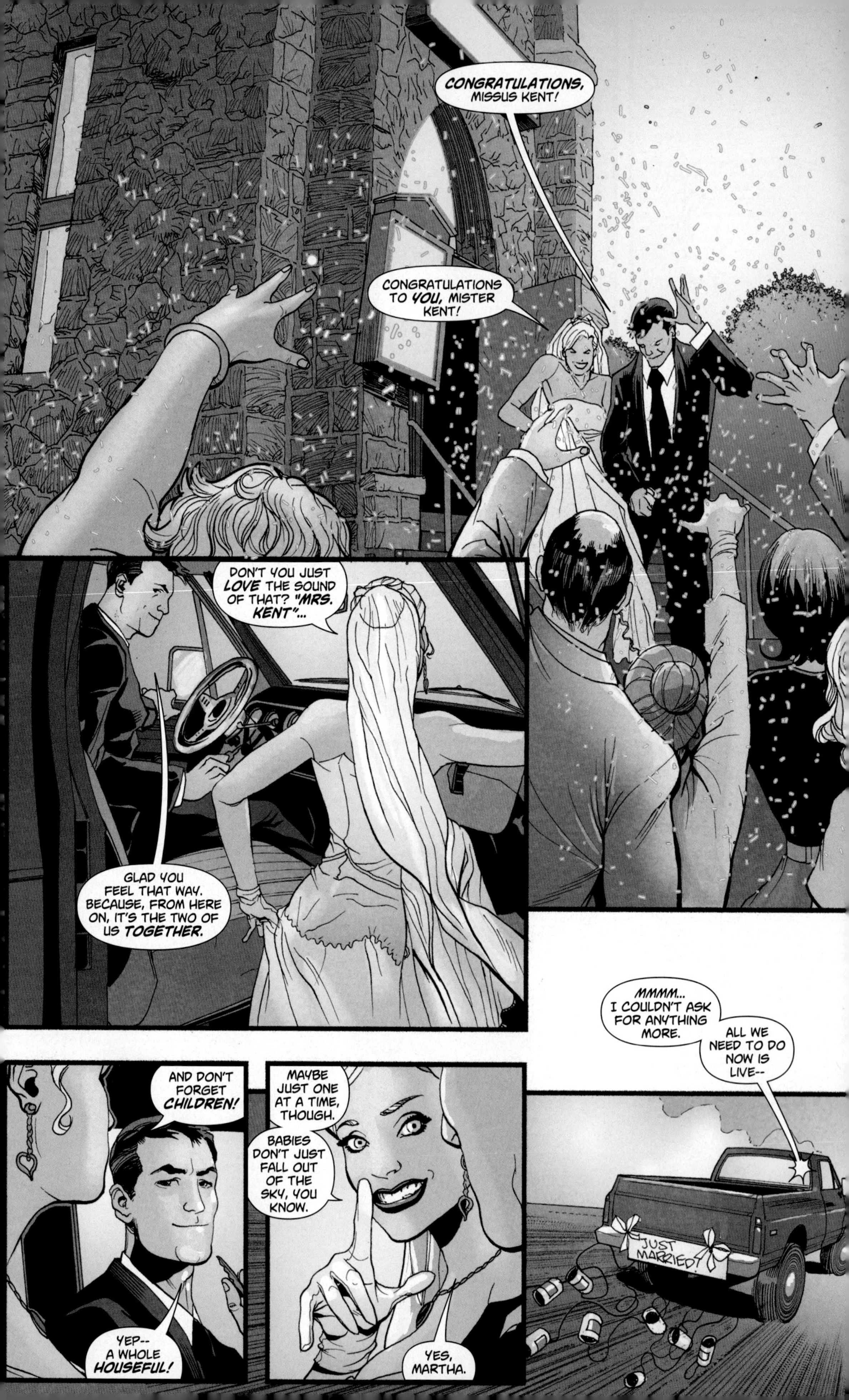
CONGRATULATIONS, MISSUS KENT!
CONGRATULATIONS TO YOU, MISTER KENT!
DON'T YOU JUST LOVE THE SOUND OF THAT? "MRS. KENT"...
GLAD YOU FEEL THAT WAY. BECAUSE, FROM HERE ON, IT'S THE TWO OF US TOGETHER.
AND DON'T FORGET CHILDREN!
YEP-- A WHOLE HOUSEFUL!
MAYBE JUST ONE AT A TIME, THOUGH.
BABIES DON'T JUST FALL OUT OF THE SKY, YOU KNOW.
YES, MARTHA.
MMMM... I COULDN'T ASK FOR ANYTHING MORE.
ALL WE NEED TO DO NOW IS LIVE--
JUST MARRIED!

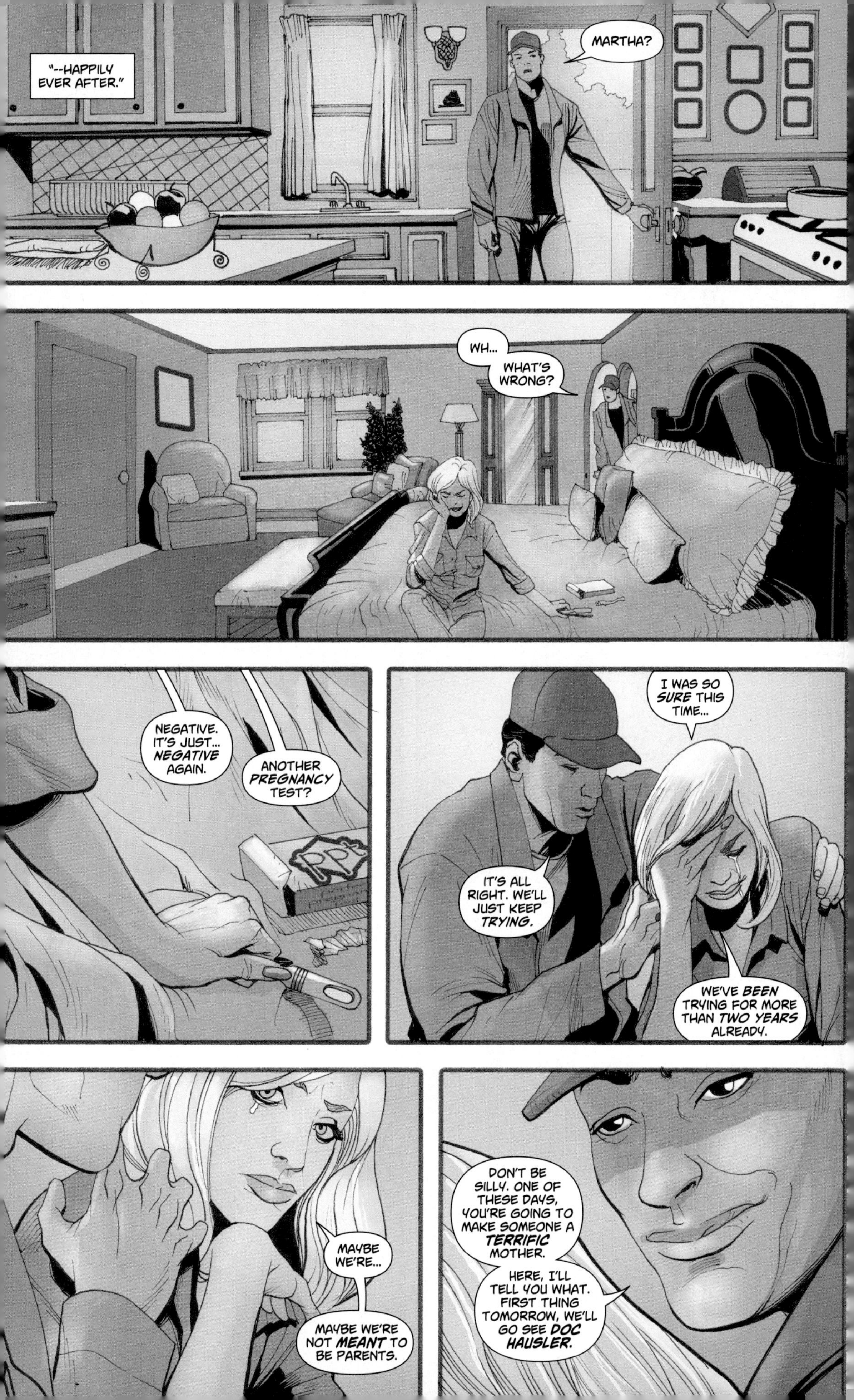
"--HAPPILY EVER AFTER."
MARTHA?
WH...
WHAT'S WRONG?
NEGATIVE. IT'S JUST... *NEGATIVE* AGAIN.
ANOTHER *PREGNANCY* TEST?
I WAS SO *SURE* THIS TIME...
IT'S ALL RIGHT. WE'LL JUST KEEP *TRYING.*
WE'VE *BEEN* TRYING FOR MORE THAN *TWO YEARS* ALREADY.
MAYBE WE'RE...
MAYBE WE'RE NOT *MEANT* TO BE PARENTS.
DON'T BE SILLY. ONE OF THESE DAYS, YOU'RE GOING TO MAKE SOMEONE A *TERRIFIC* MOTHER.
HERE, I'LL TELL YOU WHAT. FIRST THING TOMORROW, WE'LL GO SEE *DOC HAUSLER.*

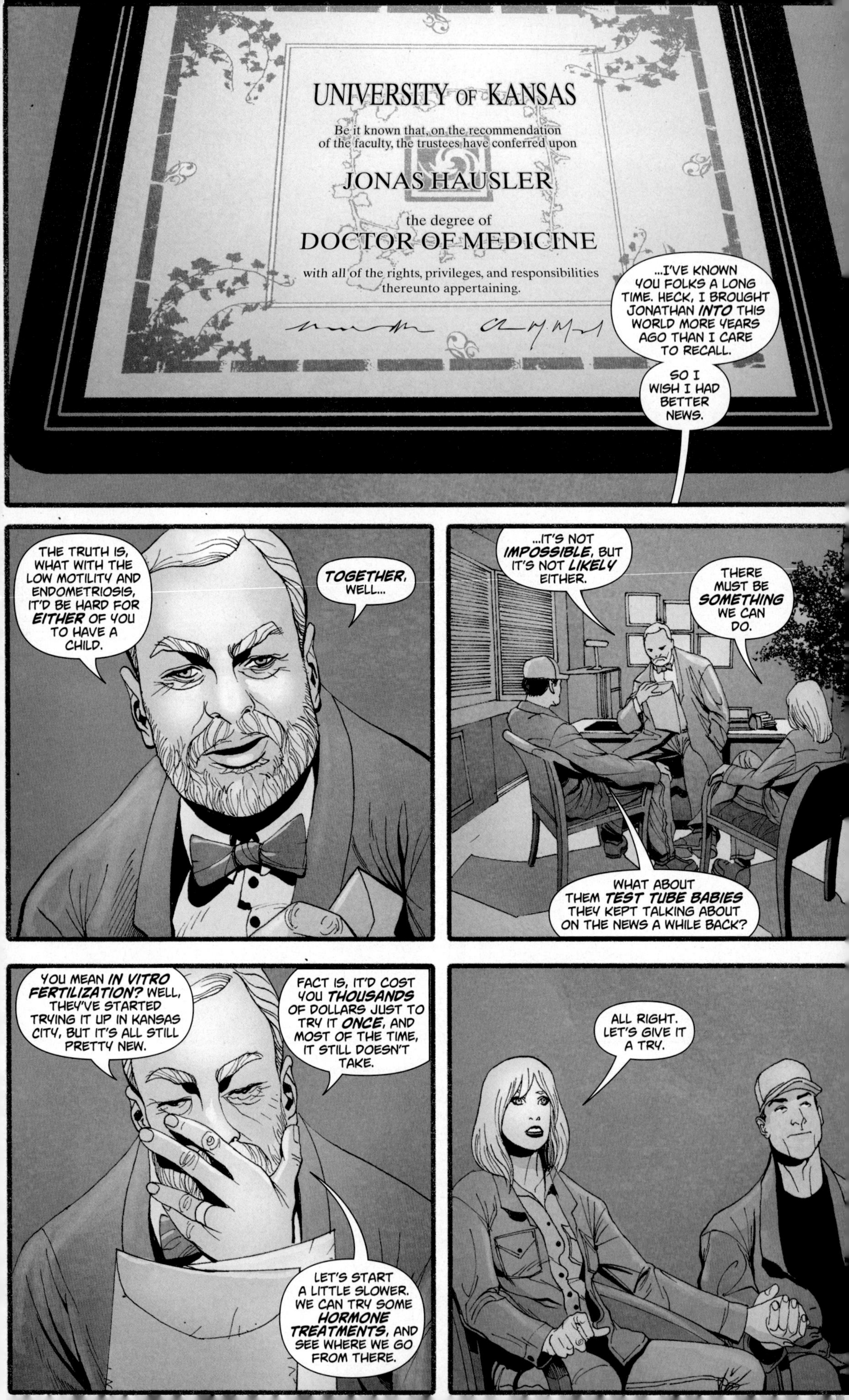
UNIVERSITY OF KANSAS
Be it known that, on the recommendation of the faculty, the trustees have conferred upon
JONAS HAUSLER
the degree of
DOCTOR OF MEDICINE
with all of the rights, privileges, and responsibilities thereunto appertaining.
...I'VE KNOWN YOU FOLKS A LONG TIME. HECK, I BROUGHT JONATHAN INTO THIS WORLD MORE YEARS AGO THAN I CARE TO RECALL.
SO I WISH I HAD BETTER NEWS.
THE TRUTH IS, WHAT WITH THE LOW MOTILITY AND ENDOMETRIOSIS, IT'D BE HARD FOR EITHER OF YOU TO HAVE A CHILD.
TOGETHER, WELL...
...IT'S NOT IMPOSSIBLE, BUT IT'S NOT LIKELY EITHER.
THERE MUST BE SOMETHING WE CAN DO.
WHAT ABOUT THEM TEST TUBE BABIES THEY KEPT TALKING ABOUT ON THE NEWS A WHILE BACK?
YOU MEAN IN VITRO FERTILIZATION? WELL, THEY'VE STARTED TRYING IT UP IN KANSAS CITY, BUT IT'S ALL STILL PRETTY NEW.
FACT IS, IT'D COST YOU THOUSANDS OF DOLLARS JUST TO TRY IT ONCE, AND MOST OF THE TIME, IT STILL DOESN'T TAKE.
LET'S START A LITTLE SLOWER. WE CAN TRY SOME HORMONE TREATMENTS, AND SEE WHERE WE GO FROM THERE.
ALL RIGHT. LET'S GIVE IT A TRY.

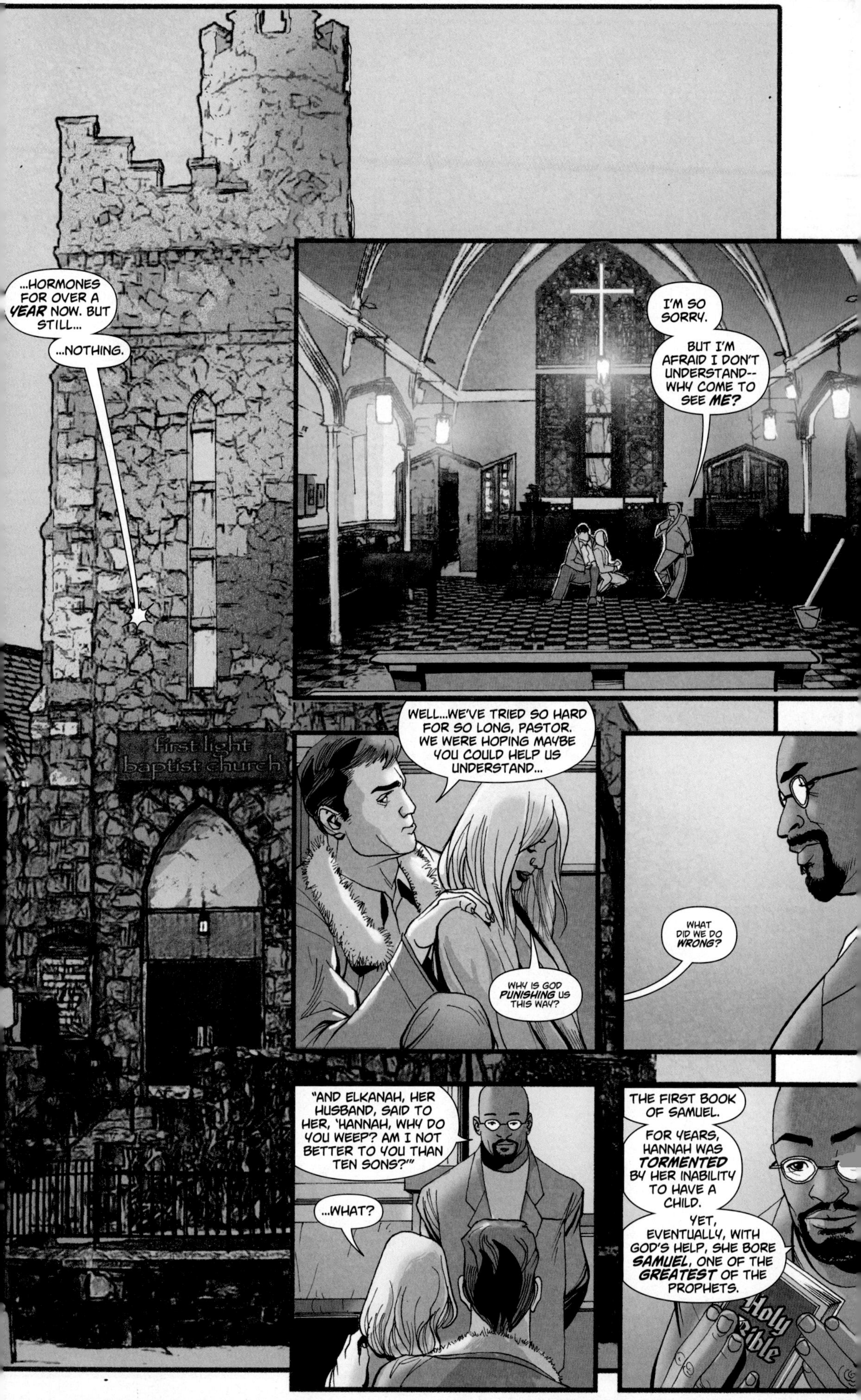

...HORMONES FOR OVER A YEAR NOW. BUT STILL...
...NOTHING.
I'M SO SORRY.
BUT I'M AFRAID I DON'T UNDERSTAND-- WHY COME TO SEE ME?
first light baptist church
WELL...WE'VE TRIED SO HARD FOR SO LONG, PASTOR. WE WERE HOPING MAYBE YOU COULD HELP US UNDERSTAND...
WHY IS GOD PUNISHING US THIS WAY?
WHAT DID WE DO WRONG?
"AND ELKANAH, HER HUSBAND, SAID TO HER, 'HANNAH, WHY DO YOU WEEP? AM I NOT BETTER TO YOU THAN TEN SONS?'"
...WHAT?
THE FIRST BOOK OF SAMUEL.
FOR YEARS, HANNAH WAS TORMENTED BY HER INABILITY TO HAVE A CHILD.
YET, EVENTUALLY, WITH GOD'S HELP, SHE BORE SAMUEL, ONE OF THE GREATEST OF THE PROPHETS.
Holy Bible

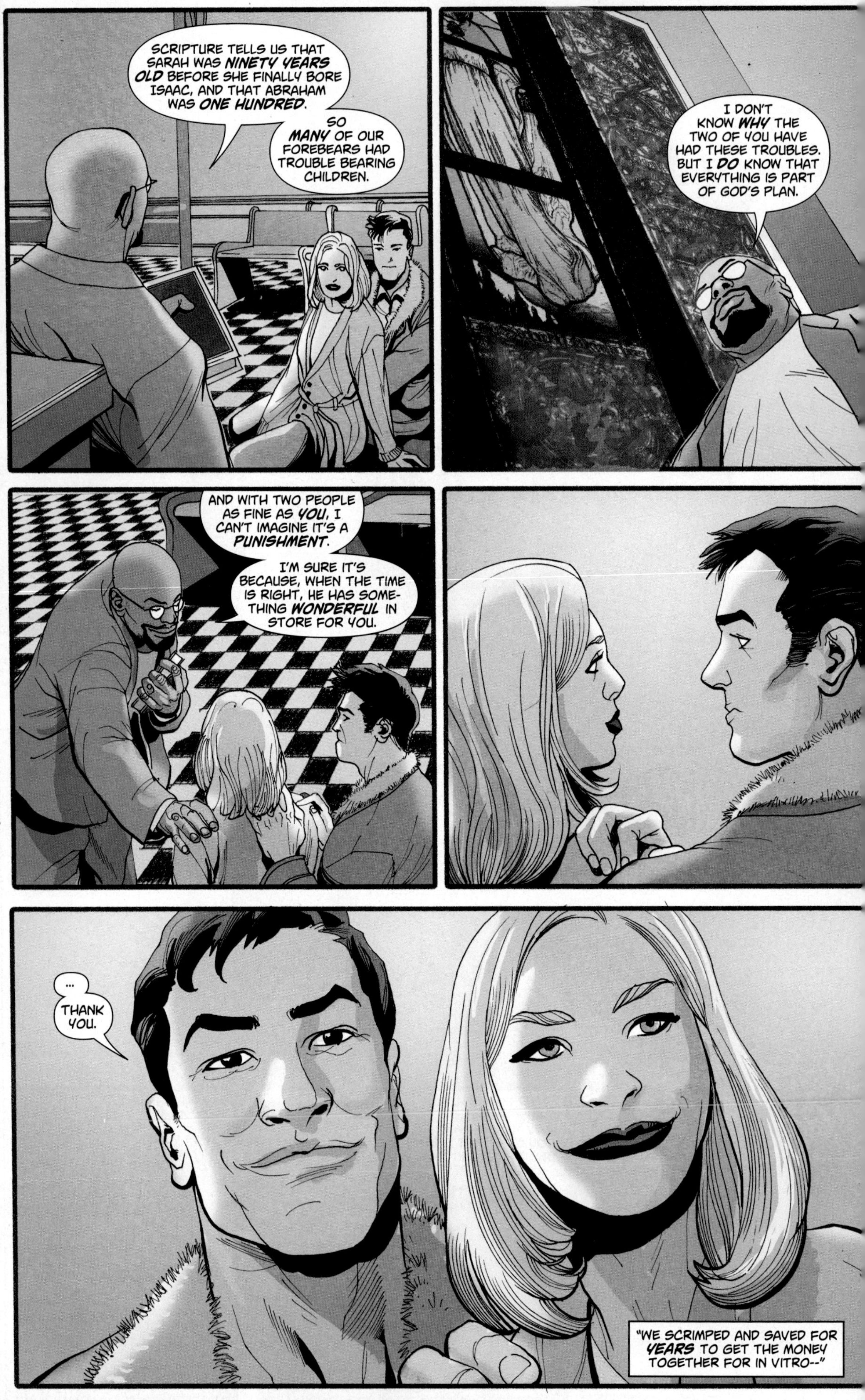
SCRIPTURE TELLS US THAT SARAH WAS NINETY YEARS OLD BEFORE SHE FINALLY BORE ISAAC, AND THAT ABRAHAM WAS ONE HUNDRED.
SO MANY OF OUR FOREBEARS HAD TROUBLE BEARING CHILDREN.
I DON'T KNOW WHY THE TWO OF YOU HAVE HAD THESE TROUBLES. BUT I DO KNOW THAT EVERYTHING IS PART OF GOD'S PLAN.
AND WITH TWO PEOPLE AS FINE AS YOU, I CAN'T IMAGINE IT'S A PUNISHMENT.
I'M SURE IT'S BECAUSE, WHEN THE TIME IS RIGHT, HE HAS SOMETHING WONDERFUL IN STORE FOR YOU.
... THANK YOU.
"WE SCRIMPED AND SAVED FOR YEARS TO GET THE MONEY TOGETHER FOR IN VITRO--"

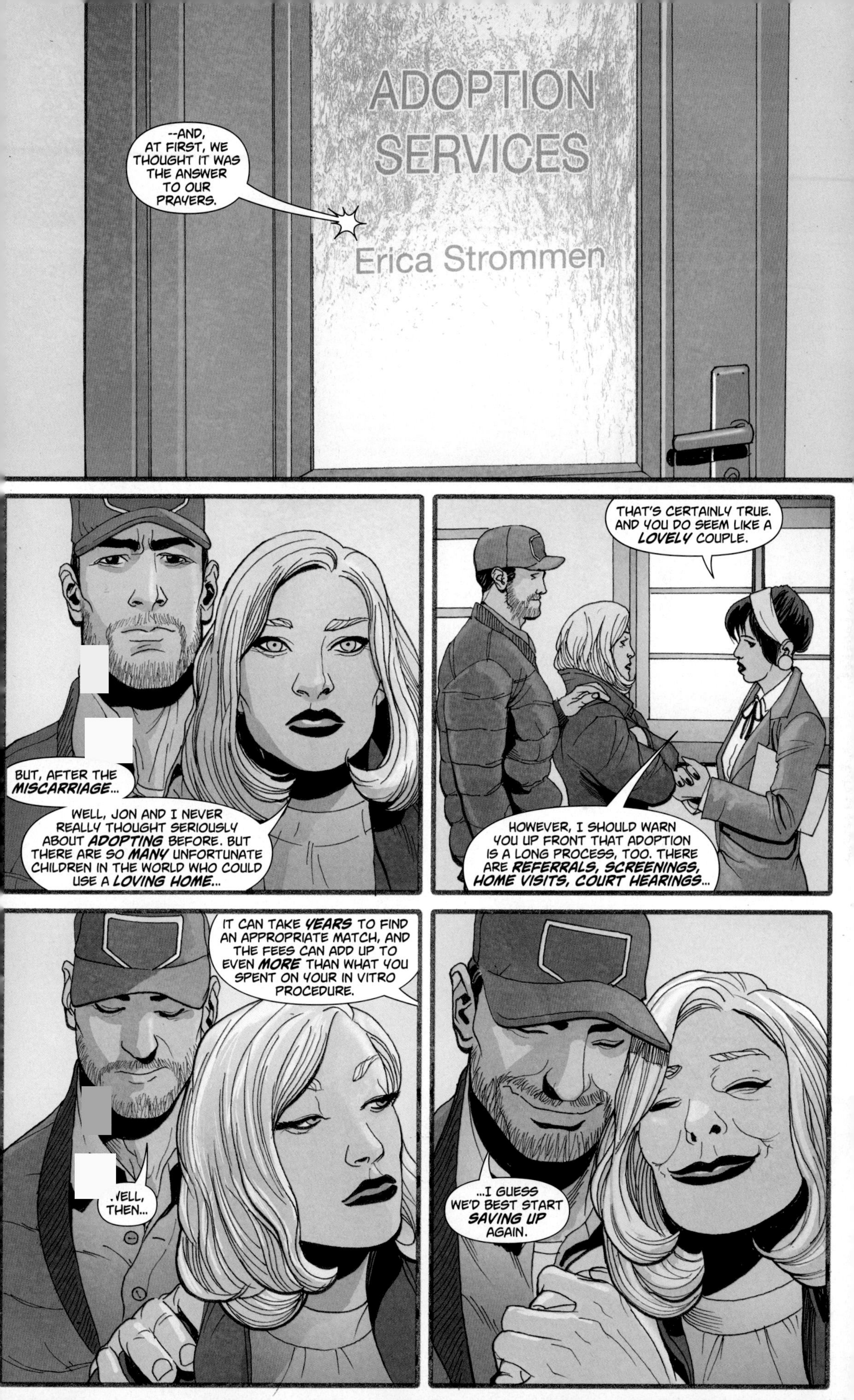
ADOPTION SERVICES
Erica Strommen
--AND, AT FIRST, WE THOUGHT IT WAS THE ANSWER TO OUR PRAYERS.
BUT, AFTER THE MISCARRIAGE...
WELL, JON AND I NEVER REALLY THOUGHT SERIOUSLY ABOUT ADOPTING BEFORE. BUT THERE ARE SO MANY UNFORTUNATE CHILDREN IN THE WORLD WHO COULD USE A LOVING HOME...
THAT'S CERTAINLY TRUE. AND YOU DO SEEM LIKE A LOVELY COUPLE.
HOWEVER, I SHOULD WARN YOU UP FRONT THAT ADOPTION IS A LONG PROCESS, TOO. THERE ARE REFERRALS, SCREENINGS, HOME VISITS, COURT HEARINGS...
IT CAN TAKE YEARS TO FIND AN APPROPRIATE MATCH, AND THE FEES CAN ADD UP TO EVEN MORE THAN WHAT YOU SPENT ON YOUR IN VITRO PROCEDURE.
WELL, THEN...
...I GUESS WE'D BEST START SAVING UP AGAIN.

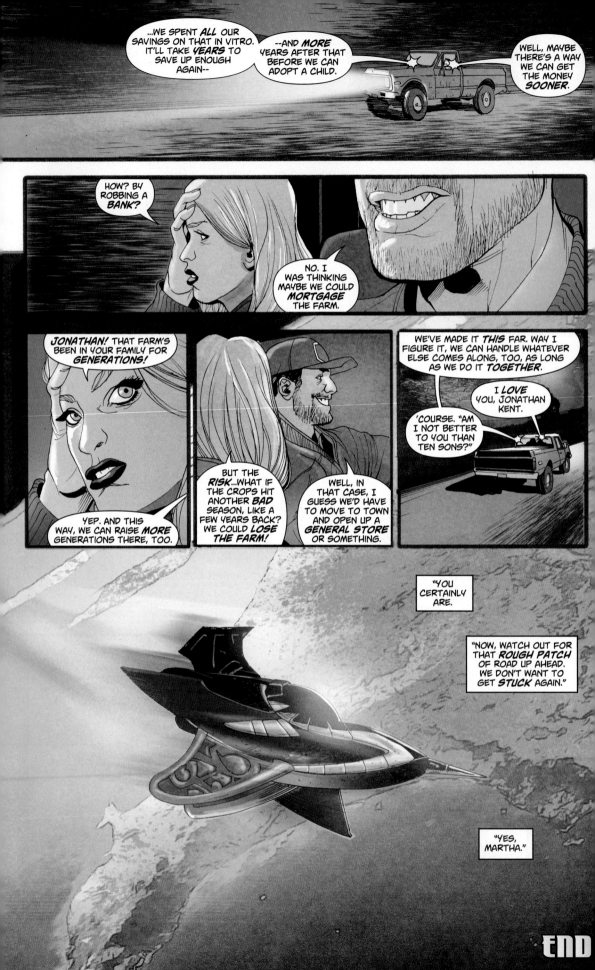

...WE SPENT **ALL** OUR SAVINGS ON THAT IN VITRO. IT'LL TAKE **YEARS** TO SAVE UP ENOUGH AGAIN--

--AND **MORE** YEARS AFTER THAT BEFORE WE CAN ADOPT A CHILD.

WELL, MAYBE THERE'S A WAY WE CAN GET THE MONEY **SOONER.**

HOW? BY ROBBING A BANK?

NO. I WAS THINKING MAYBE WE COULD **MORTGAGE** THE FARM.

JONATHAN! THAT FARM'S BEEN IN YOUR FAMILY FOR **GENERATIONS!**

YEP. AND THIS WAY, WE CAN RAISE **MORE** GENERATIONS THERE, TOO.

BUT THE **RISK**...WHAT IF THE CROPS HIT ANOTHER **BAD** SEASON, LIKE A FEW YEARS BACK? WE COULD **LOSE THE FARM!**

WELL, IN THAT CASE, I GUESS WE'D HAVE TO MOVE TO TOWN AND OPEN UP A **GENERAL STORE** OR SOMETHING.

WE'VE MADE IT **THIS** FAR. WAY I FIGURE IT, WE CAN HANDLE WHATEVER ELSE COMES ALONG, TOO, AS LONG AS WE DO IT **TOGETHER.**

I **LOVE** YOU, JONATHAN KENT.

'COURSE. "AM I NOT BETTER TO YOU THAN TEN SONS?"

"YOU CERTAINLY ARE.

"NOW, WATCH OUT FOR THAT **ROUGH PATCH** OF ROAD UP AHEAD. WE DON'T WANT TO GET **STUCK** AGAIN."

"YES, MARTHA."

END

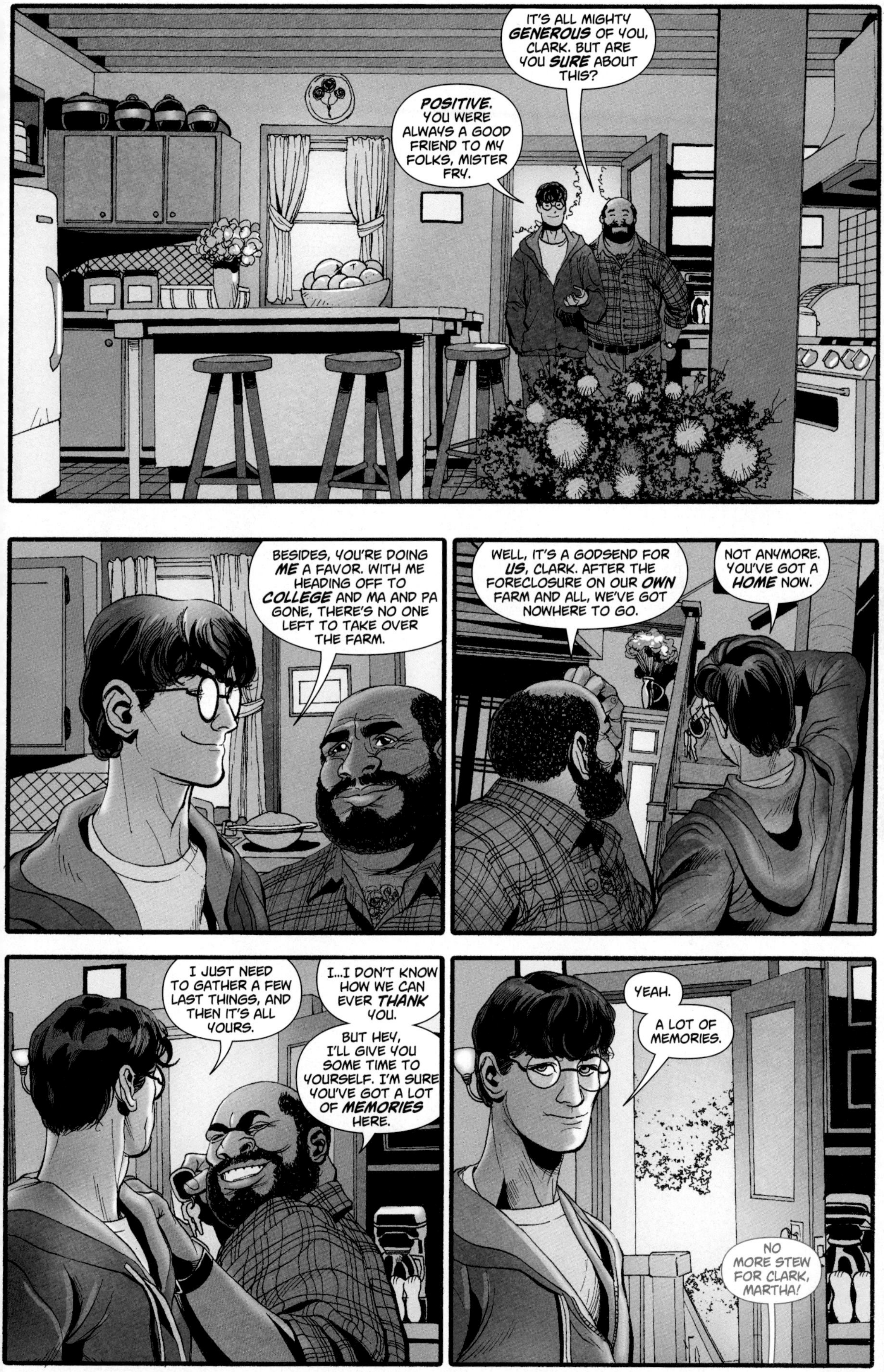
IT'S ALL MIGHTY GENEROUS OF YOU, CLARK. BUT ARE YOU SURE ABOUT THIS?
POSITIVE. YOU WERE ALWAYS A GOOD FRIEND TO MY FOLKS, MISTER FRY.
BESIDES, YOU'RE DOING ME A FAVOR. WITH ME HEADING OFF TO COLLEGE AND MA AND PA GONE, THERE'S NO ONE LEFT TO TAKE OVER THE FARM.
WELL, IT'S A GODSEND FOR US, CLARK. AFTER THE FORECLOSURE ON OUR OWN FARM AND ALL, WE'VE GOT NOWHERE TO GO.
NOT ANYMORE. YOU'VE GOT A HOME NOW.
I JUST NEED TO GATHER A FEW LAST THINGS, AND THEN IT'S ALL YOURS.
I...I DON'T KNOW HOW WE CAN EVER THANK YOU.
BUT HEY, I'LL GIVE YOU SOME TIME TO YOURSELF. I'M SURE YOU'VE GOT A LOT OF MEMORIES HERE.
YEAH.
A LOT OF MEMORIES.
NO MORE STEW FOR CLARK, MARTHA!

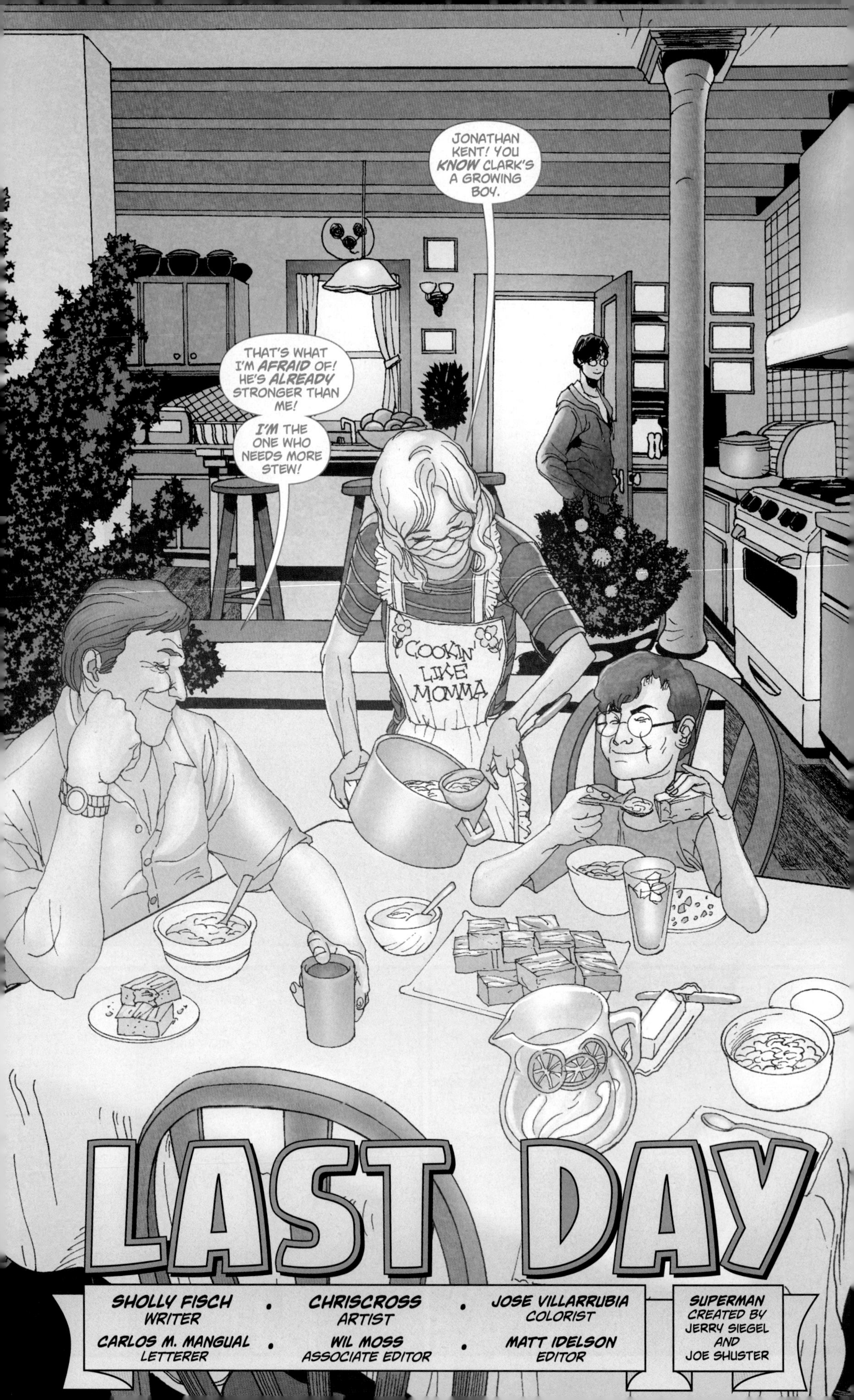
JONATHAN KENT! YOU KNOW CLARK'S A GROWING BOY.
THAT'S WHAT I'M AFRAID OF! HE'S ALREADY STRONGER THAN ME!
I'M THE ONE WHO NEEDS MORE STEW!
COOKIN' LIKE MOMMA
LAST DAY
SHOLLY FISCH WRITER • CHRISCROSS ARTIST • JOSE VILLARRUBIA COLORIST
CARLOS M. MANGUAL LETTERER • WIL MOSS ASSOCIATE EDITOR • MATT IDELSON EDITOR
SUPERMAN CREATED BY JERRY SIEGEL AND JOE SHUSTER

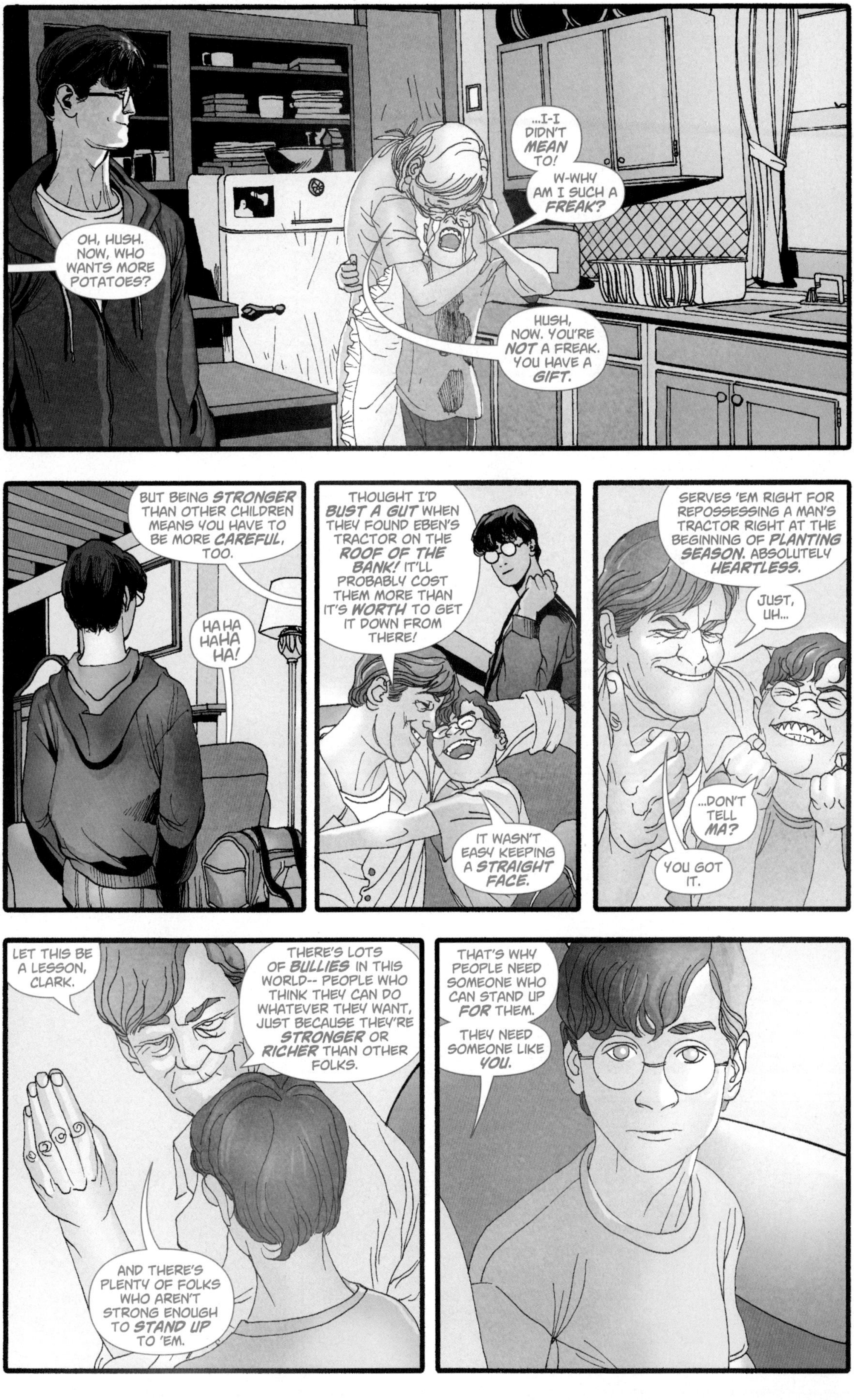
...I-I DIDN'T MEAN TO!
W-WHY AM I SUCH A FREAK?
OH, HUSH. NOW, WHO WANTS MORE POTATOES?
HUSH, NOW. YOU'RE NOT A FREAK. YOU HAVE A GIFT.
BUT BEING STRONGER THAN OTHER CHILDREN MEANS YOU HAVE TO BE MORE CAREFUL, TOO.
HA HA HAHA HA!
THOUGHT I'D BUST A GUT WHEN THEY FOUND EBEN'S TRACTOR ON THE ROOF OF THE BANK! IT'LL PROBABLY COST THEM MORE THAN IT'S WORTH TO GET IT DOWN FROM THERE!
IT WASN'T EASY KEEPING A STRAIGHT FACE.
SERVES 'EM RIGHT FOR REPOSSESSING A MAN'S TRACTOR RIGHT AT THE BEGINNING OF PLANTING SEASON. ABSOLUTELY HEARTLESS.
JUST, UH...
...DON'T TELL MA?
YOU GOT IT.
LET THIS BE A LESSON, CLARK.
THERE'S LOTS OF BULLIES IN THIS WORLD-- PEOPLE WHO THINK THEY CAN DO WHATEVER THEY WANT, JUST BECAUSE THEY'RE STRONGER OR RICHER THAN OTHER FOLKS.
AND THERE'S PLENTY OF FOLKS WHO AREN'T STRONG ENOUGH TO STAND UP TO 'EM.
THAT'S WHY PEOPLE NEED SOMEONE WHO CAN STAND UP FOR THEM.
THEY NEED SOMEONE LIKE YOU.

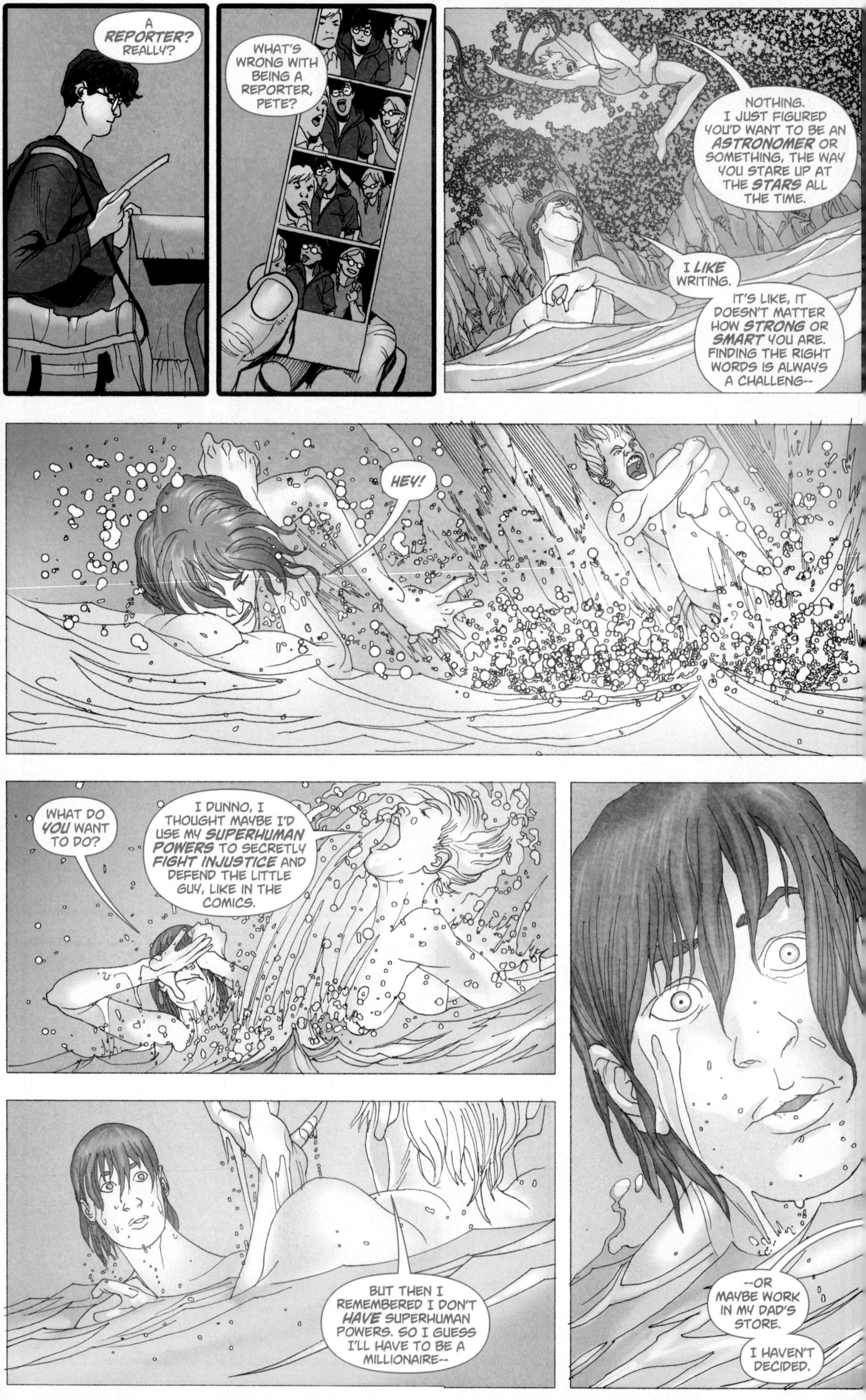
A REPORTER? REALLY?
WHAT'S WRONG WITH BEING A REPORTER, PETE?
NOTHING. I JUST FIGURED YOU'D WANT TO BE AN ASTRONOMER OR SOMETHING, THE WAY YOU STARE UP AT THE STARS ALL THE TIME.
I LIKE WRITING.
IT'S LIKE, IT DOESN'T MATTER HOW STRONG OR SMART YOU ARE. FINDING THE RIGHT WORDS IS ALWAYS A CHALLENG--
HEY!
WHAT DO YOU WANT TO DO?
I DUNNO, I THOUGHT MAYBE I'D USE MY SUPERHUMAN POWERS TO SECRETLY FIGHT INJUSTICE AND DEFEND THE LITTLE GUY, LIKE IN THE COMICS.
BUT THEN I REMEMBERED I DON'T HAVE SUPERHUMAN POWERS. SO I GUESS I'LL HAVE TO BE A MILLIONAIRE--
--OR MAYBE WORK IN MY DAD'S STORE.
I HAVEN'T DECIDED.

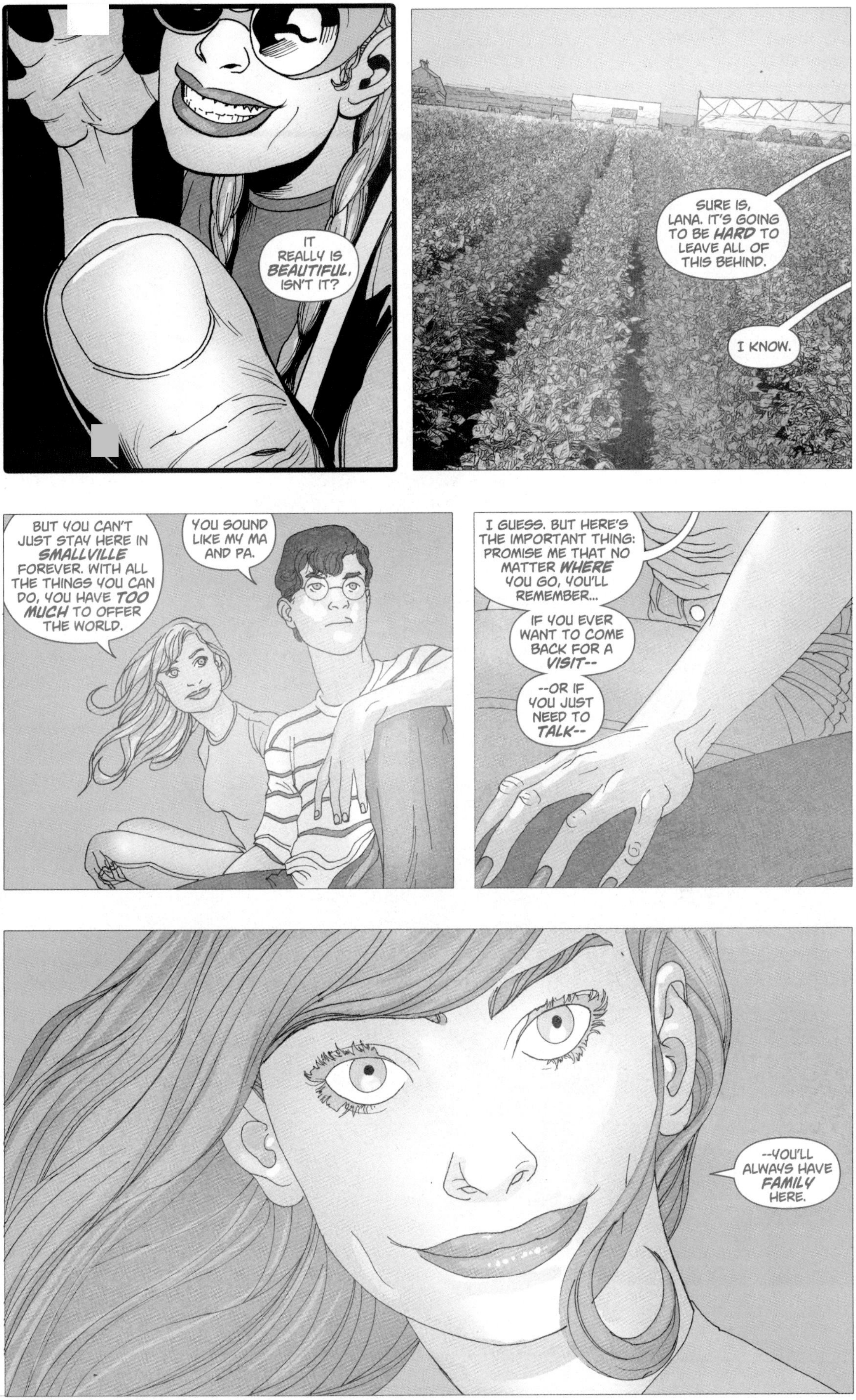
IT REALLY IS BEAUTIFUL, ISN'T IT?
SURE IS, LANA. IT'S GOING TO BE HARD TO LEAVE ALL OF THIS BEHIND.
I KNOW.
BUT YOU CAN'T JUST STAY HERE IN SMALLVILLE FOREVER. WITH ALL THE THINGS YOU CAN DO, YOU HAVE TOO MUCH TO OFFER THE WORLD.
YOU SOUND LIKE MY MA AND PA.
I GUESS. BUT HERE'S THE IMPORTANT THING: PROMISE ME THAT NO MATTER WHERE YOU GO, YOU'LL REMEMBER...
IF YOU EVER WANT TO COME BACK FOR A VISIT--
--OR IF YOU JUST NEED TO TALK--
--YOU'LL ALWAYS HAVE FAMILY HERE.

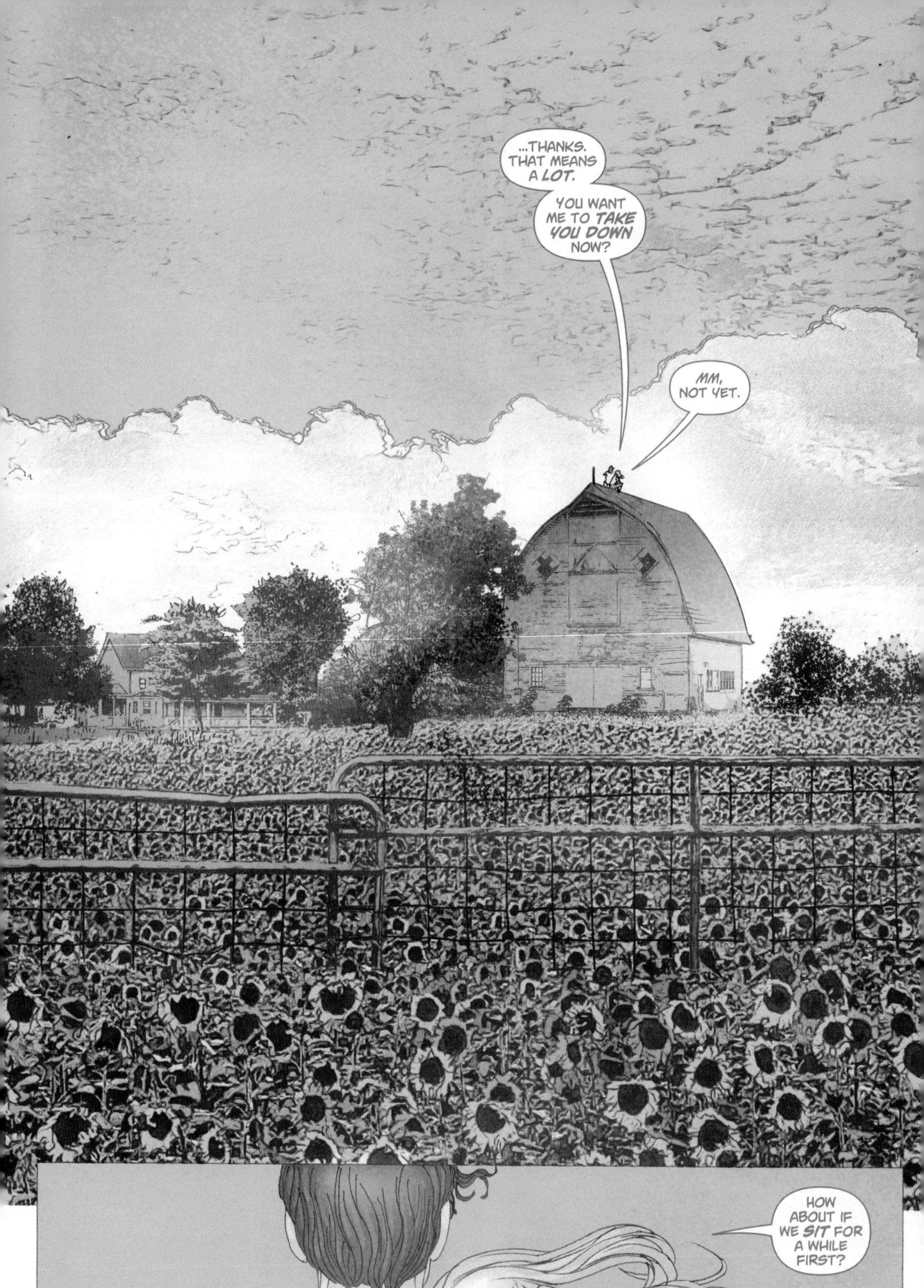
...THANKS. THAT MEANS A *LOT*.
YOU WANT ME TO *TAKE YOU DOWN* NOW?
MM, NOT YET.

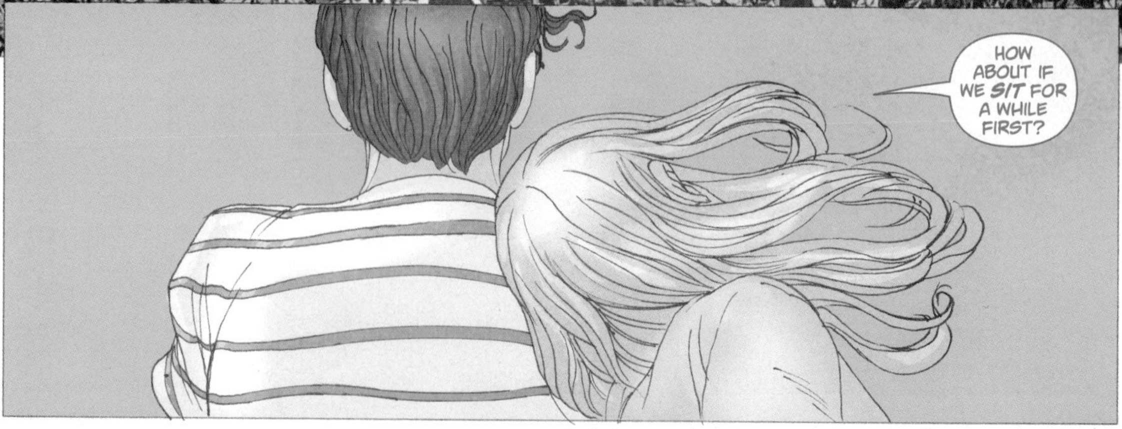
HOW ABOUT IF WE *SIT* FOR A WHILE FIRST?

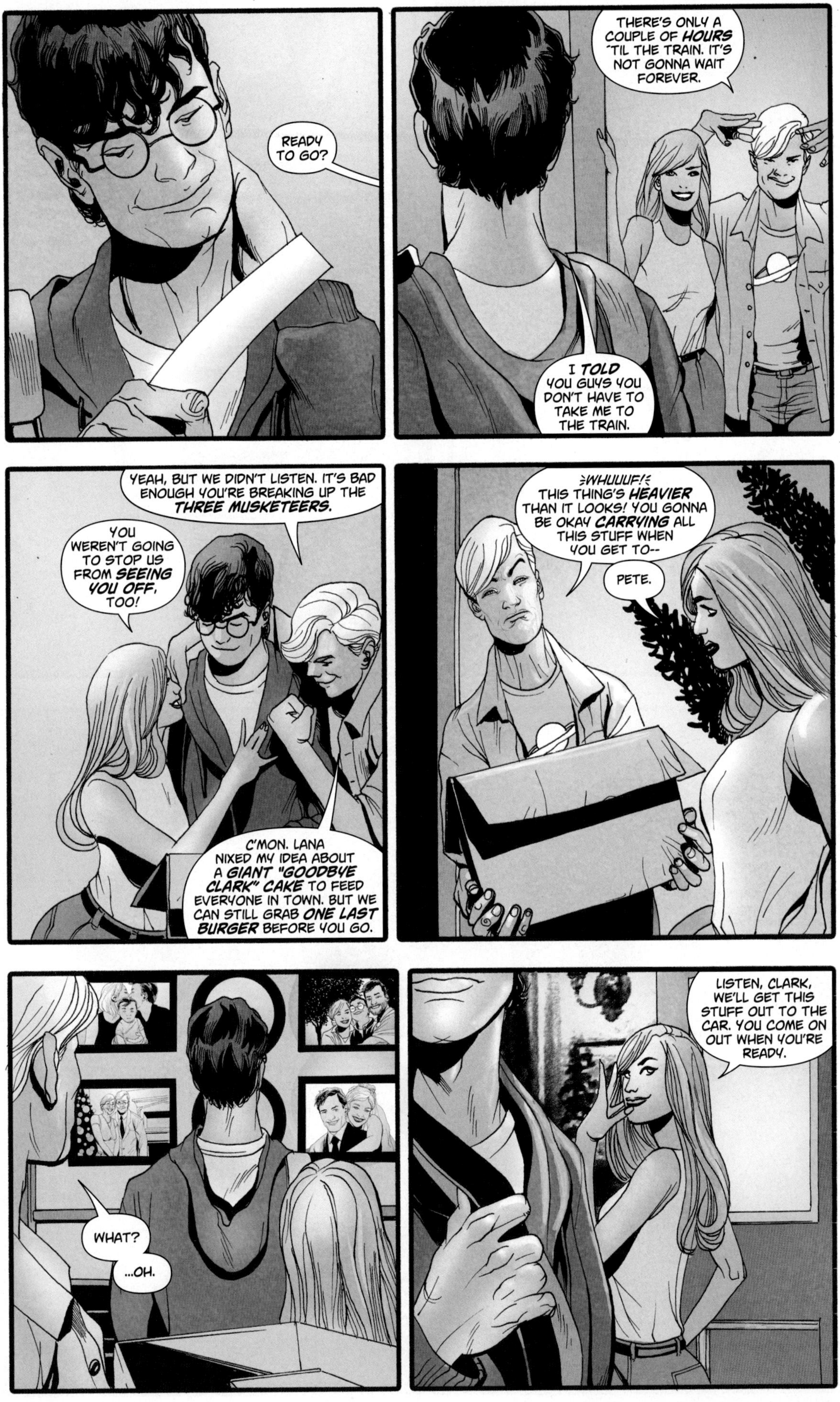
READY TO GO?
THERE'S ONLY A COUPLE OF HOURS 'TIL THE TRAIN. IT'S NOT GONNA WAIT FOREVER.
I TOLD YOU GUYS YOU DON'T HAVE TO TAKE ME TO THE TRAIN.
YEAH, BUT WE DIDN'T LISTEN. IT'S BAD ENOUGH YOU'RE BREAKING UP THE THREE MUSKETEERS.
YOU WEREN'T GOING TO STOP US FROM SEEING YOU OFF, TOO!
C'MON. LANA NIXED MY IDEA ABOUT A GIANT "GOODBYE CLARK" CAKE TO FEED EVERYONE IN TOWN. BUT WE CAN STILL GRAB ONE LAST BURGER BEFORE YOU GO.
≠WHUUUF!≠ THIS THING'S HEAVIER THAN IT LOOKS! YOU GONNA BE OKAY CARRYING ALL THIS STUFF WHEN YOU GET TO--
PETE.
WHAT?
...OH.
LISTEN, CLARK, WE'LL GET THIS STUFF OUT TO THE CAR. YOU COME ON OUT WHEN YOU'RE READY.

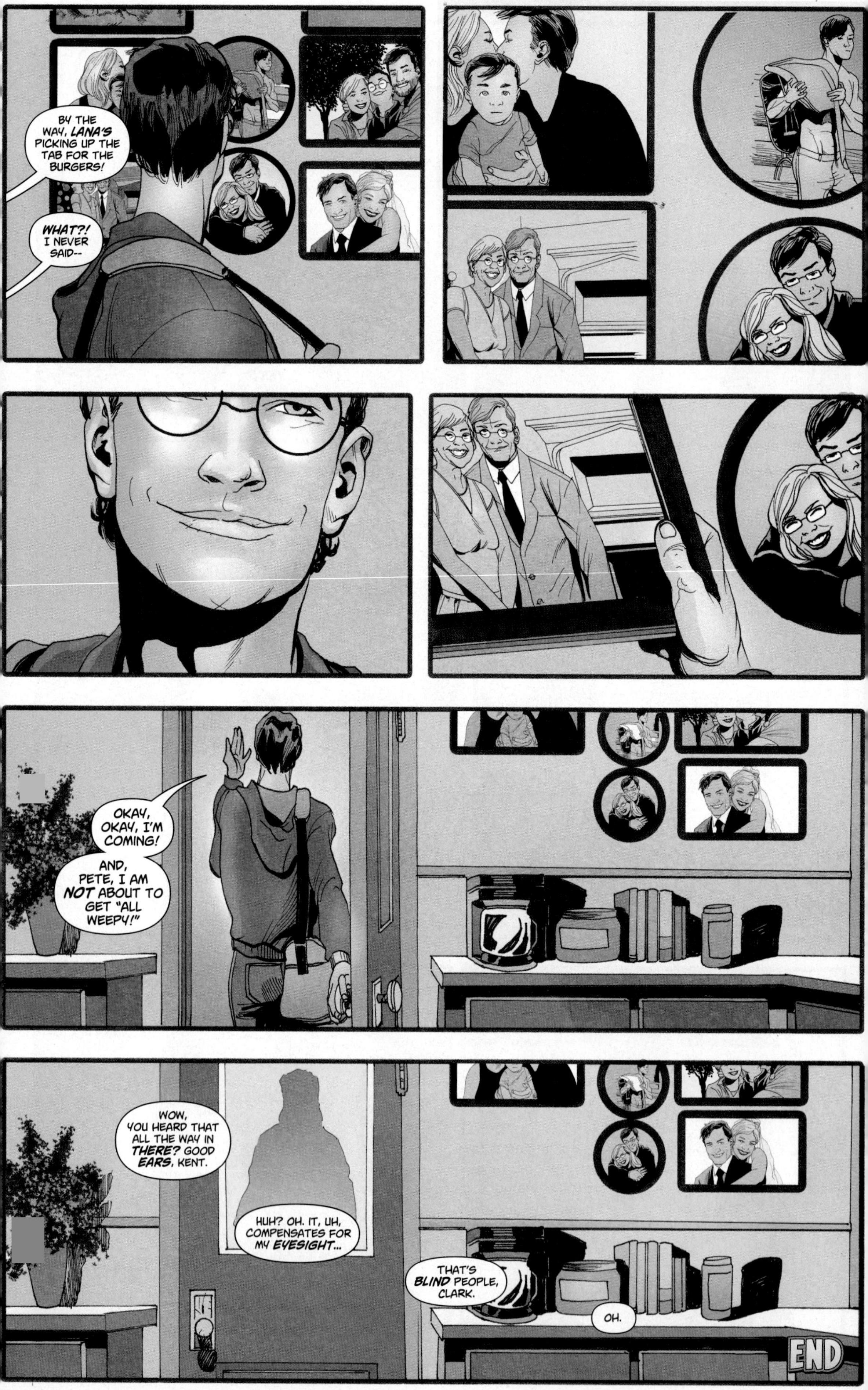
BY THE WAY, LANA'S PICKING UP THE TAB FOR THE BURGERS!
WHAT?! I NEVER SAID--
OKAY, OKAY, I'M COMING!
AND, PETE, I AM NOT ABOUT TO GET "ALL WEEPY!"
WOW, YOU HEARD THAT ALL THE WAY IN THERE? GOOD EARS, KENT.
HUH? OH. IT, UH, COMPENSATES FOR MY EYESIGHT...
THAT'S BLIND PEOPLE, CLARK.
OH.
END

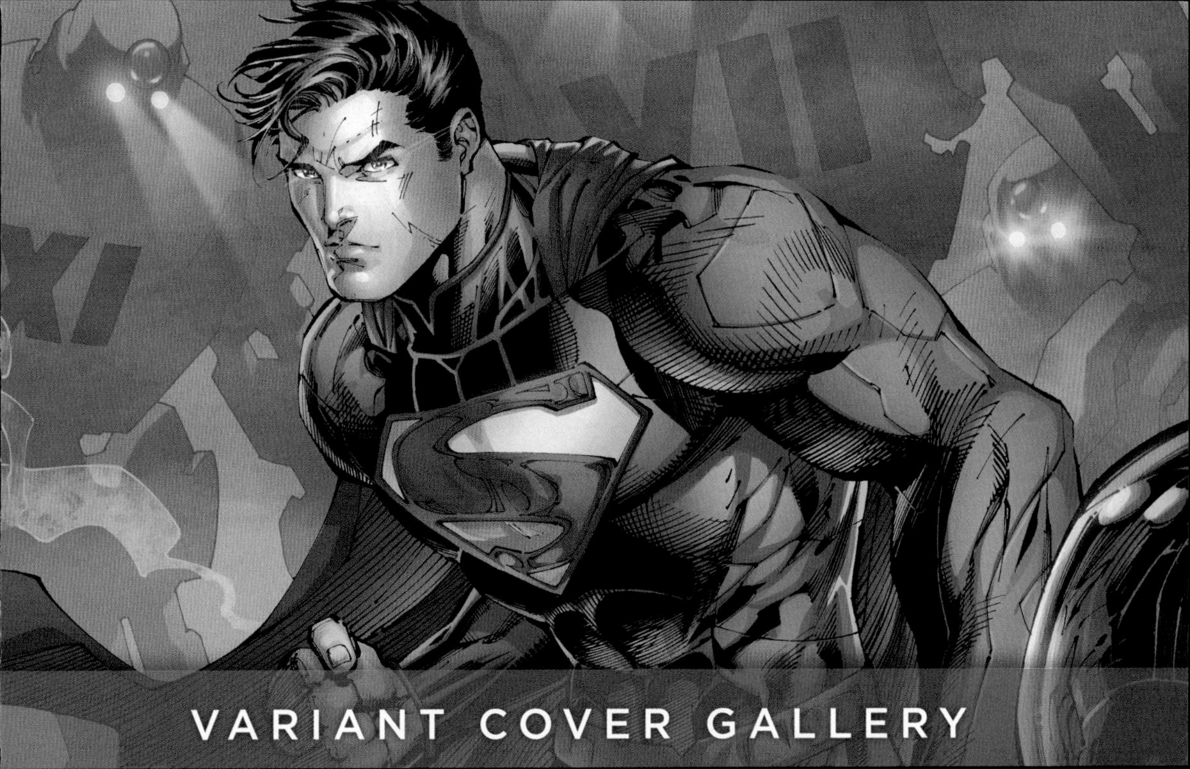

VARIANT COVER GALLERY

ACTION COMICS (promotional image)
by Rags Morales & Guy Major

ACTION COMICS 1

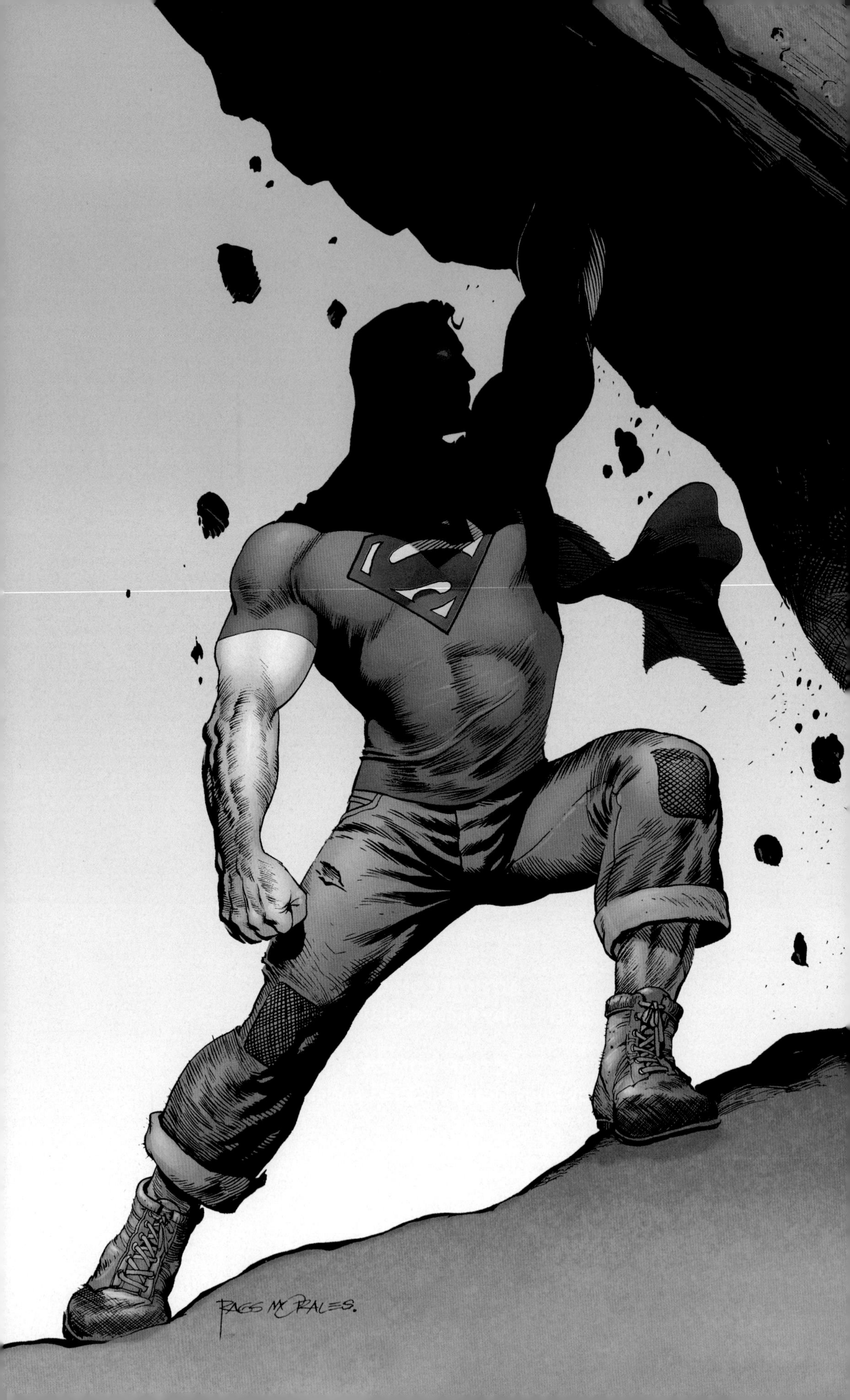
RAGS MORALES.

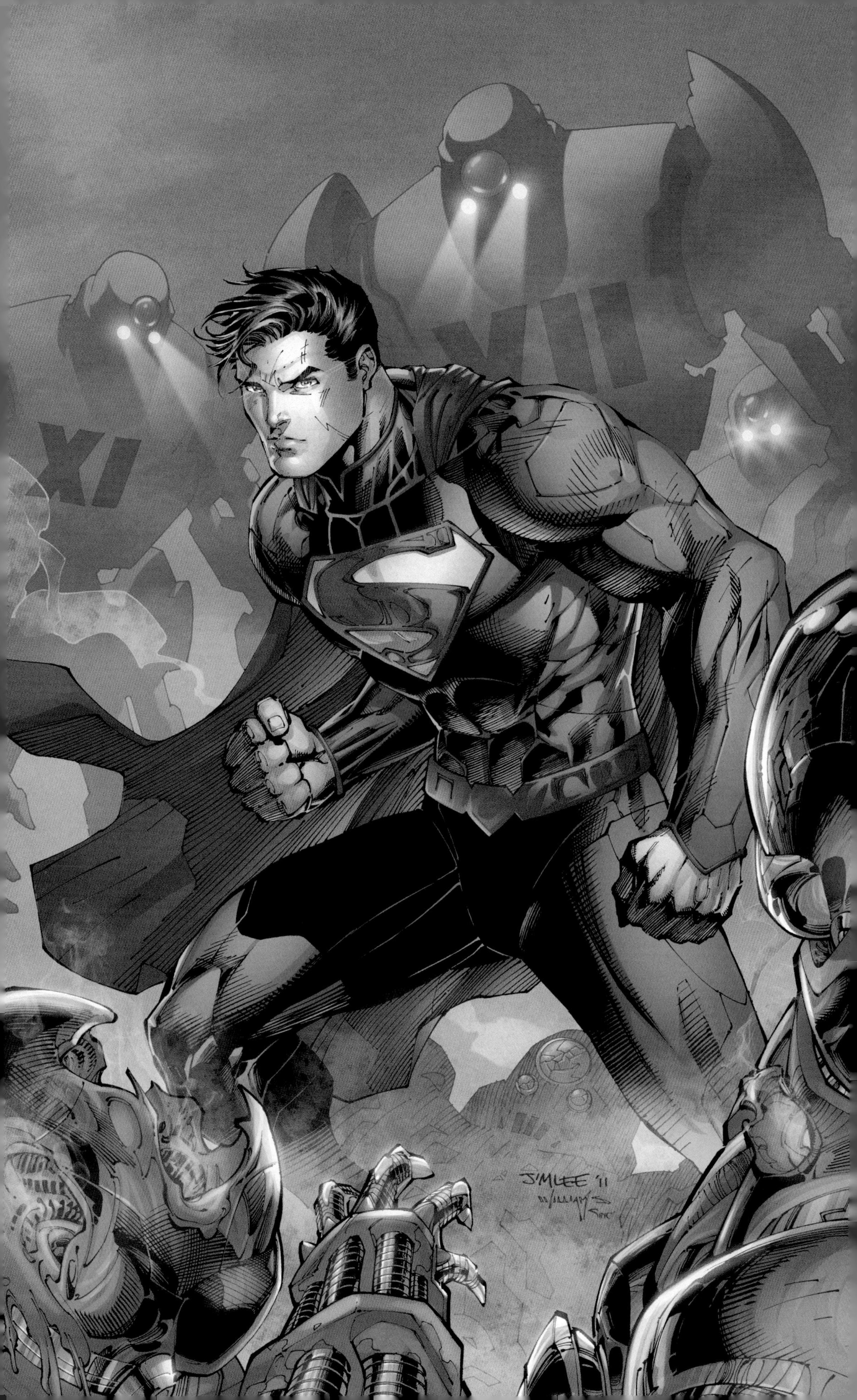

XI
VII

PENCILLER ACTION #1 COVER INKER PAGE#
TITLE ISSUE # MONTH INTERIORS

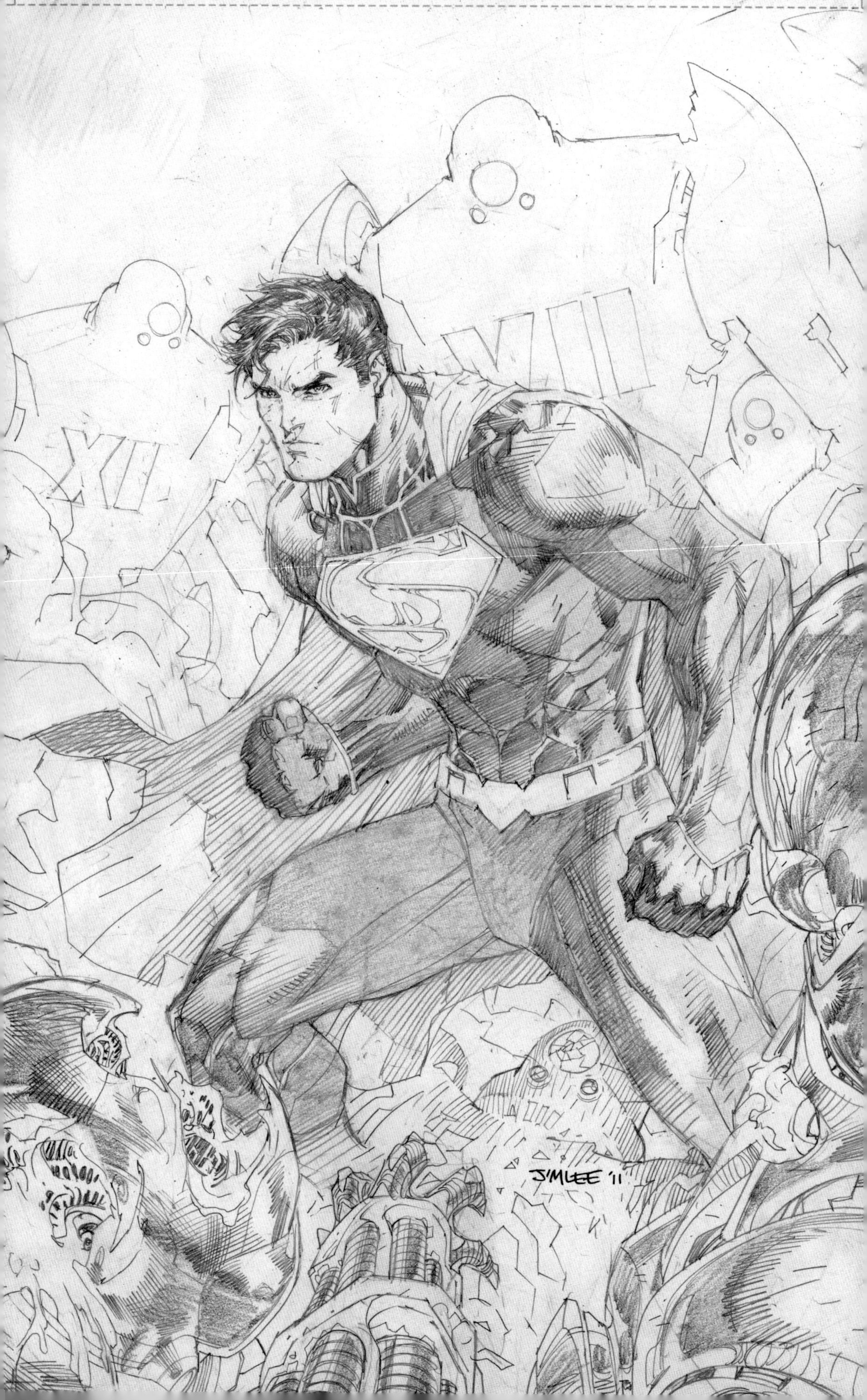

JIMLEE '11

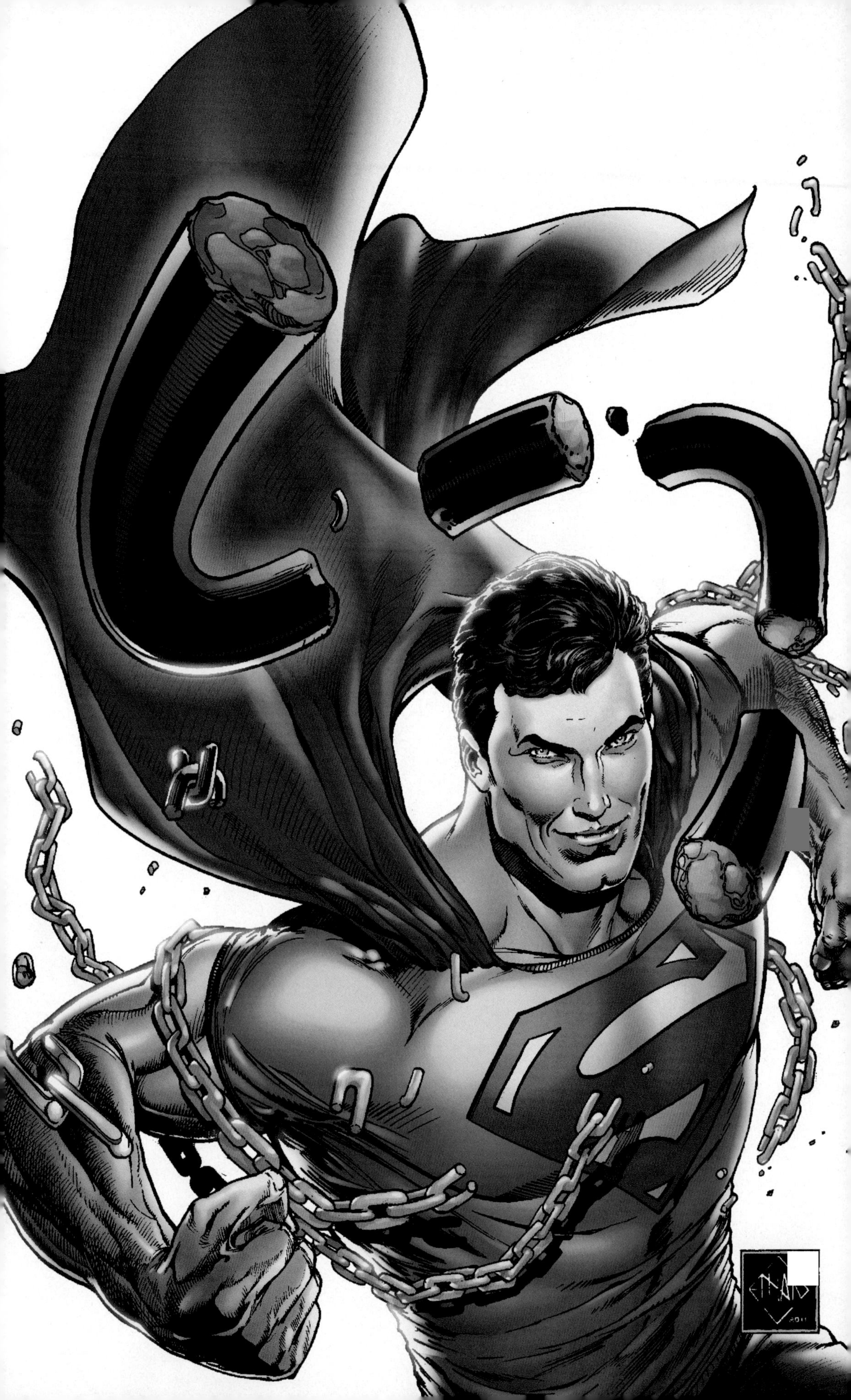

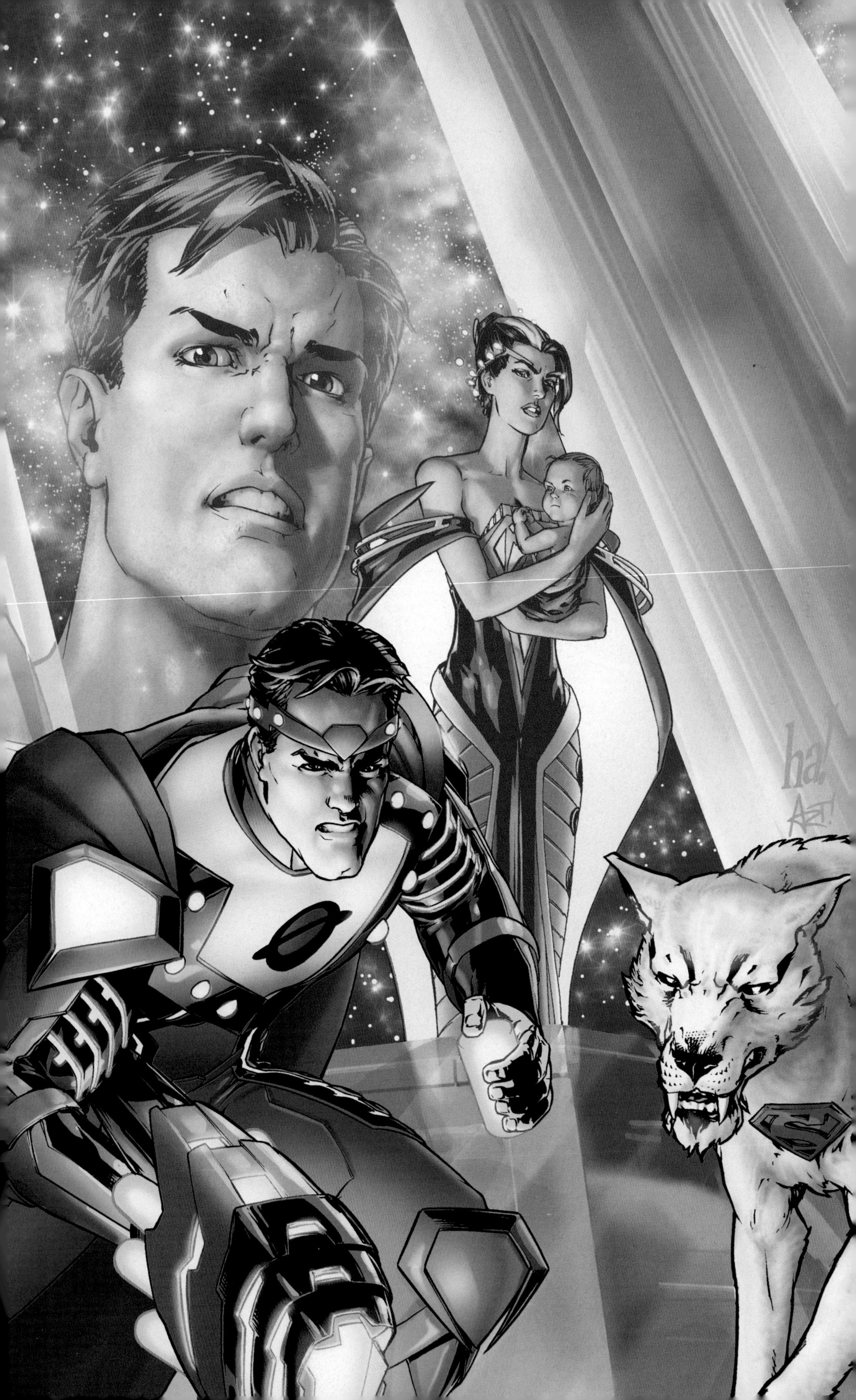

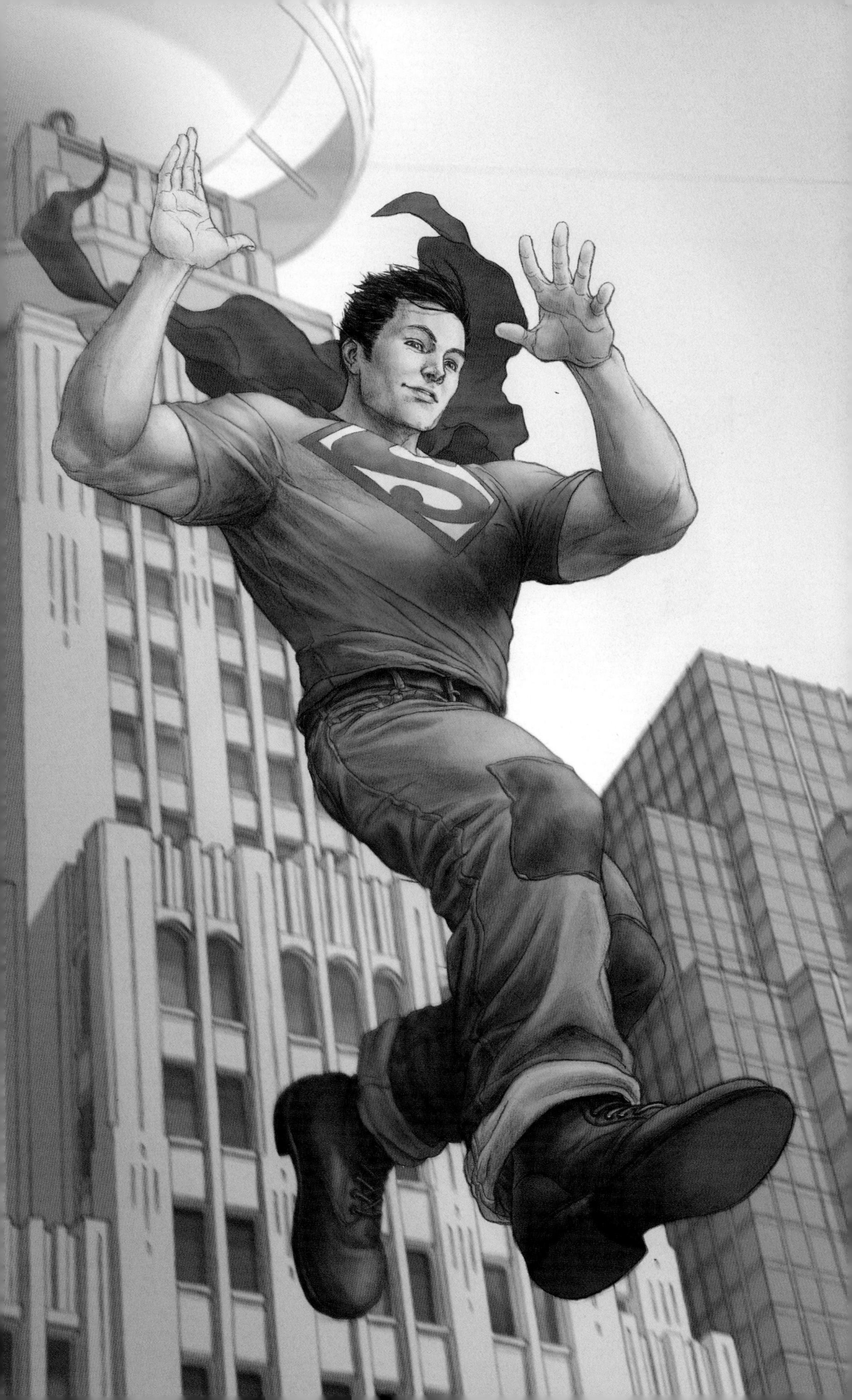

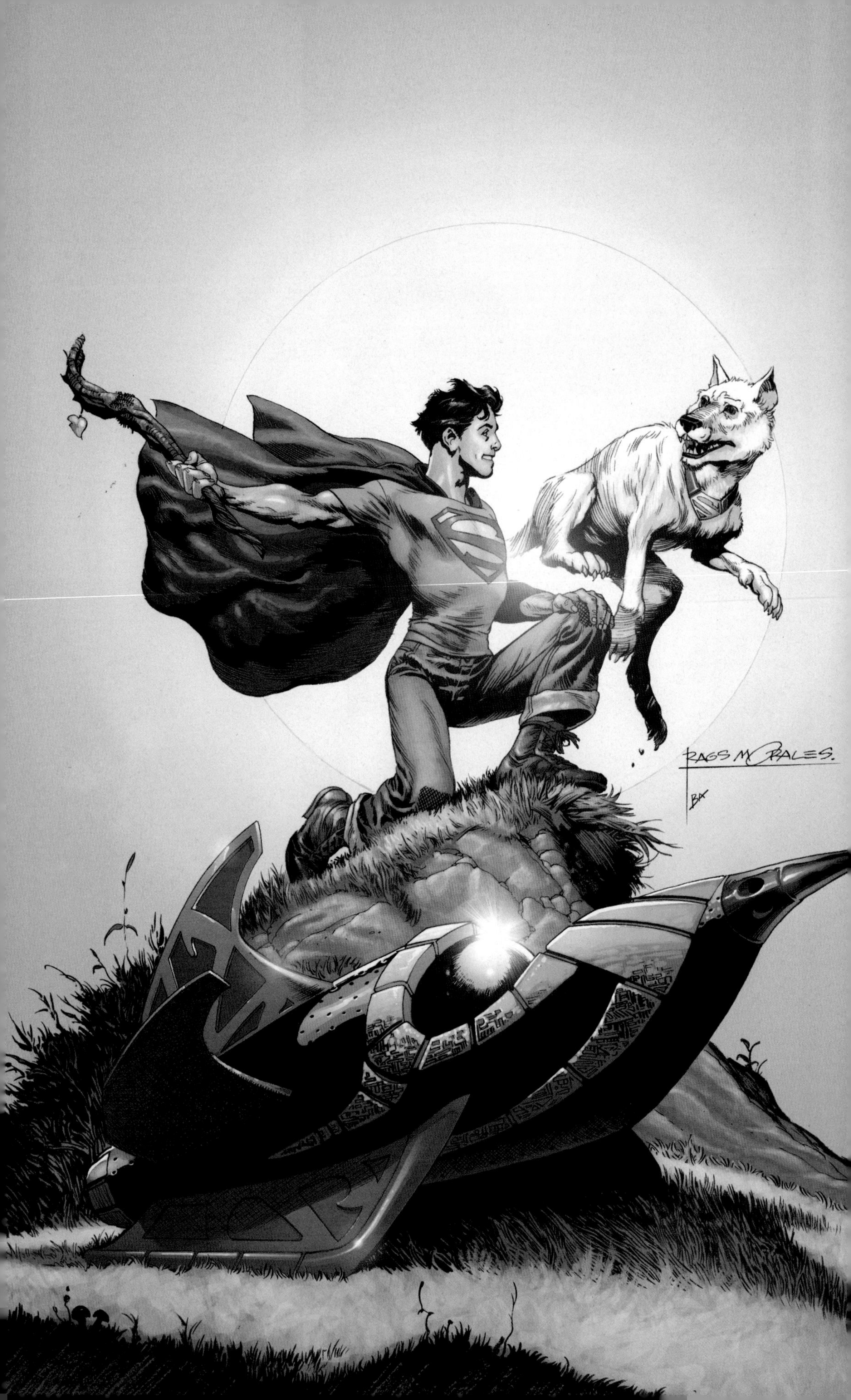
RAGS MORALES.
BIX

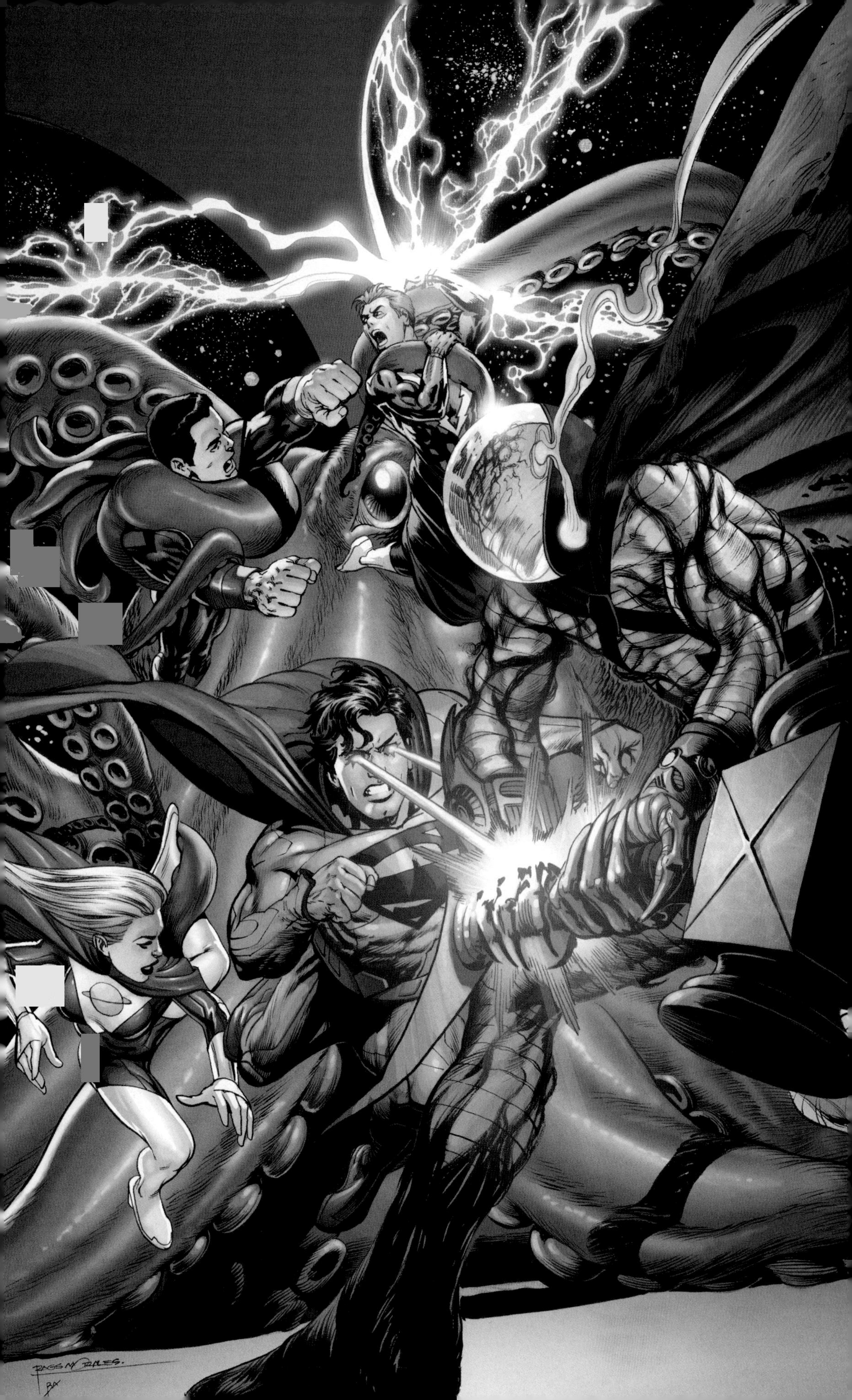

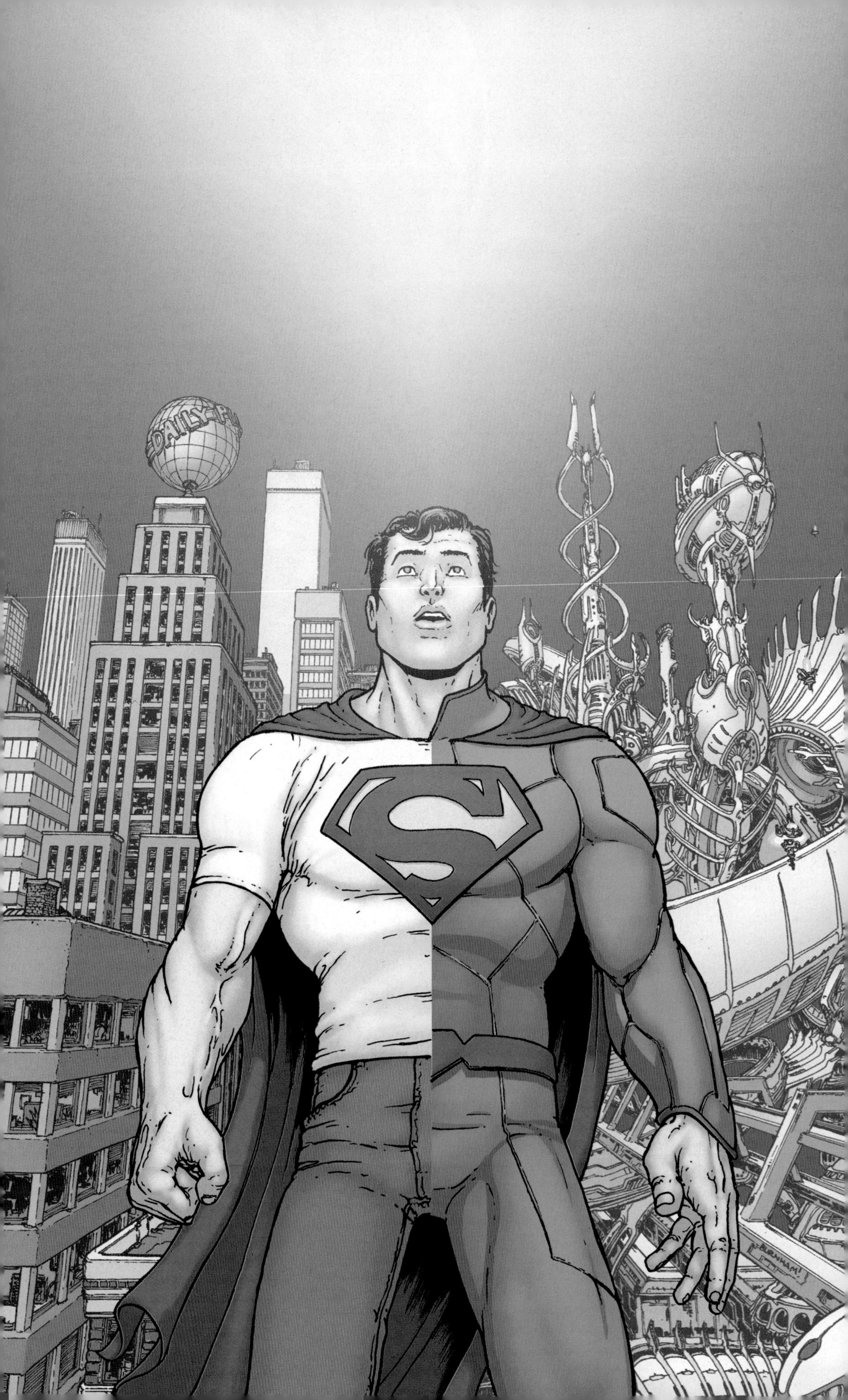

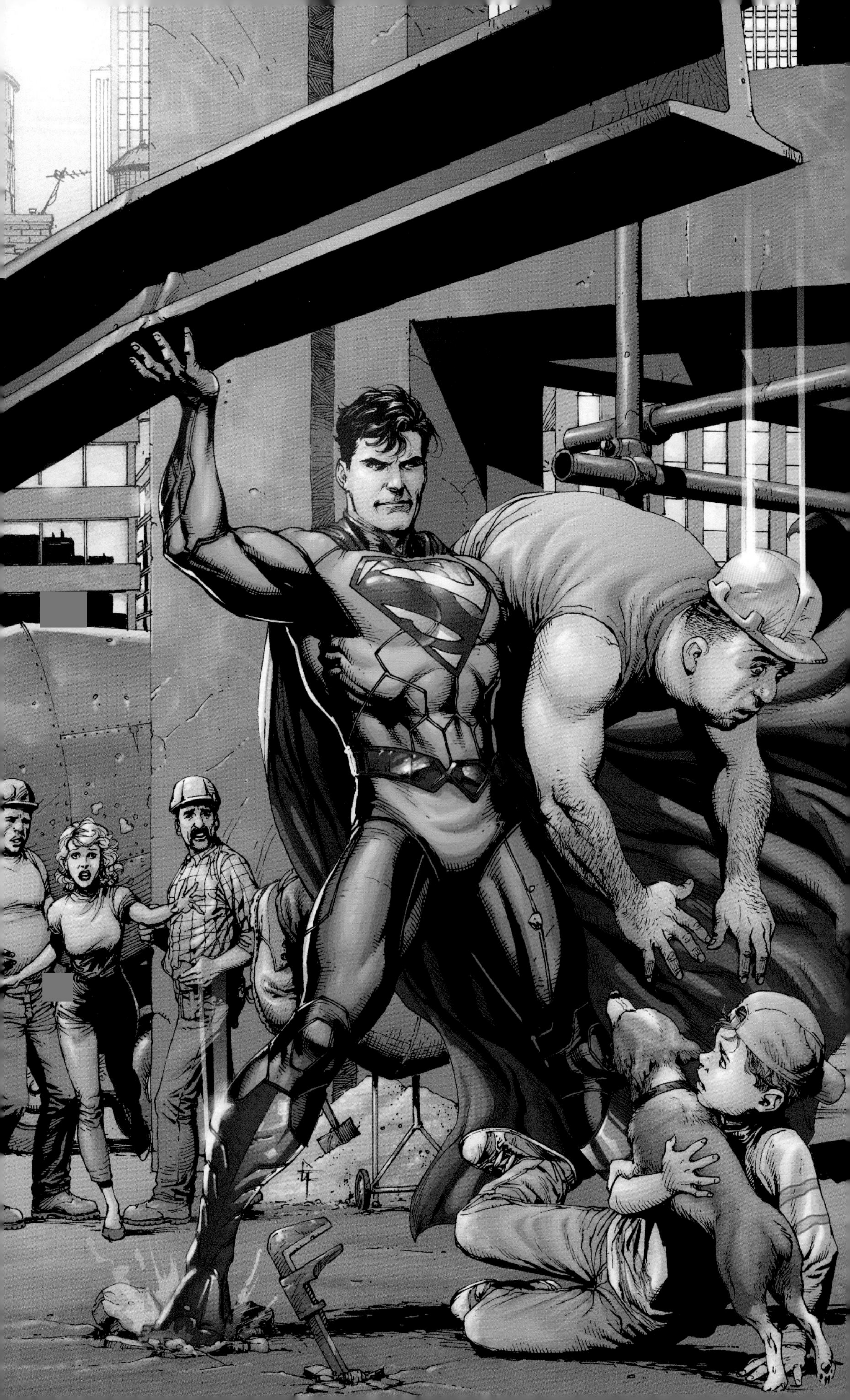

GET AN EXCLUSIVE PEEK BEHIND THE SCENES OF THE CREATION OF ACTION COMICS #1-2 WITH GRANT MORRISON AND RAGS MORALES

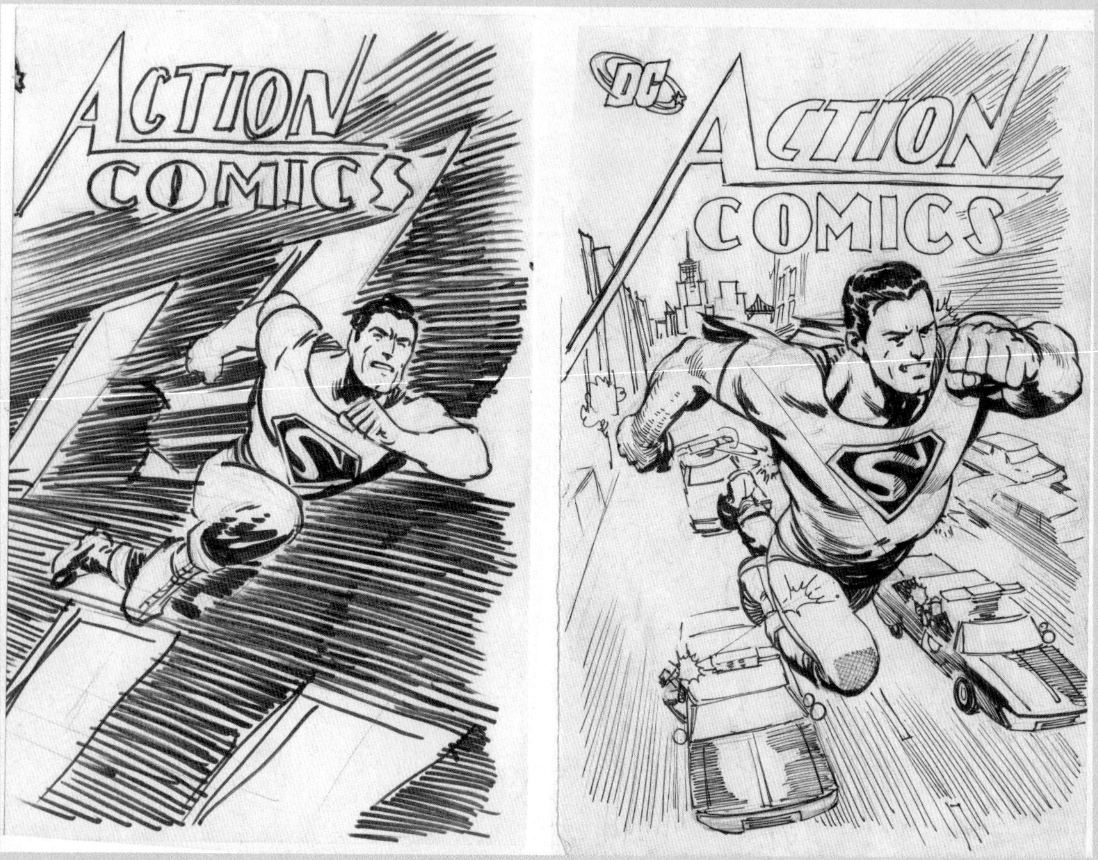
ACTION
COMICS
DC
ACTION
COMICS

Rags Morales' cover sketches for ACTION COMICS #1.

ACTION!

GRANT MORRISON: The physical things Superman does came from the first year of ACTION COMICS, where they were doing this nonstop, kinetic, muscular action. I wanted to get that into the actual form and structure of this whole run, that feeling of motion and action. It's called ACTION COMICS — let's do that!

RAGS MORALES: For the first twenty years, flying with that pose I gave him on the first cover — the one bent leg and the one straight leg, and counterbalancing with the arms — was the Superman trademark, and it made him look like he was running. Here I am trying to do an homage to it. It brought it back to the essence of that character.

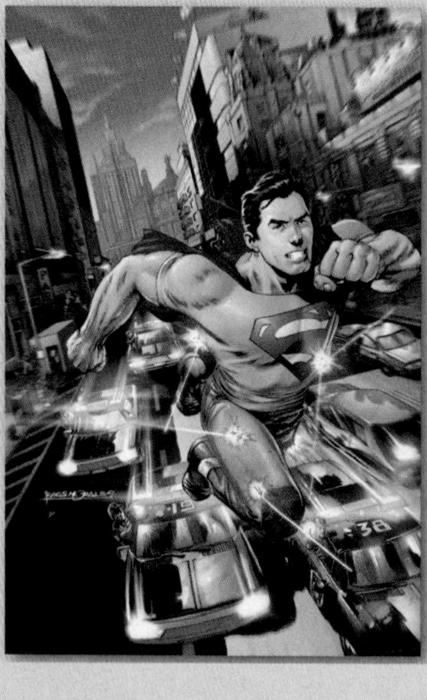

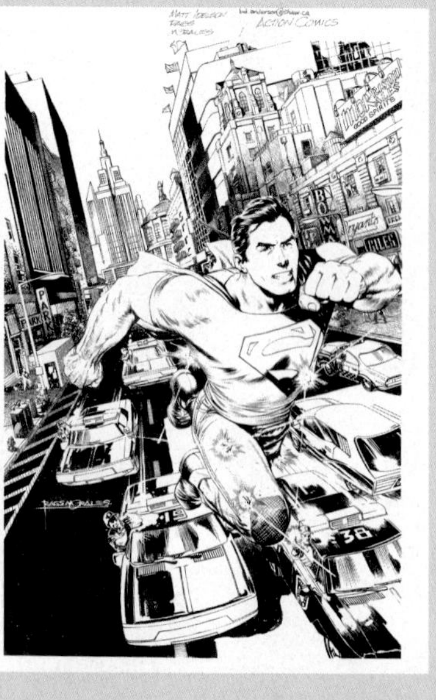

THE LITTLE MAN

MORRISON: I was thinking of the dwarf from *Twin Peaks* — a gnome-like figure, a creepy little elf.

MORALES: I relied more on the Robert Blake character from *Lost Highway*. Somehow he ended up looking a little bit like Elvis Costello, too... [Laughs]

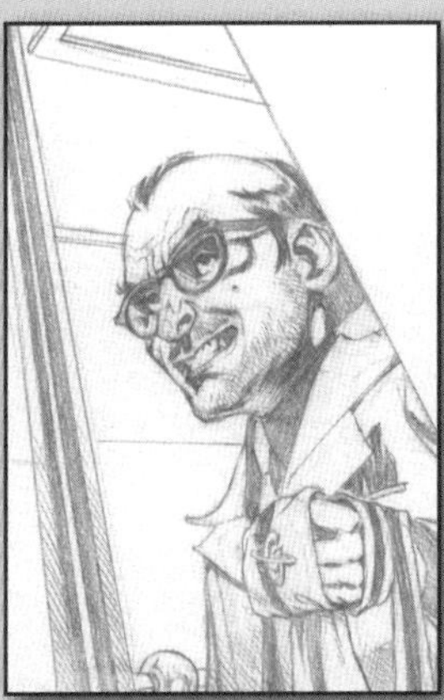

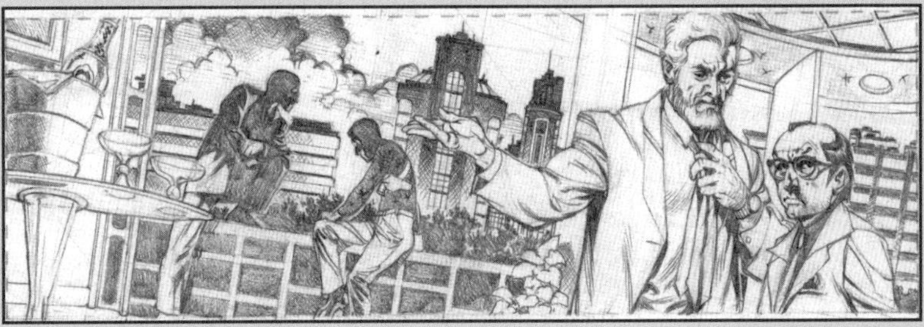

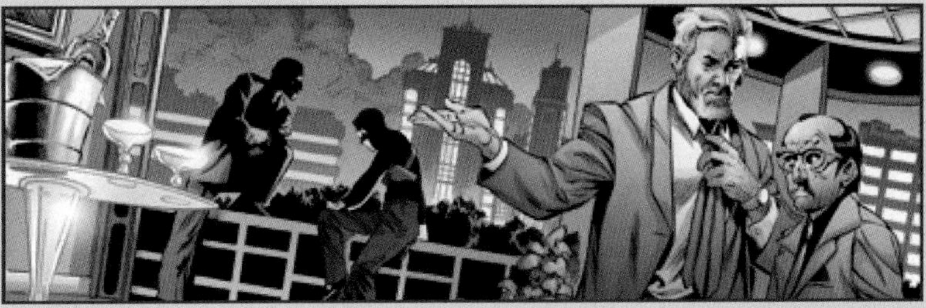

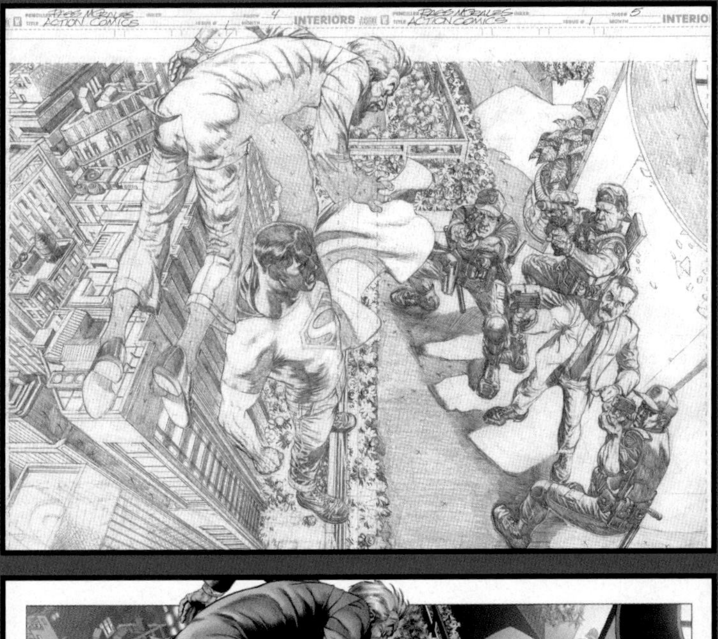

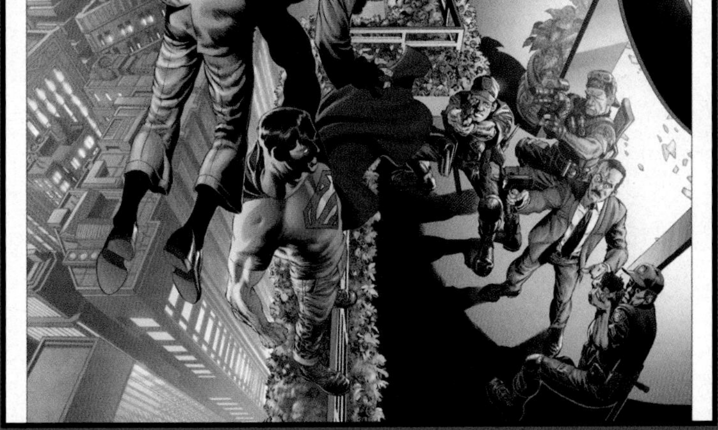

A WHOLE NEW SUPERMAN

MORRISON: Like a guitarist in a band of 17-year-olds, experience doesn't even come into it — he just does it. He's a super hero — he doesn't have to think. He's a kid who's been set free from Ma and Pa Kent. Both of them are dead, and suddenly he thinks, "I'm the most powerful thing on the planet. It's time to start cleaning up!" [Laughs] It seemed like you could get a really good story out of a young man who's not considering what he's doing — he's just doing it because it feels right.

MORALES: Honestly, I could never really get into Superman before. I even had a hard time drawing him, because he'd been done so many times by so many people. I'm glad we're going back to the beginning with him. It's a chance to do it all over again, knowing what we know now.

SUPER-SWAGGER

MORALES: I thought, "What are the two iconic things that Superman would be to me?" He'd be part Steve Reeves and part Elvis. [Laughs] When he's catching the bullet, he's got that Elvis light in the corner of his eye.

MORRISON: That swagger is part of what the rest of the world believes about America. "They're all John Wayne!" [Laughs] I wanted to put that back into Superman, that attitude of "I know what I'm doing, I'm the biggest guy on the block...but lucky for you, I'm a good guy!"

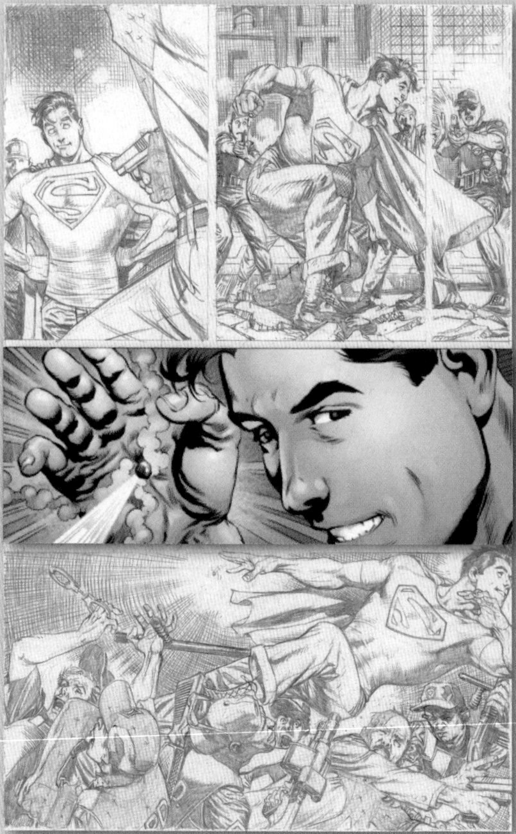

THE LABORS OF SUPERMAN

MORRISON: I constantly put Superman up against very physical objects: a wrecking ball, a tank, a train, solid stone. It was designed for the motion of that muscular, 1938 Superman — to really tie him into physical things, to big, heavy objects.

MORALES: I love that he's powered down. Love it, love it, love it, love it. I love that he's Herculean again. He's about doing the tasks. Superman back in the '40s was more relevant than Superman of recent years, because things hurt him. There was a danger to that.

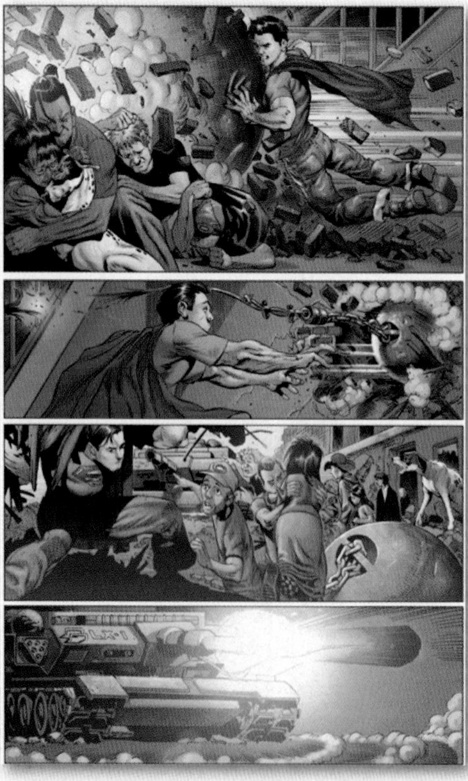

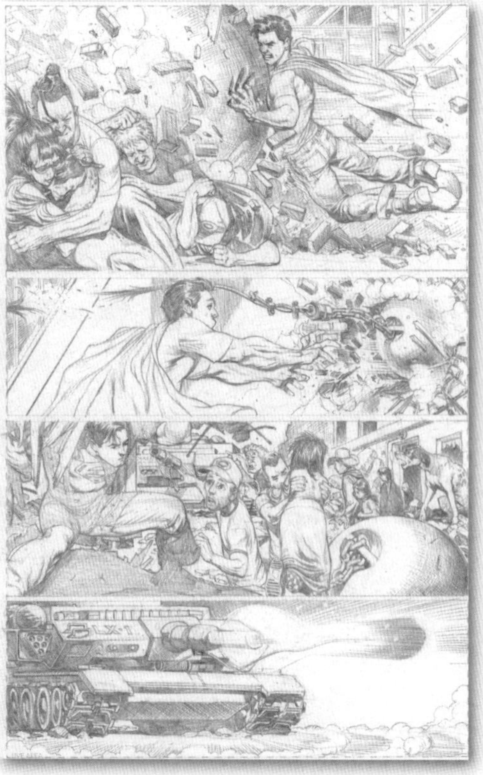

CLARK KENT

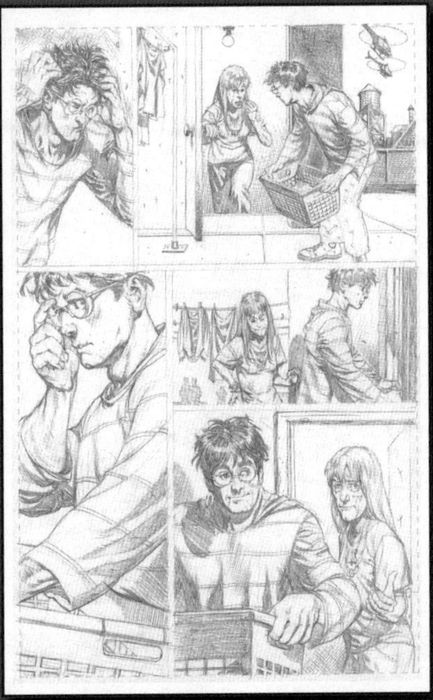

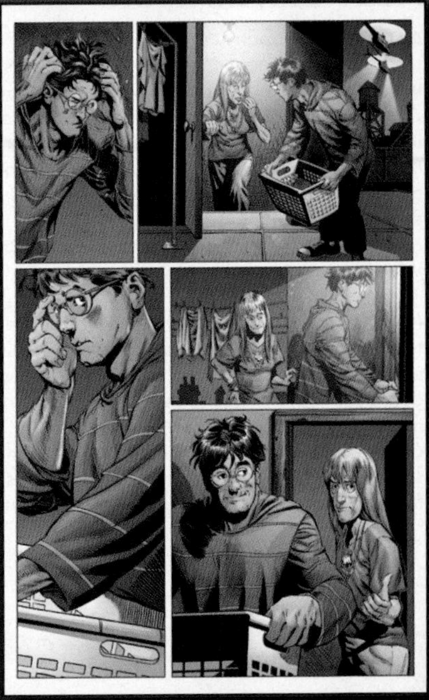

MORALES: I put him in baggy clothing to hide his muscles. Maybe stoop his posture a little bit, make him a little slack-jawed at certain moments so he doesn't look at all like a hero — more like a 22-year-old nerd, which is what he's trying to do. He's a very good actor, which is a super power I don't think many other super heroes have. And I realized that there's a certain amount of thickness to the lenses of his glasses that can help distort the size of his eyes and make them seem larger.

MORRISON: I love Rags's Clark Kent. I think it's great, this Harry Potter Clark Kent. His face is so young and pliable! His eyes get bigger, so he looks more like a kid. That's why Rags is so good to work with — he really thinks about this stuff, and it makes such a big difference to the finished product. When I saw that Clark Kent, it changed the way I wrote the character. He suddenly seemed very young, and he could be a little bit brattish. Clark's obviously this little hardcore farmer's boy who's not taking any crap from anyone.

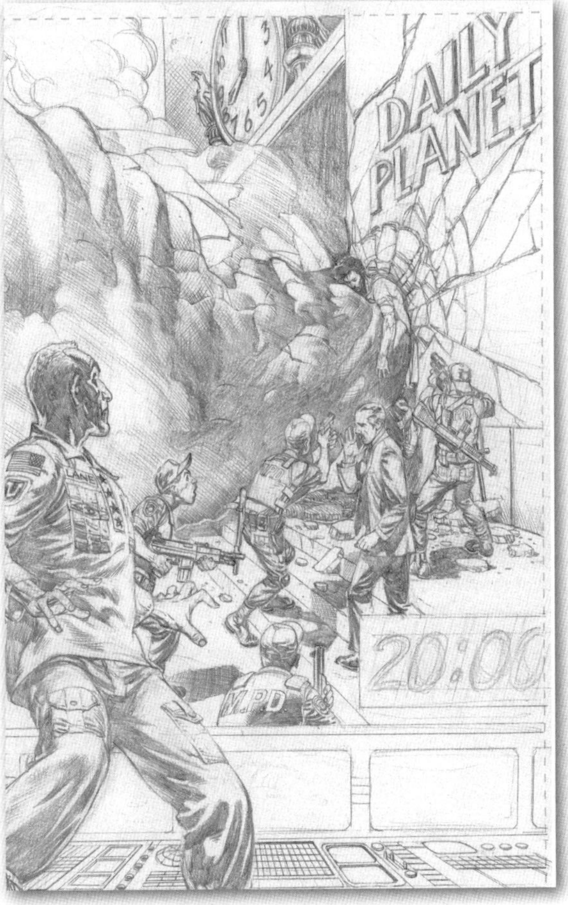
DAILY PLANET

MORE POWERFUL THAN A LOCOMOTIVE?

MORRISON: When he's hit by a train, he's not the Superman we've seen for the last 25-30 years. This is someone who can be hurt. I wanted to show he has limits. But it's also this upfront connection to the Superman legend — he's actually punched in the chest by the "speeding bullet."

MORALES: Originally, when Superman took off, he was exerting effort. To stop a train was painful. To get electrocuted was painful. He survived it much better than we could, but we forget how impossible these things are to do. I love that he's been brought back down to Earth. That's the way it should be.

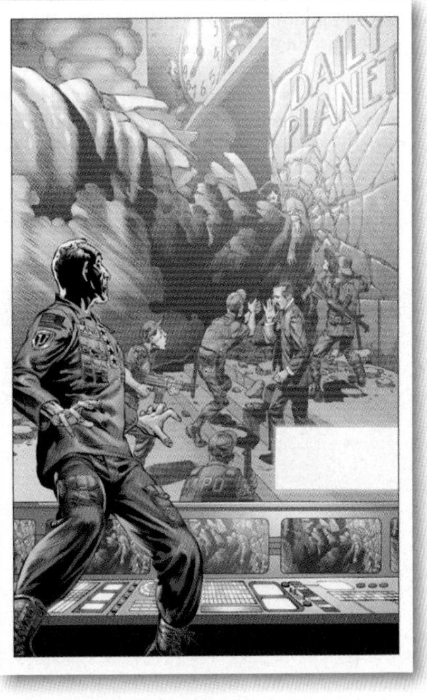
DAILY PLANET

MEET LEX LUTHOR

MORRISON: Superman is us at our best, and Lex is us at our worst...but they're both us. He's selfish, he's inwardly directed, he's greedy, he's egotistical, he pretends to hate Superman but really he wants to look like Superman, he's constantly chugging energy drinks, he talks crap...[Laughs] I wanted to make him an embodiment of all of our worst traits. They're what make us human, so that's what makes Lex human and relatable. That's why Lex Luthor's such a great villain: We all recognize those traits.

MORALES: Lex's weight is one of those little subliminal things. It adds a layer of jealousy and feeling insignificant and insecure about yourself. He's this out-of-shape, snide, condescending jerk who we're too mature now to stuff into a locker when we see him, but we still do it every time in our heads. [Laughs] Luthor's that guy from the electronics store who condescends to you when you ask about the difference between a megabyte and a gigabyte.

The following is a panel description from the script of ACTION COMICS #1:
Big pic. Now we cut to a military command center somewhere outside Metropolis. Nerve center atmosphere with military personnel hunched over computers. Big wall screen like they have at NASA. All yours, Rags. The picture is dominated by a big screen on which we see a GRAPHIC OF METROPOLIS with a pulsing circle in lower midtown east where Superman was last seen.
Silhouetted against the screen are two of our principal players — Lois Lane's dad GENERAL SAM LANE and Superman's arch-villain LEX LUTHOR. Lane is the archetypal tough American dad. Luthor, like Superman, is a little younger, perhaps a little heavier and sturdier. I like the idea that he was a little fat until his jealousy of Superman drove him to the gym to become the trim, muscular Luthor of the Silver Age and more recent stories. So he's not obese but he's veering a little more in the visual direction of Luthor's heavier build as it appeared in stories from 1941 to 1959.

LOIS LANE, REPORTER

MORRISON: Lois is an army girl, but she's become a crusading journalist to annoy her parents. She's like Clark Kent: She's crusading, she wants to do good, she's a hero in her own right. It changes the whole Superman dynamic, because Lois isn't tied to any guy. She's a party girl, she's smart, she's clever — she's Lady Gaga! She's the smartest girl on the planet.

MORALES: I think she has a poster of Woodward & Bernstein on the wall — that's what's important to her. I see her as constantly thinking. She may be saying one thing, but in her eyes you can tell she's thinking fifteen steps ahead of you.

JIMMY OLSEN, ~~SUPERMAN'S~~ CLARK KENT'S PAL

MORRISON: Jimmy's playing the role of Clark's friend rather than Superman's friend. He's the guy that Clark connected with when he first turned up in Metropolis. The two of them are geeks together, talking about movies and sci-fi. Jimmy's a young kid who's getting into this whole photography thing and is really smart. These are characters who you can imagine all have blogs, and Jimmy has his photographs up on Flickr. They're modern kids.

MORALES: He's Clark's best friend. They're buds. They're on the same level. Initially, he was all, "Well, golly gee, Mr. Kent!" But now he's just kind of like, "Hey, Clark, man — dude." If you want to make Jimmy Olsen cool, stop making him such an obsequious sycophant. You bring Clark down to him — which is perfect for Clark, too. It puts them on equal terms and instantly makes Jimmy cooler.

"THAT BEAT-UP-LOOKING KID"

MORRISON: You can tell he's in danger simply because he's no longer in motion!

MORALES: All art comes from the center. All you have to do is remember all the scraps you got into as a kid...

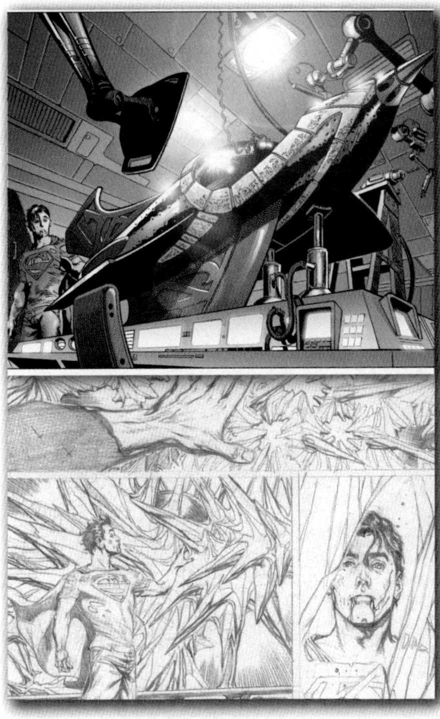

KAL-EL'S ROCKET

MORRISON: The rocket is Moses' basket, the basket that the Hindi hero Karna was placed in — the idea of people putting a child into the river of destiny. The cape, the rocket, the costume, the ship we see at the end of #2 — everything is part of the story and has character arcs of its own. Every little bit of the Superman legend is turned into something meaningful in its own right.

MORALES: Those little squiggles are designed to be hieroglyphs. If you're Kryptonian, you can read them. But it's funny: As I was drawing it, I started seeing things that reminded me of Moses' basket. Then I'm thinking, "Kal-EL— 'El' is a Hebrew word for God. The world's being destroyed, so he's being put into the basket and sent down the Nile." So I made it a little more basket-y.

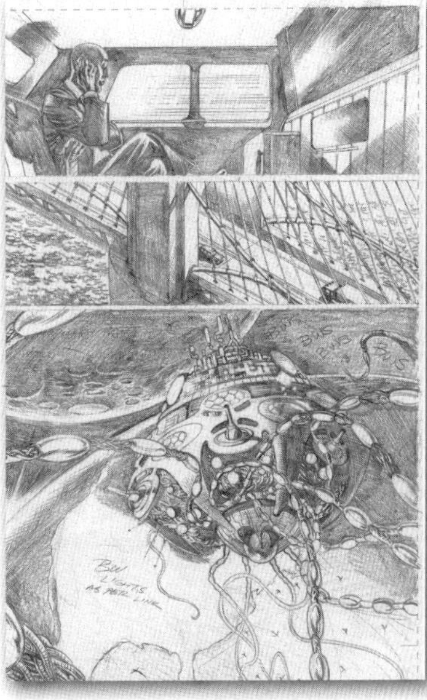

"IT CAME FROM OUTER SPACE"

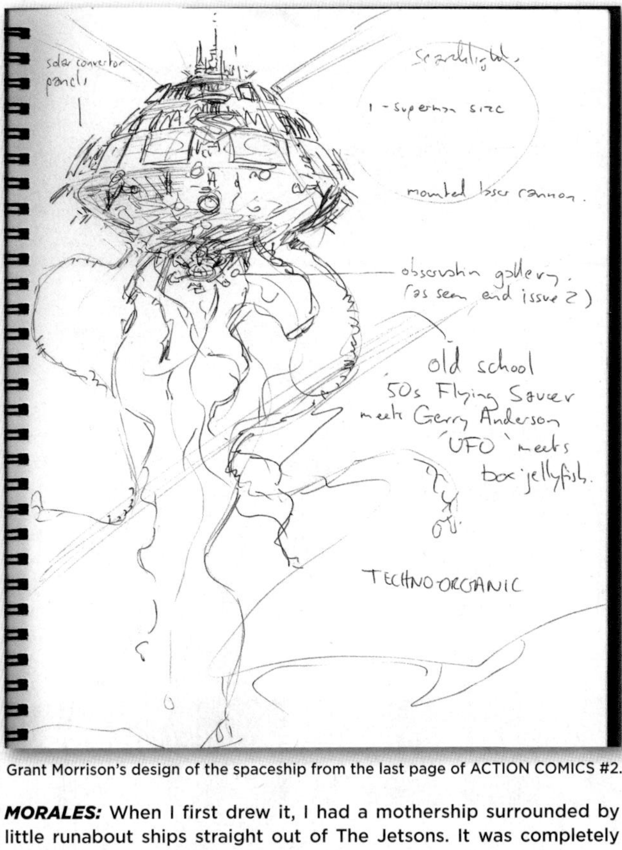

solar convertor panels
Searchlight
1 - superman size
mounted laser cannon.
observation gallery (as seen end issue 2)
old school 50s Flying Saucer meets Gerry Anderson 'UFO' meets box jellyfish.
TECHNO-ORGANIC

Grant Morrison's design of the spaceship from the last page of ACTION COMICS #2.

MORALES: When I first drew it, I had a mothership surrounded by little runabout ships straight out of The Jetsons. It was completely wrong. I sent it back and forth with the editor. Then Grant went ahead and did this jellyfish kind of design...

MORRISON: I think it's creepy that Lex is talking to something that doesn't reply, and then you see that image. That's the first hint of a bigger, overarching story to come. And tentacles are the creepiest things! [Laughs]

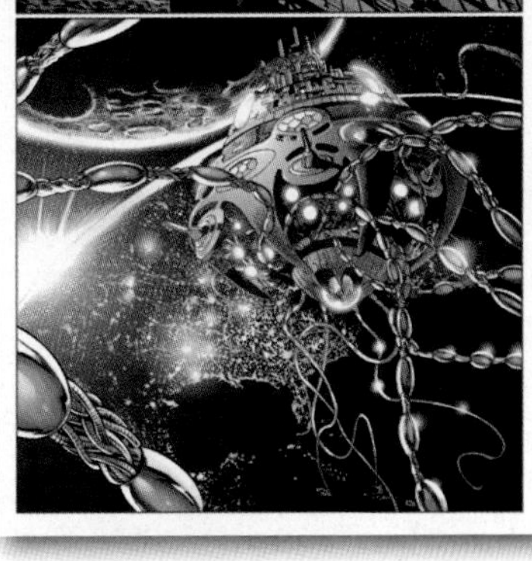

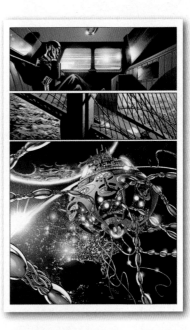

KRYPTON DESIGNS BY GENE HA!

MORRISON: It's the planet of your dreams. A sci-entific utopia. I wanted to explore Krypton as the world of super people. What would happen if they worked it all out, if they lived for 500 years with amazing technology?

GENE HA: I'm going to vary Kryptonians by standard facial features and hair texture and place-ment, mixed with very unusual color of hair and skin. A cocktail party of supermodels attacked by a god-child with god-crayons. I see Kryptonian identity as being very tied to their bodies. They always want their bodies to be more perfect, though their concept of perfection can drift into surprising directions.

MORE THAN JUST A LAMP

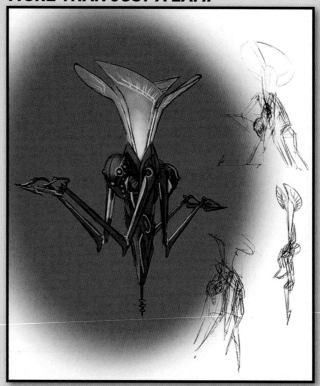

HA: The serving bots are both servants and decorative lamps with figural columns. The lily/insect wing/lampshade is their hover device. The robots are supposed to hint both at mantis arms, and also skeletons — lilies and skeletons being metaphors for the briefness of life and the permanence of death.

LIKE SON, LIKE FATHER

MORRISON: Jor-El looks just like the father of Superman should look. He's wearing an outfit that closely resembles the Jim Lee Superman suit, except in Jor-El's trademark green and red. He has the science guild symbol on his chest — a ringed planet.

THE NEW FALL (OF KANDOR) COLLECTION

HA: At the basic level, Kryptonians could have body-defying technology and clothes. I imagine Lara's snarky sister Zara wearing a gold-en face mask on the back of her head, which lets her speak to and see people behind her back. She pretty much only uses her real mouth to emote and eat and drink. Instead of drinking cocktails, they're sniffing from glass tubes. This plays with ideas like sniffing flowers, and sticking your nose into a wine glass before taking a sip. No idea what they get from sniffing: aromatherapy, mild intoxication, or even nutrition.

DANCING ON THE CEILING

HA: The party platform makes heavy use of anti-gravity and other hover technology. Each floor has normal Kryptonian gravity on each side, and people are walking on each side. It has no stairs, but instead the sun crystal columns also have their own gravity for anyone touching its surface.

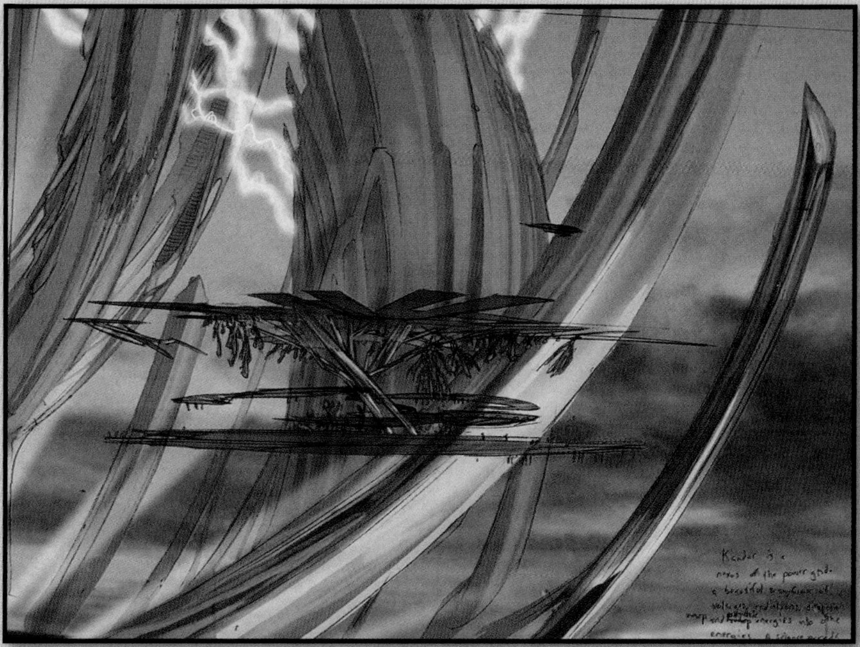

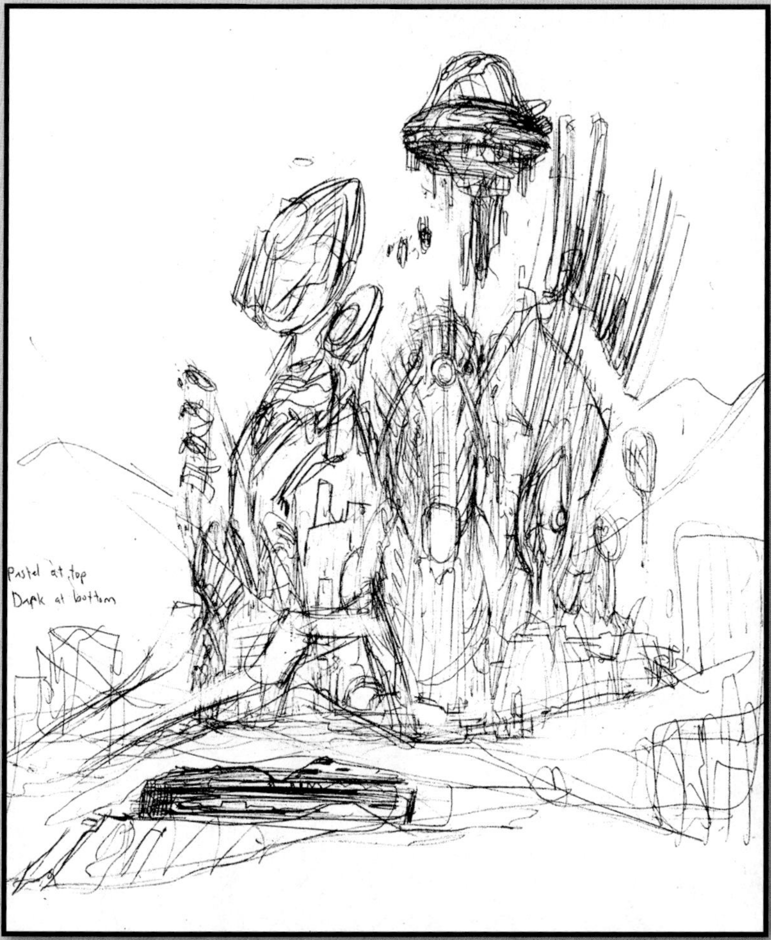
Pastel at top
Dark at bottom

CITY AS SCIENCE COLONY

HA: I'm imagining Kandor as a giant science colony. It's a mountain-sized power grid transformer, transforming and storing voltages, radiation, dimensional warps, and perhaps even information and telepathic memories. The main administration is in the floating dome at the top of the city, but various other facilities have occupant space, too.

Interviews by Sean T. Collins
Design by Rob Clark Jr.

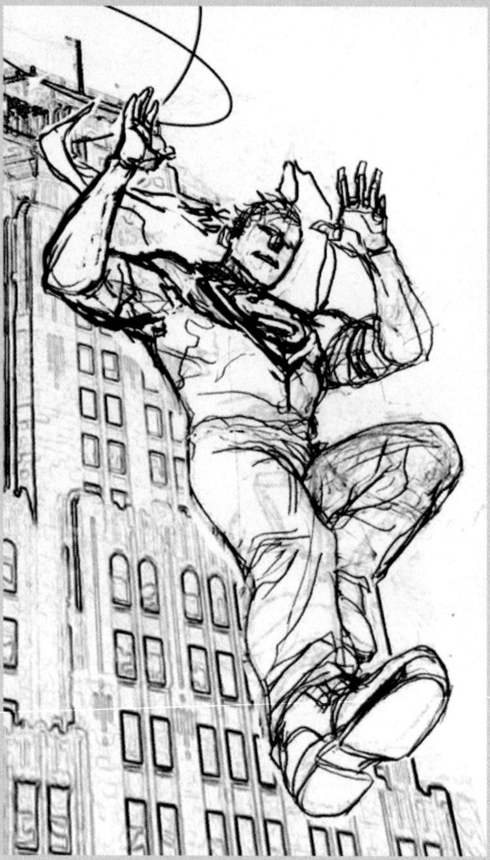

Cover sketches and pencils by Michael Choi.

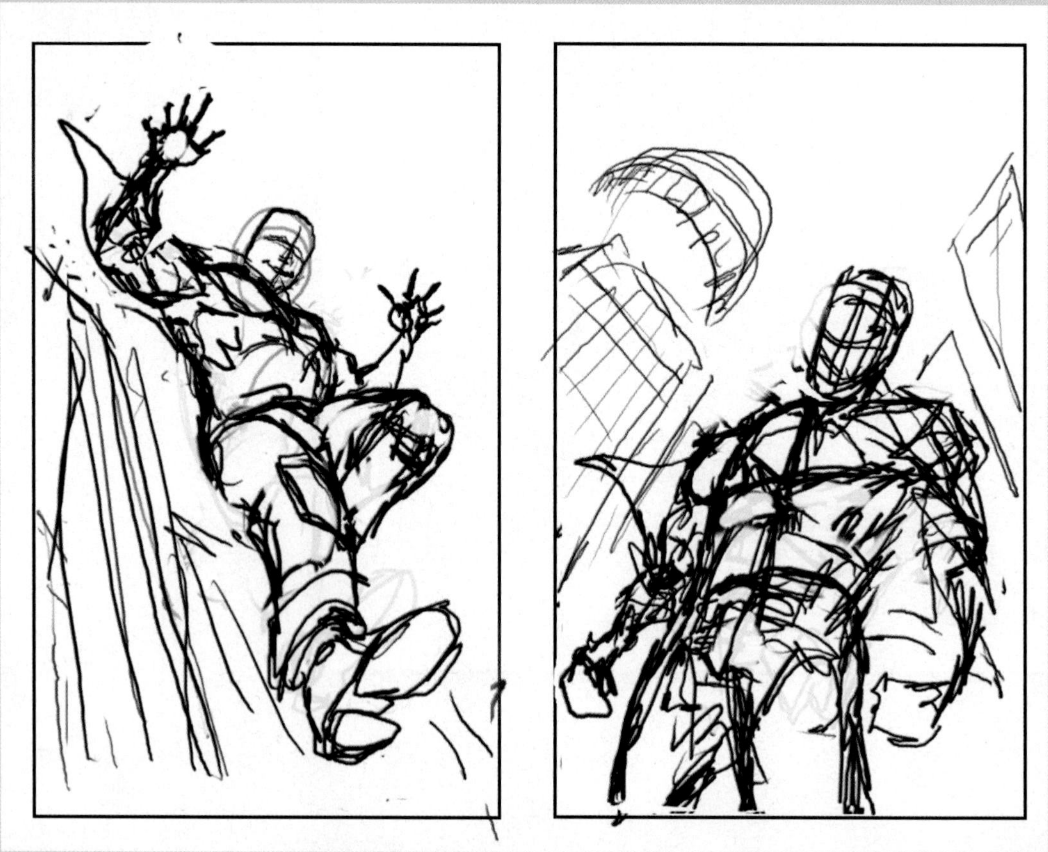

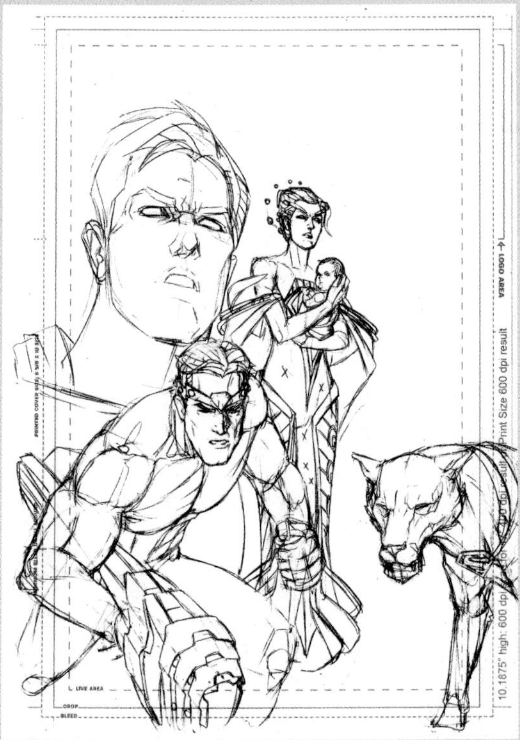
LOGO AREA
Print Size 600 dpi result
10.1875" high: 600 dpi
LIVE AREA
CROP
BLEED

Cover sketches and pencils by Gene Ha.

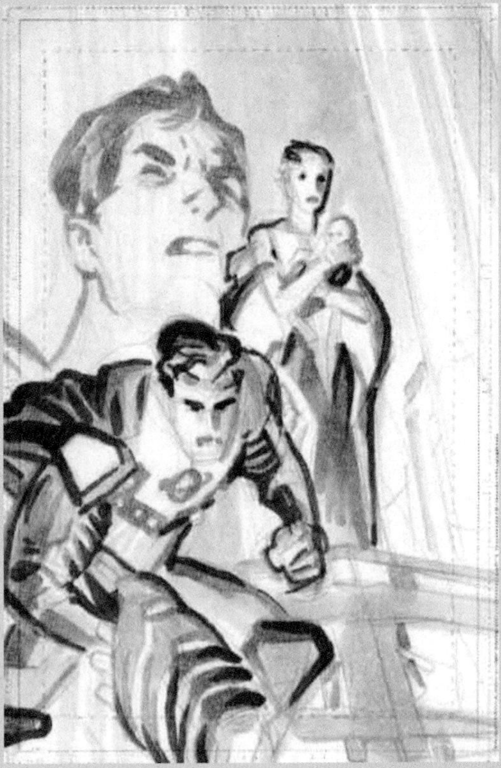

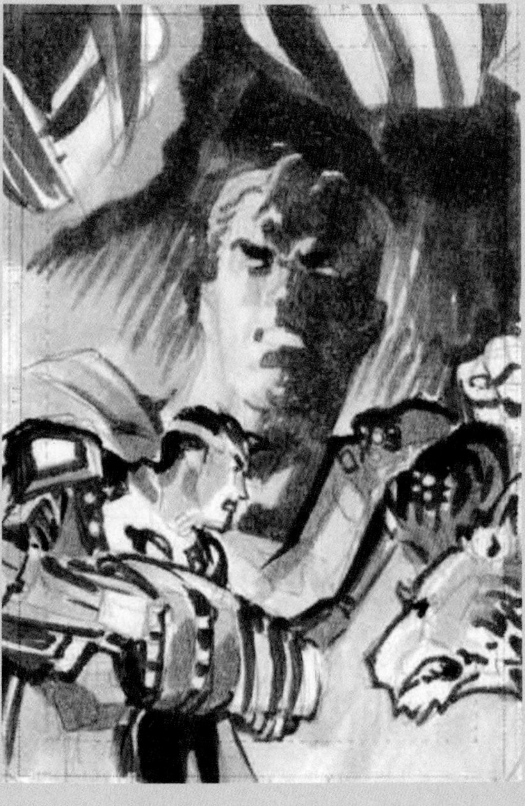

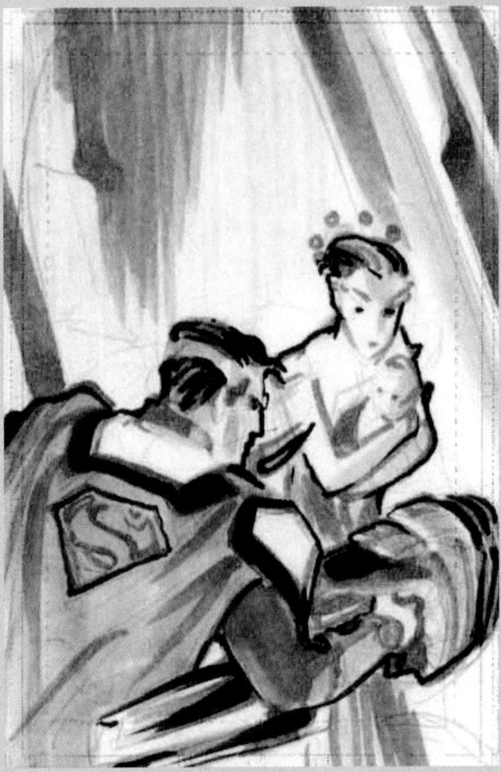

Cover sketches by Andy Kubert.

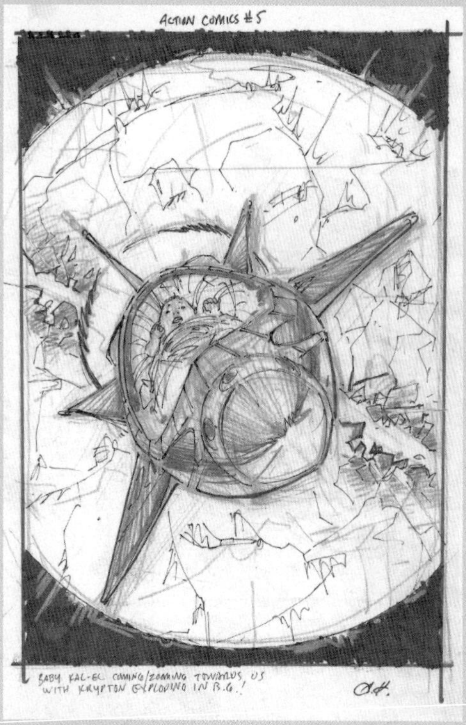

ACTION COMICS #5
BABY KAL-EL COMING/ZOOMING TOWARDS US WITH KRYPTON EXPLODING IN B.G.!

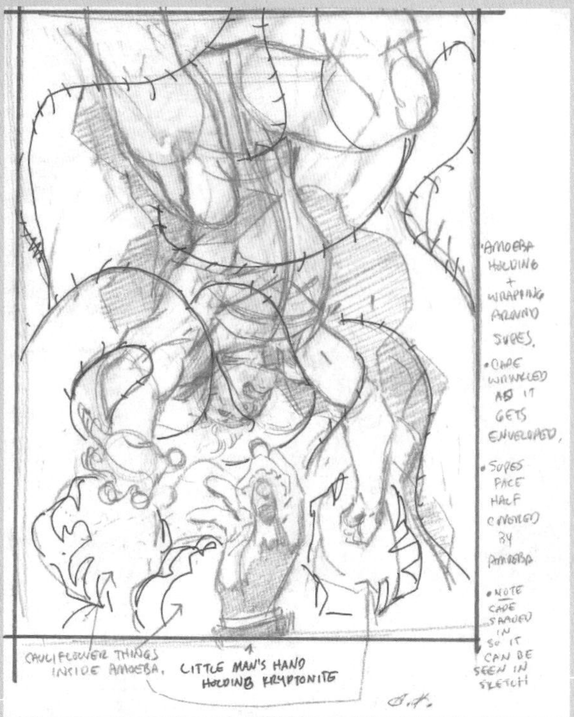

•AMOEBA HOLDING + WRAPPING AROUND SUPES.
•CAPE WRINKLED AS IT GETS ENVELOPED.
•SUPES FACE HALF COVERED BY AMOEBA
•NOTE CAPE SHADED IN SO IT CAN BE SEEN IN SKETCH
CAULIFLOWER THINGS INSIDE AMOEBA.
LITTLE MAN'S HAND HOLDING KRYPTONITE

Cover sketches and pencils by Chris Burnham.

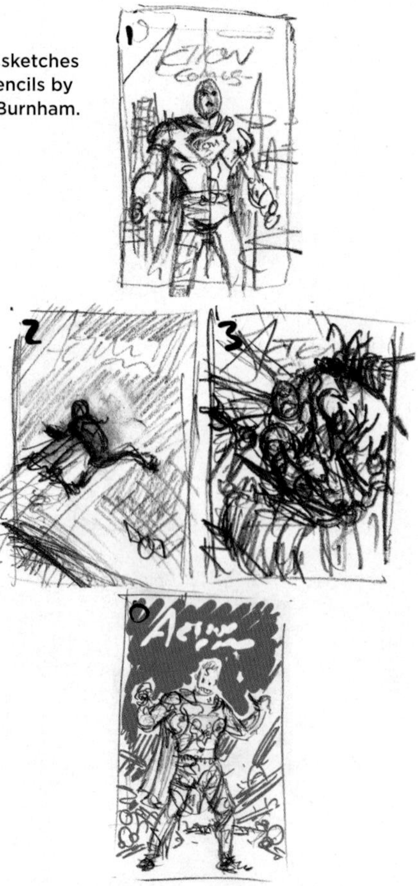

1
ACTION COMICS
2
3

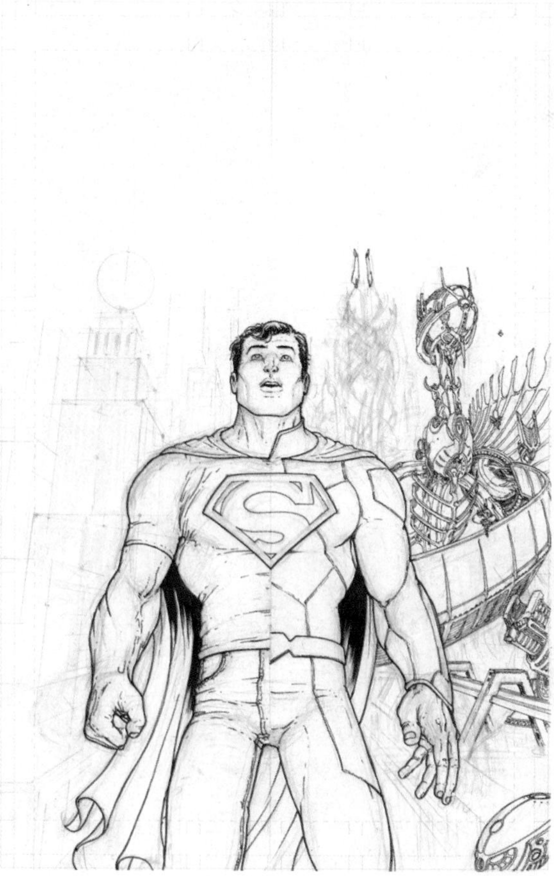